MAYFLOWER HILL

MAYFLOWER HILL

A History of Colby College

EARL H. SMITH

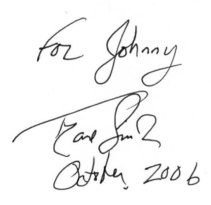

For Johnny

Earl Smith
October, 2006

COLBY COLLEGE

Published by University Press of New England

Hanover and London

Colby College
Published by University Press of New England,
One Court Street, Lebanon, NH 03766
www.upne.com

Images are used with permission. Except as
noted in the captions, all are from
the Colby College Archives.

Library of Congress Cataloging-in-Publication Data
Smith, Earl H.
Mayflower Hill : a history of Colby College / Earl H. Smith. — 1st ed.
p. cm.
Includes bibliographical references and index.
ISBN-13: 978-1-58465-604-3 (cloth : alk. paper)
ISBN-10: 1-58465-604-2 (cloth : alk. paper)
1. Colby College—History. I. Title.
LD1061.C72S65 2006
378.741'6—dc22   2006018623

University Press of New England is a member of the Green Press
Initiative. The paper used in this book meets their minimum
requirement for recycled paper.

TO BARBARA

CONTENTS

PREFACE

The years following the full settlement of Colby on its new campus were marked by vibrant growth and daring change, leading to an institutional prominence unimagined by its founders. The rapid evolution came in no small measure from the move itself—uprooting an entire institution and taking it across town, building a handsome new campus, and inviting broad support and encouragement. It also came from a succession of remarkable leaders who took inspiration and courage from the old story and carried Colby to a place among the finest small colleges in the land.

Colby's history has been written twice before. Edwin Carey Whittemore, pastor of the Waterville, Maine, Baptist Church, wrote *Colby College, 1820–1925: An Account of Its Beginnings, Progress and Service*, in 1927, on the centennial of the first year of classes. Ernest Cummings Marriner, beloved dean and Maine historian, completed *The History of Colby College* in time for the sesquicentennial celebration in 1963. Both volumes are indispensable to the full understanding of a remarkable institution, its people and its place.

This book is centered on the last half of the twentieth century, but it cannot begin there. The period from 1950 forward, after all, is barely more than a quarter of the entire history. This history begins with a retelling of the early tale and is woven with the story of Waterville, a Maine village that became a flourishing city of immigrants. It recalls the College's Baptist creation by righteous men who sought religious peace in the wilderness and were willing to hang the fate of a new institution on little more than a prayer or two. It tells of a tiny place—half college, half seminary—facing doom at the end of the Civil War and saved at the eleventh hour by a man whose hope for a theological school was never realized. Finally, the early story tells of a visionary president and of Waterville citizens, joined by hundreds of friends and strangers, rising up to rescue a college choked by the community's own success and, in the midst of war and depression, moving it, lock, stock, and barrel, to the heights above the city.

This prologue sets the stage for the tale of a new campus and, in all but name, a different place with a rich new purpose. It is the story of the move from religious focus to secularism, from "coordination" to coeducation, and from provincialism to global notice. It is the story of an ever-stronger faculty, willing to make innovative changes in the ways of teaching, and of trustees daring to revolutionize student life and shed ill-fitting traditions. It is the story of students with new and louder voices, changing old rules, protesting an unpopular war and demanding, on campus and in the world, equality and social justice. And it is the story of a college slowly reversing its role from the protected to a protector of the city that once saved it. It is the story of Mayflower Hill.

MAYFLOWER HILL

PROLOGUE

ORIGINAL OWNERS

For ten thousand years all of the land in the sprawling river valley—150 miles from the large lake to the sea—belonged to the eastern Wabanaki, "people of the dawn," proud tribe of the Algonkin. The headwater lake was named for its shape, the head of the moose that had fed in its shallows since the beginning of time. The river was named Kennebec for its "long quiet waters" below the falls in the smooth tidewater where the Sebasticook tributary runs alongside. At the river joining was the Wabanaki village of the Caniba, extending more than a mile along the east bank of the Kennebec between the two rivers. Here the Caniba named the falls for their Chief Teconnet and took his name as well. They lived on the abundance of salmon, sturgeon and, in the salty water below, clams and cod. In winter they drew back from the water, sheltered in bark cabins and longhouses and sustained themselves with smoked fish and the bounty of the forest.

The first European intruders did not stay, coming only to fish and explore the edges of their discovery. Sebastian Cabot poked along the inlets in the summer of 1498, and took the land for King Henry VII, and for England. In 1530 Jacques Cartier sailed under the French flag of King Francis I and claimed the place as well. Samuel Champlain reinforced the French claim in 1604 and broadened the territory to include everything from Cape Breton to the Hudson River. He named it Acadia. The next year Captain George Weymouth anchored off Monhegan and insisted the place belonged to England. It took two centuries to sort it out, and through that time the natives suffered far more than either nation.

In 1606, some fourteen years before the Pilgrims arrived at Plymouth, a British colony was established at the mouth of the river. The settlement, led by Raleigh Gilbert and George Popham, failed in the first winter. Captain John

Smith returned in 1615 and gave the name New England to the whole territory between New Found Land and the Hudson River. That same year the Indians of the Penobscot and the Kennebec began a ruinous two-year fight among themselves. Everyone lost. When it was over the English seized the land and began to move in among the remaining Wabanaki, settling a Plymouth Company tract of land fifteen miles wide, spanning the bank of the Kennebec from Topsham to Cornville.

The natives had more to fear from the white man's illnesses than from his guns. Deadly infections spread among them even before the English came to stay. Passing fishermen gave them a mysterious fatal disease as early as 1564 and typhoid fever twenty years later. In the decade before the English arrived at Plymouth, three epidemics ravaged the eastern Wabanaki. Where once there were as many as twenty thousand native people east of the White Mountains, barely a quarter of them survived and the illnesses kept coming—smallpox, influenza, diphtheria, and measles—continuing for two centuries until their population all but disappeared.

The land at the confluence of the Kennebec and Sebasticook was in private hands in the autumn of 1675 when the natives first took arms against the English (King Philip's War). The following summer, the entire river valley was in flames. The Wabanaki had run out of patience with the harsh English who saw them as infidels and swindled them out of fur and fish. The French, hoping to make them Catholics, treated them more kindly, and a dozen years later joined as allies against the English (King William's War). The English prevailed and in 1692 the trespassers burned the Teconnet settlement to the ground, captured the warrior Bomaseen and scattered the surviving natives into the wilderness. The homeless Teconnet continued their alliance with the French and by 1693 had a powerful, unappointed leader, Father Sebastian Rale, sent by the Catholics of Quebec to Norridgewock to establish a mission. Rale opposed the building of forts and annoyed the English by denouncing the proposed treaties. In 1717, over Rale's objections, a peace pact was signed with the governor of the Royal Court of Massachusetts, ruler of the troublesome District of Maine.

Fifty years passed, and heirs of the original Plymouth Company Kennebec tract, anxious to provide safety and bring new settlers, petitioned the court to build a fort at Teconnet Falls. The Indians objected and sent a delegation to ask Massachusetts Governor William Shirley to build no forts above the one in place at Richmond. They were willing to have the foreigners live among them, but they did not want them garrisoned inside a fort. He ignored them. A century later, when the immigrants arrived, there was no one left to argue against the colonized neighborhoods that were commonplace along the Kennebec and throughout the new country.

In dismissing the Indian pleas, Shirley declared that if the Plymouth Company would construct a fort in Cushnoc (Augusta) he would build one at the falls fifteen miles up the river. Cushnoc got Fort Western, and a wagon road was cut along the river to the confluence of the Sebasticook, where General John Winslow built a second fort called Halifax. The commander at Richmond, William Lithgow, was sent to lead a garrison of eighty men. Many died from starvation and illness in the first winter of 1755, but even so, the Indians were no match for them. On May 18, 1757, the Teconnet made a final desperate skirmish before evaporating into the forest, never to fight again.

In April 1771 the English settlement at Teconnet, first called Kingfield, was incorporated by the Massachusetts Court as the fourth town in the District of Maine and renamed in honor of General Winslow. Four years later, almost to the day, the first blood of the American Revolution was spilled at the Concord Bridge; and in autumn 1775 the central house of the unmanned garrison at Fort Halifax, by then a town hall and tavern, greeted Benedict Arnold's doomed expedition on its faltering way to Quebec. The feisty Arnold had convinced George Washington and the new Continental Congress in Philadelphia to accept a plan to surprise the British garrison at Quebec. He would avoid the predictable route of the Saint Lawrence River and take the back door through the wilderness, up the Kennebec and down the Chaudiere. On September 11 Arnold marched eleven hundred men from Cambridge to Newburyport, where schooners carried them to the mouth of the Kennebec and up to Pittston to collect two hundred new wooden bateaux. They were tested in the short, calm journey to Winslow. The 20-foot boats, made of green pine and ribbed with oak, were sodden and heavy—four hundred pounds without provisions—and the carry beyond Ticonic Falls was near impossible. At Five Mile Rips the boats began to crack. When they met the first ice and fast water at the Great Falls of Norridgewock the men began to desert. The expedition faced a great deal in the way of disaster and treachery in the months ahead, but it got its first taste of ruin at the falls below Winslow.

The river place that confounded Arnold's troops also hindered the governing of the growing town. There were difficulties in the collection of taxes and in the provision of schools and preaching; in 1791 town fathers petitioned the Commonwealth to be rid of the bothersome west bank place they called Ticonic Village. Although the cross-river land had never been at the center of things (the Indians used it only as a burial ground) townspeople were reluctant to give it up, and the petition was delayed for five years while they experimented with alternating town and religious meetings between the Lithgow meetinghouse on the east bank and the Sherwin Street home of Silas Redington across the river. It was impossible. Petitioners claimed that "in the spring season, at the annual meetings held in said Town, the Inhabitants thereof living on the opposite side from where the said meeting is to be held are frequently prevented by the particular situation of said River from crossing the same to attend said meeting." In 1801, with eight hundred of Winslow's 1250 inhabitants now living west of the river, the ruling court was again asked to cut the town in two. On June 23, 1802, the petition was granted, creating the town of Waterville and, by local decree, a place called West Waterville (Oakland).

Under the safe flag of the new nation, Maine families prospered. Farmers became sailors, and a burgeoning Kennebec shipbuilding industry soon dominated the world. Lumber and potatoes and, from the river itself, fish and ice became lucrative barter for foreign riches. Merchants, flush with unfettered free enterprise, began to build great homes on the high cliffs above the river.

The upriver twin towns of Winslow and Waterville flourished as well. From 1794 until the steamships came in the 1830s, a number of schooners, brigs, and ships were built at Waterville. The shipbuilding fostered more new shops and mills along the riverbank and beside the fast-moving Emerson Stream (later called Messalonskee for its giant muskellunge fish) draining seven lakes and feeding the Kennebec. A thriving manufacturing center grew all around it.

1. ALONG THE RIVER

HOME FOR A BAPTIST COLLEGE

It was an unlikely place to put a college. While the same might be said for most towns where the early colleges grew, the obstacles to a new institution at Waterville were especially daunting. Bowdoin had a head start and was closer to the population center of Portland and the city's well-heeled Congregationalists. The Waterville location was remote; travel was slow and awkward; the climate was harsh; the surroundings were rustic; and financial support, limited at first to Baptist followers, was scarce. Soon, new College buildings and promising industry popped up along the river, and the population began to grow. In time, everything improved but the weather.

In the colonial towns, family and community life centered on the power and politics of religion. The Baptists, moving north from Rhode Island and Massachusetts, were separatists, not reformers, insisting on absolute freedom and bent on proselytizing and missionary work to spread the word of God. Their aggression was both feared and persecuted by churches of the "standing order." The first Baptist church in the District of Maine opened in Kittery in 1682 and was quickly closed by pestering town magistrates. It was nearly a century (1768) before a second church came and stayed at Gorham. By the early nineteenth century Waterville Baptists held sway even without a church building.

All of the churches wanted to train their own ministers and end the reliance on England for providing men of learning. It was from this need that nearly all of the early colleges were begun. Congregationalists had the first established church, and in 1636, the first college, Harvard. By the Revolution there were nine church colleges. Brown University (1765) was the first for the Baptists, but it supplied few preachers for the devout in the north woods where churches were accustomed to supplying their own preachers: independent, self-taught men, rarely of the same theological bent.

Securing a Baptist seminary in Maine was aided in no small way by the First Amendment of the new Constitution: "Congress shall make no law respecting an establishment of religion, or prohibiting the free exercise thereof." The requirement left legislators little choice but to consider granting charters, land, and money to any denomination, not just to those of the "standing order." In 1807 the Reverend Sylvanus Boardman of Livermore sent a letter to the Bowdoinham Baptist Association expressing concern that many ministers, "not understanding their mother tongue," were sorely in need of an education. Three years later the association agreed to petition Massachusetts "to incorporate an institution for the purpose of promoting literary and theological knowledge." Joined by Lincoln and Cumberland, in 1813 the Bowdoinham association submitted a plea asking for "a tract of good land, and cause it to be located as nighly in the center of the district as your wisdom may find convenient." It was denied.

Although the founders dearly wanted a strictly Baptist seminary, political reality and sensitivity to the new Constitution caused them to ask for an institution of collegiate standing offering both theological *and* literary instruction. Even so, the rapidly prepared second petition barely disguised their intent:

> Whereas Harvard College in Cambridge, as well as the other Colleges and seminaries in this state, have been liberally endowed, either by the appropriation of public lands, or otherwise, by grants of the General Court, and have been committed to the more particular direction and management of that specific part of the community, denominated Congregationalists: and whereas we have sustained a part, and not an inconsiderable part, of those appropriations, without having any particular share in the oversight and direction of such appropriations ever assigned, by authority, to that part of the community denominated Baptists, we therefore consider, and are firmly persuaded, that the General Court would do no injustice to any section of the Commonwealth, but would render more equal justice to the different sections, and largely promote the best good of the State generally, by kindly receiving and favorably answering the petition, to which we solicit the attention of your honorable body.

Legislative support was led by Representative Daniel Merrill of Sedgwick, a Congregational minister turned Baptist, and by the successful Bath merchant and Jeffersonian Democrat William King. It was an uphill fight. Despite protection of the new constitution, many were wary of embracing a faith not of the "standing order." Bowdoin College, nondenominational from its beginning in 1794 but nonetheless stoutly Congregationalist, opposed the idea, but not on issues of faith. With barely 200,000 souls in the entire district, Bowdoin was struggling for its own foothold and wary of sharing scarce students with a second college in Maine. With King's help, the petition was adopted on February 27, 1813, establishing "a Literary Institution for the purpose of educating youth, to be known by the name of The Maine Literary and Theological Institution." It was the 33rd chartered college in the new United States, and its Baptist origin influenced its teachings for more than a century.

It was two years before the new institution was granted a place: Township No. 3 on land near Bangor, purchased from the defeated Indians. It was good timberland and would provide a fine income for the new college, but the place was too remote. In 1816, the court agreed the institution could find a home somewhere in the counties of Kennebec or Somerset. Waterville was interested; so were Farmington and Bloomfield. A committee visited the three places and settled on Waterville on condition that within two years the town would provide the land. The local government promised three thousand dollars in municipal funds and citizens offered an additional two thousand dollars in subscriptions guaranteed by Timothy Boutelle, Nathaniel Gilman, and seven others. Other local Baptists were eager to subscribe. There were many who thought the place was overripe for the civilized influence of a college. Years before Dr. N. Whitaker had written his Waterville colleague, Dr. Obadiah Williams, about locating a new college in the area. Williams, a Revolutionary War surgeon and veteran of Bunker Hill, had been pushing for a seminary. "Am agreeably affected by the noble and important design of erecting a Seminary of learning in these parts," Whitaker wrote, "where little skill is required to discern a too hasty return to a state of Barbarism." The citizens' pledges ($1,797.50) were used to purchase a wooded plot a half-mile above the town, between the Kennebec and the Messalonskee. Citing "legal problems," most likely having to do with the separation of the church from the state, the town withdrew its pledge, but citizens raised $2,500 more to expand the original plot to 179 acres, including more land south along the river.

With the matter of place settled, in February 1818, trustees assigned the new institution two Massachusetts ministers: Jeremiah Chaplin as professor of divinity and Ira Chase as professor of languages. Both turned them down, but Chaplin, every inch a reflective Puritan, came to believe the position offered was "a divinely given opportunity" and reconsidered. He agreed to teach religion, nothing more, and for a time at least, the new literary and theological institution would be theological only.

Chaplin's journey to Waterville began on June 20, 1818, when he set sail from Danvers aboard the coastal sloop *Hero*. With him were his wife, Marcia, their five children,[1] and seven divinity students including George Dana Boardman who would become the institution's first graduate. They reached the Kennebec in two days; on the morning of the third the *Hero* ran aground on the shoals above Gardiner. The odd assembly walked the riverbank to Augusta, and the following morning boarded smaller blunt-ended long boats. With help from men and oxen pulling from the banks, they continued to Waterville where a welcoming committee put them up in the vacant home of the recently deceased Nathan Wood near the center of town. It was here that the first classes were held.

The Wood home was at the intersection of roads leading to Kendall's Mills (Fairfield) and the Fairfield Meetinghouse (Fairfield Center). It became a tavern in 1840 and eight years later burned to the ground. In 1850, the partnership of Seavey and Williams built an inn on the site and named it The Elmwood. It too was destroyed by fire (1878) and was soon replaced by one of the original partners, Osborne Seavey, who persuaded the trustees of Colby University to advance him $15,000 for its cost. He rented it from the College until his business failed and the College took it back, only to lease it once again in 1885 to Eben and Harry Murch for $1,400 a year. In 1891 the College got out of the hotel business altogether, and sold the Elmwood to Henry Judkins for $15,000.

They were barely settled when Chaplin took it upon himself to organize and assume the pulpit of the First Baptist Church. Eight years later he oversaw the construction of a church building, the first in Waterville, and began to take the entire College to compulsory Sunday services. (Neither did it take the sober Calvinist long to form the Sons of Temperance, an organization never embraced by the local gentry.)

Trustees had a particular vision for the shape and appearance of a new campus, carved out among the birches, away from town and near the river. As with other early colleges, the buildings were placed in a row, fronted by a park. Teaching, preaching, dining, and sleeping were combined within the same structures. There were already examples at Yale and Andover and another had

1. John, 11; Hannah, 9; Jeremiah Jr., 5; Adoniram, 2; and 4-month-old Anne.

begun at Bowdoin. It took a while to raise building funds; in the meantime the District of Maine became a state. The institution's good friend William King was chairman of a constitutional convention, held in the summer of 1819. The year before, when Maine first petitioned to leave Massachusetts, there were already twenty-two states in the union, divided 11 to 11 on the issue of slavery. Under a compromise, Maine and Missouri simultaneously became new states in January 1820. In Maine, King was elected governor.

Among the first acts of the new legislature was the affirmation of the Massachusetts charter for the Maine Literary and Theological Institution, amended in significant ways. The charter insisted no student could be denied admission or other privileges "on the ground that his interpretations of the scripture differ from those which are contained in the articles of faith adopted, or to be adopted by the institution." Without this provision, the institution might never have grown beyond a small seminary in the woods.

The legislature also claimed authority to "alter, limit, or restrain" the power of the institution's trustees, prohibiting them from applying a religious test in the selection of their own members, a change the Institution accepted willingly in order to install the non-Baptist Timothy Boutelle as its treasurer. With Boutelle in the boardroom, it was not long before men of other faiths were sitting with the Baptists in the circle of power. Lastly, the legislature added a clause giving trustees the authority to grant degrees and, with this simple amendment, created a true college.

In 1821, reflecting its now enlarged authority, trustees presented the second legislature a petition to change the college name. The board hoped to name it for a major benefactor, but none would come for another half-century. In the meantime, the name of its founding town suited well enough. On February 5 it became Waterville College. Trustees elected the Reverend Daniel Barnes of New York to become the first president, but he turned them down. The founding Professor Chaplin took the job.

Within a year the re-named College completed gift subscriptions for its first substantial building; and two Waterville builders, Peter Getchell (brick-layer) and Lemuel Dunbar (carpenter), began work on South College, an austere four-story Federal-style brick structure, 80 by 40 feet. It included thirty-two double student rooms, recitation halls, and a library. The following year Getchell and Dunbar teamed to build a near-matching building, North College, for three thousand dollars. It was fifteen years before the row was completed with the construction of Recitation Hall in the middle. With its boxy, triple-stage tower holding the College's Revere Bell, the building, later named for Colby's seventh president, James T. Champlin, was the tallest structure in

Maine. Federal in style and one of the first New England educational buildings designed by an American architect (Thomas Ustick Walter of Philadelphia), it was principally a chapel with four basement classrooms and a small library taken out of South College. The finished line of handsome buildings was a proud feature in Waterville, even something of a curiosity in a town made mostly of wood. The imposing row became known as "The Bricks."

A growing Waterville was soon to have other modern additions. In 1823 the first bridges were built over the two rivers; and five years later a steamboat, the *Ticonic,* began to ply up and down the river with Waterville as its northernmost port, but it foundered too many times on the ledges in the fast water and its terminus quickly retreated to Augusta.

Curtailment of the steamboat slowed transportation from the south, but a different kind of traffic was about to bring new riches from the north, not over the water but on horseback and on foot over an old Indian trail called the Kennebec Road. Shoved out of Maine two centuries before, the French Catholic people of lower Quebec were returning. Jean Mattheu was first in 1827, and others followed, first in small numbers and then, at the end of the Civil War, in great waves that turned the region's religious and cultural milieu upside down.

Seeking work at the expanding mills, the newcomers were not welcomed. They were insulted as "lard-eaters" and "frogs"[2] and mocked for their strange language and religion. Outwardly, none of it mattered to them. They had paying jobs for six long days, a strong faith for seven, and were ardent about both. The wiry, pomaded men moved their large families into the south of town, near the river in a place others had named The Plains, and built their own shops and churches and schools. The Yankees moved away from them, up from the river, but at the same time their young students—in town and at the College—began to learn their language.

In 1834, the College French teacher was the Reverend Samuel Francis Smith, who took the job for an extra $100 a year; his principal work was as the Baptist preacher. They were his first jobs after graduation from Andover Theological Seminary where he had written the words to "My Country 'Tis of Thee," a song he was eagerly teaching Sunday school youngsters in Waterville. At Andover, Smith worked as a translator for his organist friend Lowell

2. Mostly manual laborers, the French were slurred as lard-eaters for their energy-rich fatty diets. Their labeling as frogs derived from the time of the American Revolution when the allied French troops wore closed, short-tailed coats and were said to resemble an army of frogs as they moved through the wilderness.

Mason, a well-known publisher of public school music. Mason asked Smith to furnish him with something striking for the upcoming Fourth of July celebration. Smith liked a German song, "God Bless our Native Land," and in one afternoon he wrote new English words for a song he called "America."[3] The song became widely popular, and during the Civil War it served as a rallying hymn for the north. For a century it rivaled Francis Scott Key's "Star Spangled Banner" for honors as the national anthem, a matter not settled until Congress made its choice in 1931.

There is a Colby tie to the Pledge of Allegiance as well. Near the end of the century, James Upham, Class of 1860, was editor of the magazine *Youth's Companion.* He was determined to rekindle national pride in time for the Columbian Exposition that would commemorate the 400th anniversary of America's discovery. Upham and fellow editor Francis Bellamy lobbied President Benjamin Harrison and Congress for a national Columbus Day holiday, and were themselves put in charge of developing a special program for school children. At Upham's request, Bellamy wrote the Pledge of Allegiance for the children to read on the first Columbus Day, October 12, 1892.

Smith preached at a church that still stands at the intersection of Ten Lots and Marston roads in nearby Fairfield[4] until 1842 when he became pastor of the First Baptist Church in Newton Center, Massachusetts, and editor of the *Christian Review.* He returned to Waterville to speak in 1863, sharing the platform with Ralph Waldo Emerson at the annual gathering of the Erosophian Adelphi literary fraternity. The *Waterville Mail* reviewed the speeches of both the orator and the poet. Emerson got the worst of it: "[his] epigrammatic style of writing is no more peculiar than his oratory." And, the paper said, Smith's poem "had one great merit—brevity." Emerson got the last word. He

3. Initially Smith wrote five verses, but he never published the middle stanza as it was sharply anti-British: "No more shall tyrants here, With haughty steps appear, And soldier-bands: No more shall tyrants tread, Above the patriot dead, No more our blood be shed, By alien hands." The melody today forms the British national anthem, "God Save the King."

4. Katherine Lee Bates, who wrote "America the Beautiful," was born in a Ten Lots farmhouse less than a mile from Smith's church.

later told a reporter he found his Waterville audience "cool, silent and unresponsive."

Increased local instruction in French may have helped melt the differences of the two cultures, but the English still dominated. The College, while open to all, was training a few teachers and many Baptist men of the cloth. The Catholics, who one day would provide many of those who saved Colby for Waterville, sent their college-going sons and daughters elsewhere. The old streets kept their English names,[5] and the old-line inhabitants encouraged and embraced the Anglicizing of French family names: Roys became Kings; Levesques, Bishops; Coutures, Taylors; and Vashons, Cowans.

Many thought it would be useful if the French changed their religion as well. Charles Hathaway was one. Stern and devout, Hathaway was an annoying man, pestering friends and neighbors with religious tracts, and making endless trouble for the leaders of his Baptist church. He viewed The Plains as a ripe mission site and for a dozen years proselytized the strong Catholics there, finally seeing to the establishment of Waterville's Second Baptist Church in their very midst.

Hathaway had begun his working life as an employee of his uncle at a small shirt factory in Plymouth, Massachusetts. He found the work dull and soon left to become a printer, first in Massachusetts for E. Merriam and Company of dictionary fame and, for less than a month in 1847, in Waterville as publisher of *The Union*, on the Hanscom Block at the corner of Main and Elm. The newspaper carried barely any news at all. It was packed with Hathaway's favorite sermons, and few would buy it. He quickly sold the paper for $475 to Ephraim Maxim who named it the *Eastern Mail*. Maxim's paper carried local news and was a success.[6]

Hathaway had come to Waterville to take a wife (with the fortuitous name of Temperance); and when he abandoned the news business, the couple moved to Watertown, Massachusetts, where in 1849 he opened his own shirt factory. It was the same year the first trains came into Waterville, and the freight-carrying opportunity may have induced him to return to Maine. Three years later, with his younger brother George as a one-third, silent partner, he purchased an acre of land near the train station from Sam Appleton and built C. F. Hathaway & Company.

5. In the next century, as new residential neighborhoods expanded both in Waterville and in the mother town of Winslow, the French tipped the scales with more street names of their own.

6. It is the newspaper to which today's local *Sentinel* can be traced.

The shirtmaker with the Old Testament face lived in mortal fear, not only of the devil but also of his business competitors. His employees began ten-hour workdays with a required session of prayer; when he hired his talented cutters and makers, he forced them to sign "non-compete" agreements so he would not lose them. If a retail store made an exclusive contract with another maker, he took out newspaper ads inviting customers to swap their silver dollars for his gold ones if they traded with him. To the lasting glory of his company, he quickly learned that the prize would go to the one who made the best shirts, a credo his successors were bound to live by.

ELIJAH PARISH LOVEJOY

The issues that sparked the Civil War smoldered for decades before the 1861 siege of Fort Sumter. The northern fervor against slavery grew steadily through those years, even in remote Waterville. Elijah Lovejoy took the germ of it with him when he graduated in 1826.

Elijah was born November 9, 1802, in a simple home in Freetown Plantation on the shore of a pond named for his grandfather, Francis Lovejoy. The eldest son of the Reverend Daniel and Elizabeth Pattee Lovejoy, he got his name from the local Congregational minister, the Reverend Elijah Parish, who had tutored his father in staunch Calvinist theology. Daniel combined teaching and farming to eke out a bare existence for his family.[7] The family was poor, but the house was abundant in the instruction of the evils of humanity.

Lovejoy was home-schooled until he was eighteen, and although he showed much promise, there was no money for more learning. In 1821 he dared to write Maine's new governor, William King, asking for tuition money. "Who knows, Honorable Sir," he wrote, "you may assist one in coming forward who shall take a part in the political theater of the age." King ignored him, but in the spring of 1822 the Reverend Benjamin Tapin of the South Parish Congregational Church in Augusta found a way to send him to Monmouth Academy. That fall Elijah transferred to the nearer China Academy where a young Waterville College

---

7. Daniel suffered from depression and eventually hanged himself in the family barn. Strict church elders ordered that he be buried beneath the Albion-China crossroads. The constant rumbling of carts over his head, they said, would keep him from finding peace, fair punishment for the unpardonable sin of taking his own life. Years later they agreed he had suffered enough and allowed his body to be exhumed and taken to the nearby family cemetery.

graduate, Henry Stanwood, was principal. Stanwood encouraged Elijah to study with Jeremiah Chaplin. Lovejoy entered Waterville College as a sophomore and within a year was put in charge of the College's Latin preparatory school, precursor of Waterville Academy (later Coburn). He graduated at the top of his class in 1826. Chaplin said he was "very near to the rank of those distinguished men who have been honored by the title of universal genius."

Lovejoy did not stay long in Maine, spending less than a year as principal of his own China Academy before moving west to teach in Saint Louis, finding theological comfort and conversion at the First Presbyterian Church. He soon enrolled in its prominent theological school at Princeton. He completed his studies in 1833, and was offered editorship of the church's new weekly, the *St. Louis Observer*, the first religious newspaper west of the Mississippi. He reveled in his second vocation, and made his editorial purpose clear in the very first edition: "While the *Observer* will seek to win its way to the hearts and consciences of men by the kindness of the sentiment it breathes, it will not temporize as it goes," he wrote. His readers were forewarned.

The proponents of slavery were not the only ones who felt the prick of his sharp pen. Like other Protestant leaders of the day, he railed against Rome and the pope, but it was easier for the Catholics of Saint Louis to forgive his ranting against "popery" than to abide his unrelenting stand against slavery. In 1835 patrons of the church asked him to stop writing about slavery altogether. He replied:

> I will submit to no such dictation. If I back down, they will strike again. Today a public meeting declares you shall not discuss the subject of slavery in any of its bearings, civil or religious. Tomorrow another meeting decided that it is against the peace of society that religion be discussed and the edict goes for to muzzle the press. The next day another meeting and it goes to the end of the chapter and there are no freedoms left. The truth is, my fellow citizens, if you give ground a single inch, there is no stopping place. If the mob rules, then every man must protect himself with the muzzle of a gun. We must stand by the Constitution or all is lost.

He was endured in Saint Louis until the spring of 1836, when he roundly denounced the public lynching of a free Negro, Francis J. McIntosh, and the court's acquittal of the killers. Reaction to his condemnation was violent. Thugs came at night and destroyed his press. He fled up river to Alton, in the free state of Illinois, where he fared no better. His first Alton press arrived at the docks on the Sabbath and could not be moved. That night it was pushed into the water.

Some of Alton's citizens were outraged, and at a public meeting pledged to replace the ruined press, but their help came with the caveat that he must stop his endless call for freeing slaves. His harangue was hurting the business of shipping cotton. He ignored them, and his opposition to bondage hardened. Although he never claimed to be an abolitionist, his changing views were placing him ever closer to William Lloyd Garrison, whose call for abolition was stirring things in the east. When Lovejoy's third press arrived, he spoke out in his renamed newspaper, the *Alton Observer:*

> The groans and sighs and tears of the poor slave have gone up as a memorial before the throne of God. In due time they will descend in awful curses upon this land unless averted by the speedy repentance of us all. And as surely as there is a thunderbolt in Heaven and strength in God's right hand to launch it, so surely will it strike the authors of this cruel oppression. Slavery is a sin. It must be abolished.

Soon after he stood in a public meeting to respond to a citizens' resolution calling for him to stop.

> If I have been guilty of no violation of law, why am I hunted up and down continually like a partridge in the mountains? Why am I threatened with the tar-barrel? Why am I waylaid every day, and from night to night, and my life in jeopardy every hour?

Tension and conflict escalated on the Fourth of July when Lovejoy used the occasion of the nation's sixty-first birthday to print a notice inviting the people of Alton to form a chapter of the American Anti-Slavery Society. A month later, in the dark of night his print shop was wrecked again, and his despisers multiplied. Shortly before his final stand in November 1837 he spoke at a noisy public meeting: "You may hang me, you may burn me at the stake as you did McIntosh in St. Louis, but you cannot silence me. . . . The contest has commenced here and here it must be finished, if need be until death. . . . If the civil authorities refuse to protect me, I must look to God; and if I die, I have determined to make my grave in Alton."

The new press came by steamboat to Saint Louis and was taken twenty-five miles up and across the Mississippi to Alton. It arrived at three in the morning at a secret place south of town. Its defenders were assembled on the riverbank to help bring it ashore; but there were Lovejoy haters there as well, and they watched as horse and wagon took it to Winthrop Gilman's stone warehouse near the riverbank.

Through the long day and night Lovejoy and his allies watched from the windows, rifles at hand. On the morning of the seventh, fuming crowds began to gather in town, on street corners, and in taverns, plotting against the editor. Angry residents were going to wreck his press again, and this time they might get rid of him as well. At the Tontine Saloon, lawyer William Carr raised his whiskey glass to the good old boys who would follow him to the warehouse and ordered a round for the house. By nightfall, they became a drunk and deadly mob, first throwing stones; then, as the moon cast an eerie light on their warehouse target, firing their rifles. The defenders fought back. One member of the mob was mortally wounded, and for a time his compatriots withdrew, firing from a safe distance. In the nearby town the reverberating noise of distant gunfire frightened the Presbyterian minister's wife, and she climbed to the belfry and rang the bell to sound an alarm. The mayor, John Krum, went to the warehouse door, waving a white flag, pleading with the occupants to give up the press and save their necks. Lovejoy would hear none of it. By midnight the rioters were lighting torches. Someone carried a flare up a ladder and set the roof ablaze.

No one knew why Lovejoy went to the door, but as he stepped outside, his frame made a clear silhouette against the moonlit sky. Shots rang out. Three musket balls entered his chest, another his stomach, and yet another in the flesh of his left arm. He managed to make his way back inside and up a set of stairs to a small room where he was placed on a cot. Within moments he was dead.

Someone from inside shouted the news that Lovejoy had been killed, but the milling crowd refused to leave, threatening to kill the rest. The defenders ran out the back way and into the night, leaving Lovejoy's body behind. Some of the mob entered the building, carried the press to a window, and pushed it out onto the riverbank where it was smashed and the broken pieces hurled into the river.

All that night Lovejoy's friends were afraid to retrieve his body, but at first light a lone black freeman, William Scotch Johnston, went to get him. The next morning, November 9, Elijah's thirty-fifth birthday, a small cortège made its way through town drawing cruel shouts from onlookers. Only a few were present at the grave where they buried him in the nearby hills, and they vowed to keep the place a secret. Lovejoy's widow, Celia, was too grief-stricken to attend. She had been married only two years and was left with their infant son, Edward Payson, and a second child, still in her womb. Johnston was there. He had made the wooden casket and decorated it with the stain of pokeberry juice. He wept as he helped lower the body into the ground.

Word of Lovejoy's death stunned the fracturing nation. The *Boston Re-*

corder said the murder called forth "a burst of indignation which has not had its parallel in this country since the battle of Lexington." Abraham Lincoln said Lovejoy's killing was "the most important event that ever has taken place in the western world." President John Quincy Adams later recalled the day of the tragedy and likened the impact of the news to an earthquake. Ralph Waldo Emerson said "the brave Lovejoy gave his breast to the bullets of a mob for the rights of free speech and opinion, and died when it was better not to live."

A month after the killing, John Brown attended a Lovejoy memorial service in Hudson, Ohio. At the end of the program Brown stood and vowed to dedicate his life to Lovejoy's memory and to the elimination of slavery. Twenty-two years later, nearly to the day, he too became a martyr, hung for his daring raid at Harper's Ferry. On the way to the gallows he predicted, as Lovejoy had, that "the crimes of this guilty land will never be purged away but with blood."

In 1862, the year Lincoln issued the Emancipation Proclamation, Elijah's brother Owen came to Alton as an Illinois congressman. He was Lincoln's friend and had pressed for the executive order freeing the slaves. Some said Owen was the architect of the proclamation. He spoke for two hours and did not mention his brother until the end. "The blood of my brother flowed down these streets and mingled with the great river that flows to the sea," he told the somber crowd. "And, yea, shall so much more blood flow, 'til we achieve the dream of liberty."

Some would later say the deadly fight at Alton was the first armed battle of the Civil War.

CIVIL WAR

The greatest peril for the early American colleges came at the moments of war, when the nation was riveted on its survival and young people were called away to fight. The men of Waterville and its college served gallantly in the Civil War, but when it was over and the nation preserved, the tiny College found itself with few students to pay the bills, and its endowment, savaged by withdrawals, nearly depleted. The town itself was reeling and could do little to help. Just as the College considered whether to build a war memorial or close its doors, the answer came from an unlikely savior. The intercession of Gardner Colby was a mix of fate, religious philanthropy, and a strong dose of nostalgia.

In 1833 the College literary fraternity debated the question "Ought Congress to interfere in the abolition of Slavery?" The answer was resoundingly affirmative. That summer abolitionist William Lloyd Garrison came to speak; and students were stirred to action. On the afternoon of the Fourth of July they created the Anti-Slavery Society of Waterville College. The making of a society with such high moral purpose seemed sufficient reason enough to whoop it up, and whether students drank their toasts with water or smuggled wine no one knew, but everyone agreed a good deal of noise bounced off The Bricks that night. President Chaplin was outraged. In chapel the next morning, he said they had sounded like "the braying of wild asses." Indignant students demanded an apology. When Chaplin refused, the students walked out. The unmoved president followed with a broadside in which he threatened stern discipline. Students appealed to the faculty claiming their "character as professors of religion [to be] was injured." It was too much for Chaplin, and he resigned. Following a trustee inquiry, the College's first president was given high praise and a parting gift of one thousand dollars.

Six years before the war began, a fugitive slave named Anthony Burns was captured by Boston militia and returned to bondage. In Waterville, citizens posted a notice calling for a public meeting to see if the people "will have the bells tolled in token of their sympathy [for Burns] and also take any other measures in regard to the case." Among the protestors were the College's president, James Champlin; Joshua Drummond '46, soon to be speaker of the Maine House of Representatives; and, in the last year of his life, Timothy Boutelle, College treasurer. Church bells rang for an hour.

Local leanings against slavery were evident in other ways as well. Five months before the war, the town cast its votes for presidential electors: 504 for Abraham Lincoln, 186 for three other candidates. Local support for Lincoln was bolstered by the excitement over his Maine vice presidential running mate, Hannibal Hamlin. In late February 1861, Hamlin passed through the Waterville station on the way to the March 4 inauguration ceremonies in Washington. The College students greeted him, and "gave some vent to their enthusiasm by vigorously applauding the short, but patriotic, address."

When news came that Fort Sumter had fallen, students quickly formed their own cadre and began to drill along campus walkways. On April 18, senior Frank Hesseltine stood on the steps of Recitation Hall and yelled: "President Lincoln has called for 75,000 volunteers to save the nation. I am going to be one of them. Who else?" The following morning a recruiting office opened upstairs in the Hanscom block, where Hathaway had tried to run a newspaper. Charles Henrickson '64 was the first to enlist. Soon after, Waterville's Heath brothers, William and Francis, opened a second office in the Plaisted Block on Main Street. Some forty students, a third of the student body, joined with some eighty local volunteers to form a company that on its first drill marched to Appleton Street where Charles Hathaway gave them each a fine French flannel shirt.

It was evident to President Champlin that he would soon have no students, and at a hastily called assembly in the chapel he announced the spring term was over. On May 21 the recruits made their way to Portland where most of them helped to form Companies G and H of the Third Maine Volunteers. With little training, the two companies met their first test in the battle at Bull Run in July. The eager Hendrickson was captured and spent nearly a year in Libby and Salisbury prisons.

Six Waterville College men served in the famed Twentieth Maine Regiment under Bowdoin's honored general Joshua Chamberlain. Among them were Richard Cutts Shannon '62 and Henry Clay Merriam '64. Shannon enlisted as a sergeant in the Fifth Maine Volunteers, and was captured at the May battle at Chancellorsville. He was exchanged from Libby Prison in Richmond in time to fight at Gettysburg. Merriam enlisted at home, in Houlton, Maine, in 1862, at the end of his sophomore year, when most of his classmates had already gone to war. Joining Chamberlain's regiment, Merriam was captain of Company H, a new outfit mustered barely in time to fight the September battle at Antietam.

That month Lincoln issued the Emancipation Proclamation, and soon after met with Daniel Ullman, a Union officer who had pressed the president to allow the enlistment of the soon-to-be-freed slaves. Lincoln hesitated, then agreed, and sent Ullmann to Secretary of War Edwin Stanton for help in organizing five black volunteer regiments for Louisiana. Ullman took Vice President Hamlin to the meeting with him; afterward Hamlin turned to his friend and fellow Waterville College trustee, Governor Abner Coburn, for help in scouring the Maine regiments for officers willing to lead black troops. One of those nominated by Coburn was Captain Merriam of the Twentieth Maine, who left Chamberlain's campaign six months before the battle at Gettysburg to take command of the Third Colored Infantry in Louisiana. On April 9, 1865, only hours before Robert E. Lee's surrender in faraway Virginia, Lieutenant Colonel Merriam's regiment, renamed the Seventy-third Infantry Corps d'Afrique, was the first to plant its colors on the parapet of Fort Blakeley in the siege of Mobile, Alabama. Merriam led the charge of one thousand black troops, and for his "conspicuous gallantry" was awarded the Congressional Medal of Honor. It was the last great battle of the Civil War.[8]

8. Merriam went on to make a full military career, fighting the Indians in the American west and leading troops again in the Spanish-American War at the end of the century. He retired a major general in 1903 and died in Portland nine years later.

Except in the annals of military history, Merriam's contributions brought no public fame. The opposite was true for another Waterville College graduate, twenty-five years his senior. Benjamin Butler '38, was half soldier, half politician, and entirely flamboyant. Butler and Lovejoy were, far and away, the College's most famous alumni. Unlike Lovejoy, Butler sought acclaim. Although his reputation as a hell-raising college student was greatly exaggerated, he was indeed troublesome and enjoyed being known as brash. It brought him more votes, and he was always looking for votes. In his autobiography, written sixty years after his graduation, he told of fantastic exploits at Waterville College. He claimed to have asked to be excused from daily chapel on grounds his chances of being saved were so slim that preaching to him was a waste of time. He said he tied up the clapper of the College bell to keep it from calling students to chapel and, as pranks, stole all sorts of things, including pigs, chickens, and the College gate. It is unlikely any of it was true. Faculty records from that time when miscreants rarely escaped detection turned up no evidence of misconduct on the part of young Butler. It seems instead that he, like students before and since, could not resist embellishing college exploits in the comfortable distance of time.

Butler came to Waterville after being turned down for an appointment at West Point. He was beginning his senior year when Lovejoy was murdered. Word of the martyrdom fueled antislavery sentiment in the north, especially in young Butler who within twenty years was in a position to do something about it, using his bully pulpit to support the rights of former slaves, create black Union regiments, and press the Confederate army to recognize the military status of captured black soldiers.

A criminal lawyer and a Democrat, Butler served terms in both the Massachusetts House and Senate, and in 1859 lost a bid for governor. It was his strong support of the Union and not his party affiliation that finally got him the military appointment he wanted. Abraham Lincoln made him a brigadier general, and the Democrat Butler quickly became an untouchable maverick in a largely Republican-led army. Within days he mustered a regiment and, without a fight, led them through a blockade to capture proslavery Baltimore.

When New Orleans fell, Butler was sent as commander of the occupying forces and promptly got into trouble. In April 1862 he issued the infamous General Order 28, the "Women's Order," stipulating that southern women who insulted his troops would be treated as prostitutes. It caused an uproar on both sides of the conflict. Confederate President Jefferson Davis said Butler was an "outlaw" and would be hanged if they could catch him. Union allies abroad were incensed as well. By fall the criticism of Butler for his affront had not abated, and he was replaced as commander in New Orleans and sent to lead the troops in Virginia and North Carolina and, eventually, to deal with election riots in New York City.

Through his colorful military career Butler collected an array of nicknames, none of them complimentary. For his stern treatment of the citizens of New Orleans, including the hanging of a Confederate soldier who pulled down the federal flag, he was called "The Beast." His infamous "Women's Order" earned him an added sobriquet, "The Brute," and his alleged penchant for confiscating the silverware from New Orleans' gentry got him the nickname "Spoons." Although most historians later called him a brilliant military strategist, Commanding General Ulysses Grant thought Butler's troops too often got themselves trapped. For that, the general earned Grant's title as "Bottled Up Butler."

When Lincoln faced reelection in 1864, the Republican party rejected his Maine vice president and Lincoln sent an emissary to General Butler to see if he was interested. Butler sent an eerie and prophetic reply: "Ask him what he thinks I have done to deserve to be punished at 46 years of age by being made to sit as presiding officer of the Senate and listen for four years to debates more or less stupid in which I could take no part or say a word, or even be allowed to vote. Tell him that I said laughingly that with the prospects of a campaign before us, I would not quit the battlefield to be vice president even with himself as president, unless he would give me bond in sureties in the full sum of his four year's salary that within three months of his inauguration he will die unresigned." The party settled on Andrew Johnson, and Lincoln was assassinated within a month of his second inauguration.

Butler retired from the army in 1864, returned to Massachusetts, converted to Republicanism, and was elected to Congress where he led the impeachment of the new president.[9]

9. Butler's appetite for politics was insatiable. He ran for Governor of Massachusetts no fewer than six times, finally getting himself elected in 1882. His political career ended two years later when he garnered only 2 percent of the popular vote in a bid for the presidency under the flags of the Greenback-Labor and Anti-Monopoly parties. In 1889, at age seventy-one, Butler returned to Waterville to address an alumni gathering, when he made the somewhat astonishing proposal for a "Union of the English Speaking Peoples" by the creation of a political alliance among the United States, Canada, and Great Britain. He was, among many other things, a most unpredictable man.

At war's end, Butler's name stood high on the list of national heroes—Waterville's answer to Brunswick's Chamberlain—but there were other, albeit unsung, heroes as well. At least two Waterville College men served aboard the ironclads: Robinson Turner on the Confederate *Merrimac* and Cushman Hendrickson on the Union *Monitor*. Twenty-six students, well more than half of those who left the College to fight, died for the Union cause. Lorenzo Smith '50, a Vermonter caught in the southern draft while teaching in Arkansas, gave his life for the Confederacy. More than one hundred men of the town were killed as well.

A SAVIOR

Despite the ruinous war, there were some, like Butler, who became famous, and there were others whose fortunes grew. Gardner Colby was neither famous nor a profiteer, but the war had made him rich.

Born in Bowdoinham in 1810, Gardner was the son of a sea captain, Josiah, who died in despair two years after losing his fortune in the War of 1812. Gardner's mother, Sarah, a widow at twenty-five, brought her four young children to Waterville where she sought work. At age ten Gardner took a job at a Silver Street potash plant to help support the struggling family, now befriended by Jeremiah Chaplin, pastor and leader of the new local institute.

Colby was in the crowd of local citizens who gathered to celebrate the dedication of the South College building, the first of The Bricks, in 1821. The evening observance was marked by an "illumination" with tallow candles lit behind each of the thirty-two panes of glass on two sides of the building. Set against the dark backdrop of the forest, it was an unforgettable sight, especially for the young Colby. He remembered it all of his life.

When the family could not make ends meet in Waterville, Sarah was forced to place her children separately with local families and to move by herself to Charlestown, near Boston, where she began a small business. Gardner was sent to live in the Maine town of Saint Albans for a year before rejoining his mother. In Boston, Gardner took his first job as a grocery delivery boy and then became a dry goods clerk. In 1831 he opened his own business, selling women's fashions: lace, gloves, and hosiery. Hardworking and scrupulous, the unschooled Gardner became a success, expanding his business, first to wholesaling, then importing, and finally as a manufacturer of woolen fabric. It was the wool that made him rich. The federal government bought as much as he could make, to outfit the Union army.

On a winter Sunday morning in 1864 Colby and his wife, Mary, were in their usual pew in the Newton Center Baptist Meeting House. Samuel B. Swaim was the preacher. In his sermon Swaim recounted a chance meeting with Jeremiah Chaplin in Portland, forty years before. Chaplin had come from a meeting with a wealthy man who had rebuffed his appeal to help the College, and he was depressed. Over and over he moaned to Swaim: "God save Waterville College! Waterville College must not perish!" Swaim's retelling of the story, coupled with the lasting image of the long-ago "illumination" of South College, burned in Colby's mind. The next day he told his wife he wished to make a gift to save Waterville College.

That August Colby was guest speaker at the Waterville College commencement dinner in the town hall. Champlin was the only one who knew why Colby had come. Without embellishment, Colby stood and read the terms of his agreement. He would give an endowment of $50,000 if the College raised $100,000 on its own. The audience sat in stunned silence and then erupted into wild cheering and stomping. Waterville College was not going to perish after all. Matching money was raised in two years. Colby was invited to join the College's board of trustees, and served until his death in 1879, by which time his gifts, including bequests, topped $200,000. In 1866, filled with gratitude and flush with the promise of a magnificent endowment, trustees at last were able to name the College for a benefactor. By act of the Maine Legislature, on January 23, 1867, Waterville College became Colby University.

The original Colby gift made the once-struggling institution much more secure. Receipts in 1866 exceeded the year's budget by some two thousand dollars, and it was agreed Colby would be the first college in the north to honor its war dead with a building. In the late summer of 1866, barely a year after the surrender and two years before the first Memorial Day, trustees agreed to construct Memorial Hall. The money came from a budget surplus and from the sale of timber and stumpage rights on the Penobscot County land held from the original grant. Gardner Colby added the largest amount ($4,100) and within a year $26,000 was in hand.

The chosen location was the site of the College's original building, the wood-frame house built for Jeremiah Chaplin. President Champlin spoke at the cornerstone ceremony in August 1867, citing the great need for classrooms that for thirty years had been in the often-flooded basement of Recitation Hall. (It was unthinkable to trade space with the dry chapel upstairs.) New classrooms were to be made in space vacated by the chapel, which was moved again, this time to the first floor of the west wing of the new building. The second floor became an alumni hall for special gatherings. The smaller east wing was the new library.

Designed by Alexander Esty of Boston, Memorial Hall was made of rubblestone quarried a mile west of the campus. Woodwork in the elegantly paneled interior was by a local carpenter, J. P. Blunt. The building was dedicated at commencement, 1869, at ceremonies held outdoors, beneath the imposing belfry tower, home to a finicky winding clock. One of the dignitaries who passed the building key along the platform to Champlin was the chairman of the board, former vice president and now U.S. Senator Hannibal Hamlin of the highlands in Hamden.

It was another distinguished Hamlin, Charles '47 of the College faculty, who spurred efforts to have as the building's centerpiece a copy of *The Lion of Lucerne* by the Danish sculptor Bertel Thorvaldsen. A marble tablet memorializing the names of fallen alumni was part of the original design for the Seaverns Room in the library. Hamlin thought the plaque by itself was uninspiring. The original lion, carved on a hillside at Lucerne, honored Swiss guards killed in 1792 defending Louis XVI in Paris. Henry Burrage, pastor of the Baptist Church and a College trustee, saw it and suggested to Hamlin that Memorial Hall have a replica. Martin Milmore was commissioned to make the piece—eight feet long and thirty-nine inches high, weighing four tons—in time for its separate dedication at Commencement two years later. Milmore's rendition differed from Thorvaldsen's only in size and in the insertion of the U.S. shield for that of France's beneath the dying lion's head.[10]

Even before the war was over, the town of Waterville had begun to raise funds for its own memorial. The Soldiers' Monument Association assessed dues (one dollar for men, fifty cents for women) and the town appropriated one thousand dollars and an equal amount for a war memorial building in West Waterville. The old burial ground on Elm Street fronting Waterville Classical Institute was public land, and in 1865, with most of the graves removed, the town agreed to name it Monument Park and have the new sculpture as its centerpiece. Like the College, the association called on Milmore and selected a bronze casting of his popular Citizen Soldier, copies of which soon proliferated in towns throughout the north.[11]

---

10. Charles Hamlin was a much-admired Colby professor of chemistry and natural history and later curator of paleontology at Harvard. As a promoter of the war memorial, his credentials as a patriot were unquestioned. Twenty years before, he and a classmate had been temporarily suspended for making "a great disturbance during recitation hours" in observance of the Fourth of July.

11. Waterville's monument, honoring fallen solders from town and from the renamed College, was dedicated on Memorial Day, 1876.

The power of the great river took Waterville into the Industrial Revolution fifty years before the era even had a name. As the nineteenth century drew to a close, commerce shifted away from a declining big lumber industry to the promising future of manufacturing and its accompanying expansion of retail trade. The town, exploding with new immigrants, became a city, and the University branched out to find new students by establishing preparatory "fitting schools" and opening its doors to women.

In the early 1790s Vassalboro farmer Nehemiah Getchell and his son-in-law, Asa Redington, let it known they planned to power a sawmill by putting a dam into the ferocious Kennebec. Neighbors thought they had lost their senses, but in 1794, when the short dam from the west bank to Leeman Island was completed and their mill was built, the tiny settlement found the independence to separate from Winslow and leapfrog closer to the front of the line among the most promising communities in the District of Maine.

Seventy-six years later, George Phillips bought shore and power rights from some fifty owners on both banks and formed the Ticonic Water Power and Manufacturing Company. Their dam crossed the entire river, and when it was done its investors were nearly bankrupt. Reuben Dunn '67, maker of scythes and axes in West Waterville, bailed out the struggling company and held on until 1873, when Amos Lockwood came to save the shareholders. Lockwood, a well-known developer of textile manufacturing, paid the debtors and proceeded to build a cotton mill with 33,000 spindles. In nine years the Lockwood Company built a second, larger mill (55,000 spindles) below the falls. By the turn of the century more than 1,300 of the town's 10,000 souls were engaged in making cloth.

The dam and the mill brought its own river of new enterprise. The smattering of manufacturing, begun years before at the cascades on Emerson Stream, quickly expanded, and new mills began to operate east along the smaller waterway and up and down the river. Early mills had sawed logs and ground grain; now waterpower was used to card wool and make chairs, bedposts, wagon hubs, friction matches, toothpicks, shovel handles, and more.

Established merchants saw profits grow. Jacob Peavy of Prussia, a maker and seller of men's clothing, soon had houses in Boston and New York. Brothers Arthur and Charles Alden (descendents of Pilgrims John and Priscilla) began selling clocks and watches in 1854. The German-born Gallert brothers, Mark and David, opened a boot and shoe business in 1862. E. D. Noyes was selling cast-iron cookstoves from his foundry on Chaplin Street in 1867, and the following year blacksmith Levi Boothby joined with his son Frederick to sell insurance. The Waterville Savings Bank opened its doors in 1869 with Christian Knauff, a German dry goods merchant, as a founding director. Frederick Pooler of Saint George, Canada, opened a thriving grocery business in the south of town.

By the 1870s Waterville had outgrown West Waterville. Squabbles and competition over future development led to a petition for division, approved at a town meeting by a vote of 227 to 130. The Maine legislature granted the request February 26, 1873, and the divorce was final. West Waterville carried her original name for ten years before changing it to Oakland on March 10, 1883, the same year that the Cascade Woolen Mill, soon to be a major employer with more than one hundred hands, was incorporated.

The boom served to bolster the University as well. President Champlin spoke at the celebration of its 1870 semicentennial and declared Colby "fairly founded." But, he said, merely having the money to sustain things was not enough. "To stand still in such an age and country as this is tantamount to going backward," he said, seizing the moment to build even more. For two years the University had offered a Bachelor of Science degree without an adequate science facility, and Champlin urged trustees to remedy the situation at once. The next morning Gardner Colby and Maine governor Abner Coburn led other trustees in pledging enough to pay for the new building. It was given Coburn's name. Adding to the luster of that day was a trustee vote to increase faculty salaries by a whopping 25 percent. Things were going very well indeed.

Despite the successes, the enrollment needed a boost, and the following year, on August 1, 1871, the board appointed a committee to recommend action on a proposed resolution: "That the advantages of the course of studies pursued in this university be open to young women on the same terms of admission as to young men." Led by Champlin, the appointed group reported an affirmative recommendation that very afternoon, and it was swiftly adopted. When the new freshmen arrived the following month, a bright local woman was among them. Mary Caffrey Low had matriculated at the Classical Institute in town. In scholarly promise she was more than a match for her classmates. Two future Maine Supreme Court justices, Leslie Cornish and Henry Hudson, were among her Colby classmates. She beat out Cornish for valedictorian honors in 1875, and men began to call her admission "the mistake of '71."

Issues of fairness and equality may have had something to do with the step to coeducation (the first among all the former men's colleges in New England),[12] but the case was also helped by the need to increase revenues. Neither did it hurt the women's cause that the governor's niece, Louise Coburn, was next in line as a female candidate. She joined three other women in the class that entered in 1873.

Four lone women did not do much to improve the enrollment, and that year, the last of his presidency, Champlin again teamed with Coburn, this time to affiliate the University with a Maine fitting school or two, so as to ensure a steady annual stream of students. First, the struggling preparatory schools needed propping up. Champlin, who admired the tiny Classical Institute in Waterville, suggested to the Maine Baptist Education Society in Gray that the school be given a $50,000 endowment. Governor Coburn was the perfect choice to head a trustee committee charged with considering the matter, and it soon reported that Coburn himself would give the money on condition the same amount be raised for two additional fitting schools to be tied to the University. The Waterville Institute was named for Coburn, and supporters soon found the money to affiliate with Hebron and Houlton (Ricker) academies as well. Higgins Institute in Charleston was added later, creating a reliable system, which may have saved Colby again. Whether it did or not, it is certain that the infusion of new money and the assurance of college placement for their graduates saved the struggling academies.

The College's first black graduate, Adam Simpson Green, took his degree in 1887. Green, like many of his classmates, went on to a career in the ministry. He was nearly alone as a black man in a very white town. Another was Samuel Osborne, a former slave brought to Waterville from Virginia in 1865 by a young Colby graduate, Colonel Stephen Fletcher '59. Osborne arrived with two young children and later, under the auspices of the Baptist Church, was able to bring his father, his wife, and their baby child as well. Osborne's father worked as a janitor at the college. When he died, Samuel took his place and remained a Colby fixture for nearly forty years. In the case of Osborne, the Colby literature is replete with stories giving evidence to the sad fact that while he and his family were well treated by many at the College and within his adopted church, he was also often demeaned and ridiculed. Students were especially harsh, mocking his manner of speech and imitating his plain though insightful homilies. He was a kind and decent man, and endured the taunting with grace.

Racial integration, if uncomfortable for some, was on the whole unremarkable, in large measure because of the small number of black students

12. Colby's Maine sister college, Bates, was coeducational from the time of its abolitionist founding in 1855.

who enrolled. It was the joining of the sexes that raised the most eyebrows. Colby's official equal status of women continued only until 1890, when growing uneasiness over the academic dominance of women students—in the admissions process and in the classrooms—encouraged trustees to abandon the coeducational designation and create what would be called, though never fully achieved, a coordinate university.

Although Colby was unusual in having retreated from coeducation to coordination, in the late nineteenth and early twentieth centuries a number of institutions chose coordination as a means of bolstering enrollment without suffering the slings and arrows of their predominately male alumni bodies. Harvard had Radcliffe as early as 1879, Tulane opened Newcomb in 1886, followed by Barnard for Columbia (1889), and Pembroke for Brown (1891). Kenyon opened a coordinate college for women as late as 1965, but like Colby, declined to give it a separate name. At Colby and generally elsewhere, the systems became outdated and the distinctions all but vanished long before they were officially abolished.

Waterville's first twenty-seven electric streetlamps were turned on in 1874, illuminating shops along downtown streets. One of the first three buildings to be "electrified" was the W. B. Arnold Company, a hardware store at 109 Main. Arnold, who in 1876 bought out his only partner, Nathaniel Meader '63, wore many hats, and in the fashion of his descendants and namesakes was a leader in community service. Among his many gifts were books to begin a public library.[13]

A telephone line was soon open to Portland and within a few years the rapidly growing Maine Central Railroad began looking for a site for locomotive and car shops. Portland wanted them, but Waterville officials promised a twenty-year property tax exemption and won them over. As a further enticement, citizens joined in a gift of land adjoining the tracks—and very near the campus.

With all its growth, Waterville finally convinced itself to become a city. The legislature had offered city status as early as 1883, but citizens voted 344 to 223 to turn it down. After a bit of tinkering with the proposed charter and a good deal more discussion, in March 1887 voters finally agreed. The legislature made it official on January 23, 1888.

That spring, an outbreak of typhoid fever prompted construction of the first of many new trappings of a modern city. Frank Johnson, who would one

13. Andrew Carnegie completed Arnold's job in 1902 with a donation of $20,000 for a new free library on Elm Street.

day become the College president, recalled working his freshman winter of 1887–88, stoking the wood fires and lugging buckets of water from the "college pump" to his South College residence. In the summer the well was abandoned and the spigots of a new municipal water system, taking water from Messalonskee Stream, were turned on. The College was at the head of the line among the new customers of the Maine Water Company.

The stream was polluted with sewage from both Waterville and Oakland, and the typhoid outbreaks continued. Forty local people died during an epidemic in 1902–1903, and Dr. J. F. Hill '81 urged the construction of an entirely new water system. Local attorney Harvey Doane Eaton '87 had conceived the idea of multitown service districts, approved by the Maine legislature in 1899. The Kennebec Water District, established in 1904, was soon emulated throughout the country. It was Eaton who also suggested tapping the clean water of nearby China Lake. An 8.5-mile trench was dug and the long pipe was laid in the winter of 1904–1905. The project cost was $25,000.

At the close of the decade Charles Redington (grandson of the first dam builder, Asa) and his son Frank opened a furniture store on Silver Street and, with ready access to wooden caskets, became undertakers as well. On Western Avenue the Ursuline Sisters founded Mount Merici, an academy for girls (1889). Joseph Grondin was selling both stoves and furniture. William Levine, a Russian immigrant and itinerant clothing peddler, took his team and wagon off the road and opened a store at the corner of Ticonic and Maple streets (1891), where a small Jewish community was gathering. In ten years they built a synagogue, Beth Israel, and twenty years later Levine paid off the mortgage.

The first electric cars ran up and down from Fairfield in 1892, and the pulp and paper manufacturing giant Hollingsworth & Whitney began to build a new mill on the east bank of the river in Winslow. The biggest timber had already been taken from the north woods, but the paper mills at Madison and Winslow had an insatiable appetite for the smaller trees, rafted down the Kennebec each spring in great droves that covered the water from shore to shore.

A Waterville man, Alvin Lombard, made the wood move even faster. In 1901 he was granted a patent for a steam log hauler, as odd-looking as it was effective. With tracks that negotiated snow and stumpage, the Lombard tractor hauled sleds with as much as three hundred tons of pulp out of the woods and to the yards and rivers.[14] For a mile or more, the riverfront was filling up with industry. The Riverview Worsted Mill (later the Wyandotte) was built near the river north of Temple Street, and by 1900 employed some three hundred workers turning out top-of-the-line wool worsted men's clothing on eighty modern looms.

The new buildings, in town and on the campus, required millions of bricks, and they were locally made as well. The abundant clay and sand made brick making a small industry even before the river mills began. A new brickyard was opened below the Ticonic Bridge when the Lockwood mill was constructed; and another yard was later built on College Avenue, near Fairfield. Proctor & Flood had been making bricks on the avenue since 1892, and in about 1900, Proctor joined with Bowie to make more than a million bricks a year at a new plant on the corner by the bridge in Winslow.

With all of the new foot traffic between Waterville homes and the paper mill across the river, in 1899 the Ticonic Bridge Company commissioned Proctor & Bowie to make the piers for a short-cut pedestrian bridge at the foot of Temple Street. The 6 ft. by 576 ft. span was built on the ice in the winter of 1900–1901 and many locals watched doubtfully during the spring thaw, expecting it to be washed away. They were wrong by a year. It went downriver in the awful floods in the spring of 1902 and was rebuilt a year later at double the original price. To recover the cost, the charter of the bridge company allowed its owners to charge a two-cent toll, a fee structure that gave the bridge its name.

All of the riverfront development was good for the new city, then barely twenty years old. It was good for Colby too—except that on the campus things were getting a bit tight, especially for a place that called itself a university. When Colby made his naming gift, the title "university" was not unusual for a college without graduate study. Perhaps some thought that with its new riches it would, in fact, become a university. More likely it simply seemed a grander name, and it stuck for more than three decades until the institution, by then eighty-six years old, changed its name for the fourth and final time. Nathaniel Butler Jr. '73 arrived as Colby's twelfth president in 1896. He came directly from the University of Chicago, and he knew a university when he saw

14. The tractors slowly replaced oxen and horses; in time eighty-three of them were used in the woods of Maine, New Hampshire, and Canada. Later converted to gasoline power, they served until the early 1930s when diesel trucks replaced them. In the meantime, Lombard's invention was borrowed for the development of military tanks and bulldozers.

one. Colby was no university. He immediately pressed for a name change and on January 25, 1899, the Maine legislature obliged. Colby was again a college.

Whether a university or a college, the campus, tiny to begin with, was getting squeezed. The noise and smell of economic success were challenging the lectures of the faculty and the earnest concentration of students, and the once-pristine river was filling up with pulp. By the dawn of the twentieth century, the College found itself on an island: a growing business district to the south; a trolley line and railroad with its belching coal-fired steam engines to the west; ironworks and a locomotive shop and its clanging roundhouse switch to the north; and, looming across the river in the east, a wonderful new paper mill, stinking of sulfur.

COMING AND GOING

Despite the bustle, at the turn of the century the city was still an isolated place in the backwater of the nation. Trolleys connected the nearby farming villages of Oakland and Fairfield, and trains and newspapers were the only ties to the rest of the world. Horses drew sprinklers along tree-lined streets to quiet the dust in summer and rollers to pack snow in winter. College students found social life on Main Street, gathering at Kelly's bookstore and along the marble fountain at Hager's for 15¢ ice cream cones.[15] Silent movies were new and exciting. Without fanfare, Waterville's population slowly expanded in still another direction with the arrival of a community of citizens from southern Lebanon. Everything was in order. The future looked bright. Then, suddenly, the peace was gone.

The Lebanese called themselves Syrian. The newcomers were in fact from that region of Greater Syria that only later became part of Lebanon. Besides, Americans knew little of Lebanon, but they knew something of Syria. Like the French, the Lebanese came to find work and escape poverty. Unlike the French, they were running from tyranny as well. They were Maronite Catholics, from the Eastern Church, Christians for years in conflict with the Moslem Druze and then defeated and repressed by the Ottomans. Life for them became even more difficult when the Suez Canal opened in 1869 and traders passed them by. A national famine followed, and by 1900 more than

---

15. From recollections of Marjorie Meader Burns '14 (honorary M.A., 1948) who, under the name of Marjorie Mills, was a newswriter (*Boston Herald*, 1916–66) and radio commentator (New England Radio Network 1923–58), and whose many cookbooks remain popular classics.

100,000—fully a quarter of the population—left Greater Syria for the industrial cities of Europe and the United States.

Abraham Joseph had opened a dry goods store in Waterville as early as 1887, but most Lebanese came later to work in the mills, settling themselves north of The Plains, near the river along Front and Union Streets at a place called Head of Falls. The men came first. Hardworking and thrifty, they sent paychecks to their families until there was money enough for them to come and live together.

They organized a Maronite parish community (1927) and later built Saint Joseph's Church (1951), where masses were sung in Arabic. The church provided a great deal more than religious services, serving as a community center for the close-knit families and perpetuating their remarkable heritage. From the beginning the Lebanese, like the French, contributed a great deal to Waterville, not the least of which was the introduction of new foods—kibbie and koosa, falafel and laban, baklava, tabouleh and fatayer—dishes that soon altered the dietary preferences of the entire community. In later years, Sittu (grandmother) George opened a bakery on Union Street and, unless the humidity was high or the breeze hard to the west, the aroma of flat bread baking in her ovens mercifully subdued the sharp smell of sulfite wafting across the Kennebec.

Except for the divisions of religion, the eclectic community of French Roman Catholics, Lebanese Maronite Catholics, Russian Jews, and European Protestants of every flavor got along well, working shoulder to shoulder in the mills if not sharing schools, and mixing along the shops of Main Street if not in the neighborhoods of town. Many of them were sitting together with the College students in March 1917, when former President William Howard Taft spoke at the local Opera House. His message of patriotism and warnings of an inevitable war so stirred the editors of the *Echo* they promptly urged the formation of a campus military company. Its first drill was held April 4. Two days later Congress declared war on the imperial German government.

A resolution passed in chapel endorsed President Woodrow Wilson's action and pledged support "for the protection of our seamen and our people in the prosecution of their peaceful and legitimate errands on the high seas." By mid-May nearly a quarter of the men had enlisted and gone. The College opened late in the fall of 1917, in deference to farmers needing help in gathering crops. When the first semester began in October, two campus buildings were closed for lack of coal. By spring, half the men were in the service.

Over the summer of 1918 the conscription age was lowered from twenty-one to eighteen; when the College fall term began, again late, President Arthur Roberts announced military training would be compulsory for all of the now draft-eligible freshmen. In order to preserve the colleges while developing its armed forces, the government established the Student Army Training Corps (SATC). All fit male college students were put into military service and under military instruction. The men's division became a "war college." By government order the College divided the academic year into three sessions, including the summer, and the men were meant to receive the equivalent of a full college year in each of the three "semesters."

The Twelfth Cavalry was in charge. Its officers had headquarters in Chemical Hall. President Roberts no longer had much authority over the men's side of things, and would bide his time at the fieldhouse, watching the Colby Military Company drill. The chapel became a study hall and the gymnasium, a mess hall. Under order of the War Department, fraternities were suspended. "Considering that fraternity activity and military discipline are incompatible," the order read, "the Department deems it for the best interests of the Service that the operation of fraternities in institutions where units of SATC are established shall be suspended for the period of the present emergency." The YMCA took the Alpha Tau Omega (ATO) fraternity house and managed it, under military control, as a dormitory for soldiers.

Evan Shearman '22 (honorary D.D., 1972) later recounted life as a SATC member, mostly raking leaves, shining boots, cleaning his long Russian rifle, and drilling on the ballfield. Security was of first importance. Shearman told of one morning in the early fall of 1918 when Prexy Roberts appeared on the walkway in front of Chemical Hall, headed for his office. Thaddeus Tilton '20 was on guard duty and challenged him. "Who is there?" the young officer called out. "The president of the College," Roberts replied. "You may not enter," Tilton said, saying he had orders to admit no one to the campus but the milkman and the grocery man. Shearman wrote: "No protestation of the hearty head of the College, who had been accustomed to personally running his school in every detail, could shake Tilton or change his rifle from the port position. Nor would he call the corporal of the guard. And so the head of the college turned back toward his house, himself a victim of the war, made subordinate to a second lieutenant."

Harvey Eaton '87, director of the local exemption board, led the induction ceremonies for the entire corps in October. President Wilson sent a message reminding the students they had pledged, as had their forefathers, "your lives, your fortune and your sacred honor to the freedom of humanity." A month later it was over. The November 11, 1918, armistice prompted a first and last SATC parade, and there were nightlong bonfire celebrations in the city. The local *Sentinel* received news of the final surrender at 2:45 A.M. on November 12 and ran a special edition with a headline proclaiming:

The Greatest Day in History of Waterville

Before dawn the streets were filled with gleeful citizens beating on pots and pans and burning effigies of the kaiser. Miraculously no one was hurt, but the large gatherings were blamed for rekindling a deadly influenza that plagued the region through the fall. The College first quarantined the campus, then sent the women home. Two students died, both members of the soon-to-be-abolished corps. Before the epidemic was over more than five hundred had died in Maine.

Not a great deal of learning went on through the twenty months of war. College officials worried that many students might never come back, especially those whose unusual education had been paid for the government. Roberts wrote to them, pleading for their return. He promised financial help and, thanks to local merchants who provided them, part-time jobs in town. It worked. The College reopened in January with 364 students, a few more than there had been when classes began in 1917. The College devised ways to allow veterans to receive academic advancement and credit for their war service. In all there were 124 students in SATC, joining more than five hundred of their classmates and alumni on active duty or in supporting organizations. Eighteen of them died in service.

Three years later, in 1920, Colby celebrated its centennial. It might have been observed on the anniversary of the granting of the charter, but in 1913 the College was in no shape to celebrate. It might have marked the date of first classes in 1918, but the nation was at war. Instead, the centennial marked the date of the receipt of its charter from the new State of Maine in 1820.

Commencement a year later coincided with the fiftieth anniversary of the admission of women, and the graduation of 1922 was on the centennial of the first graduation. Ceremonies included the rededication of the Boardman Memorial Willows, planted each year since 1832 to honor alumni who had died and making a path to the river. The trees had begun to die, and students joined President Roberts in planting new twigs. Mary Low Carver wrote a special hymn, and the esteemed professor of Latin, Julian Taylor, gave a stirring address in which he spoke of the need for quiet space on any college campus. It presaged a growing threat to Colby:

The practical man is here with his scales and his measuring rod to tell us exactly how much excellent pulpwood these trees would yield, and the scholar's voice of protest is not easy to hear amid the thunder of railroad trains and the clatter of mills and factories, yet those of us here in this group will join our voice to his. Let them build, we say, their laboratories and their vocational workshops, but let them leave to the scholar this sylvan corner of the old college for his books, his meditations, his mysteries, and his Boardman Willows.

TIME TO MOVE

Franklin Winslow Johnson was sixty years old when he became Colby's fifteenth president in the inauspicious year 1929. He was well suited to move an entire college, an idea that was on his mind even before he took the job. Every inch a Maine man, at 5'8", with dark, deep-set eyes and a square jaw, he had the appearance of a bulldog. He had another characteristic of the breed as well: when he got a bone in his teeth, he wouldn't let go.

Johnson was born in the western Maine town of Jay and schooled at Wilton Academy, a Bates College preparatory school of Calvinist Baptist leanings. It was an early sign of independence when in the fall of 1887 he chose to enter Colby, tilted toward the Free Baptists.

His first job was as principal of the high school in the remote Canadian border town of Calais, where he stayed long enough to fall in love and marry a local woman, Carolyn Lord. In 1894 the couple moved to Waterville where he became principal of Coburn Classical Institute, spending eleven years before being lured west to head Morgan Park High School in Chicago. In 1907 he signed on as principal of the prestigious University of Chicago High School where he was a colleague and cautious disciple of the controversial innovator in secondary education, John Dewey. During World War I Johnson served as a major in the Army Medical Service, and afterward he followed Dewey to Columbia University where he taught at Teachers College and gained notice as a consultant. In 1920, Colby invited him to join its board of trustees.

In the spring of 1928, while Johnson was still at Columbia, colleagues at Teachers College were hired to staff a Maine higher education survey, conducted by the Maine Development Commission. Johnson was a friend of Harold Boardman, University of Maine president and instigator of the study. Boardman worried that higher education in Maine was developing helter-skelter, without attention to the state's economic needs. Boardman went to

Governor Ralph Owen Brewster, who in turn convinced the commission to fund a study.

At the time, Colby was without a president. When President Arthur Roberts fell ill in autumn 1927, he appointed a faculty committee to run the college while he took a medical leave. He was gone nearly two years. In 1929, while in New Jersey seeking a cure, he died. Known alternately as "Old Rob" (even as a young president) and as "Prexy Roberts," Colby's first nonpreacher president had served for nineteen years, the longest tenure of any of his predecessors, and was admired by generations of students and the people of town. Hundreds of mourners lined the Waterville railway station platform when his body was returned for burial.

Trustees didn't have to look long or far for his replacement. Johnson was well known, respected, and already in their midst. His appointment in November was greeted with enthusiasm all around. He took office in June 1929. His wife Carolyn had died only weeks before Roberts's death, and his inauguration was a somber, private affair at the president's house on College Avenue.[16] The ceremony was further dampened by the concurrent public release of the *Maine Higher Education Survey Report.* The survey was the work of an advisory committee whose members came from the four state university colleges, the private colleges (Bates, Bowdoin, and Colby), the normal schools, and the junior colleges of Westbrook and Ricker. Johnson knew most of its members, including the Colby representative, board chair Herbert Wadsworth; and Bowdoin's president, Kenneth Sills, to whom Johnson often turned for advice.

The report included a detailed examination of each of the institutions: physical plant, teaching staff, organization and administration of instruction, size and composition of student bodies and alumni, and certain aspects of the financial affairs. In the measurement of the physical plant, Colby got 377 out of a possible score of one thousand.[17] The physical plant at Bates was declared "complete enough," although the report fretted about an encroaching Lewiston and urged trustees to "obtain control of the additional land surrounding

16. A year later he married Imogene Hall, the widow of his Colby roommate, Dana Hall. The Johnsons and the Halls had been friends for years, spending summer vacations at their nearby homes in Robbinston, Maine. The new couple moved into the Elmwood Hotel while the old president's house at 33 College Avenue (once the home of Nathaniel Boutelle) was being renovated. The pipe-smoking president-elect became a deacon of the First Baptist Church, and he and his wife were regulars in the pew reserved for Colby presidents for more than a century.

17. Bates had 618; Bowdoin, 644; the University of Maine, 567.

MAYFLOWER HILL

the present campus." The survey team had visited Bowdoin during a heavy shower and the road in front of Moulton Union was "a small lake." The report recommended improved drainage, but overall found the oldest of Maine's colleges "favorably located on a desirable and adequate site."

The assessment of Colby's site was complete in its damning:

> The campus is located on a small plot of land bounded on three sides by railroad tracks, the station, and railroad yards, and on the other by the Kennebec River, with one of the largest pulp mills in the State directly across the river from the campus—near enough to cause annoyance from smoke and unpleasant odors. The prevailing winds come from the direction of the railroad yards and shops, and there are always smoke and soot laden to such an extent that it is practically impossible to keep buildings or equipment clean. Added to this, there is the noise of the trains, and the danger from crossing the tracks. The above list of disadvantages is made even more impressive when it is realized that the present central campus contains only about 28 acres and that a college like Colby should have from 60 to 75 acres as a minimum for the development of a modern college program of activities. The worst feature is that the possibilities for expansion are shut off by the river and the railroad.

Concern about trains was not exaggerated. Civil War historian John Pullen '35 (honorary M.A., 1958) later wrote that "west winds blew clouds of smoke and soot through the campus; east winds brought sulphurous fumes from the paper mill across the Kennebec." Sleeping in the "ram pastures" (attics) of North and South College, Pullen said, "we were often lulled to slumber by the monotonous thundering rumble of a potato train (it must have been five or six miles long) that went through about midnight." The trains, of course, kept the "boys and girls" on opposite sides of the tracks, making for many anxious foot races to beat the locomotive to the College Avenue crossing.

The assessment of campus buildings was no more cheerful. It found no evidence "that a plan of any kind has existed for the future development of the college's building program." Commissioners worried that six of the ten buildings were more than fifty years old (two were more than one hundred) and poorly maintained; that there was no central heating plant and the individual furnaces increased the fire hazard, not only from the old equipment but also from the coal stored in the basements. The negative marks piled up: poor artificial lighting, inadequate ventilation in the toilets, no drinking fountains, not enough baths or showers, not enough telephones, too few faculty offices, inadequate athletic facilities, and on and on.

Unmentioned, but still among the stark deficiencies of the old campus was the lack of dining facilities for men. The women ate at Foss Hall, but from the beginning the men fended for themselves. Many took their meals at the YMCA behind the railway station, and at the tiny "Quick 'n' Dirty" north of the tracks. Private boardinghouses had sprung up near the campus, including one operated by "Ma Frost" on Center Street, near the post office, where Colby men were served family-style meals for seventy-five cents.

The conclusions and recommendations for Colby reflected the despair of the surveyors. It began simply enough: "It is difficult to make recommendations for Colby College." That said, the section went on to make a rather startling one:

It is the opinion of the surveyors that its present site and present physical plant are so far below the desirable standards for a college with Colby's standing that the site should be changed before any more capital is invested in the present plant, most of which has given worthy service for a long period. It is a matter of only a relatively few years until more than half of the present buildings will have to be replaced. It will cost no more to build these buildings on a new site than on the present one. . . . The recommendation is, then, that Colby College should move to a larger and more desirable site.

The popular notion, then and later, was that the report came as a stunning surprise, that it was the single trigger of discussions about a possible move. In fact, well before the report became public there were many who knew Colby was suffocating and felt the College should pick up and leave. Johnson was one of them. He had become a "move or die" adherent well before the survey was even conducted, and the surveyors must certainly have been influenced by his views.

The director of the study was O. S. Lutes, chairman of the Department of Education at the University of Maine, who assigned much of the legwork to a young graduate student, Ermo Scott.[18] Lutes was anxious not to offend or sur-

18. Scott became a well-known Maine educator, eventually serving as president of the University of Maine at Farmington.

MAYFLOWER HILL

prise Colby officials with the harsh findings, and when a first draft of the report was written he sent Scott on the train to Waterville to share it with Johnson and Dean Ernest Marriner '13. Johnson read the report in silence before passing it to Marriner. When the dean finished reading, Johnson said: "Tell Dr. Lutes to publish it just as it stands. Here is our first factual evidence which justifies our new campus."

As a trustee Johnson had witnessed firsthand the plight of the College: one thousand students cramped on a tiny campus, plagued by the new economy, and no place to go. As early as 1927 he and his good friend Herbert Philbrick '97, a dean at Northwestern, had talked about moving. Trustee chairman Herbert Wadsworth '92 was initially not interested in moving at all. Philbrick was the first to approach him with the idea,[19] and four months before taking office Johnson himself privately broached the subject to his new boss.

The moment the survey report became public Johnson wrote Philbrick (May 15, 1929): "Everything seems to be set for presenting the proposal to the trustees in June to move the College to a more adequate location." The letter went on to reveal that Johnson had gotten his fellow trustee and good friend Walter Wyman to begin to secure options on land on a ridge between Waterville and Oakland, a place called Mayflower Hill. It seemed Johnson not only wanted to move the College, he also knew precisely where he wanted it to go.

Wyman was the perfect stalking-horse. A well-known entrepreneur, his gathering of purchase options would have raised no eyebrows. He and Harvey D. Eaton had parlayed a small, local electric power firm into what became Central Maine Power Company in 1910. Wyman put together nearly twice as much land as was eventually purchased. He tied up 1,378 acres at an option cost of $166,000. They encompassed all of what was known as Mayflower Hill, and extended to Pray Field on the town side of the Messalonskee, site of the annual circuses when P. T. Barnum came to town.

Except in the inner circle, Johnson kept his thoughts to himself. First there was the matter of getting a majority of the board to agree. Then there was the court of public opinion. It wouldn't be easy. There was a great fondness for

19. Philbrick was a Waterville native; his family ran the Iron Works. Years after the move he recalled that during a 1927 visit he and his wife were sitting on the veranda of the Waterville Country Club, and "the beauty and open space all around us led us to say in chorus 'Colby must have more room,' and with it was the resolve to help bring it about." Philbrick was a new member of the Colby board. Board chair Wadsworth later said he would have opposed Philbrick's election had he known the man was a proponent of moving the College.

the old campus, no matter how crowded and decrepit. And even if there could be general support, there was still the matter of finding the money. The College had only recently beaten the bushes for two new buildings. Alumnae Hall, a recreation building for the growing women's division, was just opened across College Avenue, and a new fieldhouse, down a steep bank near the river, was set to open in the fall. The decade before, Prexy Roberts's Centennial Fund had scraped to raise a half-million, and the current development effort wasn't going well at all. There was barely enough to finish the new buildings.

Despite his zeal for moving the College, Johnson had little enthusiasm for raising the money. In discussions with trustees about assuming the presidency, he made it clear he planned to devote his time to making educational improvements, not passing the hat, and in November 1928 he inveigled the board to pass a resolution embracing that very notion: "It is agreed the main efforts of Dr. Johnson shall be directed to the building up of Colby as an educational institution rather than to canvassing funds for endowment and equipment." It was a promise soon breached.

The trustees met on June 14, 1929, the eve of Johnson's inauguration. Armed with the survey report, Johnson presented his proposal. At the same time, he revealed that Wyman was securing land options. Board members listened carefully as Johnson pressed his case. They could agree only to take a pause while Wadsworth named a special committee of six, charged with making a recommendation on the central question of a move. In July committee members took a walking tour of the old campus and then, with Wyman as the guide, trekked the length of Gilman Street and up the dirt road that continued beyond the intersection of the First Rangeway to have a look at this place called Mayflower Hill. After the tour, the group adjourned to the Elmwood Hotel, where only Wyman and Philbrick voiced any willingness to move. (Johnson would surely have been a third, but he was laid up and sore from an automobile accident while vacationing down east.) After a long discussion, the two eventually convinced the others to recommend a move.

Trustees received the recommendation at a special meeting of the board in August, and Johnson asked for another delay. Wyman needed more time to assemble land purchase options, and Johnson needed to see if he could begin to build a public consensus in favor of a move. General support would be needed if they had any hope of raising $3 million, the estimated cost of an entirely new campus. Two months later, on October 29, the stock market crashed, and the nation slid into the Great Depression.

When the stunning news began to spread, many didn't believe it. Move the entire college? A preposterous idea. The stage was set for 1930 to be a most suspenseful and chaotic year. The furor began in April when Johnson received a letter from William H. Gannett, publisher of four Maine newspapers, including the local Waterville Morning Sentinel, inviting Colby trustees to have a look at a possible new site in Augusta. If they liked it, Gannett said, they could have it, and to sweeten the deal he'd give some relocation money as well.

As a young man William Gannett bought the formula for a soft drink, similar to the popular Moxie, and claimed it could cure all sorts of troubles. He named it Oxien, bottled it on Cony Street in Augusta, and with a team and covered wagon, visited the fall fairs, selling the stuff at a nickel a glass. He later found a Boston manufacturer who made the preparation in lozenge form, and he hired agents to sell Oxien Health Tonic Tablets through a brisk mail-order business. In 1921 he took some of his earnings and bought two Portland newspapers.

Long before, in 1892, Gannett had purchased the Milliken Farm on Western Avenue in Augusta, and later built an estate, naming it Ganneston Park. He was seventy-six when he offered the park to Colby and gave the publishing business to his son, Guy Patterson Gannett. He most likely wanted to catch a prize for his hometown, and it is also possible his proposal was invited. Architect Jens Frederick Larson had developed a concept for a new Colby campus even before the decision was made to move. He recalled passing through Augusta before 1930. "I noticed a hill of large acreage opposite the airport," he wrote. "Later I found out that this land was owned by William H. Gannett." When Larson was commissioned to move ahead with plans for a new campus he remembered the Augusta property. "I suggested that an approach be made to him [Gannett]," Larson said.

It is likely Larson made his suggestion to Franklin Johnson. Whether Johnson or anyone else approached Gannett is not known. Still, the president was pleased by the attempt to lure Colby downriver. Talk of the offer would affirm that the College was serious about moving, and it might provoke a counteroffer in Waterville, where Johnson wanted the College to stay. Gannett made his offer official on June 9, 1930. The College could have the land provided it raised $3.5 million in moving money in three years. The publisher hinted he would help with the matching money as well. It was a magnificent gesture, and one that could not be taken lightly. Four days later, the trustees met and unanimously approved the special committee's recommendation with a terse resolution: "it is the sense of this meeting that the College, as soon as means can be obtained and it is feasible, be moved to a new and more adequate location."

News of the trustee decision and the Gannett offer hit at the same time, and the reaction was powerful. Around town people quickly tied the Colby president to a conspiracy with the Augusta publisher. The *Sentinel* cried out: "Keep Colby, Move Johnson"; and among alumni and in the local homes, shops, and mills the very idea of moving the College at all—never mind out of town—seemed utter nonsense. They called it "Johnson's folly."

The president's silence and his determination to keep the Gannett offer on the table had the predictable effect. Within days a Waterville citizens' committee was formed to see what could be done to keep Colby. J. F. Hill and Herbert Emery were leaders, as was a man with great credibility both in town and at the College, Herbert C. Libby '02. A Waterville native, Libby had served as the city's mayor, taught public speaking, and had been Prexy Roberts's assistant. He was now editor of the College alumni magazine, the *Alumnus,* which he unabashedly used to trumpet the Waterville case: "The immediately important step is for Waterville to organize her citizens into a large group of Friends of Colby," he wrote, "and for each to pledge so generously as to convince the governing body of the College and its 4,000 graduates that the home folks deeply desire to keep Colby within its sacred walls."

Between June and September the Citizens Committee held fifteen meetings, and pledged to raise $100,000 and give it to the College if it would stay in town. In the meantime, the College launched its own $500,000 campaign for the development of a new campus, wherever it was going to be. General Herbert M. Lord '84, director of the U.S. Bureau of the Budget, was general chairman. (His selection by Wadsworth was regarded as a prediction of success, given that he had "more experience than any other man in the country in handling huge sums of money.")

With the time for a location decision drawing near, the committee called for a final meeting of citizens and took a full-page advertisement in the *Sentinel*. "Make this the largest meeting ever held in Waterville," the ad said. "Don't depend on the other fellow, do it yourself. Sickness is the only excuse any citizen of Waterville should have not to attend." The paper's editorial page picked up the cry: "For a city of the size and resources of Waterville this is really a tremendous task and so it's well that every effort is being made to make it possible. It will need everything every citizen can do and is a real test of mettle and loyalty. There's no place for slackers or whiners in this situation."

More than one thousand gathered at the Opera House. Redington's Funeral Home loaned extra chairs. Bands played, and the glee club of the American Legion Auxiliary, "dressed in natty uniforms," sat at the edge of the stage. The Hon. H. C. Marden presided: "If it is the sentiment of this gathering that by moving to Augusta they can transpose the willows, recreate Memorial Hall, recreate the new and old North and South buildings, replace the athletic field with its invisible monuments of bitter but friendly battles, then we will step aside because we respect the will of the majority," Marden said. "But if it is the sentiment of this gathering that Colby will stay with new support and a chance to prosper on its native soil, you know that Colby can and will stay."

Dr. Hill took the podium to explain that the organizing committee hoped to educate the people as to the seriousness of the situation, secure pledges of support, engage Colby alumni, find land options in Waterville, and finally "present to the Board of Trustees the moral claims that Waterville has upon the College so that the trustees will be slow indeed to pull up the roots of a 100-year-old institution and endanger its future growth by planting it in foreign soil."

Mayor F. Harold Dubord '03 made the longest speech by far. He said people already knew his sentimental reasons for keeping Colby, but he wanted to give some practical ones. He described the negative economic impact of Colby leaving town. He said local bankers agreed property values would depreciate 25 to 30 percent and, although Colby was exempt from property taxes, the exodus of faculty and staff would leave "empty rents and empty houses." His economics lesson painted a scenario of the need for an "unprecedented increase in taxes" because if Colby moved "the city's bonded debt would surely and quickly exceed its legal limit."

Professor Libby then rose to make it clear he was no stalking-horse for Johnson. He said it was "nonsense" to think Johnson had made up his mind that the College should move to Augusta. Moreover, the eloquent speech teacher said, his presence on the stage was ample evidence Johnson had not "muzzled" the faculty to keep them from speaking out in favor of a Waterville site.

Last to speak was Professor Julian "Judy" Taylor who stunned the audience by offering the College his own landholdings in Waterville's south end, a gravel pit adjacent to the cemetery. He said he was willing to buy abutting land (known locally as Poulin's Point) owned by Dr. James Poulin Sr., for $10,000 and present the entire package if Colby would stay in Waterville. A banner headline on the front page of the next day's *Sentinel* screamed: "Taylor Offers Colby Trustees Poulin Land."

If Johnson was at the moment being much reviled, Taylor was much revered. His father, Daniel, was one of Waterville's earliest white settlers. Then in his sixty-second year as a teacher of Latin and literature, Taylor was an icon of the College. He was a student at Waterville Academy (later Coburn) in 1863 and was on hand to hear Ralph Waldo Emerson give the Waterville College commencement address. He was a freshman the following year when President Champlin announced the staggering gift of $50,000 from Gardner Colby. He had been at Colby since Colby was Colby.

Known affectionately as the "Old Roman," he was convinced the College would remain in Waterville, and even consulted a lawyer who confirmed his hunch that a move to Augusta would entail a great deal more than trucking an entire college sixteen miles downriver. The state had granted a charter to Colby in Waterville, not Augusta. To move out of town would mean relinquishing that charter and starting over. Taylor was so sure this fact would cinch the deal he bet a man one thousand dollars to one cent Colby would remain where it started.

The Taylor property of about three hundred acres became known as the Kennebec-Messalonskee site. It was an improbable place, but with the Mayflower Hill site it added a second strong card to the hands of those who wanted Colby to stay put. A third local place was also soon considered: the Mountain Farm site, on the highland north of the city toward Fairfield. All of the properties were surveyed. Wyman had the options for Mayflower Hill in his pocket.

Local forces lobbied the trustees hard. In early November the chamber of commerce of Waterville and Winslow resolved with a flourish: "Realizing the inestimable value of Colby College to this community, and appreciating the great loss, educationally, spiritually, and financially, which would follow its removal from our city, we declare for ourselves and the organization we represent, our most hearty endorsement of the action of the Committee of One Hundred and of the city government in their purpose to raise $100,000 for Colby College in the event this institution removes to another site in this community."

A second resolution scolded the city government. "The report that the city has voted $100,000 is not borne out by the record," it said. "All that the city government has done is to pass a resolution unanimously endorsing the action of a citizens' committee in underwriting the sum of $100,000 . . . it is doubtful whether the board of trustees of the College will regard this action of the city government as of any value whatever." The signer of these resolutions was Caleb A. Lewis '03, chamber president, manager of the local *Sentinel*, and a man to be reckoned with. A newsman of the old school, he ran the paper like a czar, making it a prime and powerful source of local news and opinion. Local activists knew it was well to have Lewis on their side in any fight. He was quickly made a member of the executive committee of the Committee of One Hundred, divided into myriad subcommittees, each aimed at raising money or the promise of it. Lewis wrote a well-read column under the pseudonym Ima Wanderer and he used his space to cajole in the cause of keeping Colby. His publisher, the Gannetts, had owned the *Sentinel* since 1921, and Lewis's defiant stand against the offer in Augusta must have made Guy P. and his father cringe.

The Great Depression was underway. Many families had barely enough to live, never mind help buy land for a college. Every day there was news of a bank closing. Al Capone, a man with a better reputation for taking than giving, opened a soup kitchen in Chicago. In Waterville, even as the *Sentinel* touted the fundraising effort for Colby it was giving free space to anyone with any kind of a job to offer.

> The College had become used to hard times. Peter Mills '34 remembered that era, when students got by on a mug of coffee for breakfast and a 45¢ supper at one of the boardinghouses along College Avenue. He recalled a student losing his job in the library for returning to college with a 1924 Chevrolet. If he could afford a car, he didn't need work. When the job was given to someone who owned a raccoon coat worth more than the $25 Chevy, students signed a letter of protest.

Alongside the "work wanted" ads ran daily coupons for membership in the Friends of Colby: "A pledge of $2 to $10 is required for membership. Fill out and mail to F.A. Drummond, Waterville Savings Bank." Letters to the editor alternatively cursed and praised the project—and Johnson. Welton Farrow, then superintendent of buildings and grounds at the College and later a bookshop proprietor on Main Street, wrote not once but several times, balefully claiming no one was listening to his obvious solution: move the Maine Central Railroad tracks and leave Colby alone.

Before the trustees met on November 21, the Committee of One Hundred pledged it would raise the $100,000 in a year's time. The twenty-five members of the board, meeting at the president's house on College Avenue, unanimously voted Colby would stay in town if the pledge could be met. Although trustees put on a solid front outside the meeting, the discussion in the Johnson living room was tense. There were several strong proponents of moving to Augusta who finally capitulated, in part because feelings were so strong a few of them feared those who favored Waterville would go so far as to buy the old campus and continue with their own college.

The next morning's headline in the *Sentinel* read:

Colby Remains In Waterville

Citizens rejoice in Decision

Many Statements Are Prepared

Johnson's local stock began to rise. "The action of the Board of Trustees today brings the solution of an extremely difficult problem," he said. "Happily, the heat that has developed among some of the alumni and friends of the college over the question of a change of location has not extended to members of the board who, while differing in their opinions, have been actuated solely by their desire to promote the best interests of the College . . . with all the controversial factors happily removed, it now becomes our task to capitalize on the loyalty and good will of our friends, confident that what must be done can and will be accomplished." His ending became a catchphrase for the twenty-year effort to move the College.

The *Sentinel* waxed both poetic and prophetic: "In the new Colby that is to be, we believe that Waterville is to have its full share in making for a better and finer institution which will be an honor to the State of Maine and take its place among the outstanding institutions of higher learning in the country."

Immediately, the Committee of One Hundred began to wring every spare nickel out of a city that had precious little loose change. Five pledges of $5,000 came quickly, but the rest was in small gifts. The deadline was April 12, 1931, when the trustees would meet for a final decision. With two days left, they were $2,000 short. Ima Wanderer begged for the last pennies "to save the city its greatest industry" and suggested the city print the names of donors "on parchment and hang them in City Hall so those who come after will know who of the Waterville citizens were loyal to the city in its time of peril and thus do them honor." Whether or not the city would buy parchment, the *Sentinel* printed the names for two days in a row, more than five hundred of them. "After today," the newspaper scolded, "no excuses will be in order."

The committee held its final meeting on Saturday night, April 11, at Waterville Savings Bank on Main Street. When the meeting opened Drummond reported $97,406 in gifts and pledges. Federal Trust officials promised to fill any shortfall of less than $500. Committee members made additional gifts out of their own pockets. Before the meeting ended the goal was topped at $101,376.

By prearranged signal, the Central Fire Station siren began to wail and two groups—Drews Band and the Waterville Military Band—stepped out to march down Main Street, with horn-tooting cars behind them. The bands stopped in front of the bank to serenade the committee and then proceeded to Castonguay Square at City Hall.

In the general hullabaloo, no one thought to tell the firefighters in the south end Water Street station what was going on. Believing there was a conflagration on Main Street, the firemen roared north in their 1924 Dodge hose cart nicknamed Pee Wee and met the revelers head-on. Matters were soon cleared up, and the firefighters joined the celebration. From the square, the merrymakers marched onto Front Street and up College Avenue to the President's House to play for Johnson. He had gone from goat to hero in ten months' time.

The next day trustees agreed on the Mayflower Hill site. A week later, in a grand ceremony at the Opera House, Mayor Dubord presented Wadsworth with the deed to the new campus.[20] Judy Taylor spoke at the alumni dinner that spring and took the occasion to recall his wager that Colby would remain in Waterville. He collected his penny on the platform from a man who wanted him to win: Franklin Johnson.

OLD PASTURES

In the spring of 1931 Walter Wyman sent his Central Maine Power Company engineers to survey Mayflower Hill, and in August an open house was held for local citizens. Standing in the field below where the chapel would go, the group gaped at the vast expanse: acres and acres to far horizons, a striking contrast to the cramped and dingy place by the river. It was mainly old pastureland with an occasional small woodlot, and an orchard on the steep facing slope near a place called Beefsteak Grove, where critters once fed among the trees. The fields were crisscrossed with half-fallen fences that had divided farms; here and there could be seen the ubiquitous ledge, soon to confound the construction. Growing along the edges of the woods were expanses of trailing arbutus, the fragrant flower that gave the place its name.

20. The newly acquired property consisted of about six hundred acres, less than half the amount for which Wyman had taken options. It was an assembly of lots from ten owners: Alonzo Morrell, Ralph Stanley, the heirs of W. H. Stanley, Elmore Hustus, Phillippe Poulin, Wilfred LaPointe, Roy Page, Thomas Labbe, William Lannigan, and Mount Merici Convent.

Frank Johnson led the August assembly as it passed under a crude ridgepole archway hastily constructed over the narrow, unpaved road at the foot of the hill. A sign hung in the middle:

Entering
Mayflower Hill Park
600 Acre Site of the New Campus
Colby College

Ebullient as always, Johnson pointed to invisible buildings and roadways. Many in the crowd were expected to help complete the dream, and while Johnson's enthusiasm was contagious, the devastation of Black Tuesday still rang in their ears.

Despite the times, planning for the layout of the campus began immediately. In February 1931, trustees commissioned architect Larson and hired the New York firm of Hegeman-Harris as general contractor. Best known for his work at Dartmouth, Larson had worked on more than two dozen campuses. Stanley Nicholson, administrative vice president in the 1980s, wrote that Larson was an easy choice for trustees who were attracted by his traditionalist approach, and his preference for the neo-Georgian style. As Nicholson explained, Larson chose "a pattern based on Thomas Jefferson's design for the University of Virginia—extended rectangular space, defining a longitudinal axis, with a dominant structure (the library) as a focal point at one end and subsidiary buildings along the sides." Larson took his scheme, planned for flat land in Augusta, and redrew it for the rolling Waterville hillside.

First, there was the matter of finding money to build anything at all. A Mayflower Hill campaign was launched with the help of the fundraising consulting firm Marts and Lundy, which sent Joseph Coburn Smith '24 as its principal agent.[21] (In a short while Smith left the firm and joined the College as a PR man.)

The campaign had a goal of $3 million, quite enough for a new college, and the effort was launched at the fall Colby Night dinner in the gymnasium by the river. Judy Taylor spoke. He had retired in the spring after an American

---

21. Smith had a long Colby pedigree. He was the son of former board chair George Otis Smith, the nephew of Louise Coburn, and the grandnephew of the College's seventh president, George Dana Boardman Pepper. He had a stutter, a condition triggered whenever he got excited. He stuttered a lot when he talked about Colby. As the undergraduate editor of the student newspaper, the *Echo,* it was Smith who first proposed that the College adopt the white mule as its rather odd mascot.

record: sixty-three years as a teacher and sixty-seven years involved with the College. He stunned the audience by promising $250,000 to the campaign, but when he died a year later his entangled estate, decimated by the Depression, had no funds for Colby at all.

The Taylor debacle was only the first of a series of setbacks that were enough to make the fainthearted believe in jinxes. Years later, Colby's top fundraiser, Ed Turner, wrote a short essay on the travails of the College's move to a better neighborhood. He called it "The Perils of Pauline," a name taken from the 1914 silent film episodic serial, the most enduring scene of which, ironically, was of Pauline tied to the railroad tracks and borne down upon by a train. He told of Johnson's trip to the Bahamas to meet with the multimillionaire Sir Harry Oakes, from whom he extracted a promise of $450,000 only to have Sir Harry murdered before the money found its way from his offshore account. He also told of Johnson's appointment with the New York philanthropist Edward Harkness, who died before the two could meet, and the attorney in nearby Ellsworth who wrote to say he would build a dormitory in memory of his father, but fell down his cellar stairs and died of his injuries the day after the letter was sent. Still, Johnson was indefatigable.[22]

No tale of near misses compared to the discouraging events on the larger scene that cursed much more than Colby. The national Mayflower Hill Campaign kickoff dinner was held in Boston on the evening of March 4, 1933. President Franklin Roosevelt closed the nation's banks the next morning and solicitations for the Mayflower Hill Campaign stopped.[23]

Desperate for help, Johnson and his mostly Republican board turned to Roosevelt and his New Deal. Johnson convinced his friend and trustee Henry Hilton to help in Washington. Hilton had left the board at Dartmouth to join Colby's. His understanding of Dartmouth's renowned success in getting money from graduates led him, in spite of the times, to urge Johnson to begin an annual alumni fund. Hilton, a leading partner in the Chicago publishing firm of Ginn and Company, knew Harold Ickes, Roosevelt's secretary of the interior, and went to see him with Bainbridge Colby, a fellow trustee who had been secretary of state under Woodrow Wilson. In 1935, when solicitations resumed, Colby was assigned a Works Progress Administration (WPA) program to build

22. A man once turned down a plea to give and told Johnson he had no interest in Colby. "Give us $100,000," Johnson replied, "and you will."

23. Among the closed banks was the Peoples-Ticonic Bank of Waterville, which shut down permanently, taking with it some fifty thousand dollars of the College's money. Years later, most of the funds were returned.

the main road and lay a sewer line to the campus. The year before, also with federal money, a bridge was built over the Messalonskee Stream at the terminus of North Street and, with the help of the Maine Central Railroad, a rail overpass was installed to allow safe travel from the County Road up to the "back door" of the campus.

Enthusiasm for the New Deal was not limited to College officials looking for a way to build a campus. In 1936 Roland Gammon '37 took up the cudgel for Roosevelt's reelection on page one in the *Echo:* "Now is the time for all intelligent collegians to rally to the cause that has been America's salvation—The New Deal." Without realizing, the *Echo* had become Maine's first Democratic newspaper. His editorial raging against "the outmoded Republican No-Deal . . . with its laissez-faire in business and splendid isolation in foreign affairs," created a firestorm. The local *Sentinel* and the *Portland Press Herald* called for gagging the upstart editor. Professors Galen Eustis and Curtis Morrow called for his "suppression or expulsion." Gammon later remembered a command appearance in the president's office. "As the only Democratic editor in Maine," Frank Johnson said, "you seem to be under fire as everything from a fool to a communist." Gammon waited for the axe to fall. Instead Johnson told him "free speech and a free press are as much a Colby tradition as a Constitutional guarantee." The College would not interfere with his pro-Roosevelt policy.

The full price of building a campus was not borne by construction costs alone. As annual budgets were pared to the bone to find building money, faculty members worked for sacrificial salaries. Old campus buildings were barely maintained, and students living there could only imagine what their successors might enjoy. As they waited for Johnson's dream to come true, generations of students and faculty endured inconvenience and distraction as they straddled two campuses. Graduates of those years would say that their education was not only adequate, but also remarkable. In 1939 two of the twelve U.S. Rhodes Scholarships went to Colby graduates: William Carter '38 and John Rideout '36.[24]

24. The first Colby Rhodes Scholar was Harold Soule '04. Abbott Smith '26 was the second.

The Herculean effort to turn the old pastureland into a College wore on, but not until 1937 was there solid evidence that there was going to be any building at all. In March, George Horace Lorimer '98, editor of the *Saturday Evening Post*, gave $200,000 for a chapel to honor his father, once pastor of Boston's Tremont Temple. Ground was broken for the chapel in August, and Joe Smith arranged a perfect photo opportunity. Johnson, surrounded by dignitaries on a platform down the hill, pushed the plunger igniting dynamite that exploded the hillside behind them in a mushroom of smoke and debris. At the same time, a campaign was begun to secure $300,000 for a building in memory of Prexy Roberts. Even in this worst of times, gifts sufficient to ensure the building of Roberts Union came quickly from alumni who adored the late president. Groundbreaking ceremonies were held in the spring of 1938.

Meanwhile, alumnae struggled to raise money for their own union, as yet unnamed. Work on that facility began a year later. It was eventually (1960) named for Ninetta Mae Runnals '08, dean of women and professor of mathematics (1920–49). A Dover-Foxcroft, Maine, native, Runnals had a master's degree from Columbia's School of Education and was serving as dean of girls at Maine Central Institute in nearby Pittsfield in 1919 when she got a letter from President Roberts: "I am writing to inquire if you would be at all interested in the deanship of women here for the coming year and the rest of your life." She set her terms (full faculty membership and a free hand to improve the lot of women). Roberts accepted: "The salary is more than the college can pay but I am confident that you will earn it." She did.

Most everyone called her "Miss Runnals." A devout Baptist, she was strict in the enforcement of tight rules and liberal with second chances. She knew almost every student under her care (it was said she could recite the full names of every woman in the commencement line without looking at the list) and was an unrelenting advocate for her "girls" in a world firmly centered on the men. "There was a general feeling Colby was a men's college and women were just permitted to come," she later recalled of her arrival in 1920. Still, she pressed for the women at her weekly conferences with "Rob" (Roberts) and "brought up things just a little bit at a time, until I had sort of crept up on him." Runnals worked only a brief time on Mayflower Hill but was a full partner in much of the planning of the new women's dorms. "Adjacent dorms seem to be a good arrangement with coeducational lounges and dining facilities," she said. "I expect the men's behavior at meals is better than it was when they had their own dining halls." She was recalled to College service in 1953 to serve six years on the board of trustees.

With two buildings underway, Johnson and the others despaired of finding donations for the library, the centerpiece of Larson's plan. The widow of James King '89 had given $150,000 for part of a library, but the building couldn't fly on a single wing. More than twice the amount was needed. As early as 1933 Johnson fixed on Merton Miller '90, who had made a fortune in the gold mines of the Philippines. Miller promised some $50,000 would be in his estate to build a library in memory of his parents, William and Esther. At Johnson's urging in 1937 he agreed to do even more and do it sooner. He wrote Johnson to say he wanted to keep his money "out of the greedy hands of politicians" and transferred 10,000 shares of his gold stock for the construction of the library. In 1938 the foundation was poured. At first Miller paid the construction bills as they came in, but in 1940 he began to worry about a possible Japanese war occupation of the islands and asked Johnson to slow construction. A year later, when the Japanese took the islands, Miller's mines were flooded. After the islands were recaptured, the mines were pumped out, and Miller resumed sending checks.

In 1938 the College launched the Maine Million campaign, a name describing the precise source and amount of the next push. It was focused on finding funds for the men's dormitories. Herbert Hoover sent remarks for the campaign kickoff dinner in Portland.[25] George Averill was chairman of the board and, in the fashion of leaders before and since, made the lead gift of $100,000 to be used "for any purpose the trustees deem wise." Of the many who gave to build Mayflower Hill, none were more generous than the Averills, whose philanthropy benefited not only the College but also many institutions in Waterville. Averill had begun his career as a physician in Cambridge, Massachusetts. Poor health forced him to leave medicine; and he and his wife, Mabel, moved to Waterville, where he became general manager of the Keyes Fibre Company in Fairfield, the molded pulp firm founded in 1903 by her father, Martin Keyes. Mabel died in 1918, and in 1921 Averill married Frances Moser of Bangor. He sold his Keyes interests in 1927. The fortune that had been served up on paper plates was invested in real estate and oil wells in California.

He was, by far, the richest man in town. He was also the most generous. His gifts to Colby exceeded $1 million, making him the largest single benefactor of

25. Five years after his plagued U.S. presidency, Hoover railed against intervening in a war that seemed certain to come. His personal pain of having to defend his values against public scorn was reflected in his remarks for Colby: "Not only is it the province of the small college to furnish leaders who stand firm because they individually hold certain positive principles of life and of morals, and defend spiritual values, but a larger field in liberal education is to furnish followers, citizens who will place reason above emotion."

the new campus. His generosity was felt in town as well. He spared the College further awkwardness over abandoning the old campus the same year the new Alumnae Building was opened when he put up most of the money to buy it from the College and give it to the local Boys Club he helped to found. Speaking at a luncheon meeting of the Maine Million Committee, Averill explained that his most important and useful trustee committee assignment was on the one that had induced Franklin Johnson "to give up a much higher salary" and come to Waterville. "Our greatest desire," Averill said, "is to see that dream of good Doctor Johnson's realized—that is to see that dear Old Lady safely moved to her new home on Mayflower Hill and functioning 100% in 1941."

In fact, in 1941 the new campus was not functioning at all.

WORLD WAR II

The great World War was a dreary time for colleges everywhere. Most men had gone to fight, and educational resources, scarce to begin with, were further depleted by the war effort. Frank Johnson's dream, already delayed by a crippled economy, was put on hold again, and students and faculty endured the drudgery of having to shuttle between the sorry old campus and the incomplete new facilities on the Hill.

Johnson was out of town in 1941 when war was declared. On December 8, the day after the bombings at Pearl Harbor, Dean Ernest Marriner addressed the men students. It was one of his finest Colby moments:

> Now, if ever, the nation has need of trained minds. It is for you to take a private oath of allegiance to serious college work, as our friends and relatives in the service take public oath of allegiance to military duty. Then, when the nation does call you into its armed services, you will indeed be ready. There must be no jitteriness, no confusion, no futile bull sessions about what we shall do next, when the obvious next is tomorrow's lessons. Not with fear, not with uncertainty, certainly not with indifference, we shall meet whatever call our nation makes upon us. With calm yet alert courage, as Elijah Lovejoy faced the mob at Alton, as William Parker faced the Confederate charge at Spotsylvania, as Murray Morgan faced German bayonets at Mons, we too shall meet the challenge of our day. Before we are Dekes or Zetes or members of any other fraternity, before we are Protestants or Catholics or Jews, even before we are Colby men, we are Americans, and as Americans we shall not fail.

The effort to keep men from impulsive flight was mostly in vain.[26] There were no general deferments for college men—Colby refused to join colleges that asked for them—but most local draft boards were willing to exempt those studying medicine or other natural sciences. Still there was no way to predict the likelihood of being called, and campuses swarmed with military recruiters. In the fall of 1941 enrollment stood at 435 men and 267 women. By September 1942, the number of men had plummeted by a third. Within a year the total enrollment dropped to 282.

To stem the exodus, Colby pressed for the assignment of a government military training unit and was selected for the new College Training Program of the Army Air Force. The plan, begun in early 1943, called for one hundred enlisted men to arrive each month until the detachment reached five hundred. Each group would receive four months of classroom instruction and a final month of flight training prior to reporting to the Army Air Force Pre-Flight School. It was, in fact, a mess. Colby simply turned its facilities over to the Army. Enlistees were not truly students. The Army selected them, and many were not qualified for college work. Treasurer Arthur Seepe kept separate books to protect College money. Marriner was charged to make it all work. He gave it a good fight even while continuing as dean, but his hands were usually tied in Army red tape. Only one of some twenty groups entering the Twenty-first College Training Detachment (CTD) ever completed the five-month program. Most got called to service before they were finished. Many became foot soldiers. In February 1944, after one year of operation, the CTD was disbanded. In June, a year before the German surrender, the last man in uniform left the program.

For a moment that year, trustees were tempted to surrender the new campus itself. There was no money to build and no construction materials or laborers anyway. When the Navy offered to lease the entire campus and turn it into a thousand-bed hospital, treasurer Galen Eustis and buildings and grounds superintendent Francis Armstrong were tempted. Eustis presented the proposal at the April meeting of the board. He said the deal involved "all present buildings plus completion and construction of others according to our plans." After brief consideration by a special trustee committee, the offer was rejected.

A second cooperative defense program was underway before the war. In 1939, in cooperation with the Civil Aeronautics Authority and the managers of

26. Members of the Delta Kappa Epsilon (DKE) fraternity enlisted in the Marine Corps in a body.

the local airport,[27] the College began a Civilian Pilot Training (CPT) Program. Pilots were prepared under the Air Corps Enlisted Reserve (ACER) program. Over the next three years George Gerry, the local operator, trained ten Navy lieutenants who were sent on to Pensacola, Florida, as flight instructors. From May 1942 until the end of the war all local civilian traffic was diverted to Pittsfield. In return for use of the airstrip, the federal government paved the airport road and runways.[28]

Throughout the war, the government pressed colleges to accelerate programs and allow men to finish before reaching the draft age of eighteen. It made a strange mix on the campuses where the men were mostly seventeen-year-olds who had never finished high school. Over the next two years the College abandoned vacations and recesses and added a twelve-week summer term carrying a full semester of credit. A new cadre of freshmen arrived three times a year, and there were three commencements. Volunteer faculty taught summer courses with no extra compensation in the first year and a small stipend in the summer of 1943, after which the program was abandoned.

As trustees continued to search for ways to boost the sagging enrollment, in 1943, Dr. F. T. Hill '10 convinced them to begin a school of nursing, a five-year program requiring two-and-a-half years of undergraduate study, two years of clinical study in the field, and a final year back at Colby. An adjunct to the school was a course in medical technology. Both programs were discontinued in 1950.

These were dark times in more ways than one. The academic year 1942–43 was the darkest. It was the year of double daylight savings with a second hour added to the customary summer one-hour fallback, and both hours continued into the winter. By the biological clocks of students, eight o'clock classes seemed to begin at six. In the winter of 1943 the College bus, the Blue Beetle, chugged up and down from dark mornings to darker nights, catering to two hundred women and a mere fifty-five men.

---

27. The airport had been in operation since 1931 when a prime source of business was the shipment of films for Haines Theater. Amelia Earhart landed there in 1933 to inaugurate a new Boston and Maine Airways Flight Service (Waterville, Bangor, Rockland, Portland, Boston) and Vaughn Monroe breezed through on his way to the Lakewood summer theater. Two future presidents, Richard Nixon in 1966 and Jimmy Carter ten years later, dropped by on their campaign journeys to the White House.

28. The CPT program was discontinued in 1951 when a training pilot, Paul Paulette, was killed in a crash in Fairfield Center.

Throughout the war, students made the best of it, later recalling small pleasures in a period void of anything extra. Many trudged over the tracks between classes to have coffee at the railway station where actress Dorothy Lamour had stopped to sell war bonds. Anne Lawrence Bondy '46, later a trustee, remembered the worry about loved ones overseas and having to wait as long trains lumbered over the crossing at College Avenue, lugging war supplies south and prisoners of war to containment camps in the north Maine woods. Course offerings were slim in both the classrooms and dining rooms, where "meat extender" was used generously. Bondy claimed steak was on the menu only once—when the cattle barn burned at nearby Mount Merici Convent. Jean Whiston '47 said war students knew neither campus very well. Some classes were held in the new women's union. "In winter," she said, "the degree of comfort depended on the proximity to the boiler room. But of academic merit was the fact that students nearest the wall could listen to a lesson in economics while partially sitting in on a lecture in classics being delivered next door." There were shortages of almost everything.

Johnson retired in the spring of 1942 with his campus dream far from complete. He had tried to leave when the war began, but nervous trustees convinced him to stay another year. Lorimer Chapel, Roberts Union, Miller Library, Women's (Runnals) Union, East (Small, Champlin, Butler) and West (Chaplin, Pepper, Robins) men's dormitories,[29] and two women's dorms were in stages of completion.

The women's dorms were ready first. The women's union and its attached Averill Gymnasium—the result of a second $100,000 gift from the doctor and his wife—opened first. Mary Low and Louise Coburn dormitories were rushed to readiness, and in the fall of 1942 women were shoehorned in, three in rooms meant for two and two in places made for one. Johnson joined his successor, J. Seelye Bixler, at the ceremonies. The choice of names had been easy. Mary Caffrey Low Carver was the first woman graduate, and Louise Helen Coburn, the second.[30]

At war's end in 1945, Colby counted some 1,350 of its men and women, in-

---

29. Buildings in the men's quadrangle were named for former Colby presidents: Jeremiah Chaplin (1822–33), James Tift Champlin (1857–53), Henry Ephriam Robins (1873–82), George Dana Boardman Pepper (1882–89), and Albion Woodbury Small (1889–92).

30. The Coburns were lumber barons from Skowhegan. Both her grandfather and her uncle, a Maine governor, had served on the College board. She too excelled in the classroom and worked to improve the lot of women at Colby, as founder of the alumnae association and the first woman on the board of trustees.

cluding nine faculty members, who had served the war effort. Sixty-three gave their lives. Many of those who returned took advantage of the first-ever veterans' benefits, the G.I. Bill, and once again the College jiggled the rules to give academic credit for time in service.[31] Of some 750 veterans who eventually earned immediate postwar Colby degrees the largest number (413) was enrolled in 1947–48. (By 1951–52 the veteran population dropped to twenty-three.)[32]

BUILDING AGAIN

Major construction all but halted for the duration, and the campus vaguely resembled photographs from war-ravaged cities in Europe: holes in the ground, vacant foundations, partial walls, and the shells of buildings.

With little money for construction, local crews had used the war period to begin fashioning the landscape. Larson's solution for the impossible ledge was to leave it alone. Instead he designed sloping terraces around the central buildings, made from fill taken from a boggy area west of Miller Library. The excavation exposed a number of small springs that, beginning in 1939, created a pond, soon named for Johnson. Terraces in front of the library were the most striking. Mary Curtis Bok, daughter of the publisher Cyrus Curtis (Mr. Lorimer's publisher) did not like the original sloping lawns in front of the chapel and in 1951 gave money to make it right.

Soon after the Japanese surrender, contracts were issued for $2 million in new buildings. Only a fraction of the money was in hand. Four barracks buildings were purchased from a Rhode Island shipyard and hastily transplanted on the northwest corner of the campus. Each one had eight apartments for returning married veterans. The apartments were both a blight and a blessing.

---

31. Many graduate and professional schools accepted returning veterans even though they had not received their undergraduate degrees. Nearly a half-century later Colby offered its diploma to Colby veterans who had gone on to earn higher degrees. In a special ceremony in October 1989, ten were honored in a small and sentimental private commencement attended by trustees and overseers. The event was complete with caps and gowns, Latin charges, and proud families, including many grandchildren. More veterans came to collect their diplomas at the 1990 commencement.

32. Colby names became part of the Navy during the war. In October 1943 a U.S. Liberty Ship, the SS *Jeremiah Chaplin,* sailed from South Portland. Bixler's wife, Mary, cracked the champagne bottle on the bow at its christening. The SS *Colby Victory* was launched from California two years later.

The plan was to keep them for only a few years, but they remained in use until 1958 and were not torn down until the early 1960s.

The first men's housing, East and West Quads, opened in 1946, seven years after construction began. Johnson, who had never gotten to officiate at the dedication of a new building, spoke to a commencement weekend audience that year. "A schoolmaster doesn't earn much money," he said, "but I lived frugally and made some prudent investments. I would be able to give the college more if I hadn't made some imprudent ones too." He then presented a check to Colby for $96,247.47, an amount that matched to the penny the total of his salary over nineteen years as president.

In the fall of 1947 Maine reeled from devastating forest fires at Bar Harbor and in York County. The fires raged for a week. Plans for Homecoming Weekend were scaled back and many students traveled down east to join volunteer firefighters. The football game was canceled, and weekend entertainment was trimmed to a simple, drab dance. During intermission a double quartet of men in bowties sang barbershop harmony. The Colby Eight, formed around an old, loosely tuned baby grand on the second floor of the new Roberts Union, was an instant success.[33]

Part of Miller Library was opened that fall, and the hands of the tower clock, frozen at 8 o'clock (first class) and awaiting internal works since 1939, began to turn. The four faces rarely told the same time, a fine thing for students arriving late to class. The library was the tallest building in the state (191 feet), and although there was no law to require it, two dozen blue neon lights were installed at the top of the tower to warn night-flying aircraft. The "Blue Light" soon created intriguing lore of its own.

The library's most unusual tradition, born of necessity and continued for simple convenience, was its assembly of nonlibrary functions. With buildings for classrooms and offices still on the drawing boards, spaces designed as reading and circulation areas were partitioned for temporary classrooms. Spaces planned for other uses became shared faculty and administrative offices. The English department carved offices among the carrels of the stacks; two lecture rooms were separated by a supply and mimeographing room. Still it was not enough, and faculty members found themselves teaching in unlikely places, from the tower of the chapel to the basement of Roberts Union.

Of all the odd tenants, the most incongruous was the College Spa, a snack

33. The original members of the Colby Eight (plus one) were Ed Waller '51, Dick Leonard '50, Clifford "Bump" Bean '51, Phil Lawrence '50, George Bowers '50, Tom Samuelson '50, Bob Armitage '50, Harold Wormuth '50, and Conrad White '49.

bar and gathering place sharing its tiny space with the nation's smallest college bookstore, operated by the strict and efficient Millard Trott. Within a decade, classroom partitions were removed and the administrators and a few faculty moved out, but the Spa (habitués were called "Spa Rats") remained an institution within an institution for thirty years. The management contract was let to local Army veteran Joe Joseph and his partner, Gubby Carter Sr. The two were managers of the downtown Templeton Hotel and Restaurant. Joe died of war wounds in 1954. His brother John took charge, joined by brother Pete in 1960. The Spa eventually moved out in 1975, but the practice of mingling offices in the stacks and reading rooms of the library continued.

In 1947 the Averills came to the rescue again. Before the war, Colby had received a $200,000 bequest from George Averill's first mother-in-law, Jennie Keyes, to build a much-needed building for chemistry and physics. At war's end inflation had doubled the estimated cost. The Averills pledged the shortfall, and work began on both the Keyes Building (opened in 1950) and the companion Life Science building for geology, biology, and mathematics.

Lorimer Chapel, the first new campus building begun nine years before, opened in 1948. That same year the Bixlers moved into the new President's House, having spent the previous year in a second-floor apartment in Roberts Union. The Averills had given $50,000 to build the new house, but inflated costs forced a construction delay. Four years later the College added proceeds from the sale of the old President's House on College Avenue and work on the new house continued. Bixler used his "President's Page" in the *Alumnus* to describe it:

> In both laundry and kitchen electricity is very much in evidence with buttons that produce flashing colored lights or mysterious hidden swishings and rumblings. Over the garage is a cupola, called "Howard Johnsonesque" by the students, soon to be surmounted by a weathervane in wrought iron bearing a musical staff with the notes of the opening theme of Dr. Ermanno Comparetti's *Mayflower Hill Concerto*. This is the gift of Mr. Charles Wescott of Blue Hill in memory of his son Robert, who died in the war.

Before the house could be built it was necessary to move a wood-framed farmhouse, originally the home of Josiah Morrell, from the adjacent property. It was rolled along an old road called Maple Court to a grove of trees behind the tennis courts where it was renovated and used as a home for the superintendent of buildings and grounds.

The year 1948 also saw the opening of the first two fraternity houses, DKE and ATO, and myriad athletic facilities sorely needed in order to abandon and sell the riverbank campus. A war-surplus airplane hangar was sliced in two and its pieces placed side-by-side to create a dirt-floor fieldhouse. In the winters, a portable wooden floor was laid for basketball. The building's brick front gave the hint of the Georgian theme and enclosed the entrance and staff offices.[34] In 1956 the building was dedicated to Herbert Wadsworth, chair of the board from 1925 to 1937.

Wadsworth was a bookkeeper and partner in a Livermore Falls firm that manufactured oilcloth table coverings in the days when they were used for more than picnics. A politician and respected Republican state senator, he chaired the powerful appropriations and financial affairs committee (and the committee on insane hospitals) and introduced the legislation creating the first state constabulary (state police) out of general concern about speeders on the expanding Maine highways. His leadership in building the fieldhouse on the old campus made him the logical choice for the naming of the new one. When he died, the residue of his estate, $100,000, was left to Colby, the income to be used to maintain a professorship "wherein shall be taught and expounded the practices and principles of sound and prudent business."

The first football game on the Hill was played in September 1948 (Colby beat American International College), and the new field was dedicated at ceremonies a month later and named for Charles F. T. Seaverns '01. The *Alumnus* magazine called it "the first athletic field of the Atomic Age" and, in perfect celebration, Colby beat Bowdoin, 14–0. It was the second Colby field named for Seaverns. In 1922, on the occasion of the late observance of College Centennial, Seaverns pledged $75,000 for an endowment to produce $3,500 a year to create a new Department of Physical Training and Athletics and to operate it "in perpetuity." The football field on the old campus was named "now and forever" for him. A decade later Seaverns served as a trustee leader of the Maine Million Campaign. His own gifts included the central lounge for the new Roberts Union (now the Colby Seaverns Bookstore), and in 1932 he served as chairman of the College's first-ever annual alumni fund.

Crafts Field for baseball and softball, given in memory of Oliver Crafts by his parents, was dedicated in 1948, as were tennis courts, built near Mayflower Hill Drive in memory of Walter Wales, killed in the invasion of Sicily. Neither Crafts nor Wales had gone to Colby.

---

34. The old hanger infrastructure remains, a survivor of three subsequent major renovations and a fire.

As the 1950s dawned there were fourteen buildings on the new campus.[35] Like "the little engine that could," Colby was slowly and bravely chugging up the Hill. The *Saturday Evening Post* called it "a magnificent triumph of spiritual engineering," and indeed it was. The move was without precedent.[36] Some thirteen thousand people made gifts to create Mayflower Hill, nearly half of them with no ties to Colby at all.

The cost, once estimated at $3 million, was already more than doubled, but after twenty years of struggle, Colby's place seemed more secure. Yet there was still much to do. With every new penny being devoted to construction, there was a growing self-consciousness about what had *not* been achieved. While other colleges had taken whatever extra money they could find to enrich their endowments and add new faculty and programs, Colby had been busily buying bricks.

35. The early buildings included a small pumping station at the foot of the Hill, an unanticipated structure required when it was discovered that the campus was too high to be gravity fed by the Kennebec Water District. A pump was needed to supply a large storage tank above Beefsteak Grove.

36. Wake Forest had relocated, but a single benefactor paid the cost.

2. THE 1950S

THE BLUE BEETLE

*College students were in the "Silent Generation," quietly bent on finding the op-
portunities and riches that had eluded their parents. Many came from families
nesting in the suburbs, buying stoves, refrigerators, washing machines, and other
prizes of the war-boosted technology. Television, still black-and-white and
"snowy," began to shape their lives in ways they did not understand. They trusted
their political leaders—Franklin Roosevelt was mourned, Harry Truman was a
pleasant surprise, and Dwight Eisenhower became their hero—and they revered
their teachers, still reigning in the manner of the old school. Most of the boys were
hot on the trail of making money, and most of the girls were hot on the trails of
the boys who wanted to make it. If they were "silent" it was only because there
wasn't much to make noise about. Many of them would later say that fate had
given them the best of times for growing up.*

The College still straddled two campuses, and for many students the mile-wide
gap between the two Colbys was closed by a big International school bus, the
Blue Beetle, shuttling them back and forth and serving as a convenient and curious center of social life. It had been running up and down the Hill for eight
years. By the fall of 1952 the College would be firmly ensconced on the Hill,[1]
and the bus would be retired. In the meantime, there was still circling to do.

In the fall of 1950, some three hundred freshmen arrived a week early for
orientation, and the Blue Beetle resumed its daily route. It was always jammed
beyond its listed capacity, but nobody counted, least of all Rowena Nugent, a
tiny woman who concentrated mightily on her driving. She needed to. Sitting,

---

1. The last class on the old campus was a biology lab, held in Coburn Hall on the
morning of May 22, 1951.

standing, and jostling around, students shouted above the din of the engine, to one another and out the window. Besides the perennial fall buzz about the new freshmen, there were many things to catch up on. Those who arrived by train had narrowly missed a national rail strike, averted when President Truman seized the railroads. The newspapers had begun carrying a new comic strip, *Peanuts*, and the Diners' Club was issuing intriguing new plastic things called credit cards.

On the global front the talk was mostly about communism. That spring, a million Chinese Communists had crossed the Yangtze River to run Nationalist party leader Chiang Kai-shek across the Formosa Strait to Taiwan, and the world's biggest country was split in two. The faculty began to worry that students were short of instruction on international politics, and there were hastily arranged Gabrielson Lectures (a series established in 1946 by Colby trustee Guy Gabrielson) aimed at sorting things out.

Students had barely left for the summer when North Korean troops charged south into the Republic of Korea. Seoul fell quickly and the communist threat suddenly seemed very real, as ever-larger headlines warned of another war. For the first time the United Nations agreed to fight; and, on his own, President Truman ordered forces to provide "tactical" support south of the 38th parallel. "We are not at war," he said, claiming the involvement was more accurately a "police action." He would rue the day. Some 100,000 Americans suffered casualties over the next three years, and the Republicans made hay with his remark in the 1952 presidential campaign.[2]

News of the communism threat had a local slant, tied to Maine and Senator Margaret Chase Smith from nearby Skowhegan. She had challenged the bully from Wisconsin, Joseph McCarthy, with her "declaration of conscience" speech. Earlier, in a talk containing phrases flatly stolen from the champion anticommunist, Richard Nixon, McCarthy claimed to hold the names of 205 Communists working in the State Department. The Age of Suspicion was full-blown; fingers were pointed and accusations made; jobs and reputations were lost.

Truman said privately that "the son of a bitch ought to be impeached," but McCarthy met little resistance until Smith took him on. In a speech written by hand at her Skowhegan home, she said it was "high time that we remembered

2. One of the hay-makers was lecture series sponsor Gabrielson, then chairman of the Republican National Committee. Gabrielson backed Robert Taft of Ohio at the convention. In the end the country had a new president, Dwight Eisenhower, and the GOP had a new chairman.

that we have sworn to uphold and defend the Constitution (that) speaks not only of the freedom of speech but also of trial by jury instead of trial by accusation." The next day, Bernard Baruch said if a man had made the same declaration, he would be elected president.

The Blue Beetle must also have echoed with chatter about sports. Major League Baseball had sold the All-Star Game and World Series television rights for $1 million a year for the next six years, and Red Sox fans were crushed when Ted Williams, who batted .406 in 1941, was recalled to the air force and was flying over Korea by the end of the 1950 season. And there was Jackie Robinson, the Brooklyn Dodger and the first black player in the modern major leagues, poised to become the National League MVP.[3]

The bus began its daily run from Hedman Hall downtown, and then lumbered onto College Avenue for a stop in front of old Mary Low. It stopped at the only set of traffic lights in town, where College Avenue ended, at the top of a bustling, two-way Main Street. Across the intersection sat the classic post office and on the right loomed the venerable Elmwood Hotel, exactly one hundred years old. The building had but a few not-so-good years left. (Its front yard was already relinquished to an Esso Servicenter.) Across the street the fire station blasted a curfew every night at nine, to test the horn and get the kids off the streets.

Post Office Square was the center of town; and Waterville, population 19,584, was still growing. Within two years there would be no college on College Avenue (and many fewer elms on Elm Street), but that fall the busy downtown was an inviting place. As the bus passed through the square, students could look downtown and see the marquee of the Haines Theatre where Bob Hope and Lucille Ball were starring in *Fancy Pants*.

Waterville had eleven hotels and thirty-eight eating places, ranging from competing hot-dog stands on Front Street (Jimmy Datsis ran one; Ricky Thomas, the other) to the upscale Jefferson Hotel on College Avenue, where Ma Shiro presided. Joe Pete's Little Big Store was near the rail crossing on Main Street, where Phi Delta Theta fraternity brothers hung out and bought lunch for a buck. Joe and Kay Peters carried the tab for anybody short of cash. Of the many watering holes, a student favorite was Onie Noel's place on Silver

3. Dodger coach Clyde Sukeforth from the tiny Maine town of Washington is credited with identifying Robinson for Brooklyn owner Branch Rickey who wanted the first black player to be "someone with guts enough not to fight back."

Street: a bar to the right with well-scratched booths and tables around a dimly lit room. Alice and Rollie Violette gave light to conversations and served "Dimie" beers. (Onie's became Alice's Café in 1956 although students kept calling it Onie's.) Here and elsewhere the checking of the legal drinking age was spotty. A smattering of veterans improved the general plausibility of any student being of age, and helpful local cops tipped off bar owners when the liquor inspector was in town.

At the top of Main Street, next door to the Waterville Savings Bank with its iron sidewalk chiming clock, was tiny 24-hour Parks Diner, a true railroad car that boasted of its air conditioning. Morgan-Thomas Business College was on the street too. Its name was changed that year to Thomas Junior College.

Although local neighborhoods were separated in ethnic ways, Main Street was a melting pot. Enrico Conte ran a soda shop and sold frosted mugs of root beer for a quarter. Leo Diambri had a lunch counter with "ultra spaghetti." Willard Arnold II ran the family hardware store. Saul Mandell had another. Evariste LaVerdiere's drugstore would soon become a chain. George Sterns's department store boasted the city's first store elevator and an X-ray machine for measuring feet for shoes. Dunhams sold Hathaway shirts (pricey at $3 a shirt) and did a brisk mail-order business from the back room. Tom Georgantas named his Candy Kitchen for his wife, Bea. His burly form could be seen from the sidewalk, pulling taffy from hooks hung over large copper kettles.

On the corner by Temple Street, above Bob Dexter's Drug Store and next door to a Chinese restaurant, Al Corey, fresh from the army, ran a tiny music studio, selling reeds and strings and giving lessons. Eventually he moved downstairs and then across the street where he continued the business into the next century. Corey befriended a thousand college students, and campus groups vied for bookings of his "Big Band" orchestra.

At the foot of Main Street was Levine's, "the store for men and boys." Since moving downtown from Ticonic Street in 1896, Levine's may have employed more Colby students than any other (and more than a few faculty members). For certain, it housed two of the College's most enthusiastic sports fans. The founder's sons, Ludy '21 and Pacy '27, captured and devoured generations of Colby people who came to talk and never left empty-handed. Nephew Howard Miller '41 helped manage the store and did his best to keep his uncles in check.

James Boyle, department adjutant of the American Legion, practiced law on Main Street and, at no. 131, upstairs over Fidelity Insurance and across the hall from the Waterville Women's Association, were the offices of a young lawyer recently moved from nearby Rumford. Edmund Muskie was married to Jane Gray, a clerk at nearby Alvina & Delia's, a women's store specializing in grand hats. Muskie, the law partner of James Glover, was president of the local Lions' Club.[4]

Community esprit had much to do with the local news media. Howard Gray, Jane Muskie's brother, took over the reins at the *Waterville Morning Sentinel* in 1952, when there was advertising money enough for a deep reporting staff (and 72 paid-by-the-inch area town correspondents) providing lots of local copy, including births, deaths, and hospital admissions. Students listened to the local radio station WTVL, 1490 AM, an ABC affiliate, established in 1948 by Carleton Brown '33. Don MacNeil's *Breakfast Club* was on weekdays at 9 A.M.; *Inner Sanctum,* Monday nights. Local programming included *Luncheon with Allison* (Day) and *Variété Français* with Joe Bulger. Brown had enlisted Colby dean and historian Ernest Marriner '13 to do a weekly 15-minute Sunday show, *Little Talks on Common Things.* Devoted to Maine history, especially that of the Kennebec Valley, the popular program became the nation's longest-running radio show under the same continuing sponsor: Keyes Fibre Company.

In addition to Keyes, the area had four other paper-related mills, eighteen textile and apparel plants, twenty-five food-processing places (some seasonal), and eight shoe and leather firms. Growing pains were not unlike those of similar communities across the nation. Downtown parking was a headache, exacerbated by families that liked to pile in their cars and take diagonal parking spaces on Main Street, only to watch the bustling crowd. An experiment with a rotary traffic circle at the south end of the street was causing a stir; worse, there was talk of the need to make some of the downtown streets one-way. Three local hospitals—Thayer, Sisters, and Waterville Osteopathic—having brought 447 new citizens into the world in 1950 (and treated 35 cases of whooping cough and 133 of measles), were bursting at the seams. Thayer had just gotten itself a building permit for a $1 million facility on North Street, near the College.

Growth was also putting pressure on the local airport, recently named for Robert LaFleur '44, a Waterville youngster from The Plains and a football star at both Waterville High and Colby, killed in 1943 while on a flying mission over Germany. By 1950 Northeast Airlines was flying DC3s on routes that included Waterville, Lewiston, Portland, and Boston. That summer the city added

4. Muskie had already been elected to the Maine House of Representatives (1946) but was defeated in his 1948 attempt to be mayor of Waterville. Russell Squire, owner of a popular Main Street clothing store, beat him. Muskie wouldn't lose another political campaign until twenty years later when he stood as the Democratic candidate for vice president of the United States.

MAYFLOWER HILL

to the runway, built a hanger, and installed runway lighting so the airport crew no longer needed to set flare pots for night landings.[5]

As the Beetle headed up narrow Center Street, it continued through the intersection at Pleasant Street, stopping at "Colby Corner" beside Sacred Heart Church,[6] a gathering place for students waiting to hook rides up the Hill. Farther up Gilman Street the bus passed the red brick high school, a focus of pride for a community still heady over the 1944 "Cinderella" boys' basketball team that had defeated the Somerville (Mass.) team to win the New England high school championships. Like most Maine towns, Waterville was galvanized by basketball. The 1944 team was brought up on basketball by Dutch Bernhardt at the local Boys' Club and was coached to glory by one of Waterville's and Colby's greatest athletes, Wally Donovan '31.[7] The school gymnasium was not big enough to handle the hordes of fans, and the city inveigled state government to pitch in $50,000 and paid Colby $150,000 for the College's old gymnasium, fieldhouse, Shannon observatory, and Seaverns football field. The fieldhouse was renovated, but the building had a short life. Clouds of dust rising from the dirt floor around the court dimmed the already weak lighting, and the glass roof leaked like a sieve.

Near the end of its route, the bus crossed the Gilman Street Bridge over Messalonskee Stream and headed up Mayflower Hill Drive. All summer the drive had been closed. Cars were rerouted so the Waterville Sewerage District, established in July, could lay lines ahead of the new paving. Local police warned of a "crackdown" on speeders: exceed 25 mph and pay $5. The vista from the bridge was of old farmland bristling with construction. The new campus had become a magnet for new development west of the stream. There were already a dozen houses between the stream and the campus, and work was beginning on a dozen more. As Mayor Dubord had predicted, the College

5. Mayor Russell Squire knew what more air traffic could mean and began to talk about Waterville getting together with Augusta and considering a single airport somewhere in between. He was hooted down in both cities. His vision never got off the ground.

6. The building foundation for Sacred Heart was completed in 1908 and for twenty-one years, until the plate was passed enough extra times to pay for construction of the great stone edifice, masses were held in the basement gathering hall. The city's Catholics—a majority of the population—supported four Catholic churches offering a choice of sixteen Sunday masses and five on weekdays. For the especially devout there were afternoon vespers as well. There were also a dozen Protestant churches in town, and a small Jewish synagogue.

7. In thirty-eight years of coaching at Waterville High (1934–72) his basketball and football teams won a combined five state titles.

that the community had fought to keep in town was raising new property tax revenues, hand over fist.

Near the top of Mayflower Hill, on the right, the Blue Beetle passed the white Colonial home of Franklin and Imogene Johnson. He was eighty years old, eight years retired from the Colby presidency. The land between their home and the College was still old pasture, and trees had not yet overtaken the view of the campus from their living room. Johnson waved to the students when the bus passed on the way to Runnals Union where chattering students changed places with those headed back down the Hill. He liked living near his campus where he could watch new buildings going up, walk among them, and supervise the landscaping. By 1950 he was known as the "Man of Mayflower Hill." All but forgotten was the brief time in the summer two decades before when he was called by other names and reviled by those who feared he would take their College downriver to Augusta. He died in 1956. Ten years later, on Commencement weekend, a tablet honoring his memory was unveiled in Lorimer Chapel. Neil Leonard '21 spoke at the ceremony: "in our time, while timid souls crept into nameless graves, a rash soul, Franklin Winslow Johnson, appeared, and by forgetting himself, rushed into immortality." By then the Blue Beetle had been sold for junk, and the College was nicely settled on the Hill.

J. SEELYE BIXLER

Ask anyone who ever met Seelye Bixler to tell about him and the first thing they will likely say is that he remembered their name. He not only remembered almost everybody he ever met, he went to great lengths to get acquainted with more. Sid Farr '55, who made a career at the College and came to know more Colby people than anyone of his time, was playing touch football with student friends one afternoon in the early 1950s. Crouching over the line as the ball was about to be snapped, he heard a familiar voice speak his name. Startled, he looked up into the face of Dr. Bixler: twinkling eyes; outsized, almost comic ears and nose; and a broad grin. The president had quietly slipped into the game, delighted by his own mischief.

Stories abound of meetings with Bixler, who sometimes called himself "prexy," although hardly anyone else did. Meeting "Dr. Bixler" was always the same: tall, thin frame bent to bring him face-to-face; an earnest, inquiring look; intent on the conversation. His encyclopedic understanding of students and faculty created a sense of family that was much needed in his time. His personal warmth surprised people who knew only of his great intellect. The first to come to the presidency as a recognized scholar, he had studied with Husserl and Heidegger in Germany. Albert Schweitzer, the great theologian, musician, and medical missionary, was his friend. Martin Luther King Jr. later quoted Bixler in his sermons. His grandfather was Julius Hawley Seelye, a towering president of Amherst. His father, James Wilson Bixler, was the pastor of the Congregational church in New London, Connecticut, where Bixler was born.

After graduating from Amherst in 1916, he taught at a missionary college in India, returning to study at the Union Seminary. Following brief service in the army during World War I, he resumed teaching at the American University in Beirut before returning to Harvard, and then Yale, where he took his doctorate in philosophy in 1924. He taught at Smith College for nine years, interrupted only by a year of research in Germany. In 1933 he joined the Harvard faculty; when the Colby trustees found him there he was Bussey Professor of Theology and acting dean of the Divinity School.

Boston attorney Neil Leonard '21, who became chairman of the board in 1946 and served through Bixler's term, was put in charge of the search. In June 1941, Leonard reported on the discovery of Bixler to chairman George Otis Smith '93 and other trustees who agreed that the committee should interview him and "if, in their judgment it is expedient, tender him the office of president." It was that simple. Bixler accepted the job and a $10,000 salary and waited a year while Johnson finished up.

Some wondered why Bixler even wanted the job. He might easily have gone to a place where the physical plant and the academic program were already in place. He later answered the question, recalling a meeting with the search committee—Leonard, Charles Seaverns, and Henry Hilton—on a warm afternoon at the creaky old Union Club on Boston's Park Street. The men were quickly in their shirtsleeves, each with a stein of beer:

> After about three hours of talk—and I don't know how many steins—we decided to adjourn. As we put on our coats Neil made a classic remark. "Well," he said, "this business of choosing a college president is one awful job. I do hope we haven't made a mistake." "Neil," I could only reply, "be sure my hope is as fervent as yours!" A few weeks later . . . I telephoned Neil, and the die was cast. Many of my friends were surprised—some more surprised than pleased. Colby seemed a gamble, which like the jewel box in *The Merchant of Venice* might summon the one who chose it to give and hazard all he had. But the more I became acquainted with Colby people the more clear it was that the decision was in line with some of my most deeply felt convictions.

In 1941 he was also attracted by Colby's physical promise. He wrote:

> one could feel something stirring here that offered a basis for great expectations. Incomplete as the project was, the half finished structures had undeniable grace and dignity, while the symbolism of the plan as a whole made an irresistible appeal. . . . The impression Mayflower Hill makes on me is that of a hospitable host with a cordial welcome. "Come let us reason together," it seems to say, "accept from this institution an invitation to learning." In my own case the invitation was irresistible.

It was conviction and sense of purpose that made him take the job, and a dozen years later the same two things kept him when Amherst flirted with him to be its president.

By the time Bixler arrived, the College had already lost much of its Baptist bent. In his last year Johnson told the board that Colby, "once a college attended by native sons and daughters of Maine, predominantly from Baptist families, has become cosmopolitan—geographically, racially and religiously." He proved it by providing a survey of the new freshmen: 36 Congregationalists, 34 Catholics, 33 Baptists, 29 Episcopalians, and two Jewish refugees being supported by the Society of Friends. Even so, members of the board were mindful of the condition of Gardner Colby's gift requiring that the president and a majority of the board be Baptists. Bixler was a Congregationalist, and set to be the first president out of line. Trustees gingerly asked him if he might be willing to convert, to which he bluntly replied: "It would be unfortunate to change one's religious affiliation for the sake of becoming a college president."

Soon after his appointment, the fundamentalist *Sunday School Times* sharply commented: "It is a strange proceeding to go to the Unitarian theological school at Harvard for the head of a Christian institution." The *Times* editorial was circulated among the Maine Baptist ministers, about to gather for a conference in Waterville. Frank Johnson arranged for Bixler to be their keynote speaker. Bixler talked about his friend Schweitzer, and noted Schweitzer's life was "lived against a background indistinguishable from the Unitarian." In their enthusiasm for the work of Schweitzer, Bixler recalled, "the ministers forgot to ask embarrassing theological questions and the meeting broke up happily."

The new president had exercised the wit and charm that would serve him well, from faculty meetings where discussions were not usually very funny, to sessions with irate alumni with better ideas about how to run the College. Using humor as a tool, he put listeners into his pocket, and then carried them toward the more erudite things. A young reporter covering one of his lectures for the local newspaper once wrote a story more about his riveting and humorous introduction than the essence of his talk. Typically gracious, Bixler wrote to thank him and ended by saying: "You may have missed my point." Well, of course, he had missed it—by a mile. Bixler's humor had a strong bent toward the pun (rivaled only by the elegantly mustached latter-day registrar, George Coleman, who could break up any meeting to a chorus of groans). The story went around that someone once asked the philosopher president if he thought life was worth living. "That depends," Bixler answered with a twinkle, "upon the liver."

Like his predecessor, Bixler began his presidency in the worst of times. Johnson came with the Great Depression; Bixler came in 1942, in the midst of war. But like Johnson, Bixler was well suited to his time and place. His task, as he and others agreed, was to lead the completion of the new campus and build an academic reputation to match. To help enhance Colby's standing, his wife, Mary, was a full partner, especially in the bolstering of the neglected areas of art and music. The Bixlers' love of the arts led to the development of revitalized academic departments and an infusion of the arts in the broader community. Mary Bixler, a Phi Beta Kappa graduate of Smith, held a master's degree in philosophy from Columbia. She was a gifted violist, and a driving force in the formation of the Colby Community Symphony Orchestra, in which the Bixlers were faithful participants.[8]

Given his choice, Bixler would have devoted full time to his academic interests, and engaged with faculty and students in a life of the mind. Like Johnson, he would have liked to leave the business of asking for money to others. Johnson had no choice, and paid a price. Many students of his era said they didn't know him. Bixler, with help from a fledgling development office, managed to do both.

He never got comfortable "traveling with the begging bowl." In 1984 when he was gravely ill and staying with his daughter Nancy Isaacs in Weston, Massachusetts, President William "Bill" Cotter and his wife, Linda, paid a visit. Bixler, who held his sense of humor despite failing health, told the Cotters he was being haunted by two recurring nightmares. In the

8. Ever the gracious hostess to faculty, students, and visiting alumni, Mary Bixler customarily visited the wives of new faculty members and knitted toys for the new babies. Each year the Bixlers made certain every senior was invited to the President's House for an evening of dining, lively conversation and, of course, music.

first, he said, he was taking his Ph.D. oral examination and was being asked to outline and critique the ideas of all the major philosophers from the beginning of time. In the second, he dreamed he was being asked to go on a fundraising trip for Colby.

While his era was marked by the continued development of the physical plant, he would most especially be remembered for his strengthening of the faculty and curriculum. He could make a good case for more bricks, but the case for the liberal arts was his mantra. "The real sign of a liberally educated mind," he once said, "is its freedom. Its zest for the life of free inquiry is not hampered by custom, convention, or prejudice. The liberally educated mind is inventive and experimental. It meets unexpected challenges quickly and is not afraid to blaze new trails when facing new problems." Mark Benbow (English), one of the stars Bixler brought to the faculty, said Bixler reminded the faculty always to "inquire whether what we were doing was just within the tradition of the liberal arts. This was the theme upon which he was ready to fight in word and deed, and we became better scholars and better teachers, better human beings because he encouraged us to inquire."

By the time Bixler arrived there were the beginnings of a supporting cast in the business of finding institutional support. Trustees themselves had gotten used to "high-class begging" and were already chasing prospects for the upcoming Fulfillment Campaign. On the staff were at least a few seasoned in the art of asking. Alan Lightner, the Colby point man with the fundraising firm of Marts and Lundy, signed on as assistant to the president in 1940 and, as a company man, continued to glean funds for a fledgling endowment even while getting money for bricks. In 1952 John Pollard became the first director of development; a year later Edward Turner arrived to lead the effort for another two decades and more. Lightner stayed on as goodwill ambassador, president's assistant, and fundraiser until 1961.

Working to help Bixler warm the circuits with alumni was G. Cecil Goddard '29. Until 1938 there had been a dual alumni organization. Goddard kept touch with the men, and Joe Smith's wife, Ervena Goodale Smith '24, was secretary for the alumnae. Goddard somehow managed to raise $300,000 for the Roberts Union and Ervena Smith got $100,000 from a much smaller body of alumnae for the building that became Runnals Union. In 1939 the two organizations merged into one, and Goddard was named alumni secretary. By 1950 he, like Lightner, was an assistant to the president.

Two other supporters appeared on the administrative scene in 1950 and each in his own way kept fences mended, both on and off the Hill. Ellsworth "Bill" Millett '25 was already well known when he replaced Goddard as alumni secretary. A stellar undergraduate athlete, he returned to the old campus in 1927 after two years of teaching and coaching at Waterville High. Millett's popularity reached deep to the Waterville community, making him the perfect host for summer open houses to show off the new campus. Like Bixler, he knew everybody's name, and he too was a humanist and as much beloved as any figure of his time. His work with alumni began on the campus where he was a specialist in rescuing undergraduates.[9] Along the way, someone gave him the title as "Mr. Colby" and it stuck. In 1966 the newly acquired alumni house was named in his honor.

Richard Nye "Dick" Dyer came in 1950 to fill the large shoes of both Herbert C. Libby as editor of the *Alumnus* and Joseph Coburn Smith as chief of public relations. A tireless and loyal advocate for Colby, he developed strong ties to the regional media representatives and took the quality of the magazine to new heights. Thorough and precise, he was as demanding of others as he was of himself. (In one seven-year stretch he hired and fired twenty-two secretaries.) An inveterate saver, more than anyone Dyer preserved what could be moved from the old campus. He plagued higher-ups to find money to rescue artifacts, and he pestered librarians to organize the "Colbiana" collection. His loyalty led him to serve well as an assistant and confidant to three presidents.

Bixler's aversion to money extended to the balancing of the College budget. For that, he had A. Galen Eustis '23, a giant in the task of keeping the College afloat in the precarious years when academic support competed fiercely with the need to buy more bricks, and when capturing every new class of freshmen was an anxious adventure. Eustis came from Strong, Maine, and graduated from Colby at the top of his class. With a Harvard master's degree, he returned in 1926 to lead the department of business administration. At the age of twenty-three, he was elected as the youngest member of the Maine House of Representatives (a Republican of course). He became full professor and treasurer in 1938, and in 1950 the College's first administrative vice president. Shrewd and

9. One of those he rescued was Jack Deering '55, a Korean War air force veteran who left the downtown campus and felt out of place after returning to the new campus on the Hill. He was packing his belongings into the trunk of his car to leave school when Millett appeared and convinced him to stay. Deering became Colby's principal cheerleader in the Portland, Maine, sea of Bowdoin graduates, served as a College trustee, and received numerous alumni awards, including the Marriner Distinguished Service Award.

utterly devoted, he was as important to the development of the new campus as was his friend and architect, Jens Larson. Bixler once observed that his vice president's "down-to-earth shrewdness and astute realism was the perfect foil" for Johnson's "ebullient optimism." He might have said the same thing of his own relationship with the man.

The inherent tensions between thrifty money managers and thirsty faculty and students are legendary, and Eustis must have felt like the only saver in a sea of eager spenders. If he had a reputation for being tight, it was both deserved and understandable. The faculty was always asking for more money, even as students pressed demands for a social center, "with a dance floor, juke box, card tables and a soda fountain."

Even trustees made him nervous. At a single meeting in November 1945, the board voted to complete the buildings under construction, add two science buildings, two women's dormitories, and two fraternity houses. It was a brave move that thrilled Franklin Johnson, but the College didn't have half the money. It was Eustis who arranged for bank loans and waited anxiously for contributions to come in so he could pay the mounting bills.

> If Eustis knew how to make the buffalos on the nickels of his day squeal, he also knew what motivated people. Ansel Grindall, who became director of physical plant in the 1970s, tells of a late winter day twenty years before, when he was a driver of the Blue Beetle. During a break, Grindall spotted a pile of coal outside Hedman Hall on the old campus and began shoveling it through an open window. Someone called out of the dusk: "Young man, what do you think you are doing?" It was Eustis. For one sinking moment Grindall thought perhaps he was shoveling coal into a faculty office. He explained he was simply keeping busy between runs. Eustis walked off without a word. The next week Grindall found a ten-cent-an-hour increase in his paycheck.

Against the genteel nature of the men he worked for, Eustis had the rougher instincts of a street fighter. In November 1950, the local Laborers' Union of the International Hod Carriers' Building and Common Laborers of America struck Colby and Thayer Hospital and took almost all of the construction workers with them. The organizer of the local union (no. 1284) was a Colby student, Paul Christopher '51. Christopher, who also worked as a laborer, told the student newspaper that "due to the increased cost of living in the Waterville area, one dollar per hour, making a take-home pay of approximately $37 a week, fails to keep life and limb together for the workers." Laborers were making seventy-five cents an hour. Christopher convinced the union to ask for twice as much. Eustis offered the same dime he had given Grindall. A few workers picketed the construction sites on North Street and Mayflower Hill. Christopher was surprised that his fellow students—and most people in town—seemed uninterested. He was labeled a troublemaker. Bixler scolded him for being disloyal. Christopher, who lived with his wife, Alice, in the veterans' apartments, felt threatened and feared he might be thrown out of school. Union leaders negotiated a new hourly rate of $1.25, a 66.6 percent increase. When the strike ended, Eustis seized a page of the *Alumnus*. His message seethed. "Although in excess of $5 million in construction has been carried on at Colby over a period of several years," he wrote, "the College did not have any labor troubles until November of this year." He made sure alumni knew the cost of the settlement was about $20,000.

Also at Bixler's right hand was Ernest Marriner '13. As listeners to his weekly radio program could attest, he was a Mainer through and through, and his down east accent was undiluted. He taught at Hebron for a time and represented the academies as a speaker at the Colby Centennial in 1920. Three years later he joined the College staff as librarian and professor of English. He was one of a half-dozen faculty members who ran the College during Prexy Roberts's last illness. He served as the first dean of men (1929–47) and first dean of faculty, a position he held for a decade until his retirement in 1957. Thereafter, until his death in 1983, he served as College historian. Before the era of multiple deans, Marriner was known simply as "the dean." His service to the community and the state included fifteen years on the local board of education until 1947 when he became a founding member of the state board of education. For more than two decades he was a moderator of the First Baptist Church and a trustee of the Waterville Public Library and Thomas College.

The entire senior administrative contingent was crowded into Miller Library, including the student deans, George T. Nickerson '24, who succeeded Marriner, and Barbara Sherman, twelfth in a line of deans of women that began in 1896. Until the buildings and grounds department got its own home, superintendent Willard Jennison carved out space in the library as well. Jennison resigned in 1955, and George Whalon took his place. Whalon had a remarkable campus presence, far beyond the scope of his position. He and his wife, Helen, lived on the campus. His big, green Land Rover was everywhere. A dog lover and consummate storyteller, he took care of his crew, and they adored him. He embraced faculty and staff alike, especially the newcomers, whom he sometimes supplied with discarded College furniture or shop-made sandboxes for their children. Students liked him and they amused him. One winter, short of the manpower to cart firewood to the dormitory fireplaces, Whalon put a sign near the woodpile: "Property of Colby College: Keep Off." By spring, the wood was gone. On hearing the story, a trustee quipped that Whalon ought to be made professor of philosophy.[10]

HOUSEKEEPING

Good Housekeeping magazine published an annual Report on Small Colleges in the early 1950s, naming 125 colleges recommended to parents and students. The measurements were financial stability, quality of the faculty, adequacy of the library, and the percentage of students going on to graduate school. It was the first of the magazine ratings that would soon popularize and proliferate, debunked by colleges not included and hyped to the sky by those that were. Bowdoin and Bates were on the Good Housekeeping list. Colby was not. Bixler knew why, and he struggled mightily to raise the intellectual tone of the place. It would take money, and money was in short supply. The subsidized GIs were mostly gone; the flood of "war babies" hadn't arrived. Inflation had eaten into the already meager endowment, and uncertain times and a growing tax rate had closed the wallets of philanthropists.

Bad enough the tides were running in the wrong direction, but forward progress had to be made against a growing chorus of questions about the value of the liberal arts. Traditionalists wanted the curriculum to stay put. Others were bent on change. Some thought small colleges had already sold their souls. "The ivory tower has become the irreverent symbol of a decadent system of higher education," the *Good Housekeeping* article quoted others as saying, even while claiming it wasn't so. The problem, the piece said, is that colleges had "become increasingly concerned with the development of skills and experiences essential in modern society."

Liberal arts champion Bixler knew the toughest fight was in his own backyard. "Ask a student why he chose a college of liberal arts rather than a technical school and the chances are he will be unable to tell you," he wrote, adding that the undergraduate was not alone in his embarrassment. "Even alumni have been known to quail before the effort to explain what their training did for them."

10. Three years after his death in 1970, the College established a George E. Whalon Memorial Grove surrounding Johnson Pond.

Colby's traditional curriculum always had things sticking out on the edges that were concerned with developing "skills and experiences essential in modern society." The ROTC was one, though half the requirement was centered on the liberal arts. The short-lived Division of Nursing and Medical Technology had been another, an obvious hedge against declining enrollments. Nowhere was skill-building more elegantly expressed than in the department of business administration, with its courses in accounting, finance, investments, marketing, shorthand, and typing.

While in the first half of the twentieth century Colby had prepared preachers, and by the second half it was churning out teachers, by the 1950s it was also making movers and shakers in the world of business and industry.[11] Despite the department's successes, purists saw it as a misfit. Shorthand and typing were the first to go; then, to make it sound better, the department name was changed to Administrative Science. It could run from its detractors, but it could not hide. Eventually, in 1989, it was wrapped into the strong economics department and lost its status as a major course of study altogether.

While students were eager for immediately practical instruction and flocked to get free equipment lessons offered by the Burroughs Adding Machine Company, Bixler was looking in another direction. He could get there, he knew, by improving the size, shape, and credentials of the faculty. In 1950 the highest earned degree of most of the faculty was the master's. Only 23 of 75 held the terminal Ph.D. or M.B.A. degree. Bixler wanted new teachers to have Ph.D.'s, and hiring doctors was pricey.

Thirteen newcomers arrived in the fall of 1950, a fifth of the full faculty, and the number of replacements and additions accelerated through the decade. Gone were names tied to the earlier campus: William "Wilkie" Wilkinson, history; George Parmenter, chemistry; and Webster "Bugsy" Chester, the "father" of Colby biology. A few of the old-timers made it up the Hill, but they were no more than settled when they too began to leave. Carl Weber, renowned Thomas Hardy scholar, stayed on a bit to build the College's impressive collection of rare books and manuscripts. Retirements included Edward "Eddie Joe" Colgan, at Colby since 1924 and the educator of hundreds of secondary school teachers; Herbert "Pop" Newman '18, beloved director of religious ac-

---

11. Business-trained graduates came to rank among the most ardent and active alumni. At the end of the century, more than a dozen of the alumni serving on the board of trustees were trained in the world of commerce. Six were business administration or administrative science majors: Lawrence Pugh '56, Douglas Schair '67, Joseph Boulos '68, John Zacamy '71, Edson Mitchell '75, and Andrew Davis '85.

tivities and the last strong official tie to the College's Baptist roots; Lester Weeks, a stalwart in chemistry; and Gordon Gates '19, a short-timer (1948–51) whose reputation in the classroom was exceeded only by his fame as the world's finest expert on the unlikely subject of earthworms.

Older veterans stayed at the expanding center of power. Weber, who led the English department for three decades, issued control to Alfred King Chapman '25, the last true despotic chair. When the Division of Languages, Literatures and Arts was renamed the Humanities, "Chappie" ruled there as well. He lived for a time in Roberts Union where he could keep an eye on his beloved DKE house across the street. His rotund figure, cigarette ashes collecting on his generous shirtfront, was a morning fixture in the Spa, sipping coffee, surrounded by students.

The English department claimed two of the faculty's thirteen women. Luella Norwood was the only female full professor when she retired in 1953. Alice Comparetti had been teaching since 1936. Mark Benbow, arriving in 1950, was the first among more than a half-dozen newcomers in English. Before long, upper-class students and alumni were saying a Colby education was incomplete without having taken Benbow's course on Shakespeare. John Sutherland and Richard Cary came within two years, followed by Irving Suss, whose great contribution was in the inspiration of spectacular student theater. Ed Witham '52 came to help Suss two years after his graduation. The English department was further enriched with the arrival of Colin MacKay and Eileen Curran.

Although Galen Eustis worked full-time as vice president, he continued to lead the teaching of business administration. Arthur Seepe, who replaced Eustis as treasurer, taught with him. Walter Zukowski was a new instructor and was a popular figure in the department for more than thirty years. Eustis died of a heart attack in 1959, his death hastened by the strain of work. When the new administration building was opened the following year it was named, perfectly, in his memory. Ralph S. "Roney" Williams '35 took Eustis's three roles as Wadsworth Professor, chair of the department, and vice president. While he reflected the frugal approach of his mentor,[12] he kept stronger ties to the faculty and exercised a lesser influence over the presidents he served.

Walter Breckenridge had come to Colby with his dear friend Chappie in 1928 and played a similarly strong role in economics and as chair of the social sciences. "Eccy with Brecky" was not for the fainthearted—or for anyone up

12. In the early 1960s Williams took out foul-weather insurance to protect against lost revenues from home football games, and for a couple of rainy autumns made more than would have come through the gate.

late the night before. He arrived for morning class with a single piece of chalk and lectured nonstop for the full fifty minutes. Bob Pullen '41, heir apparent as vice president, was Breckenridge's partner in economics. Robert Barlow was the new star. Kingsley Birge led sociology, a discipline then tied with economics. Newcomers were Frederick Geib and Jonas Rosenthal, who in ten years became dean of students.

The study of sociology was by then barely fifty years old, and Colby claimed a tie to its founding. Albion Woodbury Small '76 returned to teach five years after his graduation and in 1889 became Colby's ninth president, the first Colby graduate. It was Small who established the co-ordinate college, against the wishes of a growing faction in 1890 that wanted to get rid of the "girls" altogether. He served only four years before being lured to the University of Chicago where he led the nation's first department of sociology. His work there earned him the honorific "Father of American Sociology."

John McCoy taught German and chaired the modern language department, his clout multiplied by the power of his additional job as the dictator of class and exam scheduling. Veteran colleagues included Everett Strong and Gordon Smith (French) and Philip Bither '30 (German). Newcomers were Richard Kellenberger (French) and Henry Schmidt (German), soon followed by Archilles Biron (French) from Rutgers where he directed the Colby-Swarthmore School of Languages, Henry Holland, and Francisco Cauz (Spanish).

In the beginning, the art and music departments got by with only two teachers. James Carpenter came from the Harvard faculty to replace department founder Sam Green and worked alone until 1956, when William Miller joined him. Ermanno Comparetti, recruited from the faculty at Waterville High School, handled all of the music until Peter Ré arrived in 1951 to be College organist and director of the glee clubs and choir.

Archibald Allen came to teach classics in mid-decade and, with the help of a single instructor, offered two dozen courses in Greek and Latin. Norman Smith comprised the entire education department, picking up from Eddie Joe Colgan and teaching five courses and a seminar. Psychology soon tripled in size. Parker Johnson, a mover in the arena of curriculum innovation, joined the department in 1955 and later became dean of faculty. James MacKinnon Gillespie arrived in 1951 and resided in a faculty apartment. Gillespie ("Mr. G") was a favorite with students. He ended his career as associate dean of students; from his tiny Lovejoy office, he delighted recalcitrant students by assigning them colorful and irreverent nicknames. An opera aficionado and a talented pianist, he might have taught music in addition or instead.

Paul Fullam, supported by young instructors (including Frederick Gillum and Clifford Berschneider), offered no fewer than twenty-six courses in history and government. Harold "Hal" Raymond, a respected Civil War historian, came in 1952. The end of the decade saw the arrival of Albert Mavrinac with the rare opening appointment of full professor in government.[13] David Bridgman, a brilliant historian, signed on as an instructor; sadly, illness forced him to retire in midcareer.

Bixler himself taught courses in philosophy and religion; when "Pop" Newman retired, Clifford Osborn continued on as chaplain and teacher. John Clark and a newcomer, Richard Gilman, swung the department's weight to philosophy. Two outstanding teachers, Robert Reuman and Gustave Todrank, joined the department in 1956. Over the years each acquired legions of student disciples and taught courses also on the "must take" list that defined a complete Colby education. Adding more luster to the department was Yeager Hudson, who arrived at decade's end.

The new faculty members joined a line of predecessors with broad academic reputations, most evident in the sciences. The biologist Gates, with his thorough knowledge of earthworms, was followed by Allan Scott, a seasoned teacher from Union College with ties that continued at the Marine Biological Laboratories at Woods Hole, Massachusetts. Beloved by generations of students, Scott was every inch the measure of those who taught before. He and Robert Terry soon began to make biology one of the College's strongest departments. Evans Reid and Paul Machemer joined veteran teacher Wendell Ray to bring similar new strengths in chemistry.[14]

The math department entered the 1950s under the leadership of Wilfred Combellack and an accomplished graduate, Lucille Pinette (Zukowski) '37. The department was inspired by the preeminence of a former student, Marston Morse '14, a Waterville native recognized worldwide for his work on the calculus of variations in the large. (In addition to other more useful things, he

13. Mavrinac was a star, an example of the new breed of teacher-scholars. U.S. presidential historian and commentator Doris Kearns Goodwin '64 would later say that he was her "hero."

14. In 1967–68, while Parker Johnson was on sabbatical, Reid served a term as acting dean of faculty.

had shown that by the adroit application of the principles of dynamics, a single game of chess could be extended forever.) Morse had gone from Colby to Harvard and then to teach at various American universities before joining Albert Einstein as an associate at the Institute of Advanced Studies at Princeton. A member of the American Academy of Arts and Sciences, he was Chevalier in the French Legion of Honor and, on appointment by President Truman, a director of the National Science Foundation.

In physics, the torch was passed from Sherwood Brown[15] to Dennison Bancroft, both worthy successors of the remarkable teacher and researcher William A. Rogers. In 1890 Rogers was the first to occupy the Shannon Building on the old campus, a structure he helped to design. In the single laboratory that occupied the entire tiny first floor, he developed the standard yard measure for the U.S. Bureau of Standards (by counting wave lengths of sodium light), a noteworthy achievement made all the more enduring by the impact of the yardstick on the bottoms of generations of misbehaving American youngsters.

Donaldson Koons was the geology department. On deck since 1946, he enjoyed the respect and affection of generations of students. Charles Hickox doubled the department in 1957, and at the very end of the decade its ranks were further bolstered by the arrival of Harold Pestana. Geology (early on including geography) also had a distinguished lineage and through the 1950s was sending more students on to graduate school than any other. Ezekiel Holmes '24 opened the department in 1833. As a student he discovered some of the state's first tourmaline deposits on Mount Mica. Justin Loomis became chair in 1836 and left three years later to become president of Bucknell University. Edward Perkins[16] chaired the department while serving as state geologist, and George Otis Smith '93, chairman of the board of trustees during the early years of the move to the Hill, was for twenty-three years director of the U.S. Geological Survey before being named chairman of the Federal Power Commission.

15. Throughout most of the 1940s, Brown was a teaching colleague of William T. Bovie, inventor of the electrosurgical knife that, to this day, remains in use and bears his name. A native of Fairfield, Bovie began work on his invention at his home on Summit Street before joining the Harvard faculty as a physicist with the University's Cancer Commission. The Bovie knife was patented in 1926, and Bovie sold his rights to the invention for one dollar. When Harvard denied him tenure, he returned to Maine and taught at Colby from 1939 to 1948.

16. The campus Perkins Arboretum and Bird Sanctuary is named in memory of Perkins and his wife. The twenty acres of woodland were dedicated in 1959 and were later designated and protected by the state as a game management area.

By the end of the decade the teaching faculty swelled to 103. Although the newcomers were homogenous in many respects—all white, mostly men and mostly Protestant—taken together the faculty was in other ways enriched in scholarship (nearly half had a terminal degree); and it included many teachers whose reputations served as a magnet for attracting an ever-stronger student body. In the matter of strengthening teaching, Bixler had begun to achieve what he set out to do.

TESTING NEW WATERS

Students and faculty returning each fall became accustomed to seeing new buildings sprouting like mushrooms. Averill and Johnson Halls opened in the fall of 1950, and all the men were finally on the Hill. Mary Low and Louise Coburn dorms were almost finished. The Keyes Science Building finally opened in 1951, albeit crowded, awaiting the 1952 opening of the Life Science Building when four fraternity houses—Delta Upsilon, Zeta Psi, Phi Delta Theta, and Tau Delta Phi—were on line as well. New campus features were not limited to buildings. Summer educational programs burgeoned and the College began collecting fine art. And on top of all that, there were three white ducks.

In 1948, on the day Johnson Pond was dedicated, Frank Johnson had gleefully rowed around the man-made lake in a small boat. After that, except for the occasional splashes of veterans' children[17] jumping off a small wooden dock built at the edge near the road, the pond was calm. The only living things on the water were gulls taking a break from the local dump, a few wild mallards, and an occasional common loon, sadly off course. The newcomers were gifts of Maine author John Gould, who convinced Bixler of the ornamental attraction of having ducks in residence: Indian Runners "with a posture more like a penguin than a goose," Gould said. He wrote in the *Christian Science Monitor*: "Dr. Bixler is a highly cultured man, intellectualized right up to the last notch, and he knows more about everything than I ever will. Except ducks. He is ignorant on ducks. I knew that right away, because he said: 'I think it would be a fine idea.' The story went around the campus that Bixler had asked for bucks but got sent ducks."

Although the birds were fine bucolic props for photographs, having them around was not easy. In the fall when decent domestic ducks were in a barn, Colby's were left for B & G (buildings and grounds) workers to round up.

17. In 1950 there were a dozen.

They were always uncooperative and ungrateful, and the sight of posses with nets inevitably gave rise to speculation that some folks were getting free Thanksgiving dinners.

Not every duck on the Hill liked the pond. In 1965, Deborah Anglim '65, Marcia Norling '66, and Diane Fullerton '66 bought a duckling at a local pet store. Having taken no course in anatomy, they named him Esther. His namesake was star swimmer Esther Williams, but having been raised in the more or less dry confines of Coburn Hall, he didn't care for water. Instead, Esther bonded with his owners and followed them to classes, to the Spa, and to the bookstore. With spring vacation in sight and Esther fast becoming more than a duckling, they decided to release him in the pond. He could go to the afternoon baseball game, but after that he had to leave. They borrowed a canoe and put him overboard in the middle of the pond—several times. Each time he swam fretfully to the bank and waddled after them. At last the women escaped and walked sadly back to Coburn Hall. After supper they got a call. Esther was in the ATO house, watching television.

A better-sounding new feature of 1950 was a baroque pipe organ for the chapel. The gift of trustee Matthew Mellon, the instrument was made in Germany by E. F. Walcker. Its design met the specifications of Bixler's friend Albert Schweitzer who resisted the trend toward making organs sounding like full orchestras. Schweitzer and Bixler wanted the Lorimer organ to play music of Bach, polyphonic rather than harmonic.[18] Even with the new feature, that fall a student fussed in a letter to the *Echo* that student participation at chapel was dismal. The organ piped in one of the first special summer education programs, the Church Music Institute, cofounded in 1955 by modern language professor Everett Strong, organist of the First Congregational Church in town; and Rutgers University professor Thomas Richner, organist of the First Church of Christ, Scientist in Boston. Strong died in 1976 and Richner con-

18. Eighteen years later, with a grant from the Louis Calder Foundation, the organ was completely dismantled and all 2718 pipes, ranging in length from seventeen feet to a quarter-inch, were revoiced. Nearly half were replaced. A series of further improvements were made through the late 1990s, when the heaviest of the pipes, made of poor German postwar steel, began to show sagging feet.

tinued for a total of forty-two summers. In 1989 the program was renamed the Richner-Strong Institute of Church Music.

Summer programs had begun in 1947 when Roney Williams joined the faculty with extra marching orders to find ways to keep the plant running through the summer, to avoid layoffs and make a little money. Williams partnered with Dr. F. T. Hill to develop postgraduate medical courses. The first, the Institute on Hospital Administration, began in 1954. The most prestigious was the Lancaster Course in Ophthalmology, developed by Hill and his brother, Howard, who both had worldwide reputations as eye surgeons. Soon, medical training was offered in a variety of other specialties, forming the centerpiece of a summer enterprise sufficient to prompt the American Medical Association to make Colby the only nonmedical college in the country certified to award AMA accreditation.

When Bill Macomber '27 arrived in 1954 as the first full-time director of adult education and extension, the summer was already filling up. Macomber and his wife and Colby classmate, Peg, lived in Roberts Union and managed an expanding number of summer programs and a series of winter evening "extension" courses for area citizens.[19] Over time, additional programs ranged from Great Books to library science and from occupational safety to coaching. For undergraduates, there was the Colby-Swarthmore School of Languages, created in 1948 and comanaged by Edith Phillips of Swarthmore and John Franklin McCoy of Colby. In 1955 it became a Colby program, with McCoy as director. It was discontinued in 1968 when college students had begun to travel abroad.

The testing of new waters ranged into the undergraduate program. When James Carpenter joined the art department in 1950, he had little in the way of support beyond his own considerable enthusiasm. The College owned few works of fine art, and students studied mostly from slides and prints that Carpenter exhibited in most unlikely places. By the end of the decade there were plans for an art and music building, to include modest gallery space. There

---

19. Enrollment in the medical programs flourished through the years when the Internal Revenue Service permitted full tax deductions for the cost of educational advancement. Physicians and their families came from around the nation and the world, rented camps on the nearby lake and homes in town, and enjoyed Maine vacations while earning continuing education credit. Many of their children eventually returned as students. The IRS tightened the rules in the late 1980s, and the number of participants began to decline.

was neither artwork nor money enough for more, but there were a few who had bigger dreams. Among them were Bangor sisters Adeline and Caroline Wing who had been students of Bixler's uncle and Smith College President L. Clark Seelye. In 1951 the Wings began to make anonymous gifts of works by important American artists: William Merritt Chase, Childe Hassam, Winslow Homer, and Andrew Wyeth.

During a visit to France in the early 1950s, the Wing sisters came across a chateau in Maintenon. It was being torn down and the sisters took a liking to the fireback rescued from Madame de Maintenon's private apartment. They bought it and shipped it home. When the President's House was being built, they offered it to Colby. Bixler later quipped that as long as the house lasts Colby presidents "will look straight at the scene that greeted so often the eyes of Louis Quatorze."

In 1956 Ellerton and Edith Jetté multiplied the tiny collection with the gift of their American Heritage Collection of one hundred primitive paintings, watercolors, and drawings. The gift was intended for students to use in conjunction with courses, but there was no place to show them. Some of the primitive portraits were hung on the high-paneled walls of baronial Foss Dining Hall where their crude faces with following eyes looked sternly down upon the occasional food fight. Students were not universally fond of them, but in time the works became the core of one of the nation's best college collections of early American art.

Willard Howe Cummings and his mother, Helen Warren Cummings '11, donated a collection of American folk and fine art in 1957, and with the Harold Trowbridge Pulsifer Collection of Winslow Homer paintings (placed on permanent loan in 1949), and the Eugene Bernat Collection of Oriental Art, the College's art holdings moved into the realm of the respectable. Cummings was well known as a portrait painter,[20] and in the spring of 1959 began work on a portrait of Bixler. On one of his visits to campus he suggested to Ed Turner,

20. His many subjects included Pablo Casals, Adlai Stevenson, and the actress Bette Davis (who later gave her portrait to the College). A founder of the Skowhegan School of Painting and Sculpture, Cummings led in the development of the school as a recognized center for talented young artists.

the new vice president for development, that an organization of art supporters be formed to help develop the new College art program. Turner and Bixler
readily agreed and the Friends of Art organization was formed that year with
Edith Jetté as its first chair.

As the faculty grew in number and strength, Bixler found many allies in the
effort to improve the overall learning milieu. A Book of the Year program was
established in 1949, and the first selection was Lecomte du Nouy's *Human
Destiny*. While some thought it was a bit controversial (and heavy going), the
bookstore sold 264 copies to an enrollment of one thousand. Librarian James
Humphrey assured Bixler that each copy was certainly read by more than one
student.

The Colby chapter of the American Association of University Professors
(AAUP) was formed that year and was the genesis of a number of educational
reforms and innovations. In 1953 the chapter supported the faculty-initiated
Senior Scholars Program, providing special partnerships for top students with
faculty in writing, research, and special projects. The chapter later pressed for
a required graduation examination within the majors (comprehensives). Both
the AAUP and the Academic Council (full professors only) were forces in
shaping academic policy; by the 1970s, however, both had faded in importance. The AAUP would later revive itself with an agenda bent more toward
matters of faculty pay and privileges.

An elective cross-discipline course for freshmen, "Great Thinkers in the
Western Tradition," was created in 1954, and that year a select number of freshmen were chosen for a course in creative thinking taught by instructors of
art, chemistry, mathematics, philosophy, and sociology. A second "Thinking"
course was open to the upper classes. The required freshman English composition course was revised to develop writing skills based upon classic readings,
and the department adopted Colin MacKay's practice of requiring freshmen
to write biweekly in-class themes. Reflecting the gradual increase in admissions standards, the sophomore writing course (reserved for those receiving a
grade of D or worse in freshman English) was discontinued, and seminar sections were introduced for advanced students.

Bixler, of course, reveled in the scholastic improvements, and he loved
nothing more than an "academic party," focused on intellectual ideas and providing fodder for out-of-class discussion. He saw to it that an academic convocation was held at least once in every student generation. The celebrations
began in 1947 with the first Religious Convocation, and continued with a series of additional academic convocations. The first (1953) had as its theme

"The Liberal Arts in Illiberal Times." A second, "The Rediscovery of the Individual" (1956), was radio broadcast live over America's Town Meeting of the Air. In addition, there were three lecture series, made possible by George Averill, Guy Gabrielson, and Robert Ingraham '51, invigorating the spaces between convocations, and bringing many distinguished speakers to the campus. The convocations were highly touted, and students got the day off to attend. Some did. Bixler said they were "not as responsive as they should be to many worthwhile issues." In fact, he once told the trustees that students "while usually a joy individually, can often be a problem collectively." They did not collectively attend the convocations, and by the end of the decade the class-suspending events were abandoned.

Bixler's constant pushing for improvement of the curriculum got a boost in 1954 when the College received a grant from the Fund for the Advancement of Education, established by the Ford Foundation. The money was used for an internal study that urged broader offerings in art and music, and called for more combined majors and interdepartmental courses. It vindicated business administration, and it pressed the need to find a way to reduce the aversion of men to the foreign language requirement. It also urged faculty to eschew the "recitation" method of teaching and join the trend toward lecture and discussion.

The faculty began to chew on the recommendations almost immediately. The Division of General Studies and the former Division of Languages, Literatures, and Arts were melded into the Division of Humanities and included the department of philosophy and religion. Members also agreed to begin a separate listing of interdepartmental courses in the annual catalogue. Most sweeping was the adoption of new graduation (distribution) requirements. Previously students took two years of English, were required to reach the intermediate level in a foreign language, and took three yearlong courses in social sciences, and two in natural sciences. In the new order of things, students were expected to meet the same requirements in English and foreign language but needed only a single course in each of the divisions. The recommendations led to changes in the overall graduation requirements as well. Beginning in 1957 students needed a minimum of thirty-two grades of C or better in forty courses.

The Ford Foundation returned in 1956 with $432,000 more for faculty salaries, a handsome sum in the days when promotions and raises had much more to do with available funds than with merit. It was not the last time the Ford Foundation would favor Mayflower Hill.

When North Korean troops swarmed south to begin a war in June 1950, college students paid little attention. They believed as they had been told: World War II was the last war. Besides, if there was trouble in Korea (wherever Korea was), the United States was not alone in the fight. The United Nations was for the first time backing its peace role with men and weapons. More worrisome than Korea was the cold war against global communism. After all, there was the raging Joe Mc-Carthy warning of Reds under their own beds, stark images of atom bombs, and all those lessons on how to "duck and cover." The cold war was to last forty years. The one in Korea was over in three.

Soon after World War I, the National Defense Act (1920) created the Reserve Officers' Training Corps (ROTC). When World War II came, ROTC programs at the land-grant universities gave a more measured approach to the draft, and the government was content to build manpower reserves while cadets continued their studies. When the Korean War began, the most vulnerable students were the dwindling number of World War II veterans. Most had already passed through. Only two new GIs entered Colby in the fall of 1950; about one hundred were in the upper classes.

The College's most immediate military role was with the area civil defense program, operating the radiological section of the mobile battalion for the Augusta area. Physics professor Sherwood Brown was in charge. Waterville's city clerk, Charles "Chick" Nawfel, took on an extra assignment as CD director, writing in the 1950 *City Report:* "For the third time in the span of the lives of some of us we will again put down the plow, take up the rifle, and go to war." His local arsenal comprised a single police cruiser.

The war began with no draft, but men over eighteen were required to register with their local boards. "Ask Not For Whom the Bugle Calls; It Calls Thee," the *Echo* headlined. Twenty-three left for the armed forces at the end of the first semester, 1950. Seoul fell again and President Truman fired General McArthur. The faculty, worried that the male enrollment would plummet, once again agreed to offer a full semester of work over the summer. In the spring Truman said students in good standing would receive deferments. With patriotic memories of the last war still fresh, many did not want to be excused. Frank Piacentini '53, a popular athlete, wrote to the *Echo* to say he felt like a slacker. "Simply because a fellow doesn't have the money to go to college," he said, "is no reason why he should have to go in the service before anyone else."

The fledgling U.S. air force had by then created several campus officer-training programs and was inviting interest in more. Many Colby students thought it was a good idea. The faculty wasn't so sure, but voted (29 to 19) to support an application. Sixty-five colleges were chosen; Colby was one. In the fall of 1951 all men students were required to take two years of basic military training, and would be commissioned as second lieutenants upon graduation.

Uniforms, including all but underwear and handkerchiefs, were issued upon deposit of fifteen dollars at the treasurer's office, and the new Cadet Corps was organized into four squadrons, subdivided into flights. Offices were ensconced in the new Keyes Science Building, and drills were held on the athletic fields or, if the weather was bad, in the fieldhouse. On occasion marching units strayed from the athletic fields and onto the walkways of the central campus where cadence calls became a familiar accompaniment to classroom lectures.

In the spring of 1952 the cadets marched down Waterville's Main Street, the smartest unit in the Armed Forces Day (May 18) parade. In mock presidential elections that fall, students picked the eventual victor, Dwight Eisenhower (74 percent) over Adlai Stevenson. Eisenhower was elected on a promise to go to Korea and find a peace. On July 27, 1953, the United States, North Korea, and China signed the armistice leaving the embattled country oddly divided along the 38th parallel. Two Colby graduates, Charles Graham '40 and John Thomson '51, gave their lives in the war.

ROTC continued, strong as ever. In 1955 the program was expanded on a voluntary basis and cadets staffed what was claimed to be the only college ground observation post in the country. From the tower room of Lorimer Chapel, more than one hundred students worked in two-man shifts from midnight to dawn, looking for enemy planes. The watching post was tied by telephone to a "Filter Center" at Dow Air Force Base in Bangor that sometimes sent decoys overhead to test the student watchers.

The success of the Colby ROTC program was quickly evident. In 1956 the College was cited for having not a single graduate candidate "wash out" of flight school. In that same year air force authorities accepted recommendations from Bixler and the faculty for sweeping changes in the ROTC requirements. Separate military courses for freshmen and sophomores were combined into a single freshman course. The sophomore course, approved for ROTC credit, was the traditional introductory course in philosophy. All sophomore men (except veterans) and any woman who signed up took a course called "Logic, Ethics, and Political Theory." Bixler loved it. "We shall have more 'philosophizing' on the campus than ever before," he said. The Pentagon loved it too, and said other colleges should follow the Colby lead.[21]

In the midst of the war, Maine had a brief battle of its own. When NBC TV's *Today Show* went on the air for the first time in January 1952, its weather forecast wasn't of much use in Maine. Dave Garroway and the local *Sentinel* for Saturday, February 16, predicted "occasional light snow," good for Winter Carnival Weekend. Overnight, strong northeast winds circled a low-pressure area off the Carolinas and roared into Maine where the storm met cold Canadian air and stalled—a classic nor'easter. By Sunday morning, the storm had dumped a century-record twenty-eight inches of snow on central Maine. Heavy winds tossed flakes into drifts ten feet high and more.

Monday morning, grounds supervisor Ansel Grindall walked from his home in Winslow and to Stedman's Taxi Stand at the Elmwood Hotel. They laughed when he asked for a cab. It took him two hours to walk up the Hill, often lying down to roll over drifts. He arrived to find the College's lone plow truck, an Army surplus 6 × 6, had been left outside. The crew put chains on all six wheels and began plowing. It took four days to clear the roads and parking lots. By Tuesday buildings were low on heating oil, and Grindall plowed Mayflower Hill Drive for a delivery tanker that had somehow made its way from Searsport to Central Fire Station, but could go no farther.

Classes were suspended for two days. Students dug tunnels through snow piled up in front of entryways. Dave Roberts '55 remembers jumping out of windows on the second floor of Averill Hall. His wife-to-be, Ruth McDonald '55, fearing she might be buried and lost in the drifts, wallowed from West Quad to Mary Low where, with help from Dean Sherman, she and others prepared meals. When desserts ran low, a local ice cream maker, Whitcomb Rummel, delivered forty gallons on horseback. After the roads were opened, some braved a walk downtown to see *Snow White and the Seven Dwarfs* at the State Theater.

Students, of course, relished time off from classes, but when the sap ran in the spring they were eager for another escape. Since the early 1930s, Arbor Day had given the excuse. The observance was Frank Johnson's idea, and students pitched in with free labor to plant, rake, and clean. By the early 1950s students continued to embrace the notion of a short break, but their ardor for cleaning

21. ROTC became optional in 1959; and, with student interest dwindling, the 1965 federal Vitalization Act gave trainees the opportunity to receive commissions after only two years of training.

up and planting trees had withered. Fewer stayed on campus to work; more took the chance to lie in the sun or journey to the coast. Some faculty, whose spring lesson plans were wrecked by the blizzard hiatus, suggested the 1952 Arbor Day be cancelled. With renewed zeal for helping out, students found an unlikely ally in none other than Johnson, who told the *Echo* "a student may learn far more from a project of community cooperation like Arbor Day than he will ever lose by missing one lecture." The conflict wound its way to the floor of the Faculty Meeting, where members were trapped. A vote to rescue a precious day of classes would also be a vote against the Man of Mayflower Hill. Discretion overcame valor. Members agreed to restore the special event, and went one better in recommending the day be named for Johnson himself.[22]

The 1952 snows melted barely in time for commencement. Ralph Bunche was the speaker, a substitute for U.N. Secretary-General Trygve Lie, forced to remain in New York. That summer Waterville celebrated its sesquicentennial, and local men became Brothers of the Brush, growing moustaches, full beards, goatees, and sideburns "to honor the pioneers who built our great city." Jonas Salk had developed the polio vaccine, and nervous mothers soon began to let their youngsters return to the North Street swimming pool. A year later, the last Maine Central Railroad steam-powered locomotive, no. 470, made its final stop in Waterville, and the speedy diesel Yankee Clipper took its place. Eisenhower added the phrase "under God" to the Pledge of Allegiance, and Martin Luther King Jr. accepted his first pastorate, at the Dexter Avenue Baptist Church in Montgomery, Alabama, and began to lead peaceful boycotts of the city's buses.

Tragedy and scandal struck Colby in June 1953. The day before commencement a janitor discovered the body of a newborn baby, a cord around its neck, in a trunk in the storage room of Mary Low Hall. A senior confessed it was her child, delivered in secret the previous February. She pled innocent to a charge of murder, and on appeal in October, was fined $1,000 for concealing the birth of a child and sentenced to one to two years of "imprisonment at hard labor" at the women's reformatory in Skowhegan for concealing its death.

22. The tradition continued under its new name until 1964 when it ended. It was resurrected briefly as Strider Day in 1979.

As the economic and social worlds bubbled, so did the politics of Maine. The state Democratic Party, out of power and out of the Blaine House governor's mansion for two decades, began a revival. Two young attorneys, both navy veterans, led the recovery: Frank Coffin of Lewiston, who later served Maine in Congress and became Judge of the U.S. Court of Appeals for the 1st Circuit, and Edmund Muskie of Waterville. Coffin was elected state party chairman in 1954, and one of his volunteers and advisers was a fellow Lewiston resident, Donald Nicoll '50. While working as a radio reporter, Nicoll had interviewed Coffin and was taken by his enthusiasm for rebuilding the party. Muskie reluctantly agreed to stand for the governorship against the incumbent Republican, Burton Cross. It was a greater challenge to find someone willing to run against the formidable Senator Margaret Chase Smith. Nicoll urged Coffin to approach his history professor, Paul Fullam; and Fullam finally agreed. ("I cannot refuse the call to be a candidate without repudiating everything I have taught.") He was unopposed in the June primaries, and the party geared up for a tough run in November. Coffin got permission from the state committee to raise money to hire an executive secretary; and when the first $1,000 pledge arrived, Nicoll quit his radio job and took the job.

Fullam, forty-seven, was inexperienced as a politician, but in the classroom he was, as Bixler put it, "scintillating." As a candidate, he insisted his campaign would be conducted "on the highest principles of honor and decency," saying that victory at any other price would be "a sorry bargain." He kept his promise. Senator Smith, whose gracious demeanor belied the inner core of a political infighter, was ruthless. Muskie won. Fullam lost, and less than a year later died of a heart attack. At his funeral the new governor recalled that the professor politician "believed that there was no civilization in the world's history that held out so much hope for a better life for the average man and woman as the one we enjoy here in America."

NOT SO SILENT

There were conflicts between the "silent" label young people carried and the things that most attracted them. The generation born of war and depression was said to have no passionate causes of its own, yet many of them went to the front lines in the fight for civil rights. They favored an army general over an academic as their president, but they spawned peacemakers like Martin Luther King Jr. They were conservative in their choices of professions, but they embraced the rebellious music of rock 'n' roll and Elvis Presley, cropped from the waist down for the Ed Sullivan Show, *and they were hardly quiet at all.*

During the war, most students took their academic work seriously, and the era produced a number of fine students and outstanding alumni. (The College had five Fulbright Scholars from 1950 to 1953.) After Korea, increasing numbers viewed college as a nuisance to endure before exploring the enticing opportunities of "the real world." For these students it was hard to focus on learning. Grades of C were just fine, thank you. The American Association of University Professors at Dartmouth couldn't stand it any more. Just as James Dean's *Rebel Without a Cause* was running in the nation's theaters, the AAUP indulged in a bit of rebellion itself, charging that "deep-seated indifference, casual un-preparedness, and habitual absenteeism" threatened an institution's very effectiveness as a center of higher learning. *Time* magazine chimed in, describing U.S. college students variously as "stodgy," "docile," and "inarticulate."

Even the *Echo* crabbed about indifference. Responding to criticism that students were afraid to speak out, the newspaper created an "open forum" column and invited readers to prove the critics wrong. Ann (E. Annie) Proulx '57 jumped at the offer, but her already polished pen sided with the critics. "As disgusting as the apathetic mental stagnation of at least 85 percent of the Colby student body (5 percent are actually numb), is the similarly stagnated 10 percent group of self-proclaimed intellectuals," she seethed, claiming "this little group of the elite (of which I consider myself a passive member) cries often and loud there is no 'mental stimulation' here on campus, that there is no 'thought,' no appreciation of the fine things. It's a rather pathetic situation."

If there was a dearth of "intellectualism," there was no shortage of after-class fun. Almost all of it ran on student energy. Except for the help of a few faculty and staff, College support was limited to a general endorsement and earnest oversight. The largest of all student institutions with some four hundred members, the Outing Club was long and well established. Its offerings had expanded in 1942 when the College purchased an old resort property on the shore of nearby Great Pond. Regular trips were conducted down the coast and up the mountains. The club sponsored the grand annual Winter Carnival, and its subdivision, the Colby Woodsmen, held an intercollegiate meet as a feature of Homecoming Weekend.

The drama club, Powder & Wig, tied both fun and a bit of intellectual stimulation. Cecil Rollins first linked drama to the curriculum in the mid-1920s. It languished until Eugene Jellison '51, while still an undergraduate, pirated the thespians away, introducing theater-in-the-round, and leading students in ever more ambitious productions. The World War II veteran staged a number of plays in the early 1950s, including *All My Sons, Murder in the Cathedral, The Crucible,* and *Mister Roberts,* directed by future chair of the board

H. Ridgely Bullock '55. Plays were produced in makeshift settings (usually in Averill Gymnasium) until 1955 when the B & G department moved into its new airplane hanger and an old farm building near the tennis courts was converted into a home for Powder & Wig. Trustee Frederic Camp put up half of the $5,000 cost, and the place was appropriately named the Little Theater.

Editorships of the yearbook, the *Oracle* (first published in 1867), and the newspaper, the *Echo* (since 1877) were envied prizes as were places with a cappella singing groups, the glee club, the orchestra, and the band. The Colby Eight was flourishing, singing on and off the campus, and at many weddings, including their own. (The era produced a remarkable number of weddings of Colby couples.) Almost every appearance included a performance of their trademark number, "Mood Indigo," purloined from the counterpart Meddi-bempsters at Bowdoin. The women's answer to the Eight, the Colbyettes, began in 1951. Janice "Sandy" Pearson founded the group,[23] encouraged by the energetic glee club director, Peter Ré, who found them music ("It's a Grand Night for Singing," "Deep Purple," and so forth), and even wrote them a song, "Colbiana." The "Ettes" were beginning to perform with Ré's Glee Club and traveling with alumni secretary Bill Millett to club meetings in Maine.

Religious groups, the largest being the Student Christian Association, were expanded to include an interfaith association whose members ran the annual Campus Chest, a fund-raiser for local charities.

Students had agitated for a radio station since moving to the Hill. In the spring of 1951 physics professor Sherwood Brown worked with a new club, Radio Colby, and began testing a single-tone oscillator for a closed circuit station. Hugh Hexamer '52 was the director. Henry Fales '50, already graduated, assembled the transmitter. It was going to cost money to get things up and running, and the College dragged its feet. The *Echo* complained:

> The argument has been raised that Colby students should postpone such ambitious projects as a social center and campus radio station until the Mayflower Hill Development Fund is nearer completion, until the world situation is more clearly defined, until the Manpower Commission decides how many students will be transferred, until the future is brighter. Why didn't our predecessors wait? Were world conditions so predictable in 1939 when Roberts Union was begun? Was Wall Street a stable, reassuring influ-

23. The original "Ettes" were Pearson, Anne Fairbanks, and Carolyn English, from the Class of 1952; Virginia Falkenbury and Elaine Zervas, Class of 1953; and Georgia Roy, Dorothy Forster, Lorraine Walker, Dorothy Seller, and Natalie Harris, Class of 1954.

ence when Colby decided to move to Mayflower Hill? There is more to building a college than the symmetrical arrangement of bricks.

Still there was no station. In December 1953 Carleton Brown '33 gave students time on his local WTVL station, a half-hour weekly program "with the aim of binding firmer relationships between people of Waterville and the students on Mayflower Hill." Finally, at 7 P.M. on October 15, 1956, a bona fide campus radio station, WMHB, 660 on the dial, went live, not on the air but through the heating and water pipes. Reception was possible within 130 feet of Roberts Union, Miller Library, or the Women's Union. Peter Vlachos '58 built the system, carrying the sound through a newly laid pipeline. Bond Wheelwright '58 was the station manager. It didn't last long. There was interference from the growing number of refrigerators and television sets in the dorms, and students complained of hearing rock music over telephone dial tones. (A woman in Mary Low claimed to have picked up a hockey game on her electric toothbrush.)

The year 1956 also saw the College begin to move into the realm of educational television. The adventurer Brown pressed the trustees at Colby, Bates, and Bowdoin to head off "an interested party in Boston" and apply to the FCC for the Channel 10 license. Bates President Charles Phillips took the initiative in 1959. Colby and Bowdoin signed on as partners. WCBB (Colby, Bates, and Bowdoin) got its call letters the following year and went on the air in November 1961, only the sixth educational television station in the country, boasting of "full-scale black-and-white production" and coverage for two-thirds of the state.

Two honor societies, formed in the early days of the new campus, engaged in benevolent works. Cap and Gown came first and chose its membership from among senior women on vague criteria having to do with "contributions to the College and to the Women's Division." Blue Key, a society for men, began soon thereafter. New members were announced at an annual recognition assembly in Averill Gymnasium. New members were "tapped" one by one in the midst of whoops and cheers for those chosen and the palpable pain of those who were not. The societies were discontinued in the mid-1970s, as was the all-college awards assembly.

The Student Council was first in line to enforce the social rules: dances on Saturday night only, no alcohol, and no smoking on the dance floor. Separately, the Women's League, established in 1917, dealt with the many-times-multiplied rules for "girls." A visit to a men's college required written parental permission. Afternoon "calling hours" in the public rooms of the women's dormitories were from 1:30 to 5:00 P.M. (until 5:30 P.M. on the porches) and from 7:00 P.M. until closing in the evenings. "Chaperonage" was required for all mixed parties and in no case could the "girls" attend public dances in town. Only men could smoke on the streets of Waterville.

Then as always, parties were the business of the Greek fraternities. Sororities, with no houses and no party space, played a smaller role. By 1952, with six spanking-new brick houses facing one another on "frat row," fraternities were especially well suited for partying. Delta Upsilon (DU), Zeta Psi (Zete), and Tau Delta Phi (Tau Delt) joined DKE and ATO in 1951, and the sixth, Phi Delta Theta (Phi Delt), began the next year. Lambda Chi Alpha (LCA), struggling to raise money for a house that would not open until 1958, operated in the dormitories.[24] Two additional fraternities brought the total to ten before the decade ended. Sigma Theta Psi, later affiliated with the national Alpha Delta Phi, opened in 1955, and Beta Chi, which became Pi Lambda Phi (Pi Lam), began in 1957. Both were housed in assigned space in the men's quadrangle.

Four sororities made it to the Hill, each with a room in Runnals Union. An old Maine blue law once prohibited sorority houses, and the Baptist-leaning College never disagreed. The oldest sorority was the Alpha Chapter of Sigma Kappa, founded at Colby in 1874 and a national sorority since 1904. Chi Omega began as a local sorority, Beta Phi, in 1895. The remaining two were established in 1904 as local societies that eventually affiliated with national sororities, Delta Delta Delta (Tri Delt) and Alpha Delta Pi. (ADPi) A fifth sorority, Phi Mu, was founded in 1917. It folded during World War II.

Independent students were given the small first-floor Hangout in the west wing of Roberts Union—no competition for the fraternities, which had manpower, facilities, relaxed rules, and a greater zeal to party. Fraternities had yet another incentive. Until the late 1960s, pledging new members was a competitive business. Having the best parties was a boon in the critical game of "rushing" new members.

Under the aegis of the Greeks, 1950s social life was never more vibrant and, with an occasional notorious exception, never more healthy. Students complained little about the fare; authorities complained only a little bit more. Live bands, even at smaller parties, were commonplace. Gerry Wright, a talented local keyboard musician, played regularly at the DU House Saturdays after football games. The *Echo* touted Homecoming, Winter Carnival, and the Sadie Hawkins event for weeks in advance, building suspense over the selection of

24. The last fraternity to have a chapter house on the Hill, Kappa Delta Rho (KDR), waited until 1967 for its own place.

campus queens. Tau Delt helped with Winter Carnival, and the campus Chesterfield representative promised the queen a carton of cigarettes "either regular or the king-sized, according to her preference." The Tri Delt sorority ran the annual Sadie Hawkins Dance, an event inspired by the campus speaking appearances of Li'l Abner's creator, cartoonist Al Capp, with "Kickapoo" punch served beforehand.[25]

The work of running social events was not obstacle-free. Greeks often felt constrained by strict rules related to times, dates, and places of rushing and pledging; the topic kept the Inter-Fraternity Council fussing for years. Detailed regulations, impossible to enforce with regularity, were often bent and sometimes broken.[26] If it wasn't hard enough to manage rushing and pledging, party hosts and hostesses felt further burdened by the fact the campus was supposed to be dry: no alcohol anywhere, under any circumstances. On Homecoming weekend 1951, representatives of the Inter-Fraternity Council finagled a meeting with the board of trustees to see if students could get the rule changed. ("A more appropriate time could not have been chosen," the *Echo* observed. "While the meeting is in progress, students and alumni will be well on their way to getting fried.")

Students asked alumni to join their cause. The response was not helpful. Raymond Haskill '14 wrote: "A College is not a country club. Extended use or the misuse of liquor in a college, I have observed, affects the processes of education in just about the way that it affects the driving of a motor vehicle." Trustees refused to budge and the *Echo* took license in conveying their explanation: "The College cannot accept responsibility for 1,100 students under more liberal liquor laws. We must consider the protection of women. Parents would remove their children. Donations would dry up." And so the campus remained dry, de jure. De facto it was at least damp. Alcohol, mostly beer, was customarily well hidden, but its effects often bubbled into public view. Trustees relaxed their stand on alcohol in 1959, but not without consternation. A yearlong study had led to a proposal that undergraduates at or over the legal drinking age of twenty-one be allowed to consume liquor in fraternity houses and men's dormitories. Its use elsewhere on campus would continue to be forbidden.

25. In a 1954 Colby lecture, Capp took a swipe at the ongoing Army-McCarthy hearings: "nothing I have ever done in Abner is as wild as this!"

26. Lambda Chi, still without a house in 1953, got caught having an off-campus party that not only bruised the rushing code but also, according to local police, "violated state liquor statutes and disturbed the peace." Phi Delt got nabbed for allowing dancing on Sunday, another violation of state law.

The debate leading up to the change brought a firestorm. Benjamin Bubar, superintendent of the Maine Christian Civil League, alleged "bootlegging and heavy drinking on the campus at Colby College in Waterville." Bubar quoted Toynbee in the *Civic League Record* and reminded readers "of the 19 civilizations that have gone down, 16 have followed the liquor road to their doom." He urged "righteous thinking people" of Maine to send their objections to Bixler. The archconservative publisher of the *Manchester* (N.H.) *Union Leader,* William Loeb, did indeed write Bixler: "I may be a bit old-fashioned but I would never send my son or daughter to any college which approves of drinking in dormitories," Loeb said. "This lowering of the moral standards does no institution any good. Many of us here in New Hampshire previously regarded Colby with some esteem, but we could hardly approve of such a regulation as permitting drinking in dormitories."

Bixler wrote to calm parents and alumni in advance of the change. He confessed the total ban on alcohol was not working, and "a large majority of the students are in the habit of breaking the rule." He blamed the social mores of the day. "Many students come from homes in which moderate drinking is not regarded as reprehensible," he said, reporting a "general shift in attitudes among the modern college generation." The status quo, he said, was "intolerable."

The College had indeed found itself increasingly pinched by its own rules. In addition to insisting every fraternity hire a resident housemother, hosts were required to find at least one faculty chaperone for every event. Housemothers knew how to behave during parties. They retreated to their small apartments, closed the door, knitted, and watched flickering black-and-white TVs. Violations or not, a housemother ("Ma") was not a snitch. She might enforce rules; but when it came to reporting names of miscreants to the dean's office, she was deaf, dumb, and blind. Chaperones were only a bit more observant. Cast in the awkward role of having been chosen for their friendliness, they were at the same time expected to police the no-alcohol rule. By the middle of the decade they were complaining that they were unappreciated and ignored, with bacchanalia all around. The short list of willing chaperones got shorter. Fraternities struck on the idea of assigning brothers as chaperones for the chaperones, a change that was imperceptible except that chaperones began getting thank-you notes and the housemother apartments got more crowded.

The rule change was approved at the board meeting in October 1959. Student leaders made a plea for no celebration lest trustees quickly rue their decision. A month later the indefatigable Bubar grabbed headlines again, claiming drunkardness had reached a peak in Maine, citing specifically "excessive drinking and brawling" at Bowdoin and Colby. (At Bates, he said, things were under control.) Dean of Men Nickerson refuted half the charge. "I don't think Mr. Bubar has the facts," he said, "I've never seen any brawling or evidence of it here." As to the matter of excessive drinking, Nickerson turned to B&G superintendent George Whalon. The College was without a security department. The men who worked nights tending the boilers for Whalon were in charge of keeping the peace. Whalon, who had led the new construction at Fort Devens during World War II, doubtless knew excessive drinking when he saw it. He said he hadn't seen any such thing at Colby.

LOVEJOY REMEMBERED

Elijah Lovejoy's sacrifice was all but forgotten. Some scholars and actors on the public stage remembered him, but there were no memorials. The black people of Alton tended his secret grave from the beginning, but they had no way to share their celebration of his life. His alma mater included him on its list of famous graduates but did not otherwise mark his martyrdom. The Lovejoy home in Albion fell to rubble; the family graveyard grew over with weeds. It took a long time to make it right.

In 1890 a man named Bust Loomis, who had stood with Lovejoy at Gilman's warehouse, rescued wood from the dilapidated Lovejoy homestead on Cherry Street in Alton, Illinois, and used it to fashion a bookcase. When Loomis died the piece went to his niece, Mrs. George K. Hopkins. A Baptist minister, the Reverend Melvin Jamison, told Hopkins of the Colby connection, and in 1897 she gave it to the College. That same year a great Lovejoy monument was erected in the hills above Alton. Thomas Dimmock, who often reminded his *Missouri Republican* readers of Lovejoy, led the effort. The state legislature gave funds. The 100-foot marker with a Winged Victory bronze at its top was dedicated November 8, 1897. William Scotch Johnston, who as a young man had helped to bury Lovejoy, led dignitaries to his forgotten grave.

Two years later the Colby Class of 1899 presented a tablet honoring Lovejoy as a "patriot and a martyr" (and, curiously, as a "philanthropist"). It was placed in the old chapel and later moved to the chapel on the Hill. In 1919, Norman L. Bassett '91 had a medal struck to honor those Colby graduates who had fallen in the recent war. On its face was an image of Lovejoy. Bassett took the occasion to scold. "Until this year," he said, "neither the College nor alumni have rendered the tribute we owe him (Lovejoy). The . . . inspiration of Lovejoy should have been woven into the fiber of every boy and girl who came here . . . yet they have come and gone without a [*sic*] knowledge of that life."

In 1929, some ninety-two years beyond Lovejoy's murder, the Illinois Press Association established a Hall of Fame. The first bust placed in the new Memorial Hall was that of Lovejoy. Colby's town-and-gown leader Herbert Carlyle Libby attended the dedication ceremonies. In 1935 the hearthstone from the crumbled Lovejoy homestead in Albion was marked with a plaque and placed near South College. Colby observed the centennial of Lovejoy's death on November 8, 1937. Former President Herbert Hoover spoke in the overfilled old Baptist Church, the site of Lovejoy's 1826 commencement.[27] His address was broadcast on nationwide radio.

In 1947 President Bixler traveled to Saint Louis and to Alton to spin yet another thread in the Maine-Missouri connection. He spoke at a banquet at the Forest Park Hotel in Saint Louis and announced plans for a new Colby "Lovejoy Memorial Building," still a dozen years away. The following year the town of Albion erected its Lovejoy monument, this one on the previously unmarked site of his birthplace. The town gave the deeds for the birthplace property and the Lovejoy family cemetery to the College in 1957.

Many seized upon the Lovejoy story in their own struggles to broaden and preserve sacred freedoms. Illinois Senator Paul Simon wrote a biography, *Lovejoy: Martyr to Freedom,* in 1964 and was the keynote speaker at Colby's 150th Lovejoy anniversary in 1987. Illinois governor and two-time presidential candidate Adlai Stevenson held Lovejoy as a personal hero and often presided at occasions honoring him. The fallen editor is cited in the writings of an unending line of Constitutional journalists known for often unpopular stands on contemporary social issues: Irving Dilliard, James Russell Wiggins, Thomas Winship, Ralph McGill, Anthony Lewis, and so forth. And in Albion, Philip and Janet Dow work tirelessly to honor Lovejoy in the town of his birth.

Of all the torches that burn for Elijah Lovejoy, the brightest is in the hands of another rebel preacher, the Reverend Robert Tabscott of Saint Louis. A Lovejoy zealot and intrepid in support of Constitutional rights, the Missouri-born Tabscott is a daunting figure in the continuing Lovejoy story. Their lives are hauntingly similar, soul brothers across the ages, each one a preacher at the Des Peres Presbyterian Church in Saint Louis, each one talented with words and willing to face the issues of the day, and each one persecuted and reviled for daring to deal with them. At six-foot-six with signature reading glasses melded to his forehead, Tabscott is a colorful and compelling preacher. Inspired by liberal causes, he has lost both friends and pulpits along the way. He

27. President Johnson delighted the crowd when he introduced Hoover as "our extinguished President."

was in the thick of the civil rights movement in the 1960s, and his own mother chastised him for working with black people. Having written tirelessly on the subject, he is today the leading Lovejoy scholar. He wrote and produced the powerful documentary film *Lovejoy, The Vigil,* in 1987, with poet Maya Angelou (also of Saint Louis) as its narrator. When it is shown to schoolchildren, he often appears as Lovejoy, dressed in period costume. He relishes doing research and often walks among the graves of Alton, looking for still more connections.

Colby's first living memorial to Lovejoy was established in 1952 with the initial presentation of the Lovejoy Award, given annually to an editor, reporter, or publisher who has continued the Lovejoy heritage of fearlessness and freedom. The award, presented at a public convocation each November, was Dwight Sargent's idea. Sargent '39 had barely begun a newspaper career when he spoke at a 1944 commemoration of Freedom of the Press Week at Colby. In 1950–51, at the age of thirty-nine, he became Maine's first-ever Nieman Fellow.[28] While at Harvard he struck on the notion that his alma mater should honor both Lovejoy and the nation's best journalists. He called President Bixler and soon found himself in the living room of the President's House making the case for a Lovejoy Award before Bixler, Galen Eustis, and Richard Dyer. They agreed.

The succession of Lovejoy Award winners has become a roster of the most courageous of America's journalists. Through the 1950s many recipients brought echoes of Lovejoy himself, drawn heavily from editors who stood for peaceful racial integration in the face of hateful protests. They included James Pope, executive editor of the *Louisville Times,* the first winner in 1952; Irving Dilliard of the *St. Louis Post-Dispatch* (1953); James Russell Wiggins of the *Washington Post* (1954); Buford Boone of the *Tuscaloosa News* (1957), and John Heiskell of the *Arkansas Gazette,* who made national headlines at the 1958 convocation when he lashed out at Arkansas Governor Orval Faubus for creating "a dangerous and menacing crisis" by sending the National Guard to Little Rock's Central High School.

---

28. A self-professed "Independent Republican," Sargent became editorial page director of the Guy Gannett–owned *Press Herald, Evening Express,* and *Sunday Telegram* in 1955 and four years later was named editor of the editorial page of the *New York Herald Tribune.* At the age of forty-seven he returned to Harvard's Neiman Foundation as its curator. Colby awarded him an honorary degree in 1956, and in 1958 he joined the College's Board of Trustees. He died in 2001 having rarely missed the annual Lovejoy Convocation that he founded.

In 1974 Tabscott founded the Elijah P. Lovejoy Society of Saint Louis, which each year honors people of all walks of life "whose commitment to freedom and justice has made a difference." Two of the first three recipients were the editor Dilliard and Colby President Robert E. L. Strider. (In 1978 the Striders visited Alton where he spoke at a symposium on the 175th anniversary of Lovejoy's birth.) The third recipient was Jesse Lundon Cannon, trustee of the Lovejoy grave. The black people of Alton first assigned a trustee to care for the grave in 1885. Cannon, an Alton mailman, was only the fourth in that long line. Before him were Isaac Kelley, Henry Hunter, and Harry Coates. When Cannon died, his wife, Charlene Louise Cannon, a retired elementary school music teacher, took his place. The Cannons were honored with the presentation of a special citation at the Lovejoy Convocation in 1983. Jesse spoke for the couple and acknowledged that the Lovejoy tradition had, at last, "come full circle."

SPORTS — OVER THE TOP

Expanded facilities and an infusion of aggressive young coaches ushered in a decade of rousing success for the traditional teams. The year 1959, when every team except track won or shared a Maine State Series crown, was called Colby's "greatest year in sports." Everyone thought it was grand. Bixler did too, but he worried that athletic programs had begun to overshadow the classrooms.

Intercollegiate sports were for men only. Women's teams—field hockey, tennis, basketball, volleyball, and archery—were part of a physical education program begun in 1898. Janet Marchant, director since 1940, wanted women's athletics to avoid the "evils" of the men's programs, and the women were safely separated in Runnals Union, with two playfields close by and a third, built in 1955 across the street from the women's dorms. Marjorie Duffy Bither, a physical education instructor from 1937 to 1941, returned in 1952 and championed efforts to balance the scales. In the meantime the only way the "girls" could make sports headlines was to join the Powder Puff Football League, for which brothers of DU fraternity served as coaches of six sorority teams that competed mainly to draw a crowd and, at 25¢ a ticket, raise money for the Infantile Paralysis Foundation (March of Dimes).[29]

29. In 1953, nearly one thousand people watched Jane Whipple (Coddington) '55, later a trustee, and Marlene Hurd (Jabar) '54 lead the Sigma Kappas to a 13–6 win over Chi Omega on a modified Seaverns Field.

Although a croquet match at Bowdoin in 1860 is said to be the College's first intercollegiate competition, the oldest traditional sport, baseball, began in 1867. At the turn of the century, a pitcher from Iowa was drawing the attention of a baseball-crazy world. In 1905 Connie Mack came to watch John Wesley Coombs '06 pitch on the diamond near the railroad tracks and signed him on the spot with the Philadelphia Athletics. They called him "Colby Jack," and in his first season he pitched the longest game on record, a 24-inning, 4–1 victory over the Boston Red Sox. He won thirty-one games in 1910 (including a still-standing AL record of thirteen shutouts) and three World Series games in five days against the Chicago Cubs. In 1914 he was traded to the Brooklyn Robins (Dodgers) and two years later hurled the only Brooklyn win in a five-game World Series against Babe Ruth and the Sox. The new diamond on the Hill was named for Coombs and dedicated at Commencement 1951. Colby Jack was on hand for the ceremonies.

After retiring as a player, Coombs was a college coach, first at Williams, then Princeton, and finally at Duke University (1929–52) where among his players was a young John Winkin. In 1954, thirty-year veteran Colby coach Eddie Roundy suffered a heart attack at the outset of the season and died that summer. Winkin, age thirty-four, took his place. A former Navy lieutenant commander, "Wink" was soon recognized as one of the great students of the game; by the end of the decade the little man with a giant appetite for baseball had coached Colby teams to four straight Maine championships. In 1958 the team posted a 15–5 season before losing to Holy Cross in Colby's first-ever NCAA championships. The following year the team again qualified for the NCAA postseason playoffs, but Bixler said no. The games would conflict with final exams. Students were furious. Winkin gritted his teeth, and the team stayed home.

The decade saw a return to glory in football, played at Colby since 1892. Charles "Nels" Corey replaced Walter Homer as coach at the end of the 1950 season, and Frank Maze took over in 1952. His 1954 team (albeit 1–6) was memorable for the outstanding passing combination of seniors Don Lake and John Jacobs. Jacobs, sidelined with polio in 1952, was named All Maine the next year and in 1954 led the nation's small college pass receivers with 1,100 yards. Quarterback Lake, a mere 155 pounds, completed thirty-four passes for five touchdowns in his final season.[30] Robert "Bob" Clifford, thirty-nine, also a veteran Navy commander, followed Maze as head coach in 1956 and promptly

30. Two years later Lake was killed in an airplane crash while training at Lackland (Texas) Air Force Base.

produced the first outright State Series title since 1941. In 1958 the team stunned the University of Maine when Mark Brown '59 passed to Bob Burke '61 for a 77-yard touchdown and a 16–12 comeback win in the final minutes. (Thereafter, Colby lore claimed Pacy Levine of the sports-crazy Levine brothers beat Burke into the end zone.) The 1959 team fought through three rainy Saturdays to repeat as champs.

Interest in skiing had begun in 1946 when a group of returning veterans, all freshmen, approached Dr. Charles Vigue '20, owner of the Mountain Farm on Waterville's Upper Main Street, and asked if they could reopen the defunct slope on his property. Horatio Russ (H. R.) Dunham '86, operator of the state's largest ski equipment store on nearby Main Street, had owned the farm and built the first slope. The hill had a 400-foot vertical drop in barely 1,400 feet, and boasted a 1,700-foot rope tow—Maine's longest. A wooden jump left skiers precariously close to the Messalonskee Stream on the outrun. Dunham died during the war, and the mountain slope was closed. Ronald Brown, who shared Dunham's zeal for skiing, took over the store.[31] Vigue, the new owner, let students resurrect the place, and over the next three years they cleared the brush, laid out two slopes, reclaimed the jump, improved the road, and built a lodge with boards taken from a barn being razed to make way for Thayer Hospital.[32] The Outing Club, with Don Koons (geology) as adviser, helped, and the first ski club was formed in 1949–50. Faculty members Paul Machemer (chemistry) and Philip Osburg (biology) took turns as coaches, as did a string of students. Captain Jake Peirson '54 was invited to the NCAA national championships in his senior year and paid his own way ($200) to Reno, Nevada. The many hours of work maintaining the slope always far outnumbered the minutes of skiing, and the club all but vanished when the veterans graduated.

Something like ice hockey had been played since 1887 when students cleared snow off a piece of the Kennebec and played "polo" with a team from Coburn. There had been a real team since 1922, always at the mercy of the fickle weather. From 1930 until the move to the Hill, Bill Millett kept the precarious sport alive. Along the way Millett, once a college star himself, produced many re-

31. Although Dunham's began as a ski outfitter, under Brown it later became broadly well known as one of the country's first retail catalogue merchants, selling Hathaway Shirts both in the store and by mail.

32. John Harriman, a champion jumper, led the effort. Others included George Bowers, George Wiswell, Geof Lyford, and Dave Dobson. As a naval cadet, Dobson was killed in a fighter crash in 1951. A ski award was named in his memory.

markable players including Elbridge "Hocker" Ross '35, a member of the 1936 U.S. Olympic team. By 1951 Nels Corey's teams were making and clearing their own ice on a new outdoor rink with floodlights near the fieldhouse. The next year there was talk of abandoning the sport, but an anonymous donor pledged $1,500, and Bixler pitched in $500 to keep it going. Continuation was important not only to students but also to the local French Canadian community that revered hockey like no other sport. Bernard LaLiberte '52 went directly from being a player to coaching the team, and Romeo Lemieux and Wilfred Rancourt were local men who took turns coaching.

Fundraising began for a new covered rink in 1953 when Millett teamed with former players Gordon Jones '40 and Joseph Wallace '43, to raise $85,000. Ronald Brown championed a Waterville effort that added $14,000, and the College put in more than $100,000. Construction began in 1954 for a facility first designed with a roof only. Before the work began there was enough money in hand to enclose it. The arena was dedicated in January 1955 and named in honor of a major benefactor, Harold Alfond, who had already given five athletic fields in the area. Alfond was among the dedication ceremony speakers. He said it was the most thrilling moment of his life. "In all humility," he said, "I ask that I be granted the resources, the ability, and the life blood to enable me to continue to assist young men and women in attending Colby." Time and a generous heart would show his wishes granted.

The rink was the first and only indoor facility in the area, and Alfond wanted to be sure local youngsters could use it. There began the long tradition of giving the local Pee Wee hockey program free use on Saturday mornings and providing time for Albert "Ab" Larson's Waterville Skating Club on Sundays. That fall Jack Kelley arrived to coach. Kelley, twenty-eight, a Coast Guard veteran, had starred at Boston University and was a member of the Olympic team of the American Hockey Association. His broad assignment at Colby reflected the thin coaching ranks and the current status of hockey. He coached varsity and freshman hockey and supervised the intramural and recreational ice program.

> Except for the devout locals, hockey was still something of a mystery on the campus. The *Echo* ran a primer for the uninitiated who had not braved the outdoor cold to watch, explaining helpfully: "The idea of the game is to place the puck into the opponent's net more than they do in yours."

Basketball had been king of winter sports since 1936. Eddie Roundy coached from 1938 to the early years on the Hill, and in 1946 Lee Williams arrived to put a winning stamp on the sport for the next two decades. Colorful, aggressive, and often bombastic, Williams built winning teams and gained legions of fans. Like his coaching compatriots, he was a master of his game. His 1950–51 team (20–8) won the State Series. Ted Shiro '51 and John Jabar '52, leaders on the "Cinderella" Waterville High teams in the mid-1940s, filled the guard positions. Shiro became the all-time individual scoring leader with 1,212 points, a mark that held until 1964. Jabar captained the 1951–52 team to a 24–4 season, at the time the best ever by a Maine college.[33] By the end of the 1950s, Colby had won eight straight State Series titles, sharing the ninth with the University of Maine in 1959.

Soccer was the passion of a single man, athletics department chair Gilbert "Mike" Loebs. He arranged Maine's first intercollegiate game with Bates in 1955; four years later men's soccer became a varsity sport. He coached the teams, formal and informal, for eight years and amassed a striking 49–4–2 record. A soccer field was built across the road from Johnson Pond in 1962, and in 1966, the year of Loeb's retirement, the field was dedicated in his name.[34]

Active but out of the headlines were other teams including golf. Clifford, doubling as golf coach, saw his club team win Colby's first state title in 1957. In the dirt-floor fieldhouse, coach Andy Tryens, followed by John Coons, soldiered with sparse numbers of indoor track loyalists carrying on a tradition begun in 1895.

The overall athletic program had broad appeal. The *Sentinel*, the *Echo*, and WTVL local radio touted upcoming games in excruciating detail. Area supporters were more than spectators. Millett, Loebs, and Roundy began a Colby Junior Club for local youngsters—mostly with Colby ties—and ran Saturday clinics in the fieldhouse, borrowing coaches and players from whatever sport was in season. In the summer Millett operated a popular school for area high school coaches. Frank Lahey came from Notre Dame in 1950; Bob Cousy from the Celtics in 1956. The College built a Little League field on its own land near

33. Then and into the future, the Waterville Jabar family provided more talent for Colby basketball teams than any other: brothers John, Norman, Herbie and Paul, all '52; Tony '54, Joe '68, and Joe's son Jason '96.

34. Loebs, an indefatigable administrator, brought men's basketball (1936), tennis, and golf (1965) to varsity status, and at the same time nurtured an extensive intramural program. He spent thirty-six years in service of the College, thirty-three as athletic department chair and three at the end of his tenure as registrar.

the Messalonskee Stream in 1957, a boon to a thriving eight-team city league. Colby students were among the coaches. Meanwhile, sleep-deprived parents of Pee Wee hockey players faithfully supported the devoted Ray Lemieux who ran a program that began in the early hours of Saturday mornings, long before the winter sun was up.

Department chair Loebs had his capable hands full. The cadre of driven coaches demanded as much and often more than he could give; by mid-decade questions began to arise over the role of athletics in the full spectrum of things. The success of major sports teams developed an ever-larger army of supporters who reasoned there was no better way to broaden Colby's reputation than to dominate in sports. It was, they said, good for students, good for admissions, and good for alumni who gave the money. On the campus, particularly among the faculty, there were those who felt athletics was taking too much of the stage.

Bixler saw it coming. He loved sports—especially baseball—and was an avid fan.[35] Twenty-seven Colby teams won state championships during his presidency, yet he worried about the growing emphasis. In 1952 he wrote one of the most forceful public messages of his long tenure, published on the President's Page of the *Alumnus:*

> the will to win, important as it is, can demand too high a price for its satisfaction . . . when a college is willing to enroll athletes simply so that they can represent it in public contests it has lost all sense of what amateurism means, to say nothing of its awareness of what an educational institution requires for its own integrity . . . if the college itself allows a major share of its scholarship funds to go to students whose chief claim is that they can play games, then it seems to me that the line which divides the amateur from the professional has been crossed. . . . It is safe to say that the relations among the Maine colleges are as friendly and the athletic practices are on as high a level as anywhere in the world of intercollegiate competition. To keep them so the four colleges have now agreed to tell each other the amount of scholarship or other aid received by each boy who plays on an athletic team along with his grades in class. In a day when athletics are under such close scrutiny this is, I believe, an important step and one which our alumni will approve of and support.

---

35. During his brief Army service in World War I he once got himself back across a U.S.-held border without a passport by being able to recite the current major league baseball standings for the guards.

Some alumni approved and some didn't. Worries over "balance and emphasis" came into sharper focus in 1956 when the baseball team was made to pass up postseason play. The year before, a dilemma over drawing lines in athletics came up at sister Bates, where officials relented to a plea from the athletic department—principally concerned with football—to allow freshmen on varsity teams. Bixler refused to go along, claiming "a boy's freshman year should be free of the pressures which varsity encounters might bring." Bowdoin and UMO stood fast as well. Orono had no need to bolster its teams. There were already rumblings the university was getting too big for the State Series. Competition in football ended first, but other races held together eighteen more years until Colby, Bates, and Bowdoin decided to go their own ways entirely.

The flap over postseason baseball play and the Ford Foundation–supported study of the Colby "climate of learning" prompted a closer look at athletics in general. The faculty, in the name of the AAUP (American Association of University Professors), began to raise questions about decisions and policies in both admissions and the awarding of financial aid. The dean of men and dean of women had made all admissions decisions until 1945 when a separate admissions office was established. Two years later, when Marriner became the first dean of faculty, the job went back to the student deans who promptly got themselves an assistant to handle the task; Bill Bryan '48 became the College's first director of admissions in 1951. Earle A. McKeen '29 left an administrative post with the Maine Department of Education in 1956 to assist Bryan and double as the first director of placement.[36] Compassionate and fiercely loyal, Bryan had an unerring eye for promising students. Many under his watch would later say that without his willingness to take a chance they might never have had a college education. An avid fan in almost every sport, he readily admitted his athletic bent, and became a good friend to the insatiable young coaches.

Bixler began to apply the brakes. The Ford study paid special attention to athletics. It revealed, among other things, an astonishing discrepancy between the academic performance of men and women. In the spring of 1955 the Committee on Academic Standing dismissed twenty-seven students. Twenty-two of them were men. The superior performance of women was nothing new—

36. McKeen was well known locally, having served as assistant principal at Waterville Junior High School and as a popular superintendent of the nearby Winslow schools. He wore so many Colby hats that when an outside firm was hired to do an administrative staff survey in the 1960s, it was impossible to place him on an organization chart as he had no clear reporting line. It hadn't mattered; he did all of his jobs well and without much oversight.

women led the men in academic performance from the beginning—but the gap was widening. Women were outdistancing men by a margin of four-to-one in Phi Beta Kappa membership even while the men outnumbered them in total enrollment.

Athletics were not entirely to blame. The era produced a great number of outstanding male student athletes, but at the same time a disproportionate number of those who were electrifying the sports arenas were not lighting up the classrooms. It could not have been surprising. The wars had depleted the number of college-going men and scrutiny of admissions practices showed that, by standard measures of preparedness and achievement, the averages for admitted men were well below those of women.

The admissions process was not alone under the microscope. Soon after the Ford study's examination of admissions came the revelation that well-intentioned sports boosters, allied under the name of Mayflower Hill Associates, were hell-bent in support of athletes. The associates found "adoptive parents" in town where athletes were given room and board to avoid campus costs, and the boosters were working mightily to influence decisions on scholarship awards. Some new scholarships, in conflict with general policies, were de facto for athletes only. The faculty backed Bixler in pressing for reform, and the scales slowly began to adjust. Even so, in varying degrees of intensity, questions of athletic versus academic priorities, emphasis, and balance would come up again and again, endlessly into the future.

BUILDING AND BENDING

Construction went on at a furious pace, with more buildings and lots of moving of the earth. Visitors, accustomed to seeing only bruised ground and unfinished shells, marveled at the appearance of the place. Just as shrubbery and saplings were planted and the grass began to grow, the Maine State Highway Commission announced plans to commandeer two hundred acres and run the new highway straight through the campus. When the fight was over, I-95 had an odd, swooping bend, and the College kept on building.

It wasn't that there weren't any trees; they were simply in the wrong places.[37] Following a plan provided by John Olmsted of New York, the College began

---

37. The City of Waterville had the opposite problem: trees were too many and too big. The city health officer, Arthur Daviau, found it his duty to warn in the annual city report of 1950 that the potential threat of "damage, injury and even life present in some of the large trees that line some of our streets."

to grade lawns, install granite steps, create paths, and plant trees—lots of trees. In the fall of 1949 ten 35-foot to 40-foot elm trees were dug up, bagged, and frozen, and in the dead of winter transplanted to line the walkways to the chapel. The following year, fourteen sugar maples, weighing seven tons each, were set along the mall in front of the library. More than one thousand trees were planted, most under the supervision of the ubiquitous Frank Johnson, who horrified workmen by insisting the quarter top of each precious sapling get lopped off to assure vigorous growth.

Summer landscaping included the elimination of an old road separating the library from fraternity row; then there were the lawns and terraces, graded by hand. Many plantings were gifts. A woman in Cape Elizabeth sent one thousand tulip bulbs. A man from Augusta gave Colorado blue spruces and Norway red pines.[38]

One of the mowers and rakers was young George Mitchell who worked on the grounds crew the summer of 1954 following his graduation from Bowdoin. His father, also George, was a Colby plant foreman. Years later, George the senator often came to speak, including at two commencements (1983 and 1999). While he never told the story in Brunswick, at Colby he rarely failed to tell of his father's great pride in working for Colby, and of the time his father pointed him out to a visitor as he was working on the lawns. "You see that young man over there?" the elder Mitchell asked. "That's my son. Living proof that it takes a Bowdoin degree to work on the lawns at Colby."

If architect Larson had underestimated anything, it was the postwar explosion of automobiles. As parents bought Oldsmobiles and Buicks, students drove cast-off Fords and Chevys. Parking lots, ugly and expensive to begin with, needed expansion. When all students were safely ensconced on the Hill, trustees declared no freshman could bring a car to the campus. Dean Nickerson proffered a slim excuse: "The reason," he said, "is the College feels it has a responsibility to the students' parents to see that the freshmen get regular and balanced meals and that they are ensured adequate time for their studies."

38. The pines were planted in sensible places, but the spruces were set into a "nursery" east of the tennis courts to await the day when more plantings were needed. They were never moved and form an unusual grove near the Lunder House.

MAYFLOWER HILL

Ground was broken for Foss and Woodman dormitories in the fall of 1951. When they were finished the cost of the two, dedicated in June 1952, was almost $1 million. The identical Mary Low and Louise Coburn dorms, finished ten years earlier, had cost $430,000. The Foss name came from the old campus. The first Foss Hall, built in 1904 across the tracks and College Avenue, marked the beginning of a plan to build a separate college for women.[39] President Charles Lincoln White, charged with finding the money, went to Eliza Foss Dexter whose only Colby tie was through a friendship with William Snyder '85, a White supporter. Foss Hall, claimed to be the first building for the exclusive education of women north of the Massachusetts line, opened in 1904. By 1951 the Foss name was the logical choice for the new building. Dean of Women Barbara Sherman took part in the cornerstone ceremony; a year later, dean emeritus Ninetta Runnals spoke at the dedication. She refuted the Britannica definition of a dormitory (an institutional building furnishing sleeping quarters for pupils) and said "most pupils nowadays do not want sleep and others cannot get it."

The Woodman name was not new either. Eleanora Bailey Woodman was a Maine woman and, like Foss, did not attend college. In 1922 she gave the outdoor athletic stadium on the downtown campus, dedicated "to the undying honor" of Colby sons who served "in the cause of country and universal liberty" in World War I. Woodman, with Ninetta Runnals and Louise Coburn, were key in the struggle to achieve campus equality for women. Woodman paid the salary of the first alumni secretary, and became one of the most generous benefactors in Roberts's long tenure. When she died her will designated $200,000 to endow scholarships for women or men. In 1921 Woodman had underwritten a health and physical education program for women, and funded a women's infirmary, staffed with a full-time nurse. (There were no health services for men until 1930 when the College purchased the Bangs estate on College Avenue and made it an infirmary. It soon became coed, with Dr. John Piper in charge.)

As the Hill campus developed, space in the east end of the new Roberts Union was set aside for a men's infirmary, paid for by Bessie Fuller Perry in memory of her physician husband, Sherman Perry '01. The plan was to desig-

---

39. President White was not in favor of the coordinate arrangement. Neither were trustees or alumni. They were alarmed at the increasing numbers of women and the decreasing number of men. In 1900 the board voted to limit enrollment of women to those who lived at home in town or could fit in the meager dormitory space available for women. A committee looking into "future policy" centered its study on the battle of the sexes and, by a vote of two to one, concluded it would be best to continue the coordinate system. Colby could not afford to decrease its enrollment.

nate the small annex of Mary Low for the women, but the space proved too small and, on separate floors, the Roberts facility was made ready for both men and women. The Roberts building was already crowded with multiple uses when Thayer Hospital opened a half-mile away in November 1951. Hospital officials, led by F. T. Hill, agreed part of one wing could be designated for Colby students. It worked less than a year. A measles epidemic swept the campus in the spring of 1952, and the Roberts infirmary was reopened. Mike Loebs was put in charge and Theodore Hardy '28 led a cadre of local physicians providing coverage included Piper, John Reynolds '36, and Clarence Dore '39. Eventually Dore took the lead, and with Susan McGraw Fortuine '26 as head nurse, ran what amounted to a small hospital.[40]

With Foss and Woodman up and running, the new campus began to show its size and symmetry. The first four-year Hill class graduated in 1956 when Robert Frost gave the commencement address and read from *Birches* and *Mending Wall*. That summer new rock star Elvis Presley put *Don't Be Cruel* at the top of the hit parade. Except for shrill winds tugging at the canvas over the commencement platform, Frost's readings must surely have affirmed the bucolic splendor of Mayflower Hill—and Presley's tune could have been a theme song for Colby's fight to keep the new campus in one piece. In August the state highway commissioner David Stevens announced the new interstate highway would run between Mount Merici Academy (which that year opened a new high school) and the College, scarcely a few hundred yards in front of the President's House. It would require taking two hundred campus acres, thirty-one for the highway itself.

Frank Johnson had died only months before. Incredibly, the same encroachments that prompted him to lead the College out of town were threatening again. Never mind the sights and sounds of an express highway: future campus development to the west would become impossible, and expansion of Waterville would be hobbled as well. Earlier, Colby had joined the city in asking to bring the highway close to town, but this was *too* close.

Much of Eisenhower's greatest public works project was already built, and the highway was creeping along on a final path close to old Route 1, north from

---

40. No one ever looked less like a physician than the squatty, colorful, cigar-smoking Clarence Dore, who often wore hunting clothes to work. Seeing him for the first time students and parents were sometimes appalled—until they had occasion to experience firsthand his wizardry as a diagnostician and caregiver. He quickly became an institution within an institution, seeing Colby patients in the early morning and whenever else he was needed, and at the same time managing his own full general practice.

Miami into Maine. The line of the new system was governed by major cities and, except to avoid impossible natural barriers, was laid out by dead reckoning. If there were disputes, matters were settled by eminent domain. By the time the highway reached Maine, planners were in no mood for changes.

Board chairman Leonard called an emergency trustee meeting. Bixler and Eustis formed a war cabinet and hunkered down for a fight. Bixler wrote alumni and parents, prompting hundreds of angry messages to the Highway Commission offices in Augusta. The New England Colleges Fund sent a resolution saying: "To consider limiting Colby's development once again is in itself almost unthinkable." Mayor Clinton Clauson weighed in with a condemning city council resolution. The local chamber of commerce squawked. The Portland law firm of Hutchinson, Pierce, Atwood, and Allen took the brief, pro bono. Leonard Pierce, a Bowdoin trustee and graduate, stipulated on behalf of the firm that they accepted the job "only as a civic duty and without compensation." One of the firm's best lawyers, Sigrid Tompkins '38 was on the case.

Well-known Maine author Kenneth Roberts was furious about the plan, and the power of his pen made him a force to be reckoned with. When British historian Arnold Toynbee characterized Maine as "a backward state, rich in nothing but woodsmen, watermen, hunters and not much besides," Roberts wrote a scathing reply. Now, he said, the Highway Commission would commit "a contemptible sin" if it ran a highway through the Colby campus. If it did, he said, he would be forced to make a public apology to Toynbee.

By October the commission was holding closed meetings to see if there might be a way around the College after all. Engineers posed three alternate routes and unveiled them at a public hearing at the Averill School in town. One of their new plans (2-A) took the road farther west, in back of the campus. It required no land from Mount Merici or Thayer Hospital, but it would relocate the Second Rangeway and take a chunk of twenty-seven acres out of Colby's backyard. Fair enough.

Local agreement wasn't enough. The U.S. Bureau of Public Roads had the last word. State and other federal authorities signed on, but the bureau said no. Commissioner C. D. Curtiss wrote Eustis to say plan 2-A "would introduce considerable adverse travel distance in this important highway with resulting increased cost to vehicle operators." Eustis shot back. The plan would add a mere 44 hundredths of a mile to the highway, and add only $230,000 to the $14 million project. Colby, Eustis said, would cover the extra expense by reducing its claims for acquisition and damages. Maine authorities asked engineers to wiggle the 2-A plan to see what could be done to appease the bureau. At the same time, Bixler and Eustis wrote more letters, this time to bigwigs. Appeals for help in leaning on the bureau went to Governor Muskie, U.S. Senators Frederick Payne and Margaret Chase Smith, judges, newspaper editors, college presidents, and others. The highest reach was to Sherman Adams, chief of staff at the White House. Adams was sympathetic. Whether or not he was the one who got the job done, the bureau relented.

By late October, after fourteen months of combat, the highway war was over. In November 1957 trustees voted to accept $12,000 for twenty-seven acres of land at the rear of the campus. Eustis made it plain the amount in no way reflected the true value, and trustees seized the moment to approve the purchase of other available property between the new highway and the campus and took the further step to authorize the executive committee, forever more, to "make any and all such purchases as it deems to be for the best interest of the College."[41]

With the highway battle over, in April 1958, twenty-nine simultaneous dinners were held throughout the Northeast to launch the College's $2.5 million Fulfillment capital fund campaign. More than half was already in hand. Leonard Mayo '22 was the national chairman. Dinner sites ranged from the Pilot's Grill in Bangor to the University Club in New York and from the Officers Club at the Presque Isle Air Force Base to the Crown Hotel in Providence. A volunteer faculty member was the featured speaker at each event. Each audience heard a recorded message from Bixler, "in stereophonic sound."

The advent of "stereo" wasn't the only remarkable advance of the age. There were others, including Sputnik, the first artificial space satellite, launched by the Russians October 4, 1957. It circled the globe every ninety minutes, beeping a signal as it went. The local *Sentinel* ran a pic-

41. State Highway Department officials were grumpy about having to put a wrinkle in the new highway. Many had long tenure and longer memories. Despite repeated requests made long after there were signs for the college exits in Lewiston and Brunswick, Colby could not get markers until 1983 when George Campbell, a kindly new Commissioner, took pity and gave the order. Thomas College, suffering from the sins of its sister, had to wait as well.

ture of it on the front page—upside down. Americans sulked at being upstaged. Many blamed the nation's educational system for falling behind. Donaldson Koons (geology) said there could be no quick fix and noted that science training had diminished while the impact of science increased. He urged a return to the curriculum of a century before "when every graduate was expected to take mathematics through calculus, mechanics, optics, astronomy, chemistry, physiology, zoology, mineralogy, and geology."

On the line was money needed for three unnamed buildings: one for classrooms, one for administrative offices, and a third for art and music. In the meantime, there was tidying up to do.[42] The goal was exceeded in two years. The classroom building, named Lovejoy, opened in February 1959; the administrative building was opened a year later and named for Eustis. By then there were thirty-four buildings on Mayflower Hill. Many thought that when the art and music building was finished, the campus would be complete.

Bixler had finished much of what he set out to do, and began to consider retirement. Three years earlier, well before anyone (including the dean himself) knew Marriner was retiring as dean of faculty, Bixler and board chairman Leonard began looking for his replacement. Marriner had signaled the day was coming when he would settle into semiretirement and write a history of the College in time for the 150th anniversary in 1963. Bixler and Leonard needed to be ready for the change, and in the spring of 1957 found the man they wanted. In March they announced that in the fall the new dean would be a thirty-nine-year-old professor of English at Connecticut College, Robert E. L. Strider. Leonard later made no bones about it. He and Bixler had been looking for the next president.

At commencement 1959, Bixler announced the Fulfillment campaign was over the top. His further notice that he would retire after one more year overshadowed the fundraising news. He explained he was then sixty-five years old and "an office of this sort needs a person with the energy and vitality only youth

42. Some of the incongruous and unsightly veterans' apartments were bulldozed in the summer of 1958, and the *Alumnus* reported, "Across the vista that has opened up, Colby now has a ringside view of construction on the new expressway." The following year, the first lampposts were installed from the women's dorms to the library. With all of the utility wiring placed underground, the cost of completing the project across the campus was estimated at $75,000.

can offer." When the art and music center was opened that fall, the newly formed Friends of Art presented the College with gifts of more than one hundred works of art at a special dinner held in Foss Hall. The Jetté primitives looked down approvingly as Leonard announced the building would be named for Bixler. In matters of timing, design, and harmony, the naming choice was perfect. Bixler was deeply moved. He whimsically acknowledged he had hoped to be able to name the expensive building for Rockefeller or Carnegie, but no donor had come. (In the naming for Bixler, no one said the center was being named for Mary Bixler as well. Someone should have.) Days later Bixler posed for photographs in front of the main entrance to the center's auditorium. In the frieze over the doorway above his head was a specially designed building insignia with music icons flanked by a pair of elegant wings, a silent tribute to the publicity-shy Wing sisters whose gifts of paintings had begun a stunning collection. In the course of time the wings would take a second meaning, emblematic of a coming museum that would sprout many wings of its own.

SELLING AND SAVING

The 1929 budget showing the feasibility of moving the College included an estimate of $1 million in profit from the sale of the old property. It would be enough, they thought, to pay as much as a third of the cost of the new place. Like almost everything else associated with the move, the guess was innocently but grossly understated. As things turned out, there was barely money to move at all, much less to spend it to save the precious artifacts of the old campus.

For a while, College officials hoped the railroad company that had crowded them off the old campus might save them by buying most of the land. Even before 1941 President Johnson suggested to Maine Central Railroad that it reroute its line and buy the property. Carleton Brown joined the argument, pointing out that by eliminating the safety hazard of the crossing on College Avenue, MCRR could save the cost of guards on the avenue and on Front Street. The railroad didn't bite. Ten years later a large sign was placed on the deserted campus, facing College Avenue:

FOR SALE
Old Colby College Campus
38 Commercial lots, 8 Buildings
See your Broker
or
Supt. of Bldgs. — Colby College

Jeremiah Chaplin, president, 1822–1833

View of the early campus, showing "The Bricks," 1834

Ticonic double-barreled covered bridge and railroad bridge, from Winslow, c. 1885.
Photo courtesy of Waterville Historical Society.

Early river mills on the Kennebec River, south of the railroad bridge, c. 1870.
Photo courtesy of Waterville Historical Society.

Gardner Colby

First woman graduate,
Mary Caffrey Low,
Class of 1874

Hathaway Shirt Company
workers outside the Appleton
Street factory, c. 1890. Photo
courtesy of Waterville
Historical Society.

Two-Cent Bridge, from Head of Falls.
Photo courtesy of Waterville Historical Society.

Elmwood Hotel decorated for Waterville's Centennial, 1902.
Photo courtesy of Waterville Historical Society.

Waterville's
Main Street,
looking north,
1906. Photo
courtesy
of Waterville
Historical
Society.

Arthur Roberts,
president,
1908–1927

Between the river and the railroad, c. 1935

Presentation of the campus deed from Waterville to Colby, April 1931.
Front, left to right, Professor Julian Taylor, President Franklin Johnson,
Board Chairman Herbert Wadsworth, Waterville Mayor F. Harold Dubord.
Back row, Judge Charles Barnes, then Charles Seaverns. Behind Wadsworth is
Walter Wyman, then George Averill. Behind Dubord, Senator Burleigh Martin.
Right corner, Charles Vigue.

Franklin W. Johnson, president, 1929–1942

Inspecting Jens Larson's 1933 campus model. *Left to right,* trustees George Otis Smith, Walter Wyman, Franklin Johnson, and George Averill.

Mayflower Hill signpost marking the way to the new campus, c. 1931

World War II Cadets of the College Training Program of the Army Air Force
march on College Avenue, 1943.

Miller Library, 1945

As a publicity stunt, it worked fine. A photograph of two women students pretending to touch up the lettering was printed in newspapers and magazines around the country. Captions and stories advertised the new Colby. As a sales pitch, it was a flop. Before long the sign looked as forlorn as the crumbling campus buildings it advertised.

When the downtown campus was fully vacated in 1952, Harvey D. Eaton Jr. '16 proposed the College give it all to the city. Neither Mayor Squire nor College officials had any comment. The College needed money for bricks. Some parcels sold quickly. A piece on the corner by Front Street became a filling station. A paint store and a linoleum store went into buildings south of the station. The Phi Delta Theta fraternity house became a supermarket. Father John Holohan leased Foss Hall for a Sacred Heart parochial school. Mary Low, on the corner of Getchell Street at College Avenue, became Robert Drapeau's appliance store. Melvin and Meverett Beck bought two lots near the river on Champlin Street, expanding the family enterprise in metal roofing. Across the way, Yvonne Mathieu bought land to establish a family business, in auto repair. On the central campus a few of the buildings were used for storage. Sears, Roebuck rented part of Memorial Hall.

By mid-decade there were still nineteen parcels of land and six buildings left (Memorial, Champlin, Coburn, Roberts, Hedman, Chemical). In 1955 Governor Muskie, Mayor Dubord, Brown, city engineer Ralph Knowlton, and Keyes Fibre president Wallace Parsons proposed a study of the cost of eliminating the crossings, and that winter Dubord and State Representative Albert Bernier '50 got the Maine Legislature to approve the project. The federal government agreed to pay 90 percent of the cost. In November 1961, the Federal Bureau of Roads—which only a few years earlier had thrown a monkey wrench into the plan to move I-95—approved the $2.6 million project. A month later more of the old campus was sold and deteriorating Memorial and Champlin halls were all that remained. Although Memorial Hall had fallen to near ruin, its razing was surely a crime. Waterville Mayor Cyril M. Joly Jr. '48 tried to raise funds to save it. He might have succeeded if the building could have held together another ten years; then it could have become a National Historic Landmark. Instead, in 1966 it fell to the wrecking ball, and the nation's first college Civil War memorial building was gone.[43]

43. In 1979, Ernest Marriner scoffed at a fleeting effort to preserve the architectural integrity of old Foss Hall even though the building was no longer in the hands of the College. He wrote Dick Dyer to say that while it was by then all "spilled milk," Memorial Hall was "the one building most significant for preservation." Foss Hall, he said, "does

In 1984 the remainder of the old campus was sold to Clifford and Jacqueline Morissette who allowed the College to erect a granite monument marking its original home. It had taken four decades to finally sell it all and then only for an amount barely half the original estimate. The plaque, located near the highway on the south end of the old campus, can be read at risk of life and limb.

> Earlier, at the site of the Elmwood Hotel, local historians also installed a sign denoting the College's first home. This one was quickly taken down. "On This Site," the sign read, "Was Held the First Classes of Colby College." The short-lived sign prompted Professor James Gillespie to quip: "They wasn't English classes, was they?"

Every college knows the awkward emotional distance between alumni and undergraduates. At Colby, with the distance of place as well as time, the gulf was even wider. The campus that most alumni remembered was gone. Students arriving after 1950 had no memory of it at all, and complained they had precious little to tell them of the history of the College they inherited. Pragmatists had outnumbered sentimentalists in the matter of rescuing old campus things. There was barely money for repairs and less for preservation. Nevertheless, everyone agreed two icons had to be rescued: the Lion of Lucerne and the Revere Bell.

The College used its own crews to move the grand marble lion and its accompanying plaque. Ansel Grindall and his men were reluctant to take on the job of moving the precious four-ton sculpture out the second-story window of Memorial Hall, trucking it a mile, and putting it through a basement window of Miller Library. It took eleven days in the snowy January of 1962 for the lion to be moved onto the basement "street" of the library. Later the display was slid along the same floor to an inelegant and obscure place near the newspaper archives. It was too heavy to move any higher.[44]

No item carried to the Hill brought with it more lore than the great bell. Bearing the inscription *Paul Revere & Son, 1824*, the 700-pound instrument

---

not represent the entire college . . . and is not on the original campus." Furthermore, he said, Foss Hall was relatively new, having been built nearly a century after the granting of the College charter.

44. In 2003, at the urging of students, the old lion was again skidded along the ground floor, this time to a more prominent place.

was cast by Revere's son Joseph and purchased new by the College. In its first years it was needed to synchronize classes. A half-century later Memorial Hall got a tower clock; but, as with the Miller Library clock that was to come, it was rarely accurate, and it was the student-powered bell that served to regulate both the finicky tower clock and personal watches. If the tolling for classes was acceptable—especially in the years when it pealed above the din of steam locomotives—it was its annoying 6 A.M. clanging to rouse students for chapel that provided most of its legends. Just as latter-day students occasionally shoot the messenger by abusing bedside alarm clocks, nineteenth-century scholars took revenge upon the annoying bell. Time and again the clapper was removed, once embedded in the masonry of a building undergoing renovation and another time buried in a gravel bank near the river. Once the entire bell was taken by sleigh to Brunswick where students swapped it for the bell at Bowdoin, each one then installed in place of the other. In 1880 the bell was smuggled and shipped to the sophomores at Harvard who, in turn, sent it to the University of Virginia. The College hired detectives who found the crated relic on the deck of a sailing packet in New York, bound for London and addressed "To Her Gracious Majesty, Victoria, Queen, Defender, etc., Windsor Castle, England, C.O.D."

For a time there were plans to hang the bell in the tower of Miller Library. In one of his P. T. Barnum–like moments, publicist Joe Smith suggested rededicating it there on April 19, 1947, the anniversary of Revere's famous ride. He wrote Paramount Pictures and Fox Movietone News to invite them to come and make newsreels. Neither replied. The library plan didn't work out either. In 1951 South College Hall was rented to a furniture company, and the bell was taken from the belfry and put into the basement of Hedman Hall where it ignominiously collected dust for a year until it was installed on the second-floor portico of Roberts Union. The bell and porch got some fixing up in 1979 as part of the Fiftieth reunion gift of the Class of 1929. It rings only on special occasions and on the fall Saturdays of a football victory, a tradition assuring moderate use and preservation.

As the principal part of its 1979 reunion gift, the Class of '29 also provided for the relocation of a pair of iron gates that had once stood on College Avenue in front of South College Hall. First presented in 1927 as a twenty-fifth reunion gift of the Class of 1902, they were intended to be the first of at least five gates to entrances to the in-town campus. No other gates were ever built. Designed by Horace True Muzzy, a Waterville architect, the set was constructed by the local Horace Purington Company, headed by Cecil M. Daggett '03. They were placed at the top of the stairway between East and West dormitories, facing Johnson Pond.

In 1929, after President Arthur Roberts's death, local citizens named the square at the junction of College Avenue and Front and Chaplin streets for him. In 1964, when Roberts Square was obliterated by the road relocation, the monument was taken to the intersection of McCann Road and Mayflower Hill Drive. Sections of the granite post-and-rail fence that once traced the front of the early campus were used to surround it.

Old building plaques were easiest of things to rescue, and most were pried from the walls and brought along. Among them were tablets honoring Jeremiah Chaplin, Samuel Smith, and the martyr Lovejoy, all placed in Lorimer Chapel along with ancient pews from the two earlier chapels, first fastened on the main floor, later in the balconies. The south-wing Rose Chapel took the large wooden plaque listing of the names of early graduate missionaries. The chapel was named for Francis Rose '09 and his wife, Gertrude Coombs Rose '11, missionaries executed by the Japanese army on Iloilo in the Philippines in 1943. The Roses, who operated a small mission station and helped to found the Central Philippine College, chose to flee the Japanese invasion. They hid in the hills with native Christians until they were caught and killed.

As each of the buildings fell, the president's assistant, Dick Dyer, hounded the B & G department to retrieve cornerstones and building markers. They were piled in nearly forgotten storage until the mid-1990s when history buffs Anestes Fotiades '89 and David (Ben) Jorgensen '92 collected the bronze markers and had them installed along a wall on the bridge of the Student Center (later Cotter Union).

The Lovejoy family hearthstone was no more than settled into the ground on the old campus when it was moved to the center of the mall in front of Miller Library. The Lovejoy bookcase, handmade from wood taken from his last home in Alton, was put in the president's office. In 1986, President Cotter uncovered the abandoned practice of placing engraved stone class numerals in Memorial Hall. Dyer had saved them as well. Cotter had the old plaques installed around the fireplace of the Marchesi Pub in the new Student Center. Each year, after Baccalaureate, seniors present their own numerals to be placed with the others. Also rescued from Memorial Hall was a plaque given in 1916 in memory of Edward Winslow Hall '62, professor and librarian (1866–1910), now in the library, together with the bust of the poet John Milton by sculptor Paul Akers, given to the College in 1877 by Boston alumni.[45]

*   *   *

45. Nathaniel Hawthorne saw the work in 1858, soon after it was sculpted, and later said it inspired his *Marble Faun.*

The new campus slowly began to create memorial places and traditions of its own. Most prominent was the 10 ft. × 7 ft. replica of Chaplin's sloop, the *Hero*, a weathervane atop Miller Library. Most obscure was another weathervane, on the president's house, showing the first bars of Ermanno Comparetti's *Mayflower Hill Concerto*, first recorded in 1953. Memorial willow trees, named for Boardman, were planted around the pond, and chapel carillon bells, given by alumni to honor those who died in World War II, were renewed and automated in 1992 and named in honor of former dean of men George Nickerson and his wife, Ruth.

In a curious way the bricks the College struggled to buy became icons themselves. Architect Larson liked the color of the bricks at Harvard but feared their chemistry might be vulnerable to harsh Maine winters. He wanted a harder brick, and Alcaeus Cooley of Portland mixed it for him at the Morin Brick Company in Danville Junction, Maine. The Morin company, which made the Colby bricks in its kilns in Auburn, asked permission to name the new product for the College. It remains a popular standard in the trade.

In 1948 the flagpole on the central mall was dedicated to the memory of the more than one hundred students and alumni who died in three wars. The names are inscribed together with a quotation from the 1841 commencement address of Ralph Waldo Emerson. Nearby is a memorial stone listing the names of those who gave their lives in Korea and Vietnam.

Of the many enduring artifacts on the Hill, none is more curious than the large, tombstonelike "Anti-Gravity" monument, installed in 1960 at the request of the entrepreneur and scientist Roger Babson. The founder of Babson College had given Colby and several other colleges five hundred shares of the American Agricultural Chemical Company, valued at $12,500. He required that the stock could not be sold for thirty-five years and that the College erect a monument devoted to the discovery of a substance immune to gravity.[46] The monument was initially placed near the road on the east side of Mayflower Hill where its tempting inscription invited students to tip it over. In the 1990s it was moved into a grove of pines nearby where the force of gravity and a

46. His antigravity interest may have come from two family tragedies. His son had been killed in an airplane crash; his grandson had drowned.

good deal of concrete keeps it upright. The chemical company became Continental Oil, acquired by DuPont in 1981. When the stock was sold in 1995 it yielded $2.7 million, all of which was used, in accordance with Babson's wish, for science equipment and facilities.

Not the least of the trappings brought to the Hill was the white mule mascot, the 1923 legacy of the legendary tub-thumper Joe Smith. Live mules came and went, but the mule icon stubbornly stuck. In the early 1940s the College briefly adopted a true mule, Aristotle. In 1953 the father of Maury Turney '56 gave a stand-in mascot to the student body, creating a quandary as to who was supposed to take care of him. Louie was already famous, retired after playing a major role in *Aida* at the Metropolitan Opera. It took five men to get him off the train at the Waterville station, and at his one and only Homecoming appearance he bolted from the stadium at halftime. Students renamed him Ybloc (a fittingly backward notion) and pastured him at a local farm. By 1956 they despaired of paying the rent ($150 a year) and decided to do without a live mascot. He wasn't a mule anyway. He was a Sicilian donkey.

3. THE 1960S

ROBERT E. L. STRIDER

In the tracings of history, the turning of a new decade is most often unremarkable. Significant changes rarely align with anything as tidy as a calendar. The year 1960 was different. It precisely marked a number of beginnings. Two young and charismatic leaders moved to the center of the national stage. John F. Kennedy, forty-three, became president and promised a "new frontier." The Reverend Martin Luther King Jr., thirty-one, took the pulpit at his father's church in Atlanta, and stepped up the battle for civil rights. In Waterville, the interstate highway opened its two ramps into the city, creating new opportunities along Upper Main Street and the old Oakland Road (too soon to be named in Kennedy's memory). A crush of motorists threatened to suffocate Main Street, and the city began looking for what seemed to be the promise of urban renewal. On the Hill, the time was ripe for change as well. Seelye Bixler, president for nineteen years, had retired. Taking his place was forty-two-year-old Robert E. L. Strider.

Dan MacKnight, the College electrician, fiddled with the microphone one last time to see if he could stop the screeching. He might as well have turned the decrepit equipment off. The booming basso profundo voice of Robert Strider needed no amplification, even in the cavernous fieldhouse. Rugged and six feet tall with a flattop crew cut, the figure of the new president matched his voice. If it were not for his scholarly black-rimmed glasses, he might have been taken for a linebacker.

Strider had been dean of faculty since 1957. He became Colby's seventeenth president in June 1960, and his October inauguration was significant in any number of ways. For one, no one in the crowd had ever attended a Colby presidential inauguration. The last such ceremony was in the summer of 1908 when Arthur Roberts took an oath at the First Baptist Church. Frank Johnson's inauguration was a private affair, held at the President's House on College Avenue. Seelye Bixler took office without fanfare in 1942, in the midst of war.

Strider spoke of his plan for new academic directions. He said there would be "further development of programs in the languages and the sciences, new departures in philosophy and the study of government, and the adoption of continually more suitable educational methods and devices." He promised there would be "shifts in emphasis toward a greater proportion of individual study in all areas of the curriculum." He also talked of "maintaining a faculty distinguished for teaching and devoted to scholarship" and said there would be strengthening in standards of admission. All of it came true, and none of it surprised anyone, least of all Bixler or the trustees.

Four years earlier, when the time came to replace Marriner, Bixler consulted a Colby friend, Bill Avirett, who had been on the search committee for a new president at Mount Holyoke College. The Holyoke committee had taken a close look at a promising assistant professor of English at Connecticut College, but decided he was a bit too young. Bixler investigated and liked what he found. Strider had written a book, acclaimed in scholarly circles, on the seventeenth-century Puritan writer Robert Greville.[1] He was a popular teacher and had supported faculty-initiated reforms. He was active in Democratic politics and a member of the hierarchy of the Episcopal Church. And, to Bixler's delight, he was a musician.

Bixler also admired Strider's candor. The candidate had very nearly nixed his chances of coming to Colby at all when, at his first private interview, Bixler inquired about what he thought of the College catalogue. "Why on earth," Strider asked without hesitating, "do you have a department of business administration?" Eustis and Williams—half of the entire small department—were in the room. There was a general shuffling of feet. Eustis died before the end of Bixler's term. He almost certainly would have opposed Strider's elevation, as he saw the young dean as something of an upstart, and the two were ideologically worlds apart. Never mind that Strider looked askance at Eustis's favored department, or that the young dean was a Democrat (Strider and his wife, Helen Bell Strider, had worked on the presidential campaigns of Adlai Stevenson), Eustis was accustomed to running things, and Strider was unmanageable.[2]

---

1. *Robert Greville, Lord Brooke,* Cambridge, Mass.: Harvard University Press, 1958.

2. When Strider was first dean, Eustis came to warn of the pressure that would come from all quarters and said if he planned to succeed he'd have to stand up and be his own man. Within weeks the Committee on Academic Standing voted to suspend a prominent football player whose only appeal for reinstatement was to the dean of faculty. Eustis

The 1959 search for the new president, if not pro forma, for the first time was open. Reginald "Styve" Sturtevant '21, a trustee since 1949, was chairman of the twelve-member search committee. More than one hundred applications came in, most of them unsolicited, over the transom. Twenty-four final candidates were interviewed; only two got more than a passing glance. Strider's election was unanimous.

Neither politics nor religion were factors in his selection as dean or president. At his inauguration Strider joked that the Civil War must surely have ended if the grandson of one of General Jeb Stuart's private soldiers could be president at the college of Benjamin Butler. Whether or not he mentioned the tie to the Confederacy, his roots were plainly evident in his name—Robert E. Lee—passed through three family generations.[3] His investiture as president fell precisely on the thirty-sixth anniversary of his father's consecration as Episcopal bishop of West Virginia. Gardner Colby would have been appalled. Episcopalians are a far theological cry from the Baptists, but by 1960 the College had all but shed its Baptist mantle. Two years before trustees had delicately informed the National Baptist Convention that Colby would no longer participate in the annual campaign to raise funds for its "church-related" educational institutions. College-church ties, if not severed, were hanging by a frail thread of institutional memory.

Strider was born in Wheeling, West Virginia. His mother, Mary, died at his birth. He was valedictorian of his class at what was then the Linsly Institute, a private military school in Wheeling, and followed with a year at Episcopal High School in Alexandria. At Harvard he studied English literature and graduated, cum laude, in 1939. For a short while he thought he would make a career in radio—he certainly had the voice for it—but changed his mind.[4] Instead, he worked as an assistant undergraduate teacher at Harvard and Radcliffe and received his Harvard A.M. in 1940. That year, at joint rehearsals of the Harvard Glee Club and the Radcliffe Choral Society, he met Helen Bell, a Radcliffe sophomore. They were married in 1941, and the following year she

---

went to Strider and recommended clemency. A winning football team, Eustis said, was vital to alumni and town relations. Strider reminded the vice president of his earlier advice. The suspension stood.

3. His family considered naming him after Grover Cleveland, but fortunately thought better of it.

4. He later recalled being on the road to Pittsburgh for an audition, reconsidered, turned around, went home, and filled out an application for Harvard's Graduate School of Arts and Sciences. He was going to be a teacher.

finished her degree, Phi Beta Kappa. When war came, Strider served as an ensign and then lieutenant in Navy communications, stationed in Washington, D.C., where Helen found work at the Department of the Navy. Following his discharge, in 1946 he joined the English department at Connecticut College and taught there eleven years (completing his Harvard Ph.D. in 1950) before Bixler brought him to Colby.

The Striders were a team. Her background was in many ways more fascinating, and certainly more unusual than his. Born in Pegu, Burma, Helen was the daughter of Methodist missionaries, and lived with her family at various postings throughout the Far East. In 1934 the family returned to the United States via a jury-rigged Chevrolet camper, the *Wild Goose,* that carried them through the Indian deserts to Teheran, Baghdad, Damascus, Jerusalem, north through Turkey to Vienna, on the ferry to England, and on the ocean liner to New York. When the Bells returned to India the following year, Helen, age fifteen, remained behind for schooling, first in Idaho and then in Connecticut. In Hartford she was taken into the family of Francis Sayre, then assistant secretary of state, and soon became a permanent part of the Sayre family. She attended three high schools before graduating from Western High in Washington, D.C., where she received a scholarship to Radcliffe.

While he was dean, the Striders and their four children lived on Gilman Street. When they moved to the fishbowl of the President's House, she skillfully juggled roles as wife, mother, and gracious hostess to a steady stream of visiting lecturers and other dignitaries. (In 1960 daughter Mary was seventeen, sons Robert "Rob" and William "Bill" were fifteen and ten, Elizabeth "Betsy" was seven.) Through it all she found time to promote music concerts for area youngsters, encourage public conservation, and follow her passions for cooking and gardening. She supported her husband in countless ways, and defended him mightily, fuming privately whenever he was crossed.[5]

Throughout the search process there was some anguish, public and private, about being able to find anyone who could match Bixler. When he announced the formation of a search committee Leonard noted "Colby has had a succession of great presidents" and it was going to be "most difficult to find a man who can measure up to the quality of these men."[6] Strider himself was sur-

5. Helen Strider died on her seventy-fourth birthday, in 1995, at their summer home in Mackinaw City, Michigan. The couple had been married fifty-three years.

6. Following Bixler was, to be sure, daunting, but no more so than the thought of Bixler following the Man of Mayflower Hill, or Johnson himself coming after the beloved Prexy Roberts. Indeed, it was doubtless as difficult for the obscure Rufus Babcock after the ignominious departure of the founding president, Jeremiah Chaplin.

prised to find himself as president. In his first message to alumni, he wrote: "I still have occasionally the uneasy feeling that the trustees must have had someone else in mind to sit behind this desk . . . and that some morning the sheriff will be on the doorstep."

The decade brought not only a new president but also a virtual clean sweep in the rest of the higher echelon. At the top, Leonard, a member of the board since 1933 and chairman since 1947, gave way to his 1921 Colby classmate, Sturtevant, whose father, Chester, had founded the Livermore Falls Trust Company in 1895 and served two terms on the Colby board. The younger Styve now ran the bank. Newcomers to the board that fall were Robert Anthony '38, a teacher at the Harvard Business School, and Wilson Piper '39, a Boston attorney. Each made immense contributions to the College through the next three decades and more.

Parker Johnson was the logical replacement as dean of faculty, having already partnered with Strider in pressing for curricular change. A research scientist and a Fellow of the American Psychological Association, Johnson came from the Bowdoin faculty in 1955 to chair the department of education and psychology. George Nickerson soldiered on as dean of men, but Frances Seaman was only two years into the job as dean of women, following Florence "Polly" Tompkins, who had resigned to join the United States Information Agency. Within the year Dick Dyer became Strider's assistant. Earle McKeen was just then defining Colby's new position of director of placement and in two years took yet another new position, as director of financial aid. Sid Farr returned as an assistant to two veterans, alumni secretary Bill Millett and development vice president Ed Turner. Farr replaced Millett following Millett's retirement in mid-decade. Following Galen Eustis's death the year before, Ralph "Roney" Williams was new to the role of administrative vice president.

The new team met its first test in the spring of 1961. It did not come from within, as so many others would; instead it came, of all places, from the federal government. The National Defense Education Act of 1958 required all applicants for federal student loans to sign an affidavit swearing the recipient "does not believe in, and is not a member of and does not support any organization that believes in or teaches the overthrow of the U.S. Government by force or violence or by illegal or unconstitutional methods." President Eisenhower said the affidavit was "justifiably resented" in the academic community. Senator John Kennedy called it "distasteful, humiliating, and unworkable." Many colleges withdrew from the program in protest. At Colby, where scholarship money was dear, pressure mounted to do the same.

In January 1959, Colby joined with Bowdoin and Bates in issuing a joint statement condemning the affidavit, and with the law still unchanged, in November 1960 the faculty asked the board to withdraw from the program. In June 1961, as Strider was closing his first year as president, trustees said the College would withdraw within a year if the law was not changed. The delay was in deference to students already in the program. There weren't many— fewer than one hundred—but for those who signed the oath and borrowed, the maximum $1,000 loan represented half of the newly increased cost of board, room, and tuition. The College looked to alumni for new loan funds to cover the expected shortfall. Congress repealed the offending requirement in the fall of 1962. Colby, out of the program for less than a year, agreed to re-enter although trustees made it clear they were still opposed to sections of the amended legislation "that contain invidious non-academic discriminatory conditions" for the granting of the loans.

The first storm was weathered and the new team resumed its quest of the goals Strider and others set. Among them was the plan to raise $20 million before the end of the decade. If there were doubters, the number of them quickly dwindled. Within two years three-quarters of the goal was met and the business of curricula reform was well under way.

ACADEMIC ADVENTURES

Changes in the broad curriculum—general requirements, major areas, and programs—come only with the consent of the full faculty, and usually at the rate of retreating glaciers, requiring both pressure and the melting of strong opinions. Colby was accustomed to more rapid change all around (the new campus was evidence of that) and now the faculty began to approve a succession of curricular experiments and enrichments that changed the College forever. Through it all, the core curriculum remained untouched. New features were additions, not replacements, and included expanded opportunities and incentives for independent study, course offerings in non-Western cultures, and the introduction of interdisciplinary studies. Leading the parade was the most striking and pacesetting new idea of all: the January Program of Independent Study.

The germ of an interim study term was already growing when Strider arrived as dean. Sensing a mood for change, Bixler had assembled an ad hoc committee to look into reform. The committee, with Strider soon on board, first investigated the new three-semester, year-round program at Dartmouth. Committee members were impressed, but the full faculty was not. Bixler dismissed the informal group and promptly created an Educational Policy Committee

(EPC), chaired by the dean. He gave the EPC the same charge as before: explore ways of making constructive change in the academic program. In the spring of 1958 a delegation of faculty members urged Strider to have the EPC think more about independent study, and see what could be done to fill the listless academic period between the December recess and first-term examinations in late January.

That fall the committee sketched a program that would end the first semester before the holidays and begin the second semester in early February. They called it a Jan Plan. The idea, fleshed out by Strider, went to the faculty for a test drive.[7] The reception was lukewarm, but the idea survived. The following summer (1959) Colby was one of thirty colleges invited by the Danforth Foundation to send a team to a three-week workshop at Colorado Springs. Each team was to have a project. Colby's delegation—Strider, Mark Benbow (English), Harold Raymond (history), and Robert Reuman (philosophy)— chose to work on the Jan Plan. Their proposal, approved by the EPC that fall, required freshmen to participate in one of a number of classes on special topics. Sophomores would generally work within the division in which they expected to major. Upper-class students would undertake faculty-supervised projects of their own choosing. There would be no grades; students would either pass, pass with honors, or fail. A Jan Plan would be required for each of the four years. ("Otherwise," Strider said, some students "might consider the month a gratuitous opportunity for skiing and little else.")

On the edges, concessions were made. The modern languages department worried students would lose momentum over January, and so the proposal included language refresher sessions. The EPC knew it would be hard getting the votes to approve the proposal in the first place, and in a barefaced political move, agreed that faculty members would teach only every other year. In December 1960, after long and intense debate, the faculty adopted the plan (53 for, 31 against, and 3 abstaining),[8] and the Jan Plan began in January 1962. Colby was the first to have an interim (4–1–4) program, although Florida Presbyterian College (later Eckerd College) had a Jan Plan from the time of its

7. Strider was, by then, president-elect. A colleague, wary of the proposal, asked if perhaps Strider would follow the tradition of Colby presidents and refrain from debate when the Jan Plan idea came up at the Faculty Meeting. Strider had invested far too much in the idea to sit on the sidelines. "Hell no!" he said.

8. The vote may have swung on the plea from Everett Strong (modern languages), most conservative and customarily reticent, who stood to say that, on principle, he generally opposed any changes at all, but that he liked the Jan Plan idea and was going to vote for it.

founding in 1958. Months after Colby approved its plan, Smith College ratified one as well, only to abandon it after 1963.

Over time, no facet of the Colby academic program has been more highly touted—or more often revisited and revised—than the Jan Plan. Critics cite an overall lack of academic rigor. Defenders point to myriad examples of scholarly work. Deans fret that students have too much free time on their hands, and the student activities office works to fill the January calendars with after-class events and other entertainment, rarely well attended. In January, the road to Sugarloaf Mountain is busy with Colby cars, but admissions officers delight in the program attracting creative students who seek opportunities for independent study.

The faculty was let out of its year-on / year-off contract in the mid-1980s when teaching loads were reduced to provide extra time for research. By century's end, less than 15 to 20 percent of the faculty was taking January duty. The Jan Plan requirement was reduced from four years to three and—making a curious disincentive for independent study—January internships and compressed regular courses began to come with conventional letter grades. Although the plan has strayed from its original concept, it has survived with an ever-growing line of students and alumni who will testify that the January experience gave them a new appetite for learning, the discovery of major fields of study, and the opening of unexpected life paths to graduate schools and careers.[9]

Not every venture into more independent study worked. One venture, Program II, was not a complete failure, but its greatest profit may have been its lesson on the limits of student academic independence. The plan called for granting a select number of entering freshmen a full four years of independent study, free from class requirements, without examinations or letter grades. Patterned after the system in place at Oxford and Cambridge for centuries, the idea appealed to officials at the Ford Foundation who thought it was worth a try in the United States. Beginning in 1965 the Foundation funded experiments at Allegheny, Colorado College, and Lake Forest in Illinois. The following year, Colby, Pomona, and Florida Presbyterian (Eckerd) were invited in.

At Colby, there was controversy from the get-go. The grant was made in February, and the Foundation pressed to have the program begin that fall. The admissions cycle was about to end, and there was no time to wait for the next faculty meeting. From his sabbatical leave abroad, Strider sent word to accept the grant and begin the student selection process immediately. Many faculty

9. By the end of the century there were more than 160 American colleges with January programs.

members bristled; some sat on their hands and refused to participate. A few signed on to help. Thomas Easton (biology), James Carpenter (art), Eugene Peters (philosophy), Robert Reuman (philosophy), Eileen Curran (English), and Charles Quillin (associate dean of students) formed a committee that chose twenty-three students from the entering class of 1970. Easton, one of the few scientists willing to wade into uncharted academic waters, was the Program II director. Curran replaced him in the second year, and stayed to the end. A Victorian scholar, she had studied at Cambridge and knew the open system. Moreover, she had a zeal for working with the most eager students, and they, in turn, admired her.

In the first two years, participants came and went. "The best bet," Curran said, is the student "who has the gumption to be different at an age when belonging is of supreme importance." The lack of grades made assessment difficult. Students wrote weekly papers that faculty advisers marked up but did not grade. (Curran agreed it was a problem, noting "No amount of red ink has quite the shock value of an 'F' on a student's first paper.") The downside also included the extra expense of intensive one-on-one faculty oversight, far more than the cost of traditional teaching. Without Ford's money, Colby could not have experimented at all. Program II was abandoned after one generation of students. Of the twenty-three original enrollees, fourteen graduated on schedule (1970). Two others finished late. Seven transferred or withdrew.[10]

Although experiments in independent study grabbed headlines and brought Colby an ever-broadening reputation, independence was not the only umbrella under which change was taking place. Program offerings were branching out as well. In his 1961 commencement address, Supreme Court Justice William O. Douglas chided all colleges for failing to reach out to the rest of the world, and the U.S. government for not embracing Western philosophy in its foreign policy. "We have been possessed with the idea that if we fill underdeveloped nations with refrigerators, bathtubs and tractors the battle against communism will somehow be won," he said. He feared foreign students at U.S. colleges (Colby had fewer than twenty foreign students in 1961–62) would return home thinking of America as "a callous place," and he pointed to racial discrimination as one of the reasons.

10. Experience was similar at the other five colleges, ending after a single student generation. Most called their ventures the Ford Independent Study Program (FISP). Lake Forest called it Operation Opportunity. At every college there were faculty reservations, even resistance, and, while there were many student success stories, there were too many instances where students were unable to handle the freedom or were traumatized by it.

The Douglas remarks did not prompt Colby changes—they were already under way—but they reinforced a growing view that students needed a broader understanding of the world. Until the 1960s the major academic divisions operated in relative isolation. There were only two combined major opportunities, one in history, government, and economics; the other in American civilization. Soon combined majors grew to seven (American civilization; classics combined with English or philosophy, geology, and chemistry; psychology and math; and math with philosophy or psychology), but the first adventure outside these traditional offerings did not begin until 1967 when George Elison (history) came to teach Japanese. A year later a new combined major in East Asian studies was added.

Most noticeable among the gaps in the general catalogue was one that came to be called, for the lack of a better name, non-Western studies (the Far East, Middle East, Africa, and Latin America), the absence of which, Strider pointed out, came from an illusion in higher education "that the history of the world is the history of Europe and its cultural offshoots." In 1961, under an exchange program made possible by Fulbright Fellowships, John Clark (philosophy) taught in India, and an Indian philosopher, Amar Nath Pandeya, came to teach at Colby. The lectureship continued, and in 1964 Vishwanath Naravane established the first course in Indian thought and aesthetics. In mid-decade the College offered Japanese and Chinese history, and African politics. The continuation and expansion of non-Western studies was ensured by a 1965 grant from the Jacob Ziskind Trust.

The worldview also broadened with the burgeoning of foreign study and improvements in the study of foreign languages. In 1961 Archille Biron (French) was named director of a Junior Year in France program sponsored by Sweet Briar College. Colby students joined more than one hundred others from forty-five U.S. colleges for a year of study in Tours. Eileen Curran (English) was off-duty for January 1965 and planned to do research in London. Some students asked if they could tag along and make the trip a Jan Plan. She agreed.[11] The students attended thirty-seven London plays, wrote their papers, and got Jan Plan credit. Soon after, Curran became chair of the faculty's new foreign study committee. At the same time, Jean Bundy (French) took language instruction into the new era with a most modern laboratory on the top floor of

11. Three men and three women signed up, and Curran found a house where they all would live. Campus coed living had not yet been approved. Someone in the dean's office (a "pipsqueak" she said) thought the close sex mixing in London was dangerous and threatened to squelch the plan. Curran prevailed.

the Lovejoy building, where students practiced oral skills at their own pace, mimicking tape recordings of native speakers.

One foreign language initiative involved the introduction of the Spanish language and culture in the local schools. Archille Biron (French) spent a sabbatical leave observing successful foreign language instruction programs at elementary schools throughout France. He encouraged a replication of these programs in Waterville, and in 1960 Henry Holland and Francisco Cauz began teaching Spanish as volunteers at the North Grammar and Myrtle Street schools. Spanish was chosen instead of French to avoid "extraneous influences" on the children.

Expansion of opportunities for hands-on work in the sciences included an instrumental analysis laboratory in chemistry, named in honor of retired Merrill Professor Lester Weeks (1966), and an unusual outdoor science laboratory given via the Maine Nature Conservancy by Hallowell, Maine, conservationist Dorothea Marston (1967).[12]

The term "interdisciplinary studies" was still new in 1966 when Leonard Mayo '22 came as professor of human development and began to bring faculty and students together across departmental lines. He was well suited to his new role. An internationally known social worker, he was director of the Association for the Aid of Crippled Children and served as an adviser to five U.S. presidents.[13] His credentials and warm personality broke down old departmental barriers, and his work, "free from the fetters of precedent," paved the way for many interdisciplinary initiatives. Human development expanded to a major offering (1974). As interdivisional courses grew more commonplace, the major itself was abandoned, but his work made it possible to mount new programs by borrowing faculty members from various disciplines instead of hiring new ones. The scheme worked well in filling the voids.

The old American civilization combined major was in the main a compilation and tweaking of existing courses; none of them centered on the American black experience. Nationwide, many felt the omission, together with dis-

12. The Colby-Marston Preserve, a twenty-acre glacier-formed sphagnum "kettlehole" bog in nearby Belgrade, is named in honor of her late father and Maine educator, Walter Marston, Class of 1871. In 1975 the National Park Service declared the preserve, which holds plant life typically found in the tundra of northern Canada, a registered natural landmark.

13. He had been vice chairman of Truman's White House Conference on Children and Youth, chairman of Kennedy's Panel on Mental Retardation (together with respected Waterville pediatrician Edmund Ervin '36), and a member of Johnson's Committee on Employment of the Handicapped.

tortions in the existing curricula, contributed to racial strife. One small Colby remedy, an exchange program with Fisk, a predominately black university in Nashville, began in 1960, but with few takers in either direction. In his first year on the faculty (1963–64), Patrick Brancaccio offered a Jan Plan in African American literature, the first of its kind at Colby. His course opened the door a crack, but it would be another six years before the study of black history and culture found its way into the regular program.

In 1969 the EPC formed a black studies subcommittee with Brancaccio as chair; Jack Foner came as a sabbatical leave replacement and taught the first regular term course in black studies. At the end of the year Strider, Johnson, and history and government department chair Al Mavrinac urged Foner to stay on to help build a new program.

Foner had been out of work as a teacher for nearly thirty years when he came to Colby. He had begun his career in 1935, on the downtown campus of City University of New York (now Baruch College). In 1941 he and some sixty of his colleagues were called before a state legislative committee looking into suspicious activities in the educational system of New York. Foner was suspect because of his support for anti-fascist forces in Spain and for U.S. trade unions. It also seemed to investigators he was doing altogether too much teaching about the role of blacks in American history. He and the others refused to answer the committee's questions, were labeled as communists, and fired. In 1981 the New York City Board of Education apologized to the victims, acknowledging an "egregious violation of academic freedom." Foner retired from Colby in 1976. In 1982 the College awarded him an honorary degree for his pioneering work in African American studies.

Within a year Colby had a fledgling Black Studies program, one of the nation's first. Foner taught three period courses and a seminar; Brancaccio, black American literature; and Lewis Lester, black psychology. The ten-year effort to mount the new study area was a difficult and often noisy struggle against those who felt the specialty would be too costly, overnarrow, or even unnecessary. And while no black studies program would be for blacks only, there was the unrelenting problem of having precious few blacks in the student body and only an occasional black person on the faculty. In 1971, Charles Bassett (English) led the program in American civilization, soon renamed American studies. It became one of the College's most popular majors. The following year Afro-American studies, by itself, became a major.

A proposal for creating an experimental "living-learning" complex was first floated in 1967 when a committee working on coeducational living urged the creation of a "sub-college" that would provide "a new milieu, which more closely relates living with academic affairs." The following spring, Strider's administrative assistant, Howard Koonce (English), was asked to head a Colby project, funded by the Braitmeyer Foundation, aimed at exploring residentially-based units of faculty-student associations at other colleges. Koonce traveled to some twenty colleges with "sub-college" units and returned convinced Colby should have one of its own. In the spring of 1969 his committee proposed a program focused on interdepartmental courses that would encourage more faculty-student interaction and create a pervasive learning environment. That fall, ninety-three members of the Class of 1973 signed on to live in Woodman and Foss Halls, newly constituted coeducational living units. The hope was to transform these places from "sleeping chambers," into "vital centers of learning." It was named the Center for Coordinated Studies (CCS). Koonce was its director.

The first initiative of CCS was to enliven what many felt had become a moribund freshman experience. Students could choose among four "cluster" areas of interdisciplinary study: bilingual and bicultural studies (French and English), Western civilization (classics, history, English, and biology), human development (biology and English), and an amalgam called "music and the other arts." Within four years the "clusters" expanded to eight, and in 1974 the center offered its first fully coordinated course when Bassett and Louis "Sandy" Maisel (government) joined two courses into a single six-credit course they taught together. Other coordinated courses soon followed. It wasn't long before CCS experimented with a college within itself. CXC ("X" for experiment) enlisted volunteer teachers—faculty, students, and others—offering free courses on both academic and nonacademic subjects. In 1976 a government grant made it possible to include area citizens as both students and teachers.

Like Colby's early Baptist missionaries, Koonce sang the praises of living and learning to students and proselytized colleagues to teach in the program. Many students were attracted. Many faculty members, whose participation was voluntary, were skeptical.[14] At the core of the program was a changing cast of a few faculty associates who worked half-time in the center. Over time, a

14. The direct budget for CCS was never more than $350 a year, although the green

larger group of some thirty faculty affiliates (one-fifth of the faculty) taught occasional courses, without course relief.

By standard measures (SATs, grades) the CCS students were similar to their counterparts elsewhere on campus. In other ways they were perceptibly different. With few exceptions they were not involved in athletics and had a marked tendency to eschew fraternities and sororities. In the selection of majors they tended to choose English or interdisciplinary studies over economics or administrative science. They were, in the main, idealists.

Attempts to extend CCS involvement beyond the freshman year were largely unsuccessful, but the center's influence reached the entire campus. The CCS Academic Planning Board, heavily influenced by students, played key roles in the 1973 acceptance of interdisciplinary majors in both human development and Western civilization, and the center's successful social and residential component became a model for the move to self-governance in other dormitories.

The initial enrollment of ninety-three was never again matched. By 1974 the number dropped to forty. Idealism was, by then, on the wane. Students were eager to find work, and some worried employers would be wary of credentials earned by interdisciplinary studies. Moreover, for those who wanted them, interdisciplinary courses and programs could be found elsewhere. Faculty members, pressed by increased demands of teaching and scholarship, no longer wanted to overload schedules by volunteering in CCS, and support withered. In February 1978, it was simply announced at the Faculty Meeting that the Center for Coordinated Studies would be discontinued in the spring.

Before it ended, CCS broadened and added a new dimension to a campus split that had existed on the Hill since the days of coordination, when student life was divided in both real and artificial ways: women living south of McCann Road, men to the north. Coming on the heels of coeducation, CCS attracted some men south (a few women moved north), but the fraternity houses and the athletic facilities remained powerful male magnets. Not only did the gender balance stay skewed, but now the ideological scales slipped out of balance as well. Conservative elements of the campus lived mainly to the right of the library. Only the bravest and most idealistic men volunteered to live in the south. Like the nation at large, the campus had a New Left (in campus folklore, the phenomenon was un-gently labeled "the jock-freak split"), and CCS became the liberal wing of the campus, a perfect incubator for the discontent and protest that rumbled into the next decade.

---

eyeshades pointed to some $40,000 of lost revenue from the occasional course-relief for faculty and the use of student bedrooms for faculty offices.

Given Colby's precarious beginnings, reaching its sesquicentennial was remarkable all by itself, but the occasion was much more than that. By 1963, Colby had come of age. Faculty and students were getting comfortable in the clothes of the new campus, and, like a debutante, the College began to catch the eyes of a growing world of college-goers. Looking back, if anyone were asked to pick the precise moment Colby moved into the big leagues of small colleges, they would have to choose June 26, 1962. On that day the old Paul Revere Bell rang out across the campus when Strider announced the Ford Foundation had chosen Colby for what was, far and away, the biggest gift in the College's long history.

Word was out that the Ford Foundation planned to make a series of "accomplishment" grants "to develop selected independent institutions of higher education as regional and national centers of excellence." Colleges could not apply; they would be chosen. Any hope Colby might be included in the first round of grants in 1960 was dashed when the Foundation said places with new presidents would not be eligible. But in January 1961, with Strider in office for barely eight months, he received a call inviting him to a meeting with Foundation officials at the upcoming Association of American Colleges (AAC) meetings in Denver.[15] A number of Ford representatives were in the room when Strider arrived. He held forth for an hour or more, and left the room with no promises and a briefcase-load of forms.

A Ford representative visited the campus in the spring of 1962, and several weeks later called Strider to say he wanted to meet some College trustees. The meeting was arranged at Boston's Union Club, where the discussion centered on how much money Colby could raise. At least two dollars would be needed for every one awarded. Ford was giving grants as big as $2.5 million, but only to heavy hitters with strong records in fundraising, and then only with a 3-to-1 matching requirement: $7.5 million. Colby was eligible for between one and two million dollars and would have to raise double the amount. Several trustees speculated the College would do well to come up with a match for the minimum $1 million. They were taken aback when the Ford official said their president had already asked for twice that much. The Foundation settled on

---

15. The meeting was held at the Brown Palace Hotel. A cowboy convention was also in town, making an odd mixture of humanity in the hotel's grand lobby. As Strider rode an elevator to the Ford meeting, a cowboy noticed the tag on his briefcase. "Does Colby have a rodeo?" the fellow asked. "Nope," Strider said, "just a three-ring circus."

$1.8 million, an amount nearly six times more than any gift the College had ever received. The Ford largesse to thirty-five institutions nationwide totaled $114.7 million. Colby was the only Maine college and one of only four New England colleges (with Amherst, Mount Holyoke, and Hamilton) on the full list. In selecting Colby, Foundation officials noted the "vitality" in its curriculum, its strong teaching, and its educational experimentation (Jan Plan). They also cited Strider's leadership and the "strong participation and support" from the local community.

The morning before the public announcement Strider called an employee assembly in Given Auditorium. Faculty and others left the meeting buzzing about the enormity of the gift. Bixler wrote to say the grant was comparable only to the historic occasion in 1930 when the trustees agreed to move the campus. The *Sentinel* called it "a shot in the arm" for the economy of the Waterville area, as the grant would "make it possible for Colby to contribute to the community's social, cultural, and economic life in even greater measure in the years to come."[16] The gift also had a major impact on the $20 million Blueprint for the Sixties campaign, voted on the 1960 fall weekend of Strider's inauguration, and now quickly integrated with a new Ford Challenge Campaign to make the $3.6 million match. Trustees took the lead. Neil Leonard, board chair from 1946 to 1960, was named national chairman. Gordon Jones '40 was general campaign chairman, and Ellerton Jetté was put in charge of major gifts.

It was not a difficult sell. More than one thousand people attended a February kickoff dinner in Boston, the largest-ever off-campus Colby gathering. A full 100 percent of the faculty, administrative staff, buildings and grounds, and food service employees (311) made early contributions. Robert Rowell '49 and Henry Rollins '32 were chairs of a local campaign that raised more than $200,000, twice what was given to keep Colby in Waterville. Alumni giving topped $1 million; parents chipped in $270,000. Through his foundation, Connecticut philanthropist Charles A. Dana gave $300,000 at the end of 1963—the second largest individual gift ever—and it was applied to the cost of a new $1.4 million women's dorm, the nation's seventh college building to bear the Dana name.

The Ford money came without restrictions and provided, as Strider said, "the opportunity to determine our own destiny and pursue our own way." A

16. Strider's elder son, Rob, momentarily dampened the exuberance when, at an evening party at the President's House, he spoke up from a corner of the room to caution there was little time to celebrate. He had calculated that if Colby were to meet the challenge, his dad would have to help raise $137 an hour, day and night for the next three years.

down payment of $400,000 had to be spent in the first year. The boom in student applications prompted trustees to plan an increase in enrollment from 1,200 to 1,500 by mid-decade, and some of the first money went for preliminary work on the new dormitory, a women's playfield, laboratories and equipment in the sciences, and library improvements. The rest was for faculty salaries and financial aid. In June 1964, the pot had reached $3 million. Two months before the end of the campaign, a bequest of $400,000 from the estate of an old Colby friend and English professor, Florence Dunn '96, put the effort over the top. On June 30, 1965, with all counted, the College exceeded the challenge by $1 million. A total of $4,622,950 had been raised in three years. Strider borrowed from Lewis Carroll, and called it "a frabjous day." Colleagues and other friends celebrated with champagne and strawberries in the back yard of the President's House.

Dunn grew up in a home opposite the President's House on College Avenue. Her grandfather, Reuben '67, made his fortune as a developer of the Lockwood cotton mills and as founder of the Dunn Edge Tool Company along the Messalonskee Stream. An accomplished writer and teacher of English, she served on the Colby faculty and the board, always working for the equal recognition of women. (Judge Cornish once said "she fought for the girls without making a nuisance of herself.") In the early 1920s she made a key gift of $25,000 for a women's gymnasium on the old campus, and in 1939 another to build the Women's Union named for her friend Ninetta Runnals. Four decades after the campaign-making bequest of 1965, in the midst of the kickoff phase of yet another Colby capital campaign, her estate yielded a second bequest. This one was for $1.6 million.

In five years, faculty salaries rose 39 percent and the financial aid budget vaulted 191 percent. Success in meeting the Ford challenge brought riches beyond what the money could buy, and the occasion of the sesquicentennial provided a perfect opportunity to show it off. Observances began in October 1962 with an academic convocation centered on the topic of the influence of machines on the life of man. Speakers were Frank Stanton, president of CBS; Gerard Piel, editor and publisher of *Scientific American;* and Oscar Handlin, Harvard's Winthrop Professor of History. Barnaby Keeney, president of Brown University (the only Baptist-founded New England college before Colby), spoke as well. Marriner's *The History of Colby College* was released in November; and on February 27, 1963, the dean spoke on the precise anniversary of the signing of the charter and the creation of the College. Strider ordered a birthday cake, and he and Marriner cut it for the photographers.

Some thirty colleges and universities sent delegates for the grand finale in the spring. Over two days, the fieldhouse was jammed to hear addresses by Stuart Udall, U.S. secretary of the interior; Earl Warren, chief justice of the United States; and Thomas Storke, editor of the *Santa Barbara News-Press* and the 1962 Lovejoy fellow.[17] Birthday celebrations ended on Alumni-Commencement Weekend with the largest crowds ever. Bixler returned to give the Commencement address.

It was a remarkable year, but when the clamor and speeches were over, the most enduring feature of the observance was an exhibition of Maine art. The Ford grant gave the College itself new prominence; the show vaulted the tiny art museum onto the national stage. The idea of mounting the ambitious sesquicentennial art show came from inveterate promoter Joseph Coburn Smith, by then a trustee and consultant on public affairs. Three years before the anniversary he was asked to propose how best to celebrate. As usual, his suggestions were over the top: invite the president of the United States to speak, give honorary degrees to Albert Schweizer and Charles de Gaulle, commission Leonard Bernstein to conduct the Colby orchestra. His proposal also included the notion the College might "gather a really notable exhibition on 150 years of American art, or something similar."

The College took the "something similar" idea. With only a part-time curator, Christopher Huntington, plans were made for a survey exhibition, not of American art but of two hundred years of art in Maine, a state rich in art and artists. The exhibit, "Maine and its Artists, 1710–1963," opened in May 1963. Thousands came to see it. *Time* touted it as one of the world's twelve most outstanding international shows of the year. The magazine recited the places to visit: New York, Paris, London, Brussels and . . . Waterville, Maine.

17. The Sesquicentennial Committee had wanted President Kennedy as the featured speaker; the chief justice was an alternate choice. Warren spoke on the morning of the second day, May 17. That afternoon he took a stroll on the campus and stopped for a rest and to enjoy the view from the steps of Runnals Union. Within minutes, nearly one hundred students gathered around, and he chatted with them for nearly an hour. The serendipitous gathering was one of the warmest and most memorable moments of the entire anniversary celebration.

A book by the same name was published in conjunction with the show (Viking Press, 1963); for collectors and dealers, this book remains the definitive work on the art of Maine. After its Colby closing in the fall, the show traveled to the Portland Museum of Art, the Whitney Museum in New York, and the Museum of Fine Arts in Boston.

Just as the building of the Bixler Center provided the impetus for more ambitious undertakings in the visual arts, so too the facility made possible new ventures in music. Under the leadership of Mary McGowan, and with help from Helen Strider and Willard and Helen ('11) Cummings, the Friends of Music group was founded in 1961. Four decades later, subscriptions of the Friends made it possible to open the annual music series to the public without charge.

The Summer School of Music was established in 1963. Under the direction of Colby composer and conductor Peter Ré (music), the school began with the world-famous Juilliard String Quartet as faculty-in-residence. The following summer the Hungarian String Quartet began a nine-year run as teachers in the monthlong program offering master classes and public summer concerts.[18] The following year Ré began an eleven-year stint as conductor and music director of the Bangor Symphony, the nation's oldest community orchestra.

Two of the principal benefactors of the arts were Ellerton (honorary L.L.D., 1955) and Edith (honorary M.A., 1962) Jetté. By 1960, the Jettés were already prominent Maine art collectors. Their American Heritage Collection gift to Colby in 1956 was the core of the College's holdings. The Jetté success came from shirtmaking. A Connecticut native, he left his studies at Boston University to serve in World War I and never returned to school. In 1932 he was the lead investor in the purchase of C. F. Hathaway, the country's oldest shirtmaker.

The new Hathaway president was as elegant and gracious as the fine shirts he sold. He made friends easily and never seemed out of place driving the only Rolls-Royce in a town where all the Cadillacs were counted. Like the company's namesake, he was obsessed with quality; unlike Hathaway, however, Jetté had a bent toward the flamboyant. Hathaway didn't like buttons at all; Jetté liked them king-sized, and, for added distinction, with three holes. His

18. In 1966 the quartet included in its final summer concert Ré's own three-movement Quartet no. 1, first performed by the Juilliard Quartet in the opening summer. The score became part of the Hungarian's repertoire.

innovations included the introduction of oval collars, square-cornered cuffs, single-needle stitching, and one-piece sleeves. He led the shirt industry into the world of exotic fabrics and color: silk and Madras from India, gingham from Scotland, prints from France, broadcloth from Japan, and Lochlana from Switzerland. At heart, he was a marketer and a promoter. Under his leadership the old company flourished as it never had before and never would again.

The advertising icon for Hathaway shirts was the famous "man with an eye patch." David Ogilvy of the prestigious New York advertising firm Ogilvy, Benson & Mather took credit for creating the branding image often cited as the epitome of advertising genius. In fact, it was Edith Jetté's idea. One evening in the winter of 1950 as she and Ellerton were traveling on a cruise ship, an elegantly dressed man with an eye patch entered the state dining room. Edith whispered to her husband that they had found the Hathaway man. The following September "The man in the Hathaway shirt"—gray mustache, white shirt and tie, black eye patch— first appeared in the *New Yorker*. Sales of Hathaway shirts soared. (Ogilvy client Rolls-Royce saw a similar profit jump in 1957 with use of the slogan: "At 60 miles an hour the loudest noise you can hear is the electric clock." The line, almost verbatim, was first used in 1933, to sell the Pierce-Arrow.) When Jetté became trustee chairman at Colby, he convinced Ogilvy to join the board. It was not a good match. Ogilvy thought many of his trustee colleagues were too "Victorian." He quit.

When Warner Brothers acquired Hathaway in 1960, Jetté stepped down as president. In 1965 he retired from Hathaway altogether and agreed to follow Sturtevant as chairman of the Colby board. Although Strider and Jetté came from different worlds, they were in many ways soul mates. Jetté was a Renaissance man, with interests and talents ranging from manufacturing and marketing to the fine arts. (Fellow trustee and former chair Neil Leonard called him "a creative businessman turned humanist.") He supported Strider through thick and thin, and throughout his tenure (1965–70) there was plenty of the thin. The two men found the most common ground as visionaries. Jetté, in fact, wanted to add a "dreaming committee" to the list of otherwise traditional and functional trustee committees. It didn't happen, but at least twice Jetté called selected trustees and key administrators to brainstorming retreats.

The Jettés were engaged with Colby well before he took his turn as board chair. Together, they helped to make their dreams for a noteworthy museum come true. When the College decided the new Bixler Center should have a real museum, the Jettés scoured the circuit looking for someone to make a naming gift. They were not successful. On the eve of the sesquicentennial show, Strider announced that the new gallery would be named for them.

"TIMES THEY ARE A-CHANGIN'"

Young people began to gather on the new road even as the decade opened. By the time Bob Dylan gave them an anthem in 1964,[19] they were already joined in the crusade for social change and civil rights. It was, most certainly, a battle that "shook the windows and rattled the walls."

For many, ugly memories of the integration battle at Little Rock High School had faded. In February 1960, a small group of protestors staged a sit-in at the segregated lunch counter of the Woolworth Store in Greensboro, North Carolina, and when at the same time the Reverend King took his new pulpit in Atlanta, the demonstrations multiplied. Nightly television carried stark pictures of the conflicts, and the nation again became anxious. As the tide of confrontations rose, students at Jackson State University in Mississippi passed a simple resolution favoring integration. The college's president abruptly abolished the student governing body. Many students were suspended and five were beaten in the melee that followed.

Colby's student government sent a telegram to President Kennedy and his brother Robert, the attorney general, protesting the abridgment of academic and constitutional freedoms. Students at Harvard and MIT formed an Emergency Public Integration Committee (EPIC) and began picketing Boston's Woolworth stores. In March, Colby students created their own EPIC, with the philosopher and pacifist Robert Reuman as faculty adviser, and called a public meeting for "anyone who ever felt disgust at the way the southern situation is handled." Some 150 gathered in Lovejoy Auditorium, and for more than two hours talked of ways to respond.[20] Someone suggested one or more of the sus-

19. "The Times They Are A-Changin'," Bob Dylan, 1964.
20. By coincidence, the following week United Nations Under Secretary Ralph J. Bunche came to give a Gabrielson Lecture on Africa in the U.N. Bunche knew of the EPIC meeting and encouraged the local committee. "Significant material and moral support is needed," he said, "for those who are combating discrimination in our country." He came to speak again, in April 1965, a month before his son, Ralph Bunche Jr., graduated from Colby.

pended students be brought to study at Colby. Jackie Lee '63, one of a half-dozen black students, warned it might not be such a good idea, that Colby was not altogether free from discrimination itself.[21] A white student from North Carolina cautioned students to move slowly. She blamed the Civil War for the southerners' "dislike" of Negroes, and Eisenhower for perpetuating the problem by sending troops into Little Rock. "Southerners like to feel superior to Negroes," she wrote in the *Echo*. "Isn't that human nature? Don't Maniacs feel superior to French Canadians?"

The idea of staging a sit-in at the Waterville Woolworth store was rejected out of concern that it would "further unfriendliness and misunderstanding." Instead, EPIC sent a letter to the local manager protesting his company's discriminatory policies, and agreed to raise scholarship money and send it south. A work project was scheduled for a Saturday afternoon in April. Thomas Junior College students pitched in and local clubs and churches agreed to find work raking leaves and taking down storm windows. EPIC raised $539.65 and sent it to the NAACP. Thurgood Marshall, director and counsel to the association, wrote to say thanks.

Although the topic of discrimination had been swirling for some time, there was little evidence of racial discrimination among the fraternities or sororities. Of the small number of minority students enrolled, a few were pledged to Colby chapters, almost always in defiance of the national organizations. Many local chapters had begun to pester the nationals to abandon onerous membership requirements.

Jacqueline Ruth Nunez of Freehold, New Jersey, was a sister of Chi Omega, a writer for the *Echo,* and a member of Student Government. In May before her 1961 graduation she introduced a Stu-G motion calling for the abolition of discriminatory clauses in the charters and constitutions of all campus organizations. She felt pressure from Stu-G might assist the local chapters in their efforts to force the change, and she acknowledged that a student initiative would take the heat off an administration likely to face resistance from alumni if it took that road by itself. The Nunez Proposal was part of a rising tide of pressure on the national organizations from colleges across the country. The "grand worthy chief" of Alpha Tau Omega (ATO) explained the organization

21. A classmate, Camilo Marquez, later recalled that there were too few black students for generalizations to be made about the campus climate. He said he was not discriminated against because of his color and, besides, black students were not looking for recognition as a community, "just acceptance on our merits."

was a "Christian fraternity," and freely acknowledged both racial and religious discrimination. The local chapter ignored the rule. Lambda Chi Alpha (LCA) eventually removed membership restrictions (1964), but held that brothers "must believe in the principles of Christianity." Efforts to eliminate restrictions at both the national and local levels of Phi Delta Theta (PDT) were routinely overruled by the majority vote of its national members. The sororities had no written rules, but local presidents feared expulsion from the national organization if they sought to admit a Negro.

In the fall, Student Government embraced the Nunez Proposal, giving it extra teeth by calling for a deadline of June 1963. The Faculty Meeting concurred. Strider added his own endorsement and in November took the proposal to a board of trustees laden with fraternity alumni. Trustees took aim, but did not pull the trigger. Although they expressed opposition to any fraternity or sorority that discriminated, they gave no deadline for compliance. Strider was horrified by the trustee inaction. He told his wife, Helen, that perhaps they had made a mistake in coming to Colby. Student leaders were enraged. The *Echo* charged that bigotry had played a role in the board's decision, and that trustees were clinging to an "old Colby," and running against the tide. "There is nothing quite so touching about an Old Regime," an editorial said, "as its death." Board Chairman Sturtevant replied in an open letter in which he confessed the omission of a deadline was in deference to alumni, "whose contributions are largely responsible for Colby's establishment, maintenance, and future growth."

The first board vote had been a narrow one. Bixler, now a life trustee, might have turned the tide. Instead, he did not speak up and later confessed to Strider he had been asleep at the switch. He had not seen the ambush by those who lined up ahead of time to oppose a deadline. Sturtevant, Neil Leonard, Dwight Sargent, and a handful of others led an effort to have the trustees revisit the question, and a year later, in November 1962, the board finally gave the Greeks an ultimatum. They had until Commencement 1965 to satisfy the requirement or be banned from the College.[22] More than a dozen other colleges had by then taken a similar stand.

Slowly, the national fraternities gave in, but there were casualties along the way. Williams College abandoned its fraternity system altogether, citing a waste of energy in its efforts to erase the "rigors and humiliations of the caste system." The ATO chapter at Bowdoin, protesting the "whites only" rule, dis-

22. The extended deadline was in deference to the national organizations, some of which had tri-annual general meetings.

affiliated. At Colby, the ATOs and other chapters hung on until the national organizations relented. In 1964 the national sorority Delta Delta Delta (Tri-Delt) ended its fifty-six-year association with the College. Its national president wrote Strider to say Colby's criteria "cannot be reconciled with our organization." Colby's Tri-Delts formed a new local sorority, Delta Alpha Upsilon.[23]

It took ten years to heal the rift between the student body and the trustees, and by that time there were new divisions. At the end of his tenure as Stu-G president, Frank Wiswall Jr. '62 wrote a letter to Sturtevant in which he cited "a tremendous lack of rapport" between students and trustees, caused in some measure by the board's "slight" in ignoring the student position on the fraternity/sorority matter.

Student mistrust of the established order, growing since the beginning of the decade, turned to despair and disillusionment on a cloudy Friday in November 1963, the day John Kennedy was killed. Many of them, like their teachers and others, wept openly. That night, Strider called students and faculty to Lorimer Chapel to "share a common grief." He said "the emptiness we feel tonight will never leave us" and that Kennedy had "reaffirmed our faith in the dignity of man, at the same time that he has shared with us our common condition, in triumph and in suffering." Five days later, classes on the Hill and in the local schools were canceled as millions watched the televised funeral.

Although ten million Americans who hadn't voted for him would later say they had, claims of an affinity with the fallen president in Maine and at Colby had some validity. The College gave his father, Joseph P., an honorary degree in 1946. Following the Democratic National Convention in the late summer of 1960, candidate Kennedy made his first campaign stop in Bangor. In the fall, David Buston '60 organized Colby Young Democrats to greet him on a Sunday night in Portland. Dean Nickerson gave permission for the women supporters to be out after eleven. Henry Wingate '61 bodily carried the back-ailing Kennedy from

23. Jackie Nunez graduated at the top of her Colby class and went on to earn a master's degree at Harvard. She was teaching at Bedford Hills (Massachusetts) High School when she became ill and died in 1966, at the age of twenty-seven. Led by her former roommate, Gracie Hall (Studley) '61, classmates established an all-College award in her memory. The Nunez Prize is given each spring to a senior woman who has demonstrated "academic excellence and personal leadership."

MAYFLOWER HILL

the airplane to a waiting flatbed truck. In the month before the 1960 election, the *Echo* ran a political advertisement from the *Harold Poll* of Cambridge that harshly played upon Kennedy's religion: "If we elect a creature that does not worship once in a church other than his own without the permission of his religious boss, will we have a man or a mouse in the White House?" Response to the ad was immediate and damning. The price of the ad was $1.90, and the editors said they wished they hadn't taken it. When Kennedy made his last Maine appearance at the University stadium at Orono a month before his death, many Colby students were in the huge and enthusiastic crowd.

The summer after the assassination, college students composed a majority of the quarter-million people who marched on Washington and heard King speak of his dreams. After King's speech and Kennedy's death, the commitment of college students to find racial justice became unshakable. Although many students came to revile Lyndon Johnson for the lingering war in Vietnam, for now they stood with him as he embraced his own convictions and the Kennedy legacy in the fight for civil rights. Before the 1963–64 year ended, Colby students formed chapters of the national Student Nonviolent Coordinating Committee (SNCC) and the Northern Student Movement (NSM). Each group worked to raise money in support of efforts to register Negro voters in the South and pressed for passage of the new Civil Rights Act, slowly moving through Congress.

Despite Colby's remote location, students were well informed on world issues, helped in no small measure by a steady string of prominent visitors who came to teach and speak. Besides the headliners who added sparkle to the Sesquicentennial, the 1960s brought a succession of notables including Bunche, and former Kennedy advisers Henry Kissinger, Adam Yarmolinsky, and Zbigniew Brzezinski. In 1962, James Jackson, editor of the communist newspaper *The Worker* squared off in a colorless debate with Senator Muskie.

The year 1964 opened with two lectures, each more significant in retrospect than at the time. In January Michigan Congressman Gerald Ford came at the invitation of Student Government Association president Stephen Schoeman '64. Ford had been named to the Warren Commission, investigating the Kennedy assassination. The subject was off-limits. On the whole, his lecture was uninspired, although students listened carefully when he borrowed from Thomas Paine and said it was "no time for summer soldiers and sunshine patriots." A final bit of advice, while portentous, would in a short while seem unnecessary. "It will be an evil day in this country," he said, "when it is wrong to say no."

Four days later a crowd jammed into Averill Gymnasium in Runnals Union to hear James Meredith, who two years before had tested the federal school desegregation laws and under the protection of federal troops became the first Negro student at the University of Mississippi. Meredith, self-effacing and outwardly shy, warned the current crisis in race relations was "more explosive than the issues of slavery," and unless a solution could be found "another Civil War could very well be in the making."[24]

In the spring, as Meredith graduated from Ole Miss and the Reverend King began a march from Selma to Montgomery, the Colby chapter of NSM staged "a peaceful picket" in Post Office Square, denouncing a Senate filibuster of the Civil Rights Act. Colby's commencement speaker was the U.S. ambassador to the United Nations, Adlai Stevenson, who spoke lightheartedly to the matter of student activism:

> I think we older people ignore students at our peril these days. While sometimes their emotion exceeds their judgment, student demonstrators have even been toppling governments all over the world. . . . It is getting so that old-fashioned dictators can't enjoy a safe night's sleep any more. Happily for us, students have not tried to overthrow the Government of the United States, but they certainly are making their views felt in public affairs. I think especially of the participation of American students in the great struggle to advance civil and human rights in America. Indeed, even a jail sentence is no longer a dishonor but a proud achievement. Perhaps we are destined to see in this law-loving land people running for office not on their stainless records but on their prison records.

At the same time Stevenson exhorted students to "fight against injustice and for its victims" and, "above all, do not wait too long, for time is about the only commodity in America of which we do not have enough."

---

24. In the minutes before Meredith's lecture, as he was being interviewed in a second-floor room by *Echo* editor Jan Wood (Parsons) '65, a pickup truck pulled up the loop road in front of the Union. A man got out and bounded up the front steps, threatening and yelling racial epithets from the back of the packed gymnasium. There was a brief scuffle before he was subdued and arrested. Police found a 30-30 rifle and ammunition as well as handmade racist posters in the back of his truck. Meredith did not know. Two years later, during a freedom march in Hernando, Mississippi, a sniper succeeded in wounding him.

In July 1964, with King at his side, President Johnson signed the Civil Rights Act and a month later received the Democratic nomination to face Barry Goldwater in the fall elections. That summer Bobby Vinton sang *Roses are Red* at the Skowhegan Fair, WTVL Radio brought Don McNeil and his Breakfast Club to Waterville, and the literary giant E. B. White came to Colby to receive the Presidential Medal of Freedom. White had been on Kennedy's prize list at the time of the assassination. Johnson wanted to honor the late president's choice, but White's wife, Katherine, was too ill to travel to Washington. The Striders and the Whites were friends, and so it was arranged for Senator Muskie to make the presentation in a brief, private ceremony in the boardroom next to Strider's office. When it was over, White commented that during the drive from his home in North Brooklin, he had pondered the significance and current relevance of the names of several Maine towns (Union, Liberty, Hope), including one he had driven through that morning: Freedom.

BREAKING THE MOLD

Circumstances, events, and new regimes of leadership called urgently for changes in the old order, at home and around the world. Nikita Khruschev had put up a wall in Berlin, and in Waterville a battle raged over an urban renewal project that would rearrange the face of downtown. A slumping Maine Central Railroad discontinued its passenger service to Waterville and Northeast Airlines removed LaFleur Airport from the list of stops for its DC3s. On the Hill, the first wave of baby boomers altered the size of the student body, and in the midst of it all, Strider was launching his own fight to escape the monotony of treasured campus architecture.

Colleges saw the postwar babies coming, and administrators smacked their lips at the prospect of greater selectivity and of added money for strained budgets. Faculty members, always happy to teach brighter students, were not eager to have larger classes. Bowing to temptation and demand, trustees agreed to admit 150 additional students for the academic year 1964−65 and push up enrollment to 1,500.

Except during World War II, the men had always outnumbered the women, and the capacity of the fraternity houses only widened the gap. To balance the scales (and, as a bonus, to improve the academic profile markedly), all of the new students were to be women. The newest 210-bed dormitory was meant to handle the increase. Groundbreaking ceremonies for Dana Hall were held in the fall of 1963. Doris Kearns (Goodwin) '64 spoke for the students. The building wasn't quite ready the next fall when the first wave of extra students arrived. As a temporary fix, some women were moved across the previously sex-dividing McCann Road and into Averill Hall. Rooms for sixty-eight displaced men were rented at the Elmwood Hotel and for another fifty at the Hotel Cassini (once the James) in town. Ninetta Runnals spoke at the opening the following September. In October, Charles Dana brought the gift of his own portrait for the dedication ceremonies.[25]

Strider was happy to have the new building, but unenthusiastic about the way it looked. The large, prominently placed structure was the last neo-Georgian building on the original Larson plan. Strider had gingerly suggested that perhaps it was time for an architectural change. Trustees would hear none of it. Any architectural changes were bound to be hard sells. College tub-thumpers had never lost opportunities to tout the striking, unified appearance of the new campus, and the bragging was contagious. As far as many were concerned, Larson's red brick village with its magnificent towered library was what made Colby most distinctive. For them, any variation was unthinkable.

Although Larson's buildings were certainly impressive and easy to look at, those who lived and worked in them knew the inherent difficulties. The repetitive and strictly defined spaces were monotonous, and torturous when time came for the inevitable renovations. Dana Hall became a model of the worst features of the Larson style. Until major renovations were made more than three decades later, the dormitory was the dead-last choice of students.[26]

In 1965, even before Dana Hall was open, Strider enlisted no less an ally than the eminent American modernist Edward Durrell Stone. Stone knew Colby (he received an honorary degree in 1959); and when he returned to give a public lecture, Strider seized the chance to ask his advice on campus planning. The man who had designed the original Museum of Modern Art and was soon to be at work on the Kennedy Center agreed a change was in order.[27] Later that spring the board began to lay plans for new athletic facilities and more dormitories. To deal with the design of the new buildings, Strider con-

25. The philanthropist was by then quite old. No one, including his chauffeur, dared tell him his fly was unzipped. All photographs of the occasion are cropped, like Elvis on Ed Sullivan, from the waist up.

26. Dana Hall never ranked as the most ugly building on the campus. That prize went to the three-story, cinder-block press box that first offended the landscape in 1961. No amount of repainting or lettered decoration could ever disguise it.

27. Meanwhile, the College acquired a classical New England structure on the edge of campus. A fine house, modeled after the old library in nearby China Village, was purchased by the Alumni Council and named for Bill Millett.

vinced a committee of trustees, faculty, and administrators to depart tradition, and the board gave the dormitory design contract to another modernist, Benjamin Thompson of the Harvard School of Design. In no time at all, Strider began to get letters and calls from irate alumni. The yelling got louder when the Thompson dormitories popped out of the ground.

Strider's reply, on the President's Page of the *Alumnus* had the tone of strained patience. He reminded readers of the announced decision to hire Thompson. "It was thoroughly understood at that time," he wrote, "that such a decision would mean a modification in the classical red brick Georgian style of architecture." His defense was simple, and he repeated it throughout his presidency. While the planning objective was to create a campus with "harmony, balance, and beauty," even a good thing could be overdone. "If a pattern, no matter how lovely, is too long continued, monotony rather than harmony will be the inevitable result," he wrote. He also hinted Colby was getting behind the times:

> We are two-thirds of the way through a century marked by exciting architectural development. We think of Colby as a college in tune with its century in every sphere of its activity. With our handsome and dignified nucleus of 18th century buildings, typifying the age of rationalism and the enlightenment, is it not appropriate for us now to expand upon this nucleus with visible symbols of thinking in our own time?

From many, the answer was plainly no.

The new project, including four dormitories and a chapter house for Kappa Delta Rho (the last fraternity house), was assigned space in the woods, west of the library, overlooking the pond. Its location was a concession to those who wanted it hidden, but it turned out to be the perfect spot: striking white buildings nestled into the hillside with native landscape restored and embellished under the supervision of Carol Johnson of the Thompson firm. Construction—delayed three days to accommodate a nesting woodcock—was completed in time for the opening of school in 1967.[28] The buildings were called the first "coed" dorms, although connecting staircases safely separated the men and women. They were named for former board chairs and 1921 Colby classmates Sturtevant and Leonard, for Ernest Marriner, and for the late Pro-

---

28. That summer, in a gesture to the past, an outdoor music shell, named for its donor, Ralph T. Gould, was set up near the Coombs baseball field. The structure, a war memorial, was moved from the grounds of South Portland High School where it had stood for thirteen years.

fessor Julian Taylor. When fraternities were closed in 1985, the KDR house took the name of its brother, benefactor, and vice president successor to Eustis, Ralph Williams. Collectively, the buildings were called the Hillside Dorms.

Complaints over the new architecture slowed to a simmer when the places opened in 1967 and the new Maine Commission on Arts and Humanities gave a special award to the College "not exclusively for the excellent architectural and landscape design," but for the "courage in bringing contemporary architecture to Central Maine—an area not renowned for its 20th century architecture." Further vindication came when the American Institute of Architects (AIA) chose Thompson and his Colby project for one of twenty national Honor Awards, the only one in New England. Students also gave high marks, although early on many were asking when the room ceilings were going to be finished. The poured concrete had been simply whitewashed, leaving the imprint of the wood knots, seams, and fasteners of construction forms. Thompson said it was exactly what he wanted, and to leave it alone. What Thompson and others had not considered was that the expansive lounge windows faced directly north, into the bone-chilling winter winds. Much of the glass was unartfully sheathed over during the energy crisis of the 1970s. The playfully decorated lounges became a whole lot darker but a good deal warmer.

The temptation to increase enrollment had not ended. Even while the bulked-up classes were working into the cycle, trustees considered whether there might be an educational advantage to adding three hundred more students. In 1967 they concluded there was no advantage at all. It would require too much new construction. Instead, goals were set to reduce the teaching load of faculty from four courses to three and improve the student-faculty ratio of 15 to 1.

It was hoped the four hundred new beds of Dana and the Hillside dorms would provide student housing aplenty, but they didn't. Harry Carroll came from the University of New Hampshire as the College's first experienced dean of admissions in 1964, and his marching orders were never to undershoot the planned size of an entering freshman class. He never did. At the same time, the ratio of admitted-to-enrolled students kept going up, and the place often overflowed for the first semester, sometimes for the full year. Whenever students outnumbered campus beds, the College simply rented space in town. The Elmwood Hotel was on its last legs when the men stayed there waiting to reclaim Averill Hall. Afterward, the Hotel Cassini got used once more, and in 1966 Robert Sage '49 opened his Fenway-Maine Motor Hotel at the I-95 interchange on Upper Main. Sage, unfailingly helpful to Colby (and Colby people), rented satellite rooms there as well. And, to further relieve the pinch, the num-

ber of students given permission to live in their own rented off-campus apartments was allowed to grow.

> Being sent to live off campus had many disadvantages, but there were
> bonuses as well. Among the plusses was the increased opportunity for
> mischief. One warm fall night some students consigned to the Hotel
> Cassini climbed to the large, blinking, red-neon rooftop sign of the
> same name and shorted out the last two letters of HOTEL and the first
> and last three letters of CASSINI before retreating to the building's in-
> terior, padlocking the heavy roof hatch behind them. Traffic moving
> north along College Avenue quickly slowed to a crawl. Drivers honked
> their horns in merriment. Someone not among the honkers called the
> cops. It took nearly an hour to break onto the roof and pull the plug.

Downtown Waterville had its own share of crowding, and the old order of
things was changing there as well. In cities and towns everywhere, too many
automobiles were competing for too few parking spaces. Even as the federal
government helped finish the interstate highway, it was providing money to
revitalize the in-town areas where the highway had stolen business. Democrat
Albert Bernier '50 was mayor (1958–61) when the city first applied for a local
project. His successor, conservative Republican Cyril Joly '48, preferred to have
Waterville pay its own way, but the scheme was already too far along and too
expensive. When the first federal check arrived in 1962, the wrecking balls
began to swing. By the time Democrat mayor Malcolm Fortier took office in
1966, the shape of the project was cast in concrete. It took another thirteen years
to complete and, as on the Hill, controversy followed it every step of the way.

In the end most of Temple Street was gone, and, with it, all of Charles Street
and the apartment buildings of adjacent neighborhoods where tenants had
once walked to Saint Francis for mass and to Cottle's store for groceries. All
that was left was the red brick *Sentinel* building (later pale yellow), too big
and too expensive to move, a looming ark in a sea of asphalt. Casualties along
Temple Street included the YMCA and the grand old New England–style
Congregational church. The "Y" was replanted at the corner of North and
Pleasant, where George Keller presided over a new, single-story building with
a flat roof (yes, it leaked). The altar and stained-glass windows of the Congregational church were rescued and installed in a new building, with architecture mimicking the nearby College, on the corner of Upper Main and a new
parkway named in memory of Galen Eustis.

Alice's Café, né Onies, in business since Prohibition, also had to go. When it closed in the spring of 1965, its wooden booths were saved and ensconced in the Zeta Psi house on campus. Uprooted merchants were variously angry and pleased. George Desmond's Ford garage and Dakins's sporting goods store went out of business. Eddie Vlodek's dry goods store and Leo Diambri's restaurant traded up, moving from their quaint Main Street roots into new cinder-block, plate glass, and Formica-furnished quarters on the Concourse. The K-Mart came as the centerpiece, their rooftop logo sign both the smallest of any K-Mart in the country and the largest ever seen in town. A plea for a few trees and an occasional grassy strip was roundly nixed in favor of extra places to park.[29] The following year, amid the local frenzy to tidy up, two other great landmarks—the Elmwood Hotel and Memorial Hall—fell as well.

While new projects on the Hill led to better days, urban renewal could give only a brief reprieve to the health of downtown Waterville. At best, the re-arrangement of the Main Street environs produced more parking spaces. At worst, it destroyed some of the very things that might have made downtown a more attractive destination in the years to come.

MULE TRAIN

At Colby, as with many American colleges, football was the icon of sports, a gal-vanizing force at the opening of each school year that, if fates allowed, could carry a special campus spirit the whole year through. In the 1960s, football fortunes began to dwindle, and sports fans began to find pride at different venues: the ice arena, the baseball field, and the track. A new athletic facility broadened recre-ational opportunities all around, and the doors began to open ever so slightly to a more comprehensive and competitive program for women.

Invigorated by a talented young coach and a parcel of stellar athletes, men's ice hockey began to play the role of David in matchups with the Goliaths of the Northeast. Jack Kelley's teams were mesmerizing. Sold-out home seats were rarely sat upon. Fans rose howling to their feet when the team skated onto the ice to the throbbing strains of their theme song, Vaughan Monroe's "Mule Train," and didn't sit down until the game was over.

29. The bleak parking lot remained unchanged until the mid-1990s when, in a valiant attempt to attract shoppers, it was broken up by plantings, a maze of roadways, and curbing. A controversial steel sculpture was set in the middle. The changes brought a tiny bit of charm and a great deal of traffic confusion.

In 1960–61 the front line of Ron Ryan '62, John Maguire '61, and Sandy Boardman '61 gathered 222 points in an 18–5 best-ever season to become the highest scoring line in the history of U.S. collegiate hockey. The following winter, the Mules took an 18–1–1 record against U.S. opponents into the Eastern College Athletic Conference (ECAC) tournament, losing to Clarkson in the semifinals. Victims included Boston University, Boston College, Northeastern, and Providence. Ryan led the nation's scorers (104 points), and he and theatrical goalkeeper Frank Stephenson '62 were All-Americans. Kelley, 34, was NCAA U.S. Coach of the Year, and promptly got lured away by his alma mater, Boston University.[30] Charlie Holt, Kelley's teammate on the U.S. team in the 1949 World Championships, took his place and the Mule train rumbled on, winning both the NCAA and ECAC Division II championships in 1965–66, and entering postseason play every year to the end of the decade.

Basketball victories were harder to find. It began well enough, with a 1962 crown in the nine-game State Series. The brightest light was Ken Stone '64 who went on to score a College and state record of 1,500 career points. In 1965, Coach Lee Williams was given his leave to become executive director of the Basketball Hall of Fame at its new home in Springfield, Massachusetts. In nineteen seasons he had won a dozen state titles, including nine in a row. Verne Ullom, a Christian Scientist who read from Mary Baker Eddy in the locker room, followed Williams. His squad won the Maine Intercollegiate Athletic Association (MIAA) in 1966 and again in 1967 before he was succeeded by Ed Burke '60 whose teams struggled for two years until walk-on Doug Reinhardt '71 netted 469 points as a sophomore, on his way to breaking Stone's career record.

When spring came, John Winkin's baseball teams were the customary State Series winners, having taken five titles in six years by 1961. The following year he added the role of athletic director, and his teams continued to win. "Wink," who prayed with his players before each game (and cursed a bit during them), took his 1965 squad (15–5) into the regional NCAA tourney in Yankee Stadium; the following year the National Association of Baseball Coaches made him Coach of the Year. In ten years, his Colby teams amassed a record of 153–81–7. The 1966 squad was the most successful in the ninety-nine-year history of the sport at Colby, finally losing in the NCAA District One playoffs in Boston's Fenway Park. Eddie Phillips '66 threw a no-hitter at UMO that year;

30. At BU Kelley won six Beanpots and two NCAA championships before moving on to coach and then manage the professional Hartford Whalers. He ended his career as president of the Pittsburgh Penguins of the NHL.

Jim Thomas '67 was the nation's RBI champ (forty runs, twenty games), and captain Sal Manforte '66 was a first-team All-American.

The fate of football seemed to shift in an instant. In 1961 Bruce Kingdon '62 was an All-American, but by season's end coach Bob Clifford had only twenty-three players, and eight freshmen had to be brought up to play the final game. Clifford resigned that winter to coach at the University of Vermont, which soon abandoned the sport altogether. John Simpson, later a coach at Boston University, stepped in and the player shortage continued. Bowdoin and Bates took the giant University of Maine off their football schedules after 1964. Colby hung on for two more years before throwing in the towel and joining a new Colby, Bates, Bowdoin (CBB) rivalry. Even in the decline, there were moments to celebrate. Quarterback Bill Loveday '67 completed sixteen passes against Bates in 1965, setting a national collegiate record, and Steve Freyer '68 caught forty-four season passes for a new Colby high. In 1967 Dick McGee came from nearby Lawrence High in Fairfield where he was Maine high school coach of the year, and replaced Simpson. Through the end of the decade, McGee's tiny squads were devoted to him, but regularly got less than they gave, losing every game in the 1968 season.

Some blamed Strider for the nosedive, but he was following a course set by Bixler and a faculty bent on broadening and enriching the student academic profile. The College was beginning to attract new strains of students, and for many of them, athletics was not at the top of the list. At the same time, the shrinking pool of student athletes was being further diluted by new sports options.

Men's soccer, varsity since 1959, was among those sports that began to steal a share of those who might have played football. UMO fielded a soccer team in 1963, and a State Series competition began the following year. With Winkin as coach, Colby took the first title. A lacrosse club, formed in 1965 with Jim Wilson '67 as volunteer coach, grew to varsity status in 1972. As a club, the golf team (later to be coed) won the MIAA championship in 1960 and 1961, and was on its way to becoming a varsity team in 1965. Men's tennis began in 1965; women's, in 1969; and even before, as clubs, both were accustomed to winning state titles. Other clubs were emerging in squash, swimming, and cross-country, all soon to become varsity as well.

Skiing was resurrected in 1963 when Mildred Vigue gave Colby the old up-and-down ski slope at Mountain Farm in memory of her brother Charles, the man who had welcomed the GI skiers years before. The College resurrected the area for a third time. A rope tow provided intermittent skiing until 1964 when a small lodge, a 1,280-foot T-bar, lighting, and snowmaking equipment were added. It was rededicated as a community recreation area, and alumni used it on the first of many annual Winter Weekends in 1965. Season tickets were sold to the public ($30 for adults, $15 for students). Despite the hard work, with shortages of both snow and customers, it was a struggle to keep the slope running. Unlike Thompson's Hillside dorms, the slope faced the winter sun. There was rarely enough snow on the two south-facing trails, or on the outrun of the ancient 32-meter jump. Ansel Grindall, Norman Poulin, and their crews tinkered with a half-dozen new-fangled "snow guns" through endless cold nights. Even with plenty of snow, the 1,200-foot main slope was a steep menace for recreational skiers, and too short for the ski team. Sugarloaf Mountain had been operating ski trails since 1951, and by 1960 Alpine and Nordic skiing were gaining increased recreational popularity. Silas Dunklee signed on as the first paid skimeister in 1965, and in 1967 the men's club joined Sugarloaf as hosts to the NCAA national ski championships. A year later, the club won Colby's first Maine championship.

The slow expansion of recreational opportunities for those who were not athletes at all jumped several notches in 1967 with the opening of a 103,000-square-foot athletic complex, paid for in part by yet another grant from the Dana Foundation. The Wadsworth Field House became a permanent gymnasium with a varsity floor and room for three intramural courts.[31] A new fieldhouse boasted a state-of-the-art eight-lap artificial surface track, and a new swimming pool (175 × 75 feet) was advertised as "Olympic size." The Dunaway Charitable Foundation of Ogunquit gave money for squash courts, and there were new men's lockers and showers. A physical therapy center (for men only) in the new facility honored the late Mike Loebs. Carl Nelson, on board since 1959 as the College's first athletic trainer, presided. The popular Nelson was much in demand, covering practices and competitions by himself, while assuming Loebs's place as director of the Roberts Union infirmary.

The new fieldhouse brought resurgence in the ancient sport of track and field. Ken Weinbel came to coach in 1964, and two years later Colby got its first win over Bowdoin in forty years. A young Ethiopian runner, Sebsibe Mamo '70, provided the edge. Mamo ran a 3:45.8 1,500 meters for Ethiopia in the 1964 Tokyo Olympic Games, and Peace Corps volunteer Joseph Woods persuaded

31. The new gym worked fine for athletics, but was dismal as a place for musical performances. In 1977 a portable music shell was acquired to improve the acoustics, and was named in honor of Alma Morrissette McPartland '07, a generous lifelong contributor who in 1903 had helped to found "the ladies glee club."

him to enroll at Colby. In 1966 he broke the ECAC freshman cross-country record, and the following year he won six college meets. In the spring (1968), Colby won the MIAA track championship for the first time in the association's sixty-nine-year history. Earlier that spring Weinbel staged a fieldhouse grand opening invitational meet. More than three hundred competitors came from throughout New England and a crowd of some 1,500 spectators packed every corner. Mamo beat archrival Amby Burfoot of Wesleyan in the two-mile race, destroying the College record with a time of 8:48.3.[32]

> The last event of the night was the high jump, and the final two competitors were Colby's Bob Aisner '68 and John Thomas of Boston University, a national hero who held both world and Olympic trials records. The popular Aisner, a two-sport, same-season, track and basketball standout, matched Thomas at 6'-7", and the bar went up an inch. Thomas, who as a freshman set a world mark of 7'-3¾" in the Olympic trials, cleared easily. Aisner waited at the head of the runway as Thomas approached him to offer encouragement and advice. The two shook hands, and when Aisner cleared the 6'-8" jump, the crowd exploded. No Maine collegian had ever jumped that high. Thomas and Aisner, in shared elation, embraced each other for a long moment in the pit. With the bar at 6'-9", Aisner missed. Thomas skimmed over the top.

Cobbling together the many parts of the new complex had been an architectural challenge. There were weak points. On February 2, 1969, a snowstorm piled six-foot drifts onto the flat roof connecting the Alfond Arena to the gymnasium. The roof collapsed at 4:30 in the morning, showering the south stands of the arena in debris and creating an implosion that broke glass bricks at the far end of the rink. The storm had forced cancellation of a game with Bowdoin the night before. Engineers said the uproar of the game almost certainly would have brought the roof down on the crowd. Bowdoin offered its rink for the remaining two games of the season.

32. The indoor track was surfaced with Tartan, all the rage in a time when artificial surfaces were new. The "healing" nature of the material allowed runners to use short spikes. If it was a marvel, in fact the surface was too hard, and the corners of the short track were not banked. The combination spawned an epidemic of shin splints, and by the 1980s the track began to be used mostly for practice, rarely for competitive events.

The central lobby of the new athletic facility was adorned with a stainless steel sculpture by Maine artist Clark Fitzgerald. Its title, *The Whole Man,* spoke volumes about the status of women in athletics. For now, they were consigned to continue operating their reduced athletic program on the other end of campus, with locker rooms and meager facilities in Runnals Union. Marjorie Bither took Janet Marchant's place as director of women's physical education in 1965. The *Alumnus* announced the change, and said that going forward it would "find some way to include the athletic doings of coeds." It didn't. Two years later, the editor apologized again. With the College by then officially co-educational, a column headed "The Girls" again promised to do better. Bither began to improve things, if the magazine didn't. The decade saw the addition of four new women's sports. Making golf coeducational when a varsity team was created in 1965 was not gratuitous. The first full women's team, basketball, came in 1968. Field hockey began the same year, and in 1969 the venerable tennis club went varsity as well. All students had a physical education requirement, and although the men's list was longer, the program had twenty-five activities for women including dancing, swimming, and a semester's worth of individual sports elected from a menu including fencing, judo, track and field, squash, hiking, and gymnastics. The new pool brought the addition of synchronized swimming. The magazine managed to boast that Cynthia Paquet '67 had represented the College in two national intercollegiate golf tournaments, and that Mary Walker '69 was the mideastern champion in badminton.

RIGHTS AND RULES

The sexual revolution was under way and students were well pleased to be a part of it. At Colby the revolt came on the same tide with the residential mixing of the sexes and true coeducation. Students eagerly took up arms against institutional regulations that no longer reflected their social attitudes—or their behavior. The itch should not have surprised anyone. Students were only mimicking their elders who, from the president's office to the shared office of the newest instructor, were doing a good bit of tinkering with the old order of things themselves. Indeed, when the time came to tackle a general revision of the Student Handbook, members of the faculty gleefully joined in. It was never a question of whether new freedoms were needed. There was some agreement on that. The questions were about where to draw the lines.

Many single-sex institutions were talking about coeducation. It took another decade, but when they made the shift they did it in the safety of numbers. Women entered Williams and Wesleyan in 1970; Bowdoin, 1971; Dartmouth,

1972; Amherst, 1974. Men broke into Connecticut College in 1968 and Vassar, a year later. Harvard had been engaged to women since 1943 when Radcliffe women first came to class. They were officially married in 1972. In the meantime, Harvard's president, Nathan Pusey, liked to say the old college was not coeducational at all, "except in fact." By the 1960s, women had been enrolled at Colby for nearly a century, but Colby was a little like Pusey's Harvard. Strider and others aimed to take the next steps, to eschew the strange system of coordination and make Colby coeducational—in law and in fact. At a place everyone already thought was coed, the switch was harder than it looked.

Except for the forces of culture in the self-selection of courses (fewer women in the sciences, fewer men in the humanities) classroom mixing was taken for granted. Outside of class, authorities worked hard to keep the sexes apart. Library stacks were closed at night to prevent necking. Women's dormitories were locked at 10:30 P.M. on weekdays and the residents were carefully counted. Student guards staffed entryways to women's dorms; bells and loudspeakers announced a "man on the floor!"[33] Hoping for safety in numbers, officials designated a "coed room" (201 Runnals) as a place for couples to meet. Students called it a "mass necking room," but it never was. As quickly as a single couple commandeered one of the couches, others respectfully declined to enter. A good deal of the overflow "making out" went on in automobiles. Watching the movies was a secondary matter at the Augusta Road Drive-In Theater, and parkers regularly lined bumper-to-bumper along the road by Johnson Pond.

High schoolers and other local lovers caught on fast, competing for pondside parking spaces. Boys from town would sometimes stalk the parkers at night, beaming flashlights into the darkened, fogged-up cars for eye-popping glimpses of what was going on inside.

Even as students looked for rules to delete, someone was always adding more. When fraternities began adopting canine mascots, Dean of Men George Nickerson banished dogs. After a rash of accidents, Strider declared the campus off-limits to motorcycles. Student apartment renters in town were given

33. The barriers were not impenetrable. Since the beginning of the new campus, men had avoided the bell desks by crawling through first-floor windows and climbing the exterior fire escapes.

the same rules for visitations as the dormitory dwellers. The faculty limited class cuts to two per semester, and imposed a $25 fine for missing the last class before a vacation.

Those who argued the College could not move to true coeducation without plenty of rules, or thought students should not write them, did not lack supporting evidence. When the Class of 1964 arrived, Henry "Hank" Gemery, assistant director of admissions,[34] announced that the women came from the top 10 percent of their high school classes; the men, from the top 20 percent. Despite an edge in the classroom, the "girls" on the south end of campus were still having a fine time hazing new classmates, getting them out of bed at odd hours, making them sing the alma mater. (The men had about given up the hazing of freshmen. Their hands were full with fraternity pledges.) And even as the *Echo* complained of a "paternalistic" administration and a "Victorian" social code, it advertised a 1961 protest favoring Johnson Day as a "panty raid." The event in fact featured loud chanting: "We want Johnson Day!" and (although it was unclear what they intended to do with him) "We want Strider!"

Despite occasional lapses, men and women students were changing their views of each other. The Kinsey reports on *what* was going on in human sexuality had been well digested. By the mid-1960s, William Masters and Virginia Johnson were detailing the *how*, and Betty Friedan gave light to the question of *why* women were victims of a system of false values subjugating them in their various roles in the workplace and at home. Friedan's book *The Feminine Mystique* was already a best seller when students (mostly women) jammed Averill Auditorium to hear her warn that the insecurity of young women made them vulnerable to brainwashing. Her message set a buzz. Panty raids were nearly finished.

The first brush with near anarchy was yet to come, but lines of authority were getting fuzzy. Who was in charge? Students yelled for the power to make instant changes, and shifting factions of the faculty were always willing to join them. Trustees distanced themselves, their reputations soiled by their initial refusal to put teeth into the Nunez Proposal. Strider seized his best weapons— education and the written word—to see if he could put things straight. From 1965 to 1966 he wrote a series of four articles on the roles of various constituencies in the governance of the College. The trustees, he said, knew it was not their function to "run the college" but instead "to see that the college is

---

34. Gemery, a newcomer in the economics department, was persuaded to take a tour as an admissions officer in order to give some counterweight to director Bryan's bent toward prep schools and athletes.

properly run." His piece on the faculty and administration underscored the paramount role of the faculty in setting the academic direction, and the place of the administration in supporting them. In his essay on alumni roles, he cited their importance in development and in helping to identify new students. He knew from his mailbox many alumni were grumpy about change, and he had already given them a good deal to be grumpy about. He wrote that the most helpful alumni were those "who recognize the inevitability of change and are receptive to it," adding, for emphasis, "if, as I understand, it is occasionally true in some institutions, the alumni regard themselves as apostles of a past that is no longer viable in a changing world, their contribution is necessarily limited. The ancient war cry, *Come weal, come woe, / my status is quo,* is inappropriate."

In the last and longest piece, Strider gave his view on of the role of students who, he said, had quite enough to do without trying to run the place. Even so, he acknowledged students "not only have something important to say but are also uncommonly anxious to say it." Their voice, he said, "might make some of their elders uneasy, but we had better give them a chance to speak." He said he very much favored student participation in governance "although ultimate decision on far-reaching matters of policy should not be theirs."

Students first sat with rule-makers in January 1965, when members of Blue Key and Cap and Gown joined a daylong "conversation" to discuss the plan to mix up the dorms. The administration wanted to put men and women in separate wings of Mary Low-Louise Coburn and Foss-Woodman, and let women into Averill and East Quad, on the men's side of campus. Students weren't much interested, and in April, Strider announced the plan would not go forward. Instead, the administration would press on the possibility of coed dining.

Merely mixing the sexes in the dining halls or by adjacent dormitories wasn't what students really wanted. The system of room selection that gave students choices of what they considered the best dorms would continue to plague proposals for housing changes for the next twenty-five years, until the dorms were systematically renovated to create more parity in overall quality and space.[35] Students' real passion was for the chance to get out of the parked cars, and for men to be able to visit women in the cozy confines of the dorms. American institutions couched the debate in the eloquence of ancient Latin, passed on through the European universities. "Parietal hours" was the label for relaxed visitation rules in the women's dorms (never the other way around),

---

35. Nothing, of course, could change location. Cold winters would always make proximity to the library a prize.

and "in loco parentis" described an institution's behavior as surrogate parents. Students wanted parietal hours; they did not want the College in loco parentis.

Clifford Osborne retired as chaplain in the spring. Frederick Hudson replaced him. Hudson was a Baptist reformer. The cellar of Lorimer Chapel soon became a coffeehouse; the annual religious convocation was discontinued, and one of his first sermons was titled "The Death of God." In his valedictory Osborne blamed his own "grandfather generation" for failing the current students. These "victims of two generations of 'lostness,'" he said, "are for very good reason an enigma to their elders—who don't know what to do with them." He said the culture was delayed in its development, perhaps not ready for a sexual revolution, and warned, "Until the American male gives up his attitude toward sex as an exploitation of the female, promiscuity is likely to increase." Many who feared allowing parietal hours would send the pregnancy rate over the blue light in the library tower shared his views. It didn't turn out that way at all.

Coed dining began in the fall of 1965. Women who wanted to eat in Roberts (few did), and men who wanted to eat in Mary Low or Foss (many did) needed to sign up in the Spa a week ahead of time. The *Echo* warned, "Men students eating on the girls' side will be responsible for learning the individual rules for their respective dining halls and will be required to adhere to them."

Strider took a well-earned leave that winter, and he and his family made a four-month trip around the world. He returned with "a clearer recognition on my own part of where Colby stands and what Colby might do to make itself an even better institution." His reflections convinced him that, despite a growing awareness of the world beyond the Hill (including concern in the struggle for civil rights), the College remained far too insulated.[36] Part of the difficulty, Strider felt, was a failure to integrate the social and intellectual lives of students. He began to frame solutions in a document, "Certain Proposals," issued that fall, and sent in draft to board chairman Ellerton Jetté. "I have taken the position that just shuffling people around on the campus coeducationally is not enough," Strider wrote, explaining his proposals were "pointed toward an alteration of the social structure, without which mere increase of coed opportunities doesn't add up to much."

Jetté knew something about students. He was the first chairman in mem-

---

36. At the opening fall assembly in 1966, he reminisced about his trip. He told students that being away made him see the often-celebrated campus issues as rather trivial. He said it was "illuminating to read, as I did one bright afternoon in Athens, a copy of the Colby *Echo* in the shadow of the Acropolis."

ory to join students on their own turf when, in the midst of the debate over parietal hours, he accepted an invitation to attend a meeting of Student Government. It wasn't long before he was calling for another of his "dreaming sessions" with fellow trustees. In preparation, he offered his own views of the future. He saw needs for an ever-stronger faculty, more classrooms, and a better library. Not surprisingly, he dreamed of a true art and culture center. "I am not sure about [the need for] a student union," he wrote to Strider, and neither was he sure of the need for an athletic complex "as I have an idea that in 10 or 15 years colleges like Colby will not be playing intercollegiate athletics."

"Certain Proposals" called for a mixing of living accommodations, complete coeducational dining, and the discontinuance of the men's and women's divisions in all of their manifestations. All of these things soon came to pass. He further proposed a division and reorganization of the living system itself, suggesting the College be organized into four or five residential units, each with fewer than five hundred students, and each with its own academic focus, faculty affiliates, and social governing body.[37] Strider's proposals were the focus of a campuswide "congress," held in mid-November. Students were already in a bad mood, and in the middle of it all, Strider turned down a request for a trial run of parietal hours because, he said, it lacked an honor system. In fact, the parietal hours plan proffered by students was not entirely without creative controls. It was suggested a woman's door be left open a crack when she had a visitor, and the man signal his presence by hanging a necktie on the doorknob. The safeguards presumed too much (not the least of which was that the men owned neckties), and although there was general student crabbiness over the rejection, Strider was heartened by the reaction of some. He wrote Jetté to report quite a few students had told him that "they applaud this firmness of purpose on the part of the administration, and they are relieved to be able to get back to work and forget about the entreaties of the fire-eaters."

The congress was a flop. Averill Gymnasium was packed for a faculty/student panel discussion that was drowned out by a three-hour free forum of complaints. The biggest problem with Strider's proposals seemed to be that he had made them. By and large they were criticized, ignored, or summarily dismissed. A frustrated faculty panelist, Tom Easton (biology), called the blasé attitude of students "creeping coolth."

In the aftermath, the Campus Affairs Committee (CAC) and Student Gov-

37. Twenty years later, with the abandonment of fraternities and sororities, the Commons system would strikingly resemble Strider's reorganization plan. For now, it was too much, too soon.

ernment set up subcommittees to come up with recommendations on a number of issues, including an honor system, coed living, and student-faculty relations. The CAC, with Strider's assistant Howard Koonce as chairman, held open hearings in the spring. Many students used the hearings to complain of an administrative failure to communicate. Koonce fumed. "It is," he said, "nothing short of astonishing to hear college students clamor for 'communication.' After all, they have as much of their day free from any real necessity of mind-boggling labor as they wish to make free; they have as much contact with articulate instructors as they wish to use; and they are asked to attend sessions at which every one of us charged with the responsibility of teaching them damn well wishes most of them *would* do their work and *would* start communicating meaningfully and intelligently."

In January 1967, trustees declared Colby coeducational, de facto and de jure, and by spring the plan for mixing the dormitories got sorted out. Freshman dormitories were abolished; women moved into Averill Hall, men into Coburn,[38] and an elaborate system for selecting rooms, seniors first, was put in place. That fall, students on their own abandoned the ancient hazing practice of requiring freshmen to wear beanies and signs around their necks.

Chaplain Osborne's fears about the sexual attitudes of males were made manifest in April. Just as the CAC was sorting out the final plan for coeducational living, twenty-six members of Tau Delta Phi fraternity and eight others were accused of sexual misconduct with a local young woman in a downtown apartment. Dean Nickerson sent the messy affair to the Inter-Fraternity Council, which imposed sanctions on the fraternity: a fine, probation, and public service. Strider said it wasn't enough. Members involved could not hide behind the fraternity; they must be disciplined as well. Hundreds of students marched around the Eustis Building, protesting Strider's decision and threatening to strike classes and hold sit-ins. Strider agreed to convene an independent committee and reopen disciplinary proceedings, and Stu-G and the IFC called off further demonstrations to await the outcome. In the end, there were sanctions for both the fraternity and the individuals involved.

---

38. When the first male residents moved into Louise Coburn Hall, they climbed above the entry doorway and pried the "e" off Louise.

In June, a joint committee of the American Association of University Professors, the National Student Association, the Association of American Colleges, the National Association of Student Personnel Administrators, and the National Association of Women Deans and counselors gathered in Washington, D.C., and wrote a *Joint Statement on Rights and Freedoms of Students*. The comprehensive document set forth new standards for the protection of student rights in the classroom, in the keeping of student records, in student affairs, and in off-campus activities. It also established procedural standards for disciplinary proceedings. The Colby faculty adopted the statement in November 1970. It remains the definitive document on student rights.

The move to full coeducation was more than mere ceremony. There were structural changes as well. The divisions of men and women disappeared, a single-student judicial system was created, and various student records and lists were blended. The offices of dean of men and dean of women were abolished. Dean of Men Nickerson retired and Dean of Women Frances Seaman became the first dean of students and served a year. When Strider assistant Jonas Rosenthal became dean in the fall of 1968, he had two associate deans and a new office of student activities.

A trained sociologist, Rosenthal was open to new ideas in residential life and to extending the new rights and freedoms, but he was caught in a time warp. Students often saw him as being too conservative; some of his colleagues, above and below in the pecking order, thought he was too liberal—and soft on crime. Others, like Gene Peters (philosophy), thought the administration should back off and let students decide things for themselves.[39] Peters spoke from the left. He wrote that if the College felt obligated to provide for the social and moral cultivation of students [and it did], then it should satisfy this obligation "by yielding its authority and giving students the opportunity to cultivate themselves." Quite likely, he said, "The social habits and moral standards the students will adopt will not coincide with those the College would have struck upon. Why should they?" Rosenthal replied that it was not that simple. "Students should have plenty of responsibility for their own social and moral development," he wrote, but the College "should also accept the responsibility to pass on to students guidelines and models for methods of making decisions."

The new system was made manifest at Commencement 1968. Graduates marched to the platform to claim their degrees in a single line, alphabetically,

39. Peters left teaching to study medicine and later practiced as a respected Waterville obstetrician.

by surname. A woman, Jessie McGuire of Fanwood, New Jersey, led the parade as the first all-senior valedictorian and class marshal.

"STOP, CHILDREN, WHAT'S THAT SOUND?"

Rock 'n' roll became rock, and Buffalo Springfield warned to look around and see what was going down. Battle lines were being drawn. Once-docile baby boomers were becoming disillusioned, confused, and angry. The nation was building a nuclear ability to destroy the world ten times over, and there was a troubling and deepening war in Vietnam. In a seeming instant, many young people turned away from the established order and began to assert themselves in ways their elders did not comprehend: their music, their drugs, their hair, and the clothes they did and did not wear. Like so many others, they faced the inner conflict between patriotism and a war they found absurd. At the end of the day students forced their government to stop the fight. Along the way, they were often grim and quarrelsome.

Shortly after the ill-fated 1961 invasion of Cuba, President Kennedy sent three thousand military advisers to help the South Vietnamese in their long war against the Vietcong. At home, there was little notice or objection. Providing help for South Vietnam was nothing new. The United States had been sending advisers there since 1956 when the French, tired of the ten-year Indochina stalemate, simply went home.

The war did not come into national focus until August 1964, when the new president, Lyndon Johnson, claimed North Vietnamese PT boats had fired on U.S. destroyers while they patrolled in the Gulf of Tonkin. Within two days Congress gave the president authority to take "all necessary measures to repel any armed attack against forces of the United States." Whether the gulf attack actually occurred—most said later that it hadn't—the door was open to a larger war. In early 1965 two battalions of Marines went to protect the American air base at Da Nang, and almost overnight the country had eighty thousand troops at war. College students knew many of them. They were high school classmates who, by choice or circumstance, had not gone on to college.

At first there were only a few Colby antiwar activists, mere yeast in a bowl of uncertainty. Within five years their numbers swelled to a clamoring majority. U.N. Secretary-General U Thant of Burma was the commencement speaker in the spring of 1965. He told seniors there was a whole range of scientific, political, and economic activity "which cry out for youthful vigor and intelligence." They already knew it. Over that summer students were part of demonstrations in cities across the country. In August, Johnson signed a law criminalizing draft card burning; in November protesters encircled the White House and burned them just the same.

By Christmas, U.S. combat troops reached 385,000. Six thousand had been killed. More troops were needed, and when 1966 began, Johnson called for an end to deferments. Students would be measured by their academic standing; those with the lowest grades would be called first. The *Portland Evening Express* said the government was "playing God," creating privilege for those who scored well and finding "cannon fodder" among the rest. The Colby faculty concurred. Dean of Faculty Parker Johnson wrote General Lewis Hershey, director of the Selective Service, to criticize any deferment for college students at all, and especially the new policy of protecting only those who tested well. All the while, the College supplied local draft boards with class standings. A year later (1967) the draft was reorganized again. This time the youngest would go first, chosen by lottery from among eligible eighteen-year-olds. Registrar George Coleman explained the new rules in the *Echo,* where editorials reflected the sullen mood of students and acknowledged there was no sign of the kind of patriotism that had ignited past generations in time of war. The war, the paper said, "seems to arouse a feeling that more closely resembles resentment than loyalty."

Although few students were ever drafted, at the time their fate was uncertain, and they began to scramble for ways to avoid or delay being sent into combat: ROTC, the National Guard, graduate school, or even flight to Canada. The College staff soon included a part-time draft counselor.[40]

The war was coming home in more powerful ways than by the looming draft. In September 1967, sixteen months after his graduation, Marine lieutenant Philip McHale '66 returned to campus to speak. The platoon leader had been wounded in combat a few months before. Ten of his men were killed. He told his former schoolmates the war could not be won. A month later, two dozen students and faculty joined 100,000 antiwar demonstrators at the Pentagon. David Dillinger and Jerry Rubin organized the Washington rally where 10,000 students gave up their draft cards. On the campus, a silent vigil was held around the war memorial flagpole near the library. Jerry Boren and Tom

40. The best-known resistor and antihero was the world heavyweight boxing champion, Cassius Clay, who became a Muslim, changed his name to Muhammad Ali, and declared the war violated his religious principles. Denied status as a conscientious objector, he refused induction into the army and was imprisoned. The World Boxing Association stripped him of his title. Ali had a strong Maine following. Two years before he had fought in Lewiston, knocking out Sonny Liston in defense of his title. Maine governor John Reed now said he should be "held in utter contempt by every patriotic American."

Jenkins, 1969 classmates, reported back to Colby, saying the Washington crowd represented a cross-section of young America, and they were not, as reporters described them, all "hippies" and "wild-eyed extremists."

The stomping around was not always about war. The year before a group calling itself CORA (Colby Organization for Roses in America) marched on behalf of Maine Senator Margaret Chase Smith's campaign to make the rose the national flower. Smith, who wore a rose every day, was at the moment doing battle with Everett Dirkson, the gravelly-voiced Illinois senator who wanted the marigold. (Twenty years later, President Ronald Reagan signed a resolution making the rose the "national floral emblem.") A group of some one hundred, led by sophomore class and CORA president Philip Merrill '68, marched to the Blaine House in Augusta, rang the doorbell, and tried to present a red rose to Cora, the wife of Governor John Reed. She wouldn't let them in, and so they crossed the road to the governor's office where security guards agreed to admit only one, Thomas Rippon '68, who presented Reed a small bouquet. Abbott Meader (art) chastised organizers for making light of the serious and effective tool of protest. Robert Hughes '68, one of the CORA conveners and soon to be Navy serviceman aboard the U.S.S. *Intrepid*, later noted the "spoof" was mounted just before students began to realize the horror of Vietnam.

Robert Reuman (philosophy) knew more than a little about civil disobedience. He had declared his status as a conscientious objector during World War II, and while he strongly opposed the Vietnam War, he thought the students were unfocused, and their causes, undefined. Resentment, frustration, and hostility, he told an *Echo* reporter, were leading them to pick the wrong targets and express themselves in the wrong ways. He said local authority figures, including Strider, were merely "accidental targets." Reuman blamed the unrest on the war, Kennedy's death, and disappointment in Johnson's leadership. He also blamed television, noting that the first TV college generation was accustomed to being entertained, expected instant dramatics, and needed to experiment in vivid ways.[41]

41. Television had more than a sociological impact; it was the principal purveyor of a growing sense of the horror of war as well. Just as Vietnam began getting bigger pieces of the evening news, a satellite transmitted the first transatlantic television signal. On

War opinion on the campus was still sharply divided. In November 1967 half the Colby faculty and administrative staff (seventy-one) signed a statement in opposition to the war. A month later, a Stu-G poll showed only 27 percent of the students wanted "unequivocal withdrawal" of American troops. An equal number thought the United States should invoke a ceasefire for six months "to bring Hanoi to the peace table." The local *Sentinel* construed the poll results to mean Colby students were more hawkish than the faculty. The antiwar faction added the student numbers together, claiming a majority opposed the war.

In January 1968, a small group carried protest signs outside the Eustis building, while inside students interviewed for jobs with Dow Chemical Company, makers of napalm; in March, student and faculty demonstrators held a sit-in at an army recruiting booth in the lobby of Roberts Union. Counterdemonstrators, many of them on their way to lunch on the ground floor, blocked the door to the union, chided the protestors, and dropped bars of soap on their heads. (A prevailing stereotype placed war protestors among the unwashed.) Deans worried not only about what the dissidents had up their tie-dyed shirtsleeves, but also about their safety. Navy recruiters, slated for an information session the next day, said they feared violence and canceled.

The counterdemonstration was predictable. Some students wanted to inquire about signing up. Most others, including those who were adamantly against the war, agreed they had the right. Just as recruiters converged on the campus, student friends of Leslie Dickinson Jr. '67 were mourning his death. The Patten, Maine, student left college in the middle of his junior year to join the Marines, and on January 31, 1968, a day before his twenty-third birthday, he was mortally wounded near Quang Nam. He died three days later.

The spring brought more assassinations. The Reverend Martin Luther King Jr. was killed on April 4. Strider and student Stu-G president Henry Thompson '69 spoke at memorial services in town and on the Hill. "Our hearts go out to those who have labored, black and white, for Dr. King's cause," Strider said. "This is America's cause, and we are failing." Strider led a campus-community drive to raise money for the United Negro College Fund in King's memory. Some $16,000 came in, at the time the largest contribution of any educational institution. Students marched solemnly from the campus to the packed Opera

---

July 10, 1962, European viewers saw a picture of an American flag waving at Telstar's U.S. earth station in Andover, Maine, and stations in England and France sent signals back. The war was soon seen live in American living rooms. If that wasn't vivid enough, in 1965 the networks added color.

House service in town, where Thompson, the first black president of the student body, warned that while "advocacy of violence is a nullification of the identity of Dr. King," the killing nonetheless would cause many "to cross over to the militant policies of violence." He was right. A month later, Robert Kennedy, a front-runner for the Democratic nomination for the presidency, was killed as well. The two deaths and the war touched off a summer of urban riots, and in the fall, students returned to college itching for a fight.

Lyndon Johnson had withdrawn from the presidential race, and with Robert Kennedy gone, war opponents turned to Eugene McCarthy, and worked through the summer for his nomination. They felt betrayed when Democrats, slugging it out at a violence-filled convention in Chicago, narrowly chose Hubert Humphrey to oppose Richard Nixon in the fall. Peace activists had little use for Nixon or his vice presidential candidate, Spiro Agnew. Humphrey had been forced on them, and even in Maine the choice of the state's junior senator, Ed Muskie, as his running mate made little difference. (Nor did it make much difference to students that in Maine, Democratic Party head George Mitchell made Strider the chair of the state's party platform committee.)

On Election Day, with hordes of national reporters tagging along, the Muskies cast their votes at the old South Grammar School. Student protestors lined Silver Street, one hundred yards away, chanting "free elections now," and "one, two, three, four, we won't fight your dirty war." Across the street, a smaller group of counterdemonstrators heckled the protestors and yelled at them to take baths. The past summer of demonstrations had proven that a police presence only made things worse. During the Election Day face-off in Waterville, Mayor Donald Marden kept the cops around the corner, out of sight. That winter he asked the city council to buy them riot gear.

On the Hill, authorities were worried. Dean of Students Rosenthal assembled a group to puzzle ways of dealing with trouble that was sure to come. He circulated a confidential discussion paper describing protest scenarios, and outlining rules for response: avoid violence at all costs, listen carefully to the protestors, call in outside authorities only as a last resort, offer no amnesty, and leave all public comment to the president's office. The guidelines were needed. The uprisings were unpredictable. Whenever demonstrators headed to the Eustis building, secretaries in the ground-floor business office lowered and locked the steel curtains at the service counter and hid. Protestors knew there was nothing to fear, but the hysterical reaction was pleasing just the same.

In late October, some suspected antiwar sabotage in the burning of the makeshift Little Theater, one of two remaining wooden buildings on the Hill.

The blaze was discovered during a Powder & Wig play rehearsal, and it raged on as firemen from four local departments searched in the dark for the hydrant (foolishly painted dark green so as not to offend the landscape). The fire started in an attached shed, housing a 1966 Ford station wagon belonging to the Air Force ROTC.[42]

Through the winter American forces reached a war-high peak of 350,000. Casualties and war resistance mounted at the same time. In April, a new English instructor, David Stratman, encouraged the formation of a Colby chapter of Students for a Democratic Society (SDS), a national counterculture organization formed ten years before. Its manifesto, written mostly by the University of Michigan student newspaper editor, Tom Hayden, called for a fully participatory democracy, and initially focused on the fight for civil rights and the battle for free speech. By 1966 it had become more radical, mounting antiwar demonstrations on nearly one hundred campuses across the country. The Weather Underground, a SDS splinter group, was formed that year, preaching the violent overthrow of the government. The Colby SDS chapter did not flourish. While its leaders were often at the center of local demonstrations, the events themselves were not centered on SDS.

When their offspring acted up, many parents kept their own counsel, but there were others who were unafraid to move into the fray and set things straight. In January 1969, some seventy-five black students took over the communications center at Brandeis, making "non-negotiable" demands, including that the university hire more black teachers. As the standoff entered the second day, the mother of one of the protestors came out of the crowd, walked through the front door into the building, and returned with her son in tow. At Colby, the president of the new SDS chapter appeared one day in the dean's office, slumped in a chair, and said he was going to quit his SDS post and needed some advice. He wanted to know how to break the news of his resignation to fellow radicals. He worried they would laugh when he said his mother made him do it.

42. The worst Colby tragedy of the year occurred in February 1969. Two students were examining a pistol in their room on the second floor of the Phi Delta Theta fraternity house when the gun accidentally fired. Across the room their roommate, sophomore Robert Crowell, was killed instantly. A grand jury ruled the death accidental.

In the fall of 1969, faculty joined students in a nationwide October 15 "Vietnam moratorium," aimed at compelling Nixon to end U.S. involvement in the war. Students from Colby, Thomas College, and Waterville High School held meetings on the Hill and in town, where some one thousand people attended an afternoon rally in Coburn Park. Students marched from the Hill, carrying a flag-draped simulated casket. Ken Eisen '73 and Joan Katz '70 read from the list of war dead. The moratorium was followed by yet another "march on Washington" a month later. Students and townspeople gathered in the chapel for a "sympathy vigil," sponsored by the Colby moratorium committee and local churches. Organizers were intent on protest until the war came to an end.

REBELLION AND CON CON

"The trouble with revolutions," Roland Thorwaldsen said, "is that you don't get enough sleep." Religion instructor and head resident of Louise Coburn Hall, "Thor" was right about a lot of things; Strider would soon make him College chaplain. The sleepless second half of the academic year 1968–69 began with a testimonial to the boundless creativity of the Jan Plan as students found faculty advisers for a project focused on unionizing the cafeteria workers. In February, a small demonstration was held at the bookstore to complain about the cost of books (the average price of a college textbook had risen to $9.86). Later that month, the student government submitted to Strider a list of nine proposals. It led to a minor rebellion and from there to a constitutional convention that gave students seats in the boardroom.

None of the nine proposals had anything to do with war. Six were about College rules. They asked that dorms be permitted to govern themselves; that upper-class students be allowed to live and eat off campus if they wanted to; and that students living in town be free from campus authority. They addressed complaints of scholarship students who were prohibited from having cars on campus and required to maintain higher grade point averages than their nonscholarship counterparts. They called for the creation of a rules committee, with student membership to match the number of faculty and administrators. Finally, they insisted night security officers be given radios, that the switchboard remain open twenty-four-hours, and that the College provide clinics on birth control, drugs, and mental health.

The proposals came through as demands and with the assertion that previous attempts to effect changes through the usual channels had been "futile." Strider was not inclined to deal with demands. Neither did he think recent initiatives for change had been futile. He said Colby prided itself on rational process and respect for orderliness—"a tradition and spirit to which the peremptory tone of your letter is alien"—and took his time in responding. Days later he sent word the proposals would be parceled out to special committees and warned he would reject and resubmit any recommendations the committee reached "without adequate discussion, with significant dissent, or with a significantly narrow quorum." It was the procedural caveats that caused the trouble.

Student Government seemed willing to talk, but glaring in from the outside were students who felt the administration was slow and unresponsive and that Stu-G was incapable of speeding things up. They formed "the Chapel group," a shifting small crowd of dissidents that wrote its own proposals and planned a vigil in the chapel to force their adoption.[43]

On March 12, some three hundred students attended an early evening meeting of Student Government in Given Auditorium where Stu-G president Thompson urged students to attend the upcoming committee meetings and work on the original proposals. John Sobel '70 spoke for the dissidents, and announced the unveiling of the new proposals at a mass "celebration for a new Colby" later that night. When the Stu-G meeting ended, about fifty students walked across campus to Lovejoy Auditorium, hoping to attend the faculty meeting. After two inconclusive voice votes, on a show of hands the faculty voted not to let them in. In the midst of it, a dog wandered through the auditorium and a professor remarked loudly that apparently a student had gotten in anyway. Behind closed doors, the faculty endorsed Strider's handling of the nine proposals, but an attempt to introduce the newest proposals for debate was summarily declared out of order.

43. The Chapel group had plenty of examples of the effectiveness of building sit-ins. By that time there had been building occupations at more than a dozen campuses elsewhere. They began at Columbia University the year before, when several buildings were taken over in separate protests, resulting in the rejection of ROTC and the end of construction of a disputed gymnasium. At the University of California at Berkeley, a fifty-day student strike on behalf of minority studies resulted in the occupation of campus land that was turned into a "peoples' park." Students at the University of Chicago held an unsuccessful sit-in demanding the reinstatement of a radical sociology professor who had been fired. The National Guard was called to squelch a ten-day demonstration for an Afro-American studies department at the University of Wisconsin, and at Swarthmore a ten-day sit-in at the administration building resulted in an agreement to increase the enrollment of black students. In the midst of it, Swarthmore's president and Strider's friend, Courtney Smith, suffered a fatal heart attack in his office.

MAYFLOWER HILL

Some faculty members carried the news of the faculty meeting—including the unfortunate aside comparing students to dogs—to a late-night student meeting in Roberts Union where the angry pot boiled. At midnight, more than one hundred students took over the chapel, lit candles, and danced for the "new Colby." The next morning other students awoke to find copies of the "new Colby" proposals slid under their doors, the chapel under siege, and a letter from Strider in their mailboxes, inviting them to sign up for service on the committees that would work on the original nine proposals. Again, the president reiterated his right to veto any committee recommendations, and again the bottom line did not sit well.

That afternoon, chapel occupiers sent a delegation to the president's house, inviting him to meet that night with a few dozen students and clear things up. He agreed. When he arrived shortly after 10 P.M., more than six hundred howling students were jammed in the sanctuary, throbbing to the music of the Motor City Five. It was an ambush. Strider stood on the steps in front of the altar and began by addressing the battle cry for a new Colby. "The College," he said, "is renewed every year." Someone in the balcony yelled "bullshit." Strider said he wasn't interested in having a conversation at that level. Someone on the main floor apologized.

They were not all revolutionaries. The place was divided between those who supported the more deliberate committee approach and did not much care for the dissidents, and the noisier protestors, bent on rebellion. When Thompson pressed the president on whether he would in fact reject any committee recommendation on procedural grounds, Strider stuck to his guns and went on to explain the roles of president and trustees. Students began to walk out. Thompson said he felt betrayed, and resigned as Stu-G president. Two student leaders of the new committees quit on the spot as well. Dismayed, Strider left by the side door and walked to his car.

The confrontation left him deeply hurt. After that night, to the end of his presidency, he was never the same, often keeping the door to his office closed, and avoiding unscripted meetings with students. (In times of trouble, a plain-clothes local policeman sat in the parking lot of the administration building, watching the windows of the president's office. A drawn shade meant trouble, to come at once.)

The chapel vigil continued for sixteen days, with occupiers ebbing and flowing, all the while conducting negotiations between hard- and soft-liners and having an occasional party in between. Elsewhere, the new committees worked to churn out recommendations on the proposals. Some of them—a twenty-four-hour switchboard and radios for the campus watchmen—were easy, but other issues dragged on through the spring. With the exception of the proposal that students be allowed to live off campus willy-nilly, all of the others, in one form or another, were eventually adopted.

Spring recess came, and the vigil-keepers abandoned the chapel and headed down the hill. When they left, the dean's office collected their belongings, and Dean Rosenthal wrote them letters, explaining their possessions could be retrieved at the buildings and grounds office. "We have decided," he said, "it is time for the Colby College chapel to be restored to its proper functions." Rosenthal offered to set aside a lounge if they wanted to continue discussions after vacation, but there were no takers. When they returned, there were better things to do. In April it was time to defend faculty members whose contracts were not being renewed. (To some students, the short list seemed lopsided with faculty dissidents.) In May, the 1969 yearbook came out, replete with counterculture art and precious little else. As students headed off to the summer of a moon landing and Woodstock, some 150 seniors stopped long enough to build a bonfire on the front steps of the library and, in a smoky protest against the protestors, burned their *Oracles*. It was that kind of year.

Trustees watched the smoldering from afar; and as the ad hoc committees struggled with the various proposals, the board assembled a few administrators, faculty, and students for a rump meeting in Boston, where trustee Eugene Struckhoff '44 suggested mounting a communitywide constitutional convention. Jetté and Strider agreed. The convention's purpose would be "to scrutinize the existing organizational structure and its inter-relationships, with a view toward possible restructuring of the divisions of authority, representation in the decision-making process, and the process of decision-making itself." Jan Hogendorn (economics) and Jeff Silverstein '70 worked through the summer to make arrangements.

There were many skeptics, on campus and off, who saw the convention as simply a device to head off further troubles. Avoiding more trouble was reason enough, but the convention was by no means a sop. Strider and others were hopeful the fractured lines of communication could be improved. Acknowledging "a minority of dissident students and some faculty whose purpose may not be entirely constructive," Strider said that, nonetheless, "the best protection is the establishment of a realistic governmental structure."

The planned convention roused many faculty members who were again bitter at not being consulted. At a special faculty meeting in mid-September they rose up against what one of them called the board's "arbitrary use of power." They were also jittery about possible tinkering with their authority in matters of academic policy. After the fuming, at their regular meeting in September, the faculty passed a resolution giving an after-the-fact blessing to what was by then called Con Con, and followed it with a second resolution making it clear all recommendations would have to be approved by both the Faculty Meeting and the student body before being passed along to trustees. With that settled, the six constituencies of the College set about to choose 108 convention delegates who were assembled in Averill Auditorium on Friday, October 3. They chose the new professor of human development, Leonard Mayo '22, one of only a few on the broad scene who enjoyed full confidence and respect across all constituencies, as chairman. More than once over the next three days, his wisdom and unfailing good humor kept the proceedings from falling apart. Strider greeted the delegates and promptly checked himself into nearby Thayer Hospital, suffering a physical ailment his doctor said (to no one's great surprise) was brought about by stress. Silverstein ferried bulletins and messages to him.

Early on, delegates dismissed the idea of creating a faculty-student senate, a governing mechanism gaining favor on campuses elsewhere. A proposal introduced by Professors Koonce, Mavrinac, and Koons titled "Principles of Governance and Accountability" occupied much of the discussion, and semblances of it found their way into the final report. The train nearly went off the track at the very end when students moved a "corporate override" resolution that would have given final authority in nonacademic matters to an all-campus referendum. At the brink of collapse, the motion was withdrawn. After two days of debate and faced with the hopelessness of finding word-for-word agreement on final recommendations, the several issues on which there was general consensus were sent to an overnight drafting committee. On Sunday, October 5, with only a smattering of dissenting votes, the convention approved a sketch of the final report that got brushed up over the next month and given a final blessing when Con Con reconvened in November.

When the dust had settled, the clear headline among the many approved recommendations was that students could elect two of their own to the board of trustees. The faculty had been given two nonvoting seats in 1955, and the convention asked for voting privileges for both faculty and the new student members. Ultimately, the board agreed to seat two students, but neither faculty nor students were given votes. At the same time, students, like faculty, would have seats and votes on most committees of the board

Faculty-student tensions that had become full-blown during the spring contretemps were addressed with the agreement that Stu-G would send the seven members to the faculty meeting without vote, and in turn, the faculty would choose two of its members to attend meetings of Student Government. (The faculty did not press for more seats. It would be hard enough to dragoon *two* members to attend Stu-G meetings, which often exceeded the Faculty Meeting in the matter of rambling.) In addition, students would have voting seats on the standing College committees, including a new committee on student affairs. Where sensitive personal student matters were discussed (e.g., financial aid, academic standing, and later, admissions) student members could participate and vote on policy matters but would be excluded from the discussion of individual cases. Thereafter, both students and faculty would approve changes in the committee system and the two bodies would share committee minutes.

Although it would provide a long-continuing source of debate and controversy, it was also agreed students could participate in academic department planning and in the evaluation of courses and instruction. To catch what was left, the convention created the short-lived position of College ombudsman, who was supposed to resolve nonjudicial complaints; and a faculty-student conference and review board, designed to give oversight to administrative policies. In December, both the faculty meeting and a student referendum voted by a two-to-one margin to send the recommendations on to the board where, in January, they were adopted.[44]

Strider was heartened by the friendly spirit of the convention, and said he could not have been more pleased with the outcome. Ben Kravitz '70, Stu-G president and a convention leader, said Con Con had brought "significant changes" and was not, as some had feared, an act of mere "tokenism." For a blissful moment that winter, the campus greeted the new decade with a note of harmony. By spring, however, the music had again gotten badly out of tune.

44. Colby was not alone in heeding student demands for a greater voice in campus decision-making. That same year, Harvard formed a committee on governance analogous to Con Con, and students joined committees and governing boards at other colleges, including Stanford, Wesleyan, and Oberlin. At Yale, president Kingman Brewster said he was not convinced that more representation was the key to university improvement; he warned, "If it is carried too far it could lead to disaster."

4. THE 1970S

BACK TO THE CHAPEL

The baby boomers became the Now Generation, a loose tag for an age that defied description. College students were divided among themselves, not just over politics and views of the war, but also over matters of lifestyle and values. If they had a unifying label, it was only because they shared an impatience with the world they were poised to inherit, and a frustration with "the establishment" that, from top to bottom, was painfully slow in making things right. By 1970 a growing college counterculture was engaging power centers in fierce debate, building fires against them, and often taking matters into their own hands. The dominant focus of conflict was the escalating war in Vietnam, but prominently on the edges were other issues begging for settlement as well. The long assault on the nation's environment had taken a frightening toll, and the young were determined to reverse the destruction. The new status of women lacked definition and acceptance, and a growing feminist movement was making the old order uncomfortable. And there was the enduring struggle for minority rights, with the nation's students again marching at the front, pulling and tugging others to follow. Colby students were engaged along all of the revolutionary fronts, and the noise was sometimes deafening. In early March, before the winter snow had melted, eighteen of the College's tiny black population found a way to be heard above the din.

On Monday evening, March 2, President Strider drove to Bangor to appear on a WABI television interview program on student protests. It was a topic on which he was reluctantly becoming something of an expert. Later that night he returned to Waterville to find student dean Jonas Rosenthal on the front steps of the president's house with news that a group calling itself the Student Organization for Black Unity (SOBU) had gone into Lorimer Chapel, tying the doors shut behind them. The protestors—ten men and eight women—issued a two-page mimeographed statement reciting five "demands" that they said must be met before they would come out.

After the chapel occupation of the previous spring, officials from Strider on down resolved to put down future illegal disruptions with dispatch. Moreover, Strider's position on dealing with "demands" from any quarter was well known. He would have none of it. Proposals for change must be dealt with through the committee process, established by the recent constitutional convention. But advance crisis planning had not anticipated the current dilemma. Even the appearance of heavy-handedness in dealing with SOBU, representing most of the College's twenty-five black students, was bound to smack of racism. For the moment, there was little to do but talk.[1]

The SOBU demands called for one hundred enrolled minority students by the fall, and a 10 percent black enrollment in freshman classes going forward; a special orientation program (sub-freshman week) for new black students; a black studies program taught by a black professor; and the elimination of the C+ grade point average (GPA) standard for receiving financial aid. All five issues were already under discussion in various committees, but in the short campus lives of students the committee process always seems to drag, and in the case of the Chapel 18, the dragging had gone on too long.

Colby began its concentrated minority recruiting efforts in 1965. Two years later twenty-three minority students, including thirteen black students, were enrolled. This year (1969–70) there were forty-two minorities, twenty of them black. Admissions dean Harry Carroll and his staff had already recruited seventy-eight black applicants, the largest number ever, for the class set to enter that fall. Even so, it was evident that the actual count of final enrollees would be a far cry from one hundred, and from the chapel SOBU revised its demand down to fifty. The future target of 10 percent minority enrollment was ambitious but not out of line with the College's own aspirations, and the Student Affairs Committee was even then mulling over the idea of a preorientation program for minority students.

The demand to eliminate the GPA guidelines for receiving financial aid fed two unfortunate stereotypes: that black students were less well prepared than their white counterparts, and that all minority students were in need of finan-

---

1. The Ethiopian track star Sebsibe Mamo '70 was one of the Chapel 18. Otherwise, the small number of black Africans eschewed the protest. They came from entirely different cultures, where they were among the majority (and where dissent was often not tolerated), and many of them did not understand what the fuss was all about.

cial aid. Neither was true. Further, the demand annoyed many, on and off campus, who complained that the chapel occupiers were squandering their financial aid, even though they were no different from white classmates who were regularly skipping classes to protest. The Academic Affairs Committee had recently addressed the controversial financial aid rule and, with the concurrence of the faculty and trustees, upheld the C+ standard, but allowed for exceptions. Exceptions were routinely being granted in cases where students, black and white, were making demonstrable efforts to achieve. (Registrar Coleman said if there was any discrimination at all, it was only against "the motivationally disadvantaged.")

The demand for a black studies program with a black professor reflected the rarely stated but deeply felt frustrations of being black at an almost-all-white college. There were no ranking black faculty members.[2] During his temporary appointment, Jack Foner had made small inroads in developing black studies—the catalogue listed two courses in Afro-American history—and he had agreed to stay on and continue the work. A five-course black studies program was set to begin that fall.

The general climate that spring was bleak for black college students across the country. The assassinations of Martin Luther King Jr. and Robert Kennedy had left them disheartened, and the war had shoved civil rights activism into a distant second place. President Richard Nixon was pressing private employers to hire minorities, but his "southern strategy" catered to whites by slowing school desegregation. Court-ordered busing was still a year away. At Colby, black students faced even greater challenges. Although they were generally well accepted on the campus, it was always less comfortable in the all-white environs of town, and they avoided Waterville streets and businesses. Shops did not offer many of the products they were accustomed to; local barbers and hairdressers did not know how to serve them. Most local children had never met a black person, and they stared. On the campus, even in classrooms, blacks were often asked to express the black view on various issues, as if there were single views and as if they knew them. While at first they were patient and willing to explain, they quickly grew weary of the silly questions,

2. The first black faculty member was Gladys Forde, who taught English from 1960 to 1962. Marie-Ange Cassol was an instructor in modern languages in 1970–71; Marion Brown was a visiting professor of music in fall term 1973; and Kenneth McClane, a Cornell graduate student, taught English in 1974–75. Wayne Brown (De Ponton D'Amécourt) '73 worked as an assistant in admissions for more than a year following his midyear graduation.

even from well-intentioned classmates. They griped that they had come to *get* an education, not to give one.[3]

The leader of the Chapel 18 was Charles Terrell '70, a history major. Strident and outspoken, he was also articulate and unfailingly polite. He met well with students and faculty across the campus and now with a rising tide of reporters who began to call the chapel telephone for interviews. On Tuesday, with the occupation one day old, Strider sent a warning that the students were illegally trespassing. Terrell and the others replied, "The matter of illegal trespass is pitifully irrelevant when compared to the matter of man's illegal trespass against human dignity." They would not move. Instead, they called for the support of a general class boycott the following day. It fizzled and a spokesman from the chapel called the inaction "essentially racist."

Many empathized with the black students and agreed with their demands. The *Echo* said the demands were reasonable and that rather than "violating the treasured channels of Con Con," the protest merely "dramatized the need for rapid action on black problems." White students smuggled food into the chapel and the owner of a local restaurant (taking pains to remain anonymous) sent in hamburgers and milkshakes. On the afternoon of the failed class boycott, some 350 people gathered to show support at a rally on the slushy lawns in front of the Chapel. With soul music blaring from loudspeakers in the tower, students carried signs and cheered as several demonstrators spoke from the front porch. That night, after a heated four-hour discussion, Student Government passed a resolution embracing the sit-in and calling for the administration to reevaluate its priorities. It allocated one hundred dollars to cover the cost of campuswide circulation of the messages from SOBU, and Stu-G President Kravitz rented the occupiers a film, *The Battle of Algiers*. Kravitz, who worked to negotiate a peaceful end to the protest, was a leader in establishing a "disadvantaged fund," later called "Project Open Door," which quickly raised $13,560 in gifts and pledges for minority student scholarship funds.

At the same time, others were suggesting that the administration cut off the chapel phones, barricade the building, and "starve them out." Many students signed a letter to Strider saying they did not agree with the Stu-G resolution.

General reaction off the campus was harshly critical of the sit-in. The pub-

3. Black students at Bowdoin and Bates had similar complaints. The Colby blacks were in close touch with their fellow students at Bowdoin where confrontation was avoided when President Roger Howell met with black students and agreed to a demand for thirty minority students in the upcoming freshman class. It was a goal Bowdoin could not meet. Bates, the Maine leader in minority enrollment, had twenty black students.

lic had little enough patience with any student protests, much less with the current uprising. The *Sentinel* accurately observed there was "more sympathy for and understanding of their (the protestors') frustrations among the people they are fighting than among the public at large." Although a bluntly racist letter to the *Sentinel* editor drew a flurry of scolding replies, much of the local grumbling had uncomfortable racial overtones. Not all of the criticism was pointed at the protestors. The *Portland Sunday Telegram* saved its strongest rebuke for the College leadership, declaring "If the administration surrenders to this nonsensical revolt, then it won't be able to complain at whatever demands, from whites or Negroes, are made in the future. . . . All over the country colleges are in trouble, but those most troubled are institutions whose officials abdicate their responsibility." So too, many alumni were seething.

On Wednesday, as angry letters and phone calls piled up, Strider called protest leaders to a morning conference in his office. By noon the negotiators moved to the chapel, where nobody blinked. The sit-in continued. Throughout the week the only disruption of the building schedule was the College-run basement nursery school for children of employees. A handful of mothers who showed up with their tots on the first morning of the occupation were politely turned away. As the weekend approached, Chaplain Thorwaldsen announced that his usual Protestant service, Father Leopold Nicknair's Catholic Mass, and Rabbi Phillip Goodman's Friday Jewish Sabbath observance would be combined in a single Sunday service in Given Auditorium. While worshipers prayed for the swift reclamation of the chapel, Strider again drew the weapon with which he was most comfortable. He wrote and distributed a six-page document detailing the College's minority recruiting efforts and its position on each of the demands.

On Monday morning, March 10, local attorney Robert A. Marden, a trustee and legal counsel for the College, led a small delegation of senior administrators to the Chapel door and delivered a message from Strider. Protestors had until 12:30 P.M. to vacate the building or face legal action. At 12:15, Terrell gave their reply: "We will not get out until we are taken out."

In the seat of authority and elsewhere, time and patience had run out. Marden had already set the wheels in motion for a temporary restraining order, and in Augusta Superior Court Justice James L. Reid quickly agreed, saying he had "adequate reason to believe a riot of serious proportions might result" if the building occupation was allowed to continue. He was wrong about that, but the College had the clout it needed to end the stalemate. The order, addressed to the students by individual name, gave them until 10:30 P.M. to leave or be held in contempt of court. It fell to acting Kennebec County Sheriff

Horace Drummond to deliver the order, and with visible trepidation, he took it to the side door of the chapel shortly after 6 P.M. Rosenthal was with him. Some three hundred students gawked from the nearby lawn, and several state troopers waited in Lovejoy Hall. Terrell greeted the frightened sheriff politely, shook his hand, thanked him, and evaporated into the building, locking the door behind him. The crowd, expecting a confrontation that never came, slowly drifted away. By 9:30 only a few onlookers were left when the side door of the chapel opened again and the students emerged silently and in single file, tossed their sleeping bags and other belongings into a nearby station wagon, and dispersed across the campus. The seven-day occupation was over.

Strider knew the last resort use of law would not sit well with the protestors or their sympathizers, and he quickly issued a statement saying the decision to seek a court order had been difficult: "The ultimate objectives of the students in many ways were resonant with College policies and goals," he said. "But the decision became inevitable as it appeared more and more likely the occupation of the chapel, with its attendant dangers, could be ended in no other way. The task of the College now is to press rapidly for appropriate action in the areas that reflect these concerns." He took the moment to clearly warn against any future building occupations. Any such actions, he said, "will bring legal action as quickly as it can be arranged, whether the objectives—immediate or ultimate—are noble or otherwise."

The following day, SOBU issued its own statement, decrying the use of the courts. That afternoon Strider met with the black students in his office. He said he understood their resentment and explained the choice of seeking a restraining order, which carried civil penalties, was "vastly preferable" to seeking a warrant for criminal trespass. He reiterated that procedures established by Con Con must be followed and pledged that he would "encourage discussions and do my best to expedite them" and work to "eliminate the divisiveness" of the past week. As the meeting wore on, some two hundred SOBU sympathizers milled in the hallways of the three-floor building and 150 more picketed at the President's House. For an hour or so it looked as though Strider's freshly issued promise of swift legal action against protestors was going to be tested. Deans and others stepped gingerly among the bodies and backpacks, reminding students of the new edict, and when the offices closed at 5 P.M., the students quietly walked out.

The president was caught squarely between those who felt he had been hasty in calling in the cops and others who wished he had allowed the peaceful occupation to drift on. Both the *Echo* and Student Government railed against the legal action. The management of WABI-TV, which earlier in the month had called Strider to comment as an expert on student protests, now scolded him for coddling the protestors, saying he "reacted badly" in the crisis by not moving quickly enough to put it down.

On March 21, as various committees began working on minority issues with renewed vigor, the junior class sponsored a lecture by Muhammad Ali. The gymnasium was overfilled, and those turned away lined the walkways outside and listened over loudspeakers. Ali, stripped of his heavyweight boxing title and free on bail after being convicted of draft evasion, did not expound on the recent local crisis. Instead, he preached against racially mixed marriage: "No white person in his right mind and no black person in his black right mind wants integration to the extent of intermarriage," he said. "Every man wants a son who looks just like him. You folks don't even know yet what people on other planets look like," he scolded, "but you've already decided that Miss Universe is going to be white."

Later that month the executive committee of the board met in special session at the Union Club in Boston, endorsed Strider's handling of the crisis, and directed a new trustee committee on equal opportunity and the relevant College committees to address the issues raised by SOBU and report to the board in June. On the campus, Dean Johnson implored the faculty to allow the protestors to make up their missed classes and called a special faculty meeting where, after nearly four hours of discussion, a resolution embracing the board's charge was adopted.[4] As students headed into the last weeks of classes before final exams, the mood on campus was sullen and tense. Although the end of the school year was only days away, the tumultuous spring of 1970 had only barely begun.

4. Colby accepted forty-five minority students for admission in the fall following the chapel occupation. Only three, two of them black students, enrolled. A sub-freshman orientation program began that fall, and under a new exchange program with predominantly black Saint Augustine's College (Raleigh, North Carolina) eight students from St. A's visited Colby for a week in March 1971. The ad hoc committee reported in June, calling for renewed minority recruiting efforts to create a "viable" black community within the College (estimated at fifty). For two academic years, 1972–74, the number reached sixty-six, including thirty-eight blacks, then declined again.

As the war droned on and the death toll mounted, the antiwar movement began to collect converts hand over fist. By the spring of 1970, most Americans wanted out, no matter what. President Nixon wanted to end it too, but only if there could be "peace with honor" and the communists left first. The year before, barely a month after his inauguration, he ordered secret bombings of Vietcong and North Vietnamese sanctuaries in Cambodia. Taking the war to a neutral country was illegal, and the move broadened the war he had promised to end. Campuses roiled in protest. Ignoring the dissidents and emboldened by the "silent majority," on April 30 the president announced ground troops were being sent to protect the new pro-American Cambodian government. Student protests mushroomed. Nixon called them "bums." In one of hundreds of outbursts across the country, students at Kent State University in Ohio buried a copy of the U.S. Constitution, claiming Nixon had "murdered" it. In four days of upheaval, students pelted police cruisers with bottles and fires were set in the streets of Kent. On the campus, students cut fire hoses and an abandoned ROTC building was burned to the ground.[5] The governor sent the National Guard with orders to prevent any assembly. On Monday, May 4, some 1,500 demonstrators gathered on the campus commons. Guardsmen, armed with tear gas and loaded M-1 bayoneted rifles, dispersed them. When the commons were cleared, the guard fell back and watched as the most militant of the protestors jeered from a nearby parking lot. Many students thought the confrontation had ended and began walking back to classes. Suddenly, inexplicably, guardsmen turned and fired into the crowd. Within seconds, four students lay dead. A dozen more were wounded. The news brought instant revulsion across the country.

Campus elections are held every spring, with the new government taking office in the fall. In 1970, Ben Kravitz relinquished the Stu-G presidency after the April voting. His role during the chapel occupation had taken a toll on his studies, and graduation was looming. His replacement came from the left. Stephen Orlov '71 was a new activist. The son of working-class parents, he came from mainstream America: played football as a freshman, joined Kappa Delta Rho fraternity, and made plans for summer training as an ROTC officer. His early Colby experience changed him. As a sophomore he read Alex Haley's *The Autobiography of Malcolm X.* He took a seminar on pacifism from the

---

5. In the first two weeks of May, more than two dozen ROTC buildings were burned nationwide.

philosopher Reuman, and a course on political change from a young China expert, Yun-Tong Pan. Years later he could still recall the "sheer excitement" of attending their classes. Before the summer came Orlov abandoned his ROTC plans and let his hair grow long. His election as Student Government president reflected the rapidly shifting political mood of the student body and made him an anomaly in the long line of otherwise conservative, buttoned-down presidents.

When Nixon announced the Cambodian incursion, the National Student Association (NSA) sent a letter calling for a student strike; it arrived in the Colby Stu-G office on the same day as the killings at Kent State. It urged mobilization of local and national support for three causes: to force the U.S. government to "end its systematic repression of political dissenters and release all prisoners, such as Bobby Seale and other members of the Black Panther Party"; to cease the expansion of the Vietnam War into Laos and Cambodia and "unilaterally and immediately withdraw all forces from Southeast Asia"; and to make universities "end their complicity with the US war machine by an immediate end to defense research, ROTC, counter-insurgency research and all other such programs."

That night some five hundred students jammed an emergency meeting of Stu-G and cheered at an agreement to call a "peaceful and nonviolent" shutdown. "It is not our intention at this time to strike *against* the college," it said; "this is a strike *by* the college." The resolve made no mention of saving Bobby Seale[6] or of an end to ROTC, but it did ask the student body and the faculty to approve a strike. The next morning Orlov telephoned student government heads of ten Maine colleges and the six campuses of the University of Maine, collecting endorsements of a telegram to Maine Senators Edmund Muskie and Margaret Chase Smith insisting they "return home and address yourself to the people whom you represent." The telegram left little room to wiggle. "Give the students of Maine the opportunity to confront you," it said. The meeting was set for Sunday afternoon, May 10, at Colby.

Orlov and two of his friends, *Echo* editor Robert Parry '71 and Kenneth Eisen '73, set out to engineer the command senatorial performance, forming the nucleus of a small band of radicals committed to nonviolent civil disobe-

---

6. Seale was a founder of the Black Panther Party, formed in 1966 to guard against police brutality in black communities. It quickly became militant. Seale was in jail in 1969, charged as one of the Chicago Eight with initiating the riots at the 1968 Democratic National Convention. The charges were later dropped and his subsequent trial for the murder of fellow Panther Alex Rackley ended in a hung jury.

dience and bent on hauling both the student body and the faculty into action.[7]
At a noontime rally in front of the library the flag was lowered to half-staff in
memory of the dead Kent State students. Four faculty members spoke. Reuman and Eugene Peters (philosophy) talked of a shared sense of sadness and
frustration. George Elison (history) decried Nixon's description of the college
dissenters. ("You have been called 'bums' by the highest authority in the land,"
he said, "and I suspect you feel it right down to your toes.") The radical David
Stratman (English) said Colby itself was part of the problem, "owned and controlled by representatives of big business." Stratman was not widely popular,
even among the dissidents, but as faculty head of SDS his participation was
obligatory. He invoked the issue of ROTC, and called for its elimination.

After the rally more than three hundred students began a "march against
death," carrying four mock coffins, one draped with the U.S. flag, into town.
Police chief John MacIntyre had issued the parade permit and arranged for police cars to bracket the marching protestors.[8] The crowd gathered a number of
local supporters as it wound its way down Mayflower Hill to Post Office Square,
down Main Street to Silver Street, and back up Elm Street to the post office
where someone lowered the U.S. flag. It was raised again when postal workers
objected, and the marchers wandered away, leaving the coffins on the lawn.

Strider called a special faculty meeting for Wednesday night. Dean Johnson
circulated the notice, explaining the need to discuss the position of the College "vis-a-vis what appears to be an escalation in violence and confrontation." There was certainly no violence, but even as faculty members plucked
meeting notices from their Lovejoy Hall mailboxes, protestors were sitting in
at the ROTC offices on the ground floor. The students knew better than to
shut down a federal installation, and despite the milling protestors, Lt. Col.
Don Harris and his three-member staff were left alone to do their work.

The student strike vote came at a mass gathering in Wadsworth Gymnasium that night. The margin was a whopping 1040 to 117.[9] Concurrently, at the

7. Orlov, Parry, and Eisen joined Washington, D.C., antiwar demonstrations that
summer and the next. The three were among some 1,500 arrested outside the Justice Department in Washington, D.C., during the 1971 May Day demonstrations aimed at shut-
ting down the government. Throughout the capital, some 13,000 were arrested in four
days of angry protests.

8. MacIntyre had some experience with college protestors in town. A month before,
on April 15, a dozen or more students had peacefully picketed the Internal Revenue
Office on College Avenue, opposing the use of tax money to finance the war.

9. Students' strike votes passed by slimmer margins at Bowdoin and Bates. Bowdoin's
youthful president, Roger Howell Jr., spoke at a prevote rally and urged the college to

faculty meeting in Lovejoy, a strike resolution introduced by Robert Pullen (economics)—a far cry from a radical—passed 71 to 21 with ten abstaining. Classes were canceled until Sunday night, when the faculty would meet again. A second, four-part motion introduced by Stratman called for the end of ROTC, and the secret ballot vote ended in a tie (50 to 50). By rule, Strider cast the deciding vote and the motion failed. A further resolution from Robert Jacobs (government) said the College should not punish the students occupying the ROTC offices. Strider said student discipline was none of the faculty's business, and the motion was defeated.

By Thursday, the campus radio station WMHB—still on 610 NHZ—was hooked into national strike headquarters at Brandeis University, broadcasting around the clock. Muskie wired Orlov accepting the Sunday invitation and commenting hopefully on the students' "determination to proceed with a positive dialogue aimed at developing a constructive course of action." Senator Smith dithered. As a lonely supporter of the Nixon administration, she knew it would not be a pleasant occasion, nor was Colby her favorite destination.

Never mind that Colby's president was a liberal Democrat; Smith's annoyance with Colby had begun many years before. In 1943, three years after she was elected to fill her late husband's seat in the House of Representatives, Colby was the first college to award her an honorary degree. She had no earned college degree and, as was custom, she got the short-sleeved master's. Over time she collected a closet full of honorary degrees (ninety-five in all), and all but this one were doctorates. It stuck out like a sore thumb on her résumé, and her colleagues never failed to remind Colby of the slight. The College made it right in 1991. Four years before her death at age ninety-seven, Colby awarded her a doctor of laws.

A series of strike events began Friday with a memorial service for the students at Kent State. Much energy went into the hasty development of a "counter curriculum" of workshops, led by faculty and others, on an array of pressing topics including militarism, racism, feminism, the military-industrial

"put pressure on President Nixon so that he knows the sentiments of the country." During a strike event at Bates, president Thomas Reynolds, who held a truck driver's license, got behind the wheel of a dump truck and led a clean-up caravan along the streets of Lewiston.

complex, and the cold war. Students flocked to support a blood drive; Tau Delta Phi held a benefit band concert; SDS presented *Salt of the Earth,* a film story of striking zinc miners in New Mexico; and Sunday Cinema showed *I Love You, Alice B. Toklas* (tickets 75¢, profits to support the strike).

On Friday night, with Strider and the deans sending strong signals they were about to send in the sheriff, protestors left the ROTC offices, still asserting the legitimacy of their action but claiming the threatened legal action "could only result in a loss of time." A second all-campus meeting that night provided an update on Sunday's rally, including news of Senator Smith's late acceptance. Strider spoke to the overflowing crowd in the gym and complimented strike leaders for "the constructive tone and high level of exchange of views." For the first time in public he revealed his view of the war. He called the recent expansion into Cambodia "depressing," and said the Nixon administration "has failed to take into account the deadening impact the war is having on young people and especially on college students." At the end, he could not resist sharing his anxiety about all those missed classes. He said he hoped the College could soon "get back to more orthodox forms of study."

Sunday, May 10, was a bright, spring day, and Colby was, for the moment, the center of Maine's antiwar universe. It was Orlov's twenty-first birthday and he had inadvertently arranged a whopping party. By early afternoon the central mall—from the Eustis Building to the science buildings and from the library to Mayflower Hill Drive—teemed with some three thousand people, most of them students. From a distance the scene resembled a county fair. Up close the mood was somber.

At 2:30, Muskie walked out the front doors of the library to a podium on the steps. The crowd cheered when Orlov introduced him.[10] Muskie was already touted as a Democratic presidential candidate for the 1972 election (he announced in December of that year), and his opposition to Nixon's conduct of the war was well known. He spoke from an eight-page text and used the friendly forum to announce his intention to introduce a Senate resolution requiring the immediate withdrawal of all U.S. forces from Cambodia. He said the purpose of the war had been to buy time for the people of Vietnam to build a country, and it was not worth it "if the price is the destruction of fundamental values and relationships in our own country."

Some of the crowd had drifted away before Smith appeared at four. She was tiny and frail, and her gray head could barely be seen above the podium. Orlov

10. In January 1971, Orlov served as a student intern in Muskie's Washington office.

loomed over her like a giant bodyguard. She had no prepared speech and immediately invited questions. She would have fared better had she read something. Asked about Cambodia, she defended Nixon's decision, adding she was confident he would keep his promise to withdraw troops by June. Students howled. Someone asked if the nation's youth had been consulted in the making of the Gulf of Tonkin Resolution. She said the question should be directed to former President Johnson. Asked to comment on the treatment of the Black Panthers, she said she didn't like the Black Panthers or the Minutemen. A black student responded: "I don't like you, or Nixon, or any of you, but I have to deal with you because you are the establishment."

The most stunning moment came when Smith was asked if there were American troops in Cambodia's neighbor country Laos. She turned to her aide, General William Lewis, and in a voice all could hear, repeated the question. He said no, and she turned back to the microphone and said she was not aware that there were any U.S. troops in Laos. Several in the crowd cursed, and some could be seen encouraging a young man as he made his way to the podium. He stood beside the senator, introduced himself as Brownie Carson, a Marine infantry platoon commander, and said he had recently been wounded in Laos. Turning to the senator, he asked how the ranking member of the Senate Armed Services Committee could not know that Americans were fighting in Laos, "and if you do know," he said, "how could you lie to us?" That was enough for Smith. As the screaming got louder, she turned abruptly and skulked back into the library, the dutiful general close behind.

Carson was a twenty-two-year-old Bowdoin graduate. Two years after chastising Smith on the Colby stage, he made an unsuccessful bid to unseat Maine Congressman Peter Kyros (1967–75) in the Democratic primary. He became one of the state's leading environmentalists and executive director of the Natural Resources Council of Maine. On the day of the Colby strike rally, another Bowdoin graduate, G. Calvin Mackenzie, twenty-five, was with the U.S. First Cavalry as it invaded Cambodia. Parts of the division had been in that neutral country months before, and Mackenzie and his comrades were irritated to learn politicians back home were saying it wasn't so. Mackenzie subscribed to the *Maine Times*, and a week later when he received the issue carrying the story of the Colby rally, he read the account of the confrontation with Senator Smith to members of his platoon. They cheered for Brownie Carson.

Mackenzie went on to earn a Harvard Ph.D. and joined the Colby faculty in 1978. He became a nationally recognized expert on the transition of power following U.S. presidential elections.

Aside from hurt feelings, little had gone wrong. Fears of confrontation and violence proved unfounded. The anti-antiwar people stayed away, and a cadre of some one hundred arm-banded volunteer student marshals kept order and cleaned up afterward. A "M*A*S*H" tent set up on the mall by the student health center (the sign said "Carl Nelson, Chief Cutter") had no customers. There were lots of beer cans smuggled in backpacks, and the smell of pot wafted in the spring air, but there were no arrests. An impending drug bust was narrowly averted when a local undercover cop, comically dressed as a hippie (bandanna, tie-dyed shirt, torn jeans, and sandals), was "outed" by a young Colby staff member who knew him and greeted him loudly as "sergeant." The officer glared in dismay, and the already popping pupils in the eyes of the pot smokers grew larger as they scurried into the milling crowd.

When all the visitors had gone, students gathered again in the gym and voted to continue the strike "to display our shock and disapproval of the further expansion of the war." The resolution asked the faculty to modify its requirements for term-ending papers and exams. From the beginning of the strike an ad hoc committee of faculty, administrators, and students had been puzzling over procedures for dealing with missed classes and, in particular, with how the Class of 1970 was going to meet its graduation requirements.

At a special meeting Sunday night, the faculty voted to resume classes the next day but left an odd escape for students who wanted to continue striking. A bare majority ruled they could simply stop going to class and take either a pass or fail grade, based upon their status in a course when the strike first began. They were given until Friday, May 15, to make up their minds. Strider seethed. Bad enough that course requirements were compromised, but he knew having students hanging around with little to do for the remainder of that angry spring was bound to be an administrative nightmare.

In fact, the worst was over. The final brush with disaster did not come until two weeks later. Early on Saturday morning, May 24, a night watchman investigating a broken window in the Lovejoy building discovered the unexploded remains of a Molotov cocktail inside the ROTC offices. A wine bottle filled with kerosene had been thrown through the window (it was a poorly made bomb; the contents ought to have been the customary oil and gas) and the burned wick, apparently cut off as it passed through the glass, merely charred the sill. Fuel from the smashed bottle spread through the office but did not ignite. Still, it was a federal crime, and the FBI investigated. Six months later, with fingerprints taken from the reassembled bottle, George Cameron '68 was arrested, convicted, and sentenced to prison.[11]

The engagement of the FBI was pro forma, as the ROTC offices were federal property. At the same time Nixon was asking Congress for one thousand additional federal agents to investigate any kind of violence on campuses receiving federal aid. Following the spring protests, student activists around the country were pressing to interrupt academic calendars with "political recesses" to allow students to campaign for peace candidates in the fall midterm elections. At Colby and elsewhere faculties squelched the idea when the Internal Revenue Service warned that electioneering could risk loss of an institution's tax-exempt status. And in Congress, Democrats blocked a bill that would have increased federal support for higher education out of fear that it would be used as vehicle for amendments aimed at curbing campus violence.

Commencement finally came. The principal speaker was South Dakota Senator George McGovern, already the darling of the antiwar movement. His message resonated with many students who carried protest signs and eschewed traditional caps and gowns, donating the rental fees to war relief. McGovern, soon to be thrust upon the national scene as the ill-fated 1972 Democratic presidential candidate, called for "a second American revolution—not a revolution of violence, but a quiet determination to square the nation's policies and priorities with the ideals of our founding documents."

Steven Cline, class president, arranged war discussion events around the customary program, and Gregory Carbone, class speaker, spoke for many of his classmates when he admitted he felt "lost" as he viewed an American society where "dishonesty is sanctioned" and "lies are an accepted part of advertising, and politics is treated openly as the art of public deception." He said he despaired of finding ways to effect change.

Everyone was exhausted, none more than Strider who clung to an annoyance that academic standards had been compromised to accommodate a prolonged strike. On that score, he did not mince his words, and when he spoke at the baccalaureate service, he threw a bomb of his own: "This year, unhappily,

11. Thirty years later, in 2001, the felon sought a pardon for his crime. The process required the forgiveness of his victim: Colby. President William Adams, a Vietnam Army veteran, agreed.

even though it was occasioned for the most part by forces beyond the control of any of us, the Colby degree for some members of this class is not as good a degree as this board and this faculty have always wanted it to be." His scorn was pointed not so much at the students, but at the faculty who had let it happen. He agreed students were free to attend class or not, but faculty members were obliged to meet their contractual obligations. Some students, he said, "have received credit in courses in which the instructors have not lived up to the obligations they accepted when they agreed to be appointed." Whatever else the president said to the graduates that morning was soon forgotten, but his assertion that their degrees were sullied rang harshly in their ears for years to come.

CEASEFIRE

There were a few new faces on the upper floors of the administration building when the College opened in the fall of 1970, and in the faculty a handful of the more rebellious members had evaporated into the mists of academe. Strider was calling for a new look at what the College was to become and for brighter lines in defining how far it would go. While no one could imagine greater upheaval than that of the spring just past, tension lingered over the ongoing war in Vietnam. Strider called for a local ceasefire, but it would be another sixteen months before the final volley was fired.

The exodus of leadership began at the top. Ellerton Jetté (who must have marveled at the differences between running a shirt company and a College under siege) stepped down as chairman of the board. Albert Palmer '30, a vice president of New England Telephone & Telegraph Company, succeeded him. Jetté and Strider had gotten along well; Palmer and Strider would not.

Parker Johnson, dean of faculty for a decade, returned to teaching. A beleaguered Jonas Rosenthal, who had trod the fine line between firmness and flexibility in dealing with the new breed of students, relinquished his dean's post and went back to the classroom as well. There wasn't time for a full search for either post, and Strider coaxed two of the most broadly respected faculty members to stand in. Mark Benbow (English) became dean of faculty; Albert Mavrinac (government), dean of students. Within a year, both jobs were filled. Paul Jenson, a psychologist like Johnson, vice president at Temple Buell College in Denver, became dean of faculty. Willard "Bill" Wyman '56, who knew something of student unrest from a tour as special assistant to the president at Stanford, returned as associate professor of English and dean of students.

Administrative vice president Roney Williams went on a year's leave and Robert Pullen '41, chair of economics, took his place. The move presaged Pullen's eventual permanent appointment in 1973 when, after a year as acting president during Strider's own sabbatical, Williams retired. Pullen was a veteran teacher. He earned his doctorate at MIT, where he taught for a time before joining the Colby faculty in 1945. Like his alumni predecessors, he was a fiscal conservative. Unlike either of them, he was liberal in his politics and longer on patience with an ever more demanding faculty.

Across the campus, the most prominent division was over ROTC, a favored target of antiwar protestors. Nationwide enrollment in the military training programs had plummeted even though college students were eligible for the draft. Many who might have enrolled as a means of finishing college were put off by peer pressure. At Colby, the number of new cadets fell into the teens. If the question had been left to students alone, ROTC would have been abandoned. In the heat of the spring of 1970, Student Government represented a majority opinion in voting for its abolition. In the midst of it, Jan Hogendorn (economics) squared off with the philosopher Reuman on the question, "Should Colby Discontinue ROTC?" Hogendorn took the negative, asserting that if the United States was to have an intelligent and sensible military, there ought to be some Colby officers alongside those from Texas A&M and the Citadel. The audience was clearly not on his side. Strider had used the same argument—"military officers ought to have read some poetry"—to convince a narrow majority of the faculty to retain the program. Under the rules of Con Con, the disagreement between the two bodies had to be settled by the newly constituted Conference and Review Board (CRB).

The CRB recommendation was to go to the trustee Educational Policy Committee on the way to the full board; as it waited for the CRB to report, the EPC met in Boston to have its own discussion. One question was going to be whether credit for ROTC courses should be counted in the number required for a student's graduation (reduced from 120 to 105 hours two years before). Pat Brancaccio (English) argued against the Strider-Hogendorn position, questioning whether the ROTC courses were truly free of distortion and asserting that the instruction might not be liberalizing the military at all. Tony Maramarco '71 (who within a few years returned as Strider's administrative assistant) said the military courses did not fit the College's overall academic program at all. Anne O'Hanian '72 (later a trustee) said removing the credit would merely "condemn ROTC to a slow death."

The CRB, with Paul Perez (psychology) and Charles Hogan '73 as cochairs, took its time, and at its fourth marathon meeting in December, agreed to recommend that ROTC courses become an extracurricular activity with academic rank withdrawn from ROTC personnel.[12] The EPC signed on and the board approved in April 1971. That fall Bill Rouhana '72 (also later a trustee) resurrected the ROTC issue before Student Government, arguing that students should have the option of choosing ROTC in order to complete college before being drafted. Stu-G agreed and reversed its 1970 vote.[13] For those who opposed the training program on moral grounds, the new Stu-G support was irrelevant. By 1971, Nixon was bringing home ground troops and at the same time stepping up the air war in hopes of forcing a peace. In protest of the increased bombings, Hanoi negotiators walked out of peace talks in Paris and prepared for an invasion of the south. The National Student Association again summoned the campuses to action.[14]

After lunch on Friday, April 21, 1972, more than a dozen students marched into the ROTC offices (relocated the year before from Lovejoy to Averill Hall) and said they would not leave "until ROTC is evicted from Colby or until we are arrested." A protestor told a crowd gathered outside that the office was a "center of death," prolonging the war by producing fliers who "commit murder" from the sky. Wyman, fresh in his post as dean, was decidedly against the war, and he sympathized with the determined students.[15] With Strider, he led a parade of officials who visited the protestors, reminding them of the consequences of civil disobedience and breaking the law. They wouldn't budge.

The next move was the dean's, and it was not made, as most had expected, in the civil jurisdiction. Instead, Wyman gave the students until 5 P.M. to vacate the premises or face charges before the Student Judicial Board. They did not leave, and later that evening Chief Justice Swift Tarbell '72 convened the

12. In fact federal law required that the assigned instructors be accorded faculty rank in aerospace studies.

13. The softening view of Student Government was made further evident that year when it overwhelmingly rejected a proposal to reorganize a local chapter of SDS. The Stu-G president was by then again a moderate, William Mayaka '73. As a government minister in his native Kenya during the 1990s, Mayaka became the highest-ranking government official in the Colby alumni body.

14. No Maine colleges went on strike. Classes were made optional at Bowdoin, and at the University of Maine at Portland, Maine Representative William Hathaway (Dem.) refused to accept a petition signed by some three hundred students calling for the impeachment of President Nixon.

15. Wyman's father, Willard Sr., was a four-star army general and on D-Day in 1944 was the first general on the Normandy beaches. While attending his son's Colby graduation in 1956, he officiated at the annual spring commissioning of ROTC officers.

board that obligingly cited protestors for violating the civil rights of Harris and his two-man ROTC staff. In the hope that the students could be jawboned out of the offices over the weekend, the order gave them until 7 A.M. on Monday morning. If they weren't gone by then, they would be suspended. The order was ignored. Instead, protestors issued a statement calling for support. On Thursday more than three hundred filled the auditorium in Runnals Union, where representatives of Vietnam Veterans Against the War spoke and showed a film of war veterans discarding Vietnam medals at a Washington protest. Stu-G met on Saturday and voted 10 to 3 not to support the sit-in.

At seven on Monday morning Wyman delivered a notice to the seventeen students still in the offices. If they did not leave by 7:30 A.M. they would be suspended, at least until September 11, 1972. The number of protestors dwindled to ten, nine men and one woman. C. Patrick Lynch '74 had become their leader. He kept his promise of a "dignified and non-violent" protest, but it was evident that the holdouts wanted to assume a classic civil disobedience stance and be arrested. By this time the College was ready to oblige. At eight o'clock Wyman verbally issued the suspensions, and seven Waterville police officers, accompanied by Chief Ronald LaLiberte and Assistant Kennebec County Attorney Marden, entered the building and arrested the students for "refusal to vacate," a misdemeanor under Maine's new, untried "sit-in law." A small crowd of some 150 students and faculty watched as the students raised their fists on their short escorted walk to a nearby school bus.[16] At their booking in City Hall they discovered that sympathetic faculty members had already passed the hat and raised bail money of one hundred dollars for each. Later that day, in light of "the dignity and concern" with which the protest had been conducted, Wyman shortened the suspensions and gave the students a chance to finish the semester. He said they could come back on May 8.

The concession did not sit well off the campus. Waterville's colorful and outspoken mayor, Richard Carey, felt duped. He and others had quietly agreed that in return for the lengthier suspension the trespassing students would be cited for a misdemeanor rather than a felony (criminal trespass). Carey called Wyman's reprieve a "wrist-slap" and a "hoax," and said that next time the College could call Oakland. He said he would send the College a bill for three hundred dollars to cover the cost of supplying the officers.[17] The next day, as

16. While waiting for the cops, the protestors did some tidying up. Before the deadline, newspapers and sandwich wrappers were thrown out, and the office rugs were vacuumed.

17. Carey was, nevertheless, a vocal opponent of the war. Later that day he wrote a

College and city officials met to smooth the town-gown waters, some two hundred students milled throughout the Eustis administration building, protesting the war and complaining about the "double jeopardy" of the students who had been both arrested and suspended. In early May District Court Judge Roland Poulin fined each of the students one hundred dollars and sentenced them to ten days in the Kennebec County Jail. He suspended the jail sentence, but warned that it was "no joking matter" and that he would put them away for ninety days if they broke the law again.

It was the ceasefire Strider had long been looking for. The protests wound down, at Colby and elsewhere, not because the colleges had found a way to quiet the angriest students, but because the war was ending. Three months later, in August 1972, even as Nixon tried to force a peace with increased bombings, the last U.S. ground forces withdrew. The following January national security advisor Henry Kissinger proclaimed, "Peace is at hand," and the air bombing stopped as well. As the last U.S. troops left Saigon in 1975, the communists swept down from the north. Neither the Congress nor the country itself had the stomach to weigh in again and stop them. Saigon became Ho Chi Minh City and the long war ended almost where it had begun.

Colby ROTC enjoyed a brief resurgence after the 1972 sit-in, but the program was never again as large as it had been before the war. With only two seniors enrolled, fourteen freshmen signed on the fall of 1972, including the first three women cadets.[18] The following year, Thomas College made a joint venture with Colby and began a companion AFROTC program on its new (1971) West River Road campus. The struggle of Strider and others to keep the military training program at Colby was made moot in February 1974 when General F. M. Rogers, commander of the Air University in Alabama, wrote to say that the postwar zero draft had taken its toll, that the program at Colby could not be sustained, and that it would be discontinued after commencement. The general thanked Strider and Colby for the many fine officers the College had sent to the air force over the past quarter-century.

In 1987, a dozen years after the war, the populist *Boston Globe* columnist Mike Barnicle gave the commencement address and called for graduates to be on guard against politics and privilege. The politics of the Vietnam War were

---

letter to Strider in which he said that while he had strong feelings about law and order, he was well aware "that a large majority of our citizens share the feelings of that small band of students." The bill for police costs was never sent.

18. Cathy Worcester of Lincoln, Maine; Joanna Pease of Lisbon, Portugal; and Carol Houde of Nashua, New Hampshire.

"obscene," he said, and privilege played its own role with the "fighting and dying being handled by kids whose fathers came out of firehouses or Local 114 or the MBTA" and whose mothers worked as "waitresses, if they worked at all." He said he had called the College to ask how many graduates died in the war, and was not surprised when he was told there were none. The answer was incomplete. Robert Lloyd '68, a Vietnam veteran, helped set the College straight. Four Colby men, three of them undergraduates, were killed in the war: Specialist David T. Barnes '68, Capt. James H. Shotwell '62, Lt. Leslie A. Dickinson Jr. '67, and Lt. Robert C. "Mike" Ransom Jr. '66.

Their names were inscribed on a tablet placed near the other war memorials on the central campus mall, and dedicated June 11, 1988. These four had made the supreme sacrifice, but there were many other students and graduates whose lives were unalterably changed because of their service. And on the battlefields at home there were patriots of a different sort, often scorned and despised, who never wanted to diminish the sacrifices of their brothers and sisters in arms, but who used the tools of a democracy—peaceful dissent and protest—to turn the heads of an entire nation toward believing that this war, despite the virtues of stemming communism, was not worth its cost in lost and ruined lives.

QUIETER REVOLUTIONS

The nation was more culturally divided and disillusioned than it had been since the Civil War. The young, emboldened by their own voices, rejected entrenched middle-class values and sought new lifestyles of their own. Their elders clung to an unrecoverable past and could not close the generation gap. As always, changes began on the campuses. Students no longer received their education as supplicants and were eager to shape the rules of how they lived and what they studied. Sometimes administrators went along for the ride; more often they fought to stay the old course, dodging potholes and applying the brakes wherever they could.

Conflict and change was evident in Waterville as well. The new highway had divided the city into smaller parts and old neighborhoods were breaking down. Crime was on the rise. In the years Colby and Waterville had shared the same few acres, borders of the campus blended into neighborhood streets, and students were very much a part of town. Now, the old ties were stretched. Some were broken forever. Never was the long mile from the Post Office to the Hill more staggeringly apparent than in November 1971.

Katherine Murphy, a freshman, only eighteen, was reported missing by her roommate on the night of November 2. College officials went looking in the early morning hours, calling her name through the rain, checking with her newfound friends. They could not find her. At dawn a jogger discovered her body in a ravine at the bottom of the hill, some thirty feet from the road. That same day a twenty-two-year-old Waterville man, Alan Pelletier, walked into the police station with his father and said that as he drove his pickup truck up Mayflower Hill Drive the night before, he had seen a man beating on a women at the edge of campus. He said he went to the top of the hill, left his truck in the parking lot opposite Mary Low Hall, and walked back to the scene of the fight. The man was gone, he said, but he found the woman and she was dead. He said he rolled the body over before running back to his vehicle, vomiting along the way.

Pelletier was known to police as one of several local men who often gave rides to Colby women, up and down the Hill. He also followed fire alarms and was rarely far from local incidents when police were called. Whatever local officials thought of his story, Assistant County Attorney Donald Marden said the death would be investigated as a hit-and-run motor vehicle accident. Two days later, pathologist Irving I. Goodof said Murphy had been murdered. Responsibility for the investigation shifted to the state attorney general, and only then was the crime scene roped off and scoured for evidence. It was too late.

State police detectives set up an office in Roberts Union. Women students came forward and identified license plate numbers and sometimes the names of a dozen local men who had accosted them during rides to and from the campus. After twenty years of gathering at the iron rail fence at Sacred Heart Church to hitch rides to the campus, "Colby Corner" was closed. The director of student activities, John Zacamy '71 (later a trustee), resurrected the Blue Beetle in the form of a nine-passenger Volkswagen bus, and the new "Jitney" ran up and down the Hill, taking passengers for ten cents a ride. The murder went unsolved, and the mystery was frightening. For a long time, students would not go out of doors alone. If there was any innocence left among them, it was fast disappearing.

The homicide investigation remained active for fifteen years, largely because of the obsession of Waterville Police Detective Norman Quirion. He was familiar with the local underworld and he believed its people knew a lot more than they were giving up. In November 1980, nine years after the murder, Assistant attorney general Pat Perrino ordered an investigative grand jury. After the proceedings he criticized the work of the investigators, and concluded there wasn't enough evidence to seek an indictment. In March 1983, *Sentinel* reporter Bill Nemitz wrote a prizewinning account of the case, and for the first time revealed the prevailing rumors of a police cover-up, a sadly botched investigation, and the mysterious deaths of two men closely tied to it. Three years later, in March 1986, an indictment was brought against Pelletier, the man who said he had seen the murder. In January 1987 the case went to a jury trial before Superior Court Justice Morton A. Brody. Assistant attorney general Michael Wescott led the prosecution, but the trail was cold, memories of key investigators had faded, and evidence (including blood samples, Waterville police arrest and investigation records for 1971, and the 1980 grand jury transcript) had gone missing. After a twelve-day trial, the jury deliberated for two days and returned a "not guilty" verdict.

Students' views of the world changed in other ways as well. The 1969 constitutional convention had decreed a second "Con Con" in 1972 when 108 delegates met for a three-day session in April, charged with "continuing, modifying, or abandoning" the changes resulting from Con Con I. Two agenda items were easy. The office of ombudsman had been established as a safeguard against heavy-handedness on the part of the administration, and to cut through red tape that might get wound around the new governance structure. Strider assigned the role to professor emeritus Alfred "Chappie" Chapman, one year retired and living nearby. Before long Chappie was advocating the abolition of his own job. Other than dealing with students unhappy with the outcome of disciplinary matters, he had seen little business. Second, the Conference and Review Board (CRB) had proven unwieldy. It had reviewed only three academic departments, and then only because each volunteered. Moreover, it wasn't clear what to do with the departmental reviews once they were finished. Con Con II quickly scratched the ombudsman and the CRB.

To hammer out details of its new creations, the convention established a Committee on Committees and Governance. Its first charge was to unravel the spool of twenty-two accumulated College committees, nearly half of which were redundant or moribund, or both. Streamlining the lumbering committees was without controversy. It was in dealing with a new system of governance that the enclave nearly collapsed. Charles Hogan '73 had spent the fall working with Profesor Sandy Maisel (government) preparing a convention proposal for establishing an all-powerful College senate. The senate idea had been part of Hogan's campaign platform (under the ambitiously titled Save America party) for his successful bid for election as Stu-G president, and it had support, even among some old guard faculty. The only problem was a clause that would have allowed the senate to override, with a two-thirds vote, any decision of the administration or the trustees. As Con Con II wore into the second day, a motion by Professor John Dudley (physics) to scrub the offending clause altogether passed 55 to 43, whereupon twenty-three of the student delegates declared the whole thing a farce and walked out.

Remaining delegates hung on through the end of the third day, when alumni representative Charles Barnes '54 brought an amendment saying a new senate could do as it pleased as long as it did not interfere with the bylaws of the corporation. The debate had come full circle, and the stalemate was broken. Con Con II adjourned leaving a full plate for the CRB: consolidate the committees, design a College senate, and develop a philosophy for shared responsibility in governance. On its own, Con Con II called for voting privileges for student and faculty representatives to the board (trustees said no); revise the bylaws to make the ancient and once-powerful Academic Council an advisory board (trustees said yes); and open the College budget to the inspection of any member of the community (trustees said no, but a summary budget could go to the new Financial Priorities Committee).

A year later trustees approved the new committees,[19] creating a scheme of shared governance that had driven the idea of a College senate. The structure of the Educational Policy Committee preserved the primacy of the Faculty Meeting, but also included student voices. The same was true for the Student Affairs Committee, charged with guided proposals for major student life changes from the grassroots to the boardroom. With that done, the idea of a senate seemed an extra layer of decisionmaking, and it died of its own weight.[20]

Much of the student interest in making policy was in the lingering debate

19. Ten committees were eliminated (Architectural, AFROTC, Campus Natural Environment, Commencement, Examinations and Schedules, Foreign Study and Student Exchange, Freshman Week, Honorary Degrees, Professional Preparation, and Safety), nine were continued (Administrative, Admissions, Athletics, Bookstore, Educational Policy, Financial Aid, Library, Senior Scholars, and Academic Standing), and three were added (Financial Priorities, Interdisciplinary Studies, and Special Programs). Students were given seats on all but Admissions, Financial Aid, and Academic Standing.

20. It would be another decade before the system for reviewing academic departments got figured out. In the meantime, the Con Con II recommendation that departments have an annual sit-down with graduating seniors was adopted as a general rule.

over coeducational living. The 1967 integration of the sexes into proximate buildings was old and uninteresting. Now students were pushing for *real* coed living: men and women housed by separate corridors, if you please (or by adjacent rooms, thank you very much.) The College had experimented with coeducational living in Roberts Union for two years before the new College Student Affairs Committee entertained a proposal from the Center for Coordinated Studies to make the largest dormitory, Dana, coed by corridor. The new committee wasn't interested, but by June 1970 was willing to recommend students be given the right to make some of their own rules for residence hall living. (The term "dormitory autonomy" was misleading because of its sweeping inference, but it stuck as a worthy battle cry.) Trustees weren't about to surrender full management of dormitories to students, but did agree to delegate some authority to each unit "for the purpose of establishing and enforcing its own hours, visiting privileges, and the conditions under which these may occur."[21] As for coed living, the board endorsed the committee's negative recommendation:

> We do not think this is an appropriate or desirable mode of living . . . nor do we wish the college to project the type of image which such housing arrangements would create . . . we feel the risks to psychological, emotional and physical health are sufficient to deter us.

In the face of the board decision, acting dean Mavrinac ordered the much-abused fire doors between Foss (women) and Woodman (men) halls firmly shut, and a student wag put up posters announcing the only coed dorm would be on Runnals Hill: "bring your sleeping bags." Within eighteen months trustees reversed themselves, their minds changed not so much by students as by the new dean, Bill Wyman. In the fall of his arrival in 1971, Wyman accepted the invitation of the board Student Affairs Committee to make a comprehensive study and recommendation on coed living. His fifty-page report addressed the points that had been made on both sides of the two-year debate. It contained findings of a survey of eight Colby-like colleges (including Bowdoin and Bates) that already had coed living and didn't regret it, and results of a Colby poll showing a whopping 88 percent of students in favor.

In denying the initial request, trustees had been frank about their concern

---

21. When college opened in the fall of 1970, all seventeen dormitories (eight women's, nine men's) and all eight fraternity houses voted for "24 parietal hours." Only two dormitories set "quiet hours." The rest agreed to an ill-defined practice of "mutual consideration."

for the College's image. Admissions dean Harry Carroll wrote for the report that with twenty-four-hour dormitory visiting privileges already in effect, the move to coed dorms couldn't do any harm. Fundraising steward Ed Turner said that while some alumni would be "deeply disturbed" and might withhold support, he thought if the College made its case most would continue to give. Although the polar arguments were often couched in lofty terms, underlying the opposition was a fear of bacchanalia and unbridled sex. Wyman said no, that adolescent behavior would decline and male/female relationships would be dominated less by sexual interests. "More and more young people today accept the idea of premarital sex," he wrote, "and there is no reason to believe this attitude would change one way or the other."

Robert A. Marden '50, chair of the board Student Affairs Committee, led the trustee cheering section on behalf of the report, and in January 1972 trustees made it official. The dean's office was licensed to set up coed arrangements in the fall, subject to certain conditions: single-sex housing for all who wanted it, men and women separated by corridors, a guarantee of privacy for all, mixed classes in all dormitories, and, to the extent possible, an integration of faculty associates and house-taught courses. The *Echo*'s response was sour grapes: "The arguments and protestations of various student groups during the past two years have been of little avail, yet the dean's office succeeded in moving the committee in only two months."

In September, Foss-Woodman, Dana, Johnson, and Averill became coed. There wasn't space to meet demand (50 percent of students requested it), but it was a start. The separate corridor arrangement worked without need of building renovations except in Dana, where a windowless swinging door was installed on the second floor to separate the only male/female split corridor.[22] A freshman resident on the floor, Martha Dewey '76, said the curiosity traffic made it seem "like living in a museum." A mother, speaking up on Freshman Parents Weekend, said she hoped the place didn't turn into a summer camp. The change never did bring the problems its detractors had predicted (the pregnancy rate did not increase), but the new system was not without surprises. With twenty-four-hour visiting privileges and the newly mixed dorms, the College despaired of keeping rooms clean and gave up providing maid service, and the new attraction of the dormitories created a vacuum in fraternity houses, where there were suddenly fifty empty beds.

22. The door got heavy use. After a number of black eyes and bloody noses, a frosted glass pane was installed. Even so, the door was usually left propped open. After two years, it disappeared altogether.

To accommodate the dormitory overflow, the College rented rooms on the old Thomas College Silver Street campus, then under lease to the fledgling Maine State Police Academy. Colby students shared Parks Hall with police cadets who were trying to sleep at night when students partied, and were up for calisthenics at 5 A.M. when students were sleeping. Head Resident Bruce Cummings '73 (director of student activities the following year) struggled to keep the disparate groups from coming to blows. Coeducational living also dramatically changed the noise level. Adherence to the rule of "mutual consideration" was in the ears of the listener, and it wasn't long before students clamored for a quiet place to live. (The request was problematic. If all that wanted quiet moved into one place, wouldn't the other places get noisier?) Still, associate dean for housing Doris Downing '69 found a place, and in the fall of 1974 Averill Hall, near the hushed library, became the first "quiet dorm."

Coed living was merely a product of a greater awareness of the need to dispel antiquated practices and old myths that applied to women.[23] In the fall of 1972, just as the College was thinking it had balanced the scales between the sexes, Bernice Sandler came to speak. The executive associate of the Association of American Colleges said there was still much work to do in achieving sexual equality. She urged women to denounce stereotypes about their sex, at home and in the workplace, and asserted, "The hand that rocks the cradle can indeed rock the boat." That fall the catalogue included its first course in women's studies, "Social Roles of Women," developed through the initiative of Rebecca Ross '71, who had spent a Jan Plan at Wesleyan University's pioneer women's studies department. Dean Jenson and Charles Bassett (English) managed the course, centered on a series of guest speakers. A year later Bassett coordinated the team-taught course "Women in American Society." More than eighty students enrolled; a full third were men.

The Colby Women's Group was organized in 1973, the same year the student body elected Martha Bernard '74 the first woman president of Student Government. That spring the group sponsored a Women's Festival Week, aimed at "educating the women of Colby to the problems and issues of the Women's Movement." It was a quiet reminder, a group leader said, "that we are here and we are not going to go away."[24]

23. Students were good at smashing stereotypes themselves. In 1970 they elected William "Tim" Glidden '74 as the first male Homecoming "queen." The old fall tradition never recovered.

24. The formation of the Women's Group emboldened Colby's gay and lesbian students to establish an open-to-all organization of their own. In February 1974, seniors

The group soon began agitating for improved and expanded campus health care for women. Among other things, it wanted the infirmary to dispense the birth control pill. Ten million American women were already using the pill, but the College hierarchy was hesitant. Alumni and others hadn't fully digested the idea of coed living, and it was too soon to ask them to swallow the Pill. After a flutter of meetings and petitions, in 1976 Strider approved increased physician coverage and a new sex education program. He sent the remaining issues to a task force (no more new committees), led by the respected young faculty member Arthur Champlin (biology). In 1977, about the time Miss became Ms., the growing number of feminists had their own headquarters in Roberts Union. Led by a determined and popular new assistant professor of English, Phyllis Mannocchi, they continued to press for a full-fledged women's studies program.

Yet another revolution was aimed at rescuing the environment, a cause in which students found plenty of allies and role models, from the nation's capital to the full breadth of the campus, all the way to the President's House. The best national example of environmental leadership was in their own backyard. As the conservation champion of the U.S. Senate, Waterville's Edmund Muskie had earned the sobriquet Mr. Clean after writing the Water Quality Act (1965) and the Clean Air Act (1970), bedrocks of the nation's air and water quality legislation. During his ill-fated run for the Democratic nomination for the presidency in 1972, he continued his environmental leadership by writing the companion Clean Water Act, adopted that same year.

Donaldson Koons, chair of the geology department and Maine's powerful Environmental Improvement Commission (later the Department of Environmental Protection), spoke at a campus rally on the first Earth Day, April 22, 1970. He warned students "the environmental bank is already calling its note" and said the regulations promulgated by his department could only treat the symptoms, not the disease. "The disease," he said, "is people." A small number of students had begun to take an environmental stand even in the din of larger protests. During preparations for the 1970 Smith-Muskie antiwar rally they passed out leaflets with a comprehensive list of drinks in "returnable, refundable, two-way bottles," and of the local stores that carried them.

Under the aegis of the venerable Outing Club, that fall Joel Ossoff '73, Nat Woodruff '71, and others formed the Environmental Council, an affiliate of

-----

Barbara Badger and Nancy Snow formed The Bridge, a group with tentative beginnings that slowly grew in numbers and campuswide acceptance.

the Natural Resources Council of Maine. It had its own newsletter, the *Colby Eco*, and was soon handing out birth control handbooks and a call for trustees to limit the College's tuition benefit to two children per family. It got snowmobiles banned from the campus. It urged students to refuse junk mail and begged them to conserve fuel, electricity, and water: "take short showers, use as little soap as possible."

The council did more than preach. Members collected tons of newspapers and sold them for recycling to Keyes Fibre Company. From the President's House, Helen Strider, a founding member of the Waterville Conservation Commission, partnered with Mayor Carey to arrange a regular citywide newspaper collection program. Proceeds, matched by the state, were used to buy trees to replace the city's dying elms. Students conducted a study for the Keep Maine Scenic Committee in the winning effort to ban billboards, and they lobbied for the successful passage of the state's returnable bottle bill. Stephen Palmer '75 led volunteers who collected trash along sections of Maine highways and presented the legislature a scientific estimate that unless the law was passed, there would be "a foot high wall of litter" along all of the state's roads by the year 2000.

In 1972, before bottles and cans were returnable, the Maine Liquor Commission worried young people were drinking too much from kegs—mainly because they could not bear to leave a single drop—and banned the sale of beer kegs. A bill requiring the commission to reverse its stand was introduced into the Legislature's Natural Resources Committee. Colby juniors Kenneth Gorman, Robert Diamond, and Stephen Higgins appeared at the legislative hearing carrying trash bags filled with empty cans equivalent to the volume of a single keg. Committee members laughed as hundreds of empty beer cans rattled over the hearing room floor. The liquor commission backed down.

The College launched its Environmental Studies Program in the fall of 1971–72, cobbling together courses in five disciplines in the natural and social sciences to create a major offering led by biologist William Gilbert. It was the first program emphasizing hands-on outreach projects, and it soon had a major impact on local and state conservation efforts. (Within four years it would have nearly sixty majors.) That fall students conducted a well-received survey of lakes near Readfield. The following summer "Homecoming Queen"

Glidden and Carol Majdalany '75 surveyed the shores of several of the nearby Belgrade chain of lakes. Property owners welcomed them, but town officials in the lake-bordering town of Oakland were less than enthusiastic. Glidden later recalled that town fathers thought all the talk about the need for zoning was "vaguely communistic."[25]

The students' recommendation of grassroots citizen involvement was the impetus for the formation of the many formal lake associations. Two faculty newcomers, David Firmage (1975) and Russell Cole (1977) paired to develop the special study area, and it quickly grew to become the College's most prominent service learning program.

Nothing gave the environmental movement more momentum than the "energy crisis" that began in mid-October 1973. Egypt and Syria invaded Israel (the Yom Kippur War), and as punishment for supporting Israel, the new Organization of Petroleum Exporting Countries (OPEC) stopped the flow of oil to the United States and its Western European allies. Spoiled by cheap energy and stunned by the sudden embargo, Americans waited in long lines for gasoline that within a few months rose from 38¢ to 55¢ a gallon. The highway speed limit was lowered to 55 mph and the sound of chain saws filled neighborhoods as residents cut firewood for winter.

Members of the Environmental Council held dozens of meetings, puzzling out ways to conserve. Most Northeast colleges responded by shortening their calendars. Bowdoin ended its first semester a month ahead of schedule. Colby adjusted its Jan Plan from January 3–31 to January 15–February 7. The customary interval between the end of Jan Plan and the beginning of the second semester was eliminated.[26]

The tight schedule helped only a bit. Spring Brook Ice & Fuel, suppliers of the fuel for Colby's aged furnaces, said it could promise deliveries only through February. Thermostats were set below 70 degrees and students, accustomed to opening windows to release the sweltering heat of unregulated boilers, closed them, put on sweaters, and took short showers. Office work schedules were

25. Glidden served as deputy director of the Natural Resources Council of Maine, and then as director of the Land for Maine's Future Program. Majdalany (Williams) worked for the Environmental Protection Agency in Washington, and later was a director of the Litchfield, Connecticut, Inland Wetlands Commission. Other preservation leaders of the era included Earle Shettleworth '70, director of the Maine Historic Preservation Commission and later Maine State Historian; and Kent Wommack '77, director of the Nature Conservancy of Maine.

26. When the crisis ended, many northeastern colleges continued the shortened calendar. Colby did not.

adjusted to match daylight hours. Every other light bulb along the building corridors was unscrewed from its socket, and in a symbolic gesture the "blue light" in the library tower was extinguished.

SHAKE YOUR BOOTY

The vacuous tune by KC and the Sunshine Band was but a mild reminder of the ever-widening generation gulf in the social sphere. Like kids in the back seat on a long ride, students annoyed and needled their elders. In the 1970s, it was about sex, drugs, and disco. Drugs were worrisome, and "sensound" music could cause permanent hearing loss. Sexual exhibitions were harmless enough but shocking all the same. At the beginning of the decade the Echo *briefly imitated* Playboy *magazine, and it wasn't long before students began taking off their clothes and streaking around buck-naked.*

Throughout the coed dorm debate, the *Echo* had taken the side of change. An October 9, 1970, edition had an article by former dean Jonas Rosenthal explaining the trustee opposition to mixed dorms. Next to it was a piece by Ken Eisen '73 in which he claimed that as there were virtually no rules being enforced in the dorms anyway, nothing much would change if men and women lived together. Illustrating the articles was a large photograph of the rear ends of a nude couple, sauntering down a dormitory corridor.

The callipygian view did little to bolster the case of those who claimed students should be able to live close together. While most eyes fixed on the nude photo, in the same edition could be seen a report on the Student Government election successes of a coalition named F.U.C.K., an acronym reflecting the group's intentions for "Camp Kolby." (In later defense, the *Echo* said it was only reporting the news and had nothing whatever to do with the naming of the group.) The "f" word was by then crawling out of dark places, together with crude names for previously unmentioned body parts and functions being thrown into the bright light of a world that wasn't ready. Strider observed there were no fewer than seventeen "f" words in a single recent edition of the *Echo*. He had counted them, and opined that whatever dubious shock value the word held, it surely lost any useful literary purpose by repeating it so many times.

Strider had for some time been fretting about the newspaper's "deterioration of taste and tone." In that same hurly-burly spring he had addressed alumni on the limits of freedom along the full range of College endeavors, including the newspaper, and asked rhetorically: "Is the uncontrolled barbarism, with its obscenities, libel, and innuendo, of the campus press, no concern of ours?" College of Elijah Lovejoy or not, Strider answered his own question. He wanted no part of censorship, but he was not about to abide what he called "a deplorable continuation of the downward spiral" of the newspaper's taste and tone. He wrote editor Robert Parry to say delicately the time had come to explore steps that could lead to institutional disassociation from the *Echo*. In the meantime he asked them to "cease immediately" using Colby's name.

The newspaper printed Strider's letter on page one of the next edition under the customary Colby *Echo* masthead (which now included a curious caveat stating that the opinions contained therein were not necessarily those of the College or, for that matter, even the student body). An accompanying editorial, illustrated with somber images of Lovejoy, countered: "While our editorial policy emerges as not always 'objective,' we do strive to be fair." As for the nude photograph, editors observed that readers could find the same sort of thing in *Time, Newsweek, Look,* or *Life.*

At the October meeting of the board, trustees affirmed Strider's action but declined to yank Colby's name or its support from the newspaper. Instead, they appointed a study committee headed by Dwight Sargent '39, curator of the Nieman Foundation for Journalism at Harvard. (Other trustee members included Jean Gannett, president of the Guy Gannett Publishing Company, and Thomas J. Watson Jr., CEO of IBM.) Meanwhile, in an effort to calm angry alumni, secretary Sid Farr sent Strider's letter to regular donors. In a cover note he apologized for the *Echo*'s transgression, and—overoptimistically—thanked them in advance for continuing "loyalty, support, and understanding."[27]

By spring 1971 the newspaper had changed editors (Michael Havey and Timothy Carey '72). Promises were made to behave, and the howling stopped. Sargent's committee said the *Echo* could keep the College name (it never gave it up) and recommended the formation of an editorial board to stand in on behalf of the College, the true publisher. The editors agreed.

It was not by any means the *Echo*'s first trial. By 1971, the paper was already ninety-four years old. Its first issue was published in March 1877. Joseph Files, later editorial writer for the *Portland Press,* was editor. It was a monthly pub-

---

27. Benjamin Bubar, superintendent of the Maine Christian Civic League, got one of Farr's letters and fired back: "Where has been the concern for other *Echo*'s?" he asked. "Why just this one?" Bubar, six years later on the ballot in nine states as the National Prohibition Party's presidential candidate, called Strider's letter "sick." He said it reflected "the administration's inability to cope with some deep-seated moral-social problems."

lication until 1886, when it began appearing twice a month. It became a weekly in 1898. For six years (1913–17) Professor Fred Fassett taught journalism. Beginning in 1920, editors were given credit for an advanced course in English composition. The faculty supervised the selection of editors until 1925, when the *Echo* chose their own, without consultation. In that year an English professor spoke at a faculty meeting and said he had found the new editor "completely incompetent and ignorant of the most elementary essentials for conduct of such a publication." The practice of granting academic credit was withdrawn. No woman ran the paper until Vivian Maxwell '44 took the job during World War II. In the hope of improved training, after the flap over the nude photo the practice of granting academic credit (English) to *Echo* staffers was resumed, and continued until the late 1980s when it was discontinued again.

The *Echo* might have planted the germ, but the paper was not responsible for the streaking craze that began on the warm campuses of Florida and California four years later. The pioneers were in fact political protestors. Students at the University of Washington held a streak for the impeachment of Richard Nixon (to "bare the truth" on Watergate), and in Hawaii a student romped through the state legislative chamber, claiming to be "streaker of the house." New sexual freedoms had uncorked a consuming fascination with the naked body. Miniskirts, having reached their peak in the 1960s, had come and gone, but there was still more to reveal: while most fads were slow to move up the turnpike, in the matter of streaking Colby was ahead of the curve. Risking frostbite, students were soon streaking over the cold and snow of the library quadrangle, at athletic contests, and through an occasional classroom.

The exhibitionist sport was not limited to men, or for that matter even to students. A seasoned secretary in the Eustis building quit her job when no one would make her young coworker wear a bra. A woman student immersed herself in a tub of green dye and streaked through You Know Whose Pub on Saint Patrick's Day.[28] At a disco dance in the Runnals Union gymnasium, a couple took off their clothes and danced in the nude. In the heat of the moment the display became infectious, and other couples joined in. A horrified and perplexed housemother chaperone fled to her tiny apartment, closed the door,

28. Located in the basement of the defunct and once elegant Emery Brown Department Store, the pub had its own titillating history. Owner Norton Webber had wanted to name it *Emery Brown's Bottom*. When Emery and Brown heirs objected, he named it simply *You Know Whose*.

and called for a dean who arrived simultaneously with the return of sanity. The lights went up, the music went down, and the clothes went on.

Sociologists were intrigued by what it all meant. Writing for *Change* magazine, Dean Wyman marveled at how much student culture had changed, and contemplated "the chasm that has grown between these solitary bursts of freedom and the kind so many of us marched for" a few years before.

Student use of drugs, both legal and illegal, was by no means a passing fad, nor was it amusing or always harmless. The legal drinking age in Maine had dropped from twenty-one to twenty in 1969, and in 1972 it fell to eighteen.[29] Two years later the College got a liquor license for its new Spa in Roberts Union. Even with most students able to purchase and consume alcohol in the open, the recreational use of marijuana was increasing. For a generation bent on experimentation, it was another thing to test. Their parents used and often abused alcohol and tobacco, they argued, and pot was no different—except in the eyes of the law.[30] College students bore the brunt of criticism for using drugs, but it was in fact a national phenomenon among the young. By the end of the decade, more than half of all students acknowledged that they had used illicit drugs before they entered college. The debate began in the late 1960s when students went back and forth on the merits of the hallucinogen LSD. In a 1967 Colby student poll, 64 percent wanted marijuana decriminalized and for its abuse to be treated, like alcohol, as a health problem.

The first local "bust" was in 1968. The student culprit claimed he had smoked the stuff to relieve his asthma. The *Sentinel* report said he was "owl eyed" at the time of his arrest. The College responded by issuing a statement in which officials tentatively expressed concern "over apparent use of marijuana by a limited number of students." Limited indeed: by the 1970s, use of pot was widespread. Students knew who used it and where to find it, and certain sections of the dorms and fraternity houses reeked of the familiar smell, especially on weekends. Marijuana plants grew on windowsills and under grow lights in closets. At the ATO house, brothers asked the maid if she would kindly water their cannabis while they were on spring break. A pot plant left on the fire escape at Woodman Hall caught the attention of passing police and thirty more plants were confiscated in the ensuing raid. Brownies laced with marijuana (from the *Alice B. Toklas Cookbook*) were sold to raise money for

29. The legal drinking age was raised to 20 in 1978, and back to 21 in 1985.

30. Although it had small favor, the use of marijuana had been legal in the United States until 1937.

The Blue Beetle in front of the Women's Union (Runnals)

Onie Noel's Café, Silver Street, c. 1950. Photo courtesy of Waterville Historical Society.

The Josephs' Spa

J. Seelye Bixler, president, 1942–1960

Galen Eustis, treasurer, 1937–1950; vice president, 1950–1959

Ellerton and Edith Jetté

Seelye and Mary Bixler

Robert E. L. Strider II, president, 1960–1979

Jacqueline Nunez '61

Deans of Faculty from
the first through 1979.
Left to right,
Robert Strider (1957–60),
R. Mark Benbow (1971–72),
Ernest Marriner (1947–57),
Parker Johnson (1960–71),
Paul Jenson (1972–81), and
Evans Reid (1967–68).

Lion of Lucern Civil War memorial removed from Memorial Hall
en route to Miller Library, January 1962

Memorial Hall is razed, 1966

Election-day protests along Silver Street, November 1968

Black students occupy
Lorimer Chapel,
March 1970

Antiwar strike rally, May 1970

Helen and Robert Strider, 1979

the antinuclear Clamshell Alliance. A faculty member found to have used drugs with students was dismissed. Local police became weary of running squad cars up the hill to retrieve confiscated pot, and made an agreement with the deans that they could take the stuff into their offices, and deliver it to the station in batches themselves.

> In February 1978, in the middle of a disciplinary hearing for several Lambda Chi Alpha fraternity members in the dean's office, someone called to report a bomb had been placed in the building. Although the origin of the call was no great mystery, bomb scares were not taken lightly. When local police searched the vacated building they found several bags of marijuana in the bottom drawer of Dean Smith's desk (along with a hypodermic syringe and several packages of illegal fireworks). The stuff had been collected for surrender to the police, and then forgotten. No charges were filed.

The "hard" drugs—amphetamines and, later, cocaine—were far less popular, but at Colby as elsewhere, they took some toll in tragic, ruined lives. Although there was always a spike of exotics when students returned from vacations, Colby's location, away from the urban centers of high drug traffic, helped lessen the scourge. Students who found themselves badly hooked on drugs could not manage both their habit and the rigors of their classes, and flunked out or withdrew. As the sports program began to expand for both men and women, Colby also had the phenomenon of the body-conscious athlete, with growing numbers of students eschewing dangerous drugs. By the end of the decade, marijuana use had diminished, but it was never to end. Although it gained a permanent foothold, even at the height of its campus popularity it never seriously challenged beer, the undisputed champion student drug of choice.

WHAT'S IN A NAME?

There was a time when "Watergate" meant a hotel and "Colby" might have conjured thoughts of cheese,[31] *but by the fall of 1972 Watergate was a burglary that*

31. There is in fact a tie between Colby the college and Colby the cheese. When Gardner Colby retired as a wool merchant in 1870 he became president of what was to become the Wisconsin Central Railroad. Most of Wisconsin was a frontier, and it was no small

would bring down a government, and Colby, with a reputation worth protecting, was dealing with a theft of a different kind. New Hampshire's Colby Junior College for Women was trying to swipe its name.

Joseph Colby and his son Anthony, later governor of New Hampshire, established an academy for women in New London in 1837. Anthony's daughter Susan was its first principal. In 1878 the small school took the Colby name, and a half-century later became Colby Junior College for Women. By 1972 it had been awarding bachelors' degrees for three decades and its enrollment of six hundred included five men. In October of that year trustees voted to change the name to Colby College–New Hampshire. Colby in Maine said, oh no.

Strider wrote his counterpart, Louis Vaccaro, in New Hampshire to say the name change would cause no end of confusion and asked if they would give it up. Vaccaro said no, and in April 1973 the Maine Colby asked the U.S. District Court in New Hampshire for help. In June Judge Hugh Bownes denied the temporary injunction saying he was not persuaded "that a prospective student who desires to go to Colby College in Waterville, Maine, will be misled for long enough to actually enter the defendant institution or even to seriously apply to it." The new sign—Colby College–New Hampshire—went up. Undaunted, Maine's Colby pressed for a permanent injunction "for the protection of its distinctive name and the good will that attaches." On May 6, 1974, Judge Bownes denied the permanent injunction as well, noting in his ruling that while Colby in New Hampshire was "definitely inferior from an academic point of view," that fact was not reason enough to make them give up their new name. President Vaccaro was pleased with the decision but called the judge's observation on his school's scholastic standing a "full-handed slap in the face."

Three weeks later, Colby of Maine appealed Bownes's decision to the U.S. Circuit Court of Appeals in Boston. Strider claimed that in the first year of similar names "instances of confusion have multiplied in number and severity . . . beyond the merely ludicrous to the potentially very serious." Colby attorneys cited cases of mix-ups in applicants and of SAT scores mailed to the wrong college. Vaccaro countered that the confusion was minimal and that

---

task to run new rails four hundred miles through the territory. When the job was done a small township on the border of Clark and Marathon counties was named to honor Colby. Ambrose and Susan Steiwand moved there in 1875 and in 1882 built a small cheese-making factory. A few years later their eldest son, Joseph, experimented with the development of a new cheese, milder than cheddar. He named it Colby.

Colby's anxiety about names had "tinges of snobbishness."[32] Everett Ingalls, a plaintiff lawyer, said the problem was not the use of the Colby name, but the juxtaposition of "Colby" and "College." He said there was "no objection to their jumping into the four-year college market, but we do object to their jumping in with our name."

In an effort to help, Maine's Colby sent a couple of name suggestions: Colby, New Hampshire, College; and Susan Colby College after founder Anthony's daughter. Vaccaro said thank you just the same, but they didn't need any help. (The joke went around New Hampshire that perhaps Susan Colby College was a good name inasmuch as the other Colby had already provided a nickname: Sue Colby College.)

Students on neither campus were much interested in the name fight. They were fixed on a broader battleground. The Watergate hearings began in May 1973, and the newly reelected President Nixon, who had called student protestors "bums," now claimed he wasn't a crook. Vice President Spiro Agnew resigned in August (law students at George Washington University brought the suit that took him down), and when college opened in the fall, the *Echo* joined eighty-four other college newspapers in calling for Nixon's impeachment. "He is no longer a legitimate leader," the editorial said. "No amount of legal double-talk or political timidity can obscure this fact." In November, Averill Auditorium in Runnals Union was overfilled to hear Lovejoy Award–winner Katharine Graham rail against the "espionage and sabotage" of the recent Nixon campaign. The *Washington Post* publisher said the Watergate story her newspaper first broke "traces the whole affair to the doors of the Oval Office." Nixon resigned eight months later.

In January 1975, twenty months after the name battle began, the appeals court cited errors in Bowne's decision and said the name Colby College–New Hampshire could not stand. Senior Judge Bailey Aldrich rubbed salt in the wound. "Without intending invidious comparison," he wrote, "we note that plaintiff outdistances defendant in size, reputation, and achievement."

32. All along, the New Hampshire college had made the point that there were sixty-two colleges with identical names, including Saint Joseph and Notre Dame (six each); Union and Trinity (five); Loyola and Westminster (four); and even another Colby: Colby Community College in Kansas.

The fight was far from over. Within weeks trustees of the New Hampshire institution thought they had finally settled the matter when they put up another campus sign with their choice of a third name: Colby Women's College. From Waterville came the reply that this name wasn't going to work either. Not only did it deny the fact that there were fourteen men among the 686 women at the New London school, but also people would quickly be calling the place "Colby." In February Maine's Colby went back to Bownes's court. Strider said he hated to do it, but the newly chosen name did not appear to abide by the findings of the court. Bownes, now tied to the opinion of the higher court, could only agree. At the same time he let off a little steam at having been overruled. It seems, he wrote, that Colby in Maine had veto over any name in which "Colby" would be the first word. "It disturbs me," he went on, "that the Court of Appeals has found that colleges compete for students and money in the same manner as commercial enterprises compete for customers, and that the law imposes the standards on higher institutions of learning that apply to the marketplace."

After only six weeks of display, the second new sign came down, and for a brief time the New Hampshire college had no name at all. The deadline for making commencement arrangements was fast approaching, and the place had no name to print on the diplomas. Switchboard operators answered the phone with a hesitant "hello." The stalemate was broken by a simple hyphen. In mid-March trustees in New Hampshire agreed to change the name again, this time to honor H. Leslie Sawyer, a native of Madison, Maine, who had been their president from 1928 to 1955. Colby College went along. In the spring, up went the fourth campus sign in two years, this one announcing the new Colby-Sawyer College.

In reversing the lower court, Judge Aldrich had said that allowing the New London college to use the direct Colby name would be "an intrusion on the interest of the plaintiff in its own identity and good will, and the interest of the public in preserving the integrity of individual accomplishment and reputation." If there had been wariness about Colby's name recognition and comparative standing when the fight began, some of it was dispelled by the time the battle was over.

A PLAN FOR COLBY

In the lull following the years of political protest Strider and the trustees felt it was time for a grand assessment of where the College stood and of what could be done to improve. A Committee to Study the Future of Colby (CSFC) broke itself into a dozen task forces to examine nearly every nook and cranny of the College.

Francis Parker was the perfect choice to lead. A senior teacher when he came to Colby in 1971, he had already posted a distinguished career as chair of philosophy at Haverford and Purdue. His junior colleagues saw him as an uncle. In June 1974, Parker's committee returned a ninety-page report, including sixteen recommendations dealing with educational programs and resources that combined "adherence to rather orthodox requirements with an openness to innovation and flexibility." They included opportunities for independent study and "academically sound" field experience. The committee affirmed both the size of the College (1,500 students, more or less) and the established calendar of a Jan Plan sandwiched between two semesters. It called for a shake-up and expanded facilities at the library.

The "future" committee also said it was time to think about having an annual computer budget. The first computer course had been offered in the fall of 1970 when William Taffe (physics) taught "Introduction to Computer Science" for two credits under the aegis of the Natural Sciences Division. The following year the College bought time on a PDP-10 computer at Bowdoin, tied to remote terminals in the Keyes and Lovejoy buildings. Elementary math students were taught BASIC computer language, and all students could receive instruction on "terminal use." The treasurer's office churned out its payroll on a finicky Burroughs E-4000, and a clanking Addressograph machine took care of alumni mailings. Registrar Coleman, unimpressed with the small market of administrative software systems, was renting time on the C. F. Hathaway computer ($65 an hour) and "bootstrapping" his own system. Within a year he had put together a student class registration program and was beginning to figure out a way to sort for conflicts, make class sections, and do grade reporting. In 1973 Colby joined the New England Library Information Network, and by the fall of 1976, the College would have its own PDP-11/50, overfilling (and overheating) the basement of Lovejoy. At the end of the decade, Strider said the day was coming "when every Colby graduate in whatever discipline will have learned something about what the computer can contribute to our understanding of the world we live in."

In its findings the CSFC noted that the admissions milieu was changed, that the train of baby boomers had passed through and the pool of qualified applicants was shrinking. Both the College and its prospective students were getting more selective at the same time.[33] New students were shoppers. Reputation mattered. Thomas Morrione '65 (sociology) used his research methods

33. Of the 3,434 applicants for the class entering in 1973, exactly 815 were accepted. One in four enrolled.

class to take a measure of student satisfaction and found that 91 percent now liked their campus living arrangements. A narrow majority agreed Colby was providing them a good all-around education. It was time to reexamine student services, the committee said ("with due regard for the disappearance of the philosophy of in loco parentis") and for a new look at the role of athletics. The most exhaustive of the studies dealt with the physical plant, where the committee found there were "obvious and pressing" needs for a health center, science facilities, a theater, and a makeover of Roberts Union to create a student center. On top of it all, more money was needed for faculty salaries, financial aid, and the endowment, which stood at $32 million.

In 1969–70, even before the study began, the College had launched the Plan for Colby, beginning with a five-year capital effort to find $6.7 million. It hadn't been easy. The decade began in a recession, and while the economy had rebounded the student contretemps did not set well with many alumni donors. In the development shop, Ed Turner had but a single aide, All-American goalie Frank Stephenson '62. Alumni Secretary Ed Burke '60 completed the team.[34] (Sid Farr '55 had moved on to manage the still-combined financial aid and career services office.) President Emeritus Bixler was the national campaign chairman. Trustees Jetté, Joseph Smith '24, Robert Sage '49, and Robert Lee '51 held leadership posts.

With the details of the Plan for Colby fleshed out by the CSFC, the College headed into the final year of the campaign. The biggest surprise came at the end. Connecticut schoolteacher David K. Arey '05 had received the Alumni Council's highest honor, the Colby Brick, at the 1963 commencement. On the return home he and his wife, Mary (Stafford), also a schoolteacher, agreed they would amend their wills to include a small gift for Colby. He died a few days later. She died in April 1974 at age ninety. At the reading of her will in June it was learned they had provided Colby a $25,000 trust fund for scholarships. Various nieces and nephews received similar amounts. The residue of the estate, the will stated, should go to Colby. What was left was more than $2 million, the largest single gift in the history of the College. A month later Strider announced that the Plan for Colby effort had brought in $10.5 million, nearly $4 million over the goal. The Arey gift was used to seed a second phase of the campaign, this one for an additional $4.5 million to strengthen the sciences, a need highlighted by the CSFC report. By mid-decade there were nearly 350 science majors pressing at the seams of the two science buildings, Keyes and Life—already thirty years old.

34. In 1975 the professional development staff mushroomed to five.

The science effort was finished in two years. In December 1975, a grant from the Seeley G. Mudd Fund of Los Angeles provided a new building for physics, geology, and mathematics. A year later both the Dana[35] and Kresge foundations chipped in challenge grants, and the matches were made in less than two years. The old Life Science was renovated for biology and psychology and, in 1977, renamed for the Areys. A year later the newest science building for physics, geology, and mathematics was opened and named for Seeley G. Mudd.[36] For a moment the College had come close to satisfying the insatiable appetite of science teaching, with facilities and equipment to match a growing, talented faculty.

The College's rapidly expanding real estate very nearly got reduced in July 1976 when a laboratory assistant, cleaning closets in the Keyes Building in advance of renovating crews, discovered two old cardboard boxes containing seven six-ounce vials of nitroglycerin. Buildings were evacuated while local police called for a bomb squad from the Brunswick Naval Air Station. Squad members made three slow trips gingerly carrying the vials to a nearby gravel pit off the County Road where they were detonated. The deafening explosions ricocheted off the surrounding hills, sending huge clouds of white smoke into the air.

Alumni-giving goals for the Plan for Colby campaigns had been set at three times the estimated maximum potential of alumni to give. It was a reach that few colleges dared to make, but Colby had already made a name for itself for its audacious fundraising. It had, after all, set out to build an entirely new campus with barely a nickel in sight.

35. The latest Dana grant raised the foundation's total giving to Colby to more than $1 million. In addition to Dana Hall it had provided the major gift for the renovation of the athletic complex, endowment for the Dana Scholarships, and four named professorships.

36. Seeley G. Mudd's father, Seeley W., made his fortune in the copper mines of Cyprus. Seelye G., a graduate of the Harvard Medical School, was a researcher of radiation and X-ray therapy. He taught at the California Institute of Technology and was later dean of the medical school at the University of Southern California. He died in 1968. His estate created the Seeley G. Mudd Fund, which provided funds for many college science buildings and facilities throughout the country.

As a replacement for the Maine State Series, the three-college CBB rivalry wasn't enough. Colby, Bates, and Bowdoin went looking for a bigger league that would match both their educational philosophies and their athletic ambitions. They found it in fine company and in the awkward name of NESCAC—the New England Small College Athletic Conference. At the same time, improved and expanded playing schedules came just in time to handle an explosion in intercollegiate athletic programs that resulted from a federal law called Title IX.

The CBB conference was formed in 1966 when Colby was the last to abandon its football rivalry with the University of Maine. Although the State Series continued in other sports for eight more years, Bowdoin had begun looking for a new athletic home in 1955, when it joined a small league with Amherst, Wesleyan, and Williams. In 1971 the four signed on with NESCAC, organized "to link colleges of similar academic and athletic programs in the fight against increasing financial pressures and the burdens of extensive recruiting." The new conference included the vaunted "Little Three" of Amherst, Wesleyan, and Williams, the three Maine colleges, and Hamilton, Middlebury, Trinity, Tufts, and Union.[37]

NESCAC prohibited athletic scholarships and off-campus recruiting by coaches, limited postseason play, and required the exchange of financial aid and admissions information. It also insisted athletic programs be "in harmony" with the educational purposes of the institutions, that all athletes be representative of their student bodies, and that the presidents control athletic policy. The conference framework was built with men's sports in mind, but it leveled the playfields for women as well—and there were plenty of women on the way.

Colby's first intercollegiate women's competition was a ski meet in 1954, when no scores were kept lest it would seem too competitive. Five years later a women's badminton squad went to Boston for a match, and in the early 1960s field hockey teams began to win round-robin tournaments with Bates and Bowdoin. Progress was excruciatingly slow, and in 1966 physical education instructor Marjorie Bither assembled a statewide committee to speed things up. The committee said there should be at least three competitive sports

37. From the beginning Union was uneasy with regulations limiting participation in postseason championship play (ECAC), and in 1977, following a violation of recruiting rules, withdrew from the Conference. Connecticut College joined in 1982.

for women, and students chose tennis, bowling, and badminton. The committee became the Maine Association for Intercollegiate Athletics for Women, with Bither as its first president. In 1973, the College joined the newly formed Association for Intercollegiate Athletics for Women, a counterpart to the male-centered NCAA.

Women's needs had not been part of the 1967 planning for the athletic complex renovations and additions. Their programs, including gymnastics and fencing, remained in Runnals Union until 1973. The first two teams—field hockey, then basketball—came in 1968, the year the new facility was opened. Tennis, long a club, was added the next year, and in 1970 the new pool brought swim teams for women and men. In the winter of 1971–72 skater Susan Yovic '73 teamed with alumni giving director Frank Stephenson to begin a women's ice hockey club. It played and lost three games but continued the next winter with JV (junior varsity) goalie Herrick Drake '75 as volunteer coach. In 1974– 75 the schedule expanded to sixteen games and the twenty-five-member squad finished 8–8. The opening contest with Brown University was the nation's first intercollegiate women's ice hockey game.

Following the adoption of the federal Education Amendments of 1972, Title IX languished without enforcement for two years, waiting for the Office of Civil Rights to write regulations. The law said that on the basis of gender no one could be excluded "from participation in, denied the benefits of, or be subject to discrimination under any education program or activity receiving federal financial assistance." It was as plain as these kinds of things ever get, but the nation's all-male athletic directors didn't believe the law was aimed at them. The regulations, saying that schools and colleges must provide equal financing, facilities, schedules, and sports for both men and women, were sent to President Nixon for approval in the spring of 1974.

Colby's athletic director, John Winkin, was president of the National Association of Collegiate Directors of Athletics. Surrounded by the male leaders of many of the nation's athletic organizations, he held a press conference in Cambridge, Massachusetts, and read from a letter he was sending to Nixon. "We cannot exist with these burdens," he wrote. "Redistribution of budgets would force instant elimination of many if not all existing male sports." The Feds were unmoved, and on July 21, 1975, Title IX went into effect. Winkin had no more than entered the Title IX fray when he was lured away by the University of Maine at Orono, where baseball was a prince among sports and the flame of gender equity was slower to kindle. Dick McGee took his place, still coaching football while taking the role of athletic director in an all-new era.

Despite the foot-dragging, at Colby there were forces already at work to secure the equal treatment of women. Physical education coordinator Bither told her male colleagues they were in denial, and worked to get ready for the coming explosion of women's teams. Frank Stephenson was an ally, and his ice hockey club was an attention-getting example. Sandy Maisel (government) pressed for equity from the faculty side. He went to Strider who agreed that Colby should balance the scales whether or not it was required, and Maisel and others prepared "affirmative action" guidelines, put in place in advance of the new law.

Women's ice hockey was the first new varsity team in the winter of 1975–76, but it would have moved up anyway. That spring, softball won ten of twelve games in its first season. Cross-country arrived a year later, and in 1978 women began intercollegiate schedules in lacrosse and indoor and outdoor track.[38] In 1979 the boom continued with new teams in soccer, squash, and—parallel with the men—Alpine and Nordic skiing. Seduced by the magnet mountain of Sugarloaf, more than half of all students owned skis, cluttering dormitory hallways and causing the local fire marshal to complain. The nearby Mountain Farm ski slope was closed, and the College made a deal with Sugarloaf to take in the new teams for a fair price.

By the close of the decade the gender score was even: fourteen teams each for men and women,[39] and Colby found itself a clear national leader in the speed and fullness of its Title IX compliance. Other colleges—especially universities—would work for the next thirty years to meet the letter of the law. The greatest struggles were on campuses where the participation numbers and costs of football programs kept statistical measures out of balance. Small colleges had the easiest time of it, but it wasn't until the end of the century that the averages of the numbers of varsity sports and expenses among all Division III schools began to reach equity.

The gloomy predictions of the demise of intercollegiate athletics never came true. Instead, as was intended, Title IX advanced gender equality, not only in athletics but also along the full range of programs and policies, from grade schools to colleges.

Title IX cut both ways. In 1974 Ronald Ayotte '76, claiming an interest in gymnastics where there was no men's club, turned to the women. True Title Niners, they took him in. A specialist in the uneven bars, he entered

---

38. The women runners nicknamed themselves "The Striders."
39. Golf, the twenty-ninth, was coed.

> a meet with UMO but failed to place. Even so, he got hugs from team-
> mates and wild applause from onlookers. He hung up his leotard after
> that one outing, claiming satisfaction at having proven "a man is capa-
> ble of competing in this women's sport."

The explosion of new sports dramatically changed the way college athletics were viewed. Many of the new teams were more appealing to participants
than to fans. Squad sizes often exceeded supporters, a phenomenon that
alarmed the old guard, accustomed to crowded stands at venues of established
men's sports. And while new opportunities arrived in a rush, women were not
so quick to show up to play. (An effort to form a women's lacrosse team failed
when five came to try out for a squad needing twelve or more.) By 1977, only
10 percent of 695 women were varsity athletes as compared to half of the eight
hundred men. McGee wondered if the women were more interested in grade
point averages than in sports, but that was not the case. There were many reasons for their ambivalence and wariness, not the least of which was that the
athletic complex, long the bastion of male jocks, was off-putting in image and
in fact.

Carl Nelson, director of the health center, worked to make things more
inviting by opening the doors of the most exclusive male club of all, the training room (injured women athletes were accustomed to hobbling up to the
second-floor Roberts Union infirmary) and both the budget for towels and
the general tone of the place improved simultaneously.[40]

Nelson had come to Colby as the only full-time athletic trainer in 1959,
when trainers were armed with little more than kits filled with scissors and
ankle tape. His career overlapped the rise of his profession, and together with
a small handful of contemporaries, he led its growth. In 1966 he replaced Mike
Loebs as director of the health center where he became the perfect foil for the
affable but sometimes gruff college physician, Clarence "Doggie" Dore. Students adored Nelson for his kindness, patience, and skill. In most cases he
could accelerate their healing; when it was slow, he manufactured devices to
protect their injuries. His word was law, and aggressive new coaches soon
learned that he was the lone arbiter of when an injured athlete could return to
play. He freely gave care and advice to local high school athletes and others,
and for nineteen summers directed the Pine Tree Camp for Handicapped

---

40. Susan Zagorski '77 was the first woman student trainer.

Children on nearby North Pond. Nelson was named head athletic trainer for the U.S. Olympic teams at the 1972 winter games in Sapporo, Japan, and again in 1976 at the games in Innsbruck, Austria. In 1980 he supervised training clinics for the Olympic Organizing Committee for the games at Lake Placid, New York. The National Athletic Trainers Association inducted him into its Hall of Fame in 1986. In 1991, two years before his retirement, alumni contributions came easily to build an expansive new athletic center training facility bearing his name.

Title IX also applied to physical education programs where the College clung to requirements that made all but varsity athletes pass tests in swimming, leisure-time sports, fitness, and posture. Bither, who became one of the country's first women senior athletic administrators when she was named director of the combined physical education programs in 1973, proceeded to make changes in the unpopular mandates. After two tries, she convinced the faculty to eliminate the swimming test, and in 1977, to jettison the loathed proficiency tests altogether.

Although sports headlines still focused heavily on men, women began to earn a bigger share, most noticeably in tennis. For six years in a row the Maine women's singles championships devolved to Colby versus Colby. Carolyn Estes '75 won the title four years running, three times facing teammate Janet McManama '76 (also a founding player of ice hockey), who took the prize herself as a senior. Under professor-coach Guy Filosof (French) the men were near consistent winners of state titles as well.

When women's ice hockey began, sportswriters were fixed on the notion of women playing a "men's sport." (The sports editor of the *Bangor Daily News* said the squad had "cute dimples" and that even with shin guards their legs were "slimmer than those of Brad Park.") By the end of the decade Lee Johnson '79 had proved the women's game was not frivolous at all. Through the winter of 1978–79 she scored thirty-one goals and sixteen assists on the way to becoming the first Colby woman to have her game jersey retired.[41] With more teams than available coaches, many women's squads had male mentors who doubled on assignments. Gene DeLorenzo '75 coached women's basketball and softball, each one to winning seasons. After some lean years, the field hockey team, under Debbie Pluck, emerged in 1978 with a state championship.

In the men's division, one of the era's most remarkable teams was in the entrenched sport of football, where the loss of success and fan support had been

41. Curiously, the first woman to win a varsity letter was not varsity. Bernice Smith '75 received a C Club jacket in 1972 as "distaff manager" of the men's cross-country team.

most evident. After six losing seasons, the magic returned. Led by tailback Peter Gorniewicz '75, McGee's 1972 team posted a 7–1 record, the best since 1940 and the third best of all time, to win its first outright CBB title.[42] Gorniewicz went on to gain 4,114 career yards, a New England college record. In 1974 he, like George Roden '60 before him, won the Boston Gridiron Club's Swede Nelson national award for sportsmanship.

Baseball dominated until Winkin left after the 1974 season, the year Bain Pollard '76 continued the string of All-Americans. In twenty years Winkin's teams had a win-loss record of 292–244. When he departed in midcareer he had established the College as a regional baseball power and himself as one of the nation's finest baseball scholars and coaches.[43]

In 1976 men's hockey fans were heartened when Jack Kelley resigned as general manager of the New England Whalers and returned to the Colby job, vacated by Ken Mukai '68. Kelley stayed but a single season and returned to the Whalers. The switch, he said, had been a mistake. Mickey Goulet took his place and promptly took the team to its fourth ECAC postseason playoff (1977–78) of the decade.

Overall, gains in coaches outweighed losses, as the period saw the arrival of three of Colby's finest ever: Dick Whitmore in basketball (1970), Mark Serdjenian '73 in soccer (1976), and Jim Wescott in track and field (1978). Whitmore, like McGee, came from the high school ranks (Morse High in Bath, Maine). He would become one of the nation's most successful college coaches, and with little dispute, one of Colby's most colorful. If his ranting was sometimes incoherent, his tone was abundantly clear, and his antics helped fill Wadsworth Gymnasium once again. Dressed in jacket, tie, shiny loafers, and garish plaid trousers, he removed almost everything but the trousers before the game was minutes old. His shoes sometimes ended up in the stands, and in a pique of emotion he once broke his foot while making a fleeting tour of the bleachers.[44] Through the 1970s, his teams took two of the last three State

42. The 1972 team was compared to the 1914 state champion team, and Gorniewicz, to its captain, the legendary Paul "Ginger" Fraser. In 1914 Colby beat Bowdoin (48–0), Maine (14–0), and Bates (61–0) before losing its fourth and final game to the U.S. Naval Academy at Annapolis (21–31).

43. Winkin did the same for the state university, where he took six teams into the College World Series. More than fifty of his players, at Colby and UMO, were drafted into the major leagues.

44. John "Swisher" Mitchell had been Ed Burke's basketball assistant for three years before Whitmore arrived, and continued into the next century as Whitmore's alter ego. A basketball star at Waterville High and the University of Rhode Island, locally "Swisher"

Series championships (1970–71, 1972–73), the first five CBB titles (1974–78), and entered the ECAC postseason tournament three times. In Whitmore's first coaching season Doug Reinhardt '71 took the career scoring record, and four years later another All-American, Brad Moore '75, collected 1,935 points to take the scoring crown and eight other records. Soon enough, Paul Harvey '78 moved the record up to 2,075 points, and was twice named to the All-American first team, joined in 1978 by teammate Mike McGee (later a successful coach at nearby Lawrence High), the College's first sophomore All-American in any sport.

During the 1970s the athletic ranks filled with outstanding students, both men and women. Basketball captain and playmaker Matt Zweig '72 was a premier example of a new breed of scholar athlete. Elected to Phi Beta Kappa in his junior year, he was a senior scholar and principal violist in the orchestra. In 1972 he received national recognition from the NCAA, including a scholarship for postgraduate study. The previous year two Colby seniors, football star Ron Lupton and two-time state singles tennis champion Frank Apantaku, received the same NCAA recognition.

In the still-young sport of men's soccer, Serdjenian quickly surpassed his coaching predecessors, and in 1978 his team won the ECAC Division II–III New England championships, setting many records including one for most wins (11). Serdjenian at first coupled his coaching assignment with teaching at a local grade school; in 1982, however, he began working full-time on the Hill, managing both the varsity soccer program and his new role as associate dean of students. As a coach, he established himself as one of the best in the burgeoning sport of soccer. As a dean he earned broad popularity among students, despite having chief responsibilities for discipline.

Track and cross-country coach Jim Wescott was among the last holdouts in a coaching profession fast filling with specialists. He understood athletics in the liberal arts, and his passion for physical education was equal to his zeal for coaching. All the while, he enjoyed the same measure of coaching successes, and when he retired in 2003 nearly every track and field record had been set under his watch.

The Committee to Study the Future of Colby had urged a close look at athletics, and it was getting hard for the faculty to get its arms around a program that had exploded in so many directions. It was again time to do some tuck-

---

is the self-declared and agreed-upon most famous of the Mitchell brothers—including George, the U.S. Senate majority leader.

ing in,[45] and the stern Paul Machemer (chemistry), chairman of the Athletics Advisory Committee, was charged with making a review. At decade's end, a new statement of philosophy made things as clear as NESCAC and Title IX:

> It is axiomatic that the academic program . . . has the highest priority, but in athletics, Colby's intention is to achieve the same high standards of performance. With regard to intercollegiate athletics . . . the most important consideration . . . must always be the value of the competition to the student participants. We hope Colby teams can be competitive with other teams, but most of all we hope athletics will add a healthy dimension to a vigorous educational program.

NEW DIRECTIONS

The College and the city planned a joint observance of the nation's Bicentennial, and beyond the spirit of patriotism there were many reasons for each to celebrate. Waterville was comfortably weathering a sagging national economy and still growing. Driven by different forces, Colby was emerging from the years of raucous unrest to find its strength and reputation stronger than ever. As campus life returned to more customary chaos, the College's longest-serving president elected to take his leave.

By mid-decade the country was in its worst recession since the 1930s. Inflation rampaged and unemployment broached 10 percent. Waterville was faring better than most small cities, but there were already ominous hints of change in the patterns of trade and competition. Executive Airlines called it quits and Air New England filled in briefly then stopped coming as well. The two fiercely competitive allopathic hospitals—Thayer, the creation of Protestants, and Seton, established by Catholics—could no longer afford to go their separate ways, and officials met secretly with the monsignor to create a unified 349-bed Mid-Maine Medical Center. Although Seton's Chase Avenue plant was newer, Thayer had the political clout, and the new hospital centered services and improvements on North Street.

45. Strider had to put his foot down in 1978 when nearly every member of the baseball team signed up for a Jan Plan in Cuba. The objective of the trip was to give students a firsthand look at the economic, social, political, and cultural institutions of Cuba. Instead, it looked to Strider and Machemer very much like a boondoggle to get a jumpstart on the baseball season. Strider called it off.

Some five thousand citizens still worked along the river. A thousand made paper plates at Keyes Fibre. At the city's oldest factory, 750 people were stitching four million Hathaway shirts a year. Scott, with 1,300 workers, was building a $185-million pulp mill above Skowhegan, and the Wyandotte textile mill at Head of Falls, razed by urban renewal, moved to a modern plant on West River Road. Entire streets disappeared under the urban renewal wrecking ball, and families moved into neighborhoods away from the center of town. The A&P came to anchor a Kennedy Memorial Drive shopping center on the site of the old Meader horse farm, and a fire department substation opened on Western Avenue to protect the expanding population west of the Messalonskee. Mayor Carey experimented with a free municipal bus service, but as with the trains twenty years before, citizens preferred their cars.[46] As the population inched up, the city built a new Brookside Elementary School (later named for Senator George Mitchell), and the old schools on Brook and Myrtle Streets were abandoned. Sacred Heart School was closed, and the replacement Waterville Catholic Consolidated School lasted only four years. A new Notre Dame Church, with two assigned priests, opened on Silver Street.

On Main Street, Woolworth closed and Central National Bank went into the abandoned space, joining a list of city banks that soon numbered a dozen. There were still fifty downtown merchants, each one with a wary eye on the outskirt plazas. The Jefferson Hotel near the old campus went bankrupt, but the city still had eight hotels and motels and more than two dozen thriving restaurants. In 1979 the newest was a "fast food" place called McDonalds.

Bob Kany, a historian and Strider's assistant before becoming director of Special Programs, led the Bicentennial committee. Ernest Marriner, who two years before had made his national record one thousandth WTVL radio broadcast of *Little Talks on Common Things*, was honorary chair. Celebrations began in May 1976 with a communitywide convocation. Dartmouth president John Kemeny spoke. He said he'd had a nightmare in which an "evil genius" set out to ruin higher education by creating a recession, double-digit inflation, a Dow Jones tumble from 1,000 to 600, and quadrupled oil prices. He woke up, he said, to find it was all true.

46. There are no local monuments to buses, but there is one to trains. In 1970 Maine Central Railroad bequeathed its last steam locomotive, no. 470, to the city. First run between Portland and Bangor in 1924, it made its final trip through Waterville on June 13, 1954. Sixteen years later former Mayor Donald Marden, who had led the effort to preserve it, rode in the cab for the last few yards to its resting place near the railroad shops on College Avenue.

Colby had a hand in three days of July 4 celebrations in Waterville; throughout the following year the campus was host to some twenty public events, each with a national history theme. A December symposium, sponsored by the Colby chapter of Phi Beta Kappa, featured scientist Linus Pauling, economist Robert Heilbroner, architect Paolo Soleri, and actress Ellen Burstyn.

Douglas Nannig '77, a high-ranking chemistry major, was given the honor of driving Pauling and his wife to a postsymposium luncheon. Days before, moments after he locked his Toyota Corolla in the Delta Upsilon parking lot, he watched in horror as it slid out of gear and rolled backward across the road, broke through thin ice, and floated out on Johnson Pond. Nannig followed the car into the cold water and pushed it to the shore. Anxious not to miss his chance to escort the Paulings, he let the car run around the clock with its heater on for the next several days. It was still damp and musty when the time came to chauffeur the two-time Nobel Laureate and his wife, who rode to the Dana Hall lunch on layers of towels draped over the back seat.

In the spring, Conservation Commission chair Helen Strider and Mayor Carey dedicated a new Bicentennial Trail and Park, north of the old Wyandotte mill site, one of three commission projects that included Arnold Park, west of the failing Two-Cent Bridge; and Ticonic Park, an observation site east of Castonguay Square.

A central attraction of the birthday celebration was the exhibition *Maine Forms of American Architecture*, a largely photographic display assembled by historian Earle Shettleworth '70. Hugh Gourley, the museum's first full-time director (1966), was the catalyst for many new acquisitions with barely space to show or store them. In 1971 the College acquired a full collection of the work of internationally known Maine artist John Marin. Two years later the museum received forty-eight works by Charles Hovey Pepper '89, son of Colby's ninth president, George Dana Boardman Pepper, who painted in the picturesque northern Maine village of Attean.[47] That same year, Russian-born American expressionist sculptor Louise Nevelson gave thirty-six of her early works.

47. The Marin works were given by his son and his son's wife, John Jr. and Norma, and their daughter, Lisa. The Pepper paintings came from his children, Stephen Coburn Pepper and his sister, Mrs. Frederic (Eunice) Langenbach.

Other gifts included the Lee Fernandez '55 collection of Winslow Homer graphics and a fine print collection from A.A. D'Amico '28. The tiny facility was bursting at the seams by 1973 when the Jettés gave a new 6,500 square-foot double-storied wing. Two years later the couple made their third major gift,[48] a priceless collection of ninety-eight American Impressionist paintings. Their exhibition was launched with a nineteenth-century garden party (guests came wearing boaters and carrying parasols); when the show closed, the collection began a three-year tour of national museums.

In his centennial convocation remarks, Kemeny said he worried American colleges had overexpanded and predicted many would now have to fight for survival. He was right. Most colleges struggled. Some were forced to close. Colby did not escape the economic strife (many graduates had a hard time finding jobs, and annual budgets were tighter than usual), but by mid-decade the College was in the midst of the largest building project since early construction on the Hill. The centerpiece, headed for completion in the spring of 1978, was the unified science complex, expanded by the Seeley G. Mudd building, and improved with the renovation of Life Science (cum Arey) and a new second story "greenhouse" bridge tying Keyes and Arey together.

Science building renovations brought the first sign that the "new" campus wasn't still new, a shocking revelation to alumni and others whose image of a fresh, young Mayflower Hill was frozen in time. Now some $5 million was earmarked for tearing out and rebuilding. Runnals and Roberts Unions had already seen thirty years of hard use when $1 million was assigned to transform the old women's union into a theater and another $900,000 to make the men's building an all-student union. All of the building and rebuilding brought lively discussion and controversy, but none more than the planning for a new infirmary where naysayers could be found all the way from the dormitories to the board of trustees.

The existing infirmary, shoehorned onto two floors of the east wing of Roberts Union, was inadequate. Students were climbing the stairs to find medical help at the astonishing rate of more than nine thousand a year, and in early spring, when influenza was raging, there were never enough beds. Strider argued a freestanding infirmary was a logical step in the domino game of expansion planning; besides, it made no sense to keep sick students in a building being retrofitted for loud parties. The "future" committee had urged improved health services, and the board had approved the development of

48. Previous gifts were the American Heritage Collection in 1956 and American eighteenth- and nineteenth-century portraits through the 1960s.

building plans. In January 1975 it was time for a final trustee blessing. Strider was unable to attend the meeting where a few trustees, including chairman Al Palmer, convinced the others to table the project. They said the plans were too grand (twenty-four beds), too expensive (almost $1 million), and the proposed site in the middle of the campus too precious for anything as ancillary as a health center. Maybe, they said, a modern infirmary could still be made to fit in Roberts, or if there must be a new building, then it could be smaller, and put elsewhere. Perhaps, with Thayer Hospital a half-mile away, it wasn't needed at all.

Strider fired a letter off to Palmer saying he was "deeply troubled" by the turn of events and asking for a special trustee meeting to get things back on track. Inflation had already increased the earliest building estimates by $300,000, and any savings from further trimming would only be eaten up by the delay. Besides, the president lectured, "Colby does not wish to engage in any second-rate enterprises." The infirmary had to get out of Roberts because the College wasn't going to build a new student union, he said.

When the board reconvened in February, trustees took their medicine, and the project got a green light, but troubles didn't end there. Students had gotten wind of the fray and gleefully joined in. At a groundbreaking event in May, Student Government president Robert Anderson '76 declined to turn the ceremonial shovel. Some two hundred onlookers cheered when he said the building wasn't necessary. (It was not the customary student demonstration. Spencer Aitel '77 said the "conservative"-spirited Student Association planned "none of that sign-carrying stuff students pushed in the 1960s.") The new building opened in the fall of 1976.[49]

It was time to make Roberts a bustling student union, but it never bustled. Off the beaten track, the place could not shake its male image. An improved coed dining room appealed mostly to the men on Frat Row. Centralizing the post office didn't help, as women came at noon to pick up their mail, and then made their way back up Frat Row to the south campus. The feature designed to be the most appealing, turned out to be the most controversial. The Josephs—John and Pete—opened the first beer-selling Spa pub in 1975, covering the windows on the first floor of the west wing of Roberts Union, once the

49. The building was named for Fay B. Garrison and a former trustee, Alfred D. Foster. Garrison, general sales manager of the A. J. Tower Company of Roxbury, Massachusetts, died in 1955. Through his friendship with Foster (a trust officer of the Merchants National Bank of Boston), he named Colby as recipient of $475,000, the residual assets of his estate.

place of the independent hangout called The Paper Wall. Three years later the Spa was moved to new underground space at the front of renovated Roberts. Although the Josephs took the familiar stained brown plastic coffee cups and a new beer license with them, business plummeted by half. Not even the familiar, chirpy voice of waitress "Dot" Hurd could bring them back. The underground architectural feature was more blight than blessing, and monitoring the legal drinking age was a nightmare for the easygoing owners.

Some renovations resulted in new names for old places. The first-floor north-wing library room, once the office of the president, was named in honor of emeritus professor Alfred King Chapman. In 1977 the only original structure left standing on the Hill, the farmhouse once occupied by building and grounds superintendents, became the Hill Family Guest House, honoring three generations of Hills.[50]

The makeover of Runnals Union into a performing arts center was more successful than that of its counterpart across campus. The second floor became a springy-floored dance studio and Averill Gymnasium, a theater. Some wished it were larger, but as a workshop for the thespians, homeless since the Little Theater burned eight years before, it was welcome. In 1977 the new theater was fittingly named in honor of the Striders. The following spring the president announced he would retire at the end of the next school year.

Strider had been at Colby as dean and president for twenty-one years, and like his twentieth-century predecessors, he was leaving the place far better than he found it. Facilities on the Hill had matured—some were saying the campus was finally complete—and the first round of building renewal was nearly over. In two decades the physical plant had almost doubled. The College had grown from regional to national appeal, and with the admissions bar being raised every year, alumni had begun to complain that their children, some with academic profiles better than their own, were being turned down. The performance of men had risen from the doldrums and now closely matched the achievement of women. The College was among the nation's leaders in enrolling students with advance placement (AP) courses, and as one of the few elite invited into the fellowship program of the Thomas J. Watson Foundation, began to garner a disproportionate list of impressive recipients.[51]

50. James "J. F.," instrumental in the move itself; Frederick Thayer "F.T." '10, a founder of Thayer Hospital and a trustee and leader in the development of summer medical programs; his brother Howard '19; and Howard's adopted son Kevin '50, a trustee who founded the summer postgraduate course in ophthalmology, later named for him.

51. Thomas J. Watson, the son and heir of IBM, received an honorary degree at Com-

In 1977 English major Jennifer Barber '78 was named one of thirty-two national Rhodes Scholars, the first at Colby since 1938.

Through the 1970s the faculty examined nearly every inch of the academic program, including the often-scrutinized Jan Plan. Although many colleges succumbed to pressures to jettison traditional requirements, Strider and the faculty had resisted wholesale changes. While the catalogue listing of courses nearly doubled (from 300 to 590), new offerings had not come at the expense of the core curriculum. In the end, student work got harder. In 1975 the door was opened for students to create their own independent majors, but the old distribution requirements, including English and foreign languages, were reaffirmed. In 1977, despite yelps from students, the option of taking courses pass or fail was limited, but as a salve to ever-increasing student grade anxiety, in 1978 the faculty agreed to weigh plusses and minuses in the calculation of grade point averages.

Since 1960 enrollment had grown (from 1,200 to 1,600), while the size and quality of the faculty kept pace. The number of faculty increased (from 86 to 136) as did the percentage of them who held terminal degrees. There had been only modest growth in the number of women teachers (twenty-two in 1979), but they became a disproportionate source of strength in the new wave of exceptional teachers who came and stayed, defining the Colby experience for students through the 1980s and beyond.

By the end of the 1970s, transition had already begun in the senior administrative staff and would continue in the early years of the next presidency. Faculty dean Paul Jenson and admissions dean Harry Carroll remained in place. Robert Pullen, administrative vice president since 1973, delayed his retirement as a courtesy to the new president. After leading the College's development effort for a quarter-century, Ed Turner retired and the versatile Sid Farr, director of financial aid and career counseling since 1971, replaced him as vice president. Bill Wyman, dean of students through the rocky years, left in 1975 to become headmaster at the swanky Thacher School, under the pink clouds of California's Ojai Valley. Earl Smith took his place. Smith, who had joined the staff as a publicist in 1962, was the first director of student activities in 1968. He later served as an associate dean (1970–74), and then for a year as assistant to the president. His appointment to replace Wyman was delayed while he completed a stint as director of communications for the science campaign. Popular Jim Gillespie was dean in the interim.

---

mencement in 1991. During the proceedings he took a shred of paper from his pocket and made a note: "More Watsons for Colby."

Trustees began looking for a new president in the summer of 1978. Robert Anthony '38, vice chair and a twenty-year veteran of the board, led the search committee. Anthony was counted among Colby's most distinguished alumni. A Navy lieutenant commander during World War II, he taught for more than forty years until his 1983 retirement as the Ross Graham Walker Professor of Management Controls at Harvard's Graduate School of Business Administration. He was the author of twenty-seven accounting textbooks including the most widely used programmed text on the subject. From 1965 to 1968 he was assistant secretary of defense under Robert McNamara. In 1996 he and his wife Katherine gave the lead gift for a dormitory that bears their name.

As the search began, it was a time for reflection and transition, and for honoring the Striders for their long service. Both on and off the campus, he had earned prominence as an educational innovator and as a public servant.[52] At Colby, the new theater had already been named for the Striders, and alumni raised money to endow an annual Strider Concert.[53]

Not everyone was sorry to see the veteran president leave. Through the many fractious moments over two decades, he had assembled a full share of detractors, divided among those who felt changes had come too fast, those who thought they had not come fast enough, and those who preferred no change at all. The majority, including those who watched most closely, felt he had charted a course through the roughest of waters to bring the College to a place of prominence in the matter of good teaching and learning. For these many admirers, the most poignant final salute came from the members of the Class of 1979 who asked him to be their speaker at commencement. Although his legacy would least be measured by tenure, it is nonetheless remarkable that he served longer than any other Colby president, and that the man who so treasured orderliness and reason had endured, even triumphed, through the single most turbulent period in the history of American higher education.

52. He had been a leader of the Association of American Colleges, which he chaired in 1973. In 1979 the Maine Bar Association presented him with a Distinguished Service Award for his work as chair of a select commission that made recommendations to the state Supreme Court on governance of the bar and its ethical responsibilities.

53. Waterville joined in honoring the Striders as well, but no permanent tribute was made until the turn of the century when, in the process of tidying up for an enhanced 911 emergency system, the city found it had two streets honoring Franklin Johnson: Johnson Heights and Johnson Avenue. The avenue south off Mayflower Hill, just below a street named for President Roberts, was renamed Strider Avenue. Concurrently, campus roads serving their eponymous buildings were named for Seelye Bixler and William Cotter.

5. THE 1980S

WILLIAM R. COTTER

Many posses were sent to look for a new president: a search committee charged with bringing in finalists for the trustees to pick from, a campus advisory committee to help the search committee, the faculty educational policy committee and the executive committee of the Alumni Council to scrutinize the final suspects, and the executive committee of the board to watch over the whole roundup. For good measure, a broadside was sent to alumni and parents, asking them to keep a sharp eye for anybody who might have slipped through the fences. The process began with a good deal of soul-searching and rumination over the qualifications the new president should possess. When the long lists were finally made, the groups found solid agreement on only two items for their "Wanted" poster: the person had to have a Ph.D., and needed to have had some solid experience at a small liberal arts college. William R. "Bill" Cotter had neither.

Robert Anthony, about to be chair of the board, was the search director. In the summer of 1978, soon after Strider announced his impending retirement, Anthony put together the principal search committee, appropriately lopsided with seven trustees and including two faculty members, two students, and the chair of the Alumni Council. Deans Harry Carroll and Earl Smith wrote Anthony to complain there were too few faculty and students and that the administrative contingent had been left out altogether. Anthony responded by creating a Campus Advisory Committee of seven faculty members, two administrators, and two students. Now there were two posses in the hunt, each one amply filled with egos. The double-barreled approach might have gone wrong had the two groups, in the end, not agreed.

Despite the official searchers, it was a parent who found the new president. Sol Hurwitz and Bill Cotter were Harvard schoolmates and friends. The two were playing squash at the New York Harvard Club one afternoon in the late fall of 1978 when Hurwitz suggested to Cotter that he consider the Colby job. Hurwitz's daughter, Linda, a talented violinist, was a satisfied freshman, and her father, a strong Colby supporter. Cotter wasn't looking for new work, but he let Hurwitz put his name in the hat and figured that would be the end of it.[1]

By the time the committees had seen Cotter's résumé, the list of two hundred candidates had already been carved to twenty. By January there were only five survivors. Cotter was one of them. Each candidate and his spouse came for a two-day campus visit. When it was over, the searching groups found broad consensus on a first choice. No one agreed on a runner-up. It wasn't necessary. At a special meeting on February 25 the trustees unanimously elected Cotter as Colby's eighteenth president.

Cotter's background, while impressive, did not follow the track of most college presidents. In presenting his name to the trustees Anthony acknowledged the president-elect had never been a faculty member or an administrator of a liberal arts college, did not have a Ph.D., and was not, in the conventional meaning, a scholar. "None of this," Anthony said, "bothers us in the slightest."

Born in Detroit, Cotter was eleven when he moved with his family to Tarrytown, New York, where his father, Fred, was director of industrial relations at General Motors.[2] After graduating from Washington Irving High School, Cotter went on to Harvard for both his undergraduate (1958) and law (1961) degrees. As a young attorney he served for a year as clerk for U.S. Federal Judge Lloyd McMahon in New York (Southern District) and in 1963 began a long association with the affairs of Africa when he was chosen as an MIT Fellow and assigned as assistant attorney general of Northern Nigeria. He returned to the United States and worked briefly for a New York law firm before being selected for the prestigious White House Fellows Program in 1964–65, where he was assigned as special assistant to Secretary of Commerce John T. Connor. He then spent four years as a Ford Foundation representative for Colombia and Venezuela before joining the African-American Institute (AAI), the country's largest private organization concerned with African development and African-American relations. He had been president of AAI for nine years when Hurwitz turned him toward Colby.

1. Cotter was forty-two, the same age Strider had been when he became president. Cotter's mother, Esther, ever delightfully candid, questioned whether he should even take the job, telling him he was "much too young to retire."

2. Cotter drove mostly Chevys during the time he was at Colby.

Linda Kester of Brooklyn was every inch his match. The two met when she was at Wellesley. Still too young to vote, in 1956 she headed the Massachusetts student committee for Adlai Stevenson's last, futile presidential campaign. Along the way she called upon the head of the Harvard Democratic Club, Bill Cotter, for help. They both graduated in 1958, each with honors, each with majors in political science, and each with acceptance to Harvard Law School. Linda eschewed law school and instead took a prestigious graduate fellowship at Columbia University. Following Bill's first year in law school, the couple married. Living in Cambridge while teaching school in Lexington, Massachusetts, she earned a master's degree at the Harvard Graduate School of Education.

In the fashion of many women who came of age in the 1950s, she gave up her own career opportunities to raise a family and follow her husband. When the call came from Colby, she left work as a foundation official and in the summer of 1979 moved from the Cotter home in Oyster Bay, New York, into the President's House on Mayflower Hill. David, thirteen, was a high school freshman. Deborah was eleven, Elizabeth, seven. It was a long way from Oyster Bay—a distance measured in many more ways than miles—and there was no primer for spouses of college presidents, certainly not for the end of the twentieth century. Linda Cotter wrote her own script, juggling roles as wife, mother, volunteer, and professional, and as a behind-the-scenes assistant to the president with an unfailing antenna for the needs of the broader Colby family and the details of public and private presidential events.

Local reaction to Cotter's appointment was wide-ranging. Early on, rumors circulated in town that the new president was black. The whispers were based upon readings of his résumé and had the tinge of racism. Quoting Strider's assertion that the trustees had chosen the new president wisely, a *Sentinel* editorial wryly observed that only time would tell whether they had been wise or not. A well-known local Republican politician, discouraged that the College had once again selected a left-wing Democrat president, curtly refused Cotter's invitation to get acquainted over lunch.[3] On the campus the

3. The rift came in the summer before the inauguration, when Cotter spoke to the local Rotary Club and defended Andrew Young, whose behind-the-scenes meeting with the Palestine Liberation Front prompted President Carter to dismiss him as U.N. ambassador. Cotter, who had worked with Young, said Young was being unfairly depicted as a "radical" and was not given credit for his work to shift Third World alliances from the Soviet Union to the West. The Rotary Club was not just then the perfect setting for finding agreement with Cotter's view.

new president was greeted warmly, if quizzically. There was the customary transitional phenomenon of pent-up private agendas being pressed from every quarter, and a scramble for football bleacher seats near where Cotter chose to sit. The *Echo* opined that one of his first acts should be "to clean the dead wood out of Eustis [administrative office building]."

Despite the many other adjustments, there were no sudden religious conversions. Unlike all the times before, in the recent search the matter of religion had not come up at all. Bixler, who had broken the string of Baptist presidents, raised enrollment at the local Congregational church. Strider had improved the lot of Episcopalians. Cotter was brought up Catholic but had let his membership lapse.

Inauguration ceremonies were held in late September 1979. Some three thousand filled the gymnasium to watch the parade of 150 delegates from colleges, universities, and the learned societies, arranged in order of their founding from Harvard (1636) to the Maine Law Enforcement and Criminal Justice Academy (1972). Harvard's delegate, President Derek Bok, gave the principal address, observing it was "an inescapable sign of advancing age and decrepitude when you start installing your favorite students as presidents of colleges."

The platform held the customary trappings. The new board chairman, Anthony, gave the oath of office on Hannibal Hamlin's Bible, but Cotter declined to use the old, high-back President's Chair (he was barely 5'10" and it would have dwarfed him), and it sat as an empty ornament on the stage.[4] Bixler spoke, calling Cotter "a young man with the courage of an innovator, a sensitive conscience, with concerns that are intercontinental." Maine Governor Joseph Brennan brought greetings, as did Waterville mayor Paul LaVerdiere '59, Morgan State University President Andrew Billingsley, Professor Lucille Zukowski '37, and Student Government president Scot Lehigh '80.

In his address, Cotter spoke of his ambitions for Colby, many of which would ring out as themes for the next twenty years. He emphasized a "clear preference for the teacher-scholar over those publisher-scholars who neglect students." He said there must be more women and minorities on the teaching staff, and more racial, ethnic, and geographical diversity in the student body. He announced he had formed a new scholarship program named in honor of the late Ralph Bunche (LL.D. '52), with Ralph Bunche Jr. '65 as honorary chair. He said he would establish regular overseer visiting committees to academic

4. The chair was a gift to President Roberts from Leslie Cornish '74, classmate of Mary Low, Maine Supreme Court justice, and chairman of the Colby board. It was first used at the rededication of the chapel on the old campus in November 1924.

and administrative departments; increase cooperation with Maine sister colleges; and lay the groundwork for a new capital campaign, to include either a rebuilding or a remodeling of Miller Library. He also proclaimed—ever so delicately—that he would reexamine Colby's officially sponsored church services "to ensure they meet the needs of students and faculty." (He had chosen both A. H. Freedman, former rabbi at Beth Israel in Bangor, and Edward O'Leary, Catholic bishop of Portland, to offer benedictions.)

Toward the end he said he was "not sure that women, although equal in numbers at Colby for some time, have been fully equal in rights," and went on to warn: "We must be self-conscious about attitudes that connote second-class citizenship." His determination in that regard was symbolically made manifest at the conclusion of the ceremony with the singing of the alma mater, "Hail, Colby, Hail!" He had changed the words. For a half-century, the song, set to the tune of "O Canada" and written by mathematics professor Karl Kennison '06, began with the line: "Hail, Colby, hail, thy sons from far and near." "It is time to recognize that we have had daughters for 108 years," Cotter said. The new line, printed in the inaugural program, read: "Hail, Colby, hail, thy people far and near." The new words seemed strange at the first singing, but the crowd loved it, especially the field hockey team, which Cotter had been following as a fan and whose members arrived in game uniform.

By the spring of 1980, Cotter had examined every corner of the College. As part of an ongoing curriculum review, he ordered a survey of alumni and students, and in his first baccalaureate address was able to announce a broad consensus that Colby was on the right track. A whopping 88 percent of alumni (2,500 responded) and 70 percent of students thought graduation requirements should be left alone, or perhaps expanded. Both groups believed Colby's greatest strengths were in the "quality of teaching" and "student-faculty interaction."

Cotter also offered seniors some advice that faculty would hear him give at baccalaureate exercises again and again over the next twenty years. When you leave here, he told the seniors, go directly to the nearest public library and take out a card. Second, take a good book with you whenever you travel. "I continue to be disappointed," he said, "when I fly from Boston to Waterville and encounter unprepared Colby students thumbing aimlessly through *Air New England Magazine*."

The alumni-student affirmation and the faculty's own sense of things prompted the Educational Policy Committee to recommend only minor changes in requirements (distribution courses in the sciences should include a laboratory experience, and courses in the humanities and social sciences should stress methodology and include "hands-on" work). The 120-hour graduation requirement of 105 basic credits in traditionally graded courses plus 15 credits in regular courses, pass-fail courses, or field experience was let stand.[5] The biggest change was in the often-criticized Jan Plan. Both students and faculty liked the twenty-year-old program, but fully 90 percent of alumni said students were not working hard enough during the month (many were in a good position to know). The faculty voted to drop the required number of Jan Plans from four to three and to allow students to substitute independent plans with regular credit courses.

While campus affairs seemed for the moment to be tucked in, there were mounting outside pressures threatening all colleges. Bixler had begun his tenure in the face of a world war. Strider had endured a cultural revolution and Vietnam. Cotter faced external battles of a different sort. Rampaging inflation had driven college costs up while the numbers of eighteen-year-olds, whose stretched parents had to pay the bills, were headed down. To make matters worse the twin crises warmed up the endlessly simmering debate over the value of the liberal arts.

In March 1980, not yet a year in office, Cotter wrote a *New York Times* op-ed piece in which he said "faculty salaries have slipped dangerously behind the cost of living and competitive salaries outside the academy." He said he feared that both inflation and rising energy bills would force a radical change in the kind of education colleges could offer. To press his point, he explained that while average family incomes had risen 20 percent in the 1970s, faculty salaries had fallen behind by almost the same amount; and endowment income, which had once produced more than 20 percent of educational costs, was now covering less than 10 percent. A month later he sent his first annual

5. Colby changed from a 40-course (five a semester) requirement to 120 credit hours (216 quality points) in 1968. Varying credits (two to five) were assigned to courses according to rigor and time in class. At the end of that year the faculty began to phase in new rules, dropping the requirement to 105 credits (while requiring eight semesters of full-time study) on the premise that the lower number would be treated as a floor, rather than a goal, leaving students the flexibility to take extra courses without risk. It did not work. Too many seniors were graduating with the bare minimum of credits. In 1972 the requirement was again moved up to 120 credits, of which at least 105 had to be in conventionally graded courses.

letter to parents and students announcing the largest increase in fees in history. Trustees approved a $1,120 jump for 1980–81 ($6,510 to $7,590), a whopping 16 percent hike.

The cost crisis was deepened by the demographic reality that the number of college-age students was plummeting. The baby boomers had passed through, and a 22 percent decrease in high school graduates was predicted over the next fifteen years. The heaviest decline was going to be in the Northeast, from which Colby was drawing 70 percent of its students. The struggle to find both new money and new students was set against the backdrop of a trend toward vocational training and the concomitant assault on the liberal arts. President Bok had warned of it in his inauguration remarks. Liberal arts colleges had always been in a precarious position, he said, and now they were "moving to a strange and disquieting contrapuntal melody." He pointed to the rash of books and articles "on the growing irrelevance of liberal arts to the practical problems of daily life."

History was repeating itself. In 1981 the Alfred P. Sloan Foundation issued a startling report claiming the liberal arts were dead, and calling for the creation of "the new liberal arts" with the inclusion of applied math, technological literacy, and the computer. In November, soon after the Sloan Report set the college world abuzz, Colby launched its own defense. For the first time ever, three Colby presidents were together on the same stage. At an alumni gathering in Dedham, Massachusetts, Bixler, Strider, and Cotter sat for a discussion of both the past and the future of Colby.[6] Strider called the Sloan Report "astute," but said the debate was not about the nature of the liberal arts but about "the avenues toward fuller understanding of man's role in the universe." Bixler had no quarrel with technological literacy, but said it ought to be taught in the secondary schools, and "if we teach computer, mathematics, or science in college, let's teach it in a liberal way rather than in a vocational way." Cotter said the report made the error of "assuming the liberal arts are somehow disconnected from the real world." A look at the Colby catalogue, he said, would show that sciences had already become an important part of the curriculum.

As many colleges retrenched—curtailing building, reducing faculty and programs—Colby trustees agreed with the new president's plan to go in the opposite direction, to take a calculated risk and forge ahead. The prize, they knew, would go to those colleges that could attract and keep the strongest fac-

6. Peter Vogt '63 made a film of the three presidents event that became a centerpiece of Cotter's first round of alumni club meetings.

ulty and bring the very best students from a diminishing pool. The decade had barely begun when the College embarked on the quiet phase of a new $20 million–plus capital campaign to meet critical physical plant needs of renovation and new construction, and to rebuild the contribution of endowment earnings for faculty support and scholarship aid. In the meantime, before any money came in, ground was broken for an expansion to double the size of the library, and construction began on a modern new dormitory.

A new dorm was certainly needed. Each new school year students were arriving in vans, sometimes with U-Haul trailers, bulging with ski equipment, bicycles, microwave ovens, television sets, and (soon) computers. It was an annual fall miracle to watch as it all disappeared into rooms built for a time when students came to college on a train, with a single trunk. Now there was never enough room. Students rejected standard-issue furniture in favor of the things they'd brought with them. They built precarious sleeping lofts of 2 × 4s and plagued the buildings and grounds department (and the local fire marshal) by piling beds, desks, and dressers in the corridors. By the fall of 1979 the student body had overflowed again. Nearly one hundred students were temporarily housed at the health center, in dormitory lounges, and at a local motel.

The newest dorm had no major donor and was built on borrowed money ($3.6 million). Named for its place above the chapel, the hundred-bed Heights was designed by Philip M. Chu, and boasted spacious rooms—singles, doubles, four-person suites—a faculty apartment, and ample lounges. It was equipped with alarms and sprinklers for safety; for energy efficiency its double- and triple-pane windows faced mostly to the south and east. Computer-operated oil burners were convertible to coal, and it had a stand-by generator and wood-burning boiler. With Cotter exhorting contractors and checking every detail of the construction, the building went up in a record 410 days.[7] When it opened in the fall of 1981 it took the standard of dormitory living up another notch.

STAR SEARCH

Hippies dressed up and became Yuppies. Hip-hop was their music; Rubik's Cubes, their worry beads. They cared about the same things the aging activists had fought for—peace, and the causes of minorities, women, and the environment—

---

7. The Thompson dormitories, although individually named, were still being called the "new dorms" when people began to call the Chu building the "new, new dorm." In the summer of 1981, with students about to move in, Deans Seitzinger and Smith met and, without benefit of committee, unilaterally named Thompson's dorms "Hillside" and the Chu building "The Heights."

but they pressed their battles in quieter ways. If the Me Generation deserved to be called selfish it was in some measure because they worried about finding work. The economy was in the tank, and inflation had two digits. All the while the College was reshaping its top leadership, moving ahead against the tide, and struggling to find the best students in a shriveling pool of candidates. Everybody was looking for stars.

The thinning ranks of antiwar activists hitched their cause to a star in their own backyard. The Soviet army had invaded Afghanistan, and by the spring of 1980 President Jimmy Carter was worried that more help might be needed by the Muslim guerillas in their jihad against the communists. He asked Congress to renew the law, abandoned since 1975, requiring all eighteen-year-old males to register for the military draft. Just as the Senate considered the bill it was also preparing confirmation hearings for Senator Edmund Muskie, nominated to be secretary of state. Students thought a tie to Muskie might turn a national spotlight on their opposition to the draft. They were right.

On Monday, May 5, some fifteen students staged a sit-in at Muskie's Main Street Waterville offices. The senator's field representative, Beverly Bustin, sent out for coffee and doughnuts and explained that Muskie was in a delicate spot and would not be getting into the fray. Outside on the sidewalk, draft supporters marched with American flags. When a few protestors left the next day, one of them took the food, and the sit-in became a hunger strike. Eight vowed to stick it out. On the campus several hundred held a sympathy rally and chanted: "No draft, no war, no way!" On Thursday, with the media in rapt attention, students were told the cops were coming, and the three-day occupation abruptly ended.[8] Benjamin Barlow '81 said he and the others gave up "to avoid any kind of a senseless martyrdom." Muskie was confirmed secretary of state that night, and soon Waterville's George Mitchell left the U.S. District Court bench to take his Senate seat.[9]

On the campus, officialdom was looking for some of the spotlight as well and at the same time trying to get over an inferiority complex. The lingering self-consciousness stemmed from the long struggle to build everything at once and from years of looking over the shoulder at other fine old places that

8. A similar protest in the offices of Massachusetts Senator Edward Kennedy had ended the day before when U.S. marshals hauled the protestors off to jail.

9. Congress approved the draft registration requirement and required colleges to certify that their students had signed up. The colleges balked, but complied. The certification requirement was dropped within a year, but the registration law continued.

had been better longer and steeped in traditions unbroken by not having to move their entire roots. Since the early 1960s, when the Ford Foundation affirmed Colby as a center of some excellence, frustration had grown over the gap between the reality of that quality and the stubborn perception that the College was somehow only average. Nobody was more determined to close that gap and move to a higher constellation among the best colleges than Bill Cotter. In pursuit of that goal, in January 1982 he marched himself into the offices of the *New York Times* and demanded an extra star.

In the competitive marketplace for students, guidebooks had a special niche. Publishers and parents gobbled them up. Bookstores gave them separate sections. Whenever a new one came out, admissions officers winced. Most guides included straight facts (which were often misleading), but editors also insisted on including essays and ratings based on little else but whimsy. The newest guidebook, *The New York Times Selective Guide to Colleges,* written by education editor Edward Fiske, was set for the newsstands. An advance copy was sent to the College. Colby's entry began: "On a mountaintop in picturesque Waterville—only an hour's drive from Sugarloaf Mountain—Colby College offers much more than a playground for rugged preppies." It went on to say students were "more interested in their skis and their books than in any activity that smacks of the real world, including job-hunting." The cute and breezy text wasn't the problem. Every college got a taste of that. The problem was that in rating the quality of the academic program, Fiske gave Colby only three stars, a mark he declared average. Bowdoin had four. A handful of the most elite places had five.

The book and its star rating system brought loud yelps from presidents across the country (especially at places with three stars or fewer), but before the full, angry storm hit Fiske's office, Cotter went to see the editor face-to-face. In advance of their meeting he sent a seven-page letter with multiple supporting attachments in which he made the case that Colby ought to have gotten five stars, four at the very least. He told Fiske flat-out that the College had been "damaged" (a startling word when a lawyer uses it) and was entitled to a letter acknowledging the mistake and a higher rating in the next edition.

Fiske had no wiggle room. Within a week of the meeting Times Books sent Cotter a telegram: THIS IS TO CONFIRM THAT A LETTER REGARDING THE REVISION OF ACADEMIC RATING FOR COLBY, DISCUSSED WITH TED FISKE, IS IN THE WORKS AND WILL BE SENT TO YOU AS SOON AS POSSIBLE. The follow-up letter from Fiske said Colby would receive four stars in the next edition. Cotter was only a bit happier, and steamed that the *Times* was "more careful when they review restaurants or plays than they are when they rank colleges." He told a reporter that the newspaper's name gave "a special credibility that this particular book doesn't deserve." He also fretted that there were still nine thousand copies of the three-star version in bookstores across the country.

Fiske went on NBC-TV's *Today Show* to defend himself, claiming the Colby change (Colby's was the only concession he had given) was made necessary because College officials had not returned the original questionnaires. In fact they had, but it didn't matter. The fight was over. In March, buried in complaints about errors of fact and judgment in the Fiske guide, *Times* publisher Arthur Ochs Sulzberger said future editions would not carry the imprimatur of the venerable Gray Lady.

Significance of the star war was not simply in setting the record straight, or even in protecting Colby's attractiveness to all prospective students. There was no need for that. Some three thousand applications were coming in every year, with fewer than 450 slots to fill. The quest for a fourth star was all about the importance of being properly placed in the market for the very best of stars in the shrinking galaxy of students. Inching up the quality of the student body was going to be difficult enough without having misinformation in guidebooks.

Not long after, *U.S. News & World Report* published its first rankings of the nation's top twenty-five liberal arts colleges. Colby was slighted again. The choices were based solely on a poll of five hundred college presidents (Cotter had thrown his out). Once again, the president launched a protest, and wrote to suggest the magazine couple the popularity poll with some objective indicators. The magazine changed its rating scheme, included objective criteria, and in the next year Colby was on the list to stay.[10]

Never mind counting stars; Fiske's claim that students cared more about skiing and books than finding jobs was also dead wrong. Against the background of general student contentment were persistent grumbling noises about whether all the money they were spending was worth it, and whether they were going to be able to find useful work. Cotter had by then established a new board of overseers, an advisory body comprising of alumni, parents,

---

10. Lisa Birnbach, author of the popular *Preppie Handbook*, released its most infamous edition in 1984. Everybody felt the sting, and the section on Colby included references that exaggerated both the remoteness of the College and the drinking habits of its students. Taking a cue from Cotter, the president and vice president of Student Government, Tom Claytor and Cory Humphreys, traveled to catch Birnbach at an appearance at Boston College and protest the Colby references. They offered to pay her way to Waterville so she might see for herself. She didn't come, and subsequent editions of her book were nearly as slanderous.

and other friends of the College. The board swiftly became a principal source of candidates for the governing board of trustees, and its members were chiefly engaged as participants on the new departmental visiting committees. It was not by chance that the first-ever round of overseer visiting committees (in 1980) included the office of career planning. In the time when many seniors could pick among several jobs, it had been called a "placement" office. When Sid Farr took over in 1971 the name was modified to "career counseling," reflecting a changed focus from sorting jobs to finding them. Even then the office continued to include the management of financial aid. The twin functions were not split until 1978, when Farr left to become development vice president.

By the time the visiting committee took a close look, both students and parents were complaining loudly. After the visit, James McIntyre (German) took leave from the faculty to head the department. Renamed Career Services, it was a place where the emerging uses of computers had broad application. McIntyre took full advantage. His task required a realignment of expectations and a scouring of the world to find new opportunities to match with graduates. He made progress in both directions. In 1982 Linda Cotter volunteered as coordinator of the Jan Plan internships sponsored by alumni and parents and, two years later, signed on as a paid part-timer. Summer and January internships often led to job offers and careers, and she set out to find more of them. Some 1,800 alumni responded to her plea for help, and it wasn't long before Colby had a menu of internship opportunities that rivaled the "old boy" networks of the Ivies.

Anxiety about finding jobs included fretting about the College's advising system. Parents, especially, wanted to know about what kind of advice their students were getting (if they weren't listening to them, who *were* they listening to?); the College responded by tinkering with an advising system that stubbornly defied full repair. In order to get personal attention up and the individual workload down, one solution was to require every faculty member to advise students. It was a scheme that worked better in form than function. Then, as always, students persisted in taking important advice from those in whom they had the most comfort and trust: mostly other students, sometimes faculty members (whether they were assigned as advisers or not), and occasionally custodians or even deans.

The change of presidents led to the inevitable realignment of top leadership, and time and circumstance soon had Cotter searching for stars for an almost entirely new senior administrative team. The shuffle began at the very top, even before Cotter arrived. As chairman of the board, Al Palmer '30 let his great passion for Colby get mixed up in the chain of command and had taken to making late-night telephone calls to senior administrative people, sometime plotting against Strider. Trustees agreed to make the next president the gift of a new board chair, and just as Cotter's term was about to begin, arranged for Palmer to step down in favor of Robert Anthony '38. Anthony led the board until 1983 when he retired from teaching at Harvard.

Anthony was replaced by H. Ridgely Bullock '55, a Renaissance man and unlike any other in the long line of board chairs. An entrepreneur and attorney, he was a partner (with Richard Nixon and John Mitchell) in the New York City law firm of Mudge Rose Guthrie Alexander & Ferdon. He was CEO of Uni-Dynamics Corporation, a manufacturing company in Stamford, Connecticut, and was later chief executive officer of Montchanin Management Corporation, an investment bank and consulting firm. He became expert in rescuing enterprises on the verge of collapse (for example, Bank of New England), and his varied special interests took him from producing Broadway plays to making wines in California. Bullock was no more loath to take a hands-on role at the College than was Palmer (especially in the matter of fundraising), but there was a difference. He was firmly in Cotter's corner.

The exodus of senior administrative leaders began quickly. In 1980, Paul Jenson, dean of faculty for nearly a decade, resigned to become the second president of nearby Thomas College.[11] A national search found his replacement, Paul Dorain, chair of the chemistry department at Brandeis, who stayed less than two years before taking a research position at Yale. Sonya Rose (sociology) minded the store as acting dean before Cotter turned inside and tapped Douglas Archibald, a scholar in Anglo-Irish history and culture and a specialist in the poetry of W. B. Yeats, as vice president and dean. As chair of the large and often fractious English department, Archibald came into his new job already seasoned. Having a colleague and an insider in the front faculty office suited the members, and it suited Cotter as well. Archibald's natural instincts and good humor enabled him to coalesce the faculty around prickly issues and to heal bruised egos after the frays. Under his watch student foreign study opportunities exploded and the curriculum at home was strengthened. He partnered with Cotter in the fight to improve salaries even as the size of the overall faculty grew, and in the process began to balance gender scales and make small inroads in the hiring of faculty of color.

11. The first president of Thomas College was John L. Thomas Jr. (Colby '42), son of the founder of its predecessor business college. The younger Thomas died in April 1980.

Robert "Bob" Pullen '41, administrative vice president since 1973, stayed with Cotter for a year before retiring in 1981. He had given Colby thirty-six years of yeoman service ranging from economics teacher and department chair to, for eight years, vice president. His replacement was the first in the half-centurylong line of vice presidents without a Colby pedigree. Stanley Nicholson earned his undergraduate degree in his home state, at the University of Montana. His doctorate was from Duke. He had been at the U.S. International Communications Agency, where he was director of the office of academic programs. His résumé also included stints with the U.S. Agency for International Development and the Ford Foundation, where as an economist with the Harvard Development Advisory Service he had worked with Cotter in Colombia and later served as the foundation's representative in Brazil. He came to Colby from the prestigious Brookings Institution, where he had been administrative director. Bright, easygoing, and creative, Nicholson was a perfect match for Cotter who, unlike his immediate predecessors, was fascinated with figures and read budgets with the same facility and eagerness as he went over the college guides. Douglas Reinhardt '71 helped watch the money, stepping up to become treasurer while keeping his role as controller.

The 1981 semiretirement of Dick Dyer, assistant to three presidents, led Cotter to invent a new senior post for Earl Smith, dean of students since 1976, who became dean of the college with oversight of an eclectic assembly of services reflecting his Colby experience: the dean of students office, public affairs and publications, safety and security, the health center, and (for courage) the College chaplains. The new dean of students was Janice Seitzinger, who would keep the post into the next century, becoming the College's longest-serving dean of any sort. Already a seven-year veteran as associate dean, Seitzinger took the lead position just as the elite colleges moved into the buyer's market for students. If deans were once disciplinarians whose largesse was principally forgiveness, they were now agents for all kinds of new and appealing services. The ancient concept of in loco parentis, squelched in the 1960s when students demanded new freedoms, slowly crept back into vogue; while student rights remained protected, their expectations of what deans might do for them knew no bounds.

Seitzinger's small physical stature belied a giant inner force (a colleague once referred to her as "General Patton in drag"). Eyeball-to-belt buckle, she could wither the spirit of the biggest miscreant, but she just as quickly stood up against the world in support of one of her students. She was at the jail when they were arrested and at the hospital when they were hurt. Her hands-on style and natural penchant to supervise everything within her reach worked well in the new era of deaning. Within five years of her appointment the Carnegie Foundation cited the College for having "an exemplary residential life system," and a nationwide survey of some fifty chief student affairs officers ranked Colby, Grinnell, and Oberlin as having the best small-college student services in the country. Other colleges began to copy.

The tragic death of Harry Carroll in the summer of 1982 prompted Cotter to turn inward again. There was neither time nor need to look far for a replacement, and he asked Robert McArthur to leave his teaching post in philosophy and religion and lead the newly invigorated admissions effort. He consulted experts for a crash course in admissions marketing, and in a short time embarked on a flutter of new initiatives with pamphlets, posters, strategic visits to high schools outside Colby's customary cache, and close oversight of those pesky college guides.

Capitalizing on Colby's two chief attractions—quality and location—McArthur ordered up a giant poster with a photograph of the majestic moose at a remote pond. Its tag line said "Excellence in Maine." The offbeat poster became an irresistible adornment in high school placement offices around the country and for a time provided a backdrop on the news set of one of Maine's TV stations. Some said the poster wasn't academic enough. McArthur tried drawing in eyeglasses and a book.

Sid Farr, who once made the third man in the combined alumni and development shop, soldiered on as vice president and began to gear up for the eleventh capital fund drive in the College's long history. A growing staff was anchored by a Colby cast including David Roberts '55, on deck since 1977 as director of the then new planned giving effort; Charles "Penn" Williamson '63, a designated hitter who became director of development in 1983; Sue Conant (Cook) '75, in alumni relations; and Eric Rolfson '73, a campaign specialist.

The Colby 2000 Campaign (a name some later wished had been saved for the next one) began in April 1982, with goals of $20 million plus another $5 million in the coming five Annual Fund appeals. Bullock, soon to lead the board, was the chair. Twelve million dollars were earmarked for new endowed funds (principally for faculty salaries and financial aid), and another $8 million for new construction, most of it ($6.7 million) for doubling the size of Miller Library, a project already near completion. The library project was finished by the fall of 1983. At groundbreaking ceremonies two years before, the new president had misjudged even his own ambitions for Colby when he declared the structure would make the new campus "finally complete." The finished building, still with forty-nine faculty offices, had study places for 620 students and space for a half-million volumes. That summer, with the economy creeping out of the cellar, the College had forged ahead with the first of the dormitory renovations (Averill and Johnson) that would continue for more than a decade.[12]

By 1983, the planets were aligned to face the most contentious debate since 1929, when the question was first raised as to whether Colby dared to move itself to a new campus.

OMEGA

The Cotters came to visit in March 1979, shortly before he took office. He spoke to curious students in Given Auditorium, and then invited questions. ("Do you have a nickname?" "Call me Bill. If it's going to be anything else, please ask me first.") At the end a student asked what he thought of fraternities. He explained that where he had gone to college there weren't any, and that he'd reserve judgment. The entire audience applauded, and he was mystified. What he did not know was that some in the crowd—including a string in the front row wearing Greek emblems—were cheering his promise to wait and see. The rest were warmed by the thought of a college without fraternities. Within five years he would be criticized (and credited) for presiding over the ending of fraternities, but in truth there were clouds hanging over Colby's secret societies well before he was even born.

In the 1930s, when time came to move up the hill, there was a moment when trustees considered leaving the six fraternities behind.[13] There were philosophical objections to the exclusive societies, but in the end the decision was driven by more practical considerations. The College did not have money to build residences for men, and fraternity alumni did. A committee studied the question and voted (19 to 2) to recommend letting the fraternities come along.

12. With all the planning and construction, much of it supervised by the College itself, the name of the old Buildings and Grounds Department (B & G) no longer applied. In 1982 it was renamed the Department of Physical Plant.

13. Delta Kappa Upsilon was founded in 1848. Zeta Psi began as Alpha Omega in 1850, Delta Upsilon as Equitable Fraternity in 1952, Phi Delta Theta as Logania in 1882, Alpha Tau Omega as Beta Upsilon in 1881, Lambda Chi Alpha as the Colby Commons Club in 1912, Kappa Delta Rho in 1818, Tau Delta Phi as Gamma Phi Epsilon in 1932, and Pi Lambda Phi as Beta Chi in 1957.

Trustees agreed, but they were determined to keep them on a tight leash. The College would lend each of the corporations half the building costs, but the houses would be built on College land, with deeds that gave the College ownership if they should cease to exist. The seemingly harmless caveat simplified matters when the day came that they all closed at once.

A second condition was not benign at all. On most campuses fraternity members dine together. Sharing meals is at the center of the bonding experience, and bonding is at the core of fraternities. Delta Kappa Upsilon (DKE), Phi Delta Theta (PDT), and Kappa Delta Rho (KDR) had dining rooms in their houses in town. The rest ate at local boardinghouses. The new houses, trustees said, would have no kitchens. Members would eat at the common trough, in Roberts Union. The decision made the Hill fraternities different from the very beginning.

Fraternity house construction had to wait for the war. In the pause there were further doubts. At the 1943 Commencement meeting of the board, Dr. F. T. Hill inquired into "the possible desirability of eliminating these [fraternity] organizations."[14] Another committee was formed, and after a daylong meeting at the Eastland Hotel in Portland that October, the conclusion and conditions were the same as before. Although the estimated cost of building a house had risen through the war from $45,000 to $100,000, by 1948 Fraternity Row had begun. Eight houses were built between 1948 (DKE and ATO) and 1967 (KDR), and for hundreds of men in that period, fraternity life was at the center of their Colby experience. There was value in the growth and development that came from fraternal membership, and many lives and careers were improved by the leadership skills they acquired. Fond college memories and long friendships were created by the intimacy and support of the brotherhood. Despite the good, fraternities could not shake the ageless, nagging issues of discrimination, exclusivity, and sexism, all part of the very epoxy that held the fraternal orders together. As society and cultural values changed, the Greeks could not keep up. Even through the glory decades brothers often had to circle the wagons to fend off mounting critics, including fellow students.

At Colby, there was never any systematic fraternity discrimination on the basis of race or religion. There were few minorities in the first place, and when time came to fight the racist policies of national organizations, local chapters joined the fray against them. With the student body centered in urban Massa-

14. The proximity of Hill's College Avenue home (later the Salvation Army headquarters) may have diminished his affection for fraternities, but more likely his opposition was philosophical.

chusetts, it made no sense to discriminate against Catholics, and after World War I, when the national hierarchy called for the exclusion of Jews, the Colby chapters ignored them. (When Jewish students formed Tau Delta Phi in 1918, the faculty ruled its members could not be chosen "on religious or racial lines.")

Fraternities and sororities did, however, discriminate in more general ways. Members were chosen in secret, with selections based on little more than the whimsy. For freshmen looking in from the outside, the exercise of inclusion and exclusion had nothing to do with any known criteria and everything to do with whether or not someone liked you. On a small campus where Greeks dominated social life, the pain of rejection was magnified. Making matters worse, fraternities had squatters' rights on prime real estate, the likes of which were not available to the rejected men—or to any women at all. Sororities, with fewer members and no houses, had a lower profile. Some said the sisters were tossed out with the bathwater when the Greek system was abandoned. It wasn't true. They too were single sex, and controlled by national organizations whose charters were often at odds with local principles of decisionmaking. And in the matter of exclusivity their behavior was the same. Each annual pledge season reaped a full share of women who suffered at being turned down. Deans and faculty members, unable to make things right, could only hand out tissues and fend off angry parents.

Most early fraternities had been founded as literary societies. Teachers drilled students in classes by day, and students gathered to read papers by themselves at night. Teaching methods changed, and the literary societies evolved into social clubs and bastions of after-class parties. In his "Certain Proposals" paper, fodder for the 1966 Colby Congress, Strider urged stronger ties between a "rather barren" social life and the intellectual pursuits of students. He predicted fraternities had a "limited future" unless they helped make the connection. Students began to speak out as well. At a 1968 Alumni Weekend seminar, Robert French '70 called the fraternity system "alien" to the intellectual life of the College and recommended that "serious thought" be given "to executing a change in the social structure of the College." As SAT scores rose, the indictment of being anti-intellectual was getting louder. By 1970 Strider was publicly asking "if the time-honored exclusiveness" of the fraternities and sororities was any longer "a relevant part of college life."

With some radical adjustment, fraternities might have survived, but by the end of the 1960s chapters began to devour themselves. The slide began with the antiestablishment fervor that swept campuses during the Vietnam War, when nothing (except perhaps the evil administration) was more entrenched and established than the craggy old fraternities. New crops of entering freshmen began to see Greek membership as an alternative, no longer a single, almighty goal, and students began making rooming choices based upon lifestyle preferences. Housing on the Hill had always been eclectic—big and small, old and new, near and far—and when twenty-four-hour dormitory visiting privileges were granted in 1970, fraternity houses were no longer the only places with relaxed rules. Two years later true coed living multiplied the opportunities for social life. The dormitories, including the roomy new Hillside dorms, began to look better than the aging houses, where membership losses had begun to translate into deferred maintenance and shabbiness.

As fraternity beds began to empty, the cost was borne not solely by the corporations but by other students as well. Unlike most colleges where fraternities border the campus and are autonomous, at Colby they were an essential part of the housing stock. Annual budgets relied on every bed being filled. College officials met a half-dozen times with fraternity members and their alumni prudential committees to try to stem the exodus. The honored tradition of strict rushing and pledging rules was abandoned. New members could be recruited at any time. Fraternity leaders were supplied lists of new freshmen in the summer. In most cases, if men wanted to join all they had to do was ask. Brothers who wanted to live outside the houses were required to get written permission from the fraternity, and in 1971 the dean of students agreed to assign transfer students to fill the empty fraternity beds.[15]

Nothing seemed to work, and in 1972 the Alumni Council formed an all-fraternity committee. Its recommendation, approved by the board, said each house would have to achieve 80 percent of its housing capacity. Missing the target would bring probation, and a second year of failure would result in the building's being taken for dormitory use. The capacity of the eight houses was 260.[16] In 1972–73 occupancy was 218 (171 members, 47 nonmembers). To make up the difference the College rented off-campus facilities for forty nonfraternity men. The next year fraternities opened with 206 residents, the lowest occupancy since all the houses had been open.

Through the period, alumni support dwindled. The cultural sea change of the 1960s had turned away many of them. They would return for Homecoming with memories of standing around the fireplaces with crew cuts and in

15. The agreement was rescinded the following year. The hapless transfer men were not generally welcomed. One was assaulted.

16. The ninth fraternity, Pi Lambda Phi, had no house of its own. Its members resided in Chaplin Hall where vacancies in their assigned space were automatically filled by the housing office.

sport coats, singing college songs and drinking beer. Now they discovered long hair, tie-dyed T-shirts, acid rock, and pot. The only thing that hadn't changed was the beer. When time came to convene the prudential committees to plan a resurrection, several chapters had to scurry around to find alumni volunteers. The Inter-Fraternity Council (IFC), founded as a governing body in 1938, had been dead since 1970, when it met only once, and then without a quorum. The abandonment of rushing and pledging rules, the relaxing of regulations, and the broadening of the social scene left the council with little to do. Its successor, the Presidents' Council, fared no better. The national organizations were no help at all. The bulwark fraternities were in the south, still strong and traditional. Agents coming north found themselves in a strange land. Their pleadings seemed like Greek to most members, who treated the traveling secretaries as annoying bill collectors.[17]

By 1977 empty beds were costing the College $200,000 in annual lost revenue, and qualified admissions applicants were being turned down for lack of a place to put them. The eight fraternities had accrued an annual operating deficit of $56,000, and their collective debt to the College was broaching a half-million. Nervous trustees asked Strider for a full review, and he asked the dean of students, Earl Smith, to prepare it. The report was gloomy. Over the previous four years there had been an average of thirty-eight empty fraternity beds. Five houses had bounced on and off membership probation. Alpha Tau Omega (ATO) was going under. With only nine members and a minimum requirement of twenty-one, ATO had become the first Colby fraternity to accept women. Three occupied the deserted housemother's suite in 1976–77. The next year the entire third floor was to be given over to women, and eleven had signed up. The prudential committee despaired and asked the College to run the place through 1977–78. Since 1973 the College had required the houses to meet state fire codes with alarm systems, emergency lighting, and stairwell enclosures. None had complied. Regular deferred maintenance—wiring, roofs, woodwork, chimneys, and bricks—was piling up.

Social misconduct was always at the top of the public list of fraternity indictments, but on the campus authorities knew there would be plenty of mischief in any population of eighteen to twenty-one-year-olds, fraternities or not. The root of disruptive behavior was alcohol. Even so, the majority of Student Judicial Board cases involved fraternity men. Hazing, the unique province of the Greeks, continued despite state laws and prohibiting College rules.

17. Ten members of Lambda Chi Alpha (LCA) were thrown out of the chapter house following the assault of a traveling secretary in 1978.

At the end of his report Smith recommended that "all fraternities at Colby be abolished." With Smith's unsolicited advice removed, Strider forwarded the report to the trustees. The board was not far distant, in time or temper, from the one that had voted to reject the Nunez Proposal, which dealt merely with discriminatory practices. Its membership was still filled with fraternity supporters who would have been apoplectic at the idea of abolishing them.[18] Instead, they fumed about the safety deficiencies and promptly advanced the houses $75,000 each to make improvements. (Two months later ten women died in a dormitory fire at Providence College.)

When Cotter arrived in the fall of 1979, PDT and Delta Upsilon (DU) had failed to reach minimum capacity for two years running but were allowed to continue. Smith had launched three task forces to consider the overall residential life and the advising programs. As part of his "wait and see" promise, the president called for the development of fraternity guidelines. How could the organizations live up to expectations, he reasoned, if they didn't know what the expectations were? Trustee Kevin Hill '50 (Zeta Psi), nephew of F. T. Hill, who had questioned the need for Colby fraternities thirty-five years before, chaired a committee that worked eighteen months putting them together.

The renewed fraternity discussion brought the general student population into the fray. In the fall of 1980, on the eve of homecoming weekend, an *Echo* commentary blistered the fraternity system as "discriminatory and elitist," and called on the College to make their houses available to all students. The authors, seniors Jane Eklund and Whit Symmes, began a "Ban Frat Row" campaign. That spring, the Student Affairs Committee of the College, acting on a recommendation of the residential life task force, proposed a statement of philosophy blithely calling for equal access to all housing, regardless of race or sex. Race once again wasn't an issue, but sexual integration was another matter. Beleaguered IFC president Douglas Terp '84 said the problem was not the principle of women in fraternities, but in getting everybody to buy in. Few women were interested in joining fraternities, and few men were eager to have them. Cotter appointed a Select Committee on Housing to figure things out. Robert McArthur (philosophy) was chair until he became dean of admissions and trustee Hill took over.

The guidelines went into effect in June 1981. Standards were set for membership numbers, academic performance, financial health, social service, building

18. Strider was right. A dean of students should not offend an important segment of the student body, least of all that segment that brought him the most daily business.

maintenance, safety, and housekeeping. There would be inspections and re-port cards. Everybody signed off: the barely breathing IFC, the prudential com-mittees, the student affairs committees of the College and the board, and the board itself. That fall, the president and others met with each house president and its prudential committee to explain things. A budget workshop was held for the chapter house treasurers.

At the end of 1982, new dean of students Janice Seitzinger wrote a report on how the fraternities were faring under the guidelines. Her inch-thick report card showed that while some houses had improved (the revival of ATO was a marvel), on balance things remained bleak. There were still empty beds (fifty), and four of the houses were on probation for falling below the minimum oc-cupancy requirement. The all-fraternity GPA average (2.6) was only a bit below the all-student average (2.8), but KDR and DKE were in serious academic trouble. Some inroads had been made in catching up with budget deficits and maintenance, but most were still in the hole. McArthur, now in the admissions business, wrote a piece for Seitzinger's report and cited the findings of a recent visiting committee to the admissions office, which said consideration should be given to "admitting women to fraternities, as a minimum, and abolishing the fraternity system as the other extreme."[19]

In April 1983, with KDR suspended, DKE on probation for guideline defi-ciencies, and TDP in deep trouble for a well-publicized incident of sexual mis-conduct, Hill's Select Committee on Housing made its report. By a vote of 6 to 2 it affirmed the right of every student to have access to all types of housing, and recommended fraternity members be evicted so houses could be turned into dorms. Six people weren't nearly enough to steer the fate of the long-established fraternities, and in June board chair Bullock named a seventeen-member trustee commission to make "a comprehensive inquiry into residen-tial and social life."[20] He acknowledged the timing was driven by the "burning issues" surrounding fraternities, expressed in the charge itself, which called for

19. McArthur cited instances of campus tours where "prospective applicants and their parents had been yelled at from the windows of fraternity houses, including phrases such as, 'Go to Bowdoin' and worse."

20. Members were President Cotter; trustees Ridgely Bullock '55, board chair; Law-rence Pugh '56 (DKE), commission chair; Anne Bondy '46 (Sigma Kappa), Levin Camp-bell, Kevin Hill '56 (ZP), Wilson Piper '39 (DU), and Richard Schmaltz '62 (DU); Alumni Council members David Marson '48 (TDP) and Josiah Drummond Jr. '64 (DKE); fac-ulty members Arthur Champlin (ZP), Jane Hunter, L. Sandy Maisel, and Robert Reu-man; parent Sylvia Sullivan '53 (Delta Delta Delta); and students Sheila Ryan '84, Patri-cia Shelton '84, Douglas Terp '84 (TDP and IFC president), and Gregory Walsh '84.

an inquiry into "whether fraternities and sororities are still appropriate for the College." Greeks were well represented on the commission. Eleven were fraternity or sorority members.

Lawrence Pugh '56 (DKE) took the bold assignment as chair. Already an iconic Colby success story, Pugh had worked his way to the presidency of Samsonite Luggage and was now chair and CEO of the V. F. Corporation, the world's largest apparel firm, which he would soon lead into the ranks of the Fortune 500 companies. A stout Colby supporter and deft consensus builder, he was the perfect choice, but for him and other alumni members the assignment carried the risk of losing long friendships. Student members flirted with campus recriminations.

There were 254 fraternity members in the student body when the commission began its work that fall; 182 lived in the houses, the rest (including nineteen members of Pi Lambda Phi) in the dorms or in town. Of the five sororities that had come to the Hill, only two were left: Sigma Kappa and Chi Omega. Membership names and numbers were private, but by now the Greeks represented less than 15 percent of the student body.

Sworn to keep their minds open and their thoughts to themselves, commissioners set out in three directions for the most comprehensive inquiry the College had ever made. Subcommittees conducted a general alumni survey, held public hearings, and visited other campuses in quest of information and ideas. Separate fall polls of faculty and students affirmed a split that had been there all along. Three-quarters of the faculty wanted fraternities abolished; three-quarters of the students wanted to keep them. Although the results were not surprising, fraternity support from women students was at least curious. Leaving aside the exclusion of women from the fraternities and their prize housing, the bill of particulars in the case against fraternities also included charges of harassing treatment of women in the context of social events and in their passage along Frat Row. (A most notorious incident involved a woman captured in a net thrown from a second-floor fraternity porch.) Although individual women spoke against fraternities, the collective Women's Group—otherwise never loath to cry out for important changes for women—remained silent.

At the end of their work, the three subcommittees filed lengthy reports with recommendations that equivocated on the central question of whether fraternities should stay or go but included suggestions for improving residential life. Threaded throughout were calls for more social space away from the fraternity houses, stronger ties between the intellectual and social lives of students, reforms of the confused student judicial system, and improvements in dining services.

The surveys subcommittee, chaired by Hill, sent a questionnaire to 3,800 students, faculty, staff, and a sample of alumni. Nearly one thousand replied. Members also conducted personal interviews with key campus and alumni figures, and read some ninety letters that came over the transom (90 percent from men, 90 percent of them in favor of keeping the fraternities). Trustee Anne Bondy led a subcommittee on visits to ten other campuses, and trustee Wilson Piper chaired the group that held open hearings in five cities and, for two days, on the campus.[21]

Fraternities had been on their best behavior since the close scrutiny began, but as the investigation drew to a close, members sensed the mood swinging against them. At the eleventh hour, only days before the commission report was to be issued, Lambda Chi Alpha rediscovered its roots, and put up posters advertising the creation of a new literary society and plans to provide the place "where the community can meet in an intellectual yet casual atmosphere." The suggested reading for the first meeting was George Orwell's *1984*. Alas, senior members may have forgotten that the work had already been assigned and discussed as their freshman book of the year.

Cotter did not tip his hand until the commission's penultimate meeting in November, and then his advocacy was more for a new system of residential commons than for the necessarily coupled step of abolishing fraternities. He knew and liked the house system at Harvard, and the commons plan was largely his invention. All but one commissioner agreed it was time to replace fraternities with the broader scheme.[22]

Trustee and parent Levin Campbell (Eleanor '81) wrote the final report. As chief judge of the U.S. Court of Appeals for the First Circuit, he knew the ingredients of a persuasive brief, and his skill shone through the document that would be, for most alumni and others, the only thorough explanation of the

21. Commissioners visited Amherst, Bates, Bowdoin, Hampshire, Haverford, Middlebury, Swarthmore, Trinity, Wesleyan, and Williams. Hearings were held in New York, Boston, Hartford, Washington, D.C., and Portland, Maine.

22. The outlier, David Marson, wrote a "concurring opinion" in which he said he would like to give the guidelines more time, but as chair of the Alumni Council he went on to urge those who shared his view "to actively support and serve the College."

decision they would ever read. The punch line was on the first page: "After thorough appraisal . . . we recommend, sadly, but with great conviction, that Colby withdraw recognition from its fraternities and sororities." The report went on to outline the skeleton of a new residential commons plan, and discuss the commission's analysis of the fraternity question. It described several options that had been considered and why they were rejected.[23]

Lost in the shadows and unrelated to either the fraternities or the anticipated Commons were recommendations having to do with institutional values and traditions, diversity, the orientation of new students, greater faculty involvement, the student judicial system, health services, the College chaplain program, and programs to stem the abuse of alcohol.

When trustees met in Boston for a final vote on Saturday, January 14, 1984, the commission's recommendations were discussed for more than two hours before being unanimously approved by secret ballot. Fraternities and sororities would close at the end of the coming spring term. Members could continue their affiliations, but no new members could join. The new Residential Commons Plan would be put into place, and the trustees would pony up for a new student union that students would help design.

The report was mailed to all alumni, and on Sunday morning Cotter, Pugh, and Bullock met with fraternity officers to give them the news. That afternoon, as the three entered the Chapel for an all-campus meeting, they were greeted with hisses, catcalls, and a shower of confetti made from hastily shredded copies of the report. "Look what you've done," someone yelled from the balcony. "Our fraternities were like a tree, nurtured and fed for years, and as soon as a few branches begin to die, you cut it down." Of course, that is exactly what had happened. Not everyone was angry. Some braved the heat of the moment to praise the new plan, and to ask questions. Cotter urged everyone to help make it work. Toward evening, as Bullock's private jet circled the campus on its way south, the campus was abuzz. Spontaneous small parties of celebration were held in the south side dormitories, and in the north a bonfire was started in the middle of Frat Row. A crowd began to gather. The fire, fueled by wooden shutters, beds (presumably the ones that were empty) and other furniture, including a piano from Zeta Psi, began to grow. The fire department was called. So were the deans. When Smith and Seitzinger arrived they en-

23. Other considerations were: press for coeducation (as with Trinity, Bowdoin, and Amherst), take some of the houses and make them College-run coeducational dormitories, acquire all of the houses and let fraternities and sororities go on as special interest groups, and allow the Greek organizations to exist simply as extracurricular clubs.

couraged the firemen to let the bonfire burn itself out. Fewer trips to the dump would be needed in the spring.

The angry scene was surreal, the blaze at once a vent for disappointment and anger and at the same time a defiant last gasp of the dinosaur the grand old fraternities had become. The next morning photographs of the bonfire appeared in the nation's newspapers alongside the story of the first fraternity closings since Williams had abolished them twenty years before.[24]

COMMONS SENSE

Many had predicted ruin for the College if the Greeks were disbanded. (A few prayed for it.) They said students would become divided and troublesome, admissions applications would drop, and alumni support would wither. The skeptics and the ill-wishers were wrong. They had miscalculated the resilience and optimism of undergraduates, the preferences of coming crops of new students, and the unshakable devotion of alumni, even of those who hated to see the fraternities go.

The commission had already named the new Commons for the founding president Jeremiah Chaplin, the martyr Elijah Lovejoy, the first woman student Mary Low, and the "father of Mayflower Hill" Franklin Johnson. Residence halls were geographically grouped in the Commons, each with some four hundred students and a dining hall. More than 160 students signed up to serve on the Residential Commons Advisory Board (RCAB) and its seven committees that worked through the spring, creating a new student-faculty Judicial Board, rewriting the Student Government constitution to make room for Commons governing boards, and engaging students in the management of the dining halls.[25]

Two key elements of the envisioned system fell apart in an instant. The architects wanted sophomores to choose a Commons and stay put until graduation. They also wanted students to take evening and weekend meals in their own dining halls. RCAB wanted none of it. The choice of campus housing was too varied to have anyone saddled to a single building for three years, and students had come to like grazing among the dining halls. Cotter and the deans acceded.

---

24. Trustees at Amherst College followed suit a month later.

25. Other committees delved into the arcane system of student room selection, overall social life, faculty-student interaction, class and College identification, and orientation programs.

Much attention was focused on the new student center. Some thought the construction could be tacked onto Roberts Union (perhaps a "bubble" on the backside) but Roberts had already failed as a gathering place. It was not in the center, and furthermore, it abutted the well-stereotyped Frat Row. It was agreed the new building would go in the middle of campus, east of the chapel, across the McCann Road from the Lovejoy Building. Jefferson Riley of the Essex, Connecticut, firm of Moore, Grover & Harper (later Centerbrook), was principal architect. The patient and clever Riley moved his office onto the campus and worked with students through the days and nights until Commencement, preparing plans for the new $3.5 million facility. Construction began that fall.

Enthusiasm was not universal. Labeling the commission's work a "witch hunt," the campus Coalition for Fraternities organized to fight the decision, but its call for a student boycott of the Commons planning was not contagious. (More than thirty members of the Greek societies were on RCAB.) In February an alumni group, including a handful from other colleges, formed the Committee on New England Campus Life. Using chapter mailing lists, it sent a letter to all fraternity and sorority alumni expressing "shock, anger and frustration" at the abolition decision. The harsh broadside placed the blame on Cotter, claiming he had made fraternities a "scapegoat" for campus problems of vandalism and alcohol abuse, and asked alumni to send money to mount a fight. Some recipients forwarded their letters to the College, warning of trouble. The committee also wrote board chair Bullock, urging him to have the trustees reconsider. Bullock obliged, and in April wrote back to say the board had voted again and was "firmly and unanimously committed to the January decision," and there was "no possibility" that fraternities or sororities would be retained.

The College proceeded to press the fraternity corporations to fulfill the terms of their original contracts. The near uniform agreements said if any chapter ceased to exist, the fair market value of the buildings,[26] less any debt, would be put into an endowed fund for College purposes (most were scholarships) honoring the fraternity. All of the national organizations except Zeta Psi respected the trustee decision. Local chapters of DKE and ATO quickly signed final agreements. In May, days before Commencement, Zeta Psi, on behalf of all of the others except DKE, asked Superior Court Justice Robert Browne for a preliminary injunction to keep the College from following

26. Outside appraisers placed values on the "row" houses ranging from $191,300 (DU) to $200,000 (Phi Delt). The newer KDR house was appraised at $607,000.

through on the closings. The motion was denied. Browne said it wasn't an urgent matter and that the College had "good reason" for its action. LCA, TDP, PDT, and DU pressed on for the permanent injunction.

Most of the stuffing went out of the fraternities' legal case that same month when, in an odd coincidence, the Maine Supreme Court found in favor of the Greeks in their four-year-old property tax fight against the city. The fraternities had been paying taxes under protest since 1980 when the city claimed their buildings were privately owned and not protected under the College's general tax exemption. The Superior Court agreed with the city; on appeal, however, the Supreme Court overturned the ruling saying that the College owned the fraternity buildings and had "an absolute option to turn these buildings at any time into dormitories." The Court wrote: "The integration of the fraternity houses geographically, structurally, architecturally, and historically into the development scheme of the College and its campus is strong indication of Colby's ownership status respecting these buildings." The tax money would have to be returned. In the confusion over the status of fraternities, City Solicitor Bill Lee didn't know where to send the $84,404 refund. Superior Court Justice Donald Alexander ruled that although the tax bills had been paid by the College, the money belonged to the fraternities. It all came out in the wash.

In its tax decision the Supreme Court had all but ruled on the new fraternity closing case (Chi Realty Corp. *v* Colby) where the plaintiffs' principal hope rested on turning the tax case finding on its head. Where fraternities wanted to say they were part of the College in order to share the tax exemption, soon the fraternity plaintiffs would try to claim the College had no ownership at all. In Superior Court, Justice Alexander denied the permanent injunction on the closings, and on its own, Zeta Psi appealed to the Maine Supreme Court. Two years later (August 15, 1986) in a 4 to 1 ruling in favor of the College, the high court said that the Colby decision "to more fully integrate the housing units into the academic program of the college was one way in which the president and trustees discharged their duty to evaluate the policies and to change them from time to time to achieve the educational goals of the college."[27]

27. The College's annual budget for legal services was getting bigger by leaps and bounds. Early in his tenure Cotter scoured the state for a College attorney. With the help of John Cornell '65, chair of the Alumni Council and later a trustee, he found Hugh G. E. MacMahon, a specialist in higher education law, of the Portland firm of Drummond Woodsum and MacMahon. MacMahon was the lead attorney in the fraternity cases and, with his colleague, Jerrol Crouter '78, continued to provide legal counsel for the College.

Justice Alexander, who in 1998 was named to the Maine Supreme Judicial Court, presided over several of the Superior Court fraternity cases. As a student at Bowdoin in the early 1960s, he had for a time been a fraternity man. It was then ten years before Bowdoin became coeducational, and 90 percent of the student body belonged to fraternities. Uncomfortable with the "Animal House" atmosphere and other issues, Alexander resigned his fraternity membership in his junior year and become a maverick independent.

By the summer of 1984 plans for the Commons were mostly finished, and work began converting the fraternity houses into dormitories. In a final act of defiance, some houses were left in shambles. Truckloads of books went back to the library, and cartons of catalogued old exams were carted to the dump. Electricians removed pennies from the fuse boxes (and a few bags of marijuana from behind the light switches at ATO), and the buildings were rewired, repainted, and refurnished. When the buildings were spruced up that fall the only clue as to their former life came on damp days when the places gave up the unmistakable odor of stale beer.

The rest of the campus was tidied up as well. Cotter, his reputation for tidiness already legendary, was behind it. Broken windowpanes and empty beer cans in the bushes annoyed him. The grounds crew took to making early morning patrols, picking up trash before he could see it. Budget-tender Nicholson liked to joke that any one of the Cotters' frequent evening campus strolls could cost the College $10,000 in improvements. When the Student Center was finished and the McCann Road repaved, Cotter thought the bright yellow curbs were offensive. He ordered them painted over, in gray. No one could tell parking wasn't allowed.[28] Alan Lewis, a Mainer through and through, came on as director of the physical plant department in 1984. Like his predecessors, George Whalon and Ansel Grindall, he was popular with those who worked for him, and they did twice the work of an ordinary crew. The College soon had no deferred maintenance at all.

That fall the College opened without crowding for the first time in years.[29]

28. Smith had the curbs stenciled in dignified Latin: *Noli Restare.* Scofflaws multiplied.

29. The following year a whopping entering class of 480 freshmen overfilled campus beds by forty.

All 1,558 beds were full; 138 lived off campus. Half the faculty had signed on as faculty advisers to the Commons, and some two hundred students applied for positions on the dormitory staff. More than a thousand students voted in campuswide elections, choosing the 38 members of the new Board of Governors (there were 105 candidates), and a string of officers for each of the dorms. Nearly half of all students ran for one office or another. The election of women to leadership posts was sudden and never again remarkable.

The following spring, on Alumni Weekend (June 8, 1985), the eight fraternity houses were renamed and rededicated in a two-hour series of ceremonies at KDR and up and down old Frat Row. The names were taken from recommendations of the corporations of the several fraternities and sororities:

Drummond (Delta Kappa Upsilon)
> Josiah Hayden Drummond '46 (LL.D, 1871) was founder of the DKE chapter, Colby's first fraternity. Attorney general of Maine (1856–64), he was a Colby trustee and chairman of the board. His family held the record for having the most Colby alumni. (His namesake, Josiah Drummond '64 was a member of the trustee commission.)

Goddard-Hodgkins (Alpha Tau Omega)
> Cecil Goddard '29, a retired local insurance executive, was Colby's first alumni secretary and founder of the Alumni Council. Theodore Hodgkins '25, a former trustee and benefactor, had been president of Forster Manufacturing Company in Wilton.

Grossman (Tau Delta Phi)
> A former trustee and a charter overseer, Nissie Grossman '32 was CEO of the building supply company that bore his name. In 1976 he established the Grossman Professorship of Economics.

Perkins-Wilson (Phi Delta Theta)
> Norman "Cy" Perkins '32, a stellar athlete as an undergraduate, was a beloved ten-year coach of men's cross-country and track teams. C. Malcolm Wilson '33, also a standout athlete, was a longtime fraternity adviser and member of the Alumni Council. Each had received the prestigious Condon Medal at his graduation.

Pierce (Zeta Psi)
> A former trustee, T. Raymond Pierce, 1898, was the largest benefactor of the ZP house.

Piper (Delta Upsilon)
> A trustee, Wilson C. Piper '39 (LL.D. '75) was founder and longtime president of the Boston Colby Alumni Club. He had taken a major

role in every capital fund campaign since his graduation and was a recipient of the Ernest C. Marriner Distinguished Service Award.

Treworgy (Lambda Chi Alpha)

As president of his fraternity, Charles Treworgy '22, a native of Surry, Maine, died in a vain attempt to save four of his fraternity brothers who died in a fraternity house fire on the North Campus in December 1922.

Williams (Kappa Delta Rho)

Long-serving professor and administrative vice president (and later a trustee) Ralph S. Williams '35 was instrumental in arranging for the construction and financing of the KDR house, the last fraternity building on the Hill.

Many public rooms in the fraternity houses were named to honor distinguished alumni brothers as well. In Runnals Union the marching dignitaries dedicated the Chi Omega sorority room to Mary Rollins Millett '30, widow of the beloved alumni secretary, Ellsworth "Bill" Millett; and the Sigma Kappa room to the late Frances Mann Hall, 1877, who with Mary Low, Louise Coburn, Ida Fuller, and Elizabeth Houg founded the alpha chapter at Colby in 1874. A plaque was installed at the union entrance, marking these two chapters as well as Delta Delta Delta and Alpha Delta Phi, which once occupied rooms in the building. Additionally, the main lounge of Chaplin Hall was named in honor of Thomas Gordon '73 and in memory of Kenneth Thompson '63 and John Bernier '61 for their service to the Pi Lambda Phi fraternity chapter, which was never able to build a house on the Hill.

The Colby 2000 Campaign stood at $17 million when the fraternities were closed, and the goal of $25.5 million was increased another $3 million to pay for the Student Center and cover the Commons plan extras. Trustees passed the hat to post a $1 million one-for-two challenge to meet the added needs. Although trustees feared bitterness over the fraternity decision would impede fundraising, there was a glimmer of optimism. The national economy began to improve, and there was evidence that alumni, writ large, were not going to punish the College for making the change. Worries over alumni reaction and the needs of the ongoing campaign had prompted an all-out effort to improve giving. The popular Sid Farr returned to his former post as alumni secretary, and Penn Williamson became director of development until Calvin Mackenzie left the government department to become vice president in 1985.

Mackenzie's organizational skills and his appeal as an academic broadened outside support. Annual gifts the year before the fraternity decision were $2.6 million, of which $615,000 was from alumni. By 1986, annual giving had nearly doubled ($4.6 million), including $717,000 from alumni. The participation numbers took a brief dip, but the amount given went up. Many wrote to say they first gave or gave more to compensate for those who were disgruntled and didn't give at all. The Class of 1985 began a tradition of making a senior class gift to the annual fund and nearly half the members pitched in. In 1988 alumni giving topped a million for the first time and increased every year thereafter.

Worries that Colby's popularity with prospective students would diminish without fraternities proved unfounded as well. Robert McArthur, standing in as admissions dean, said quality of life was an issue of growing importance to high school students and that their counselors saw the change "as an indication of Colby's commitment to improving residential life." In 1985, the first full admissions cycle after the decision, application numbers went up by nearly one hundred (to 3,174) over the previous year, and they continued to climb steadily until 1989 when they totaled 3,547 before the full impact of the declining college-age population hit. While there were undoubtedly students who wanted fraternities and did not apply, of those who applied and entered, many said their choice was based in part on the College's new, fraternity-free system of residential life. SAT scores went up, geographic diversity broadened, and student retention improved. Volunteerism and attendance at campus events increased as well. A student survey showed that 63 percent felt that with continuing adjustments the Commons system was going to work.

In 1985 McArthur returned to full-time teaching and Parker Beverage took his place. An Augusta, Maine, native, Beverage was a Dartmouth graduate and former associate admissions dean at Stanford University. Despite a growing staff of aides and increasing numbers of applicants, he read every admissions file, and years later could remember the names of and details about almost every Colby student he ever admitted.

The new Student Center opened in December 1985. It had been built in 437 days, a pace that pleased Cotter. *Architecture Magazine* called it "one of the most engaging and delightful new buildings in New England" and "one of the best—and one of the most student sensitive—buildings of its kind anywhere." It won one of two architectural prizes in a competition of some one hundred entries sponsored by the *American School and University Magazine*.[30]

30. The building generated so much foot traffic that for safety reasons the city and the College agreed to close the McCann Road as a throughway in 1987.

In the spring, more than 750 filled the large Page Commons Room to hear the distinguished Holocaust survivor and writer Elie Wiesel, who that same year won the Nobel Peace Prize.

For many whose Colby experiences were enriched by ties to the fraternal groups, memories of the older system would remain bright and positive; still, after the closings most accepted the decision and moved on. Yet there were some who refused to give up. Underground groups calling themselves fraternities plagued the College into the next decade.

Long before they were closed, several of the established fraternities had evolved into dormitories for athletic teams: DKE, hockey; Lambda Chi, football; Zeta Psi, basketball. The postclosing imitations had few of the virtues of the originals and almost all of their sins: exclusivity, coercion, initiations, and hazing. Parents wrote anonymous letters, complaining their sons were being pressured to join the underground groups. The College advertised itself as being fraternity-free, they said, and the College had better keep its promise.

In 1986, during a routine dormitory inspection, officials discovered a pledge list marked LCA and a dues book for Zeta Psi. They were in plain sight, but when the dean's office set out to investigate, students on all sides yelped that their privacy rights had been abridged. (One filed a police report, charging the College with theft.) The students had a point. The deans backed off and pledged a review of search and seizure rules. The next year the newest Zete dues payers, mostly basketball players, were caught stealing Christmas decorations in town. It was initiation hazing. They paid the piper in district court. On campus, amnesty was offered in return for a pledge to sever fraternity ties, once and for all. The formal surrender came at a hastily arranged ceremony in the basement coffee room of the Eustis Building. The solemnity of the occasion was the students' idea. Cotter was there, with a color guard of deans. As colleagues bit their lips and stared hard at their loafers, Dean McArthur gave a longish talk on the ancient origin of secret societies. When it was over, the students filed by an open, coffinlike trunk, depositing remnants of the chapter archives, bound for the national headquarters.

Thereafter, coaches made team members sign pledges swearing they would not perpetuate or join fraternities, and the next edition of the *Student Handbook* contained the caveat that anyone caught participating in fraternity activity would be subject to automatic suspension. There were some who weren't paying attention.

The old cash register–maker IBM introduced the first personal computer in 1981. A good deal bigger than a breadbox, it ran on an operating system created by Bill Gates and a company with the funny name of Microsoft. Learning MS-DOS required instruction, and most folks clung to their familiar calculators and typewriters. Three years later when Apple Computer made the Macintosh, a friendly, magical mouse took center stage in the panoply of new technologies, seducing even the most timid and creating new academic opportunities that sent the College scurrying for money. In the span of a single decade, the campus was introduced to new and faster communication, easier methods to record and to create, and intriguing new ways to study the old subjects.

Welcoming the new age first required being open for business. Bill Cotter had been in the corner office only a few weeks when he inquired of a colleague where everyone went at noontime. They were off to lunch he was told, although in Maine some still called it "dinner." Everything closed from noon to one or so, including the College switchboard, recently converted from spaghetti cord plug-ins to actual switches. Do you suppose, Cotter gently asked, people might be willing to stagger lunch times in order to keep the offices open, just in case someone called? It was a citified idea; but it made sense, and it was done.[31]

When the decade turned and Ted Turner's all-news, all-the-time CNN went on the air, Colby owned fourteen shared computer terminals. Sandy Maisel (government) was chair of a new ad hoc computer committee, charged with sorting out the growing demand for more. Long-range planning was impossible—even looking ahead two years was a stretch—but the committee was able to recommend that the goals for the Colby 2000 Campaign include a half-million dollars for computers. It wasn't nearly enough, but it was a start. Going forward, the insatiable demands of new technology would eat a frightening, ever larger share of annual budgets.

As computers came into more common use some worried they would, Godzilla-like, rise up and devour the academic program. A task force of the Educational Policy Committee planned the defense, bravely setting a goal of "universal computer literacy" but insisting that computers would be only the

---

31. The switchboard had been covered by a succession of all-Maine women who answered the phone in the same clipped twang: "Kobe Kalige." Callers from away often thought they'd gotten a wrong number.

means, not the ends, of learning. "Our approach," Cotter underscored, "is to integrate computers into the liberal arts curriculum." The College was not about to "bolt on" a separate computer science program, disconnected from the core mission. In fact, use of computers as an aid to instruction had already begun. By the mid-1970s, computers were being used in the natural sciences, and students in introductory psychology courses were marking test answers on IBM cards that could be sorted and scored within a day or two. Computer application beyond the sciences came, of all places, in philosophy and religion. Biblical scholar Thomas Longstaff and Thomas College mathematician Elizabeth Tipper began work on Colby's first computer-produced book in 1975, created on the balky PDP 11[32] and published in 1978. For most others, the introduction of computers began with the expanding ability to store typed material on magnetic media—memory typewriters—and word processing. Although few were interested in learning how to operate the noisy machines,[33] lots of people wanted the speedy, clean results. Faculty members and others queued up to get their words processed onto eight-inch floppy discs by overworked experts at a half-dozen sites around campus. Administrative Services Director Ken Gagnon offered a crash course on word processing but cautioned that the new machines would never replace typewriters, the machine of choice for making memos, letters, and short reports. Gradually, as personal computers were assigned according to painfully constructed priority lists, folks began to process their own words. Only then did typewriters, in vogue for more than a century, slowly become obsolete. Although computer neophytes at first kept the old machines close by—a hedge against both personal and equipment lapses—typewriters were soon relegated to the far corners of offices, and then to the dump.

In 1982 the College replaced the two PDP 11 minicomputers with a new PDP 11/44, using the original operating system designed around the inflexible BASIC language. More complex programs were developed on the still new and six times bigger VAX 11/780. Printing terminals could make 180 characters a second. That fall faculty members began receiving computer-generated student papers, the usual errors now cleverly hidden in the flawless, handsome type. That fall, the Lovejoy Fellow, West Virginia publisher William Chilton, predicted newspapers would be subsumed by television and its computerized offspring.

Electronic mail arrived on the Hill in the fall of 1983, barely ten years after

32. *Synoptic Abstract,* vol. 15 of The Computer Bible series, 1978.
33. DECmates, made by Digital Equipment Corporation, cost $5,350 in 1982.

its invention. Everyone got a colby.edu address whether they wanted it or not. The informality and ease of the new messaging did nothing to improve the use of the language, but it sped up the discussion and saved postage.[34] Using e-mail had a learning curve. Novice users got confused, sometimes hitting the "send" button without first checking the "to" line. The subject of a slanderous message was occasionally also the unintended recipient, and the retelling of the mishap would bring gales of laughter to coffee rooms around campus. It wasn't long before a Computer Ethics Subcommittee was making policy to safeguard the integrity of the network and promising banishment for anyone copying software, invading files, or sending obscene or threatening messages.

Oddly enough, e-mail arrived before the offices had their own telephone numbers. Direct Inward Dialing came in 1984, and with the soon-to-follow voice mail feature (Audix), also required lessons. The first FAX machine was not installed until 1988, and then only at the urging of board chair Bullock. After several campus huddles, it was agreed that a single machine would suffice. It was placed at the Eustis basement switchboard with Allen LaPan, one of the few who knew how to make it work.

When Apple set loose the mouse, Computer Center director Jonathan Allen worried that without some purchasing discipline the proliferation of incompatible machines would swamp both the budget and his five-person staff. (The multiple brands were also creating vast, unwieldy libraries of floppy discs.) He said the day was coming when there would be microcomputers on every desk and in every dorm room and the machines ought to match up. After testing the options (Apple, IBM, and AT & T's entries, Data General and Tandy), in 1985 the committee chose the Mac as the single Colby platform. Those who wanted anything else would have to maintain it themselves.[35]

Over that summer Seaverns Bookstore advertised 512K Macs and an Imagewriter for $2,392.20. Ninety students bought the package before school opened. A year later there were six hundred PCs on the campus. Students owned more than half of them. Bill Pottle, a one-man sales and service department at the bookstore, was relieved that two out of three purchasers actually knew how to use them. Students were in fact the fastest learners. In a short while, office staffs and faculty members were calling on student workers to solve their computer mysteries, and the College began to pay a premium

34. E-mail helped undermine the U.S. Postal Service. By 1985 the price of a first-class stamp rose to 22¢.

35. By 1998 the growing popularity of Windows machines forced a change of policy. Thereafter, computer services bought and supported both machines.

hourly wage for the most skilled among them. By the end of the decade, most entering students were computer savvy before they arrived.

The inner records of the College itself were trusted to the newest technology in 1987, when personnel and payroll data got plugged into the College Administrative and Records System (CARS). The earlier Wheaton Information System for Education (WISE), written in BASIC, was no longer being developed by its parent, Digital Equipment Corporation, and the PDP 11/44 was running day and night to keep it going. The new database management system, operating on UNIX, provided only the tools of a new system. Construction had to be done at home. Registrar George Coleman, who had been building his own student record system all along, worked with Beth Hallstrom (later Schiller), tweaking and tacking on features to make CARS do things it was never designed to do.

That same year the library began making its ancient card catalogue system redundant and obsolete. Since 1976 librarians at Colby, Bates, and Bowdoin had allowed reciprocal book borrowing among faculty and students; in 1980 they began working with the University of Maine to develop a statewide library network. Ohio libraries had been automating and linking catalogues since the late 1960s; by the mid-1970s regional consortia, including one in New England, had formed a national network. Now the Maine college librarians were out looking for $1.5 million to install a computer-automated system that before decade's end would double the number of titles immediately accessible on all of the campuses.

Aside from the growing number of technology firms, colleges constituted the fastest-growing segment of computer users in the country. In 1987 the *Chronicle of Higher Education* listed seventeen colleges where microcomputers were required or even supplied and seven other places, including Colby, where they were "strongly recommended." Some of these colleges worried they had gone overboard and began to retreat. Students were using computers mainly for word processing, and as technology costs began to rise they were reluctant to require students to own "expensive typewriters." There was concern at Colby as well, but by the end of the decade computers were being used in more than half of all courses, and a growing number of them required computer skills beyond the making of words. There was no turning back, even though technology expansion on the Hill carried the extra expense of putting the infrastructure underground. The College bought a mechanical trench-digger and plowed ahead, making intricate subsurface cobwebs of endless miles of conduit and wires. The sods barely healed before they were sliced up to make replacements: from twisted pair, to coaxial cable, and then to fiber optics. (Only in the next decade, when most of the latest wiring was safely planted, was there talk of going wireless.)

The full force of the Internet did not come until the next decade, but its promise had been evident since 1985 when Steve Case unveiled the service America Online. In 1989 Tim Berners-Lee invented the World Wide Web while working at CERN, the European partical physics laboratory. Four years later Longstaff, by now chair of a permanent computer committee, worked with the computer center staff to create Colby's first Internet pages to support his archaeological research.[36] Anestes Fotiades '89 soon became the College's "Webmaster," and by 1998 Colby's Web site exceeded 30,000 pages served to a worldwide audience.

In ten years, the College budget for computers, related equipment, and salaries had jumped from $80,450 (1979–80) to $1,261,465 (1989–90). The support staff had grown from two to thirteen, and director Ray Phillips was able to report that almost every faculty member and fully a third of students had their own microcomputers—more than a thousand. Each one of the small machines had the same power as the mainframe computer that had served all members of the campus a mere eight years before.

WORLDVIEW

"Globalization" was a word in vogue. The end of the cold war and the rush of new technology brought an era of unmatched political and economic interdependence among nations; at home expanding minority populations were making the world seem smaller still. New college graduates were entering neighborhoods and workplaces vastly different from those their parents had known. Educators adjusted policies and programs to make them ready. Lessons were offered both in and out of class. The campus stood with the president to fight racism halfway around the globe, and foreign study opportunities were expanded to satisfy a growing student hunger to see the world. On the campus, a vow was made to make the racial and ethnic enrollment of entering classes more closely mirror the changing population of the country. It was an uphill struggle.

Colby was not immune to the prejudice that had triggered unrest and embarrassment on college campuses for years. On the weekend of Bill Cotter's inau-

---

36. John Beaulieu '89 is believed to be the first to offer a computer bulletin board in Maine. In 1988 he began using a telephone modem to connect his Mac-based system with other computers.

guration someone scrawled "KKK" on a wall of the library. The ugly sign may even have been directed at him. His well-studied résumé was replete with evidence of his work for social justice, and his public pronouncements made clear his commitment to broader campus diversity.

Even when students behaved themselves, the general climate did not favor more diversity. The national battle for equality had long been out of the headlines, and there was a vacuum of leadership at the top. President Ronald Reagan, first elected in 1980, opposed the Equal Rights Amendment and turned a deaf ear to the demands of civil rights proponents. Local support was thin as well. As the admissions bar kept rising, the number of enrolled area students went down.[37] Although it wasn't true, many thought that accepting more minorities would result in lost places for others. In fact, the minority community hadn't yet taken many places at all. Ten years had passed since black students occupied the chapel demanding that their numbers increase. When the 1980s began, Colby's ALANA[38] enrollment stood at an anemic forty-nine in a student body of 1,660 (only 2.9 percent). The newest freshman class had no black Americans at all. Only eight were in the upper classes.

The renewed commitment was not driven by guilt. Colby had never discriminated. Instead, Cotter said colleges had a "national obligation to help empower minority youth" and "a strong self-interest in providing each student the wonderfully enriching encounters . . . with those whose backgrounds are different from our own." The effort was also driven by simple reality. By the end of the decade minorities were set to dominate the nation's largest public high schools (72 percent in Boston) and to keep growing. Through the 1980s the U.S. population would grow by 72 million. Whites would constitute barely 6 percent of the increase. The greatest jump would be among Asians (107 percent), followed by Hispanics (53 percent), and African Americans (13 percent). Standing still on the admissions front would amount to falling behind.

The board led the way, setting admissions goals that would match the student body with the racial mix of the nation's new college-going population. Most on the campus agreed, but the work to create a more inclusive and inviting campus climate was still plagued by displays of racism. The hateful incidents (always the work of one or two; never a group) would invariably be followed by reinvigorated efforts to educate, although most of the preaching was to the choir. One generation of students would no more than complete their

37. Maine students constituted barely 10 percent of the class that entered in 1980, the lowest percentage ever.

38. African American, Latin American, Asian American, Native American.

tolerance lessons when a new class of freshmen, nearly a third of the resident population, would arrive with their baggage of ignorance and racism.

The academic year 1983–84 was devoted to "Celebrating Diversity and Confronting Intolerance." Academic departments and student groups mounted lectures and programs centered on the theme. Seelye Bixler's beloved book of the year program, dormant for a decade, had been resurrected the year before with Garry Wills's *The Kennedy Imprisonment.* The next theme-year book, assigned to entering freshmen and encouraged reading for everyone, was *Hunger of Memory,* the autobiographical account of Richard Rodriguez's childhood in an immigrant home. Thereafter, the annual book became a device for enlightenment on the broad topic of minority issues. The choice of each book included the caveat that the author had to come to the campus and speak. Although generally successful, the scheme closed options on much of the world's great literature whose authors had not only chosen different topics but were also decidedly dead.

Rodriguez was but one of a number of the year's lecturers that included *Roots* author Alex Haley; former chair of the Equal Employment Opportunity Commission and newly elected Washington, D.C., congressional delegate Eleanor Holmes Norton; and well-known black activist Angela Davis. The Davis appearance brought howls from those who thought the College had jumped the limits of free speech. An avowed revolutionary, Davis was at the time the Communist Party candidate for vice president. The author of *Women, Race, and Class* told an overflowing audience that the women's movement and the fight for civil rights were often tied together. She called for Reagan's defeat in the fall elections. Davis was not the only campus speaker to cause a stir. The Watergate ex-con G. Gordon Liddy spoke in 1984. Abbie Hoffman and Jerry Rubin, founders of the radical 1960s Youth International Party, debated in 1985. Hoffman was still a Yippie. Rubin, no longer antiestablishment, brandished his American Express Card. A year later Timothy Leary, the former director of the Psychedelic Research Project at Harvard and an LSD advocate, gave what most found an uninspired lecture. Students thought perhaps he was still on drugs.

The decade marked the beginning of the celebrated national clash between free speech and multiculturalism, when the new pejorative "politically correct" (PC) first began to appear. The ensuing war over words was prompted by many new initiatives, most of them prominent on the college campuses: affirmative action in employment and admissions, multiculturalism in the classroom, and the changing vocabulary used to define minority groups. Colby tested on every front. Even the matter of selecting a name for the yearlong diversity and tolerance theme was contentious. The meaning of "diversity" applied along the full range of race, class, religion, and gender. It wasn't always clear what group was being talked about. A special Mayflower Hill Scholars financial aid program, established in 1981, recognized the minority status of some Maine students, who were by now culturally as far from home as black students from the Bronx. The word "tolerance," with its minimalist inference, was inadequate for those who preferred something more ambitious, like "embrace."

Even the attempt to change the erroneous name of the College magazine raised the specter of PC. When the magazine was first published in 1911, editor and librarian Charles Chipman had named it the *Alumnus,* the Latin word for a male graduate. He ought to have known better. The alumni body was already filled with women. If any of them objected, there is no record of it, and a succession of later feminist fighters had bigger fish to fry. It was a man who finally complained. In 1986 Perley Leighton '43 wrote the editor, Lane Fisher, wondering why there had been no "alumnae uprising." Former editor Ian Robertson '51 wrote a letter for the next issue, saying he was embarrassed and urging the name be changed "right off."

Leighton should not have been surprised. The name had set in, and moreover, the campus had not been brushed up on its Latin since the days of the Old Roman, Judy Taylor. Not so fast. A handful of alumni leaders, including a few trustees, balked, claiming the editor was caving in to political correctness. The *Alumnus* name had been good enough for seventy-five years, and besides, there had been enough changes (fraternities) to the old place already. A 1987 survey of magazine readers showed that most didn't care about the name. Only five percent said to change it. Never mind. It wasn't "political" correctness so much as it was simple correctness. With the approval of the development committee of the board, editor Robert Gillespie brought out the *Colby* magazine in the spring of 1988. The word *alumnus* was not in sight, and that fall, the board amended the College by-laws to eliminate all gender-specific (he, him, his) language.

In 1986 Cotter greeted the incoming freshmen by spelling out where the College stood:

we stand today for diversity, without which we become parochial; for tolerance of varied lifestyles and beliefs, without which we become mean-spirited; and for the protection of every individual against discrimination on account of race, ethnic origin, religion, sex, sexual orientation, physical handicap, or political belief.

His mantra (thereafter included in the annual catalogue and *Student Handbook*), coupled with the closing of fraternities and the accompanying new standard of opening all opportunities to all students, emboldened even the most reticent. Colby's gay and lesbian students had a small organization as early as 1974 when seniors Nancy Snow Littlefield and Barbara Badger (later Euan Bear) formed The Bridge. In 1988, with its acceptance slowly growing, The Bridge sponsored the first BGLAD[39] Awareness Week. The bravest students wore yellow ribbons in support. Among the handful of faculty and staff whom the students could adopt as models, none was more popular than the far-out-of-the-closet gay manager of the switchboard and student post office, Allen LaPan. In the 1980s he had only just begun a sideline career of service, using wisdom and warmth (and outrageous humor) to reassure the uncertain and cure the homophobes.

Although numbers were only part of the equation, by the end of the decade there were forty-two minority freshmen (including ten African Americans) in the entering class. New minor courses of study had been launched in both African American and women's studies. Still, exhibits of prejudice, diversity's hateful alter ego, often accompanied the gains. In January 1988 someone burned a cross near the Arey Building, marring the Martin Luther King Jr. Day observance; the following winter the campus was horrified when racial epithets were shouted in the heat of a home men's basketball game. That spring Cotter launched a task force on racism that, among other things, quickly arranged a week of "racial awareness days" that included a rally, a march of some eight hundred faculty and students to an all-campus convocation, and roundtable dinner discussions.

All the talk of human rights and the importance of diversity slowly raised the general level of awareness and concern. Students began to say the campus was in a protected "bubble," insulated from a world where the struggle for justice carried life-or-death consequences. By 1985, nowhere on earth was the fight for racial justice more apparent than in the Republic of South Africa. Objections to the apartheid policies of the white Afrikaner government had been fermenting for a long time. Many believed the only peaceful weapon against the repression of the majority blacks was the almighty American dollar.

39. Bisexuals, Gays, and Lesbians Against Discrimination.

In 1977, the Reverend Leon Sullivan, a black member of the General Motors board of directors, had developed the "Sullivan Principles," calling on American multinational corporations to train and pay whites and nonwhites equally and insisting on a climate of racial tolerance in the workplace. In his final year at Colby, Strider had created the Committee on Investment Responsibility of faculty, students, and administrators; on the committee's recommendation the College became one of the first to subscribe to Sullivan's principles. In September 1980 the College divested more than $750,000 in stock owned by noncompliant companies. Broadening participation in the principles brought positive changes: by 1982 black workers had organized and work conditions had improved. Yet despite the gains the overarching system of oppression by the white government was barely affected.

The new Colby president was a recognized expert on African politics, and anti-apartheid activism remained in his portfolio when he came to Waterville. Cotter continued as a member of the board of the Africa American Institute, and served on the National Council of the South African Education Project.[40] He wrote and spoke frequently about African politics and the crisis in South Africa, always with the caveat that his views were personal and separate from either Colby or the AAI. Speaking in Pennsylvania in 1982 at a Yale University–sponsored conference attended by executives of some sixty U.S. corporations, Cotter faulted the U.S. government, not only for "doing nothing" to help fight apartheid, but also perhaps even working against reform. The Reagan administration had relaxed export controls, and Cotter feared the arms being shipped to South Africa would be turned on black protestors. "Change is inevitable," he said, "whether through violent revolution or peaceful negotiations. The question is, will change occur fast enough to avoid a holocaust?"

The long-serving chair of Colby's Investment Responsibility Committee was Thomas Tietenberg (economics), who knew a thing or two about the power of economic investment in shaping public policy. Trustees followed the lead of his committee in making divestment decisions, and by 1985 Colby had sold shares worth nearly $3 million in nine companies that had failed the Sullivan test. Fifty more companies were on a watch list. Although the number of participating colleges grew, South African authorities remained intransigent, and violence continued.[41] In the fall of 1985 Tietenberg's committee called for

40. The project had by then brought nearly three hundred black South Africans to study in the United States, including three to Colby.

41. At the time Peace Corps alumnus Robert Gelbard '64, (honorary LL.D. 2002) was the U.S. State Department's director of southern African affairs.

an open campus meeting to discuss next steps. Cotter announced the meeting at the opening assembly for freshmen and said the time had come to consider whether partial divestment was an adequate response. In October, in a near unanimous vote, the faculty called on trustees to immediately divest all of the College's assets in corporations and banks with holdings in South Africa.

An anti-apartheid rally held in the week before the trustee meetings drew more than four hundred people who stood for nearly two hours to hear dozens of speakers. Veteran observers of campus rallies and protests were amused to see the president of the College standing on the library steps beneath a banner proclaiming "Power to the People," and making a lawyerly, measured case for social change. The crowd loved it.

Cotter was not so much tempting an uprising as he was risking some of the goodwill he had built. Most faculty and students agreed with him on the divestment question, but there were others, including members of the board, who were not inclined to include social causes in the formula for making investment decisions. The College's endowment stood at just over $40 million, some 15 percent of which was at stake in the apartheid discussions. Colby's portfolio was small in comparison to its elite competitors and, to a greater extent than most, endowment earnings were needed to moderate tuition charges. Faced with a divestment decision, fiscal conservatives worried about the "slippery slope." If they divested in South Africa, what was next? Tobacco companies? Environmental polluters? (A 1971 Student Government request to divest General Motors stock had been rejected out of hand.)

Cotter said the precedent had already been set with the 1978 signing of the principles. Moreover, internal U.S. social ills could be addressed in other ways. The problem in South Africa was unique and urgent. Divestment might be the only way to avoid a revolution. Trustees held open hearings before they voted. More than sixty people testified, most of them in favor of immediate, full divestment. In the end, the board voted 20 to 0, with two abstaining, to take a more moderate course. It set a divestment deadline for spring 1987, a time frame recommended by the Reverend Sullivan and the general secretary of the South African Council of Churches, Desmond Tutu. If the dismantling of apartheid did not begin by then, trustees said, the College would fully divest. In the meantime, decisions would be made on a company-by-company basis.

Following the trustee decision, Cotter joined fifteen other American educators and African scholars in calling on the giant retirement fund firm TIAA to join the boycott and "help end our unwilling support of apartheid." Two weeks later TIAA said it would file shareholder resolutions in favor of the principles at the annual meetings of targeted portfolio companies. By 1986, eighty-one American colleges and universities had divested more than $315 million. A year later, on the Sullivan-Tutu deadline, Colby trustees determined that insufficient progress had been made toward ending apartheid. Unanimously and without debate it resolved to get rid of all South African holdings, worth some $6.5 million, by December 31. The divestment strategy eventually worked. There was never wholesale bloodshed and no coup d'état. Free elections were first held in 1994, and South Africa quickly became one of the most stable democracies on the continent.[42]

Even as students on the Hill were learning about international affairs, increasing numbers were getting to see the world for themselves. It was all part of the plan. Cotter privately wished for a mandatory national Peace Corps–like program requiring a year of foreign or domestic public service between high school and college. It would, he said, provide much needed social work around the world and at the same time elevate the general maturity level of the campuses. He settled instead for pressing his dream that the experience of every Colby student would include foreign study.[43]

Small numbers of students had been hitching rides on other colleges' study abroad programs for years. By 1980 there were students joining the Associated Kyoto Program at Doshisha University in Japan and at Manchester College in Oxford, England. Colby's first full junior year program of its own had begun in 1970 when Jean Bundy (French) took thirty students aboard the S.S. *France* to study at the Université de Caen, near Normandy. The program withered and was restructured and renewed in 1980 under Arthur Greenspan (French), in a collaborative effort with Washington University in Saint Louis. It was a success. Students returned with tales of worthy experiences and high adventure, and the demand for foreign study opportunities increased. Two more JYA offerings were added in 1985, when Francisco Cauz (Spanish) joined Colby with Washington University to begin a satellite school at the University of Salamanca in Spain and Dan Cohen '75 (philosophy) led a new program at

42. In October 1993, Colby was among the first to respond to a plea to investors from African National Congress president Nelson Mandela "to remove immediately all South Africa related constraints in the investment choices by portfolio managers."

43. Michael Metcalf '68 was at the time bent on seeing the entire world at once. The former Air Force pilot was a schoolteacher at Hazen Union High School in Hardwick, Vermont. In 1985 he became one of ten finalists among eleven thousand teachers who applied to fly in the *Challenger* as the first civilian in space. In the final days of the selection process his stomach objected to the flight simulator and he was eliminated. The National Aeronautics and Space Administration (NASA) chose Concord, New Hampshire, teacher Christa McAuliffe instead.

University College in Cork, Ireland. New half-year programs included a London program offering exposure to British theater.

By decade's end, there were additional programs designed especially for students, including entering freshmen, wanting or needing intense language instruction. Henry Holland (Spanish) had opened a school in Cuernavaca, Mexico, in 1982, and quickly forged close ties with the affiliate Center for Bilingual Multicultural Studies. In 1985 the Cotters traveled to Cuernavaca to help dedicate a new library building, honoring Holland and named for Colby. That same year Bundy began a French program in Dijon and Hubert Kueter (German), one in Lübeck. A year later Charles Ferguson (Italian) opened a Colby program in Florence. Students were given a semester's credit and certified as having completed their foreign language requirement. Many who thought total immersion would be an expedient way to be rid of the onerous requirement found themselves eagerly enrolling in advanced language courses when they returned.

Yet Colby-sponsored offerings only scratched the surface. By now the College was inviting students to sign on with the Council on International Educational Exchange in the People's Republic of China, the Intercollegiate Sri Lanka Education Consortium, and a cooperative program in the Soviet Union. Arrangements were in place for student enrollment at most British universities, and the College had blessed programs operated by other American colleges in Austria, Germany, Italy, and Canada. For scientists, Colby joined the West Indies Laboratory College Association, the Williams College Mystic Seaport Program, and Boston University's Sea Semester. Harold Pestana conducted a geological Jan Plan in Bermuda. Study in Washington, D.C., was available through Colby's own program and various Washington Semester offerings organized by American University. (Certainly not foreign study, although it may have seemed like it.)

Student concern about the world wasn't all focused on distant shores. The so-called Me Generation was serious about giving to others. Perrin Boyd '86 was the first to coordinate a comprehensive volunteer effort, spending her 1986 Jan Plan identifying groups of greater Waterville agencies needing help. Hundreds took assignments from a new Colby Volunteer Center. Some stayed on campus during vacation breaks to work. Beneficiaries included the full range of local help enterprises, from the soup kitchen at Sacred Heart Church to the Child Care Center at the Congregational Church, and from the Rape Crisis Center to the Salvation Army.

The balance between foreign students on the Hill—thirty-nine from eight countries in 1989—and Colby students studying abroad quickly became lopsided. At the turn of the decade fully 20 percent of Colby graduates were having some sort of foreign study experience.[44] The large numbers brought both surprises and challenges. Faculty program directors found themselves training on the job as deans on the satellite campuses, handling student housing, counseling, advising, discipline, and security as well as teaching. News of the Mexico earthquakes in September 1985 caused concern for the safety of Holland and his troop of forty-four. In the third round of calls to anxious parents, the home dean's office was able to report that Cuernavaca had escaped damage. A year later terrorist threats to Americans in Paris prompted Greenspan to move his thirty charges out of the city and back to the program's base in the Normandy countryside.

There were curious adjustments on the Hill as well. Each fall brought new wonder at where the junior class had gone. Members who went away were not available for the leadership positions in clubs, organizations, and athletics that they had once dominated. Underclass students ruled. Moreover, when students who had seen the "real world" returned to the Hill they were often disinclined to live in the sophomoric dormitories. The comings and goings of students wreaked havoc in the matter of counting beds on the Hill. The true annual enrollment outdistanced the campus population by the number of those who were earning credit elsewhere. In making study plans, students dithered as students do: too many choices, too much paperwork, and too little time. Deadlines helped a little. Otherwise, it was left to housing dean Paul Johnston to keep the campus beds filled. His system used little of the new technology. He called up each of the ditherers and then hand-counted every Colby student, name by name.

FITNESS CRAZY

The nation was nuts about sports. Credit or blame—depending on who got asked on a weekend afternoon—belonged to television. Colby students were not just watching. Half of them were varsity athletes and most of the rest were working to stay in shape. A nationwide fitness craze had delivered waves of weight-conscious calorie-counters who bought running shoes and Gore-Tex clothing at L.L. Bean, turned nearby roads into congested jogging loops, and demanded more salads in the dining halls.

44. Within ten years the number of students studying abroad would jump to 80 percent, one of the highest foreign study participation rates in the country.

Aerobics were in. Male athletes, once sole proprietors of the scant exercise equipment at the gym, were asked to share, and still there wasn't enough. Board chair Ridge Bullock gave a set of Nautilus machines to the nonathletes and joked about his rotund figure at the 1987 dedication at Mary Low. Intercollegiate athletes and fans were by now scattered in twenty-seven team directions, and there were more stellar individual performers than ever before. The decade produced thirty-two first-team All-Americans.[45] Beyond the teams there were nine athletic clubs, an intramural program with more than one thousand participants, all those pesky PE classes, and abundant recreational activities, including a booming outing club and its marvelous coed woodsmen's division.

The fitness obsession helped settle some old health concerns and raised new ones. Anorexia and bulimia, long-hidden diseases on the campuses, were finally exposed, but the cure-defying illnesses were already epidemic. Other things stayed the same. Alcohol abuse, the most public of the campus health problems, only appeared worse. In order to keep federal highway funds, Maine raised the legal drinking age to twenty-one in 1985, making scofflaws of those who had been drinking all along and doing little to stem the tide of beer flowing up the Hill. The state cracked down, increasing its staff of inspectors from three to seventeen, and assigning one of them to the troublesome local area full-time. Students enjoyed playing cat and mouse with her, but she did a brisk business handing out citations, making a dozen or so arrests during a notorious Winter Carnival weekend in 1987.

On the never-legal side, there was marijuana aplenty, and even more exotic things. For those who went looking, the amphetamine Ecstasy and hallucinogenic "mushrooms" were most popular. Despite a national rise in illegal drug use, Colby went in the other direction. Fitness and drugs did not mix. Whether they paid attention to Nancy Reagan or not, most just said no. When the president declared his war on drugs, Secretary of Education William Bennett asked college presidents to help enforce the ban. Cotter replied tartly that he was not a cop. "Students are told what the laws are, and they are expected to abide by them," he said. "Parents don't arrest their children and put them in

45. Basketball: Kaye Cross, Harland Storey, Therese Langlois, Matt Hummel, and Matt Hancock. Cross-country: Kelly Dodge, Rob Edson, Karen Boomer, Jill Vollweiler, and Todd Coffin. Ice hockey: Walter Edwards and Vin Paolucci. Lacrosse: Emily Batchelder, Kevin Plummer, and Margaret Mauran. Soccer: Mark Burke. Swimming: Sally White. Track: Todd Coffin, Terrie Hanna, Kristen Johnson, Eleanor Campbell, Tom Pickering, Kevin Farley, Kristin Hoitt, Heidi Irving, Robin Blanchard, Mike Misner, Mark Pagnano, Tracey Morrow, Bill Derry, Debra MacWalter, and Jill Vollweiler.

jail, and we don't either." Even so, he asked the deans to step up alcohol and drug education programs.

> The booze battle had been going on since the beginning. It brought down the first president, straitlaced Jeremiah Chaplin, and in 1887 President George Dana Boardman Pepper had to deal with a prolonged incident as reported in the *Echo:* "Cider has been just as free as water this fall. It only required a stolen wagon, a hired horse and a dark night for the sophomores to import a 43-gallon cask of the apple juice. It was sampled on the afternoon of the freshman-sophomore ball game, and was found to be potent. Certain seniors showed that they know how to drink cider, even if they are members of the Good Templars. Cider drunks and Indian war dances were in order for a number of nights, till at last the cask ran dry and consumed itself in a bonfire."

The most remarkable intercollegiate teams of the decade were among the oldest. Near homeless track and cross-country squads took several strides forward in 1980 with the opening of a campus cross-country trail system, the gift of trustee Levin H. Campbell and his wife, Eleanor, parents of Eleanor '81. Two miles of paths in the Perkins Arboretum on the east side of campus provided regulation courses for cross-country running (3.1 miles for women, 5 miles for men) and cross-country skiing (7.5k for women, 15k for men). In 1988 Harold and Bibby ('38) Alfond improved the lot of runners by replacing the crumbling forty-year-old cinder oval at Seaverns Field with an eight-lane all-weather synthetic track, the first in Maine. The trails and track were instant hits, not only with student athletes but also with folks from town who, by the hundreds, were up in the early morning to their turns as walkers.

The Campbell trails had barely opened when a trio of All-Americans set them ablaze. The cross-country team won the NESCAC title in 1981, when Kelly Dodge '83 became Colby's first All-American runner. Robert Edson was the second a year later, and Todd Coffin '83 joined them in his senior year after winning the 3,000-meter steeplechase to become Colby's first modern-day individual national champion in any sport. Coffin was Maine cross-country and

46. Dodge joined the development staff in 1999 and became director of annual giving. Coffin replaced his mentor Wescott as coach of men's cross-country and track and field in 2004.

3,000-meter champ as well.[46] The team was a conference champion again in 1987. Under Rick Bell, women's track won three NESCAC titles before 1984, when it went 11 for 1, taking both NESCAC and ECAC crowns. Debbie Aitkin became the first woman coach in 1985 and quickly gave the women a tradition as rich as the men's. Her 1986 cross-country squad was one of the nation's best, taking first in the NCAA New England championships; the 1989–90 team won the New England title when runner Jill Vollweiler '90 became the team's first All-American, taking the honor twice more in track.

In winter, men's basketball regained center stage. Fans who had shifted to the ice in the era of hockey dominance returned to the warm gym to watch coach Dick Whitmore and a succession of outstanding teams. All-American Harland Storey '85 led the 1984–85 squad to a 22–3 season, finishing second in the nation, the highest-ranked Colby team ever. The 1988 team went all the way to the ECAC championship game before losing to Amherst in the final. Another All-American, Matt Hancock '90, obliterated the career-scoring mark with 2,678 points on the way to becoming the country's highest scorer and national player of the year in his final season. Whitmore's son Kevin '91 joined Hancock and the All-American team in 1989–90, when for the first time the Mules were ECAC champs.[47]

Patricia Valavanis '80 brought women's basketball to prominence in a hurry, collecting a dozen team records while becoming the first 1,000-point scorer. A follow-up star, Kaye Cross '84, led coach Gene DeLorenzo's team to a 23–4 season in 1981–82, the best ever. From 1983 to 1985 the team won back-to-back conference titles. Cross, a sophomore and junior Academic All-American, bumped the career scoring mark to 1,452. Despite their successes, the women did not play for packed houses.[48] Cross said that for some the concept of excellence in women's athletics was still startling. It was true. Many viewed women's athletics as merely meeting the obligations of Title IX.

With half the students playing so many sports, there were fewer left to sit and watch. Although athletic interests were more intense, the focus of fans was

47. The 1988 semifinal against Wesleyan was played at home. Extra bleachers were installed and a record crowd of some four thousand watched as Nick Childs '90 hit a long baseline game-winner in the final seconds. Fans swarmed the court. The college president led the way, headed for the exuberant coach. The two met at midcourt. Whitmore, a bear of a man, swept Cotter into the air. The sight of the twirling president, legs dangling in midair, was as indelible as the buzzer-beater moments before.

48. With the exception of men's basketball, there were no packed houses at all. In 1986 Colby stopped selling tickets for regular season sporting events. The NCAA required gate audits and the auditing cost of $2,000 exceeded annual gate receipts in all sports.

shifting, most noticeably in the fall, when soccer routinely outdrew football. Neither soccer team won a championship, but spectators still flocked to watch the exciting play. Mark Serdjenian's men's team had the best player Colby had ever seen, three-time All-American Mark Burke '86.

New athletic interests extended even to the matter of the mascot. Some began to agitate to replace the white mule with the majestic moose. In 1983 *Echo* coeditors Rick Manley '83 and Carla Thompson '85 editorialized for the switch, calling the native moose both "intelligent and self-procreating." The Save-the-Mule federation called it nonsense. That summer, omenlike, a cow moose visited the lawn of the President's House. In the fall Maine voted to have an open season on the animal. (The hardest part of shooting one was getting a license.) There was some name-calling. Moose pushers called mules "stupid." The College physician, Clarence Dore '39, said moose weren't all that bright either, as he had shot one and eight others stood around to watch him clean it. The next year a fitness moose joined student joggers on the three-mile loop. The moose campaign continued through the decade. In early 1990 the *Echo* and editor M. F. "Chip" Gavin '90 made a last-ditch effort to send the mule packing, but in 1993 the Class of 1943 settled the matter by presenting the College a mule statue and installing it near the athletic center. Moose people applied makeshift antlers once or twice, then surrendered.

As players on the newer teams graduated, the athletic focus of the alumni body spread to the full gamut of sports. Cotter began to carry team summaries when traveling to meetings across the country. Even so, for every alumni inquiry about field hockey, squash, or tennis, there were many more that zeroed in on the fall fate of football. Dick McGee had dropped his coaching assignment in 1979 to devote full time to directing the department. Tom Kopp, who had come from Dartmouth as McGee's assistant the year before, took the job for four seasons before moving on to the admissions department. His replacement, Harold "Chris" Raymond stayed three years and left ignominiously after a 0–8 season in 1985. Catching heat for the recent grim showings, Cotter said he was "committed to a competitive football program" and took the lead in finding a new coach. That same month Lou Holtz left the University of Minnesota. Cotter, who rarely thought anything was impossible, called Holtz in Saint Paul to ask if he might be interested in the Colby job. Holtz politely said he would think about it, but called back three days later to say thanks just the same, but he'd decided to go to Notre Dame.

Colby did better in hiring Tom Austin from nearby Bridgton Academy. Austin and his staff worked nonstop on recruiting, and to compensate for the thin ranks introduced multiple formations on both sides of the line. In 1988, teams began a nine-year stint of winning or sharing (with Bowdoin in 1993) the CBB title.

There were bright moments elsewhere, and more individual stars. The women's tennis team, coached by just-graduated player Beverly Nalbandian '80 (later Beverly Madden, a trustee), took the state title in 1980, the same year women's hockey under coach Bob Elwell '71 had goaltender Stephanie Vrattos '81 to help assemble an eleven-game winning streak. Sara Bunnell '81 led Deborah Pluck's new varsity teams of lacrosse and field hockey to rapid prominence. The women's Nordic and Alpine ski team won the Eastern Intercollegiate Ski Association titles in 1986–87 with coach Jeff Meserve, in 1987–88 with Richard Tonge '78, and again in 1988–89 with Jeff Clark, when both the women and the men were NCAA Division II champs. Gene De Lorenzo made CBB champs of the softball team in 1985 and 1986 and took the baseball team to the finals of the Division III playoffs in 1987. Coach Sid Farr's golf team was one of New England's best in 1989, taking the Maine title.

Many alumni were engaged in the burgeoning sports industry as well. Jan Volk '68 was general manager of the Boston Celtics. Tom Whidden '70 was tactician and crewmember for *Stars and Stripes,* the winning U.S. entry in the 1986 America's Cup races. Ken Nigro '60 was director of public relations for the New York Yankees.

Multisport athletes were mostly a thing of the past at the universities. Small colleges still had a few.[49] Valavanis led in softball as she did in basketball, finishing her career with a 35–4 pitching record and becoming the first Colby athlete, man or woman, to be named scholar-athlete of the year by the Maine Sports Hall of Fame. Bunnell earned a dozen varsity letters as captain of lacrosse, field hockey, and ice hockey. Paul Belanger '81 made eleven in football, basketball, and baseball. James "Jamie" Arsenault '88 was a team captain in the same three sports.

The mushrooming sports culture brought with it the age of specialization.

---

49. The book *The Game of Life* reported that among all athletic participants, multisport male athletes in liberal arts colleges declined from 37 percent in 1951 to 20 percent in 1989. Women remained the same at 27 percent. At Colby the multisport numbers for both men and women slid below the norm.

Coaches, who had always haunted admissions officers for players, were now looking for position players, and there were twenty-seven rosters to fill. Although it wasn't stated, when academic qualifications were met, the elite colleges were giving an admissions edge to accomplished athletes, and hopeful candidates knew they could no longer afford to present themselves as general athletes. Parents caught on. To be noticed, their students needed to stand out in a single sport. From an early age, youngsters began to play the same sport year-round. Sports camps flourished. Little Leaguers got batting coaches. Soccer moms proliferated. Grandfathers got disgusted.

At Colby the craziness pressed the limits of both budgets and patience. Whitmore took over as athletic director in 1987 (even then an anomaly as department head and coach of a major sport) in time to preside over fusses about NESCAC's tough stand on postseason championship play and the skyrocketing cost of athletics. From 1980 to 1990 the athletic budget rose from $384,000 to $1,130,000. Students were demanding more and there was little more to give. The expensive sport of crew, begun as a club in 1984, was beating its oars for varsity status. Volleyball wanted in, too.

Rugby was a different matter. A men's club had been formed in 1975. Women began in 1980. Neither had any interest in varsity status or the restrictions that went with it. The relaxed rugby culture, which included its own form of postgame entertainment, was by the end of the decade attracting more than one hundred students. College physician Clarence Dore was appalled at the lack of training and safety regulations. Maine college presidents cancelled the spring 1986 season to borrow time to insert some rules.

Cotter announced plainly that "the constant expansion of the number of varsity sports and the athletic budget cannot continue," and he appointed a twenty-three-member committee to examine things. Sandy Maisel, perennial chair of the Athletics Advisory Committee, led the group that worked through the spring of 1989 and returned seventeen recommendations. They reaffirmed the College's support of the NESCAC philosophy and rules and set additional, Colby-only, limits. The new rules, approved by the faculty, harnessed the time commitment of athletes (two hours of practice a day, six days a week), and made tests for club teams wanting varsity status. Crew was turned down and volleyball was made to wait as well. Because underground clubs had infested one or two major men's teams, athletes were required to make written promises to their coaches that they would not participate in fraternitylike activities. The committee also called for more women coaches of the women's sports, and recognized the general student thirst for health and fitness by urging invigorated intramurals and a revised physical education program centered on wellness.

In 1988 the College was 175 years old, and Waterville had been a city for a century. The two celebrated birthdays together. Over time the flourishing city had often propped up the struggling college. Now, roles were reversing. Foreign competition was gnawing at Waterville's manufacturing base, and the city was feeling an economic chill. At the same time Colby was winning in the stiff competition for the best students in a diminishing national pool. Application numbers soared and the education world was calling the place "hot."

As Colby's fortunes improved, city leaders were struggling to hang on to what they had. The great industries, wounded in the 1950s by competition from southern states, were being threatened anew, this time by economic forces from abroad. A national tide of bankruptcies, takeovers, buyouts, and mega-mergers had begun. The century-old Wyandotte Worsted mill, which had drawn and sustained hundreds of immigrant families, was already closed, and the giant Kimberly Clark had its eye on Scott Paper, the biggest sustainer of them all. Up the road, officials at the molded pulp–maker Keyes Fibre warned that electricity costs were driving them out of business.

The outlook wasn't any brighter along Main Street. Sterns Department Store, the anchor at the center, closed its doors and empty storefronts multiplied. The post office moved into modern quarters on College Avenue, and the classical old building, once the proud greeter at the top of Main Street, was sold for $112,000 and went mostly vacant. Waterville was becoming a service center, with colleges, hospitals, lawyers, doctors, and all those banks. On weekdays the city's population could quadruple, hiking demands for services even as tax revenues went down. An influx of subsidized housing made it worse. In each budgetmaking season a few licked their chops at all the tax-exempt property. The decline wasn't good for anybody. Colby and Waterville were tied together in more ways than by good feelings and proud histories. The College relied upon a healthy and vital community to entice students and encourage the best teachers to come and make a home.

In 1981 Waterville elected its first woman mayor. Ann G. "Nancy" Hill took office during the worst recession in forty years. Unemployment and interest rates were skyrocketing. (The United States would go from being the world's largest creditor to the biggest debtor in that single decade.) Bright and aggressive, she was well suited to break the gender barrier in a city still deeply political. Hill managed the city through three terms (1982–86) and declined to run again. Thomas Nale, an energetic Republican, took over for 1986–87.

The economy began to improve, and Waterville was building again. There were five hundred new jobs in town, and more housing starts than ever. The electoral pendulum swung back to the Democrats before decade's end, and Waterville elected its second woman mayor, a colorful and hardworking state and local politician, Judy Kany, who served in 1988–89.[50]

> During Nale's term, on April Fool's Day 1987, the Kennebec River left its banks in the worst flooding in a half-century. Damages exceeded $63 million. Many Colby students came back from spring break early to help families and local authorities clean up. Alan Lewis loaned College trucks to the beleaguered Salvation Army. The 233-year-old Fort Halifax, the last wooden blockhouse of its kind, was washed down the river. Stanley Mathieu and Donald Carter, 1957 Colby classmates, were put in charge of the restoration.

In the year of the birthdays, *U.S. News & World Report* used some of the objective measurements urged by Bill Cotter, and Colby finished twenty-first among the nation's best colleges. All such rankings were suspect, but they nevertheless suggested a growing reputation. Behind the headlines, there were more valid affirmations. The ten-year reaccreditation report of the New England Association of Schools and Colleges said the place was "competently managed," and that there was "a sense of pride and pleasure in the school . . . a sense that the College is on the move."

The moving had been going on for some time. The College had first drawn prospective students with its movie-set campus and its place in the middle of the Maine outdoors, and then with the distinctive offerings of independent study and the Jan Plan. Now students were also coming for the international study opportunities, the new residential life program, and leadership in the use of computers. Trumping it all was the appeal of an ever more prominent faculty, and the clear testimony of students who said Colby's very best feature was the supportive friendships of their teachers. Part of the charm was also in the balance between independent study and the old core curriculum. The Jan

50. Hill's husband, Kevin, was a local physician and Colby trustee who led the fight for equal housing leading up to the disassociation with fraternities. Her son, Michael, was graduated in 1986. Kany's husband, Robert, was Colby's director of summer and special programs.

Plan first included mini-courses for regular credit in 1982, and while the change diminished independent study adventures, there were many more student-faculty research partnerships, most notably in the sciences but in the other divisions as well. The one-on-one projects, begun in the 1970s, now multiplied and inspired students to follow their interests into graduate schools.[51]

Beyond their teaching, faculty members were gaining more public notice than ever before. In 1982 Susan Kenney (English) won the prestigious O. Henry Award for her story "Facing Front." Kenney, Peter Harris, and Ira Sadoff were pioneers of what soon became a distinctive creative writing wing of the English department. Students clamored to get in. The arrival of James Boylan in 1988 increased offerings but made the demand even greater.[52]

Students were also queued up for classes in the economics department, cited by *Change* magazine as one of the best among the undergraduate institutions, comparing it with Dartmouth, Amherst, Wellesley, and Williams for "exceptional dedication to teaching." James Meehan was chair. Members included Jan Hogendorn, winner of a Guggenheim Fellowship in 1986; Henry "Hank" Gemery, who would win the Jonathan Hughes Prize for excellence in teaching economic history; and Thomas Tietenberg, already a renowned expert on regulatory reform, including emissions trading in air pollution control. (His book *Environmental and Natural Resource Economics* remained a standard for students in economics and environmental policy.) As president of the Association of Environmental and Resource Economists, he was a frequent government consultant and a source for reporters seeking to translate the arcane theories into popular understanding.

Government department chair Sandy Maisel had lost in the race for the Democratic nomination for Congress in 1978,[53] but the experience and his subsequent books, *From Obscurity to Oblivion* and *Parties and Elections in America: The Electoral Process,* gave him credibility as an expert on congres-

51. A 1986 study conducted by Franklin and Marshall ranked Colby seventy-eighth among the country's 839 four-year private colleges in the number of graduates receiving doctorates, and seventieth in science doctorates.

52. In 2002 Boylan, a successful author and popular teacher, came out as transgendered and took the name Jennifer. The change was a bit of a sensation off the Hill, but faculty colleagues and students were mainly supportive, even nonchalant. Her memoir, *She's Not There: A Life in Two Genders,* was the first best-selling work by a transgendered American. It drew attention to Colby as a place supportive of diversity.

53. Of his congressional bid, Maisel wrote: "If I could honestly think that a young, liberal, Jewish college professor from Buffalo could win a primary and then beat a popular incumbent (David Emery) in Downeast Maine, any level of delusion is possible."

sional elections. His insightful commentary made him a favorite source, and his signature bow tie (and later a fine Stetson hat) added pizzazz. The department also boasted Lee Feigon, a much-quoted China expert, and Cal Mackenzie, whose specialty in public personnel management and the American presidency put him in quadrennial demand as a consultant to presidential staffs and congressional committees. Through the 1970s Mackenzie worked with several commissions, studying the organization and workings of Congress. Now he led a special project on presidential appointments for the National Academy of Public Administration. Senators were seen carrying copies of his book *The Politics of Presidential Appointments* during the contentious confirmation hearings of John Tower as secretary of defense in 1989. Anthony Corrado, a scholar of political campaign financing, joined the department in 1986 and gathered as much ink and airtime as the rest.[54] In 1989 the Council for the Advancement and Support of Education (CASE) named Maisel Maine's first Professor of the Year. Tietenberg took the prize the following year.

Trustees guarded the faculty well, sometimes against their wishes. In 1980, when the board voted to retain the merit pay system, the faculty noisily objected. It didn't matter. Most members were given the regular merit pay anyway, and the result, together with an infusion of new money, helped double the overall average salary from $13,900 to $27,500, in ten years. Trustees scrutinized the tenure policy in 1982, but declined to assign a quota. Who got tenure was more important than how many. As quid pro quo, the faculty took hold of the promotion and tenure process and made it both fair and rigorous.

Faculty Dean Douglas Archibald monitored every new search, pressing for diversity. Nearly half of the decade's new teachers were women. Several were minorities, three were African American. The talent piled up, in quality and in number, and the tenured and tenure-track faculty increased from 112 to 128 in the decade, taking the student-to-faculty ratio down from 12:1 to 10:1.

The effort to improve the number of women faculty got a lift in 1988 when Colby was named as one of fourteen institutions to participate in the Clare Boothe Luce Fund, created under the terms of Luce's will "to encourage women to enter, study, graduate, and teach" in scientific and technological fields where they were historically underrepresented. Colby got $3 million. Luce's only tie to the College was her honorary doctor of letters degree, re-

---

54. There were alumni making headlines in the political arena as well. Class of 1964 classmates, the presidential biographer and commentator Doris (Kearns) Goodwin and the public opinion pollster Peter D. Hart, were always in the news.

ceived in 1941. Many of the 1980s' newcomers, men and women, shaped the face of the faculty for generations of coming students[55]:

Seelye Bixler died in 1985, the day before his ninety-first birthday, but he had lived long enough to see the expansion of student interest and the matching addition of splendid new teachers in his beloved fine arts. The music faculty added four places all at once in 1986 when Cotter twisted arms and scraped for money in order to make the Portland String Quartet affiliate members. An agreement was made for the musicians; Cotter called them a "Maine treasure." Bixler's friend Jeré Abbott, the first associate director of New York's Museum of Modern Art and former museum director at Smith College, left in his estate a $1.8 million endowment for museum acquisitions in 1982. Plans were soon underway for a $3.1 million renovation and expansion of Bixler's building.[56]

By decade's end the catalogue bulged with more than seven hundred courses, a new division of interdisciplinary studies, and several new area concentrations (not quite minors). Although the faculty had expanded, it was hard for members to keep up with all those courses and monitor off-campus and independent study, advise freshmen and majors, and stay apace in their disciplines. In 1986 the annual teaching load was reduced from six courses to five and the student standard of five courses per semester was dropped to four, with the caveat that the scope and intensity of courses would be bolstered to keep the rigor. Although the liberal heart of things did not change, the foreign language requirement was reduced from a four-course series to three. English composition remained, but as a requirement the English literature introductory course was jettisoned.

Many of the adjustments were made to make room for a pilot freshman seminar program, first opened to half of the Class of 1990. Students could

55. Many of those who joined the faculty in the 1980s were later chosen by students as recipients of an annual distinguished teaching award established by the Class of 1993 and named in honor of the never retiring Charles Bassett, the first recipient. They were Cedric Bryant (1994), Robert Weisbrot (1995), David Findlay (1995), Paul Greenwood (1997), James Boylan (2000), Tony Corrado with Dasan Thamattoor (2002), and David Simon (2005). Other recipients were Robert LaFleur (1998), Laurie Osborne (1999), Margaret McFadden (2001), Jeffrey Kasser (2003), and Jonathan White (2004).

56. Teaching facilities for the growing faculty were magnified a bit in 1988 with the construction of the Collins Observatory with its 400-power 14-inch Celestron telescope, the gift of Anthony Cramer '62 in memory of his classmate, Lawrence Walker Collins III. The observatory would become the domain of Murray Campbell, an astrophysicist who began working with students on infrared astronomy in 1981.

choose among four course "clusters," each centered on an interdisciplinary theme and taught by a team of five. Cobbling together grants from the Pew and Mellon foundations and the National Endowment for the Humanities, Archibald made it a worthy experiment, but it was also expensive. In four years the money ran out and the seminars ended.[57]

The mostly conservative students adored their mostly liberal teachers, but in 1987 some on both sides had a falling-out over whether the Central Intelligence Agency should use the offices of the College to recruit seniors. The faculty said no, resolving that "as a result of its illegal incursions into Nicaragua, its role in illegal arms sales, its illegal investigations into the lives of private citizens," the CIA should be banned from campus. Most students took the opposite view, and the division was not surprising. Students were toddlers during the Vietnam War when the CIA was first accused of violating its own charter at home and human rights abroad. Many of the faculty had protested the war, and their disdain for the CIA had not waned.

The confrontation began in October with a "die in" staged during a recruiting visit, followed by a faculty vote calling for a ban of the agency from the offices of career services. The Student Board of Governors promptly adopted a counterresolution that underscored students' concern for freedom of choice. (They were also worried about getting jobs.) The debate lasted until April 1988 when trustees came for their regular meetings a day early in order to attend an open forum and a debate between John Stockwell, a former CIA agent who later criticized the agency, and Admiral Stansfield Turner, CIA director under President Jimmy Carter. The ensuing discussion lasted long into the night, and in the morning the trustees approved a two-page statement that said they had "weighed the very real concerns regarding the CIA against Colby's historic commitment to free speech and freedom of choice for its students" and had concluded, "the latter considerations must prevail." Guidelines accompanying the decision said that any campus group of twenty-five could petition to require a prospective recruiter to hold an open information session prior to conducting interviews.

The nationwide publicity of the Colby-CIA flap prompted Secretary of Education William Bennett to put Colby on a short list of colleges he considered

57. In 1997, with grants from the Christian A. Johnson Endeavor Foundation, a similar semesterlong program in integrated studies was offered to all classes. Students investigate a single era or an aspect of world civilization from the perspective of multiple disciplines.

hostile to conservatives. (Others included Stanford, the University of California at Berkeley, Harvard Law, Dartmouth, Barnard, and the University of Massachusetts.) Bennett bemoaned a "rising tide" of "left-wing intolerance" to conservative views. Cotter fired back. "I have always been offended by the very idea of list-making in the context of such criticism because it allows the critic to violate the very principles he presumes to defend." He explained Colby's Lovejoy tradition and went on to say "since bluntness can be as much a part of the Maine tradition as freedom of expression, let me conclude simply by saying I find Colby's inclusion on your list outrageous."

By 1988 Archibald had led the faculty for two four-year terms, and he returned to full-time teaching. Robert McArthur, a logic professor who eighteen years before had ridden into town in a Volkswagen minibus sporting a "Question Authority" bumper sticker, was put in charge of herding the faculty cats. He had already handled questions of his authority as a stand-in admissions dean following the death of Harry Carroll, and as Archibald's sabbatical replacement in 1985–86. While filling in for Archibald he had rallied the faculty to support the adjustment of teaching and student course loads, and now he wanted to get members to agree on a description of the principal elements of a Colby education. It was no simple task. The assembled faculty—any faculty—can rarely agree on the wording of a single sentence (entire meetings are joyfully spent debating a word or two), and McArthur wanted the endorsement of a full document reflecting the temptingly debatable educational principles of the institution. It worked. In the spring of 1989 the faculty adopted the Colby Plan, a list of ten precepts meant to serve as a guide for students in making course selections and measuring their four-year educational development. It was also expected that the tenets would help graduates frame their postcollege continuing education.

The Colby 2000 Campaign ended in January 1987. Like all the ones before, it was the most ambitious ever. First set at $25 million and hiked to $28.5 million to pay for the new commons plan, at the end it topped $30 million. The endowment, which began the 1980s at $23 million, reached $74 million by decade's end. Board members, many of them dipping twice into their own pockets, gave nearly $5 million of the total. Cotter planted trees near the south steps of the library to honor campaign cochairs Bullock and Pugh.

Cal Mackenzie, who led the drive during the final, hectic year, also returned to the classroom and was replaced in 1988 by Peyton "Randy" Helm, a Yale graduate who came to Colby via the University of Pennsylvania where he had been director of development at the School of Arts and Sciences. Helm took over a staff of a dozen fundraisers, a number soon to burgeon and press on the walls of the Eustis administration building from the basement to the attic. Fundraising on the Hill had once relied mainly on charm and a special ability to call forth institutional loyalty. The presidents, together with Alan Lightner, Ed Turner, Bill Millett, and Sid Farr, were successive stars. Now, development work was big business with most colleges fielding full squads of players, each one a position specialist. Helm, with strategic plans and spreadsheets, was the prodding and cheering manager. Cotter, the essential presence, was the closer.

The Portland String Quartet played at a gala campaign victory in Boston, although there was little time for celebration. Helm had no sooner arrived than trustees approved a series of mini-campaigns, beginning with a two-year, $15 million drive to find money for professorships, programs, scholarships, and unrestricted endowment.

The period between campaigns was a time for Cotter to consider his own future. He was fifty-two and it might have been his last chance to consider a career change. Although he hadn't tested the waters, he had many options. His friend Derek Bok had presided over Harvard for eighteen years, and was talking of retirement. With his success at Colby and his Harvard pedigree, Cotter might easily have been in the inner ring among candidates for the job. Trustees wasted no time in getting his agreement to stay and then voted him a well-earned sabbatical leave. The Cotters spent from November 1989 through March 1990 in London, where he pursued his passion for the law, doing research related to the course he taught in government.

The city's centennial observance was subdued, not like the exuberant birthdays of the past. Colby's 175th anniversary[58] was quiet as well. The grandest moment came January 22, 1988, on the precise anniversary of the granting of

58. All through the decade, Colby wrestled with names: the delicate renaming of the fraternity houses, the premature naming of the Colby 2000 Campaign (which ended a decade before the new millennium), the fuss over politically correct labels in the arena of diversity, and the controversy over renaming of the College magazine. A committee planning the 175th anniversary invited suggestions for its name. Sue Conant Cook '75, director of alumni relations, suggested "Semisemiseptcentennial." It was called the 175th.

the College charter by the Commonwealth of Massachusetts. To the fanfare of trumpets, the 1813 charter presentation was reenacted in the chamber of the old Boston State House. Descendants of Jeremiah Chaplin, Gardner Colby, and Mary Low Carver were there. Massachusetts Representative Peter Forman '80 read a Commonwealth proclamation. Kany read one from Maine. Back on the Hill, when the time came to light the candles on Colby's birthday cake the place seemed quite hot enough without them.

6. THE 1990S

As the 1990s emerged Americans began to take notice that they were not mostly white; and colleges, always the vanguard of social change, worked to build populations that were microcosms of the mixed country at large. Although there was no general agreement on what diversity meant, or even how to talk about it, almost everyone agreed Colby was beginning to have some of it and wanted more. The adjustments were often uncomfortable, and there was always more work to do. First, there was the business of dispatching a troublesome ghost, lingering since the 1980s.

An entire student generation had passed through since fraternities were abolished. Left over were a few clandestine make-believe groups, centered on sports teams. Although the basketball Zeta Psi pretenders had taken amnesty and dissolved in the wake of the 1987 hazing incident, similar groups continued in football (Lambda Chi), hockey (Deke), and soccer (Phi Delta Theta). They had the worst features of the organizations they replaced—hazing and hell-raising—and none of the virtues. Worse, the underground groups were sometimes perpetuated by pressuring fellow athletes whose decisions to join were more often driven by a desire to be accepted as teammates than as brothers. Elsewhere, the self-selection in admissions had produced a majority population that had no use for fraternities at all.

Throughout 1989–90 students trickled into the dean's office complaining of fraternity activity, including late-night marauding in the dormitories. Parents wrote to say the College was violating its "fraternity-free" promise. The faculty urged that the administration "take whatever steps necessary" to uphold the complete fraternity ban, and deans and others had tried, back and front door, to convince athletes of suspect teams that they were on a collision course. The athletic department required team members to sign "no fraternity" pledges, and in early 1989 Dean Earl Smith wrote the football coach, Tom Austin, to say it was "only a matter of time" before the LCAs (Lambda Chi Alphas) were caught, and to warn that there could be no forgiving.[1]

That fall, in addition to making agreements with the athletic department, football and soccer players signed pledges for their coaches as well. The promises were mostly ignored. At the end of the football season the LCA underground group pledged seventeen new members. The undoing came during "hell week," in March 1990. LCA members rented Cambridge Valley Grange 582 in nearby Somerset County, and blindfolded pledges were taken there on two occasions, first for a "vigil" and, on March 17, for an initiation. Grange hall neighbors, accustomed to little more noise than the oohs and aahs of a fine potluck supper, were irritated by the raucous proceedings and called the cops. The responding state police sergeant thought he had come upon a satanic cult. Candles lighted the hall and a cow's head hung on each end of the small stage where several men stood around in their underwear. On the main floor were forty-five or so onlookers. Two mortified chickens scurried among kegs of beer. "Lambda Chi Alpha" was scrawled on the wall. The students politely told the officer it was a fraternity initiation. Relieved that he had not stumbled into the netherworld, he told them to pack up and leave. They returned to Waterville and a local establishment called The Plaza to conclude the initiation with the ritualistic decapitation of the birds.

The next morning the College security director drove to Cambridge and met grange leader, Clara Watson, who was perturbed at being duped by "those polite and well-mannered kids." She offered up a muddy five-page document that had been dropped in the grange parking lot in the hasty retreat the night before. It contained a sophomoric account of the year's fraternity activities and signatures of all seventeen pledges.

It took two weeks to sort things out, and in the meantime the campus screamed for retribution. "If this frat is allowed to go free," the *Echo* fumed, "the student body will have been punished more than the guys who are actually in the damn things." The newspaper said to "throw the book" at them. Dozens of students wrote President Cotter, urging punishment. In the end, on the advice of an ad hoc faculty-student advisory group, twenty-nine sophomores and juniors were suspended for the coming fall term. Seventeen were football players. A full nine played baseball. Nineteen seniors were barred

1. Janice Seitzinger was on sabbatical leave in 1989–90. Smith, her predecessor as dean of students, filled in for the year.

from Commencement. Freshmen were put on probation and assigned public service. Within a week, word spread that the soccer and hockey groups had quietly dissolved.[2]

Lawsuits were never far behind any of the College actions against fraternities, and first in the parade of new plaintiffs were several seniors barred from Commencement. The case went to none other than Superior Court Justice Donald Alexander, by then a veteran adjudicator of fraternity cases. He promptly rejected a request for a temporary restraining order, ruling that the student conduct had "direct and significant" campus impact "detrimental to the College" and that the penalties were nothing more than traditional college discipline, not an issue of civil rights.

The plaintiffs realigned. Represented by the Maine Civil Liberties Union, nineteen students pressed for trial in the more distant Cumberland County Superior Court to permanently enjoin the College from carrying out the discipline. The venue would have escaped the consistent Justice Alexander, but the suspended students asked for an expedited decision; to their chagrin, the case was shifted to Alexander's Androscoggin County court in Lewiston. The August case was brought principally under the Maine Civil Rights Act, asserting Colby had denied students their First Amendment right of free association and expression. The argument might have held water at a public institution, but Alexander ruled that "limiting the right of a private college to impose standards of civility, decorum or participation" would be a "radical departure" from the current law and not suggested anywhere in the short history of Maine's Civil Rights Act. Moreover, he wrote in his denying order, many students had chosen Colby because it did not have fraternities. For the court to authorize fraternity activity at Colby, he said, would "violate the rights of these students to associate with each other and gain an education in a fraternity-free environment."

The squelching of the underground fraternities rekindled the hard feelings of those still bitter about the initial abolition. Robert Livingston (R-Louisiana), chairman of the powerful U.S. House Appropriations Committee and a member of Delta Kappa Epsilon since his undergraduate days at Tulane, wrote

---

2. The Cambridge Valley Grange had not been painted for thirty years, and the $35 rental fees were accumulating in a fund to do the job. In mid-May, Jeffrey Cox '90 led a group of some twenty students who set out to repair both the hall and Colby's damaged reputation in the town of Cambridge (population five hundred). With College-donated equipment and materials, the students spent two days scraping, painting, and sprucing up.

the presidents of Colby, Bowdoin, and Middlebury, saying they were in violation of Title IX and hinting they were risking the federal funds his committee handed out. "Limiting free speech and freedom of association on your campus with a federal taxpayer subsidy should be avoided at all cost," the letter said. Middlebury president John McCardell Jr. fired back, saying that Middlebury did not discriminate (by requiring fraternities to admit women), and challenging Livingston to make his free speech charge public. "If . . . you choose to involve the Congress . . . in the affairs of a private institution that has existed longer than the state you represent, I for one am prepared to let the public decide, at the ballot box, the merits of the case." Cotter's reply was a single paragraph: "as the first male college in New England to admit women, we are strong supporters of equal opportunity and we share your concern that some organizations (perhaps, including many national fraternities) may violate the spirit of Title IX by their exclusion of women."

The renewed fraternity debate also gave fuel to a growing fire of critics who claimed colleges everywhere were preaching a new orthodoxy and were absorbed with political correctness. When a student at Brown University was expelled for yelling insults at minority students, the right wing cried foul. President George Bush (the forty-first) attacked the "new intolerance" on the campuses, and in 1991 Rep. Henry Hyde (R-Illinois) introduced the Collegiate Speech Protection Act that would have withheld federal funds from colleges that forbade racial and sexual harassment. Cotter was president-elect of the National Association of Independent Colleges and Universities (NAICU), and he joined others in a meeting with Hyde, arguing that regulations aimed at stopping harassment would not stifle the free exchange of ideas.[3] The bill withered and died.

Cotter, like many college presidents, took the position that the right of free speech stopped short of directed hatefulness. "People who use words as weapons against others," he said, "should find no shelter at our colleges and universities." Political correctness (PC), he said, was like cholesterol. There were two kinds: good and bad. "If one advocates that members of minority groups be treated equally and with respect," he said, one should wear the PC attack "as a badge of honor." Bad PC comes, he said, "when anyone engages in actions that abridge free speech."

A 1990 report of a Task Force on Women and Gender was a target of the PC

---

3. Cotter was succeeded as NAICU president by Widener University president Robert Bruce '59.

police. Its very first recommendation said "freshmen" should thereafter be called "first-years." Cotter called it bad PC and continued to call them freshmen. The PC debate aside, the report's sixty-eight recommendations included many that broadened the feminist perspectives in the curriculum and improved the safety, classroom climate, and health care for women. Within two years special programs director Joan Sanzenbacher (who already had the extra assignment as equal opportunity employer compliance officer), added the job of director of women's services to her repertoire.

While others jeered at what to them seemed liberalism gone bonkers, many on the campuses said it was simply the newest arm of social change for the better. Cal Mackenzie (government), director of the College's new Public Policy Program, said the "grinding noise" was "nothing more than the awkward way colleges change and progress." In 1993 Cotter debated Robert Peck, legislative counsel of the American Civil Liberties Union, and agreed with Peck that some codes were too broad, but argued that carefully drawn codes that protected individuals from words used to injure in fact broadened the opportunity for free speech and inquiry.[4]

Sensitivity antennas were up everywhere. In 1990, when veteran protestor Ann R. Kist came to speak, males were excluded from the audience. They howled in a protest of their own. What was good for the goose was good for the gander. College authorities agreed and the word went out that everything must be open to everybody.

Critics of the new orthodoxy were wrong in assuming college faculties were as one in their quest to change the world, and wrong as well in believing students were puppets on the strings of those who wanted change. Although

---

4. Colby's free speech regulation, unchanged since 1991, reads: "The right of free speech and the open exchange of ideas and views is essential, especially in a learning environment, and Colby vigorously upholds these freedoms. Similarly, the College is committed to maintaining a community in which persons of all ethnic groups, religious affiliations, and nationalities are welcome. The College will not tolerate racism, harassment, including sexual harassment, or intimidation of any kind; any student found guilty of such actions or of interfering with these goals will be subject to civil prosecution as well as suspension or expulsion from Colby."

a new international studies major (1990) led by Kenneth Rodman (government) was far less controversial than had been the introduction of non-Western studies, in 1991 the faculty debated long and hard before fiddling with graduation requirements and adding one in the broad arena of diversity. It said students must take at least one course related to issues involving two or more subjects including race, class, gender, and non-European cultures. Opponents argued that students were already taking these courses (90 percent were) and that, however noble the notion, delivering these subjects to students ought not to be done by requirement.[5] Dealing with curricular diversity in the more or less civil milieu of faculty discourse was one thing. Managing diversity in the after-class student environment was quite another. Here, a tiny number of students who posted hateful signs or hurled demeaning insults could disrupt the entire campus for days.

Solutions seemed to go in opposite directions. The discourse had to be increased, and at the same time the talk had to soften. The conversation spread to many new venues. In 1990 a campus student chapter of the national Society Organized Against Racism (SOAR) was formed and quickly had one hundred members. Two years later a faculty and staff chapter was added with Pat and Ruth Brancaccio (English) as cochairs. In 1991 Cotter formed and chaired the ad hoc Campus Community Committee, a monthly breakfast lightning rod for discussions with campus leaders and student and faculty representatives from all of the ethnic, racial, and religious groups. The Marson Club Room (gift of Dorothy and David Marson) in the Student Center was reincarnated as the Marson Common Ground, where students could gather to learn about other cultures and share their own. After a year of ruminating, the faculty approved a revision of the class schedule to open a weekday morning slot for community Spotlight Lectures. The resurrection of Bixler's academic convocations featured speakers and performances of general interest.

Even with the new opportunities for dialogue, students said there wasn't enough. In April 1992 some two hundred clogged the lobby and stairwell of Roberts Union leading to upstairs meetings of the board of trustees. A leader explained they were demonstrating frustration and concern about student voices not being heard and things not getting done. Cotter, ever eager for the facts, leaned over the railing and called for an example. Someone from down

5. Effective with the Class of '95, students needed to meet the new diversity requirement, the continuing requirements in English and foreign language, and take one course each in the areas of arts, historical studies, literature, and quantitative reasoning, and two, including a laboratory course, in natural sciences.

below yelled that despite repeated student complaints the Roberts Dining Hall had been out of strawberry jam for a week.

There was more to it than strawberry jam. Since the inception of the Residential Commons, student leadership had become so broad and decentralized that lines of student power were blurred, and the work of the many committees was not being effectively communicated to the general student body.

In the aftermath of the Los Angeles jury verdict in the Rodney King case, and as the student power movement simmered, a poster depicting the beating of King appeared as an advertisement for the annual Senior Art Show. It was intended as a statement of outrage over injustice, but it provoked outrage itself and brought what Cotter called "a storm of revulsion and hurt." Two days later a second poster appeared, this one purposefully using racial and ethnic slurs to test the right of free speech. Even as the campus was absorbing all of this, a faculty victim of sexual harassment, speaking at a rally in support of women's issues, told of her attack and revealed the name of her attacker, a faculty member who had admitted his guilt and was gone from the College. Before the year ended, the president issued an eighteen-point plan designed to "redouble our efforts to build an inclusive and supportive campus community." It expanded the freshman reading assignment to include the whole campus, incorporated material on racism, sexism, and harassment into new faculty orientation, and increased programs on multicultural issues in the dormitories.

The end of the academic year, at least, brought good humor. Comedian Bill Cosby was the speaker at what was at once the coldest (40 degrees) and warmest (Cosby shook the hands of all 462 graduates) Commencement ever.[6] His invitation was bolstered by his friendship with the late civil rights leader Whitney Young, whose grandson, Mark Boles, was a senior.

The Cosby invitation languished for a long time—a *very* long time for Cotter—without an answer. Cotter moved on and invited Georgetown University Professor Madeleine Albright, poised to be the U.S. United Nations ambassador, later President Bill Clinton's secretary of state. Two days later Cosby volunteered. For a moment the College had the potential of two Commencement speakers. Albright graciously understood

6. Angela Toms was recognized as Colby's 20,000th graduate in the College's 175-year history.

and withdrew. She was offered an honorary degree in 1993, but when senior class president Jeff Baron got Senator Robert Dole (R-Kansas) as speaker, Albright wasn't inclined to be upstaged by the country's leading Republican and withdrew. Dole was met with polite protest. Some students and faculty wore pins with a pineapple and a red slash (no Dole), and others wore various ribbons: purple for pro-choice, pink for lesbian and gay rights, green for the environment, blue for laborers, and rainbows for racial tolerance.

By the fall of 1992, diversity conversations had moved into the delicate arena of religion. For a long time Colby had been fully secular. Now, the founding Baptist influence had disappeared and the only official religious trappings were ecumenical. Although the fraternity decision had taken the headlines from the report of the Trustee Commission on Campus Life, the report also included the recommendation that the College have a tripart chaplaincy, with leadership for Protestants, Catholics, and Jews. It was Cotter's idea, and he made it clear that he expected the chaplains to support all world religions on the campus.

Episcopal priest Roland Thorwaldsen was the first non-Baptist College chaplain; after 1980 he was followed by two other Episcopal priests, professor and preacher Thomas Longstaff (philosophy) and, in 1981, the Reverend John Ineson. By 1978 the College had an unofficial Catholic chaplain, the Reverend Paul Coté, assigned and supported by the Diocese of Portland and residing on campus. With the adoption of the commission report, the College appointed three chaplains, the Reverend Ron Morrell of the China Baptist Church, Father Coté, and Rabbi Raymond Krinsky of Beth Israel Synagogue in Waterville. Coté was reassigned and replaced first by the Reverend John Skeehan (1985) and then by the Reverend John Marquis (1989) who with Morrell and Krinsky provided both religious services and counseling, sharing time and space in Lorimer Chapel.

It all went swimmingly until the Commons Presidents Council, in a well-intended gesture, called for cancellation of classes on Yom Kippur. Cotter expressed his approval of the sensitivity, but explained Colby had traditionally maintained neutrality with regard to holidays. Students and faculty could absent themselves from College obligations on their holidays, but classes and activities would not be cancelled. The Student Association jumped into the fray and sent a letter to faculty suggesting exams and papers scheduled due on Yom Kippur be postponed. Most obliged. Some didn't.

Since the 1980s the College had been displaying menorahs along with Christmas decorations and serving matzo during Passover. Beginning in 1993, a dormitory room was left empty to make space for Muslim students to hold Friday prayers. Someone removed the menorah from its place next to a Christmas tree on the library steps; in response a sign was left by the tree, deploring the emphasis on Christianity. One thing led to another, and before long the suggestion was made that the cross come down from the chapel tower. Although the chapel was by turns religious for services and secular for public events, its six hundred seats provided the only midsize venue for major programs and for the new Spotlight Lectures. A few Jewish students and faculty said they were uncomfortable attending these events under the cross of Jesus.[7] It was a good moment to pause, and Cotter formed a multifaith committee to explore the matter of religious symbols. At the same time he asked members to "find a way to honor our historical traditions." In the end, the committee agreed: "Because the cross reflects the recent architectural history of the Mayflower Hill campus and is for many an important symbol, it should not be removed."[8]

Through all the diversity contretemps, Bill Higgins '92 and Karyn Rimas '93, president and vice president of the Student Association, worked to keep lines of communication open and civil. They felt it was about time to get together for something other than demonstrations and debate, and planned a giant outdoor party for Colby's 180th birthday. On February 27, 1993, the granite steps of the library were cleared of snow and ice. Students and faculty gathered shivering in the night, laughing, singing, watching fireworks, and eating frozen cake.

OH, SO HAPPY

Despite the tensions of campus life, students were happy. In fact, it was claimed that they were the happiest in all the land. Maybe they were. After all, they liked their teachers, after-class activities were booming, living spaces were moving upscale, and strawberry jam was back in the dining halls. And all the while, planners were at work setting a course for more improvements and, to pay for them, a fundraising drive with a goal that topped all previous campaigns combined.

7. Someone suggested that the problem could be solved by installing a retractable cross, with folding arms.

8. The chapel bells, installed in 1947, relied on antiquated vacuum tubes for the amplification system that had not worked for several years. John ('52) and Carol Briggs gave new state-of-the-art carillon bells in honor of former dean of men George Nickerson and his wife, Ruth. They soon began to ring Westminster Chimes on the hour, together with recorded music of the alma mater and a selection of songs of many faiths— as well as of the Beatles.

Ridgely Bullock stepped down as chair of the board in 1990, the result of his own urging that bylaws be changed and trustees and board chairs have limited terms. Lawrence Pugh became the twenty-third in line as chair. Pugh, like Bullock, was a perfect fit with Cotter. The two shared a lofty vision for Colby, and each was aggressively committed to seeing it met. When it came to raising money, it was hard to say no to either of them.

There was only a bit of juggling of Cotter's senior team. Vice president Stanley Nicholson, who called himself the "dean of stuff," resigned that year to return home to Montana. Beyond his creative leadership in making budgets fit the aggressive growth, he and his wife, Colleen, had been an integral part of the community, leading orientation trips and, as faculty residents of Goddard-Hodgkins dormitory, advising and entertaining students. Nicholson's successor was a poet and a businessman. Arnold Yasinski held both an English Ph.D. and an M.B.A. and came to Colby from the E. I. Du Pont de Nemours Company. The fifth and longest-serving of the College's administrative vice presidents, he oversaw the construction of more new and renovated College buildings than any of his predecessors.

Among Yasinski's first tasks was to improve the food. Eating had always been first or second on the continuum of strongest student urges and cafeteria food shared a similarly lofty place among their complaints. Following the notion that one way to student contentment was through the stomach, Yasinski teamed with a succession of talented local managers of Seiler's food service (later Sodexho) to improve service and tweak the menus. Students were invited to bring recipes from home and Dana Hall began to offer "fast food." By 1992 a student poll showed a dining service approval rating of 93 percent.

The remaining senior officers stayed in place. By 1993 Bob McArthur had completed two four-year terms as dean of faculty; when local search results failed to please Cotter or the full search committee, McArthur signed on for four more. The only other senior change was in name only. In 1993 Dean of Students Janice Seitzinger married local physician Lawrence Kassman '69, and took his name.

After the Gulf War of 1991 (students tied a yellow ribbon around the library tower), the political focus of after-class activities shifted to the home front. Of

MAYFLOWER HILL

the sixty various student clubs and organizations, many were focused on public service. Jennifer Alfond '92 began the first campuswide recycling effort, gathering volunteers to collect waste paper in the offices and dormitories. The College was soon saving $7,000 a month on dumping fees as tons of paper were trucked to Scott Paper Company's recycling facility in Winslow. In 1992 Tara Estra '94 held a variety show at the local Opera House to raise money for Maine AIDS support organizations. That same year Heather Vultee '93 was recognized by President Bush as the 958th in his 1000 Points of Light program for her work with the Colby Friends program, begun in 1988, matching students with local youngsters in need of mentors.[9]

Concern for community needs covered the broad front and the campus diversity debate surfaced again in March 1994, when members of a new group called Students of Color United for Change overwhelmed a breakfast meeting of the Campus Community Committee and asked that a dormitory be set aside where students could live and support multicultural education. Trustees, still wary of special interest housing in the aftermath of fraternities, charged a committee to have another look at the Commons system "to see how well it supports the increasing diversity of our community." Trustee James Crawford '64 led the investigation. The committee had barely begun its work when Nazi swastikas appeared on walls in several of the buildings, and once again the campus roiled in protest and disgust. More than six hundred students rallied on the library steps. The College subsidized ticket prices for a special showing of the film *Schindler's List*. The hateful incidents detracted from the useful business of creating an improved climate for minority students.

Still and all, things were more sunny than cloudy. In 1994 the *Princeton Review* book, *The Student Access Guide to the Best Colleges,* declared Colby had the happiest students in the entire country. Although deans said it couldn't be proven by the traffic through their offices, the declaration tended to make things even happier. Perception became reality. Even the grumpiest students were warmed at the thought. Happiness was everywhere. "They love their beautiful, secluded campus," the book said. "They love outdoor sports even during the 'frozen tundra' winter months in Maine, and they love their classes." Else-

---

9. Bush left office in 1993 and the following year gave the Colby commencement address as the first presidential guest of the College since Herbert Hoover had spoken at the 1937 Lovejoy Centennial. Kathy McKiernan '90, Cassie O'Neill '91, and David Leavy '92 worked on the campaign of Bush's successor, Bill Clinton, and all three landed jobs at the White House.

where, Colby's name appeared near the top of short lists for having a "beautiful campus," for a faculty that "brings material to life," and for a "great library."
In fact, the happiness was measurable. Admissions applications went up on
one end and the graduation rate went up on the other. In a single year, proud
and happy students bought nine thousand Colby baseball caps from the bookstore.[10]

Although Colby had met the most formidable challenges of the 1980s, victories and happiness were not without cost, nor were future challenges less
daunting. Competition for the best teachers had stiffened, and the new technology increased demands on tight budgets. Always lurking was the need to
maintain and upgrade the infrastructure of a growing physical plant. The
gravest need was for student financial aid. Although the decline in the number of the nation's eighteen-year-olds had bottomed out by 1992, the steady
sharp rises in tuition charges in the midst of a faltering economy put a strain
on the middle class and multiplied the need for financial aid. Two-thirds of all
Colby students now qualified for full or partial grant aid. The concern was
high on Cotter's agenda during his term as president of the NAICU (1992–93),
and as the private college representative on a nine-member federal Commission on Financing Higher Education. He talked about his worry almost everywhere he went.

Preparing for the challenges of the new millennium began at a retreat of
trustees and key administrators in 1990 where the stage was set for a close look
at five key areas: curriculum, diversity, student life, facilities, and financial resources. Across the campus and beyond, more than one hundred students,
faculty, and others worked a full year to map the way into the next century.
Even before the plan was adopted in May 1991 trustees gave the green light to
$5 million in new campus construction. Included was a four-story addition to
the Lovejoy classroom building, a new building for admissions and financial
aid, and a central steam plant.

Planning for the hungry sciences had begun long before. In the late 1980s
Dean McArthur launched an internal study to figure out how the College

---

10. Some measure of extra happiness could be attributed to the new "wellness" graduation requirement, adopted in 1994 and mandated for the Class of 1998. The old
"phys-ed" requirement was modified to include required attendance at a series of ten
evening lectures on "mental, emotional, social, physical, and spiritual fitness," which met
half of the new requirement. The rest came by joining in any of eight lifetime sports activities. The wellness aspect was directed by Melanie Thompson, M.D., the College's first
woman director of the health center.

William R. Cotter, president, 1979–2000

With their wives, the three Colby presidents gather in Boston for a public conversation. William and Linda Cotter, Seelye and Mary Bixler, Robert and Helen Strider, November 1981.

Lawrence Pugh, chair of the Trustee Commission on Campus Life, and chair of the Board, 1991–1999.

Bonfire on Frat Row,
protesting fraternity
closings, January 15, 1984

Cotter speaks at
anti-apartheid rally,
October 1985

Jan Plan at the Hume Center

Dedication of Cotter Union, 1997

Johnson Pond drained for cleaning, 1997

Harold and Bibby Alfond

Ice storm destruction, January 1998

Lorimer Chapel

The Paul J. Schupf Wing for the works of Alex Katz

From the Lunder Wing, Colby Art Museum

Mayflower Hill, 2000

William D. "Bro" Adams, president, 2000–

The new Colby Green, 2005

could improve student interests in sciences, flagging nationally for more than a decade.[11] Also at stake was whether Colby could compete with colleges that had already begun to fill the need with new science buildings and equipment. Although the College's science facilities had been expanded in the 1970s, planners concluded that faculty growth and teaching changes now left Colby "two buildings short." The first modest step came in 1991–92 with a bridge between the Arey and Mudd buildings, providing needed seminar rooms and freeing space for further renovations.

Elsewhere, the admissions staff, expanded to handle a rising tide of applications and to support diversity initiatives, had outgrown its Eustis Building space. In 1991 Peter ('56) and Paula Lunder made the naming gift for the new admissions home, east of Mayflower Hill Drive, mimicking a grand Maine farmhouse with windows of the interviewing offices facing irresistible views of the central mall and the library. The Lunder House was opened in the fall ·of 1992, together with the Keyes-Arey bridge, the Lovejoy annex, and "Phase II" of improvements to the Bixler Center, including a gallery, art and music library, and additional storage space.

The central steam plant was at once the least glamorous and most cost-saving of any facility yet built on the Hill. By the mid-1980s the College was facing a choice: spend $1.5 million rebuilding and expanding the thirteen individual networked boilers or construct a central heating plant. Alan Lewis, director of the Physical Plant Department, wanted a single plant. Lewis, a frugal Yankee, was pained to watch dollars drain through a patchwork of Rube Goldberg boilers and poorly insulated steam lines that kept the overhead grass green all winter.

An engineering study concluded that a new plant would cost $6 million. Yasinski said it was way too much, and Lewis huddled with an old friend and respected Maine engineer, Seth Williams, to rescue his dream. If anyone could find the fat in the proposed plan, Lewis knew it was Williams, retired president of the Fels engineering company in Portland. (Lewis recalled that Williams once turned down a fancy free lunch because he had brought his own bologna sandwich and didn't want to waste it.) Williams concluded that Colby could be its own general contractor and, sparing extra bells and whistles, a plant could be built for $3 million, half the original estimate. It was claimed the new facility would pay for itself in fifteen years with savings that included trimming as much as 20 percent off the annual fuel bill ($360,000 in 1992–

11. The national demand for scientists was expected to exceed supply by 35 percent by the year 2000.

93).[12] Three years and 2,500 feet of new steam lines later, in the heat of August 1993, the new plant fired up, on time and on budget.

Not all of the expansion was accounted for by strategic planning. In 1991 a surprise gift from local physician Alan Hume and his wife, Dorothy, provided the College with a ten-acre satellite campus and, for many students, a new way of looking at the liberal arts. The Humes made their Colby ties through a series of students who, beginning in the early 1980s, lived with them in the summers and "shadowed" him in his surgical practice. Many went on to medical careers. At the same time the couple opened their Sidney lakefront property to the men's and women's club-status crew teams whose rowers found the long, calm waters of Snow Pond (Messalonskee Lake) more agreeable than the large, unpredictable surface of Great Pond, where they had previously practiced. The Humes built them docks, a shell storage building[13] and, with parents of team members, helped purchase much of their equipment. As "godparents" of Colby crew the couple was in large measure responsible for the teams' ability to achieve varsity status in 1993.

In 1990, when the College was having trouble finding satisfactory leadership for the health center, Hume, by then a Colby overseer, came out of retirement to serve a four-year stint as medical director. Their 1991 gift, including 450 feet of shorefront, was later expanded with one hundred more feet on the shore as well as their home, in which they retained life tenancy. Only eight miles distant from the main campus, the new Colby-Hume Center served multiple purposes, including lake-related recreational opportunities for faculty, staff, and students. The visionary and restless doctor soon built a large barn, outfitted it with woodworking equipment, tacked on a double-station forge for metalworking, and began to offer Jan Plans. Just as applied art and music courses provide lifetime enjoyment for students, Hume believed the same was true for learning to work with wood and metal. Lewiston, Maine, attorney Irving Isaacson shared Hume's belief and helped outfit the forges. Deer Isle, Maine, artisan blacksmith Doug Wilson was hired to teach. As students returned to campus with their finished work, it wasn't long before the number of applicants exceeded available January spaces in the shops.

*　　*　　*

12. In fact, the plant was paid for in savings before the end of the century. In addition a co-generation turbine, installed at the plant in 1999 to capture excess steam, makes about 10 percent of the campus electricity needs.

13. The Humes significantly enlarged the building in 1997 and trustees appropriately named it for them.

The mundane matter of financial resources was listed last in the strategic plan, but raising money was key to achieving almost all the rest. Although the endowment had crossed the $100 million mark (1993), Colby's portfolio ranked twenty-third among the top twenty-five colleges in the *U.S. News & World Report* ranking. It was clear that meeting the major goals would require a massive capital campaign, and in 1992, trustee Edson Mitchell '75 was put in charge of developing a campaign "nucleus fund." With the economy beginning to swing upward, there was reason for optimism. The development office reported a record $8.2 million in gifts and pledges for the year 1992–93, and the number of alumni donors topped seven thousand (42 percent).

Marts and Lundy, the firm that had plotted the first capital campaign for the new campus, was hired to suggest a goal for the coming one. Following some scratching of heads, the consultants said the goal should be no more than $75 million. Cotter and Pugh said no. They had bigger ideas and chose what they called "a nice round number" of $100 million. It was, they knew, an ambitious figure that would require donors to dig deeper than ever before. (Cotter recalled that only a few years before he and board chair Bullock traveled to Chicago to ask a potential donor for $5,000.) In fact the giving bar had already been raised in the establishment of named professorships. Colby began the decade with only three fully endowed chairs; in the four years leading up to the campaign, however, six more were added. The seventh, given on the eve of the public campaign, was from Pugh and his wife, Jean (Van Curan) '55, who gave a $1-million endowed professorship in economics and added $100,000 to "pad" the chair with support for the research work of the incumbent. A new standard of giving was firmly set, and before the campaign ended at the beginning of the year 2000, the Pugh gift would be replicated twenty-three times.

As plans were being finalized for a formal announcement of the Plan for Colby campaign, the F. W. Olin Foundation sent word that it would give $6.4 million for a fully equipped science building.[14] Colby had been courting the foundation since Strider's days. In the 1994 round, seventy-nine colleges had applied. Colby was one of three to succeed. The largest single grant the College

---

14. Franklin W. Olin, who played baseball for the professional Washington Statesmen (1884–84), was the founder of a small black powder factory in Alton, Illinois, where Elijah Lovejoy was martyred. The company became the Western Cartridge Company, which after World War I acquired the Winchester Ammunition Company that produced most of the U.S. small arms ammunition during World War II. Olin's oldest son, John, used the profits to build Olin Industries, an early conglomerate. The Winchester Company operated in its original factory, about a mile from the Elijah Lovejoy Memorial.

had ever received boosted the "nucleus fund" of the campaign to $48 million, and the announcement of the giant gift was kept secret to give special impetus to the gala campus campaign kick-off dinner in October. In the spring, scientists gladly surrendered their parking lot in front of the Arey Building so that work on the new Olin Building could begin. The construction marked the beginning of the largest building boom since Colby had moved up the Hill.

ECHO BOOMERS

More numerous than their parents, the children of baby boomers arrived on a tide of prosperity. Demographic and economic chart lines went up at the same time. Raised on video games, MTV, and the computer, echo boomers used the Internet to discover a shrunken and beckoning world. While their own diversity made them more tolerant than their predecessors, they too fought to find cultural harmony. The new media had also made them discerning shoppers, and colleges competed fiercely for their favor. Colby captured more than its fair share, reaching into the far corners of the nation and the world to pluck students from the top rungs of the academic ladder.

The ad hoc group Students of Color United for Change broadened its name to Students United for Change and pressed a number of ideas to meet the needs of minority students. At the core was the request for separate housing that would foster multicultural education. Students of color said they were often overwhelmed on the mostly white campus and wanted a "safe" place to live and a refuge where they could affirm their own identities. The request presented a dilemma. Most students embraced the principle of open housing, established when fraternities were eliminated ten years before. Although the group agreed new housing could be open to anyone, many feared separate places would attract only members of the identified groups. Other colleges had addressed these needs by creating intercultural campus centers, some with separated housing. Bates opened a multicultural center in 1993 but had no separate residences. Bowdoin had African American and Asian "theme" houses.

Members of the Trustee Commission on Special Interest and Multicultural Housing visited eleven colleges and surveyed a dozen more. Reports were mixed. Although most hailed the successes of multicultural centers, many of the campuses with special interest housing privately acknowledged that the separations increased the very racial divisions and tensions they had sought to avoid. The commission and trustees agreed Colby should not have separate housing, but instead have a "common ground" space. Trustees themselves raised

$500,000 toward a $1 million addition to the Student Center. Larry and Jean Pugh made the naming gift, and the Pugh Center opened in the fall of 1996.[15] It included gathering spaces and offices for a dozen student organizations centered on issues of race, culture, religion, sexuality, nationality, and heritage. Students liked it, but the continuing challenge was to have the center seen not simply as headquarters for the separate groups, but as a place for the full student body, rapidly growing in cultural complexity.

While the task of attracting African American students never ended, general campus diversity and Colby's overall attractiveness was expanding. In the three-year period following the declaration of total happiness (1994–96) admissions applications grew 60 percent. Class of 1999 applicants topped four thousand, the most ever, exceeding the previous record set in 1976 by more than three hundred.[16] The following year application numbers hit a record 4,600 for 475 places; and for the first time a majority of entering freshmen came from outside New England.

The broadened geographical reach for students was inevitably paired with a dwindling number of Maine students. Mainers had been in the minority since 1937, but by the mid-1990s Mainers represented barely more than 10 percent of the student body. Still, trustees remained determined to honor the College's roots, and the admissions office continued to give preference to qualified Maine applicants, awarding them nearly a third of the annual scholarship budget. The Maine emphasis was never a hard sell on the campus, where the faculty was quick to testify on behalf of the hardworking and overachieving Maine student. President Cotter said the commitment went beyond an obligation to heritage. A more "selfish" motive, he said, was that "the Maine students are among our most promising and productive academic investments."[17]

The College was not only reaching out; by mid-decade it was also beginning to attract increasing numbers who said Colby was their first choice. Sixty

15. The Student Center could not very well have another center and so its name was changed to the Student Union, leaving the Pugh building as the single center.

16. The 23 percent increase was tops in a survey of thirty-three of the nation's best liberal arts colleges.

17. Over a period of thirteen years, from 1984 to 1997, ten senior class marshals (valedictorians) were from Maine, a number ten times their relative percentage within their classes: Kirsten Wallace, Monmouth, 1984; Carla Thompson, Limestone, and Peter Westervelt, Waterville, 1985; Jennifer Cole, Bangor, 1987; Linda Roberts, Waterville, 1988; Stephen Rand, Gardiner, 1989; Hilda Westervelt, Waterville, 1992; Brittany Ray, Milbridge, 1993; Danielle Jamison, Gardiner, 1994; James Porter, Waterville, 1995; and Heidi Girardin, Waterville, 1997.

percent of the Class of 2000 placed Colby at the top of their list, and nearly three-quarters said the choice was made on the basis of academic reputation. (More than 20 percent said they had been influenced by those pesky college guidebooks.) The greater selectivity brought extra quality. In 1997 the College boasted two Fulbright Scholars (Hyun Jung and Morgan Pecelli, '97), two Udall Scholars (Heather Davidson '99 and Amy Lyons '98), a Goldwater Scholar (William Polkinghorn '99) and a Watson Fellow (Zahid Chaudhary '97). A year later, Polkinghorn, a chemistry major, was named one of thirty-two national Rhodes Scholars, Colby's first since 1978 and sixth ever. Classmate Jennie Oberszan came close to giving Colby two Rhodes seats.

Never mind that Mayflower Hill was where students wanted to be; most had barely settled in when they were looking for other places to go. More than three hundred (18 percent) enrolled in foreign study programs each year. Only Carleton College (20 percent) had more. Including Jan Plan excursions, by graduation nearly 80 percent of Colby students now had international study experience on their résumés. In any given semester two of every ten enrolled students were floating around the world. If they had come home to roost all at once there would never have been enough room. There was barely room anyway.

Even the campus itself seemed to shrink. Twenty years before the catalogue had claimed 1,400 Mayflower Hill acres. Ten years later the official number had dropped to 900. In 1988 Vice President Nicholson proclaimed the actual number as 570 (the number of Heinz varieties, he said, plus a zero). In 1995 Gene Chadbourne of the Physical Plant Department used a computer to determine with some certainty that the contiguous land on the Hill amounts to 714 acres.

Trustees had set the size of the College at 1,500 in 1967 and last affirmed the number in 1972. By 1995 enrollment had crept above 1,800.[18] There were fewer than 1,600 campus beds. More than 150 students were living in town; forty were in temporary spaces on the campus. In January 1996 trustees approved a $16 million, five-year plan to renovate dormitories and dining halls and to

18. The College budget had no separate contingency fund. Instead, at the end of each fiscal year, trustees used revenue from overenrollment for an annual reserve account, assigning its use to physical plant renovations, unforeseen needs, or the endowment.

construct a new residence hall. The 120 added beds would compensate for those lost in the renovation work; because of the enlargement of rooms and addition of lounges, however, the number would never be recovered.

That summer the campus was in a construction uproar. Ducks cowered on the far shore of Johnson's pond and chipmunks sought refuge under desks in the office buildings. The Olin science building was going up and the central mall was being landscaped and replanted. Work was under way on the Pugh Center and another art gallery wing. Bulldozers were making softball, lacrosse, and field hockey fields, and the fence around the football field was coming down. Obsolete boilers and fuel tanks were being yanked out and taken away; and if that wasn't enough, the Waterville Sewerage District was digging trenches up Mayflower Hill for a new pipeline.

Dorms were being renovated two or three at a time, and the projects always included the addition of new technology. Cable television, first received by satellite so students could watch CNN coverage of the 1991 Gulf War at the Student Center, was rapidly coming to the dorms. In 1992 the telephone system tripled with lines to every room. Parents, who for a half-century had been flummoxed by busy hall phones, at last had direct access to their students, or at least to their creative and often indelicate voice answering messages. Residence halls were all on the Ethernet by 1996, when the science division opened a state-of-the-art scientific computer center, a gift of trustee Paul Schupf. There was now "a port for every pillow," and with unlimited access to the World Wide Web, students accounted for a majority of nearly a half-million monthly "hits" on the College Web site. (The most popular campus sites were the dining hall menus.) In the spring of 1998, student elections were entirely "paperless." Jennifer Johnson '98 put the ballot on the Web and 70 percent of students voted, at home and abroad, electing Benjamin Langille '99 president of the Student Association, even though he was at the moment studying in Spain. *Yahoo! Internet Life* magazine again listed Colby as one of the nation's top twenty-five "best wired" colleges and universities. Ray Philips, director of computer services, acknowledged that the notion of teaching "computer literacy" was getting to be as silly as instruction in how to use a telephone. He suggested a better name for his department might be "information services."

In a span of eight days in October 1996, four new facilities were dedicated: the Olin Science Center, the Pugh Center, the Schupf Wing for the Works of Alex Katz, and the Schupf Scientific Computing Center. There were more to come. That same year former board chair and life trustee Robert Anthony and his wife, Katherine, made the naming gift for the first of three buildings in the new dormitory complex. Soon thereafter fellow trustees Schupf and Edson

Mitchell '75 named the other two.[19] The Anthony-Mitchell-Schupf complex took care of students displaced by the massive dormitory renovations but still left 150 living in town, foiling the premise of a residential college and presenting other problems as well. The board and room rebate given to students living off-campus was the topic of endless debate,[20] and many of the in-town apartments affordable for students were substandard and unsafe. Moreover, the off-campus crowd put a strain on town-gown relations by bringing noisy nightlife into neighborhoods that preferred to sleep. Even so, commuters were perfectly happy with the status quo. Many had studied abroad and, having seen Paree or wherever else, were not eager to return to the regulated dormitories, no matter what miracles the renovations had wrought. The solution was to allow the worldly seniors to have their apartments, but to put them on the Hill, and make the College mostly all residential again. Local landlords squawked, and some students were skeptical; but in 1997 trustees elected to build a twenty-two-unit, hundred-bed apartment complex on the hillside above the chapel. Construction began in the spring of 1998 and, with a naming gift from Harold Alfond, the facility was opened in the fall of 1999.

Details of the multiple projects were carefully checked by everyone from physical plant director Alan Lewis to the hard-driving clerk-of-the-works Pat Mullen, and from the bill-payer Arnie Yasinski to Cotter, who carried a notepad on his regular site visits. Surprises were rare, but at the cornerstone laying ceremony for the Alfond Apartments in October 1998, Alfond himself put an envelope into the cornerstone box. It wasn't until the event was over and masons were mixing mortar to seal the stone that he told Cotter his envelope contained a real check for $1.25 million, the final payment of his building pledge.

Students were soon calling it "the palace." Despite the illusion of its nickname, the resident seniors lived in relative anarchy, prompting senior class

19. Schupf was a private investor who adopted Colby as a result of strong ties to the art museum. Mitchell, a Colby parent (Erik '97 and Katie '00), was a successful international banker. He died in a Maine airplane crash in December 2000.

20. With the dormitory renovation projects nearing an end, the College abandoned the old practice of separate bills for tuition, board, room, and special fees. The first comprehensive fee (1997–98) was $29,190.

speaker Erik Bowie '00 to turn to trustees seated behind him on the commencement platform and quip, "What *were* you people thinking?"

FIRE

The athletic complex was spiffed up for the NCAA national track and field championships in the spring of 1992, and when late summer came all was ready for returning fall teams. Before dawn on August 28 a security officer discovered a fire near the bleachers overlooking the basketball court. The high-arcing metal roof of the original Quonset hut fieldhouse became a chimney, feeding the flames and sending black smoke throughout the building. The fire wasn't out until noon. Some seventy firefighters from seven local departments fought the stubborn blaze, managing to save the building from total destruction. Six squash courts, offices, and the press box were gone. The newly refinished basketball court was ruined by thousands of gallons of water. Everything was covered with soot. Within days the state fire marshal's office said the blaze was intentionally set. No one was ever arrested.

The expansive athletic program seemed to go on without a hitch, and another gift from Harold Alfond made things even better than before. In September the freshly scrubbed fieldhouse was the site of a lobster feed to honor firefighters and their spouses. Cotter and Student Association President Bill Higgins '92 spoke. Cotter presented a check for $1,000 to support the area Fire Attack School. Athletic Director Dick Whitmore handed out lifetime athletic passes.[21]

Insurance covered most of the $2 million damage, but a replication of the prefire building was not acceptable. Peer institutions had busily been building grander athletic places. A modern athletic plant had been on the planning list for years, but always near the bottom. Alfond, who never wanted Colby in second place—least of all in athletics—resolved the dilemma even before the cleanup was finished, offering a one-for-one challenge gift to both repair and expand the building. The Harold Alfond Athletic Center was completed by the fall of 1994. Many of the original facilities were improved, and the expansion included additional locker rooms and a popular two-level fitness, weight training, and exercise area. (It also had fire detection equipment and sprinklers.) In two years the College went from near the bottom to near the top in

21. Proving no good deed goes unpunished, some Waterville elected officials boycotted the event, claiming Colby ought to be paying taxes instead of buying lobsters.

athletic facility rankings in the posh company of the New England Small College Athletic Conference.

Other than having to shuffle locker room spaces, the fire had little impact on the 1992 fall teams. The football team, still reeling from the suspensions in the wake of the grange hall fraternity mess, had bigger things to worry about. All but one of the dismissed students returned to Colby, but the fourteen team members among them were not invited back to play. They had violated a pledge to the coach and Tom Austin said the team would go on without them. With only five of twenty-two starters returning, Austin dubbed his inexperienced squad "the blue team," and it stuck. He hired a sports psychologist to convince them they could win; and with "blue pride" they often did, taking their fifth straight Colby-Bates-Bowdoin (CBB) title in 1992. In 1993 the team won the first-ever NESCAC title with a 5–2–1 season, the best in twenty years.[22]

Before the decade ended the football team lost two of its biggest fans. Pacy Levine '27, sideline kibitzer for eighteen coaches since 1917, died in 1996 at the age of ninety-one. His brother Ludy '21 died a year later at age ninety-eight. Pacy and Ludy stories were already part of the Colby lore. In a rare televised game between Colby and Bates in 1990, former coach and then admissions officer Tom Kopp served as the broadcast color man and introduced the brothers. Minutes later viewers could see Ludy standing on the playing field, his face inches away from an animated discussion between Austin and a game official.

With some 250 women varsity players, Colby was a conference leader in meeting federal Title IX requirements, and when Tracey Theryl was hired to coach Nordic skiing in 1997, the College had fourteen women coaches of women's teams, the most of any college in the country. One of the last remaining sex barriers was broken by the careful design of the new building. Faculty dean Bob McArthur oversaw the purchase and placement of equipment in the new fitness/aerobics center so as to attract nonvarsity women to the place where men had once dominated. The "gym" soon became a bustling social center.

22. Austin retired in 2003 with the most wins of any Colby football coach (sixty-seven) and a dozen CBB titles. In 2000 he was selected the conference coach of the year. His replacement, long-time assistant Ed Mestieri, continued the winning ways.

Although women had mostly caught up with the men and the faculty had mostly caught up with the athletic program, the endless tug-of-war between academic and athletic interests continued. The new faculty-imposed athletic guidelines had achieved a more sensible balance in the time commitment of student athletes, but had failed to resolve concerns attending the growing number of postseason playoff opportunities. In fact, tournaments presented a conferencewide conundrum. NESCAC forbade team participation in national qualifying (NCAA) playoffs.[23] For men, seasons ended with the Eastern College Athletic Conference (ECAC) playoffs. Women, who had once relied on the Northeast Intercollegiate Athletic Conference (NIAC), were moving into the ECAC as well. In the mid-1980s, when the ECAC left NESCAC out of its regional men's soccer championships, NESCAC created one for itself. Soon after, ECAC playoffs in hockey and basketball became national qualifiers, creating curious moments when conference teams earned places in the ECACs but could not move on.

By 1989 coaches were pushing for a chance to aim for the national tournaments. They argued there would be no additional financial cost (the NCAA paid) and that participation would enhance the NESCAC image. Opponents feared further professionalism in amateur athletics, admissions pressure to produce tournament teams, and further loss of class time. In 1990 the presidents considered whether NESCAC might change from a scheduling conference to a playing one; in 1993, after yet another policy review, they agreed to a four-year experiment of participation in NCAA tournaments. That fall, the first Colby qualifier was coach Debbie Aitken's women's cross-country team.

When the time came for a review of the experiment in 1997, Cotter was skeptical of continuing. Colby had fought to make NESCAC schedules, especially for the women. He feared that by allowing NCAA participation, NESCAC members would begin to seek outside competition in order to improve their positions for NCAA bids. And besides, he never liked the spring tournament conflicts with final exams. Cotter's public position caused a stir among both students and alumni. Popularized by the televised Final Four in Division I basketball, NCAA championships had become the Holy Grail for athletes and fans in all sports. At the same time, faculties across the conference were calling for the protection of the primacy of academics against the frenzy of professionalism in college athletics that was producing yearlong training and out-of-season practices. To complicate matters, the NCAA was not an

23. Individual qualifiers in track and field were allowed to participate in NCAA national championship meets. Cross-country and relay teams were not.

inviting place for Division III member schools. The national association was dominated by the near professional athletics of Division I and driven by its enormous television revenues. Division III was a stepchild, and NESCAC barely fit under the umbrella at all. Not only was the conference the most admissions-selective grouping in the nation,[24] it also had the most restrictive rules regarding recruiting, scheduling, and practice of all the NCAA members. Colby, with its new athletic guidelines, was on the outer conservative edge of NESCAC itself.

According to Bowdoin president Robert Edwards, a 1997 presidents' meeting included "a long, animated discussion of the corrupting, distorting influences of the NCAA on collegiate sport." They considered taking the conference out of the NCAA altogether, so that they might remove "absurd" pressure on faculty and students and "cease being parties to the corrupt exploitation of the young we see in Division I." Some of the presidents were tempted to sever all ties with the national association, but there was no other place to go. In 1998 they found middle ground. They voted to affirm the primacy of academics in the conference mission, create a league office, and strengthen interconference scheduling. They also approved Cotter's proposal to allow NESCAC champion teams, in all sports except football,[25] to enter postseason play. NESCAC teams would no longer participate in the ECACs, except where it was "more appropriate."

Although the new rules brought NCAA playoff opportunities to all sports, chances of Colby teams getting invitations to "the big dance" were still scant. Men's basketball, long dominant in the Colby-Bates-Bowdoin mini-league, had an outside shot. Dick Whitmore's squads had been frequent visitors to ECAC tournaments, winning in 1990, 1991, and 1993.[26] Thereafter, three of his teams qualified for the Division III NCAA championships, entering in 1994,

24. The second most selective was the Centennial League of Bryn Mawr, Dickinson, Franklin & Marshall, Gettysburg, Haverford, Muhlenberg, Swarthmore, Ursinus, Washington, and Western Maryland.

25. The toughest NESCAC rules were always reserved for football. It stemmed from a fear of the excesses that had long been apparent on the national collegiate level. As presidents struggled to regulate postseason tournaments they were also adopting a Cotter-led initiative to hold football squad numbers to seventy-five and limit the growing size of coaching staffs. In 1998, the year the maximum team number was approved, Colby had only sixty-six players, fewest in the conference.

26. There may never have been a sweeter basketball victory earned before fewer fans than in 1993, when fewer than a dozen of the faithful made the trek through a blizzard to Williams College for the title game.

1995, and 1997. Whitmore, the most winning Colby coach ever, achieved his 500th victory by the end of the decade. Women's basketball joined the men in taking the ECAC title in 1991, Gene DeLorenzo's final year as coach. Carol Anne Beach '88 became the women's coach in 1991, followed by Beth Staples '86 and Tricia O'Brien, who took teams to the ECAC tournaments five times in six years, winning it all in 2001.

With a new home field, Mark Serdjenian's 1990 men's soccer team had the first undefeated season (12−0−2) since it went 7−0 in its inaugural year, 1959. It failed to get an NCAA invitation in 1993 but went on to win its first ECAC title in fifteen years. In 1997 both the men's squad and the women's squad, coached by Jen Holsten '90, finally got NCAA regional tournament bids. The women returned again the following year.

Not every Colby team fit comfortably into the Division III mold. In 1993, Laura Halldorson, Colby coach and president of the American Women's Hockey Coaches Association, was a founder of the first ECAC women's hockey league. Of the twelve incorporating members, all but Colby were Division I. For a time it didn't matter. The team gained tournament spots in 1996 and, under new coach Jen Holsten, again in 1997. Meaghan Sittler '98 and Barbara Gordon '97 were tapped for the U.S. Women's Select Team, from which some members of the first-ever U.S. Olympic women's hockey team were chosen. The following year Sittler and Courtney Kennedy '98 were named to the inaugural Women's Hockey All-American Team. After a winless 1998−99 season, Holsten's team dropped back to play traditional rivals in a better-suited NESCAC Division III league.

In 1996 Jim Tortorella, who replaced Scott Borek as head coach of men's hockey, passed up an invitation to the ECAC tournament and held out for third position in the NCAA seeding. The following year his team (18−6−1) won its first ECAC title in three decades, beating archrival Bowdoin four times along the way. The team was again filling up with stars, including defenseman Robert Koh '99, a three-time All-American.

Skiing didn't fit the Division III mold either. Since being reinstated as a varsity sport in 1986, both the men's and women's Alpine teams dominated Division II Eastern Intercollegiate Skiing. By 1992 the Alpine and Nordic women had won seven consecutive eastern championships, and over those years the men had taken three. The combined squads had won five in a row. The following year the teams moved into the strong Eastern Collegiate Skiing Division I and promptly qualified two seniors, Jennifer Comstock and Christopher Bither, for the national championships. In 1994 Colby was the host of the national event on the nearby mountain at Sugarloaf USA.

The decade saw an explosion of individual athletic stars across the full athletic spectrum. Their number included thirty All-Americans, half of them women.[27] Most were in track and field and in cross-country, where the honors are automatically awarded to top national finishers. Colby's list included several remarkable repeaters. Distance runner Michelle Severance '94, a leader on Aitken's 1991 New England champion indoor team, was an astonishing ten-time All-American: five in outdoor track, four in cross-country, and one in indoor track. Hammer thrower Jamie Brewster '00 was the College's first multiple-time national champion. He took the top place as a freshman and as a sophomore, finished third in 1999; he won again as a senior.[28] In 1997, Cynthia Pomerleau became Colby's first woman national champion, winning the heptathlon in her senior year while taking All-American honors in the shot put as well. Debra MacWalter '91 was a five-time honoree; four with the javelin and once in the heptathlon, and Sarah Toland '00 won five citations in a single year, starring in both cross-country and track.

The expansion of athletic programs had not ended. Despite new guidelines that put hurdles in front of clubs that aspired to be varsity, the decade brought two more teams, raising the total to fifteen each for men and women plus coed golf. As measured by the number of teams compared to enrollment, the NCAA ranked Colby fourth in the nation. Bowdoin, Williams, and MIT had one team more. Colby's newest, women's volleyball, began in 1991 and three years later Sheila Cain coached an exciting team into the final round of the NESCAC tournament.

Crew had begun as a ragtag "rowing association" in 1984–85, when Phil Purcell '87 joined with John Donnelly '87, Jeff O'Brien '86, Art Nagle '87, and Nancy Steck '87 to raise money and ply nearby frigid waters with a pair of wooden fours discarded by Assumption College. Scraping for money and staying in parents' homes, they carried the Colby banner into races around New England. A novelty for most observers, crew caught on quickly with both

27. Basketball: Matt Hancock, Kevin Whitmore, John Daileanes, David Stephens, and Ken Allen. Cross-country: Michelle Severance, Kara Patterson, and Sarah Toland. Field hockey: Katie Taylor. Ice hockey: Derek Bettencourt, Brian Cronin, Dan Lavergne, Robert Koh, Meaghan Sittler, and Courtney Kennedy. Lacrosse: Margaret Mauran, Kristina Stahl, and Matt Williams. Soccer: Brian Wiercinski, Patrick Skulley, and Graham Nelson. Swimming: Geoff Herricki. Track and Field: Debra MacWalter, Cynthia Pomerleau, Jill Vollweiler, Jennifer Hartshorn, Michelle Severance, Kara Patterson, Lawaun Curry, Jamie Brewster, Sarah Toland, and Farrell Burns.

28. Brewster, who became a Colby admissions officer, made his Colby record throw of 196'5" in a regular season meet.

participants and fans. After knocking on the door for ten years, in 1994 crew was admitted to the varsity ranks. One of the few sports still played for the sheer fun of it, crew allowed inexperienced but interested students willing to get up early and work hard to try out and "walk (or row) on" to the team. From the get-go it was a formidable competitor and perennial CBB champ. Within ten years the women's half became Colby's first national team champion.

AND ICE

In January 1998 the fieldhouse, spared by local firefighters in the stifling August heat six years before, became a shelter for area residents escaping an epic ice storm. Although the fire and the storm could not be compared in their enormity, each one put into sharp focus the enduring symbiotic relationship between Colby and its neighbors.

The storm began Monday, January 5. A stationary front set up low-pressure areas to the south and brought heavy rain into Maine. Temperatures in the mountains—often the coldest places in the nation—were warmer than in the frozen towns and cities below. For two days the rain made ice, some places as thick as three inches, and on Wednesday residents awoke to cannonlike sounds of trees and power poles falling under the weight. Half of the state, including most of Central Maine, was without electricity. Governor Angus King called out the National Guard.

Waterville had an emergency plan, but it had not anticipated an event of such magnitude or duration. Designated city shelters lost power and were useless. Lines from Central Maine Power's Rice's Rips Station to the underground campus wiring system were miraculously not damaged, and Mayflower Hill was an island of heat and light. When on Friday Mayor Ruth Joseph called the College for help, personnel director Doug Terp took charge of Colby's response, working with athletic director Dick Whitmore and plant crews to turn the fieldhouse into the area's principal shelter. Residents began to arrive before the cots were set up. EMTs John Michael Vore '98 and John Maddox '99 worked with the health center and the hospital to operate an around-the-clock first aid station. Craig Belanger '00, a Jan Plan intern with Mayor Joseph, was put in charge at city hall, and worked with the police and fire departments to transport shivering residents up the Hill. The College cancelled classes on January 9, the first time since the blizzard of 1952. Colby took inventory of its own employees, and physical plant director Alan Lewis sent help to those most in need.

Local power stayed out for a week (in some places nearly four) and by January 14 the shelter had seen more than a thousand area residents, some who came and went, some who stayed for the duration. Shower rooms had long lines. Dining service employees, assisted by student volunteers, served some five thousand meals. In town students scoured neighborhoods, knocking on doors, looking for anyone in distress. At least two lives, maybe more were saved.[29] Maine Senator Olympia Snowe visited and called the Colby effort "remarkable."

When the sun came out and the ice melted, a massive cleanup of fallen trees and branches began. The Colby landscape suffered miserably. More than two hundred trees were felled or torn beyond saving. Especially disheartening was the damage to the large Sugar Maple in front of Woodman hall, an iconic tree predating the Mayflower Hill campus whose brilliant red leaves were the first harbinger of fall. President Bixler had personally spared it from the axe in 1951. Cotter gave it a second presidential pardon following the ice storm, insisting it be trimmed and saved.

The city was still ahead on favors. After all, its people had given the Mayflower Hill campus in the first place, and many of its residents stood among the leaders who had helped the College grow. But now the tide of help was turning. Waterville had begun to feel the economic chill. The country had seen some $3 trillion worth of mega-mergers since 1980; and while the national economy was on the upswing, the local area—indeed, most of Maine above Portland— was sinking. In 1993 Scott Paper Company, successor to Hollingsworth and Whitney, lost $277 million and was $2.5 billion in debt. Al "Chainsaw" Dunlap took over as CEO and within a year fired some three hundred local employees, eleven thousand nationwide. The move puffed shareholder value by some $6 billion, positioning the area's largest employer to sell out. In late 1995 Dunlap made a deal with Kimberly-Clark for $9.4 billion, taking $100 million for himself. Two years later the Winslow plant was closed. At the same time the venerable Cascade textile mill on the Messalonskee Stream in Oakland surrendered to foreign competition and after 114 years of operation, closed its doors as well.

Throughout Kennebec County major closings affected nearly four thousand people. Most were factory workers. By decade's end the only remaining

29. Several deaths were caused by carbon monoxide when residents used open-flame propane stoves inside their homes. Students rescued an elderly couple, already overcome by the gas.

local industries were the Chinet Company, 1994 successor to Martin Keyes's molded paper plate factory (later sold to the Finnish company Huhtamaki), and the Hathaway shirt factory, taken over by Warnaco in 1967 and hanging on by selling cheaper shirts to Wal-Mart. In 1996 Warnaco sold Hathaway to private investors, including former Maine governor John McKernan; while the new group returned quality to the shirts, Waterville's oldest and most famous industry could not long survive. (On June 30, 2002, after 165 years in operation, Charles Hathaway's shirt factory closed for good.)

The factory closings made ripples. In 1996, with the paper mill in its last throes, the city's three remaining Catholic churches—Sacred Heart, Saint Francis, and Notre Dame—collapsed into a single Parish of the Holy Spirit, and Dunham and Levine's clothing stores, once anchors on Main Street, closed their doors. On North Street, Harris Baking Company emerged briefly from bankruptcy, only to shut down again.[30] A year later Mid-Maine Medical Center, born of the merger of Thayer and Seton hospitals, consolidated with Augusta General Hospital and became Maine General.

The once-vibrant industrial city was having a hard time coping in the postindustrial era. To make ends meet, the City Council eliminated its economic development arm at a time when it was needed the most, and the mayor's office did not fill the gap. It had too many gaps of its own. In 1995 Mayor Thomas Brazier, a Democrat (who had caused a small stir when he rejected the recommendation of a citizens' committee to hire a police chief who was black) went to jail for embezzlement of private funds. Former superintendent of schools Nelson Megna stood in for a year before the election of another Democrat, Ruth Joseph, who found herself in a political crossfire and was recalled by voters in a pique over all sorts of things including rising taxes. Thomas College professor Nelson Madore soldiered on as mayor through the end of the century.

In the second half of the decade Waterville's population dropped by 3,000 people, to 15,600. Blue-collar workers were disappearing and white-collar executives had already moved to faraway places where they knew little about the local communities, and cared even less. Volunteer civic and charitable agencies, once led by managers of local banks, businesses, and factories, began to

30. The news seemed never good. Sadly, in 1996 Waterville found itself in the national spotlight when thirty-seven-year-old Mark Bechard broke into the convent chapel of the Servants of the Blessed Sacrament on Silver Street and, using a knife and a religious statue, beat four nuns, killing two of them. The city mourned for them and for Bechard, who was mentally ill.

look elsewhere for leadership—and for donations.[31] Maine General Hospital's Waterville branch and the College, both nonprofits, were suddenly and astonishingly the city's two largest employers.

Colby's role in the community had always been strong compared to most places where colleges and towns rubbed elbows. The entwined histories had bound them in special ways. Until now the College's contributions to the general community had centered on sharing its facilities and cultural opportunities, but in the 1990s the outreach role expanded. A $1 million grant from the Howard Hughes Medical Institute in 1991 not only provided extra resources for science teaching on the campus but also included funds for a partnership program designed to improve science education in area secondary schools. At the same time the Maine Department of Education approved a Colby project to improve the skills of high school teachers of science. Biologists Jay Labov and Russ Cole led the twin efforts that provided science equipment and instruction, including replacement instructors, for teachers in four area schools.[32] The Hughes grants continued into the next century.

Community service learning, once limited to the lake quality research in the environmental course taught by Cole and David Firmage, expanded to include English classes focused on helping local schoolchildren. Andrea Solomita '92 led a succession of student managers of the Colby Volunteer Center (CVC), which had grown to engage several hundred students and become the largest people-power help group in Central Maine. Leaders of regional volunteer agencies met on the campus to coordinate efforts, and students played a role in all of them. A leading CVC mentor was poet and professor Peter Harris, long an advocate of outreach programs, who began to wrap his introductory English courses into service learning by engaging students as mentors for local schoolchildren. He used his seat as faculty representative to the board as a bully pulpit to encourage College support of outreach efforts, and his Colby Cares About Kids program was soon improving the lives of hundreds of area youngsters. More broadly, Colby Cares Day, begun in 1997 by Student Association president Josh Woodfork, sent students, faculty, and staff into the community in a kind of Johnson Day writ large, cleaning up and helping both

31. One way Dunlap had puffed up Scott shares was to eliminate its $3 million annual budget for philanthropy.

32. By 1998 Colby was cleaning up its older computers and donating them to the four area school systems that were short of money to meet the new technological demands.

agencies and local citizens in need. Woodfork said it should become a lasting spring tradition, and it did.[33]

In the arena of economic development, there was new ground to break as well. While previous Colby contributions had been in-kind, now some were made in hard cash. Colleges and universities around the country had already begun to make economic partnerships with their communities. Trinity College in Hartford and Connecticut College in New London were New England examples. In 1991 Cotter was a founding member of the Mid-State Economic Development Corporation and with Mayor David Bernier '79 was host to its initial meeting. Bernier was the son of former mayor Albert Bernier '50 and like his father, a progressive Democrat who, without a staff, puzzled out ways to plan economic growth. (Bernier brought a Wal-Mart, and half of the city's few remaining mom-and-pop shops folded in a New York minute.) The new corporation was the germ of regionalized development initiatives going forward.

Nowhere was the economic suffering more evident than on Main Street where store after store had buckled under the competition of outlying shopping centers and retail chains. The midstreet Sterns Department store, closed since the 1980s, had been reopened as the Sterns Cultural Center, but within a year the owners faced foreclosure. Colby had a vested interest in having an inviting town center, and Cotter feared a rundown Main Street with empty storefronts and tattoo parlors. In 1996 he led a group of local leaders in announcing the intent to purchase the building and turn it into the Waterville Regional Arts and Community Center (WRACC). It would take a million dollars to buy it, fix it up, and keep it going. College trustees agreed to make the lead gift of $100,000— the same amount the community had raised sixty-six years before to keep Colby in Waterville. CEO Scott Bullock said Mid-Maine Medical Center would match it, and eight others, including Thomas College, pitched in to collect more than $500,000 before a general campaign for the remainder was announced in May. Within a year some two thousand citizens signed on as WRACC members ($25 and up) and the goal was met. A year later, the College offered land near the Messalonskee Stream for a proposed new combined Boys Club–Girls Club–YMCA youth center, named for the familiar benefactors Harold and Bibby Alfond. When center officials chose a site closer to town, Cotter anonymously chipped in $100,000 of Colby funds for the project.

33. Woodfork wanted a strong student government and led the effort to separate the governing body from its unwieldy cultural-life arm. The following year, 1998, the Student Association became the Student Government Association.

As the decade closed, Main Street had recovered a bit of its vitality and elsewhere things were looking up as well. L.L. Bean opened a call center at the JFK Shopping Plaza on Kennedy Drive; Home Depot and Staples stores were set to anchor a new shopping mall on Upper Main; and above the interstate exchange, Oakland town manager Mike Roy '74 was helping orchestrate the creation of a high-tech business site named FirstPark. Cotter formed yet another community advisory committee, this one to encourage downtown beautification, new businesses, and development along the Kennebec, recently set free from the 162-year-old Edwards Dam at Augusta. Colby trustees established a $1 million low-interest loan fund to encourage new and renewed Main Street businesses. The struggle to regain lost ground was far from over, but Colby was in the game to stay.

CROWN JEWEL

The Colby art museum was but a dot on the regional map when it first opened in a tiny space of the new Bixler Art and Music Center in 1959. A larger place had been the dream of Professor Jim Carpenter; Ellerton and Edith Jetté made it come true. Elevated by an acclaimed Maine art show in 1963, the museum steadily collected friends and precious works; ten years later a tripling of the gallery space still wasn't enough. The greatest advances came in the decade of the 1990s when, with the accumulation of more riches and two magnificent new wings, it soared into the lofty ranks of America's finest college museums.

The Campaign For Colby earmarked $3.3 million for the Bixler Center and included more room at the museum, which could barely display a quarter of its 2,500 works and was not properly storing the rest. When Shaw's Supermarkets founder Stanton Davis and his wife, Elizabeth, visited they found the entire permanent collection in the tiny basement, displaced by an exhibition of Maine basketry. They agreed to build storage rooms in the open space beneath the Bixler Center and the Jetté wing, and it was Elizabeth's idea to put a new skylit gallery on top. The Davis Gallery opened in 1991, in time to show some of the finest art the central Maine region had ever seen.

The precious works were from the personal collection of Joan Whitney Payson, heir to one of America's great fortunes and popularly recognized as the founding owner of the New York Mets baseball team. Her many interests ranged from baseball and thoroughbred racehorses to the fine art that decorated family homes in New York, Florida, and Maine. Her collection was broad and included the work of Courbet, Daumier, Ingres, Monet, Picasso, Renoir, Rousseau, Sisley, Prendergast, Sargent, Whistler, Reynolds, and Wyeth. When she died in 1975 her son John Whitney Payson sent many of the works to Maine's Westbrook College, where his wife had gone to school. By the mid-1980s John Payson had determined to move the collection from Westbrook, to sell some and take the rest to a place where they would get more exposure. Although Westbrook struggled to curate and insure the art, officials there at first insisted the collection had been a gift, not a loan, and could not be removed. A compromise was struck whereby Westbrook would share in the proceeds from the sale of one of the paintings—Vincent Van Gogh's *Irises*—and the rest would be moved elsewhere.[34]

Cotter wanted the elsewhere to be Colby. The Portland Museum of Art wanted the collection too. Cotter and Payson were Westbrook trustees and with the compromise accepted, Cotter was free to approach Payson, who knew Colby through his daughter Heather, a member of the Class of 1988. Payson, intrigued by Cotter's proposal to engage area schoolchildren if the art came to Colby, decided the twenty-six paintings would be shared. The collection would be at home in Portland but it would be at Colby for a semester every two years, enough to twice catch each passing generation of students. Payson spoke at the first Colby opening in the spring of 1992. He said he was "thrilled" that the placement would allow students of all ages "to learn, to love art and each other." At Cotter's invitation more than seven thousand youngsters from northern and central Maine visited the museum in the next four months, some from as far away as Machias and Fort Kent. The parade of school buses, subsidized by the College and the Paysons, continued to roll in during each biannual visit thereafter.

The museum had an informal advisory committee all along, and an acquisitions committee was formed in the aftermath of Jeré Abbott's $1.8 million bequest for broadening the collection. In 1993 they were combined and expanded to create a museum board of governors. Its twenty-three members were drawn from the art department and the ruling board of trustees and from the broader world of artists, dealers, and collectors. Chairperson and a moving force on the new board was novelist and art historian Gabriella De Ferrari who had been director of the Institute of Contemporary Art in Boston

---

34. *Irises,* painted in 1889 at the Saint-Rémy mental asylum in France a few months before Van Gogh committed suicide, was sold at Sotheby's Auction House in 1987. After barely two minutes of bidding, it brought $49 million, more than twice the expected amount and a world-record price for a work of art.

and deputy director of the Fogg Art Museum at Harvard. She knew the art world and opened many doors for the ambitious Colby museum. (Her daughter, Bree [Jeppson] '93, later joined the board as well.)

The board was barely assembled when in 1994 word came that the estate of Edith Jetté was bringing $5.7 million for art at Colby. The last in the long line of Jetté benefactions was used to create an art professorship and endowment funds for restoration and exhibitions.[35] There was also money for acquisitions, and together with the Abbott endowment, which had nearly doubled, the new governing board would have some $300,000 a year to spend. A year later the museum received accreditation from the American Association of Museums, and the expansion was far from over. The collection that had centered on early American art was set to go in another direction.

In 1985 Colby and Bowdoin had collaborated on a joint exhibition of Paul J. Schupf's collection of the works of the modern realist painter Alex Katz. For the Colby opening, Cotter held a gala luncheon. Schupf was there. The successful investor knew little of Colby, but he was impressed with what he saw and the people he met. It wasn't long before he was wrapped up not only with the museum but also with Colby, writ large. A second major Katz show was held in 1992. The artist, who had studied at the nearby Skowhegan School of Painting and Sculpture and had painted in the state since 1949, said he felt guilty about having his paintings taken out of Maine and offered to give Colby more than four hundred works if the College would build a place to put them. Cotter and the trustees agreed, but the plan languished until in the summer of 1994, when Schupf, now an overseer and a member of the museum board of governors, met with Cotter and faculty dean Bob McArthur in advance of a governing board meeting. Out of the blue, Schupf said he would make the lead gift to build the place for Katz's work.

Katz himself made the first sketch of the new wing, drawn on a legal pad at the museum that same day. Acclaimed British architect Sir Max Gordon was commissioned to design the building but died before he could finish. Maine architect Scott Teas completed the work, and the Schupf Wing for the Works of Alex Katz opened in 1996. It was one of only two museum wings in the country devoted to the work of a living artist.[36] Condé Nast's *Traveler* magazine

35. The will specified that the exhibitions funded by the new endowment be named in honor of Ed Turner who had touted the museum throughout his long tenure as vice president for development.

36. The other is a gallery for the work of abstract impressionist Cy Twombly with the Menil Foundation in Houston, Texas.

called it one of the seven most exciting museum exhibitions in the country. The five-panel, 11 ft. × 30 ft. *Pas de Deux*[37] greeted visitors on the wall facing the entrance, and with sixty-five other major Katz works, the museum had suddenly and sharply accelerated its move into the world of contemporary art. Not everyone appreciated Katz's signature style. Just as many people had become wedded to the neo-Georgian campus architecture, there were many others that had become comfortable with the realism of earlier art and were unwilling to embrace the new. Schupf, a man who saw the future and who collected Katz's paintings before Katz was broadly admired, said no one should hate contemporary and new art. "If you see art that you don't like," he said, "just keep walking."

The often-inscrutable Schupf was not finished. He had resigned from the board at Colgate, his alma mater, soon after joining the Colby trustees. Unsolicited, he continued his impulsive generosity: a scientific computer center, then a dormitory, and then back to twenty-first-century art when he built a new museum entry courtyard to suit the commissioning of the site-specific 30-ton solid steel sculpture *4-5-6* by the leading contemporary American sculptor Richard Serra. Schupf was also with others in the front row cheering in 2002, when the Serra work was complemented with the acquisition of *Seven Walls*, a gift of American minimalist conceptual artist Sol LeWitt who had already made a spectacular mural for the museum lobby.

Despite the trend toward contemporary art, the museum still bulged with its core collection of eighteenth- to twentieth-century American art, most of it now safely in the new storage area, too little of it on public view. Before decade's end, collectors Peter ('56) and Paula Lunder, generous neighbors who had given and loaned many of the American works, built a house to put them in. The Lunders, like the Jettés, shared a love of fine art. They had been collecting art since the 1970s. It was something they did together. Living nearby, she was a museum volunteer and the first to make a catalogue of the collection on the computer. He was the president of Alfond's Dexter Shoe Company. She became a Colby trustee, and he, a life-appointed overseer. Both were founding members of the board of governors.

Like Schupf, the Lunders made a spontaneous offer, theirs a challenge grant, anonymous at first, to spark gifts for major museum improvements and a spacious, seven-gallery wing. Designed by Los Angeles architect Frederick Fisher, the building had the feel of a home in which the paintings and other artwork might once have been displayed. The Lunder wing nearly doubled the exhibi-

37. *Pas de Deux* was on loan and was later given to Colby by Schupf in honor of museum director Hugh Gourley.

tion space, making it the largest in Maine. It was able to show some two hundred works from the permanent collection and, with expanded space for the precious John Marin collection, covered nearly three centuries of American art.

With all the growth, the decade saw a mushrooming of undergraduate art students and majors, attracted in part by the museum but even more by talented and popular teachers. They too wanted more space, and soon-to-be trustee chair James Crawford and his wife, Linda, Colby 1964 classmates, gave it to them. The Crawford Art Studios, opened in 2001, provided expanded space for sculpture and painting and created a ripple that gave bigger and better places for more painting, foundation studies, and photography.

The Lunder gifts and matching money also made other improvements possible, including funds for traveling exhibits, collection conservation, and improved staffing for the museum that had until the early part of the decade run almost entirely on the energy and devotion of a single man: Hugh Gourley. Since signing on as museum director (1966) Gourley had steadily and quietly gathered friends and mounted hundreds of exhibitions, taking help wherever he could find it.

> Rarely did the extra help have any art training. When a well-meaning custodian cut his hand while uncrating a piece of precious modern sculpture, he found a rasp and promptly filed off the offending foundry leavings. The leavings were an intended and integral part of the work. The sculptor was apoplectic, and had to be teased to cast a replacement piece. The custodian was transferred.

Nearly every museum benefactor, from the beginning through to Payson, Schupf, Katz, and the Lunders, attributed much of their attraction to the museum to Gourley, a self-effacing man with an uncanny eye for art who gave the credit away and kept none for himself. In fact, he had almost single-handedly supervised the remarkable development of a museum that by the end of the decade was called "a place that's going places" by the *New York Times*. The *Maine Times* called it "the jewel in the crown of the Maine art scene."

REFLECTIONS

Even the consummate dreamer Franklin Johnson could not have imagined Colby as it appeared at the end of the twentieth century. His prayers for the mere survival of the withering institution along the river had been answered a thousandfold. Propelled by a renowned faculty, bright students from around the world, and a physical plant twice the size he had envisioned, Colby was in the elite league of the nation's best. Everything seemed to reflect the devotion and hard work of a half-century of like dreamers—everything, that is, except Johnson's spring-fed pond. The pond was barely reflecting at all.

Algae blooms and pickerelweed came earlier each spring. Fifty years of erosion had left two feet of bottom silt, lowering water volume and increasing the phosphorus. The ducks were partly to blame, peaking the Ph with their poop. "Don't feed the ducks" signs merely encouraged drive-by feedings by local duck lovers who heaved day-old bread from speeding cars. Scientists pressed for a thorough pond draining and cleaning. Cotter eventually succumbed to their pleas (and to his penchant for cleanliness); in the fall of 1997, with the caveat that all be in shape by Commencement, he ordered the job done.

When the plug was pulled the sunlit muck turned the place into a giant Petri dish. Curious onlookers prowled the banks, hoping to find misplaced refrigerators and Volkswagens. Instead they saw beer kegs and a barn-making load of cement blocks, purloined from construction sites to mark the boundaries of long-ago hockey games. Stalled momentarily by the ice storm, contractor Don Gurney, who had dug more campus holes (and uprooted more underground cables) than anybody, worked through the winter removing guck. He finished by late February. Within a month the pond refilled itself. The new water looked like coffee. Grounds supervisor Keith Stockford helpfully explained it was only silt. "Sooner or later," he said, "it will all sink to the bottom."

That spring the pond was reflecting again. The ducks and their feeders came back. The senior class custom of cheering the last day of classes on the library steps was extended to include a dip in the now somewhat clean pond, where a few celebrants got somewhat naked, startling local matrons who had brought grandchildren to picnic. When Dean Janice Kassman told the following class to nix the pond streaking, they called her a spoilsport for ruining a one-year tradition. Whether pond renewal had anything to do with it, that year the *Princeton Review* said that, behind Virginia's University of Richmond, Colby had the most beautiful campus in the country. To keep the reputation, the library tower clockworks were updated, (spoiling an honest-to-God tradition of showing irregular times on its four faces),[38] and dying sugar maples on the central mall were replaced.

38. In 2005, rotting timbers in the iconic tower itself had to be replaced, and the copper weathervane replica of the Sloop Hero, replated. The project cost nearly as much as Merton Miller had given to build the entire library.

The tidying up was a clue that Cotter was set to retire. In January 1999 he said he would leave in fourteen months, after Commencement 2000. Trustees had seen it coming. As early as 1994 they paid tribute to his wife, Linda, acknowledging her "unswerving support and wise counsel" in the leadership of the College; in the spring of 1997 the board gave the Student Center, cum Student Union, the Cotter name. It was a perfect match. Board chair Larry Pugh spoke at the surprise ceremony, noting that the most significant changes during Cotter's tenure had been the creation of new opportunities for students.

Although students did not always agree with Cotter, they almost universally admired him. Not surprisingly, the student lore held stereotypical images of him, including one that played on his custom of dressing up for any occasion (including fishing trips). At the spring 1997 Mr. Colby Pageant, a talent show of sorts, Peter Manning '98 sang a song he had written called *Bill Cotter Doesn't Wear Jeans*. Cotter laughed harder than anyone, and later asked board chair and Lee Jean–maker Pugh to send him a pair of designer jeans for the upcoming senior banquet. They were so new, so blue, and so finely pressed that when he spoke no one even noticed.

Cotter was leaving behind a great deal more than a new tower clock and a cleaner pond. In his public talks he frequently underscored the primacy of the faculty, and his convictions were evident. Since 1979 their number had grown by nearly a third, to 198—one for every nine students. Nowhere was his support for teaching more striking than in the accumulation of endowed chairs. When he arrived there were eight named professorships. Only three were fully funded. Eight paid-up chairs were added in the 1980s and an astonishing thirty-one more in the 1990s, raising the total to forty-two. Many of the decade's newcomers were quick to earn one.[39]

When Cotter first arrived he'd said the campus was nearly finished. He

39. They were Brad Mundy, who left a tenured position at Montana State to take charge in chemistry; Catherine Bevier, Judy Stone, and Andea Tilden in biology; Robert Bluhm in physics; Robert Gastaldo in geology; Elizabeth Leonard in history; Howard Lupovitch in Jewish studies; Julie Millard in chemistry; Joseph Reisert in government, and Herb Wilson in biosciences.

quickly came to know better. The addition of an astronomy classroom building (1999) brought the total of new buildings under his administration to a lusty ten, not counting eight major facility additions and a dozen renovation projects. By decade's end there were fifty-six discrete buildings on the Hill. Most people had stopped counting, and the rest could not agree on the total. (Was the Bixler Center with its auditorium and many-winged museum one building, or maybe five?)

Reflections of success were in the alumni body as well. A stream of notices proved Colby had for a long time been meeting its mission. Countless alumni were among local and national leaders in their professions and in public service. With more than two hundred graduates having served in some eighty foreign countries, the College ranked third in the country for its placement of Peace Corps volunteers, and nowhere were alumni more prominent than in the arts. In one six-year stretch, five won Pulitzer Prizes: 1991, Gregory Smith '73 for biography; 1992, Robert Capers '71 for journalism; 1993, E. Annie Proulx '57 (non-grad) for fiction; 1995, Doris Kearns Goodwin '64 for history; and 1996, Alan Taylor '77 for history.[40]

On the campus, with but a single exception, the retiring president was set to leave behind a seasoned administrative team. By 1998 Bob McArthur had been dean of faculty for ten years. Ed Yeterian, a psychologist and a member of the faculty since 1978, replaced him. As a specialist in the study of brain patterns of nonhuman primates as models for human brain function, he was well suited for his new assignment. His colleagues soon learned he would handle conflicting pleas with the equanimity of a scientist. Admissions dean Parker Beverage, who presided over the biggest applicant boom in the College's history, continued, as did Janice Kassman, who went on to serve as dean of students longer than anyone. Arnie Yasinski remained as administrative vice president, only later taking a similar post at the Rhode Island School of Design. Randy Helm raised money for Colby until 2003 when Muhlenberg (Pennsylvania) College took him as their president.

At the end of the decade the student body was in the throes of a dramatic swing toward diversity. Campus faces had already begun to reflect the world when two Colby families made even faster changes. In 1997 a $6.25 million

---

40. The string of Pulitzers soon extended to the faculty. Richard Russo began teaching creative writing in 1992 and stayed until his literary successes took him away at the turn of the century. He won a Pulitzer in literature in 2002 for *Empire Falls,* his fifth novel (later a movie made in Waterville and Skowhegan).

grant from the Oak Foundation, established by European Colby parents Alan and Jette Parker (Kristian '94, later an overseer), was the largest individual gift in the College's history.[41] It established the Oak Institute for the Study of International Human Rights, a program to bring human rights practitioners to the campus each year, and an endowment for full scholarships for ten international students. In 1999 Colby was one of five U.S. colleges chosen by the Shelby M. C. Davis family to participate in the Davis United World College Scholars Program. (Other colleges were the College of the Atlantic, Middlebury, Wellesley, and Princeton.) The family pledged full tuition and expenses for all students admitted from any of the ten United World Colleges, pre-university schools located on six continents and dedicated to promoting international understanding. Trustee Andrew Davis '85 announced the program. Within four years the College would have nearly one hundred Davis Scholars enrolled from throughout the world.

The growing sophistication raised both new and familiar debates, some needing full task forces to resolve. A 1998 task force on residential life made recommendations aimed at raising the quality of after-class life. Johnson and Chaplin Commons were folded together, leaving three units of the postfraternity living plan, each with at least one "substance free" (no alcohol, no smoking, no drugs) dormitory. And as the campus tossed and turned to get comfortable with the changing campus mix, Cotter set loose yet another task force to plan campuswide diversity training, bolster affirmative action and retention, examine related curricular issues, improve campus support for students of color, and rewrite the rules on harassment—the issue that had prompted the review in the first place. The group quickly renamed itself the Task Force on Institutional Racism, and Cotter bristled. "I was never told," he said, "what members of the task force believe 'institutional racism' means or whether they know of any institutions that are, in fact, free of it."

The report was given to Cotter in April. Three days later, with trustee meetings under way, more than two dozen students and a few faculty took over his office claiming minority student concerns were being swept under the rug and demanding action. Despite his first-responsible role as president, many felt Cotter was an odd target for the protest. For two decades he had led almost every new initiative toward greater diversity and the programs to embrace it.[42]

41. Jette Parker served for a time as a Colby trustee; Alan, as an overseer.
42. Many students who occupied his office were enrolled in Pamela Thoma's course "Gender, Race, and the Politics of Difference" with a syllabus requiring participation in a community or campus "action" and a three-to-five-page paper describing it. The pa-

The tinkering to embrace diversity continued to the end of the decade—and beyond. In 1999, the year Crayola changed the name of its Indian Red crayon to Chestnut, Colby gave fodder to those who wailed about political correctness by removing Anno Domini (year of our Lord) from its diplomas. Colby was one of only a few colleges that continued to use Latin as the language of its diplomas and in the pronouncements of the president at commencement. So too, in keeping with the Latin formulation, the degree remained the A.B. and not, like most others, the B.A. In 2004 the mother of a new graduate wrote to ask when her son would receive his "real" diploma.

For Colby, it was a rush to the end of the century. To complicate matters, as the millennium bore down, many were predicting a worldwide midnight computer apocalypse. In order to preserve limited memory space, early programmers had taught the machines to recognize years with two digits, not four, and in rolling to the year 2000 it was feared computers would either misread the date as 1900, or collapse altogether. The Y2K (year 2000) bug would, they said, eat ATM cards, tumble satellites, and turn off the power. Colby computer chief Ray Phillips was not worried. Systems had been checked and rechecked. When 2000 came, at Colby and most everywhere else, the bug was dead on arrival.

That spring, Colby held two parties. The first, in April, celebrated the successful end of the Campaign for Colby. The entire push had been nothing short of astonishing.[43] In the end, the $100 million goal had been surpassed by half again as much, twice what the experts had thought possible. It was another College record, and at the same time the largest single fundraising effort in Maine history. The College's endowment, $35 million when Cotter began, now stood at $242 million. In the afterglow of the campaign victory, board chair Pugh retired from his Colby post, and gave way to Jim Crawford, then in the midst of leading the search for the next president.

---

pers were due the following week. Cotter replied to the campus with a thirty-page action paper of his own, reciting the litany of diversity successes and citing future plans.

43. In the eighteen months following the 1994 award from the Olin Foundation, the development office built what Vice President Helm called "a house of cards," parlaying one matching grant on top of another. In that span, Linda Goldstein, a maven of grant writers, scored on twenty-seven successive requests without a miss.

The second party, a month later, was held to thank the Cotters. He had served twenty-one years, longer than any Colby president, and his legacy was reflected across the campus and beyond. He had given many things, but most enduring among them was an intangible spirit of a college that faced the twenty-first century fiercely believing in itself and in Franklin Johnson's long-ago assertion that anything at all was possible.

EPILOGUE

*This is a place that naturally aspires to be better in the fundamental
quality of what we do—in the teaching and learning that forms the core
of our enterprise, in the quality of the human relationships that create the
life of the campus, in the ways we support and are supported by alumni
and friends, and in the general aspiration to excellence.*

William D. Adams

Inaugural Address, October 21, 2000

The College began the new century ahead of the curve, riding the momentum of the Cotter years, and led by a new president, William "Bro" Adams, who already knew the ups and downs of the job. After examining some one hundred hopefuls in the most open presidential hunt in Colby history, the trustees snapped him up.

A graduate of Colorado College, Adams had served in Vietnam and, after his college graduation, earned a Fulbright Scholarship to study in France. He received his Ph.D. in the history of consciousness program at the University of California, Santa Cruz. His background as a teacher of political philosophy, as a senior administrator at Wesleyan University in Connecticut, and as a five-year president of Bucknell University in Pennsylvania made him a comfortable fit for Colby, where there would have been little patience waiting for an inexperienced leader to catch up.

Colby's nineteenth president had barely unpacked his bags when he assembled trustees, faculty, students, and others to undertake another self-examination, setting sights for the future. The centerpiece of the Plan for Colby, adopted in 2002, was an agreement to build a fifteen-acre elliptical campus district, across the road, facing the central mall. It would be the most aggressive building project since the College moved onto Mayflower Hill. With the wood-frame Hill Family Guest House and the Lunder admissions building already in place, the new Colby Green was meant to suggest a New England town commons, and its name had a second meaning. Both the land and its new buildings would express the College's long commitment to environmental stewardship and would be "green" as well.

The first building was for alumni and would house the new vice president of college relations, Richard Ammons, and his platoons of fundraisers. Champion of the project was trustee Douglas Schair '67 who, with his classmates, roommates, and ATO fraternity brothers Kurt Swenson and Thomas Watson, provided naming gifts. When the Schair-Swenson-Watson Alumni Center opened in the fall of 2005, work had already begun on a companion building across the Green. With a record $6 million gift from trustee Robert Diamond Jr. '73, and his wife, Jennifer, the three-story Diamond building would fulfill a long-held commitment to rescue the overcrowded departments of the social sciences and interdisciplinary studies.

While the Colby Green was the eye-popper, the strategic plan presented more than the prospect of moving earth and buying bricks. It also contained initiatives for preserving the College's culture of strong student-faculty ties, and for continuing the commitment to diversity and international education. The pursuit of innovative ways to refresh liberal learning was soon evidenced by the Goldfarb Center for Public Affairs and Civic Engagement, given by trustee William Goldfarb '68, father of Paula '00. While it waited for a permanent home in the new Diamond building, the center, directed by Sandy Maisel (government), began to gain prominence by engaging faculty and students in issues beyond the campus. It adopted many of the older lecture series and bolstered new ones, including the convocation associated with the Morton A. Brody Distinguished Judicial Service Award and Cotter Debate Series, established in honor of the retired president and his wife.

The Plan for Colby addressed after-class activities as well. While many students were not quick to embrace Adams's determination to diminish the role of alcohol in their social lives, there were other things about him and his strategic plan that they liked. (In 2004 the Student Government Association declared him Person of the Year, a rare treat for any senior administrator, rarer still for any president.) William Alfond '72 and his wife, Joan, were major donors for a lighted, multisport synthetic grass field, ready by 2004; David Pulver '63, his wife, Carol, and their daughter, Stephanie '93, agreed to build the Pulver Pavilion, a bridge for additional student social space, connecting the two wings of Cotter Union.

The buildings and other gifts were the nucleus of a new capital campaign, Reaching the World, named for where things were going and aimed at taking the College up yet another rung. The new chair of the board was Joseph Boulos '68, a fervent Colby supporter and successful Maine real estate developer. Campaign cochairs were Diamond and Larry Pugh, who took his third turn as a major fund-drive leader.

The newest effort was launched in the fall of 2005. Although its goal was 235 times larger than the 1937 Maine Million drive that had first firmly settled the College on Mayflower Hill, in the perspective of time and the spirit of visionaries it was no more daunting than any of the past campaigns to make Colby dreams come true.

ACKNOWLEDGMENTS

For this long project I have relied upon many friends, old and new, whose names follow in a type size that belies the measure of my gratitude. To those I may have forgotten, I apologize. I am especially grateful to Colby presidents who had the good sense and foresight to archive their papers so that others could read them. In particular I thank three among them, friends and former colleagues who cheered me on: Bill Cotter (who first urged me to write this book), Bob Strider, and Bro Adams. I am very much indebted to Mark Benbow, Roberts Professor of English Literature Emeritus, who read and commented on it all. His guidance and candor were needed and appreciated. My thanks, as well, to Sally Baker, a fine writer and editor whose counsel has made a better book. Many other Colby people helped for little more than my thanks. I am especially indebted to Robert Gillespie, George Coleman, Steve Collins, Brian Speer, Pat Burdick, and Karen Wickman who were unfailingly gracious in the face of pestering. I must also acknowledge Bill Arnold, a Bowdoin man and latter-day Ernest Marriner, who knows more about old Waterville than anyone else. And, for the final product, I owe much to the talented and helpful people at University Press of New England. Finally, I thank my wife, Barbara, to whom this book is dedicated and who has always adjusted her life to suit mine; my children, Kelly, Jeff '85, and Mike '90; and if you do not mind, my Golden Retriever, Nicholas, a pup when I began, who, through long hours of writing, kept my feet to the fire by sleeping on them.

E.H.S.
Belgrade Lakes, Maine
August 2006

William Adams	David Bernier	George Coleman
Debra Aitkin	Parker Beverage	Stephen Collins
Donald G. Alexander	Jennifer Boylan	Susan Cook
Byrd Allen	Gerard Boyle	Ellen Corey
Janice Anderson	Patrick Brancaccio	Sharon Corwin
Douglas Archibald	Jamie Brewster	William and Linda Cotter
Willard B. Arnold	David Brown	James and Linda Crawford
Varun Avasthi	Patricia Burdick	Harold Cross
Sally Baker	Maribeth Canning	John Cross
Bruce Barnard	Peter Carey	Eileen Curran
Clifford Bean	Brownie Carson	Jack and Ann Deering
David Beers	George Chadbourne	Gabriella DeFerrari
R. Mark Benbow	David Chaplin	Jeremy Degrasse
Margaret Bernier	Gordon Cheesman	Phyllis Deutsch
Albert Bernier	Russell Cole	Peter Doran

Nora Dore
Sidney Farr
Albert Federle
Joseph Feely
Anestes Fotiades
Eileen Fredette
Henry Gemery
Duncan Gibson
Robert Gillespie
Mark Godomsky
Douglas Gorman
Kelly and Greg Goulette
Elisabeth Dubord
　Goulette
Ansel Grindall
John Henderson
Ann G. Hill
Jan Hogendorn
Jennifer Holsten
Michael Howard
Robert Hughes
Paul Johnston
David Jones
Peter Joseph
John M. Joseph
Ruth Joseph
Janice Kassman
Sakhi Khan
Pat King
Howard Koonce
Donaldson Koons
John Koons
Thomas Kopp
Joanne Lafreniere
Allen LaPan
Alfred Letourneau
Patty Lettenberger
Lillian Levesque

Gus Libby
Hannah Liberty
Thomas Longstaff
Ivan Lopez
Paula and Peter Lunder
G. Calvin Mackenzie
Alicia MacLeay
Laura MacLeod
Sandy Maisel
Robert A. Marden
Donald H. Marden
Camilo Marquez
John Mazzeo
Robert McArthur
Laura Meader
Mary Beth Mills
Paul Mitchell
Douglas Nannig
Carl Nelson
Stanley A. Nicholson
Donald Nicoll
David Nugent
Kate O'Halloran
Stephen Orlov
Stephen Palmer
Anne and David
　Palmer
Chelsea Pawlek
Jackie Person
Raymond Phillips
Kelly Pinney-Michaud
Bill Pottle
Raymond Poulin
Larry and Jean Pugh
Susan Pullen
Philip Purcell
Dan Quirion
Jessy Randall

Douglas and Martha
　Reinhardt
David and Ruth Roberts
Eric Rolfson
Joan Sanzenbacher
Steven Saunders
Beth Schiller
Paul Schupf
Mark Serdjenian
Samuel and Carol Shapiro
Laura Smith
Michael Smith
Jeffrey Smith
William Sodoma
Brian Speer
Timothy Stenovec
Keith Stockford
Robert E. L. Strider
Suzi Swartz
Robert Tabscott
George F. Terry III
Frances Thayer
Thomas Tietenberg
Gerald and Betsy Tipper
Patricia Vashon
Jean C. Vashon
James Wescott
Nancy Westervelt
Richard Whitmore
Karen Wickman
Henry Wingate
Diane Winn
Gerry Wright
Willard Wyman
Edward Yeterian
Marcella Zalot
Louis and Kathleen
　Zambello

Trustees, 1820–2005

(FR) indicates Faculty Representative.

Abedon, Richard Lloyd, Tiverton, RI, 1986–94

Adams, Asa Charles, Orono, ME, 1966–72

Adams, Howard Dale, Lake Forest, IL, 1985–94

Adams, William D., Waterville, ME, 2000–

Alden, Frank W., Waterville, ME, 1918–29

Alden, William H., Portsmouth, NH, 1881–1900

Alfond, William L., Boston, MA, 2002–

Allan, Elizabeth S., Nyack, NY, 1947–53

Allen, Lorenzo B., Yarmouth, ME, 1853–58

Alpert, Joseph Robert, Dallas, TX, 1982–86

Anthony, Robert N., Boston, MA, 1959–1975; 1976–

Apantaku, Frank Olusegun, Chicago, IL, 1987–93; 1994–97

Averill, George G., Waterville, ME, 1928–54

Bailey, Dudley P., Everett, MA, 1900–1928

Bakeman, Francis W., Chelsea, MA, 1881–1919

Baldwin, Thomas, Boston, MA, 1821–25

Barnes, Charles P., Houlton, ME, 1923–28; 1929–35

Barnes, Charles Putnam, II, Cape Elizabeth, ME 1973–81

Barnes, John A., Albany, NY, 1944–47

Barnell, Elijah, Greene, ME, 1821–26

Barrows, Joseph, Readfield, ME, 1865–68

Bartlett, Francis F., Waterville, ME, 1951–54

Bassett, Charles Walker (FR), Waterville, ME, 1980–82, 1993–96

Bassett, Norman L., Augusta, ME, 1916–31

Bean, Clifford Allan, Concord, MA, 1970–76

Bean, Susan Fairchild, Glastonbury, CT, 1976–82

Beaumier, Carol M., Falls Church, VA, 1997–2003

Beede, Joshua W., Auburn, ME, 1894–1912

Belcher, Hiram, Farmington, ME, 1847–56

Benbow, Robert Mark (FR), Fairfield, ME, 1967–70

Berry, Myrtice C., Newburyport, MA, 1941–47

Besteman, Catherine Lowe (FR), Waterville, ME, 1999–2000; 2001–2002

Billings, John, Fayette, ME, 1840–43

Bixler, Julius Seelye, Jaffrey, NH, 1957–60, 1962–84

Blanchard, Lawrence Russell, Worcester, MA, 1961–66

Boardman, Sylvanus, New Sharon, ME, 1821–27

Bok, Mary Curtis, Merion Station, PA, 1936–39

Bolles, Lucius, Salem, MA, 1821–42

Bondy, Anne Lawrence, Mamaroneck, NY, 1981–87

Bonney, Percival, Portland, ME, 1876–1906

Bosworth, George W., Boston, MA, 1865–88

Boulos, Joseph F., Falmouth, ME, 1993–99; 2000–

Boutelle, George K., Waterville, ME, 1899–1918

Boutelle, Nathaniel R., Waterville, ME, 1856–69

Boutelle, Timothy, Waterville, ME, 1821–55

Bowen, Roger Wilson (FR), Waterville, ME, 1989–91

Bradbury, Woodman, Newton Centre, MA, 1907–35

Bramhall, Ralph A., Portland, ME, 1929–34

Breckenridge, Walter N. (FR), Waterville, ME, 1955–57

Briggs, Otis, Hampden, ME, 1821–42

Brown, Carlton D., Waterville, ME, 1954–60

Bruns, Robert Alan, Weston, CT, 1982–1983

Brush, John Woolman, Newton Centre, MA, 1945–51

Bryan, William Lafrentz, East Holden, ME, 1972–78

Bullen, George, New London, NH, 1893–1916

Bullock, H. Ridgely, New York, NY, 1978–96

Burke, Robert William, Somerset, NJ, 1981–87

Burns, John Lawrence, Greenwich, CT, 1978–82

Burrage, Henry S., Portland, ME, 1881–1906

Butler, John, Thomaston, ME, 1826–55

Butler, Nathaniel, Hallowell, ME, 1856–87

Butler, Nathaniel, Jr., Waterville, ME, 1898–1904

Cahners, Norman L., Boston, MA, 1969–75

Caldwell, Samuel L., Providence, RI, 1850–63

Camp, Alida Milliken, East Bluehill, ME, 1964–77; 1978–98

Camp, Frederic Edgar, East Bluehill, ME, 1941–60; 1962–63

Campbell, Alexander, Cherryfield, ME, 1870–76

Campbell, David W., Cherryfield, ME, 1896–1917

Campbell, Levin Hicks, Cambridge, MA, 1982–90; 1991–99

Carpenter, James Morton (FR), Waterville, ME, 1964–67

Carter, Clark Hopkins, Stuart, FL, 1965–80; 1981–89

Caulfield, E. Michael, Madison, NJ, 1993–96

Champlin, James Tift, Portland, ME, 1875–81

Chandler, Harrison, Los Angeles, CA, 1969–74

Chapin, Stephen, Washington, DC, 1821–28

Chaplin, Jeremiah, Rowley, MA, 1833–40

Chaplin, Jeremiah, Jr., Newton Centre, MA, 1843–49

Chapman, Alfred King (FR), Waterville, ME, 1961–63

Chapman, Wilford G., Portland, ME, 1903–21

Chapman, Wilford G., Jr., Portland, ME, 1930–35

Chessman, Daniel, Hallowell, ME, 1822–34

Chilcott, Clio N., Ellsworth, ME, 1936–37

Christy, John Gilray, Philadelphia, PA, 1984–92

Clark, Cecil W., Newtonville, MA, 1943–49

Clark, Royal, Bangor, ME, 1826–52

Coburn, Abner, Skowhegan, ME, 1845–85

Coburn, Eleazer, Skowhegan, ME, 1836–45

Coburn, Louise Helen, Skowhegan, ME, 1919–30

Coddington, Jane Whipple, Murray Hill, NJ, 1994–98

Colby, Bainbridge, New York, NY,
1932–42

Colby, Charles L., New York, NY, 1889–96

Colby, Gardner, Boston, MA, 1865–79

Colby, Gardner R., New York, NY,
1879–89

Colby, Joseph L., Newton Centre, MA,
1897–1918

Colby, Lewis, Cambridgeport, MA,
1842–50

Cole, Helen Dorothy, New York, NY,
1935–41

Collamore, H. Bacon, Hartford, CT,
1946–58

Comeau, Susan, Wellesley, MA, 1987–93;
1994–2000; 2001–

Combellack, Wilfred J. (FR), China, ME,
1958–61

Condon, Randall J., Cincinnati, OH,
1925–30

Conover, Charles W. S., III (FR),
Oakland, ME, 2002–2003

Cook, Daniel, Waterville, ME, 1832–34

Cornell, John R., New York, NY,
1997–2003

Cornish, Leslie C., Augusta, ME,
1888–1926

Corthell, William J., Gorham, ME,
1877–1907

Cotter, William R., Concord, MA, 1986–

Cowie, James E., Kenilworth, IL, 2005–

Crane, Abijah R., East Winthrop, ME,
1871–1919

Crawford, James Bartlett, Richmond, VA,
1992–

Crawford, William C., Allston, MA,
1908–38

Crowell, Merle W., New York, NY, 1937–43

Cummings, Ebenezer E., Concord, NH,
1866–81

Cummings, H. King, Guilford, ME,
1970–81

D'Amico, Augustine R., Bangor, ME,
1954–60

Davenport, Albert H., Malden, MA,
1902–1906

Davis, Andrew A., Santa Fe, NM, 1999–

Davis, Caleb B., Paris, ME, 1842–53

Davis, Isaac, Worcester, MA, 1847–55

Deans, Mary D., Keene, NH, 1940–46

Deering, John William, Portland, ME,
1978–81

Delano, Ebenezer Livermore, ME,
1821–22

Dexter, Henry V., Baldwinsville, MA,
1863–82

Dexter, William H., Worcestor, MA,
1906–12

Diamond, Robert Edward, Jr., London,
England, 1993–2002; 2003–

Dodge, Rex W., Portland, ME, 1915–42

Dolley, Mira Louise, Raymond, ME,
1937–42

Donovan, William N., Newton Centre,
MA, 1935–43

Dorros, Gerald, Wilson, WY, 2002–

Drinkwater, Arthur, Waterville, ME,
1839–70

Drummond, Albert F., Waterville, ME,
1918–29

Drummond, Joshiah H., Portland, ME,
1857–1902

Drummond, E. Richard, Bangor, ME,
1942–45; 1947–53; 1954–69

Dulaney, John Selkirk, Westport, CT,
1983–87

Dunn, Florence Elizabeth, Waterville,
ME, 1930–32; 1934–57

Dunn, Reuben W., Waterville, ME,
1910–27

Dunnell, Mark H., Owatonna, MN,
1858–67

Dunton, Larkin, Boston, MA, 1888–89

Dutton, Newton T., Waterville, ME,
1888–1900

Edmunds, Frank H., New York, NY,
1907–10; 1925–27
Emery, Edith Eilene, Haverhill, MA,
1961–66
Emery, George F., Portland, ME, 1859–62
Esters, Bernard E., Houlton, ME, 1947–53
Evans George, Portland, ME, 1837–47

Fairfield, Joseph S., Springfield, MA,
1958–63
Farnham, Roderick Ewen, Bangor, ME,
1959–65
Feldman, Samuel Robert, Springfield,
MA, 1964–65
Field, John Warner, Bridgeport, CT,
1964–70
Fife, Hilda Mary, Bangor, ME, 1958–64
Finegan, Warren John, Wayland, MA,
1981–89
Fitz, Eustace C., Chelsea, MA, 1886–89
Foss, Eugene N., Jamaica Plains, MA,
1897–1915
Foster, Alfred D., Boston, MA, 1956–61
Foster, John B., Waterville, ME, 1856–59
Friedman, Robert Alan, Scarsdale, NY,
1988–92
Frye, Robie G., Sharon, MA, 1912–15
Fuller, Robert O., Cambridge, MA,
1881–1900
Furek, Robert Michael, West Hartford,
CT, 1990–99

Gabrielson, Guy G., New York, NY,
1941–59
Gardiner, Robert H., Boston, MA,
1961–66
Garland, John Jewett, Los Angeles, CA,
1967–69
Garnsey, Samuel, Bangor, ME, 1831–41;
1847–73
Gelbard, Robert Sidney, Washington, DC,
2004–

Gemery, Henry Albert (FR), Oakland,
ME, 1991–94
Gere, Anne Ruggles, Kirkwood, MI,
1998–2004
Getchell, Everett L., Boston, MA, 1921–26
Gibbs, Emery B., Boston, MA, 1909–23
Giddings, Moses, Bangor, ME, 1852–1911
Gilman, Nathaniel, Waterville, ME,
1821–59
Gilpatrick, James, Bluehill, ME, 1834–51
Gilpatrick, Rose Adelle, Hallowell, ME,
1933–36
Goldberg, Jerome F., Portland, ME,
1989–94
Goldfarb, William Howe, Avon, CT,
1985–93; 1994–2002; 2003–
Goodman, Rae Jean Braunmuller,
Annapolis, MD, 1983–89
Goodwin, Angier, Boston, MA, 1932–34
Goodwin, Forrest, Skowhegan, ME,
1908–13
Gordon, Peter Geofferey, Mill Valley, CA,
1995–98
Gouvêa, Fernando Q. (FR), Waterville,
ME, 1997–2000; 2003–2004
Grande, Marina N., Stamford, CT,
1998–2001
Granger, Abraham H., Burrillville, RI,
1850–66
Gray, Carl R., New York, NY, 1938–39
Gray, Deborah England, Boston, MA,
1992–97; 1998–2005
Gray, Edgar H., Vallejo, CA, 1849–53
Greenough, Byron, Portland, ME,
1841–55
Gross, Otis C., New Gloucester, ME,
1842–49
Grossman, Nissie, Wellesley, MA,
1965–70; 1971–81
Guptill, Leon C., Boston, MA, 1922–27;
1928–32
Gurney, Charles E., Portland, ME,
1921–46

Haggett, William Edwin, Bath, ME,
1982–85

Hale, Eugene, Ellsworth, ME, 1897–99

Hall, Dana W., Chicago, IL, 1917–26

Hall, Richard D., Waterville, ME,
1942–55

Hamilton, Harry E., Greenfield, MA,
1930–31

Hamlin, Charles E., Cambridge, MA,
1880–86

Hamlin, Cyrus, Paris, ME, 1821–29

Hamlin, Elijah L., Bangor, ME, 1841–47

Hamlin, Hannibal, Bangor, ME, 1857–87

Hamlin, Hannibal E., Ellsworth, ME,
1899–1902

Hampton, Eugenie Hahlbohm, Topsfield,
MA, 1972–78

Hanson, Charles V., Skowhegan, ME,
1883–89

Hanson, James H., Waterville, ME,
1862–94

Harris, Mark, Portland, ME, 1821–42

Harris, Peter Bromwell (FR), Waterville,
ME, 2000–2001; 2002–2005

Hart, Henry B., Portland, ME, 1858–71

Hart, Peter David, Washington, DC,
1989–93; 1995–99

Haselton, Wallace Meredith, Augusta,
ME, 1971–77; 1978–81

Haskell, George Edward, Jr., Boston, MA,
1992–97

Haweeli, Doris Hardy, Worcester, MA,
1952–58

Haweeli, Ellen Brooks, Old Greenwich,
CT, 1993–99

Hawley, Jean Gannett, Portland, ME,
1960–72

Haydu, Nancy Spokes, Dover, MA,
1986–94

Haynes, John, Mount Vernon, ME,
1821–49

Hayward, Bertrand Williams, Waterville,
ME, 1979–81

Herrick, Everett C., Fall River, MA,
1919–24; 1928–34

Higgins, John H., Charleston, ME,
1890–1910

Hill, Frederick T., Waterville, ME,
1937–58

Hill, Helen H., Wellesley, MA, 1931–34

Hill, Kevin, Waterville, ME, 1977–83

Hill, Mark L., Phippsburg, ME, 1821–26

Hilton, Henry H., Chicago, IL, 1930–44

Hinds, Asher C., Portland, ME, 1904–19

Hodgkins, Theodore Roosevelt, Wilton,
ME, 1966–72

Holt, Daniel Ray, Everett, MA, 1956–62

Holt, Marjorie S., Portland, ME, 1948–54

Holtz, Gerald Jay, Brookline, MA,
1984–92; 1993–2001

Hopkins, Calvin, Mount Vernon, ME,
1869–80

Hovey, Alvah, Newton Centre, MA,
1869–70

Hovey, John, Mount Vernon, ME, 1821–32

Hubbard, Frank B., Waterville, ME,
1933–47

Hubbard, John, Hallowell, ME, 1849–62

Hudson, James H., Guilford, ME, 1933–44

Humphrey, Chapin, Bangor, ME, 1874–75

Huntington, Ruiel, Bowdoinham, ME,
1821–37

Hussey, Philip William, Jr.,
Kennebunkport, ME, 1981–87

Hussey, Timothy B., Kennebunk, ME,
2003–

Hutchins, Ruth Rich, Bangor, ME,
1954–70

Jack, William B., Portland, ME, 1938–41

Jetté, Ellerton Marcel, Boston, MA,
1950–86

Joachim, Nancy, New York, NY, 2001–

Johnson, Clayton Weare, Bloomfield, CT,
1965–71

Johnson, Franklin Winslow, Waterville, ME, 1920–25; 1926–55

Johnson, Kenneth Algernon, Newton Upper Falls, MA, 1973–82

Jones, Charles A., Woburn, MA, 1907–10

Jones, Gordon Burr, Needham, MA, 1956–72; 1973–82

Jordan, Archer, Auburn, ME, 1919–24

Jordan, Harry T., Lansdowne, PA, 1929–38

Judson, Adoniram, Nobleboro, ME, 1821–23

Kalloch, Amariah, Thomaston, ME, 1843–50

Katz, Audrey Hittinger, Silver Spring, MD, 1996–2001

Kearns, Doris Helen, Cambridge, MA, 1972–74

Keely, George W., Waterville, ME, 1853–55

Kennedy, Abial W., Warren, ME, 1855–60

Kennedy, Almore, Waldoboro, ME, 1877–83

Kennedy, Henry, Waldoboro, ME, 1861–75

Kenny, Edwin James, Jr. (FR), China, ME, 1982–85

Kent, Edward, Bangor, ME, 1838–47

Khoury, Colleen A., Portland, ME, 1995–2003; 2004–

King, Alfred, Portland, ME, 1898–1908

King, Cyrus, Ellsworth, ME, 1912–18

King, William, Bath, ME, 1821–48

Kingsley, Chester W., Cambridge, MA, 1888–1904

Knowlton, Ebenezer, Montville, ME, 1851–58

Knox, George, Lawrence, MA, 1858–64

Koons, Donaldson (FR), Waterville, ME, 1966–69

Labov, Jay Brian (FR), Waterville, ME, 1987–88; 1990–91

Lamson, William, East Gloucester, MA, 1852–55; 1857–83

Lawrence, Fred F., Portland, ME, 1927–32; 1939–56

Lee, Robert Spence, Beverly Farms, MA, 1975–87; 1989–92; 1992–95

Leonard, Neil, Boston, MA, 1933–68

Longstaff, Thomas Richmond Willis (FR), Waterville, ME, 1994–97

Lord, Herbert M., Washington, DC, 1920–25

Low, Robert, North Livermore, ME, 1821–38

Lunder, Paula Crane, Scarborough, ME, 1998–

Lyford, Edwin F., Worcester, MA, 1890–1909

Lyford, Moses, Springfield, MA, 1885–87

MacKay, Colin Edward (FR), Oakland, ME, 1973–75

Madden, Beverly Nalbandian, Dover, MA, 1986–92; 1994–2002

Maginnis, John S., Portland, ME, 1833–38

Magyar, Joanne Weddell, Stamford, CT, 2001–

Maisel, L. Sandy (FR), Waterville, ME, 1985–87; 2004–2005

Marden, Robert Allen, Waterville, ME, 1968–93

Marriner, Ernest Cummings (FR), Waterville, ME, 1957–60

Marson, David Marvin, Dedham, MA, 1984–93

Masters, Andrew, Hallowell, ME, 1838–58

Mavrinac, Albert Anthony (FR), Waterville, ME, 1982–84

Mayo, Leonard Withington, New York, NY, 1957–69

McArthur, Robert Paul (FR), Waterville, ME, 1981–82

McCabe, Rita Ann, Essex, CT, 1966–72; 1973–83

Pillsbury, Phinehas, Greene, ME, 1821–33
Piper, Bettina Wellington, Waterville, ME,
1964–70
Piper, Wilson Collins, Hanover, NH,
1959–74; 1976–85; 1986–1997
Pottle, Frederick Albert, New Haven, CT,
1932–59; 1967–1987
Powell, Kershaw Elias, Waterville, ME,
1982–88
Powers, M. Jane, Medford, MA, 2005–
Preble, Fred M., Ludlow, VT, 1912–28
Pugh, Lawrence Reynolds, Yarmouth,
ME, 1982–1988; 1989–
Pullen, Robert White (FR), Waterville,
ME, 1962–64
Pullen, Thomas S., Foxcroft, ME,
1860–65
Pulver, David, Palm Beach Garden, FL,
1983–91; 1992–
Putnam, Beecher, Houlton, ME, 1907–22
Putnam, Harrington, New York, NY,
1902–1903; 1911–12

Rachal, Patricia, Rye, NY, 1980–86
Record, Isaiah, Houlton, ME, 1882–83
Reid, Evans Burton (FR), Waterville, ME,
1969–72
Reisert, Joseph (FR), Waterville, ME,
2005–2006
Reumen, Robert Everett (FR), Waterville,
ME, 1974–76
Reynolds, John Franklin, Waterville, ME,
1971–77
Richards, Charles F., Rockport, ME,
1891–1906
Richards, Fred E., Portland, ME,
1906–1907
Richardson, Alford, Portland, ME,
1834–40
Ricker, Joseph, Augusta, ME, 1849–97
Ripley, Thomas B., Portland, ME, 1821–42
Roberts, Alice Linscott, South Portland,
ME, 1954–60

Robins, Henry Ephraim, Rochester, NY,
1880–82
Robinson, Hugh, West Newton, MA,
1945–48
Robinson, Thomas, Ellsworth, ME,
1849–56
Rollins, Henry Weston, Waterville, ME,
1962–68
Rose, Sarah Janney, Washington, DC,
1985–89
Rosenthal, Jonas Oettinger (FR),
Waterville, ME, 1977–79
Rouhana, William J., Jr., Greenwich, CT,
1999–
Rowell, Robert Converse, Waterville, ME,
1961–67
Roisman, Hannah (FR), Waterville, ME,
2000–2001
Rudnick, Robert A., Washington, DC,
2004–
Runnals, Ninetta M., Dover-Foxcroft,
ME, 1953–59
Ryan, William J., Cumberland Center,
ME, 2000–2005

Sage, Robert, Newton Centre, MA,
1974–1986; 1987–93
Saltonstall, William Gurdon, Exeter, NH,
1961–63
Sargent, Dwight Emerson, Columbia,
MO, 1958–64; 1965–74
Schair, Douglas, M., Falmouth, ME,
1994–2005
Schmaltz, Richard Robert, Rowayton, CT,
1976–95
Schupf, Paul Jacques, Hamilton, NY,
1992–2001; 2002–
Scott, Allan Charles (FR), Waterville, ME,
1964–66
Seaver, Josiah W., South Berwick, ME,
1821–40
Seaverns, Charles, Hartford, CT, 1919–50
Seidl, John M., Houston, TX, 1991–93

Torrey, Joseph, Readfield, ME, 1829–34

Tozier, Barbara L., Portland, ME, 1959–65

Trafton, Charles, South Berwick, ME, 1840–51

Trafton, Herbert W., Fort Fairfield, ME, 1912–29

Traister, Barbara Howard, North Hills, PA, 1988–94

Tripp, John, Hebron, ME, 1821–32

Turner, Edward Hill, Belgrade, ME, 1983–91

Turner, Beth Brown, New York, NY, 1989–92; 1993–96

Umphrey, Harry E., Presque Isle, ME, 1948–60

Van Gestel, Allan, Rockport, MA, 1999–2005

Vlachos, Peter Austin, New York, NY, 1977–80

Wadsworth, Herbert E., Winthrop, ME, 1917–37

Warner, Charles F., Springfield, MA, 1910–19

Warren, Ebenezer T., Hallowell, ME, 1821–30

Warren, Milroy, Lubec, ME, 1953–56

Washburn, Japheth C., China, ME, 1822–38

Watson, Jean Margaret, New London, CT, 1965–71

Watson, Thomas J., Jr., Armonk, NY, 1970–75

Watson, Thomas John, III, Norwich, VT, 1975–81

Webb, Edmund F., Waterville, ME, 1883–98

Weber, Carl Jefferson (FR), Waterville, ME, 1955–58

Weeks, Lester Frank, Boothbay Harbor, ME, 1972–73

Weiland, Nancy Greer, New York, NY, 2002–

Wells, Owen W., Falmouth, ME, 2000–2002

Weltman, Esther Ziskind, Cambridge, MA, 1958–74; 1975–77

Weston, Ethel H., Madison, ME, 1932–35

Weston, Nathan, Augusta, ME, 1821–53

Whidden, Charles, Calais, ME, 1868–76

White, Charles Lincoln, Waterville, ME, 1901–1908

Whitman, Beniah Longley, Waterville, ME, 1892–96

Whittemore, Edwin Carey, Waterville, ME, 1905–33

Whittemore, Ruth H., Portland, ME, 1946–52

Wilkins, Robert E., Hartford, CT, 1952–58

Williams, Ralph Samuel, Southport, ME, 1973–83

Wilson, Adam, Waterville, ME, 1828–71

Wilson, George A., South Paris, ME, 1889–1906

Wilson, Joseph K., Portland, ME, 1907–17

Wilson, William, Hallowell, ME, 1860–88

Wing, George C., Auburn, ME, 1901–31

Wolff, Anne Clarke, Brooklyn, NY, 2002–

Wood, Nathan M., Lewiston, ME, 1862–69

Wooldredge, William Dunbar, Hudson, OH, 1988–92

Woolworth, Robert Frederic, Winthrop, ME, 1965–77

Wording, William E., Plainville, CT, 1870–86

Wyman, Walter S., Augusta, ME, 1929–42

Young, Sarah B., Norton, MA, 1934–40

Zacamy, John R., Jr., Mamaroneck, NY, 1992–2001; 2002–2003

Zukowski, Lucille Pinette (FR), Waterville, ME, 1976–81

Teaching Faculty, 1820–2005

As—Assistant Professr
Ao—Associate Professor
In—Instructor
P—Full Professor
Fe—Fellow
Le—Lecturer

Abbiati, David L., Psychology, As 1975–76
Abbott, Carroll W., Business
  Administration, In 1950–51
Abbott, Cheryl L., English, Le 1976–77
Abbott, Theophilus C., Chemistry and
  Natural History and Greek and Latin,
  In 1852–54
Abe, Hideko Nornes, Japanese, As
  1993–95
Abetti, Frank A., French, In 1979–81
Adams, Charles E., Gymnastics, In
  1887–90
Africa, Catherine C., Art, In 1947–48
Africa, Philip R., English, In 1946–48
Ahmed, Zafaryab, Oak Institute, Fe 1999
Ahmeti, Sevdije, Oak Institute, Fe 2001
Airozo, James J., Spanish, As 1984–86
Ajibade, Yemi, Performing Arts, Le 1987
Albis, Robert V., Classics, Le 1990–91
Albright, Charlotte E., English, As 2005
Aldrich, Mark C., Spanish, In 1989–91
Alexander, Daniel S., Mathematics, As
  1992–93
Allen, Archibald W., Classics, P 1956–63
Allen, Christopher S., Government, Le
  1981–82
Allen, Donald B., Geology, In 1967–70; As
  1970–76; Ao 1976–82; P 1982–
Allen, Donald P., Economics, In 1948–51
Allin, John B., English, In 1927–28
Allshouse, John C., Chemistry, Fe
  2001–2002

Alvarez, Manuel A., Spanish, In 1987–88
Anderson, Charles M., Economics, In
  1939–40
Anderson, Douglas, Sociology, As 1996
Anderson, James C., Philosophy, Ao
  1985–89
Anderson, Jeffrey D., Anthropology, As
  1996–2001; Ao 2001–
Anderson, Kiyoko M., Japanese, In
  1984–85
Anderson, Lloyd M., Physical Education,
  In 1946–47; As 1947–48
Anderson, Martin B., Rhetoric, Tutor
  1841–43; P 1843–50
Andress, Reinhard, German, As 1989–90
Andrew, John C., History, Ao 1921–23
Anemone, Anthony A., Russian, As
  1985–92
Anthon, Carl J., History, As 1945–48; Ao
  1948–49
Aplington, Henry W., Biology, In
  1939–42; As 1942–47
Archibald, Douglas N., English, P
  1973–2004
Arellano, Lisa, American Studies and
  Women's, Gender, and Sexuality
  Studies, As 2005–2006
Arendell, Terry J., Sociology, Ao 1994–99;
  P 1999–
Arey, David K., Biology, In 1905–1907
Argosh, Richard, Music, As 1992–96
Armbrecht, Thomas J. D., French, As 2000

Armony, Ariel C., Government, As 1998–2005; Ao 2005–

Armstrong, James F., Music, Ao 1971–76; P 1976–83

Arnold, Marc H., English, In 1969–72; As 1972–73

Ashcraft, Thomas B., Mathematics, Ao 1911–13; P 1913–48

Ashton, Donald C., Jr., Education, In 1999

Atkins, Joseph E., Psychology, In 2002–2003; Fe 2003–2005

Atwood, Gary, Spanish, In 2005–2006

Auffinger, George H., Business Administration, Ao 1924–26

Auster, Marjorie, Physical Education, In 1944–45

Averna, Susan J., Psychology, As 2001–2002

Avrutin, Eugene, History, As 2004–

Azzaretti, Nicholas M., Performing Arts and English, In 1981–84

Babow, Barri Y., Physics, In 1991–92

Bacholle, Michele, French, As 1998–99

Bachrach, Jay E., Philosophy, In 1961–63

Bacon, Charles N., English, In 1946–49

Bacon, Roger C., English, In 1923–24

Baier, Lee S., English, In 1955–57

Bailey, Matthew, Spanish, In 1988–89

Bailly, Jacques, Classics, In 1996–97

Bancroft, Dennison, Physics, P 1959–74

Barbezat, Debra A., Economics, As 1992–95; Ao 1995–2004; P 2004–

Barden, Garrett, Philosophy, P 1991

Barkin, J. Samuel, Government and Environmental Studies, As 1998–99

Barlow, Robert F., Economics, In 1952–56; As 1956–61; Ao 1961–62

Barnard, Kellee, Classics, Fe 2001–2002

Barndt-Webb, Miriam, Music, As 1982–83

Barnes, Phineas, Greek and Latin, P 1833–39

Barnett, Dennis, Theater and Dance, As 2002

Barnhardt, Karen A., Education, As 2000–

Barr, Clarence F., Mathematics, P 1966–67

Barrett, James C., English and Anthropology, As 1995–

Barteaux, Miriam, Biology, In 1948–50

Bartlett, Harry, French, In 1924–26

Bartlett, Junius A., Tutor 1850–51

Barton, Paulette E., History, In 1999

Bass, Elizabeth, Physical Education, Director, 1909–13

Bassett, Carol H., Mathematics, In 1974–81; As 1981–94

Bassett, Charles W., English and American Studies, As 1969–74; Ao 1974–80; P 1980–2000

Bassett, Norman L., Greek, In 1891–94

Bates, John H., Gymnastics, In 1896–98

Battis, William S., Elocution and Gymnastics, In 1889–92

Bauer, Steven A., English, Le 1979–81; As 1981–82

Baum, Ellen K., Environmental Studies, In 1996–2003

Bayley, William S., Mineralogy and Geology, P 1888–1905

Beagle, Jonathan M., History, In 2002–2003

Beam, Philip C., Art, P 1976–77

Beaton, Donald J., Mathematics, Le 1981–82

Beatty, James W., Jr., Physics, In 1960–62; As 1962–63

Beck, William P., Physics, Ao 1901–1906

Beeman, Richard R., History, P 1979–80

Behr, Todd A., Economics, In 1980–82

Belcher, Jane C., Biology, In 1933–36

Belferman, Herman, Modern Languages, In 1951–52

Benbow, R. Mark, English, In 1950–52; As 1952–55; Ao 1955–62; P 1962–90

Benge, Frances, Spanish, In 1953–54
Bennett, George G., Air Science, As 1954–57
Bennett, Miriam F., Biology, P 1973–93
Berger, Martin A., American Studies and Art, As 1995–96
Berger, Thomas R., Mathematics, P 1995–
Berlinghoff, William P., Mathematics, P 1988–2005
Bermudez, Silvia, Spanish, In 1989–91; As 1991–92
Bernard, Joel C., History, As 1980–90
Berschneider, Clifford J., History, In 1949–53; As 1953–66; Ao 1966–78; P 1978–85
Bertrand-Guy, Annie C., French, As 1979–82
Besio, Kimberly A., Chinese, As 1992–98; Ao 1998–
Bessey, Merton W., Biology, In 1898–1902
Best, Barbara Anne, Biology, As 1993–97
Besteman, Catherine L., Anthropology, As 1993–98; Ao 1998–2005; P 2005–
Beusterien, John, Spanish, As 1997–98
Bevier, Catherine R., Biology, As 1999–
Bharath, Ramachandran, Mathematics, P 1999–2004
Bieber, David A., Physics, In 1958–59
Bier, Martin, Mathematics, As 1987–90
Bierhaus, Edward G., English, As 1970–72
Bikandi-Mejias, Aitor, Spanish, As 1996–98
Bilar, Daniel, Computer Science, As 2004–
Binnie, Eric A.G., Performing Arts, As 1984–85; Ao 1985–87
Birge, Kingsley H., Sociology, In 1946–50; As 1950–56; Ao 1956–62; P 1962–80
Birkel, Michael L., Philosophy and Religion, In 1984–86
Biron, Archille, French, In 1950–52; As 1952–56; Ao 1956–74; P 1974–77; Le 1980–82

Biron, Dorothy, French, In 1967–70
Bishop, Joseph W., Business Administration, In 1945–48; As 1948–51; Ao 1951–55
Bither, Marjorie Duffy, Athletics, In 1937–59; As 1959–65; Ao 1965–76; P 1976–78
Bither, Philip S., German, In 1932–40; As 1940–46; Ao 1946–73; P 1973–74
Bixler, J. Seelye, Philosophy, P 1942–60
Black, J. William, History and Political Economy, P 1894–1924
Black, Marlies, German, In 1989
Blake, Harriet, S., Classics, In 1965–66
Blake, Pamela A., Government and Women's Studies, As 1985–2002
Blake, Stanley E., History, Fe 1999–2000
Blasingham, Ann C., Classics, Le 1988–90
Blevins, Adrian, English, As 2004–
Bliss, Francis R., Classics, In 1948–52; As 1952–55
Blits, Jan, Government, In 1971–72
Blomster, Wesley V., German, As 1961–62
Bluhm, Robert T., Jr., Physics, As 1990–96; Ao 1996–2003; P 2003–
Boardman, George D., Tutor 1822–23
Bober, Stanley, Economics, In 1960–62; As 1962–64
Boccia, Michael, English, As 1994–95
Bogan, Nicholas, Mathematics, In 2001
Bonora, Alain A., French, P 1986
Boren, Jerry F., Philosophy and Religion, In 1967–68
Borgen, Robert S., History, In 1968–69
Borgerding, Todd M., Music, Fe 1997–98
Boruchoff, Judith, Anthropology, Fe 2000–2001
Botcheva-Andonova, Liliana, Government and Environmental Studies, As 2004–
Boucher, Joceline M., Chemistry, As 1995–96

APPENDIX B

Bubar, John H., Administrative Science, As 1981–86

Bucher, Jean-Marie, Modern Languages, In 1957–58

Buchner, Margaret L., German, As 1946–49

Budenz, Julia M., Classics, Le 1980–81

Bulevich, John B., Psychology, In 2006

Bunch, Ralph E., Government, Le 1983

Bundy, Ann H., French, In 1963–69

Bundy, Jean D., French, P 1963–90

Burch, Rebecca L., Psychology, In 2001–2002; As 2002–2003

Burdick, Robert V., English, As 1947–50

Burgum, George K., English, In 1922–23

Burke, Michael D., English, As 1987–2000; Ao 2000–

Burkman, Thomas W., History, In 1975–76

Burner, David, History, In 1961–62

Burns, James M., History, Fe 1998–99

Burns, Robert A., English, As 1985–86

Burns, William C.G., Government and Environmental Studies, In 2002–2003

Burr, Jean, Psychology, Fe 2005–2006

Butler, Lee A., History and East Asian Studies, Fe 2002–2003

Butler, Nathaniel, Jr., Philosophy, P 1896–1901

Butterfield, Lucius A., Elocution, In 1883–84

Cai, Rong, Chinese, As 1995–97

Calhoun, Cheshire C., Philosophy, Ao 1991–99; P 1999–

Calhoun, David H., Philosophy, In 1988–89

Campbell, Alec D., Sociology, As 1998–

Campbell, Debra, Religious Studies, As 1983–90; Ao 1990–2002; P 2002–

Campbell, Murray F., Physics, As 1980–86; Ao 1986–92; P 1992–

Campbell, William C., Pedagogy, In 1889–90

Cannon-Geary, Irene S., German, As 1978–79

Capen, Frank S., Physics, P 1884–86

Caputi, Mary A., Government, As 1988–90

Carlson, C. Lennart, English, In 1932–41; As 1941–43

Carpenter, James, Art, Ao 1950–54; P 1954–81

Carr, Karen, English, In 1993–94; As 1994–96

Carr, Wilbert L., Latin, P 1941–49

Carrick, Christopher Hamler, English and American Studies, In 2004–

Carrick, Tracy Hamler, English, As 2003–

Carroll, Harry R., Psychology, As 1964–75; Ao 1975–82

Carroll, Joseph F., French, In 1962–65

Carson, Thomas, History, As 1991–92

Carter, Benjamin E., Mathematics, As 1910–18; Ao 1918–26

Cary, Richard, English, In 1952–54; As 1954–57; Ao 1957–62; P 1962–75

Cassol, Marie-Ange, French, In 1970–71

Cassol, Sylvain L., English, As 1970–72

Caswell, Robert G., Chemistry, In 1914–16; As 1916–18

Cauz, Francisco A., Spanish, In 1957–60; As 1960–70; Ao 1970–77; P 1977–93

Chamberlain, Clark W., Physics, In 1900–1901

Chambers, George J., Jr., English, Le 1973–74

Champlin, Arthur K., Biology, As 1971–79; Ao 1979–87; P 1987–2003

Champlin, James T., Greek and Latin and Philosophy, P 1841–73

Chapin, Stephen, Sacred Theology, P 1822–28

Chaplin, Jeremiah, Sacred Philosophy, P 1820–22; 1829–32

Chaplin, John O., Latin and English,
Tutor 1828–32; P 1832–33
Chapman, Alfred King, English, In
1928–34; As 1934–46; Ao 1946–52; P
1952–69
Chester, Webster, Biology, In 1903–1905;
Ao 1905–10; P 1910–48
Chentsova Dutton, Yulia, Psychology, As
2005–
Chilcoat, A. Michelle, French, In 1995–97;
Fe 1997–98; As 1998–99
Chipman, Wilmon B., Jr., Chemistry, In
1960–62; As 1962–65
Chodrow, Don, Physics, As 1976–78
Christainsen, Gregory B., Economics, In
1980–81; As 1981–84
Christiansen, Robert E., Economics, In
1979–81; As 1981–85
Christie, C. Philip, Air Science, P 1951–55
Cimbollek, Max G., Music, In 1954–55
Claeson, Bjorn, Anthropology, In
1995–96
Clarey, Richard J., Business
Administration, In 1963–64; As
1974–79
Clark, John A., Philosophy, Ao 1946–52; P
1952–72
Clarke, Ralph T., Biology, In 1966–67
Clarke, Robert F., English, In 1956–59
Clements, Joyce M., Women's, Gender,
and Sexuality Studies, In 2003
Clifford, Robert E., Physical Education,
As 1956–62
Clifton, Kevin, Music, Fe 2001
Cluett, Ronald, Classics, Le 1991–92
Coca Senade, Javier, Spanish, In 1988–89
Coffin, Peter R., Philosophy, In 1954–56
Cohen, Daniel H., Philosophy, As
1983–91; Ao 1991–2000; P 2000–
Cohen, Paul E., Mathematics, As 2005
Cohen, Sarah, Art, As 1988–90
Cohn, Harvey, Physical Education,
Director, 1914–16

Colbert, Jaimee, English, As 1998
Colbert, Maria, Spanish, In 2004–2005;
As 2005–
Cole, Elizabeth, Religion, In 1941–43
Cole, F. Russell, Biology, As 1977–83; Ao
1983–90; P 1990–
Coleman, George L., II, Geology, In
1963–66; As 1966–76; Ao 1976–
Colgan, Edward J., Education and
Psychology, Ao 1924–28; P 1928–55
Colladay, Donald, Physics, Fe 1999–2000
Collins, Steven W., Government, As
1992–93
Colton, Cullen B., English, In 1930–34
Combellack, Wilfred J., Mathematics, P
1948–80
Comparetti, Alice P., English, In 1936–43;
As 1943–52; Ao 1952–61; P 1961–73
Comparetti, Ermanno, Music, In
1942–46; As 1946–49; Ao 1949–52; P
1952–74
Conant, Thomas J., Languages, P
1827–33
Congdon, Clare Bates, Computer Science,
As 2000–
Conly, Sarah O., Philosophy, As 2001–
Connell, Chester C., Modern Languages,
In 1945–46
Conover, Charles W.S., III, Physics, As
1990–97; Ao 1997–2004; P 2004–
Conry, Rebecca R., Chemistry, As
2000–2004; Ao 2004–
Contreras, Daniel, English, As 2003–
Cook, Charles H., English, In 1949–51
Cook, Constance, Chinese, In 1988–89
Cook, Cristanna M., Economics, Ao
2001–2006
Cook, James S., Jr., Education, In 1999
Cook, Leroy J., Romance Languages, In
1914–15
Coons, John H., Physical Education, In
1956–58
Cooper, Allison A., Italian, In 2002–

APPENDIX B

Corbin, Samuel E., Air Science, As
1951–54
Corey, Charles N., Physical Education, In
1949–51; As 1951–52
Cornelius, David K., English, In 1950–52
Corrado, Anthony J., Jr., Government, In
1986–89; As 1989–94; Ao 1994–2001;
P 2001–
Corvalán, Octavio E., Modern Languages,
Ao 1958–59
Cosdon, Mark N., Performing Arts, Fe
1998–99
Cotter, William R., Government, P
1979–2001
Courtemanche, Eleanor C., English, As
1998
Cox, Dane J., Economics, In 1965–68; As
1968–76; Ao 1976–77
Cox, Robert S., French, In 1962–63; As
1963–66
Craig, Alexander, English, Le 1964–66
Crain, Charles M., Modern Languages, In
1952–53
Crawford, David, English, In 1941–42
Crawford, William R., English, In 1957–59
Cresswell, Maxwell J., Philosophy, P 1996
Crichton, Alan, Art, In 1996–97
Critchfield, Theodore M., History, In
1970–72
Crocker, Denton W., Biology, In 1953–55;
As 1955–58; Ao 1958–61
Crocker, Lance W., Administrative
Science, Le 1978–79
Crosby, April E., Philosophy, Le 1978–79
Crosby, Atwood, Gymnastics, In 1875–78
Cross, Carolyn M., Mathematics, As
1996–97
Croswell, Mary S., Physical Education,
Director, 1905–1909
Crowell, Josephine M., Physical
Education, Director, 1913–14
Crowell, Robert W., Modern Languages
and German, As 1910–17; Ao 1917–18

Cudderback, John F., Physical Education,
In 1952–55
Cullinan, John, Mathematics, As
2005–2006
Culp, Gerard H., Air Science / Aerospace
Studies, As 1961–65
Cummiskey, David, Philosophy, Ao 1997
Cunningham, Anthony P., Philosophy, As
1989–91
Curran, Eileen M., English, In 1958–60;
As 1960–66; Ao 1966–73; P 1973–92
Curren, Erin F., French, As 2005–2006
Curry, Jane Leftwich, Government, Ao
1993–95
Cutbill, Catherine C., Anthropology, As
1993–94

Daddieh, Cyril K., Government, As
1986–88
Dadian, Christopher H., Classics, Le
1978–80
Dailey, Maceo C., History, Le 1980
Daley, Edward J., Physical Education,
Director, 1912–14
D'Amato, Paola, Italian, In 2004
D'Amelio, Alice L., Physical Education, In
1954–56
Danesh, A. Hassan, Sociology, As 1985–89
Danner, G. Russell, Biology, As 2004
Danoff, Alexander P., Modern Languages,
In 1930–32
D'Anton, Peter A., Government, As
1992–93
Das, David Hari, History, As 1991–92
Dauge-Roth, Alexandre, French, As
1999–2001
Davidson, Douglas V., American Studies,
Le 1980–81
Davies, Robert R., Physics, In 1967–69
Davis, Nina C., Spanish, In 1979–81
Davis, Ronald B., Biology, In 1960–62; As
1962–67; Ao 1967–70
Davis, Ryan M., English, In 1999–2000

Davison, Alan, Spanish, In 1991–92

Dean, Frank O., English and
Mathematics, In 1909–11

De Hart, Cor, Psychology, Le 1969–71

Dell, Harry J., Classics, In 1959–62

Dell'Olio, Michael J., Administrative
Science, As 2004–2006

Denney, Martha J., Education, As 2001–

Denoeux, Guilain P., Government, In
1990–91; As 1991–96; Ao 1996–2003; P
2003–

Dephtereos, Andrew J., English, As
1997–2001

Dersch, Virginia J., Sociology, As 1985–88

de Sherbinin, Julie W., Russian, As
1993–99; Ao 1999–

De Sisto, Michael J., Psychology, As
1970–74

DeSombre, Elizabeth, Government and
Environmental Studies, In 1995–96;
As 1996–2001; Ao 2001–2002

DeVito, Ann F., Classics, Le 1985–86

Devlin, Keith J., Mathematics, P 1989–93

Devlin, L. Patrick, English, In 1963–64

Diaconoff, Suellen, French, As 1986–90;
Ao 1990–2000; P 2000–

Diaz, Roberto Ignacio, Spanish, In
1990–91

Dibble-Dieng, Meadow, French, As
2005–2006

Dietz, Frederick C., Air Science, As
1953–56

DiGiacomo, Susan M., Anthropology, In
1984–85

Dillaha, Janis, Chemistry, In 1954–55

Ditmanson, Peter B., History and East
Asian Studies, As 1999–

Doan, Robert J., French, In 1969–73; Le
1977–78

Dodd, Anne W., Education, In 1986–88

Doel, Priscilla A., Spanish, In 1965–68; As
1968–78; Ao 1978–93; P 1993–

Doel, Robert G., Sociology, As 1965–85

Dole, Francis S., Air Science, As 1954–57

Doll, William E., Geology, As 1983–91

Donahue, Denise M., Art, In 1987–88

Donath, Jackie R., Art and American
Studies, As 1986–87

Donihue, Michael R., Economics, As
1989–96; Ao 1996–

Dooley, Martin D., Economics, In
1976–78; As 1978–81

Dorain, Paul B., Chemistry, P 1981–82

Dorigo, Andrea E., Chemistry, As
1997–98

Doss, Heidi Jo, Environmental Studies, Le
1994

Doss, Paul, Geology, As 1991–91; In
1991–97

Downey, Allen B., Computer Science, As
1997–2000

Downing, Marymay, Classics, In 1981–82

Downs, Linwood C., Administrative
Science, In 2003–

Drew, Ralph H., Chemistry, In 1920–21

Drisko, William J., Physics, Ao 1900

Drouglazet, Nathalie N., French, In
2002–2003

Drury, Asa, Greek and Latin, P 1839–40

Dudley, John M., Physics, Ao 1964–86; P
1986–92

Dufour, Charles L, Psychology, As
1990–91

Dunbar, Donald R., Philosophy, In
1961–62

Dunham, Anna L., Biology, As 1950–55

Dunham, Shari Uldrich, Chemistry, As
1998–2005

Dunham, Stephen Uldrich, Chemistry, As
1998–2005

Dunlevy, James A., Economics, As
1968–74

Dunn, Florence E., Latin and English, In
1909–23; As 1923–29; P 1929–34

Dutton, Gregory, Chemistry, In
2005–2006

Early, Benjamin W., English, In 1945–48

Eastman, Margaret A., Chemistry, As 1991–92

Easton, Thomas W., Biology, As 1960–64; Ao 1964–85; P 1985–87

Eaton, E. Perley, Chemistry, In 1927–30

Edelglass, William, Philosophy, As 2005–2006

Edwards, Beatrice E., Sociology, As 1981–86

Edwards, C. Harry, Physical Education, Ao 1921–22; P 1922–34

Ehrenreich, Jeffrey D., Anthropology, As 1987–88

Elder, William, Chemistry and Natural Philosophy and Chemistry, P 1873–1903

Elison, George S., History, In 1964–66; As 1966–74; Ao 1974–75

Ellenbogen, Paul D., Government, As 1994–96

Ellis, Donald W., English, In 1916–17

Elman, Benjamin A., Philosophy, Le 1980–82

Emery, Florence L., Physical Education, Director, 1917–20

England, Caroline R., Theater and Dance, In 2003

England, Eileen M., Psychology, As 1987–88

Engman, Bevin L., Art, As 1996–2002; Ao 2002–

Estaver, Paul E., English, In 1949–51

Estow, Sarah, Psychology, As 2001–2004

Eustis, A. Galen, Economics and Business Administration, In 1924–27; Ao 1927–37; P 1937–57

Evans, Austin H., Greek, In 1894–96

Evans, Gwenaelle J., French, As 1995

Evans, Rhodri, Physics, As 1994–95

Fadem, Brett S., Physics, Fe 2002–2004

Fairley, Arthur S., Physics, Ao 1959–66; P 1966–67

Falgout, Suzanne, Anthropology, As 1987–91

Fallaw, Ben W., History and Latin American Studies, As 2000–

Farber, Barry M., Administrative Science, As 1995–

Farnham, Jonathan E., Tutor 1833–35

Farnsworth, Robert L., English, As 1983–89

Farr, Sidney W., Government, Le 1970–78; As 1978–79

Farrell, Kevin J., Mathematics, In 1987–89; As 1989–90

Fassett, Frederick G., Journalism, In 1913–17

Faulds, Bruce D., Psychology, In 1959–61

Faw, Marjorie, Religion, In 1939–41

Fay, Derick A., Anthropology, Fe 2003–2004

Fay, Eliphaz, Philosophy, P 1841–43

Fearon, David S., Sr., Administrative Science, Ao 1984–85

Fecteau, Monique L., French, In 1987–88

Feigon, Lee N., East Asian Studies and History, In 1976–78; As 1978–82; Ao 1982–90; P 1990–97

Fekete, Frank A., Biology, As 1983–89; Ao 1989–96; P 1996–

Felger, Ralph W., Air Science / Aerospace Studies, As 1958–61

Fell, James E., Jr., Administrative Science, Ao 1992–93

Ferguson, Charles A., French, As 1967–75; Ao 1975–95

Ferguson, Lore, German, In 1968–69; As 1969–91

Ferm, Deane W., Religious Studies, P 1989–92

Fernald, Arthur T., Geology, In 1946–47

Fernandes, Chris S. T., Computer Science, As 2000–2001

Ferster, Judith I., English, As 1973–77

Fiedler, Gesa M., Music, Le 1960–63

Garabano, Sandra I., Spanish, As 1998–99

Garcia, Emma, Spanish, As 2005–

Gardiner, Jean K., Modern Languages, In 1945–48; As 1948–51

Gardner, Virginia, Physical Education, In 1939–40

Garraway, W. Dale, Mathematics, In 2001–2002

Garrett, Peter, Geology, Le 1979–80

Gassler, Robert S., Economics, In 1979–80

Gastaldo, Robert A., Geology, P 1999–

Gates, Gordon E., Biology, P 1948–51

Gaudreau, Lorraine N., Sociology, In 1961–62

Gautschi, Frederick H., Administrative Science, As 1981–86

Gautschi, Jeri B., Administrative Science, Le 1984

Gebrewold, Aklilu, English, In 1986–89

Geib, Frederick A., Sociology, In 1955–57; As 1957–66; Ao 1966–75; P 1975–91

Gemery, Henry A., Economics and Business Administration, In 1960–63; As 1963–71; Ao 1971–77; P 1977–2002

Gerber, Rebecca L., Music, As 1985–93

Gettens, Rutherford J., Chemistry, In 1923–27

Gherman, Dawn L., English, As 1975–76

Gibbons, Arthur M., Art, In 1972–73

Gilbert, J. Peter, Administrative Science, Ao 1996

Gilbert, Mary Ann, Biology, In 1970–71

Gilbert, Michael D., Government, In 1963–64

Gilbert, William H., Biology, As 1970–76

Gilkes, Cheryl Townsend, Sociology and African American Studies, As 1987–89; Ao 1989–2000; P 2000–

Gillespie, James M., Psychology, As 1951–61; Ao 1961–69; P 1969–84

Gillespie, Robert A., English, As 1971–86; Ao 1986–2005

Gilliam, Bryan R., Music, As 1983–86

Gillum, K. Frederick, History, In 1948–51; As 1951–55; Ao 1955–65; P 1965–95

Gilman, Richard C., Philosophy, In 1950–52; As 1952–55; Ao 1955–56

Gilmore, John E., History, In 1954–55

Gimbel, John G., Mathematics, In 1982–83; As 1983–87

Gimenez, Clara, Spanish, In 1994–95

Giraud, Frank H., English, In 1948–49

Glasser, Richard B., Education, As 1974–75

Gleason, Gayle C., Geology, As 1999–2000

Goetz, Nancy H., Art, As 1992–95

Gogol, Miriam S., English, Le 1979–80

Golden, Michael, Music, As 1993–95

Gonzalez-Alonso, Javier, Spanish, In 1985–87; As 1987–2004

Goodman, Philip R., Modern Languages, In 1969–70

Gordon, Jill P., Philosophy, As 1991–97; Ao 1997–2004; P 2004–

Gordon, William J., Mathematics, As 1984–85

Gottlieb, Julius, Bacteriology, P 1946–50

Gottlieb, Paul A., History, In 1957–58

Goulet, John A., Mathematics, As 1976–83

Goulston, Ralph, Psychology, As 1947–51

Gouvea, Fernando Q., Mathematics, As 1991–94; Ao 1994–2001; P 2001–

Graham, John P., Geology, As 1997–99

Grande, Sandy M., Education, In 1995–96; As 1996–2000

Gray, Jane L., Sociology, In 1989–90

Green, Allan P., English, In 1963–66

Green, Douglas E., English, As 1985–86

Green, Isaac, Jr., English, As 1976–77

Green, Samuel M., Art, As 1943–47; Ao 1947–48

Greenspan, Arthur D., French, As 1978–83; Ao 1983–91; P 1991–

Greenwood, Paul G., Biology, As 1987–91; Ao 1991–2004; P 2004–

Gregg, Karl C., Spanish, In 1963–66

Gregory, Charles J, Biology, In 1988–89

Gresson, Aaron D., Human Development, Le 1979–81

Griffiths, Thomas M., History, As 1926–44

Grim, Charles L., III, Economics, In 1985–88; As 1988

Grives, Steven M., Music, As 2002–2003

Grossman, Michele, Psychology, As 1994–95

Groth, David E., Government, In 1984–85

Grover, Frederick W., Physics, Ao 1911–13; P 1913–20

Grubbs, Daniel H., Government, In 1955–57

Guillois, Christiane, French, As 1993–

Gulick, Faith, Physical Education, In 1959–62; As 1962–63

Gullbergh, Harold W., Psychology, As 1950–51

Gunn, Richard W., Philosophy and Religion, In 1968

Gunthner, Gotthard, Philosophy, Le 1942–43; As 1943–44

Guss, Donald L., English, In 1959–61

Haas, Heather A., Psychology, As 2000–2001

Haave, Ethel-Mae, English, In 1944–45

Haffner, Rudolph E., Biology, In 1945–47

Hagens, John B., Economics, As 1975–81

Haigh, Maria, Computer Science, As 2002

Haigh, Thomas David, Administrative Science, In 2001–2003

Haldar, Mohit Kumar, Philosophy, Le 1962–63

Hale, Piers, Science, Technology, and Society, As 2005–2006

Haley, Charles T., History, In 1977–79

Haley, Jean, Biology, As 1992–95

Hall, Edward W., Modern Languages, P 1866–1910

Hall, Jon F., French and English, As 1971–76

Hallberg, Kristin M., Economics, As 1982–86

Hallstrom, Jonathan F., Music, As 1984–90; Ao 1990–

Hamilton, Kenneth G., Mathematics, In 1978–79; As 1979–84

Hamilton, Nathan D., Sociology and Anthropology, Le 1985

Hamlin, Charles E., Chemistry and Natural History, P 1853–73

Hanna, Ardele J., Spanish, In 1973

Hanna, Raouf S., Economics, As 1972–77

Hannay, Neilson C., English, As 1920–22

Hannula, Thomas A., Mathematics, Ao 1987–88

Hannum, Lynn, Biology, As 2001–

Hanson, David A., Russian, As 1991

Harada, Hiroko, Japanese, In 1995–98

Harjan, George, Modern Languages, In 1959–61

Harkleroad, Leon, Mathematics, Ao 2002–2003

Harlow, Ivan O., Chemistry, In 1913–15

Harned, Louise, Government, In 1958–59

Harnish, Joke A., Mathematics, Le 1983–84

Harrier, Richard C., English, In 1952–55; As 1955–57

Harris, Don G., Air Science / Aerospace Studies, As 1969–70; Ao 1970–72

Harris, Natalie B., English, As 1978–88; Ao 1988–

Harris, Peter B., English, In 1974–75; As 1975–83; Ao 1983–89; P 1989–

Harry, Philip W., Romance Languages and Literature, As 1914–22

Hartman, Charlie, Administrative Science, In 1987

Haskett, Robert S., History, As 1986–87

Hastings, Florence O., Physical Education, In 1914–16

Hatch, Hugh R., Mathematics, P 1903–1909

Hatch, Walter F., Government, As 2002–

Hauss, Charles S., Government, In 1975–76; As 1976–82; Ao 1982–90; P 1990–93

Hawk, Beverly G., Government, In 1985–89; As 1989–92

Haynes, Lowell Q., Philosophy, In 1925–29; As 1929–43

Haynes, Robin A.S., American Studies and Art, As 1989–94

Hayslett, Homer T., Jr., Mathematics, In 1962–65; As 1965–78; Ao 1978–88; P 1988–

Hazard, Mark, English, As 1999–2001

Hazelton, Paul V., Education, Ao 1962–63

Hedman, John, Modern Languages, Greek, and Romance Languages, In 1895–1900; Ao 1900–1901; P 1901–14

Heid, Patricia, Spanish, As 1997–98

Heinrich, Adel, Music, In 1964–67; As 1967–77; Ao 1977–88

Heitzman, Michele W., Sociology, In 1973–74

Helie, Euclid, Romance Languages, In 1918–19; As 1919–21; Ao 1921–42

Helm, Patricia B., Music, In 1990–98; As 1998–2004

Helm, Peyton R., Classics, P 1988–2003

Henderson, Liza M.B., English, In 1992–93

Hennessy, Catherine A., French, In 1967–68

Hennessy, John G., Air Science / Aerospace Studies, As 1966–69

Hennessy, Margaret H., Chemistry, In 2000–2001

Henry, Bill Conard, Psychology, As 1993–99

Hensley, Shelley S., French, In 1983

Hernandez Casado, Valentina, Spanish, In 1988–89

Hernandez-Torres, Ivette, Spanish, In 1993–97

Herold, Kirsten, English, Wallace, Kirsten F., In 1985–86

Herrmann, Gina Ann, Spanish, As 1998–2003

Herschman, Arthur, Physics, In 1954–55

Herszenhorn, Jaime, Spanish, In 1976–77

Hickox, Charles F., Jr., Geology, As 1957–61; Ao 1961–72

Higbie, Carolyn, Classics, Le 1986–87

Higgins, John T. R., Art, As 1974–78

Hileman, Douglas R., Biology, As 1981–82

Hilinski, S. Eugene, Air Science / Aerospace Studies, In 1968–71

Hirakata, Yukiko, Japanese, In 1989–91

Hitchings, Edson F., Biology, In 1897–98

Hoag, James A., Computer Science, In 2002–2003

Hoagland, Anthony, English, In 1993–94; As 1994–96

Hockridge, Marion L., Modern Languages, As 1947–50

Hoffacker, John F., Music, In 1988–89

Hogendorn, Dianne H., Classics, In 1967–68; As 1968–69

Hogendorn, Jan S., Economics, In 1963–66; As 1966–70; Ao 1970–76; P 1976–2003

Holder, Francis J., Mathematics, Ao 1909–11

Holland, Henry, Spanish, In 1952–54; As 1954–57; Ao 1957–66; P 1966–88

Holly, Charles A., Mathematics, As 1997, 2004

Holly, Jan E., Mathematics, As 1996–2004; Ao 2004–

Holman, Abigail M., Environmental Studies, As 2003

Holmer, Walter R., Physical Education, As 1947–51

Holmes, Alice M., Biblical Literature, As 1919–20

Holmes, Ezekiel, Chemistry and Geology, Le 1833–37

Holmes, Olivia, Italian, As 2001–

Holmes, Susan E., Biology, As 2004

Hoopes, Linda L., Psychology, As 1987–90

Hopengarten, Fredric J., Administrative Science, Le 1978–79

Horton, Scott L., Psychology, As 2001

Horton, Stephen H., English, In 1950–52

Horwitz, Richard P, History, As 1975–76

Hosack, John M., Computer Science, As 1981–87

Houde, Carol R., Psychology, In 1979–80

Hoverson, Katrina Goff, Spanish, In 1995

Howard, C. Leslie, Classics, P 1968–73

Howard, David C., Business Administration, In 1946–50

Howard, Malcolm Adam, Education, Fe 2003–2004

Hriskos, Constantine, Anthropology, In 1990–91; As 1991–2006

Hronek, Pamela, History, As 1990–92

Hu, Shaohua, Government, As 2000–2001

Hudnut, Richard, Art, P 1953–54

Hudson, Frederic M., Religious Studies, As 1965–69

Hudson, Yeager, Philosophy, In 1959–65; As 1965–70; Ao 1970–77; P 1977–99

Huelshoff, Michael G., Government, Le 1984

Huey, Talbott W., Government, Le 1980–81

Hughes, John, Economics, As 1986–87

Hull, Gordon F., Physics, Ao 1898–1900

Humphreys, Lester J., History, In 1966–67

Hunt, Joseph A., English, In 1968–71; As 1971–72

Hunt, Merrill V., English, Le 1981

Hunt, Raeburn S., English, In 1923–24

Hunt, Timothy A., English, As 1980–81

Hunter, Jane H., History, As 1980–89; Ao 1989–91

Hurd, Charles B., Chemistry, As 1921–22

Hurley, Donal, Mathematics, P 1996

Hutchison, Elizabeth Q., History, As 1996–98

Hwangbo, Imi, Art, As 1993–94

Hyde, Ralph W., English, In 1949–50

Iijima, Yuka, Japanese, In 1997–99

Iorio, John J., English, In 1955–57; As 1957–63

Irland, Lloyd C., Economics, As 1990–2001

Iwinski, Mark T., Art, Fe 2000–2001

Jackson, Barry B., Spanish, In 1977–78

Jackson, Henry C., Gymnastics, In 1894–96

Jackson, Laura Lynn, Music, In 1998–99

Jacob, Plamthodathil S., Philosophy, Le 1964–76

Jacobs, Charles G., Music, In 1963–64

Jacobs, James L., Psychology, As 1992–93

Jacobs, Robert C., Government, In 1965–68; As 1968–70

Jacobson, Harold A., Education, Ao 1968–77; P 1977–87

James, Kenneth R., English, As 2003

Janzen, Christopher, Chemistry, As 1989–90

Jaquith, Richard H., Chemistry, As 1947–52

Jarrett, Bret D., Geology, As 2005

Jarvis, Kimberly A., History, Fe 2002–2003

Jayne, Edward S., English, Le 1979–80

Jeffery, Clarence R., Sociology, In 1951–54

Jellison, A. Eugene, English, In 1953–57

Jensen, Erik N., History, As 2003–2004

Jenson, Paul G., Psychology, P 1971–81
Jerome Sutcliffe, Nina, Art, As 1991–92
Johnson, Clarence R., Romance
  Languages, In 1915–18; As 1918–19
Johnson, E. Parker, Psychology, P 1955–78
Johnson, Franklin W., Education, P
  1929–42
Johnson, Gerald B., English, In 1977–78
Johnson, Karen L., Biology, In 1966–68
Johnson, Keith, Biology, As 1999–2002
Johnson, Russell R., Biology, As
  1996–2002; Ao 2002–
Johnson, Samuel S., Tutor 1839–41
Johnston, Rebecca M., Biology, As
  1997–98
Jones, Randolph M., Computer Science,
  As 1998–
Jones, Rhett S., History and African
  American Studies, P 1986
Jordan, Henri A., Mathematics, Ao
  1947–49
Joseph, John M., Jr., Economics, In
  1975–76; Le 1976–2001; P 2001–2002
Joseph, Robert A., Physics, As 1983–84
Josephson, Paul R., History, Ao 2000–
Judah, Wayne M., French, In 1962–64; As
  1964–67
Juhasz, Marcus A., Chemistry, Fe
  2005–2006
Junghans, Earl A., Mathematics, In
  1960–62; As 1962–72

Kahn, Peter, Education, As 1991–96
Kamundu Batundi, Didier, Oak Institute,
  Fe 1999
Kany, Robert H., History, As 1969–78; Ao
  1978–87
Kaplan, Julius, Art, In 1966
Karbiener, Karen, English, Fe 2001–2001;
  As 2001–2003
Kassel, Barbara L., Art, As 1978–81
Kasser, Jeffrey L., Philosophy, Fe 1998–99;
  As 1999–2004

Kaster, Robert Andrew, Classics, In
  1973–74
Katagiri, Noriko, Japanese, In 1991–92
Katz, Jeffrey L., Chemistry, As 2002–
Kavaler, Peter Joshua, Biology, As 2004–
Kearney, Colbert, English, P 1995
Keefe, Robert J., Physical Education, In
  1948–51
Keely, George W., Mathematics and
  Natural Philosophy, P 1829–52
Keenan, David L., Chinese and East Asian
  Studies, In 1985–87; As 1987–91
Keene, W. Elery, Geology, Le 1976–78
Keeney, Willard F., English, In 1972–73
Kellenberger, Richard K, French, In
  1946–48; As 1948–51; Ao 1951–60; P
  1960–76
Kelley, John H., Physical Education, In
  1955–57; As 1957–77
Kelley, Wallace M., Chemistry, In
  1930–36
Kelly, Derek A., Philosophy and Religion,
  Ao 1968–69
Kelly, Elizabeth S., Physical Education, In
  1940–42
Kelsey, Howard P., English, In 1925–28
Kempers, John, Russian, As 1960–65; Ao
  1965–77
Kempton, Gay, Art, In 1990–92
Kendris, Christopher, Modern Languages,
  In 1956–57
Keniston, Ralph H., Latin, In 1904–1905
Kenneally, John E., Administrative
  Science, In 2003
Kenney, Edwin J., English, As 1968–74; Ao
  1974–82; P 1982–92
Kenney, Susan McIlvaine, English, In
  1968–69; As 1969–83; Ao 1983–86; P
  1986–
Kennison, Karl R., Mathematics, In
  1909–10
Kenyon, John, Psychology, As 1966–69
Keogh, Dermot, History, P 1998

Kerkham, H. Eleanor, Japanese, In 1967–70; As 1970–74

Kestner, Franklin M., Biology, As 1973–75

Kilic-Bahi, Semra, Mathematics, Fe 1996–97

Kim, Heidi J., Sociology, In 1999–2005; As 2005–

Kim, Linda, Art and American Studies, In 2005–2006

Kimball, John W., Chemistry, In 1912–13

Kimbrough, R. Keller, Japanese, As 2001–2005

Kindilien, Carlin T., English, In 1953–55; As 1955–56

King, D. Whitney, Chemistry, As 1989–95; Ao 1995–2002; P 2002–

King, Sallie B., Religious Studies, As 1981–82

Kingdon, Arthur M., Sociology, In 1972–75; As 1975–77; Le 1981–82

Kinnison, Li Qing, Chinese, As 2002–2004

Kinoshita, Tetsuo, Japanese, In 1988–89

Kiralis, Geoffrey W., Mathematics, In 1980–81

Kirby, Henry H., Air Science, P 1955–58

Kirk, Daniel F., English, In 1959–62; As 1962–63

Kirk, John, English, In 1999

Kirkpatrick, Maurine A., Government, In 1977–78

Kittler, Jason, Chemistry, As 1986–87

Kleemeier, Lizz Lyle, Government, In 1983–84; As 1984–85

Klein, William M.P., Psychology, As 1991–98; Ao 1998–2002

Kleinholz, Lewis H., Biology, In 1931–33

Kline, Thornton C., III, Philosophy, As 2004

Knapp, Robert C., Classics, As 1972–73

Knatz, A. Paul, English, In 1967–69

Knight, Yvonne R., Administrative Science, In 1958–62; As 1962–71; Ao 1971–79; P 1979–94

Knox, Omar E., Mathematics, In 1967–70; As 1970–73

Koch, Margaret, Physical Education, In 1898–1902

Kodama, Kenneth M., Government, In 1974–77

Kodama, Tomiko, Japanese, In 1995–96

Koike, Yuko, Japanese, As 2002–2003

Kolden, Gregory G., Psychology, As 1988–92

Kollgaard, Ronald I., Physics, In 1988–89

Koonce, Dorothy M., Classics, In 1963–65; As 1965–70; Ao 1970–80; P 1980–92

Koonce, Howard L., Performing Arts and English, In 1963–66; As 1966–73; Ao 1973–80; P 1980–94

Koons, Donaldson, Geology, As 1946–48; Ao 1948–51; P 1951–82

Koons, Peter O., Geology, In 1978–79

Korejwo, Richard J., Air Science / Aerospace Studies, In 1969–71

Kraehling, Claudia J., Art, In 1980–81

Kreiss, Deborah S., Biology, As 2002–2003

Krueger, Merle C., German, As 1982–83

Krugh, Janis L., Spanish, In 1979–82

Kueter, Cynthia M., German, In 1967–72

Kueter, Hubert C., German, As 1965–70; Ao 1970–97

Kumar, Krishna, Computer Science, As 1993–95

Kurtz, David C., Mathematics, Ao 1984–87

Kurtz, Robert A., Mathematics, As 1984–86

Kusiak, Karen, Education, In 1990–95; As 1995–

Labat, Alvin V., French, Ao 1976–78

Labov, Jay B., Biology, As 1979–84; Ao 1984–97

Ladd, George T., Psychology, As 2002–2005
Ladyko, Emil S., Physical Education, In 1951–52
LaFleur, Robert A., History and East Asian Studies, As 1994–98
Lagueux, Susan D., French, Le 1981–82
Lamson, Howard J., Spanish, In 1965–67
Lamson, William, Tutor 1835–36
Lance, Stacey L., Biology, As 2002–
Landsman, John L., Administrative Science, In 1968–71; As 1971–74
Lane, Charles D., Physics, Fe 2000–2001
Lane, Kenneth D., Mathematics, As 1982–87
Langey, Edward J., Geology, In 1947–48
Langley, Charles B., Chinese, Le 1982–83
Lansberry, Anne M., English, In 1954–55
Laparra, Camille F., French, As 1982–86
Largay, Thomas, Administrative Science, As 1996–2000
LaRiviere, Frederick, Chemistry, Fe 2005–2006
Larrabee, Stephen A., English, In 1940–41
Larson, James, Computer Science, Ao 1996
LaRusch, Michele R., Philosophy, In 1978–79
Lascano, Marcy, Philosophy, Fe 2005–2006
Lathrop, Frank W., Business Administration, In 1951–53; As 1953–56
Laws, John W., Social Science, In 1963–66
Lawton, Ellis E., Physics, As 1907–1909
Lee, Joseph, Government, P 1991
Lee, William A., Administrative Science, Le 1985–86; As 1986–
Lee, William L., English, In 1974–77
Leet, Don R., Economics, As 1975–76
Leighton, Perley M., English, In 1951–52
Lemaire, Martin T., Chemistry, Fe 2004–
Lemon, William, Biology, Fe 1997–98

Leonard, Elizabeth D., History, In 1992–93; As 1993–98; Ao 1998–2005; P 2005–
Leonard, Garry M., English, As 1985–88
Lester, Larry C., Air Science / Aerospace Studies, In 1972–74
Lester, Lewis F., Psychology, As 1970–79; Ao 1979–88
Levine, Alison J. Murray, French, As 2003–
Levitin, Alexis A., English, As 1975–76
Lewis, Daniel G., Physical Education, As 1946–47
Lewis, Jeremy R. T., Government, As 1984–85
Lewis, Lynne Y., Economics, As 2005
Lewis-Colman, David, History, Fe 2004–2005
Libby, Carol B., Chemistry, As 1985–91
Libby, Herbert C., Public Speaking, In 1909–12; As 1912–13; P 1913–44
Libby, R. Daniel, Chemistry, As 1985–92
Lichterfeld Thomas, Margrit, German, As 1985–93
Lieben, Katharyn, Sociology and Anthropology, In 1980–81
Lieberman, Gerald J., Mathematics, As 1973–76
Limm, Paul J., Air Science / Aerospace Studies, As 1959–61
Lindkvist, Heather L., Anthropology, In 2002
Linfield, Eva, Music, As 1993–95; Ao 1995–
Lipovsky, James P., Classics, Le 1976–77
Little, Homer P., Geology, In 1910–11; As 1911–14; P 1914–20
Lively, Robert, Philosophy and Religion, Le 1979–80
Livezeanu, Irina, History, As 1987–91
Livshits, Leo, Mathematics, As 1994–2001; Ao 2001–
Lo, Yuet Keung, Chinese, As 1991–92

Lockhart, Alton I., Chemistry, In
1905–1907
Loebs, Gilbert F., Physical Education, Ao
1934–55; P 1955–66
Lonergan, Francis D., Mathematics, As
1981–82
Long, Jason M., Economics, As 2002–
Long, Virginia C., Physics, As 2000–
Longstaff, Thomas R. W., Religious
Studies, In 1969–73; As 1973–79; Ao
1979–84; P 1984–2004
Loomis, Justin R., Chemistry and
Natural History, Tutor 1836–38; P
1838–52
Lopez, Claudio, Jr., Spanish, As 1983
Lougee, Richard J., Geology, As 1936–37;
Ao 1937–46; P 1946–47
Loughry, William J., Biology, As 1991
Lovemore, Frances, International Studies
and Oak Institute, P 2005
Loviglio, Jason, American Studies, In
1995
Low, Lisa E., English, As 1987–89
Lowerre, Kathryn, Music, As 1999
Lozano Robledo, Alvaro, Mathematics, Fe
2004–2005
Lualdi, Katharine J., History, As
1999–2003
Lubin, David M., Art and American
Studies, As 1983–89; Ao 1989–94; P
1994–99
Luoma, Robert G., Music, As 1979–80
Lupher, David A., Classics, Le 1977–78
Lupovitch, Howard N., History and
Jewish Studies, As 1998–2005; Ao
2005–
Lurie, Lev Iakovlevich, History and
Russian, Ao 1990, 1993
Luthar, Rajindar Singh, Mathematics, In
1965–67
Lyford, Moses, Mathematics and Natural
Philosophy and Physics, P 1856–84
Lynch, Catherine, History, In 1983–84

Lynch, Frederick, Art, As 1994–96
Lynn, Sharon E., Biology, As 2002–2004
Lyon, John, German, Fe 1998–2000

Maazaoui, Abbes, French, As 1991–92
Mabbott, Ann, Modern Languages, Le
1983–86; In 1986–89
Mabbott, Gary A., Chemistry, As
1983–89
MacDonald, Stewart, Economics, As
1917–20
Machemer, Paul E, Chemistry, As
1955–57; Ao 1957–67; P 1967–83
Machlin, Paul S., Music, In 1974–75; As
1975–82; Ao 1982–87; P 1987–
MacKay, Colin E., English, As 1956–61;
Ao 1961–73; P 1973–91
Mackenzie, G. Calvin, Government, As
1978–82; Ao 1982–86; P 1986–
Mackenzie, Sarah V., Education, As
2001–2002
MacLeod, Bruce, Gymnastics, In
1905–1906
Macomber, William E., Education, As
1954–66; Ao 1966–67
MacPhail, Fiona, French, As 1995–96
Madden, Deirdre, Administrative Science,
P 2001
Madison, James M., Business
Administration, In 1959–61
Maginn, Alison M., Spanish, In 1992–93;
As 1993–97
Mahmood, Cynthia Keepley,
Anthropology, As 1992–93
Mahmud, Ushari, Government and Oak
Institute, Fe 2002
Maier, George D., Chemistry, In 1965–66;
As 1966–74; Ao 1974–83; P 1983–86
Maisel, L. Sandy, Government, In
1971–72; As 1972–79; Ao 1979–83; P
1983–
Maisonneuve, Lise, Modern Languages,
Le 1984

Makinen, Evert, Government, In 1965–68; As 1968–70

Malz, Gertrude, Classics, P 1964–67

Manalis, Mel S., Physics, In 1963–64

Mandolfo, Carleen R., Religious Studies, Fe 1998–99; As 2002–

Mann, Margaret, Physical Education, In 1942–44

Manning, Charles, English, In 1931–33

Manning, Irene, Business Administration, In 1942–54

Mannocchi, Phyllis F., English, As 1977–83; Ao 1983–96; P 1996–

Mannur, Hanumant G., Economics, As 1970–72

Mans, Walter A., Air Science / Aerospace Studies, In 1972–74

Mansori, Kashif S., Economics, In 1997–98; As 1998–

Mansori, Meriwynn G., Spanish, In 1995–99; As 1999–2005

Mapp, Thomas G., Art, In 1967–68

Maramarco, Anthony M., English, In 1975–77; As 1977–78

Marchal, Joseph A., Religious Studies, In 2004–2005

Marchant, E. Janet, Physical Education, In 1940–45; As 1945–57; Ao 1957–65

Marcus, Richard R., Government, As 2001–2002

Marden, Donald H., Administrative Science, Le 1978–80

Margolis, Abby R., Anthropology, Fe 2003–2004

Mariner, Francis R., French, As 1986

Mark, Peter D., Mathematics, In 1992–93

Marks, Stephen R., Sociology, In 1969–72

Marlais, Michael A., Art, In 1983–85; As 1985–89; Ao 1989–95; P 1995–

Marquardt, Anton, Modern Languages and German, In 1891–96; Ao 1896–1901; P 1901–27

Marquardt, James J, Government, As 1999–2000

Marriner, Ernest C., English, P 1923–60

Marsh, James R., English, In 1922–23

Marshall, Mary H., English, In 1935–37; As 1937–39; Ao 1939–48

Martin, Carole F., French, As 1990–91

Martin, Doris E., Physical Education, In 1952–54

Martin, John L., Government, In 1990–92

Martin, Joseph A., English, In 1973–75

Martin, Michael F, Economics, As 1989–90

Massie, Pascal J., Philosophy, As 2001–2002

Mateos, Juan Pablo Ortega, Spanish, Le 1965–66

Mathes, D. Benjamin, Mathematics, As 1990–96; Ao 1996–2003; P 2003–

Mathews, Francis X., English, In 1962–65; As 1965–67

Mathews, Grace E., English, Ao 1899–1902

Mathews, Shailer, Rhetoric and History and Political Economy, Ao 1887–89; P 1889–94

Matthews, Harriett, Art, In 1966–69; As 1969–76; Ao 1976–84; P 1984–

Mavrinac, Albert A., Government, P 1958–92

Mavrinac, Marilyn S., Education and History, In 1963–76; As 1976–86; Ao 1986–95

Maxfield, Ezra K., English, In 1912–14; As 1914–16

Maxson, Joyce, Physical Education, In 1945–47

May, Martha E., History, As 1984–85

Mayberry, David W., Russian, In 1988–89

Mayers, Richard R., Physics, In 1956–57; As 1957–61

Mayo, Leonard W., Human Development, P 1966–71

Maze, Frank R., Physical Education, As 1952–56

Mazzeo, Tilar J., English, As 2004–

McAlary, Frederick D., Military Science, In 1917–18

McAleer, Brenda, Administrative Science, As 2003–

McArthur, Robert L., Philosophy, As 1972–77; Ao 1977–83; P 1983–

McArthur, Shannon, Art, Le 1981–90; As 1990–91

McAuliffe, Mark A., Administrative Science, As 1985

McCarthy, Sheila M., Russian, As 1987–92; Ao 1992–

McCarthy, Tommie V., Chemistry, P 1993

McClane, Kenneth A., English, In 1974–75

McConnell, Kent A., Religious Studies, In 2003–2004

McCormick, Karen, Economics, In 1981–82

McCoy, Alfred M., Physical Education, As 1937–41

McCoy, John F., German, Ao 1930–47; P 1947–63

McCoy, Karen P., Art, As 1987

McCue, Ellen M., History, As 1968–71

McCullagh, Ciaran, Sociology, P 1988

McDowell, Deborah E., English, In 1979–80; As 1980–85; Ao 1985–87

McElroy, Douglas M, Biology, In 1991

McFadden, Margaret T., American Studies, As 1996–2002; Ao 2002–

McGee, Julie L., Art, As 1996

McGee, Richard J., Physical Education and Athletics, As 1967–83; Ao 1983–87; P 1987–98

McGlew, James F., Classics, Le 1983–84

McGough, Philip, Administrative Science, As 1980–81

McGowan, John H., Jr., Philosophy and Religion, In 1970–71

McGrane, Bernard D., Sociology, As 1980–81

McGrath, Thomas M., English, In 1940–41

McGuinn, Patrick J., Government, As 2004–2005

McIntyre, James R., German, As 1976–81; Ao 1981–

McKeen, Don H., Modern Languages, In 1957–59

McKeon, Louise, Modern Languages, In 1943–44

McKey, Gordon W., Biology, As 1947–52

McKillop, Alan D., English, In 1914–16

McLeary, Frank B., English, In 1911–12

McNair, Wesley C., English, P 2000–2004

McPherran, Mark L., Philosophy, P 2002–

Mead, Darwin J., Chemistry, In 1936–38

Mead, Jane W., English, As 1993–94

Meader, C. Abbott, Art, In 1961–64; As 1964–72; Ao 1972–96; P 1996–98

Meader, Nancy, Art and French, In 1990–

Meckel, Timothy A., Geology, Fe 2003–2004

Meehan, James W., Jr., Economics, As 1973–77; Ao 1977–82; P 1982–

Meek, Edwin J., III, English, In 1967–69; As 1969–71

Melançon, Benoît, French, In 1984–87

Melcher, Nathaniel, Mathematics, P 1874–75

Menge, Paul E., Government, As 1970–71

Menssen, Sandra L., Philosophy and Religion, As 1984–85

Merideth, Robert D., American Studies, Ao 1974–75

Merlin, Lara C., Women's Studies, As 1999

Metz, Roger N., Physics, As 1968–78; Ao 1978–85; P 1985–91

Meyer, Daniel L., Sociology, As 1988–89

Miao, Weiwen, Mathematics, As 1997–2000

Miaoulis, George, Jr., Administrative Science, P 1994–

Michaels, Herbert S., English, In 1948–51

Milenky, Edward S., Government, In 1971

Millan de Benavides, Carmen, Spanish, Fe 2001–2002

Millard, Julie T., Chemistry, As 1991–97; Ao 1997–2004; P 2004–

Miller, Frank J., Russian, As 1978–85

Miller, George H., Philosophy, and Mathematics, As 1995, 2003

Miller, George M., History, In 1976–77

Miller, Margaret K., Art, In 1962, 1971–78; As 1978–82

Miller, William B., Art, In 1956–57; As 1957–62; Ao 1962–74; P 1974–82

Millett, Ellsworth W., Physical Education, As 1934–46; Ao 1946–66

Millones, Luis, Spanish, As 1998–2004; Ao 2004–

Mills, David H., English, Le 1980–85; In 1985–89; As 1989–

Mills, Leo T., Air Science / Aerospace Studies, As 1965–69

Mills, Mary Elizabeth, Anthropology, In 1992–93; As 1993–99; Ao 1999–

Mills, Neil B., Economics, Le 1974–75

Milton, William M., English, In 1953–55

Miracle, Gary E., Chemistry, As 1998–99

Miran, Marie H., History, Fe 1999–2000

Misrahi, Mary M., French, In 1968–69

Mitchell, Garry J., Art, As 1997–

Mizner, John S., English, In 1963–66; As 1966–74; Ao 1974–80; P 1980–98

Modell, Judith S., Sociology and Anthropology, As 1981–85

Moe, Richard L., Biology, In 1991

Mojallali, Rahim, Mathematics, In 1954–57

Moody, Jonathan F., Philosophy and Religion, In 1968

Moore, Leslie R., Science, In 1902–2003

Moore, Margaret H., Mathematics, In 1985–88

Moore, Rita D., Government, In 1987–89

Moore, Terris, Business Administration, P 1955–57

More, Tamar, Physics, In 1996–97

Moroni, Mario, Italian, As 2001–

Morrione, Thomas J., Sociology, As 1971–79; Ao 1979–85; P 1985–

Morrison, Maria K., German, In 2001–

Morrow, Curtis H., Economics, As 1920–24; P 1924–52

Morse, Junia L., Education, In 1935–39; As 1939–41

Morse, Samuel L., English, In 1942–43

Morton, Larkspur S., Biology, In 1998–99; Fe 1999–2001

Moseley, Fred B., Economics, As 1982–89; Ao 1989

Moss, Jane M., French, As 1979–85; Ao 1985–90; P 1990–

Moss, Richard J., History, As 1978–83; Ao 1983–90; P 1990–2005

Motoyama, Mutsuko, Japanese, As 1982–84

Mott-Smith, Morton C., Physics, In 1909–11; As 1911–14

Mueller, Julie Kay, History, As 1992–2000

Mullen, Laura K., English, As 1989–90

Muller, Robert E., Biology, As 1975–79

Mundy, Bradford P., Chemistry, P 1992–2003

Munns, Jessica, English, As 1983–84; Ao 1992–93

Murphy, John A., History, P 1987

Murray, James Alan, Biology, As 1998–99

Mursin, Tatiana, Russian, In 1968–71; As 1971–73; Le 1977

Nagahashi, Hideo, Mathematics, As 2005–2006

Nakagawa, Michiko, Japanese, In 2004–

Nakata, Hitomi, Japanese, In 1992–93

Naravane, Vishwanath S., Philosophy, Le 1963–64; P 1967–78

Narin van Court, Elisa M., English, As 1996–2003; Ao 2003–

Neff, Sherman B., English, In 1911–12

Neinstein, Raymond L., English, In 1974–76; Le 1977–79

Nelson, Barbara Kuczun, Spanish, Le 1978–85; In 1985–95; As 1995–

Nelson, Emmanuel S., English, As 1983–84

Nelson, James P., Modern Languages, As 1974–75

Nelson, Josef F., Romance Languages, In 1918–23

Nelson, Randy A., Administrative Science and Economics, Ao 1987–90; P 1990–

Nelson, Robert E., Geology, As 1982–88; Ao 1988–96; P 1996–

Nelson, Shelby, Physics, As 1993–99; Ao 1999

Nemer, Monique, Modern Languages, P 1983

Newhall, Richard A., History, P 1956–57

Newkirk, Cheryl Tschanz, Music, As 1995–2002; Ao 2002–

Newman, Herbert L., Religion, In 1922–26; As 1926–36; Ao 1936–45; P 1945–50

Newton, Calvin, Rhetoric and Hebrew, P 1831–38

Newton, Thomas A., Chemistry, As 1978–85

Newton, William D., Biology, As 1974–75

Nicholson, Stanley A., Economics, P 1981–90

Nickerson, George T., Education, As 1947–49; Ao 1949–67

Nickerson, John M., Government, Le 1979–80

Nitchman, Nelson W., Physical Education, As 1941–46

Noon, Peter C., French, In 1986

Norden, Deborah L., Government, As 1992–97

Norford, Don P., English, In 1966–68; As 1968–71

Northrup, James I., Mathematics, As 1990–92

Norton, Karl K., Mathematics, Ao 1987–89

Norton, Ronald N., Economics, Ao 1994

Norwood, Luella F., English, As 1943–47; Ao 1947–51; P 1951–53

Noyes, Edwin, Tutor 1837–39

Nugent, David L., Anthropology and Latin American Studies, As 1989–96; Ao 1996–2004; P 2004–

Numata, Chieko, Japanese, As 1999–2000

Nuss, Steven R., Music, As 1997–2003; Ao 2003–

Nutting, Peter W., German, Ao 1985–89

Nye, Peter L., Administrative Science, As 1983–85

Nyhus, Philip, Environmental Studies, Fe 1999–2004; As 2004–

Oakes, Karen K., English, As 1989–90

O'Bear, George B., Physics, In 1911–14; As 1914–16

Ober, John David, Philosophy, As 1989

O'Berry, Elmer E., Air Science, As 1951–54

O'Brien, David P., Psychology, As 1980–81

O'Brien, Liam, Mathematics, As 2003–

Odione, Joseph M., Biology, In 1936–39

O'Halloran, John, Biology, P 1998

Okrent, Mark B., Philosophy, Le 1982

Olivares, Jorge, Spanish, As 1982–86; Ao 1986–93; P 1993–

Oliver, James F., English, In 1955–57

Oliver, Michael J., Economics, Ao 2001

Olmstead, Robert T., Jr., English, In 1967–68

Omary, Mohammad A., Chemistry, Fe 1997–99

O'Meara, Mary E., Anthropology, In 1992

O'Murchu, Liam P., English, Ao 1989

O'Neil, William B., Economics, As
 1982–86

O'Neill, John, Spanish, In 1993–95

O'Neill, Kerill N., Classics, As 1992–2000;
 Ao 2000–

Onion, Patricia A., English, As 1974–85;
 Ao 1985–2000; P 2000–

Onishi, Deidre, Theater and Dance, Fe
 2005–2006

Opal, Jason M., History, As 2003–

Oplinger, Jon T., Anthropology, Ao 1994

O'Reilly, Kathleen M., Biology, As 1995–96

Orejudo, Antonio, Spanish, In 1992–93

Ortmann, Andreas, Administrative
 Science, Fe 2000–2001

Osberg, Philip H., Geology, In 1952–53;
 As 1953–54; Ao 1954–57

Osborne, Clifford H., Religious Studies,
 Ao 1950–58; P 1958–65

Osborne, Laurie E., English, As 1990–95;
 Ao 1995–2003; P 2003–

Ott, Walter R., Jr., Philosophy, Fe
 2000–2001

Otto, Fred B, Physics, In 1964–65; As
 1965–68

Oudin, Maurice G., French, In 1973–76;
 As 1976–79

Page, Stephen B., Elocution, In 1835–36

Paine, Henry W., Tutor 1830–31

Palermo, Silvana A., History, As
 2002–2003

Paliyenko, Adrianna M., French, As
 1989–96; Ao 1996–2004; P 2004–

Pallister, Janis L., Modern Languages, In
 1959–61

Palmer, Norman D., History, In 1933–37;
 As 1937–46; Ao 1946–47

Pan, Yun-Tong, Government, In 1966–68;
 As 1968–71

Pandeya, Amar Nath, Philosophy, Ao
 1961–62

Pardee, William Hearne, Art, As 1982–86,
 1989–90

Park, Calvin E., Rhetoric, P 1839–1843

Parker, Addison, Tutor 1824–26

Parker, Francis H., Philosophy, P 1971–86

Parker, Richard B., Economics, Le
 1976–80

Parmenter, George F., Chemistry, Ao
 1903–1904; P 1904–47

Parsons, Storer S., Biology, In 1958–60

Partsch, Cornelius I., German, As
 1997–98

Pattison, Robert E., Mathematics and
 Natural Philosophy and Philosophy, P
 1828–58

Paul, Marilyn B., Administrative Science,
 In 1979–81

Payson, Harold, III, Economics, As
 1979–83

Peck, Harvey W., English, In 1910–12

Peppe, Dee, Art, As 1999–

Pepper, George D. B., Philosophy and
 Biblical Literature, P 1882–99

Pepper, Stephen C., Philosophy, P
 1958–59

Pereira, Carlos, Government, As
 2002–2003

Perez, Francisco R., Spanish, As 1966–77

Perez, Paul P., Psychology, As 1959–60; Ao
 1960–73; P 1973–85

Perez-Pineda, Federico A., Spanish, As
 1980–83

Perkins, Edward H., Geology, Ao
 1920–26; P 1926–36

Perkins, Norman C., Physical Education,
 In 1934–44

Perry, Jeanne H., Psychology, As 1968–69

Pestana, Harold R., Geology, In 1959–65;
 As 1965–73; Ao 1973–85; P 1985–97

Peters, Eugene, Philosophy, In 1964–66;
 As 1966–73

Peterson, Harry E., Air Science /
 Aerospace Studies, P 1958–62

Pfaff, Christopher A., Art, As 1994–95
Pfitzer, Gregory M., History, Le 1982–85
Phelps, Frederick M., Business
    Administration, In 1931–33
Phillips, Darryl A., Classics, In 1995–96
Phillips, Raymond B., Biology, As 1984–
Phillips, Raymond C., Jr., English, In
    1959–61
Phillips, Richard V., Business
    Administration, In 1964–65
Pickering, Aaron T., Physics, In 1992
Pierce, James Smith, Art, P 1990–91
Pierson, Thomas C., History, In 1980–81
Pignard, Simone R., English, Le 1980
Pike, Fred P., French, In 1899–1900
Pinkow, Linda C., Sociology, As 1993–94
Pious, Richard M., Government, In 1968
Piper, Winthrop W., English, In 1953–55
Pitrat, Muriel, Geology, In 1962–63
Pittman, Thane S., Psychology, P 2004–
Pivetz, Richard K., Sociology, In 1954–55
Plasencia, Gonzalo, Spanish, In 1977–79;
    As 1979–80
Plesch, Veronique B., Art, As 1994–2001;
    Ao 2001–
Plotkin, Mariano B., History, As 1995–98
Podlecki, Anthony J., Classics, P 1987–88
Pollock, Stephen G., Geology, Le 1977–78
Polster, Sandor M., Government, In 2004
Pond, Addison C., Economics, In 1936–39
Porter, John R., Classics, Le 1985–86
Potter, Russell A., English, As 1991–95
Poyer, Linette A., Anthropology, As
    1985–86
Pratt, David W., Chemistry, As 2005–
Premasiri, Pahalawattage, Philosophy, P
    1988–89
Prescott, Francis C., History, In 1940–41
Preston, A. Wendy, Modern Languages, In
    1965
Preston, Jo Anne, Sociology, As 1983–84
Price, Camille C., Computer Science, Fe
    1997–98

Price, Kenneth H., Mathematics, Fe
    1997–98
Prichard, David C., Psychology, P 2000
Prindle, Peter, Sociology, As 1987
Prindle, Tamae K., Japanese, As 1985–91;
    Ao 1991–98; P 1998–
Prins, Harald E. L., Anthropology, As
    1988–89
Prowse, Angela, Classics, As 1965–66
Ptak, Roger L., Physics, P 1985–86
Pullen, Robert W., Economics, In
    1945–47; As 1947–50; Ao 1950–59; P
    1959–81
Pyle, Vivian K., Russian, In 1985–92

Quillin, Charles R., Biology, In 1965–66;
    As 1966–71
Quirk, Nancy C., Government, In
    2001–2002

Raag, Tarja, Psychology, As 1995–2001; Ao
    2001–
Raibley, Jason, Philosophy, In 2005
Ramirez, Arthur, Spanish, As 1977–79
Ramsey, Patricia G., Education, Ao
    1988–89
Randall, Clara R., Geology, In 1955–57
Randall, Deborah S., Art, As 1998–99
Randall, Laurence E., Air Science, As
    1954–58
Randall, Samuel, Tutor 1833–37
Rasmussen, Kenneth Eric, Art, Fe
    2001–2002
Rattey, Norman J., Modern Languages, Le
    1976–77
Rawlings, Martha M., Sociology and
    African American Studies, Fe
    1999–2000
Ray, Romita, Art, As 1998–99
Ray, Wendell A., Chemistry, In 1938–42;
    As 1942–46; Ao 1946–74; P 1974–76
Raymond, Anna R., Latin, As 1918–19

Raymond, Harold B., History, As
1952–58; Ao 1958–68; P 1968–94
Raymond, Paul B., Government, Le
1976–77
Raymond, Richard D., Economics, As
1964–65
Ré, Peter, Music, In 1951–52; As 1952–58;
Ao 1958–65; P 1965–84
Read, Jason D., Philosophy, As 2004–2005
Reed, Scott H., III, Art, As 1987–98; Ao
1998–
Reich, Leonard S., Administrative Science
and Science, Technology, and Society,
Ao 1985–95; P 1995–
Reid, Clifford E., Economics, Ao 1987–89;
P 1989–
Reid, Evans B., Chemistry, P 1954–78
Reidel-Schrewe, Ursula, German, In
1989–90; As 1990–95; Ao 1995–
Reig, Rafael, Spanish, As 1996–97
Reilly, Lisa A., Art, In 1988–90
Reisert, Joseph R., Government, As
1996–2003; Ao 2003–
Reiter, Joseph A., French, In 1973–76; As
1976–79
Renner, William D., Air
Science / Aerospace Studies, As
1959–61
Reuman, Dorothy Swan, Music, In
1961–71; As 1971–78; Ao 1978–92
Reuman, Robert E., Philosophy, As
1956–59; Ao 1959–69; P 1969–91
Reuterdahl, Arvid, Physics, Ao 1904–1905
Reynolds, John F., German, As 1978–85
Reynolds, Ross A., Physics, As 1983–90
Rice, John A., Music, As 1988–90
Rice, Kevin P., Chemistry, As 2005–2006
Rich, Jeremy M., History, In 2001–2002
Richard, Wilfred E., American Studies, Le
1980
Richards, Laurence D., Administrative
Science, As 1980–85

Richardson, Ashton F., Geology, As
1951–52
Richardson, Philip M., Mathematics, In
1926–28
Richey, Willis D., Chemistry, Ao 1962–63
Richman, Paula S., Philosophy and
Religion, In 1982–83; As 1983–85
Riihimaki, Catherine A, Geology, In
2003–2004
Rikoun, Polina, Russian, As 2003–2004
Rivera, Blanca M., Spanish, In 1987–88
Roberson, James C, III, Spanish, In
1999–2002
Roberts, Arthur J., English and
Philosophy, As 1890–95; P 1895–1927
Roberts, Edwin J., Chemistry, In 1911–14
Roberts, Robin A., Women's Studies and
American Studies, Ao 1993–95
Roberts, William H., Mathematics, Ao
1958–59
Roberts, William L., English, In 1918–19
Robertson, Frederick C., Elocution, In
1880–82
Robinet, Patricia M., Psychology, As
1998–2001
Robins, Henry E., Philosophy, P 1873–82
Robinson, Betty D., Sociology and
Government, Le 1979–80
Robinson, Judith E., Russian, In 1989–90
Rockstein, Edward D., Japanese, As
1971–72
Roderick, John, East Asian Studies, Le
1986
Rodman, Kenneth A., Government, Ao
1989–98; P 1998–
Rodney, Robert M., English, As 1945–46
Rodriguez, Julia E., History, Fe 1998–99
Roehl, Richard W., Economics, Ao
1974–75
Rogers, Karen, Mathematics, As 1993–94
Rogers, Phyllis, Anthropology and
American Studies, As 1989–94
Rogers, William A., Physics, P 1886–98

Rohrman, Nicholas L., Psychology, P 1977–

Roisman, Hanna M., Classics, Ao 1990–94; P 1994–

Roisman, Joseph, Classics, Ao 1990–94; P 1994–

Rolfson, Eric F., French, Le 1982–83

Rollins, Cecil A., Latin and English, In 1919–26; As 1926–30; Ao 1930–55

Roman, Howard E., Modern Languages, In 1937–39

Romano, David, Mathematics, As 2003–2004

Romanowicz, Edwin, Geology, As 1994–95

Romey, William L., Biology, As 1993–95

Rooks-Hughes, Lorna, English, In 1985–88

Roorbach, Bill F., English, Ao 2001–2003

Rosa, Matthew W., English, In 1926–27

Rose, Sonya O., Sociology, As 1977–82; Ao 1982–92

Rosen, Sydney H., Government, As 1971–75

Rosen, Warren A., Physics, As 1979–80

Rosenberg, Dorothy J., German, As 1983–85

Rosenstein, Nathan S., Classics, Le 1982–83

Rosenthal, Jonas O., Sociology, In 1957–60; As 1960–68; Ao 1968–83; P 1983–92

Rosenthal, Sidney, English, In 1948–51

Ross, Ann P., Performing Arts, In 1997–98

Ross, David R., Economics, As 1991–92

Ross, Stuart I., Art, As 1970–71, 1973

Rothchild, Donald S., Government, In 1957–59; As 1959–62; Ao 1962–66

Rothenberg, David J., Music, Fe 2004–2005

Rothschild, Harriet D., Modern Languages, In 1959–60

Roundy, Edward C., Physical Education, As 1934–50; Ao 1950–54

Rowe, Arthur M., Chemistry, In 1915–17

Rowe, Rebecca J., Chemistry, Fe 2003–2004; As 2004–

Roy, Anindyo, English, As 1995–2002; Ao 2002–

Rudolph, Seri G., Biology, As 1995–96

Ruefle, Mary, English, As 1991–92

Rueger, Bruce F., Geology, As 2003–

Runnals, Ninetta M., Mathematics, As 1920–23; P 1923–49

Rush, James B., English, In 1945–47

Rush, Richard W., Geology, In 1949–51

Russ, Jon R., English, As 1968–72

Russ, Raymond C., Psychology, Le 1977

Russell, Clyde E., Education, In 1941–45

Russell, Holly Labbe, Theater and Dance, As 2000–2001

Russell, Olga W., Modern Languages, Le 1981

Russo, Richard, English, P 1991–2004

Ryan, Michael J., Physical Education, In 1919–21

Rysman, Alexander R., Sociology, As 1977–78

Saadatmand, Yassaman, Economics and Administrative Science, In 1986–88; As 1988–89

Sacks, Paul M., Government, In 1971–74; As 1974–75

Sacks, Peter M., English, Le 1978–79

Sadoff, Dianne F., English, As 1980–82; Ao 1982–88; P 1988–95

Sadoff, Ira, English, As 1977–81; Ao 1981–88; P 1988–

Sagaser, Elizabeth H., English, As 1994–2002; Ao 2002–

Saint-Amand, Paul G, Education, As 1989–90

St. Clair, Katherine R., Mathematics, As 2004–

Saksena, Shri Krishna, Philosophy, P 1968–69

Saltus, Janet E., French, In 1966–67

Saltz, Laura, Art and American Studies, As 2001–

Salvo, Rosaleen, History, In 1991–92

Samaniego, Fernando, Spanish, In 1982–83

Samkange, Stanlake J. T., History, Le 1976

Samuel, L. Dean, Administrative Science, In 1975–78; As 1978–81

Sanavitis, Yvonne, Spanish, As 1996–2002; Ao 2002–

Sanborn, Jean Donovan, English, Le 1976–85; Ao 1985–99; P 1999–2005

Santos, John M., Economics, In 1985–88; As 1988–92

Sasaki, Betty G., Spanish, In 1991–93; As 1993–98; Ao 1998–

Saslaw, Ellen S., Philosophy and Religion, In 1969

Saunders, Ernest W., Religious Studies, As 1987

Saunders, Steven E., Music, As 1990–96; Ao 1996–2004; P 2004–

Savage, Carleton N., Geology, In 1942–44

Savage, Elizabeth F., English, In 1963–67

Savides, Antonio, Philosophy, Ao 1921–22; P 1922–24

Sawtelle, Henry A., Tutor 1855–56

Sawtelle, Mary Anna, French, Ao 1896–99

Scalzo, Richard C., Mathematics, As 1976–77

Schaefer, Jacqueline T., French, In 1961–62

Scheck, Raffael M., History, As 1994–99; Ao 1999–

Schempp, Edwin K., Business Administration, In 1951–52

Schiller, Jerome P., Philosophy, In 1958–61; As 1961–62

Schmidt, Heidi J., English, As 1987–88

Schmidt, Henry O., German, In 1946–49; As 1949–62; Ao 1962–74; P 1974–78

Schnare, Paul S., Mathematics, As 1974–75

Schneider, Laurel C., Religious Studies, In 1995–96

Schneider, Wayne J., Music, As 1986–88

Schoen-René, Otto E., English, P 1960

Schoenburg, Isaac J., Mathematics, In 1936–37; As 1937–41

Schreier, Joshua, History, Fe 2001–2002

Schwartz, Kessel, Modern Languages, In 1951–53

Schwartz, Matthew C., Geology, In 2001–2002

Schwartz, Ronald F., Administrative Science, In 1979–80

Sciacca, Franklin Arseni, Russian, Le 1981

Scime, Joy A., History, In 1986–87

Scott, Allan C., Biology, P 1951–73

Scott, Matthew, Environmental Studies, In 1995

Seaman, Frances F., Education, Ao 1957–68

Seeley, Walter B., Art, As 1948–50

Seelye, Laurens H., Philosophy, P 1958

Seepe, Arthur W., Business Administration, In 1937–39; As 1939–46; Ao 1946–72

Sensabaugh, David A., Art, In 1987–89

Sewell, Richard C., Theater and Dance and English, Le 1976–81; As 1981–85; Ao 1985–2004

Shah, K.J., Philosophy, Le 1966–67

Shamim, Choudhury M., Government, As 1989–90

Shattuck, Thomas W., Chemistry, As 1976–82; Ao 1982–2000; P 2000–

Shaw, Annette, French, As 1978–80

Shaw, Robert A., Psychology, As 1983

Sheldon, David N., Philosophy, P 1843–53

Shen, Lei, Chinese, In 1999–2000

Shepardson, Carl B., Mathematics, As 1973–78
Sherard, Michael L., Japanese, As 1975–79
Sherlock, Robin E., English, In 1991–94
Sherman, Barbara A., Modern Languages, Ao 1949–52
Sherwin, Jane K., French, In 1959–62
Shields, Christopher, Philosophy, As 1986–88
Shoen, Richard L., English, In 1970–71
Shosa, Jennifer D., Geology, As 2000–
Shubov, Victor I., Mathematics, Fe 2004–2005
Siamundele, Andre N., French, As 2000–2005
Siegel, Laurence, Music, In 1968–69
Sigel, Louis T., History and East Asian Studies, As 1994
Simon, David L., Art, Ao 1981–88; P 1988-
Simon, Sonia Chalif, Art, As 1982–91; Ao 1991–96
Simpson, Howard E., Mineralogy and Geology, In 1905–1907; Ao 1907–1909
Simpson, John B., Physical Education, In 1958–60; As 1960–71
Sims, Robert L., French, As 1973–74
Singh, Nikky-Guninder K., Religious Studies, As 1986–92; Ao 1992–99; P 1999–
Skadden, Michael J., Spanish, In 1983–84
Sklute, Barbro M., Sociology, In 1965–67
Sklute, Larry M., English, In 1964–66
Skoog, Sonya, Geology, In 1997–98; As 1998–99
Skrien, Dale J., Computer Science, As 1980–87; Ao 1987–97; P 1997–
Small, Albion W., History and Political Economy and Philosophy, P 1881–92
Small, Donald B., Mathematics, As 1968–74; Ao 1974–93
Smith, Arthur N., Physical Education, Director, 1916–17
Smith, Don D., Russian, As 1983

Smith, Doris C., English, In 1944–53
Smith, Duane R., Classics, In 1986–87
Smith, Earl H., English, As 1970–81, Ao 1981–95, P 1995–2003
Smith, Francis E., English, As 1947–49
Smith, Geoffrey W., Geology, In 1968–69
Smith, Gordon W., French, In 1930–37; As 1937–46; Ao 1946–71; P 1971–72
Smith, Helen M., Business Administration, In 1953–54
Smith, Marc L., Computer Science, As 2001–
Smith, Norman S., Education and Psychology, In 1945–46; As 1946–47; Ao 1947–68
Smith, Samuel Francis, Modern Languages, P 1834–41
Smith, Samuel King, Rhetoric, P 1850–92
Smith, Wayne L., Chemistry, As 1967–76; Ao 1976–83; P 1983–2001
Snee, Rochelle E., Classics, Le 1975–76
Snowadzky, Rudolph, Administrative Science, As 1994
Snyder, Harry C., Russian, Russian and French, As 1977–78
So, Chung, Chinese, As 1978–85
Soderberg, Sonja, Physical Education, In 1950–52
Soifer, Deborah A., Religious Studies, As 1979–81; Le 1984–85; As 1985–86, 1990–91, 1994–95
Solomon, Jeffrey S., Mathematics, Le 1981
Sontag, Frederick H., Government, Le 1974–75
Sorensen, Humphrey, Computer Science, P 2004
Sorenson, Alban, Philosophy, Ao 1903–1905
Spaien, Gail E., Art, As 1997–98; Fe 1999–2000; As 2000
Spark, Debra A., English and Creative Writing, As 1994–96; Ao 1996–
Spear, Morris E., English, In 1910–11

Spears, Edwin E., Jr., Biology, As 1984–85
Speel, Janis A., Biology, As 1976–77
Spiegel, Evelyn S., Biology, In 1957–58
Spiegel, Melvin, Biology, As 1955–59
Spiegelberg, Bruce, English, In 1966–69; As 1969–70
Stameshkin, Colleen A. M., Philosophy, In 1975–76
Stanley, George H., Mathematics, In 1949–54
Stanley, Winthrop H., Physics, In 1920–21; As 1921–50
Stanovsky, Derek, Philosophy, As 1993–95
Star, Leanne H., English, Le 1978–85; In 1985–88
Starker, William A., Air Science / Aerospace Studies, As 1959–61; Ao 1961–62; P 1962–64
Staub, Michael E., English, As 1988–89
Steigenga, Timothy J., Government, As 1997–98
Stein, Marc R., History, As 1996–98
Steiner-Scott, Elizabeth, Women's Studies, As 1994
Sterling, Susan B., English, In 1988; As 1992–97, 1999–2005
Stetson, Carlton B., Greek, In 1882–93; P 1893–1902
Stevens, Lauren R., English, As 1966–67
Stevens, William O., English, In 1899–1900
Stewart, Jules, Spanish, In 1968–69
Stillwell, John B., Classics, Le 1984
Stineford, Claude L., Economics, In 1927–28
Stirling, Jeffrey G., Music, In 1990–91
Stokes, Elisabeth F., English, In 2001–
Stone, Judy L., Biology, As 1999–
Stratman, David G., English, As 1969–73
Straughn-Williams, Maritza, African American Studies and Anthropology, In 1999–2001; As 2001–
Strider, Robert E. L., English, P 1957–79

Strong, Everett F., French, In 1922–27; Ao 1927–61; P 1961–62
Strong, John W., History, In 1960–61
Strong, Sarah M., Japanese, Le 1980–82
Strukov, Andrei, Russian, In 1992–99
Stuart, P. Lynn, Economics, Le 1980
Stubbs, Katherine M., English, As 1996–2002; Ao 2002–
Suchoff, David B., English, As 1992–95; Ao 1995–2002; P 2002–
Sullivan, David S., Classics, Le 1981–82
Sun, You-Li, History, As 1988–89
Suss, Irving D., English, As 1957–61; Ao 1961–73; P 1973–80
Sutcliffe, Nina J., Art, Ao 1991–92
Sutherland, John H., English, In 1951–54; As 1954–59; Ao 1959–70; P 1970–86
Swain, Stuart G., Mathematics, In 1986–87
Sweeney, Gerard M., English, P 2005–2006
Sweet, Paul R., History, Ao 1947–48
Sweney, John R., English, In 1967–68; As 1968–73; Ao 1973–82; P 1982–2004

Tabak, Leon H., Computer Science, P 1996
Tabari, Keyvan, Government, In 1962–63
Taffe, William J., Physics, As 1969–71
Talbot, John M., Sociology, As 1997–2003
Tanner, Anthony C., Chemistry, As 1983–84
Tanner, Lawrence H., Geology, As 1990–91
Tappan, Mark B., Education, As 1991–98; Ao 1998–2005; P 2005–
Tardif, Isola, French, In 1995
Tardito, Marcia, Spanish, In 1984–88
Tate, Duncan A., Physics, As 1992–99; Ao 1999–
Tatelbaum, Linda, English, Le 1982–85; As 1985–92; Ao 1992–2004; P 2004–
Tatem, David, German, As 1962–66

Taylor, Alan S., History, As 1984–85

Taylor, Ellen McCue, History, As 1968–70

Taylor, Julian D., Latin, Tutor 1868–73; P 1873–1931

Taylor, Larissa J., History, As 1994–98; Ao 1998–2005; P 2005–

Tays, Gerald W., Geology, In 1965–66

TeBrake, Janet, History, Le 1984

Tepfer, Diane, Art, In 1982–83

Terry, Robert L., Biology, Ao 1952–67; P 1967–83

Thamattoor, Dasan M., Chemistry, As 1999–2005; Ao 2005–

Thamattoor, Davida, Italian, As 2002–

Theruvakattil, Philip C., Computer Science, As 1997

Thibeault-Schaefer, Jacqueline, French, In 1961–62

Thoma, Pamela S., American Studies and Women's, Gender, and Sexuality Studies, As 1996–2005

Thomas, Ayanna Kim, Psychology, As 2005–

Thomas, Danford, Tutor 1838–39

Thomas, Harry S., Physics, In 1955–56

Thompson, Fred L., Physical Education, Director, 1908–11

Thompson, James L., Chemistry, In 1960–61

Thompson, Maynard, Mathematics, P 1977–78

Thompson, Woodrow B., Geology, Le 1977

Thorn, Jennifer J., English, As 2003–

Thornton, Saranna R., Economics, In 1989–90; As 1990–96

Thorwaldsen, Roland W., Religious Studies, In 1965–69; As 1969–79

Thory, Hans C., Latin, As 1931–33; Ao 1933–41

Thurston, James C., Theater and Dance, As 1988–96; Ao 1996–

Tietenberg, Thomas H., Economics and Environmental Studies, Ao 1977–84; P 1984–

Tilden, Andrea R., Biology, As 1999–2005; Ao 2005–

Tingey, Henry C., Chemistry, In 1922–23

Tipper, Elizabeth A., Administrative Science, In 1988–89

Tobey, Leonard, Tutor 1827–28

Todrank, Gustave H., Religious Studies, In 1956–58; As 1958–62; Ao 1962–70; P 1970–82

Tolman, Gilbert, Physics, Ao 1909–11; 1916–18

Tompkins, F. Pauline, Government, Ao 1952–57

Traill, John S., Classics, In 1964–65

Trefethen, Henry E., Mathematics and Astronomy, In 1911–13; As 1913–17; Ao 1917–31

Tripp, Ephraim, Tutor 1823–27

Tryens, Andrew L., Physical Education, In 1952–55; As 1955–56

Tsurikov, Alexey, Russian, In 1964–66; As 1966–69

Tuck, Gilbert W., Modern Languages, In 1949–51

Tucker, Melvin J., History, In 1959–60

Tuleja, Thaddeus F., Art and American Studies, Fe 1999–2001

Tulp, Orien L., Chemistry, Ao 1981–83

Turesky, Elizabeth A.F., Administrative Science, As 1985–95; Ao 1995–99

Turner, John H., Spanish, P 1986–87

Twaddle, Andrew C., Sociology, P 2000

Ullman, Urban C., Modern Languages, In 1954–57

Unamuno, Maria de, Spanish, In 1963–64

Underwood, William E., English, As 1998–2004

Weiner, William, Economics, In 1954–56
Weisberger, Adam M., Sociology, As 1989–97
Weisbrot, Robert S., History, As 1980–86; Ao 1986–90; P 1990–
Weiss, Dace, French, Le 1981–85; In 1985–98; As 1998–2001
Weiss, Jonathan M., French, In 1972–74; As 1974–79; Ao 1979–86; P 1986–
Weissberg, Guenter, Government, Ao 1965–70; P 1970–89
Weitz, Ankeney, Art and East Asian Studies, As 1998–2005; Ao 2005–
Welch, George A., Mathematics, As 1992–99; Ao 1999–
Welch, George G., Jr., Classics, In 1962–63
Wells, Wesley R., Philosophy, As 1919–21
Welsh, Kristen E., Russian, Fe 2001–2002
Welsh, Peter O., Business Administration, In 1965–66
Wentzel, Christine M., Theater and Dance and Physical Education, In 1973–76; As 1976–85; Ao 1985–94; P 1994–
Werfel, Gina S., Art, In 1980–81; As 1981–88; Ao 1988–92
Wescott, Horace B., Business Administration, In 1957–59
Westerman, David S., Geology, As 1980–82
Westervelt, Peter, Classics, In 1961–63; As 1963–67; Ao 1967–78; P 1978–86
Westlie, John D., French, As 1981–85
Whalen, Maureen C., Biology, As 1989–92
Wheeler, Evan R., Physics, In 1914–15
Wheeler, Nathaniel E., Physics, Ao 1920–21; P 1921–42
Wheeler, Noel C., Mathematics, In 1957–60
Wheeler, Norman E., Mathematics, In 1957–61; As 1961–64

Whelan, Leo A., Jr., Mathematics, In 1963–66
Whitcomb, Haroldene, Business Administration, In 1956–59
Whitcomb, Robert M., Administrative Science, Ao 2001
White, Alice H., Music, In 1909–19
White, Charles L., Philosophy, P 1901–1908
White, Clarence L., Greek, P 1902–34
White, Henry A., English, In 1908–1909
White, Howard R., Psychology, As 1959–60
White, Janis E., Mathematics, As 1997–98
White, Jonathan M., Sociology, In 2000–2003; As 2003–
Whitehead, Jane K., Classics, As 1996–98
Whitlock, Baird W., Humanities, As 1954–56
Whitman, Beniah L., Philosophy, P 1892–95
Whitmore, John, Physics, Ao 1906–1907
Whitmore, Richard L., Jr., Physical Education and Athletics, In 1970–73; As 1973–83; Ao 1983–1990; P 1990–
Whittemore, John H., Modern Languages, In 1952–53
Whittinghill, Dexter C., III, Mathematics, As 1989–96
Wickes, Margaret V., Sociology, In 1969–70
Wilkinson, William J., History, Ao 1924–25; P 1925–45
Willard, Anne H., History, In 1967
Willard, Frederick A., Chemical Philosophy and Botany, Le 1828–31
Williams, David N., Philosophy and Religion, Le 1977; In 1977–78
Williams, George B., Government, In 1963–64
Williams, Leon P., Physical Education, In 1946–47; As 1947–56; Ao 1956–66

Williams, Ralph S., Business Administration, In 1947–50; As 1950–53; Ao 1953–58; P 1958–73

Willie, Sarah S., Sociology and African American Studies, Fe 1991–92; In 1992–95; As 1995

Wilson, Blake McD., Music, As 1988–89

Wilson, Charles B., Chemistry and Natural History, In 1882–85

Wilson, Emily D., English and Creative Writing, As 2003

Wilson, Fred M., Gymnastics, In 1875–76

Wilson, Lindsay B., History, As 1985–94

Wilson, W. Herbert, Jr., Biology, As 1990–95; Ao 1995–2002; P 2002–

Wilson, Walter C., Economics, In 1940–41

Wilson, Wayne, English and Creative Writing, As 2003

Winder, Augustus M., Business Administration, In 1948–49

Wing, Joylynn W. D., Theater and Dance and English, As 1988–94; Ao 1994–2004; P 2004–

Wing, Lawrence A., Geology, Ao 1973–74

Winkin, John W., Physical Education, In 1954–56; As 1956–61; Ao 1961–74

Winn, Diane S., Psychology, As 1974–83; Ao 1983–89; P 1989–

Witham, F. Celand, English, In 1954–58; As 1958–66; Ao 1966–81

Witkin, Sylvie C., French, As 1987–90

Wlodkowski, Zinaida S., Russian, Le 1981–83

Wolfe, French E., Economics, As 1912–14; P 1914–17

Wong, Yan-loi, Mathematics, As 1988–89

Wood, Monica, English, As 1998–99

Woodard, Merritte P., Jr., Air Science / Aerospace Studies, As 1962–66

Woodin, Knowlton M., Biology, As 1947–50

Woody, Stephen R., Performing Arts, As 1976–84; Ao 1984–88

Woshinsky, Barbara R., French, As 1973–74

Wyman, Jane Fowler, English, As 1971–76

Wyman, Willard G., Jr., English, Ao 1971–76

Xu, Tao, Chinese and East Asian Culture and Languages, In 1990–93

Yalinpala, Cemal, Economics, Le 1979

Yamauchi, Hiroshi, Physics, In 1950–52; As 1952–54

Yang, Jane P., Chinese, Le 1983–85

Yasinski, W. Arnold, English, P 1990–2005

Yasumoto, Emiko, Japanese, In 2000–2001

Yates, Jennifer R., Psychology, As 2003–

Yedes, Ali, French, As 1999–2000

Yeterian, Edward H., Psychology, As 1978–84; Ao 1984–91; P 1991–

Yoder, Jennifer A., Government and International Studies, As 1996–2002; Ao 2002–

Yokelson, Elis A., English, In 1961–62

Yokelson, Joseph B., English, In 1956–59; As 1959–64

Young, David M., Chemistry, In 1907–11

Young, Patricia A., English, As 1987–88

Young, Ralph C., Physics, In 1915–16

Yusti, Tibor, Music, As 1970–72

Zalot, Marcella K., Director of Athletics, 2002–

Zernicke, Paul H., Government, In 1987–88

Zetrouer, Karen Hall, Spanish, As 1995–99

APPENDIX B

APPENDIX C
College Officers, 1820–2005

PRESIDENTS

Rev. Jeremiah Chaplin, 1822–1833
Rev. Rufus Babcock, 1833–1836
Rev. Robert Everett Pattison, 1836–1839
Eliphaz Fay, 1841–1843
Rev. David Newton Sheldon, 1843–1853
Rev. Robert Everett Pattison, 1854–1857
Rev. James Tift Champlin, 1857–1873
Rev. Henry Ephraim Robins, 1873–1882
Rev. George Dana Boardman Pepper,
   1882–1889
Albion Woodbury Small, 1889–1892
Rev. Beniah Longley Whitman, 1892–1895
Rev. Nathaniel Butler Jr., 1896–1901
Rev. Charles Lincoln White, 1901–1908
Arthur Jeremiah Roberts, 1908–1927
Franklin Winslow Johnson, 1929–1942
Julius Seelye Bixler, 1942–1960
Robert Edward Lee Strider II, 1960–1980
William R Cotter, 1980–2000
William D. Adams, 2000–

CHAIRMEN/CHAIRS OF THE BOARD
   OF TRUSTEES

President of the College, ex officio,
   1822–1874
Abner Coburn, 1874–1885
Joseph Warren Merrill, 1885–1890
Josiah Hayden Drummond, 1890–1902
Percival Bonney, 1902–1906
Leslie Colby Cornish, 1907–1926
Herbert Elijah Wadsworth, 1926–1934
George Otis Smith, 1934–1944
George Goodwin Averill, 1944–1946
Neil Leonard, 1946–1960
Reginald Houghton Sturtevant,
   1960–1965

Ellerton Marcel Jette, 1965–1971
Albert Carlton Palmer, 1971–1979
Robert Newton Anthony, 1979–1983
H. Ridgely Bullock, 1983–1991
Lawrence Reynolds Pugh, 1991–1999
James Bartlett Crawford, 1999–2005
Joseph F. Boulos, 2005–

SECRETARIES OF THE CORPORATION

Rev. Otis Briggs, 1820–1834
Lemuel Paine, 1834–1841
Rev. Samuel Francis Smith, 1841–1842
Isaac Redington, 1843–1847
Rev. Handel Gershom Nott, 1847–1848
Eldridge Lawrence Getchell, 1848–1852
Rev. Nathaniel Milton Wood, 1852–1862
Rev. George Dana Boardman Pepper,
   1862–1866
Rev. Joseph Ricker, 1866–1867
Rev. Benjamin Franklin Shaw, 1867–1875
Rev. Samuel Pierce Merrill, 1875–1879
Percival Bonney, 1879–1891
Leslie Colby Cornish, 1891–1907
Wilford Gore Chapman, 1907–1918
Rev. Charles Edson Owen, 1918–1921
Rev. Edwin Carey Whittemore, 1921–1932
Charles Edwin Gurney, 1932–1943
Cyril Matthew Joly, 1943–1960
Ralph Samuel Williams, 1960–1971
Robert White Pullen, 1971–1972
Ralph Samuel Williams, 1972–1974
Robert White Pullen, 1974–1977
Sidney Weymouth Farr, 1977–1979
Robert Hurd Kany, 1979–1984
Sidney Weymouth Farr, 1984–1995
Earl Harold Smith, 1995–2002
Sally A. Baker, 2002–

Timothy Boutelle, 1831–1832
Daniel Cook, 1832–1834
James Stackpole, 1834–1851
Eldridge Lawrence Getchell, 1851–1881
Percival Bonney, 1881–1902
George Keely Boutelle, 1902–1917
Frank Bailey Hubbard, 1917–1933
Ralph Alden McDonald, 1933–1937
Arthur Galen Eustis, 1937–1950
Arthur William Seepe, 1950–1972
Robert White Pullen, 1972–1974
Dane Joseph Cox, 1974–1978
Karl William Broekhuizen, 1978–1981
Douglas Edward Reinhardt, 1981–2002
W. Arnold Yaskinski, 2002–2005
Douglas C. Terp, 2005–

VICE PRESIDENTS, ADMINISTRATIVE
Arthur Galen Eustis, 1950–1959
Ralph Samuel Williams, 1959–1971
Robert White Pullen, 1971–1972
Ralph Samuel Williams, 1972–1974
Robert White Pullen, 1974–1981
Stanley A. Nicholson, 1981–1990
W. Arnold Yasinski, 1990–2005
Douglas C. Terp, 2005–

VICE PRESIDENTS, DEVELOPMENT/
  COLLEGE RELATIONS
Arthur Galen Eustis, 1950–1959
Edward Hill Turner, 1959–1979
Sidney Weymouth Farr, 1979–1984
George Calvin MacKenzie, 1984–1988
Peyton Randolph Helm, 1988–2003
Richard A. Ammons, 2004–

DEANS OF FACULTY
Ernest Cummings Marriner, 1947–1957
Robert Edward Lee Strider II, 1957–1960
Ernest Parker Johnson, 1960–1971
Paul Gerhard Jenson, 1972–1981
Paul Brendel Dorain, 1981–1982

Douglas Nelson Archibald, 1982–1988
Robert Paul McArthur, 1988–1998
Edward Harry Yeterian, 1998–

DEANS OF THE MEN'S DIVISION
  (ENDS 1967)
Ernest Cummings Marriner, 1929–1947
George Thomas Nickerson, 1947–1967

DEANS OF THE WOMEN'S DIVISION
  (ENDS 1967)
Mary Ann Sawtelle, 1896–1899
Grace Elizabeth Mathews, 1899–1902
Grace Ella Berry, 1902–1909
Carrie Etta Small, 1909–1910
Elizabeth Bass, 1910–1913
Florence Sargent Carll, 1913–1915
Mary Castle Cooper, 1915–1918
Anna Almy Raymond, 1918–1919
Alice May Holmes, 1919–1920
Ninetta May Runnals, 1920–1926
Erma Vyra Reynolds, 1926–1928
Ninetta May Runnals, 1928–1949
Barbara Aiken Sherman, 1949–1952
Florence Pauline Tompkins, 1952–1957
Frances Fenn Seaman, 1957–1967

DEANS OF STUDENTS (BEGINS 1967)
Frances Fenn Seaman, 1967–1968
Jonas Oettinger Rosenthal, 1968–1971
Willard Gordon Wyman, 1972–1977
Earl Harold Smith, 1977–1982
Janice Armo (Seitzinger) Kassman,
  1982–2006

DEAN OF THE COLLEGE
Earl Harold Smith, 1978–2004

LIBRARIANS/DIRECTORS
  OF COLBY LIBRARIES
Avery Briggs, 1820–1824
Ephraim Tripp, 1824–1827
John O'Brien Chaplin, 1828–1833
Jonathan Everett Farnham, 1833–1835

Samuel Randall Jr., 1835–1837
Justin Rolph Loomis, 1837–1842
Martin Brewer Anderson, 1842–1850
Samuel King Smith, 1850–1873
Edward Winslow Hall, 1873–1910
Charles Phillips Chipman, 1911–1917
Robert Warner Crowell, 1917–1919
Charles Phillips Chipman, 1919–1923
Ernest Cummings Marriner, 1923–1929
Robert Bingham Downs, 1929–1931
Joseph Selwyn Ibbotson, 1931–1935
J. Periam Danton, 1935–1936
N. Orwin Rush, 1936–1945
Gilmore Warner, 1945–1947
James Humphrey III, 1947–1957
John Redmond McKenna, 1957–1964
Kenneth Pond Blake Jr., 1964–1974
Eileen Mary Curran, 1974–1977
William Stuart Debenham Jr., 1977–1981
Suanne W. Muehlner, 1981–2002
Clement P. Guthro, 2003–

REGISTRARS
Albion Woodbury Small, 1881–1882
John Barton Foster, 1882–1888

Edward Winslow Hall, 1888–1902
Grace Ella Berry, 1903–1906
Howard Edwin Simpson, 1906–1909
Herbert Carlyle Libby, 1909–1921
Henry Emerson Trefethen, 1921–1924
Malcolm Bemis Mower, 1924–1933
Elmer Chapman Warren, 1933–1947
Frances Norton Perkins (Recorder),
    1947–1954
Rebecca Chester Larsen (Recorder), 1954–
    1964
Gilbert Frederick Loebs, 1964–1966
George Leidigh Coleman II,
    1966–2006
Elizabeth Neff Schiller, 2006–

DIRECTORS/DEANS OF ADMISSIONS
Daniel Greary Lewis, 1945–1946
George Thomas Nickerson,
    1946–1951
William Lafrentz Bryan, 1951–1964
Harry Rowland Carroll, 1964–1982
Robert Paul McArthur, 1982–1985
Parker Joy Beverage, 1985–

ABBREVIATIONS

A = *Alumnus*
AP = Associated Press
Ar = College Archives
CC = College catalogue
CCS = *Center for Coordinated Studies*
CLQ = *Colby Library Quarterly*
CM = *Colby magazine*
Chronicle = *Chronicle of Higher Education*
E = *Echo*
FYI = Employee Newsletter (1984–)
KJ = *Kennebec Journal,* Augusta
M-*HCC* = Marriner, *History of Colby College*
MS = *Waterville Morning Sentinel*
PPH = *Portland Press Herald*
PEE = *Portland Evening Express*
PST = *Portland Sunday Telegram*
W-*HCC* = Whittemore, *History of Colby College*
W-*CHW* = Whittemore, *Centennial History of Waterville*

PROLOGUE (pp. 1–4)

Captain John Smith: W-*CHW* 32; in the spring season: W-*CHW* 53–54; Soon after the Revolution: Coffin, *Kennebec,* 131 ff.

1. ALONG THE RIVER

Home for a Baptist College (pp. 5–13)

Boardman letter: W-*CHW* 2; second petition: Ar; Petition: copy of original; Boutelle would become: W-*CHW* 18; Whitaker letter: W-*CHW* 59; Chaplin accepted the position: W-*CHW* 17; Elmwood: Marriner letter, Ar, 1975; new buildings, the "Bricks": Tolles, *Maine History* 39:242–247; In the time Smith taught: *PST,* 2/28/32; the orator and the poet: M-*HCC* 459; Charles Hathaway: Marriner, *Remembered Maine,* 42–63.

Elijah Parish Lovejoy (pp. 13–17)

Elijah Lovejoy might never: Irving Dilliard, for *The Quill,* 10/52; Robert Tabscott, several writings including *The Vigil* and *Time and Again,* a history of the Presbyterian Church, 1997; letter to William King: M-*HCC* 118; The first edition: W-*HCC* 39; In the fashion of conservative Protestants: W-*HCC* 40.

Civil War (pp. 17–22)

Garrison, Anti-Slavery Society, Chaplin resignation: W-*CHW* 49–54; Henry Clay Merriam: Alumnus, spring '73, and Arlington National Cemetery Website; Benjamin

Butler, M-*HCC, Dictionary of* American Biography and Mark Boatner, *The Civil War Dictionary;* Butler for VP: *CLQ,* 10/1964 and *A* (Winter 1965), 33; Anthony Burns: W-*CHW* 72; Cutts: Fotiades, *Colby College,* 16.

A Savior (pp. 22–24)

Gardner Colby: various including W-*CHW* and *A Tribute to Gardner Colby;* his own business: M-*HCC* 164; Memorial Hall: M-*HCC,* W-*HCC.*

Growing Up (pp. 25–31)

Academies: W-*CHW* 104–110; Kennebec Water District—*S* 11/28/1904; Lombard Tractor: *The Log Haulers,* Lumberman's Museum, Patten, Maine.

Coming and Going (pp. 31–35)

Horses drew, etc.: Marjorie Meader Burns '14, "Notes from Never-Never Land," *A* (Spring 1975); Lebanese: various including Moses, *Lebanese in America;* Lebanon Youth Club: Saint Joseph's Church Web site; Shearman recounted: *A* (Spring 1975); Armistice and horse incident: *S* 11/12/1918.

Time to Move (pp. 35–40)

Franklin Johnson: from M-*HCC* and Soule, *Colby's President Roberts;* Coburn, from W-*CHW* and W-*HCC;* John Pullen wrote: *A* (Spring 1975); Scott later told: *A* (Fall 1978); Philbrick recollections: *A* (Fall 1961), 10; Of a possible score: *Survey of Higher Education of Maine* (1929); no dining facilities: David Kronquist '29, "Reminiscing," *A* (Spring 1977).

Saved for Waterville (pp. 41–47)

General background—*S, A,* M-*HCC;* Zuver, *Lengthened Shadow of a Maine Man;* Mills recalls: *A* (Spring 1975); Larson recalls: Ar 1953; prediction of success: *Rockland Courier Gazette* (1/19/1929); dressed in natty uniforms: *MS,* 9/24/1930.

Old Pastures (pp. 47–53)

Turner, *Perils of Pauline:* Homecoming banquet, 1975; From M-*HCC, MS* and Ar; *Echo,* New Deal: October 7, 1936; firestorm, Gammon remembered: *A* (Spring 1977); Runnals, Roberts letters, her recollections, coed living: *A* (Winter 1972); Florence Dunn: *A* (Fall 1964), 45.

World War II (pp. 53–57)

From M-*HCC,* W-*HCC, S* and Ar; Marriner, December 7: original text; CPT and Airport: Air Festival program, 8/31/1969; Bondy recollections to author, 2002–2003; Holden, *A* (Spring 1975); Liberty Ships: Fotiades, *Colby College,* 80; a certain immaturity: board minutes, 10/30/1943; Navy Department offer: board minutes, April and May 1944.

2. THE 1950S

The Blue Beetle (pp. 62–68)

From *MS, Ar,* Mannings Directory, Waterville City Reports, personal interviews; national and international events: Halberstam and Manchester; Margaret Smith: Smith, *Declaration of Conscience* and Matusow, *Joseph R. McCarthy;* By now the area had: "A Business Man Looks at Waterville-Winslow," Chamber of Commerce, 1950; Leonard, Johnson plaque: *A* (Summer 1966), 5.

J. Seelye Bixler (pp. 68–76)

Leonard: M-*HCC;* Bixler, search committee: After about three hours of talk: *A* (Fall 1973); one could feel, *A* (Fall 1973); Bixler, a non-Baptist: Bixler, "A Sense of Common Humanity," *A* (Winter 1974); By this time: board minutes, November 1941; Benbow: Bixler Memorial Service, 1985; If steel was held up: *A* (Fall 1973); with a dance floor: *E;* strike, Eustis seized: *Ar* 1950, Christopher letter, 3/2003; firewood: Strider, Whalon memorial service, 10/1970.

Housekeeping (pp. 76–82)

Good Housekeeping: Annual Report on Small Colleges, Hampton, 1950 otherwise undated; Dick Dyer writes: files; only twenty-three had terminal degrees: CC; retired faculty: M-*HCC* and *A;* continuing and new faculty: CC, M-*HCC* and *A;* Morse: *A* (Winter 1965), 36.

Testing New Waters (pp. 82–87)

Ducks, Gould: *A* (Fall 1950) F. T. Hill defends adult education: *A* (May 1950); Bixler, same: *A* (Winter 1974); Macomber: *A* (Spring 1964), 19; religious convocations: board minutes, April 1948.

Through Another War (pp. 88–92)

ROTC: *Ar,* M-*HCC, A* (Winter 1965), 36; forecast: *MS* (2/16/1952 and S 2/16/2002); storm: *Lewiston Daily Sun* (2/19/1952); Brothers of the Brush: Sesquicentennial flyer; Stephenson quote: Manchester, *Glory and the Dream,* 625; Fullam V. Smith: *A* (Spring 1965), 42, Nicoll letter, *E* 54, and Bixler, *A* (Fall 1973).

Not So Silent (pp. 92–99)

Time magazine: 1952; *E* editorial, Open Forum: 4/16/1954; Proulx: *E* (2/26/1954); ski slope: *MS* (12/31/1963) and *A* (Winter 1998); Mood Indigo: *Ar:* C. Bean, History of the Colby Eight; Colbyettes: J. Anderson letter, 1/17/2005; Bubar "bootlegging": Civic League Record, November 1958; Loeb: letter to Bixler, 9/16/1959; Bubar, Nickerson: *PST* (11/15/1959).

Lovejoy Remembered (pp. 99–102)

Tabscott, inspired by liberal causes: *St. Louis Post-Dispatch* (8/10/1987); Sargent, Lovejoy Convocation: Ar, Sargent recollections.

Sports—Over the Top (pp. 102–109)

Women's sports, Marchant: M-*HCC;* Sigmas, Coddington: *PST* (11/22/1953); ski slope: *S* (12/31/1963); Walter Brown: *The Boston Traveler* (12/21/1955); Bixler, freshmen: *A* (1955); performance of women versus men: M-*HCC;* Bixler, President's Page: *A* (July 1952).

Building and Bending (pp. 109–116)

Eliza Foss Dexter, Foss Hall; W-*HCC,* 209; Sherman at cornerstone: *A* (October 1951); Woodman, War Memorial: W-*HCC,* 185; Woodman, benefactor: M-*HCC;* Highway fight: Ar; Curtis to Bixler, Ar 4/17/1957; authorize land purchases: Trustee minutes, 11/2/1957; The argument has been raised: *E* (4/20/1951); Sputnik, Koons: *A* (Spring 1958); Breckenridge: original memo; Wing Sisters, Bixler, *A* (Winter 1974); Dedication, Bixler Center: *A* (Fall 1959).

Selling and Saving (pp. 116–122)

Selling and railroad: *A* (Fall 1962), 15; Afraid to move the lion: Grindall interview, 2003; Marriner, saving Foss Hall: Marriner letter, archives; bell pranks: Joseph Coburn Smith, *Portland Evening News* (4/18/1931); Roberts Square: *A* (Winter 1964), 12.

3. THE 1960S

Robert E. L. Strider (pp. 123–128)

Inaugural address: *A* (Fall 1960), 9; The identification of a new president: Bixler, "A Sense of Common Humanity," *A* (Winter 1974); Bixler loved to tell: ibid.; The standard résumé was impressive: *A* (Summer 1961); Helen Bell Strider: various, especially *Helen Strider,* a memorial, 1996; Sturtevant: *A* (Fall 1960); Leonard, succession of great presidents: *A* (Summer 1959); Even Strider: *A* (Fall 1960); Strider very nearly nixed: Strider interview, August 2002; NDEA: *A* (Summer 1961); Strider writes to alumni: *A* (Fall 62).

Academic Adventures (pp. 128–136)

Jan Plan origins: Ar and Strider recollections, July 2003; opportunity for skiing: President's Page, *A* (Spring 1961); student referendum: *E* (3/3/1961); Program II, Curran quotes: *A* (Summer 1967), 5–9; Even Curran had doubts: Curran interview, December 2003; Experience elsewhere: Jessy Randall, curator Colorado College; Lee McDonald, dean emeritus, Pamona; Jan Plan London: Curran interview, December 2003; Douglas: *A* (Summer 1961); Non-Western Studies: Strider, *A* (Spring 1962); Spanish, local schools: *A* (Summer 1960); French conference: *French Review* (October 1968); free from fetters: Strider, news release, 6/16/1966; Human Development: *A* (Summer 1956) and *A* (Spring 1966); Mayo, five presidents: Bunny Mayo Loomis, 1/6/2005; He felt passionately: *E* (11/20/1970); Foner blacklisted: *New York Times* (12/16/1999), sec. B, p. 13; subcollege for a new milieu: memo, Committee on Coed Living to Campus Affairs Committee, 5/5/1967; Its aims were: CCS brochure, 1972; The hope was: CCS announcement memo, fall 1969; first fully coordinated: CCS evaluation report, 5/19/1976.

Center of Excellence (pp. 137–143)

Time magazine: 12/02/1960; Ford grant background: Ar and Strider interview, op. cit.; Bixler wrote: letter to Strider, 6/28/1962; *Sentinel* called it: *MS* 6/28/1962; Rob calculates: Strider interview, August, 2002; the opportunity to pursue: Strider, alumni message, 6/27/1962; The College budget: College report, *Quality Costs More,* 1966; twelve outstanding shows: *Time* magazine, 6/23/1963; Edith Jetté, eyepatch: Hugh Gourley and *Goodbye Magazine* (July 1999); Rolls-Royce: ibid; Ogilvy colleagues Victorian: letter, Ogilvy to Jetté, 12/15/1965; a creative businessman: *A* (Summer 1965).

"Times They Are A-Changin'" (pp. 143–149)

"The Times They Are A-Changin'": Bob Dylan, 1964; Telegram: *E* (10/20/1961); EPIC calls meeting: *E* (4/8/1960); Bunche knew: *E* (4/22/1960); Lee warned: *E* (4/15/1960); Marquez remembered: e-mail to author, 12/8/2003; Southerners like to feel superior: *E* (4/29/1960); she blamed the Civil War: *E* (4/29/1960); would only further the unfriendliness: *E* (4/15/1960); raised $539.65: *E* (4/29/1969); Nunez felt, believed, said: *E* (5/19/1961); The Grand Worthy, to end of paragraph: Ar memo from Jonas Rosenthal to Strider, 8/1/1962; The *Echo* charged: *E* (11/10/1961); Strider was shocked . . . he told his wife: Strider interview, August, 2002; Williams abandoned: Williams *Record* (10/10/1962); cannot be reconciled: *A* (Fall 1964), 11; Wiswell to Sturtevant: *E* (4/27/1962); ten million: Manchester, *Glory and the Dream,* 890; Sunday night in Portland: Wingate to author, 2002; Strider at Kennedy memorial: Ar original text; Ford speaks: *MS* (1/10/1964); Meredith warned: *A* (Winter 1964), 11; Stephenson: Ar speech text, 6/5/1964; White pondered: author's recollections.

Breaking the Mold (pp. 149–154)
Strider's reply: *A* (Summer 1966); Commission cites: Award citation, 10/20/1967; the temptation: *A* (Fall 1967); Joly described it: *A* (Winter 1964).

Mule Train (pp. 154–159)
In March 1968: Author, *A* (Summer 1996); The *Alumnus* announced: *A* (Winter 1965); apologized again: *A* (Summer 1967).

Rights and Rules (pp. 159–167)
Runnals room: *E* (5/5/1961); Nickerson, dogs: March 1963; Strider, motorcycles: November 1963; Gemery announces: *E* 9/23/1960; hazing: 9/23/1960; Johnson Day: *E* 5/12/1961; Johnson Day protest: *E* 5/11/1961; Friedan: *A* (Fall 1964), 10; trustees' role: *A* (Spring 1965); faculty and administration: *A* (Summer 1965); alumni: *A* (Fall 1965); students: *A* (Winter 1966); Men students eating: *E* (10/1/1956), 3; Osborne retired: *A* (Spring 1965), 5; Chapel Coffee House: *E* (10/8/1965); Death of God: *E* 2/25/1966; a clearer recognition: *A* (Spring 1966), 3; it is illuminating: *A* (Spring 1966); failure to integrate: *A* (Spring 1966), 5–6; I have taken the position: Ar, letter, Strider to Jetté, November 1966; dropped by to tell me: Ar, letter, Strider to Jetté, October 1966; Jetté's own visions: Ar, Jetté to Strider, November 1967; criticized, ignored, or dismissed: *A* (Winter 1966); Peters: *A* (Fall 1967), 22–23; Rosenthal reply: *A* (Spring 1968), 38.

"Stop, Children, What's That Sound?" (pp. 167–173)
Stop Children: "For What's It Worth?" Stephen Sills, 1966; most undemocratic: *PEE* (5/5/1966); Dean Johnson wrote: letter to L. Hershey, 5/25/1966; In the meantime: Dean of Men memorandum to male students, April 1966; The *Echo* reflected: *E* (3/16/1967); Governor Reed: *Sports Illustrated* (May 1967); CORA: *S* 3/8 and 10/1966; Abbott Meader: *E* (3/17/1966); Hughes agreed: e-mail to author, 1/16/2002; McKale: *E* (9/22/1967), 1; Faculty-Administration statement: *E* (12/1/1967); Poll, a year later: *E* (1/19/1968); Boren, Jenkins report: *E* (10/27/1967); Gruening: *A* (Winter 1968); student stayed up: *A* (Spring 2000), 16; Army recruiters: *E* (3/27/1968); Dickinson: *E* (2/16/1968); Strider at King memorial: Ar, Strider text, 4/8/1968; Thompson warned: *S,* (4/9/1968); on election day: *E* (11/8/1968); discussion paper: Ar Rosenthal files, October 1968; officials suspected: Grindall interview, 2003; price of books: *National Association of College Stores Bulletin,* 8/2/1985; Nine Proposals: various, including *E* (3/21/1969), J. A. Newley; Students brought: *S* (10/16/1969); Muskie, moratorium: Ar. Poster: October 1969; Mavrinac: *PPH* (11/14/1969).

Rebellion and Con Con (pp. 173–178)

The trouble with revolutions: *E* (3/21/1969); The convention's purpose: Ar, from Trustee Executive Committee, 10/14/1969; Strider acknowledged a minority: *Boston Globe* (9/7/1968); Through the period: ibid.; arbitrary power: *E* (August 1960), special ed.; A majority of trustees believed: board minutes, 1/31/1970; brought about by stress: Strider interview, 2/19/2004; Colby was not alone: *Chronicle* (10/6/1969); Strider pleased: *MS* (2/16/1970); Kravitz: *Boston Globe* (10/19/1969); vote to deny: trustee minutes, 1/31/1970.

4. THE 1970S

Back to the Chapel (pp. 179–185)

Strider explained: broadside to students, faculty, local alumni, 3/8/1970; Coleman, no discrimination: *E* (3/11/1970); rally: *MS* (3/5/1970); essentially racist: *KJ* (3/5/1970); *Echo* said: 3/6/1970; First black faculty: Ar, Committee on Minorities report, 8/11/1975; *Sentinel* observed: editorial, 3/5/1970; *PST* editorial (3/4/1970); Reid said he had adequate reason: *PEE* (3/10/1970); Strider, difficult decision: *PPH* (3/10/1970); Strider met with evicted students: *A*, Strider digest of oral report to protestors, 3/10/1970; The *Echo* decried and Stu-G resolution: *E* (3/13/1970); The management of WABI: editorial, 3/17/1970; executive committee, special session: committee minutes: 3/20/1970; faculty resolution: minutes, faculty meeting, 3/25/1970; Ali: *A* (Spring 1970).

Strike! (pp. 186–194)

Kent State killings: May 4 Task Force report rev. April 1996; Orlov: interview, 7/8/1970; faculty members spoke: *MS* (5/6/1970); You have been called bums: *A* (Spring 1970); March: ibid; It was not an attack: signed statement of protestors, Ar 5/7/1970; at the faculty meeting: Ar faculty meeting minutes, May Day demonstrations: *Newsweek* (5/17/1971; 5/6/1970); Howell at Bowdoin: *S* (5/6/1970); Reynolds at Bates: *MS* (5/9/1970); series of events: Ar *Strike Notes*, 5/8/1970; While still claiming: *S* (5/9/1970); Strider spoke: *S* (5/9/1970); more than three thousand: AP, 5/11/1970; Muskie text excerpted: Ar, full text, 5/10/1970; Carson: interview 10/6/2004; Smith, Senate speech: *Boston Herald Traveler* (6/3/1970); McGovern, Carbone, Strider quotes: *A* (Summer 1970); Students were free, but: Strider, Alumni Banquet, 6/12/1970, *A* (Summer 1970); IRS warned, *PPH* (6/17/1970); Democrats block bill: *MS* (8/10/1970).

Ceasefire (pp. 194–199)

Strider began asking, and called for cease-fire: alumni banquet, 6/12/1970, *A* (Summer 1970); Hogendorn: to author, 7/20/2004; Strider, ought to have read poetry: *A* (Spring 2000) and to author; Brancaccio, Maramarco, O'Hanian: EPC minutes, 9/28/1970; Rouhana argued: *E* (11/4/1971); until ROTC is evicted: *MS* (4/22/1972); protestors' statement: Ar 4/22/1972; No Maine colleges, UMP: AP, 4/22/1972; Veterans Against the War: *E* (4/28/1972); Lynch kept promise: *MS* (4/24/1972); Carey felt duped: *PEE*, 4/25/1972; Carey, letter to Strider: *MS* 4/25/1972; Barnicle, *A* (Commencement 1987).

Quieter Revolutions (pp. 199–209)

Murphy murder: author's private files, news clippings of the period; Conference and Review Board and Ombudsman: Con Con subcommittee reports, 3/9/1972; new committee structure: trustee minutes, 6/2/1973; board delegates authority: *A*, Report from Trustee Student Affairs to Trustees, 6/3/1970; Wyman's report: *A*; The Echo, gift horse: *E* (12/3/1971); Dewey: *E* (9/29/1972); a mother: *E* (10/27/1972); Sandler: *A* (Fall 1962); Social Roles of Women: Ar and *PST* (9/24/1972); Women's Group: Ar and *E* (3/7/1974); Koons, Earth Day: *A* (Spring 1970); take short showers: *Eco* (March 1971); town officials: Glidden e-mail 8/28/2004 and *MS* (9/12/1973); Spring Brook: customer service bulletin, 12/12/1973.

Shake Your Booty (pp. 209–213)

Uncontrolled barbarism: *A* (Spring 1970); As for nude photos: *E* 10/23/1970); merely reporting the news: *E* (10/23/1970); Farr sent letter: Ar, 10/14/1970; Bubar: Ar letter to Farr, 10/19/1970; *Echo* history: *A* (Spring 1977); Wyman on streaking: *A* (Fall 1974); By the end of the decade: NIDA notes, 14:1 (April 1999).

What's in a Name? (pp. 213–216)

Bownes not persuaded: Ar court decision, June 1973; *Echo* calls for impeachment: *E* (November 1973); Graham: *A* (Winter 1974); annoyed with the judge: *Keene* (New Hampshire) *Sentinel* (5/9/1974); Strider said: *S* (5/30/1974); tinges of snobbishness: *PEE* (6/1/1974); Ingalls: ibid.; Sue Colby: *Athol* (New Hampshire) *News* (2/8/1975); Aldrich also rubbed: Colby College *v.* Colby College–New Hampshire, NH U.S. District Court, January 1975; does not appear to abide: *New Hampshire Star* (2/12/1975); It disturbs me: *Concord Monitor* (3/8/1975); the campus switchboard: *Newport Argus-Champion* (3/12/1975); Aldrich said that by allowing: Colby *v.* Colby, op. cit.; a study commissioned: Appeals Court transcript, Colby *v.* Colby 74–1178, 1975.

A Plan for Colby (pp. 216–219)

Committee to Study the Future of Colby recommendations: *A*, CSFC report, 6/1/1974; Parker an uncle: *A* (June 1986); E-4000 broke down and Coleman bootstrapping: Bowdoin, Bates, Colby Computer Consortium report, 3/5/971; Strider said, computers: *Colby in the 70s*, 7, 6/30/1979; Morrione research: *A* (Spring 1974); Alumni giving goals: Turner, Appeals Court transcript, 70; ricocheted off the hills: *S* (7/28/1976).

Equal Play (pp. 220–227)

No person shall: preamble, Title IX, 1972; did not believe, *Boston Herald American* (3/9/1974); declared war, predicted: ibid.; press conference: ibid.; Before Title IX: *A* (Spring 1979), 6–7; The smaller colleges: Daniel L. Fulks, *Revenues & Expenses of Division III Intercollegiate Athletics Programs*, 2001; feasible and proper: Bowdoin News Service release, 6/20/1974; NESCAC, ibid.; Ronald Ayotte: *Sports Illustrated* (4/29/1974); athletic participation 1975–76: Sarah Bryan, *E* (5/6/1976); McGee wondered: *E* (5/6/1976), op. cit.; PE requirements: CC 1974–75, 83; sports editor said: Osborne: *Bangor Daily News* (1/29/1976); Cuba trip: Ar Strider statement: 12/6/1978; philosophy: Ar January 1979.

New Directions (pp. 227–234)

Waterville in the 1970s: various, including City Reports; more than nine thousand a year: Ar, Program for New Health Center, January 1975; never enough beds: Ar,

Occupancy Report, 11/14/1974; Strider wrote Palmer: Ar, letter, 1/27/1975; simply pro-
hibitive: Strider memo to the board, 2/6/1975; Anderson, Aitel: S (5/13/1975); Delegation of senior women: Ar, memorandum, Strider to author, 10/1/1977; Spa business
plummeted: John Joseph to author, 11/12/2004; Watson note: author peeking; Language requirement Bundy report : Ar, March 1977.

5. THE 1980S

William R. Cotter (pp. 235–242)

Never expected to hear: Cotter to author, 1/29/2005; Time would tell: S (2/27/1979);
Echo opined: 2/26/1979; Bok, Bixler, Cotter at Inauguration: Ar, 9/29/1979; in presenting, not bothered: board minutes, 2/24/1979; Rotary Club: S (8/21–22/1979); Survey
results: A (Spring 1980); Post-Colby survey: A (Fall 1981); Cotter wrote: A College
President's Lament, *New York Times* (3/31/1980); Diminishing number: Breneman,
The Coming Enrollment Crisis, 1982; Three Presidents remarks: Ar texts; campaign
goals: Ar, Cotter to Executive Committee, 8/8/1980.

Star Search (pp. 242–250)

Antidraft protest: United Press International A Wire, 5/6–8/1980; Barlow said: *New
York Times* (5/9/1980); Cotter letter to Fiske: Ar, 1/22/1992; telegram: Ar, P. Filley to
W.R.C., 1/29/1982; more careful with restaurants: *Chronicle* (2/24/1982); without
Times imprimatur: ibid., 3/17/1982; *U.S. News,* first rankings: 11/28/1983; General
Patton: author; exemplary residential life: *FYI* 3/23/1987; best student services:
FYI 7/23/1987; campus complete: Ar, Cotter speeches, March 1981.

Omega (pp. 250–260)

Committee of 21: M-*HCC,* 470; boarding houses: ibid., 472; Hill inquired: board
minutes, 5/21/1943; Tau Delta Phi, ibid., 468; Strider was asking: A (Summer 1970);
Certain Proposals: A (Winter 1967); Koonce, an awful thing: A (Spring 1967); French
popped eyes: A (Fall 1968); report was gloomy: Ar, Dean of Students *Report on the
Status of Fraternities,* August 1977; board not far removed: letter, Strider to author,
9/18/2005; The court wrote: Finding, Alpha Rho Zeta of Lambda Chi Alpha, Inc.,
et al. *v.* Inhabitants of the City of Waterville, Decision 3512, 5/25/1984; Terp:
S 3/4/1982; *Echo* Commentary: MS 10/25/1980; burning issues: A (June 1983); 254
members: memo, A Fraternity Occupancy, Johnston to Cotter, September 1983.

Commons Sense (pp. 260–267)

Witch hunt: Peter Simpson, *Chronicle* (3/7/1984); scapegoat: Committee on New
England Campus life letter to alumni, February 1984; firmly committed: Bullock to
Committee, 4/25/1984; absolute option: Supreme Court opinion, p. 19, Alpha Rho
Zeta of Lambda Chi Alpha et al. *v.* Inhabitants of the City of Waterville, 5/25/1984;
to more fully integrate: Supreme Court decision, Chi Realty Corp. *v.* President and
Trustees of Colby College, 8/15/1986; Alexander at Bowdoin: Alexander to author,
3/2/2005; student elections: *FYI* 9/27/1984; some wag: author; feared bitterness:
trustee minutes, 1/14/1984; Annual Fund, alumni contributions: A (March 1986);
McArthur, counselors saw the change: *Chronicle* (3/17/1984), volunteerism, etc.:
author, Fraternal Law Conference, Cincinnati, Ohio, 11/4/1988; 63 percent felt:

Echo survey, *A* (September 1985); most engaging: *Architecture Magazine,* from *A* (October 1987).

The Mouse that Roared (pp. 268–272)

The Mouse That Roared: Leonard Wibberley, *Saturday Evening Post* (1959); Cotter, computer approach: *A* (Spring 1982); Gagnon warned: memo to Nicholson, 10/15/1982; Allen told committee: committee minutes 9/25/1984; librarians out looking, instantly doubled: request for proposal for integrated library system, 2/1/1987; Pottle, two of three: *A* (Winter 1986); *Chronicle* listed: *FYI* 2/6/1987; Beaulieu: *A* (January 1988); Phillips, *CM* (Fall 1989).

Worldview (pp. 272–281)

Dominate high schools: Cotter, President's Report, *CM* (June 1989); prevalent student rumor: Associated Press, Harkavy, 4/16/1980; national obligaton and self-interest, President's Report, op. cit.; Cotter called on the faculty: *A* (Winter 1980); his motive and quotes, Harkavy, op. cit.; Davis: *A* (May 1984); Hoffman-Rubin: *A* (March 1986); Leary: ibid.; Leighton letter: *A* (June 1986); Robertson reply: *A* (September 1986); survey: *A* (December 1987); we stand for diversity: *A* (December 1986); government doing nothing: *E* (9/30/1982); avoid a holocaust?: ibid.; Power to the people: *A* (December 1986), 15; most tension-filled: Tietenberg to author, 4/28/2005; faculty vote: faculty meeting minutes, 10/9/1985; Cotter's dream: Plan for the 90s, 1989.

Fitness Crazy (pp. 281–287)

Liquor inspectors: *A* (June 1987); Bennett: *A* (December 1986); Students are told: *A* (June 1987); Cross said: *A* (May 1984); 83 *Echo, A* (June 1983); 90 *Echo, E* (2/22/1990); Cotter committed: College news release, 11/20/1985; mischievous administrator: author; Cotter announced: President's Report, 1989.

Hot School (pp. 288–296)

Seven Days: *FYI* 5/13/1988; NESCAC report: June 1988; economics best: *Change* magazine (September 1981); Senators carried book; *FYI* 3/9/1989; Maine treasure: *FYI* 10/20/1986; CIA: *CM* (Fall 1988); faculty vote: minutes, 11/11/1987; Bennett bemoaned: *FYI* 4/29/1988; Cotter fired back: Ar, Cotter to Bennett, 4/27/1988.

6. THE 1990S

Strawberry Rhubarb (pp. 297–305)

Faculty urged: faculty meeting minutes, 11/16/1987; Smith wrote: memo, 2/16/1989; satanic cult: Opinion and Order, Androscoggin Superior Court, Jeffrey Phelps, et al., *v.* president and trustees of Colby College, William R. Cotter and Earl H. Smith; 8/22/1990; polite and well-mannered: *MS* 5/14/1990; Grange description: Phelps *v.* Colby, op. cit., exhibit 36; *Echo* fumed: *E* (4/12/1990); rejected temporary restraining order: *MS*, 5/25/1990; Maine Civil Rights Act: M.R.S.A. 4681–4683; Alexander ruling: Phelps *v.* Colby, op. cit.; Opponents argued: *CM* (August 1991); Livingston wrote: Ar, Livingston to Cotter, 7/25/1995; McCardell fired back: Ar, 8/4/1995; Cotter wrote: Ar, 8/8/1995; words as weapons: Cotter, *Nieman Reports* (Fall 1993); like cholesterol: President's Forum, *CM* (August 1994); Task force, women: Report and Recommendations, April 1990; Mackenzie said: *CM* (August 1991); aftermath of LA verdict: author, for President's Annual Report 1992; religious holidays: *FYI* 10/8/1992.

Oh, So Happy (pp. 305–312)

Pugh described: *FYI* 10/15/1991; it wasn't long: student poll of eight hundred, *FYI* 6/10/1992; happiest: author from President's Annual Report, 1994; planning needs: Cotter, Approaching the Year 2000, undated Plannning Committee Report, circa 1993; national demand for scientists: Report, Science Planning Committee, January 1991; two buildings short: ibid.; heating plant: author, *CM* (November 1993); nice round number: Cotter to author, August 2005; Cotter recalled, ibid.

Echo Boomers (pp. 312–317)

They wanted: *Black Issues in Higher Education* (10/6/1994); generally ignorant: *Maine Times,* Beem, April 1994; led a survey: *FYI* 1/24/1995; Survey, Class of 2000: Higher Education Research Institute of California Survey of College Freshmen; Cotter acknowledged, Maine students: Colby Maine Event, 9/23/1983; Only Carleton: Institute of International Education, *Chronicle* (11/10/1995); Philips acknowledged: *CM* (March 1994).

Fire (pp. 317–323)

Six hospitalized; Cotter letter to trustees, 8/31/1992; Cotter acknowledged: *MS* 9/23/1992; Colby had 250: *FYI* 3/3/1993; most women coaches, NCAA report, August 1997; most selective: NCAA, February 1996; Conference presidents: NESCAC 1971–97, "A Retrospective," Karin Vélez, Williams College, 1997; Cotter skeptical, letter to students, 2/9/1999; animated discussion: memorandum from President Robert Edwards to Bowdoin athletic staff on meeting of NESCAC presidents, 4/28/1997; stemmed from a fear: Vélez, op. cit.; ranked fourth: NCAA, Ankrom Index, 1996.

And Ice (pp. 323–328)

Snowe, remarkable: *MS,* 1/14/1998; Scott had lost: Business Economics, January 1998; $3 trillion: Megerstat Review, 1997; Countywide: *CM* (September 1999); population dropped: 2000 U.S. Census; bully pulpit: *CM* (Spring 2002); feared tattoo parlors: Cotter to author, August 2002.

Crown Jewel (pp. 328–332)

Elizabeth's idea: *CM* (May 1991); Payson said: *FYI* 2/13/1992; knew little of Colby: Schupf to author, August 2005; always felt guilty: *CM* (August 1992); seven most exciting: *Traveler* (September 1996); Schupf said no one should hate: Faculty-Trustee dinner, May 2005; place going places: Grace Glueck, *New York Times* (9/1/2000); jewel: Edgar Allen Beem, *Maine Times* (9/14/2000).

Reflections (pp. 332–338)

Pond cleaning: author's essay, *CM* (April 1998); most beautiful: *Princeton Review: Best 331 Colleges,* 1999; I was never told: Cotter response to report of the task force on racial concerns, 4/30/1999.

BIBLIOGRAPHY

Blank, Carla. *Rediscovering America: The Making of Multicultural America, 1900–2000.* New York: Three Rivers Press, 2003.

Chafe, William H., and Harvard Sitkoff, eds. *A History of Our Time: Readings, in Postwar America.* New York: Oxford University Press, 1995.

Coffin, Robert P. Tristram. *Kennebec, Cradle of Americans.* Illustrated by Maitland de Gogorza. Camden, Maine: Down East Enterprise, 1937.

Fotiades, Anestes. *Colby College: A Venture of Faith.* Augusta, Maine: Alan Sutton, 1994.

Halberstam, David. *The Fifties.* New York: Villard Books, 1993.

Heikes, Nelson Miles. *Sketch of the Life of Rev. Elijah Parish Lovejoy.* Albion, Maine: Ladies of the G.A.R., 1923.

Lovejoy, Joseph C., and Owen Lovejoy. *Memoir of the Rev. Elijah P. Lovejoy: who was murdered in defense of the liberty of the press, at Alton, Illinois, Nov. 7, 1837.* Edited by Robert C. Holt Jr. Foreword and annotations by Robert W. Tabscott. Saint Louis, Mo.: Lovejoy Press, 2002.

Manchester, William. *The Glory and the Dream: A Narrative History of America, 1932–1972.* Boston: Little, Brown, 1974.

Maramarco, Anthony M. *The Presidency of E. L. Strider.* Waterville, Maine: Colby College, 1979.

Marriner, Ernest C. *The History of Colby College.* Waterville, Maine: Colby College Press, 1963.

———. *The Man of Mayflower Hill: A Biography of Franklin W. Johnson.* Waterville, Maine: Colby College Press, 1967.

———. *Remembered Maine.* Waterville, Maine: Colby College Press, 1957.

———. *The Strider Years: An Extension of* The History of Colby College. Waterville, Maine: Colby College, 1980.

Matusow, Allen J., ed. *Joseph R. McCarthy.* Englewood Cliffs, N.J.,: Prentice-Hall, 1970.

Moses, John G. *The Lebanese in America.* Utica, N.Y.: J.G. Moses, c. 1987.

Reeves, Thomas C. *Twentieth-Century America: A Brief History.* New York: Oxford University Press, 2000.

Roosevelt, Nicholas. *Conservation: Now or Never.* New York: Dodd, Mead, 1971.

Rowe, Amy E. "An Exploration of Immigration, Industrialization and Ethnicity in Waterville, Maine." Honors thesis, Department of Anthropology, Colby College, 1999.

Shulman, James L., and William G. Bowen, in collaboration with Lauren A Meserve and Roger C. Schonfeld. *The Game of Life: College Sports and Educational Values.* Princeton: Princeton University Press, 2001.

Sleeper, Frank H. *Around Waterville.* Dover, N.H.: Chalford, 1995.

Smith, Margaret Chase. *Declaration of Conscience.* Edited by William C. Lewis Jr. New York: Doubleday, 1972.

Soule, Bertha Louise. *Colby's President Roberts.* Waterville, Maine: Colby College, 1943.

———. *Colby's Roman: Julian Daniel Taylor.* Waterville, Maine: Colby College, 1938.

Strider, Robert E. L., and Elizabeth Strider Dain. *Helen Bell Strider.* Boston: privately printed, 1996.

Survey of Higher Education in Maine. Orono, Me.: University of Maine, 1929.

Tabscott, Robert. *The Vigil: the Enduring Legacy of Elijah P. Lovejoy.* Forthcoming.

Tolles, Bryant F., Jr. "The Colby Bricks." *Maine History* 39 (2000–2001).

A Tribute to the Memory of Garner Colby. Boston: Franklin Press; rand, Avery, 1879.

Whittemore, Edwin. *The Centennial History of Waterville.* Waterville, Maine, 1902.

———. *Colby College, 1820–1925.* Portland, Maine: Southworth, 1927.

Zuver, Dudley. *The Lengthened Shadow of a Maine Man: A Biography of Guy P. Gannett.* Freeport, Maine: bond Wheelwright, 1956.

later manifestations and demise of, 325; "man with an eye patch" icon of, 142

Hathaway, Charles, 19; life and careers, 12–13

Hathaway, Rep. William, 196n14

Hawthorne, Nathaniel, 120n45

hazing, 161, 165, 254, 267

Hebron Academy, 27

Heights Residence Halls, 242, 242n7

Heilbroner, Robert, 229

Helm, Peyton "Randy," 294–295, 335, 337

Hendrickson, Cushman, 22

Hershey, Gen. Lewis, 168

Hexamer, Hugh (class of 1952), 94

Hickox, Charles, 81

Higgins, Bill (class of 1992), 305, 317

Hill, Mayor Ann G. "Nancy," 288, 289n50

Hill, Dr. Frederick Thayer "F. T." (class of 1910), 55, 84, 232n50; fraternities and, 251, 255

Hill, Howard (class of 1919), 232m50

Hill, Dr. James "J. F.," 29, 42, 232n50

Hill, Kevin (class of 1950), 232m50, 255

Hill Family Guest House, 232, 339

Hillside dorms, 242n7

Hilton, Harry, 49, 69

History of Colby College, The (Marriner), 140

hockey. See field hockey; ice hockey

Hoffman, Abbie, 274

Hogan, Charles (class of 1973), 195, 201

Hogendorn, Jan, 176, 195, 290

Holland, Henry, 79, 280, 281

Holmes, Ezekiel (class of 1924), 81

Holsten, Jen (class of 1990), 321

Holtz, Lou, 285–286

Holy Spirit, Parish of the (Catholic church), 325

Homecoming, 96; first male "queen," 205n23

Homer, Walter, 103

Homer, Winslow, 85, 230

Hoover, President Herbert, 52n25, 307n9

Hopkins, Mrs. George K., 99

Hospital Administration Institute, 84

Hotel Cassini, 152, 153

Houlton (Ricker) Academy, 27

Howard Hughes Medical Institute, 326

Howell, President Roger, 182n3, 188n9

Hudson, Frederick, 163

Hudson, Henry (class of 1874), 26

Hughes, Robert (class of 1968), 169

Hume, Alan and Dorothy, 309

Humphrey, James, 86

Humphries, Cory, 245n10

Hungarian String Quartet, 141, 141n18

Hunger of Memory (Rodriguez), 274

Huntington, Christopher, 140

Hurd, Dot, 232

Hurd, Marlene (class of 1954), 102n29

Hurwitz, Sol, 235–236

Hutchinson, Pierce, Atwood, and Allen (law firm), 113

Hyde, Rep. Henry, 300

ice hockey, 104–105, 154–155, 225; All-Americans, 282n45, 321, 322n27; underground Deke fraternity and, 297, 299; women's, 221, 222, 224, 286, 321

ice storm (1998), 323–324, 324n29

Ickes, Harold, 49

Ineson, Rev. John, 304

infanticide/filicide case, 91

infirmary: Garrison-Foster Health Center, 230–231, 231n49; in Roberts Union, 111–112, 230

influenza epidemic, 34

Ingraham, Robert (class of 1951), 87

Inter-Fraternity Council (IFC), 97, 165, 254

Internal Revenue Service, educational deductions, 84n19

international studies, 247, 279–281, 281n44; high participation in, 314; major, 302